THE
BEDFORD
HANDBOOK

Sixth Edition

THE BEDFORD HANDBOOK

Diana Hacker

BEDFORD/ST. MARTIN'S

Boston ◆ *New York*

For Bedford/St. Martin's

Developmental Editors: Leasa Burton and Ellen Thibault
Production Editor: Anne Noonan
Senior Production Supervisor: Joe Ford
Marketing Manager: Richard Cadman
Associate Editor: Sara Eaton
Editorial Assistant: Christine Turnier-Vallecillo
Production Assistants: Thomas P. Crehan, Helaine Denenberg
Copyeditor: Barbara G. Flanagan
Text Design: Claire Seng-Niemoeller
Cover Design: Hannus Design Associates
Composition: Monotype Composition Company, Inc.
Printing and Binding: RR Donnelley and Sons Company

President: Charles H. Christensen
Editorial Director: Joan E. Feinberg
Editor in Chief: Karen S. Henry
Director of Marketing: Karen Melton
Director of Editing, Design, and Production: Marcia Cohen
Managing Editor: Elizabeth M. Schaaf

Library of Congress Control Number: 2001087439

Manufactured in the United States of America.

6   5   4   3
f   e   d

For information, write: Bedford/St. Martin's, 75 Arlington Street, Boston, MA 02116 (617-399-4000)

ISBN: 0–312–39317–2 (Instructor's Annotated Edition)
     0–312–41280–0 (hardcover Student Edition)
     0–312–41281–9 (softcover Student Edition)

Acknowledgments
The American Heritage Dictionary of the English Language, Fourth Edition, from the entry "regard." Copyright © 2000 by Houghton Mifflin Company. Reprinted by permission of the publisher.

Acknowledgments and copyrights are continued at the back of the book on page 849, which constitute an extension of the copyright page. It is a violation of the law to reproduce these selections by any means whatsoever without the written permission of the copyright holder.

Preface for Instructors

This book is grounded in my many years of teaching first- and second-year composition to a wide range of students: young and mature, mainstream and multiethnic, talented and underprepared. As I've drafted and revised *The Bedford Handbook,* my goal has never been to sell students on my personal views about language and politics — or to endorse popular trends in the teaching of English. Instead, I've tried to look squarely at the problems students face and come up with practical solutions. Many of this book's charts and some of its text and exercises began as handouts I prepared for my own students or for the writing center at Prince George's Community College.

While preparing this sixth edition of *The Bedford Handbook,* I had little difficulty understanding the problems confronting today's students, for I have seen them firsthand: in the classroom, in the writing center, and in my own research and writing. Many of these problems stem from technology, which has proved to be both a blessing and a curse. Yes, students in this new century are privileged to have easy access to information in databases and on the Web, but evaluating sources is now a major challenge — and documenting them can be a nightmare. Today's students are also lucky to write in networked classrooms and to experiment with new forms, such as Web sites and hypertext. Along with these new writing environments, however, come fresh challenges and temptations: the challenge of organizing Web links, for example, or the temptation to rely too heavily on the grammar checker or to ignore grammar conventions altogether.

Technology offers many opportunities for textbook authors, and I have tried to take advantage of them. *The Bedford Handbook* is now integrated with its companion Web site, and both the Web site and *The Electronic Bedford Handbook* offer more electronic exercises than before. Here is a description of the book's features, new and old, along with a summary of resources available at <http://www.dianahacker.com/bedhandbook> and a list of ancillaries, both print and electronic.

What's new

Most of my revisions respond to technological change. In addition to updating the book for the digital age, I have improved the sections on critical thinking and made the book more useful for writers across the curriculum. Here, briefly, are some highlights.

Integration of the book with its companion Web site. Because most students are now working online, I've extended my book beyond its paper covers by linking it explicitly to its Web site. Throughout the book, "On the Web" boxes take students to locations on the Web site, where they will find a variety of supplements to the book: electronic grammar exercises, exercises on avoiding plagiarism and integrating sources, a links library, essays called Language Debates, and so on. Because the Web site is an extension of the book, I have written nearly all of its content myself. For more about these Web features, see pages xi–xiv.

Updated advice on finding and evaluating sources. With the help of reference librarian Barbara Fister, I have revised the sections on finding and evaluating sources with the awareness that the library and the Web now depend on one another. I encourage students to enter the Web through a library's portal or another "juried" venue that assures some sort of quality control. Also, I emphasize the need for evaluation throughout the research process — from choosing a search engine or database to selecting reliable sources to reading those sources.

The sections on finding and evaluating sources are more cross-curricular than before: They are now illustrated with examples linked to the topics of the book's MLA, APA, and *Chicago* papers.

Discipline-specific rhetorical advice for MLA, APA, and Chicago styles. Handbook advice on drafting a thesis, avoiding plagiarism, and integrating sources has traditionally been illustrated only with MLA examples. To make the sixth edition of *The Bedford Handbook* more useful for students writing APA and *Chicago* papers, I now present discipline-specific examples on these important matters in three color-coded sections: MLA, APA, and *Chicago.* Students in social science or history classes no longer need to "translate" the examples, mentally replacing MLA's in-text citations with APA's quite different in-text citations or with *Chicago*'s notes. In all three sections, examples are tied to topics appropriate to each discipline.

Expanded MLA guidelines especially for Web sources. Because many Web sources have corporate or unknown authors and because most lack stable page numbers, I now pay special attention to authorship and pagination in my presentation of MLA's in-text citations. It is easier for students to document both print and Web sources if they focus on a clear first step: identifying the author of a source. Once students grasp that the author's name links an in-text citation to an entry in the list of works cited, they can better understand the intricacies of MLA style: how to handle multiple authors, for example, or corporate authors or unknown authors. As for the issue of page numbers, I explain the MLA guidelines, along with their implications, in more detail than before.

The works cited models now cover a wider range of multimedia and Web sources because students are relying more heavily on such sources in their papers.

New sample papers. A new MLA paper that advocates regulating the use of cell phones while driving is paired with a paper opposing such regulation; the second paper appears on the book's companion Web site. Each paper draws on both print and electronic sources. One of the book's two literature papers is new (an analysis of "A Jury of Her Peers"), as is the history paper illustrating *Chicago* style (on the topic of the Fort Pillow massacre).

A new model paper in Part I is titled "Hooked on Credit Cards." In the section on writing about texts, both the sample summary and the analysis are new.

Thoroughly revised sections on critical thinking. The section on writing about texts now includes the full text of an article annotated by a student writer, along with the student's outline, summary, and analysis of the reading. The section on argument devotes more attention to audience and the need to build credibility. A new section on evaluating arguments shows students how argumentative tactics, such as generalizing and appealing to emotions, can work either to build or to undermine a writer's credibility.

More attention to writing in online environments. Part I offers a new sample paper with peer review comments from an online classroom, and Part II includes new advice about writing scannable and online résumés as well as updated and expanded advice about writing e-mails and designing Web sites.

What's the same

Although technology has led to a number of changes in the book, many of the book's features will be familiar to users of the previous edition. The features that have most contributed to the book's success are detailed in this section.

A brief menu and a user-friendly index. Designed for student use, a brief menu inside the front cover displays icons representing the book's eleven parts and lists only the numbered sections. The traditional, more detailed handbook menu, which is useful for instructors but too daunting for many students, appears on the back endpapers.

The handbook's index (which I write myself) helps students find what they are looking for even if they don't know grammatical terminology. When facing a choice between *I* and *me*, for example, students may not know to look up "Case" or even "Pronoun, case of." They are more likely to look up "*I*" or "*me*," so I have included index entries for "*I* versus *me*" and "*me* versus *I*." Similar user-friendly entries appear throughout the index.

An uncluttered page design. Created by award-winning designer Claire Seng-Niemoeller, the book's pages lay out complex material as simply as possible. Because grammar rules and hand-edited examples are highlighted in a second color (red), students can easily skim the book's central sections for quick answers to questions. The book's third and fourth colors (teal and khaki) appear in charts and boxes; these charts and boxes are easy to find and, just as important, they are easy to skip.

Quick reference charts. Many of the handbook's charts help students review for common problems in their own writing, such as fragments and subject-verb agreement.

Other charts summarize important material: a checklist for global revision, strategies for avoiding sexist language, guidelines for evaluating Web sites, and so on.

Charts encouraging reflection. In twenty "Looking at yourself as a writer" charts, I encourage the kind of self-reflection that leads to those occasional moments of recognition that help us all grow as writers. When we experience a problem repeatedly, often our difficulties can be traced to root causes: false or half-learned rules, fossilized habits, confused motivations, or needless fears. For example, we may fall into the dangling modifier trap because we fear using *I* in a sentence, or we may turn to the passive voice because we have seen it modeled so many times by our supervisors at work. By reflecting on the causes of our problems, we writers can often take appropriate steps to cure them.

Grammar checker boxes. In fifty boxes, I show students what grammar and spell checkers can do—and what they can't do. As you have no doubt discovered, students sometimes produce strange errors because they have taken the advice of a grammar checker without thinking first. And many students believe that once they have run a grammar checker, their problems are over.

To discover the capabilities and limits of current grammar checkers, I have run a large bank of exercise sentences (many containing errors), along with some student drafts, through two commonly used programs. The results, summarized in boxes throughout the book, show that grammar checkers help with some but by no means all of the typical problems in a draft.

Help for culturally diverse students. More than ten years ago, I was the first handbook author to write a special section for students who speak English as a second (or third or fourth) language. Over the years, I have expanded the section and added a number of ESL boxes throughout the book. ESL students are of course my primary audience, but many instructors and tutors who work with culturally diverse students have also found this material helpful.

Extensive exercises, some with answers. At least one exercise set accompanies nearly every section of the book. Most sets begin with five lettered sentences with answers in the back of the book so students can test their understanding independently. The sets then continue with numbered sentences whose answers appear only in the *Instructor's Annotated Edition.* Students who need more practice can go to the book's companion Web site (see below for details).

To help students learn to use the handbook independently as a reference, I have included five tutorials in "How to Use This Book."

What's on the Companion Web Site

The features described here are intended for students. Instructor resources, both print and electronic, are listed on pages xiii–xiv.

Language Debates. The companion Web site's Language Debates are brief essays in which I explore controversial issues of grammar and usage, such as split infinitives, by citing experts and weighing their arguments. The inspiration for these essays came from e-mails I've received from student users of my books: queries about passive verbs, *that* versus *which,* and so on. My goal in the Language Debates is to encourage such students to think about the rationales for a rule and then make their own rhetorical decisions.

Electronic grammar exercises. I have nearly doubled the number of grammar exercises on the handbook's companion Web site—from 600 to about 1,000 items. As always, I have played an active role in creating the exercises and writing the feedback for correct and incorrect responses.

Most of the exercises are scorable. Exercises that call for editing are not scorable because answers may vary; these exercises, on topics such as parallelism or dangling modifiers, which have a rhetorical dimension, are labeled "edit and compare." They ask students to edit sentences and compare their versions with possible revisions.

Electronic research and writing exercises. Using material from pencil-and-paper research exercises that I put together for my own students, I have created scorable electronic exercises on matters such as avoiding plagiarism, integrating sources, and using MLA documentation. Many students have a hard time understanding these matters just by reading the book; when they work through a couple of exercises, I've found, they begin to grasp the issues. At the very least, they can't tell me later that they had no idea copying was wrong!

To accompany Part I, The Writing Process, I've written a few electronic exercises on thesis statements, peer review, point of view, transitions, and the like. These too are scorable.

Links library. Throughout the handbook, students are directed to relevant portions of a links library on the companion Web site. For example, from the companion site students can go to resources such as online writing centers, tutorials on creating Web sites, and online libraries.

Model papers. Model papers for MLA, APA, *Chicago,* and CBE styles illustrate both the design and content of researched writing. Annotations highlight important points about each paper's style, content, and method of documentation.

Research and Documentation Online. As its title suggests, this online resource helps students conduct research and document their sources. Reference librarian Barbara Fister has updated her advice on finding sources and provided new links to resources in a variety of disciplines, and she continues to maintain the research portion of the site. My role has been to update guidelines for documenting print and online sources in MLA, APA, *Chicago,* and CBE styles.

Ancillaries for students

Both print and electronic ancillaries are available for students.

PRINT RESOURCES
Developmental Exercises to Accompany THE BEDFORD HANDBOOK

Answers to Exercises in THE BEDFORD HANDBOOK

Research and Documentation in the Electronic Age, Third Edition

ELECTRONIC RESOURCES
The Electronic Bedford Handbook 6.0

The Bedford Handbook companion Web site (see the On the Web box on page xxiv)

Ancillaries for instructors

Practical and professional resources for instructors are available in print form. Other resources appear on the instructor portion of the book's companion Web site.

PRACTICAL RESOURCES FOR INSTRUCTORS
Instructor's Annotated Edition

Quizzes and Diagnostic Tests to Accompany THE BEDFORD HANDBOOK

Transparency Masters to Accompany THE BEDFORD HANDBOOK

PROFESSIONAL RESOURCES FOR INSTRUCTORS

Background Readings for Instructors Using THE BEDFORD HAND-BOOK

The Bedford Guide for Writing Tutors, Third Edition

The Bedford Bibliography for Teachers of Writing, Fifth Edition

WEB RESOURCES FOR INSTRUCTORS

The Bedford Handbook instructor site <http://www.dianahacker.com/bedhandbook/instructor>

— *Exercise Masters,* print-format versions of all of the exercises in the book

— *Quiz Masters,* print-format quizzes on key topics in the book

— *Electronic Diagnostic Tests,* a test bank for instructors to use

— *Transparency Masters,* useful charts, examples, and visuals from the book

— *Preparing for the CLAST*

— *Preparing for the TASP*

Acknowledgments

No author can possibly anticipate the many ways in which a variety of students might respond to a text: Where might students be confused? How much explanation is enough? What is too intimidating? Do the examples appeal to a range of students? Are they free of stereotypes? To help me answer such questions, over one hundred instructors from more than ninety colleges and universities contributed useful insights based on their varied experiences in the classroom.

For their many helpful suggestions, I would like to thank a perceptive group of reviewers:

Dorothy Arnett, Central Missouri State University
Mary Balkun, Seton Hall University
Thomas Banks, Ohio Northeastern University

Laurie Bernhardt, Portland Community College, Sylvania
Gene Booth, Albuquerque TVI Community College
Sheree Brown, College of Mount St. John
Donna Campbell, Gonzaga University
Elizabeth Chiseri-Strater, University of North Carolina, Greens-
  boro
N. Bradley Christie, Erskine College
Mattie Collins, Angelina College
Phil Condorelli, Bunker Hill Community College
Dachang Cong, University of Texas at Dallas
Elizabeth Davis, Southern Arkansas University
Rosemary Day, Albuquerque TVI Community College
Susan Delagrange, The Ohio State University
Matthew DeVoll, Washington University
Janet Dizinno, St. Mary's University
Martha Downs, Montgomery College, Takoma Park
John Doyle, Quinnipiac University
Robert Dunne, Central Connecticut State University
Jane Mathison Fife, University of Tennessee, Chattanooga
Seth Frechie, Cabrini College
Michael George, Ohio Northern University
Christine Goffette, Valparaiso University
Barbara Goldstein, Hillsborough Community College
Heather B. Graves, DePaul University
Carol Hansen, College of San Mateo
Mary Hocks, Georgia State University
Lee Honeycutt, Iowa State University
Carol Howard, Warren Wilson College
John Jebb, University of Delaware
Kathleen Kiefer, Colorado State University
Deborah Kinder, University of Wisconsin, Platteville
Deborah Kirkman, University of Kentucky
Craig Kleinman, City College of San Francisco
Anne Kress, Santa Fe Community College
Mary Otto Lang, Wharton County Junior College
Michelle LeBeau, University of New Mexico, Valencia
Dara Llewellyn, Asheville Biltmore Technical Community Col-
  lege
Daniel Manheim, Centre College
Donald Markos, California State University, Hayward

Steven May, Pikes Peak Community College
Victoria McLure, South Plains College
Patricia McNaney, Buffalo State College
Terry Miller, Indian River Community College
John Noell Moore, The College of William & Mary
Maggie Mulz, Clark College
Kathleen O'Shaughnessy, Portland Community College
E. Suzanne Owens, Lorain County Community College
Amy Pawl, Washington University
Henrietta Pearlman, Adelphi University
Virginia Perdue, Indiana University of Pennsylvania
Carolyn Poor, Wharton County Junior College
Eric Rabkin, University of Michigan
Eugene Richie, Pace University
MeMe Riordan, City College of San Francisco
Zan Robinson, Erie Community College
Cheryl W. Ruggiero, Virginia Polytechnic Institute and State
    University
Leigh Ryan, University of Maryland
Edwin Sams, San Jose State University
Sandra Schroeder, Seattle Central Community College
Beth Shepard, St. Mary's University
Martin Simpson, University of Florida
Gerard Smith, Clark College
Wayne Stein, University of Central Oklahoma
Luther Stripling, Tarrant County College NE
Laurie Stuhlbarg, Bridgewater State College
Jenny Sullivan, Northern Virginia Community College
Susan Swan, Lane Community College
Marjorie Task, University of Dayton
Patricia Terry, Gonzaga University
Sharon Thomas, Lane Community College
Thomas Thompson, The Citadel
Lynda Vannice, Umpqua Community College
Joann Wasik, Syracuse University
Stephen Wilhoit, University of Dayton
Rosalie Winston, California State University, Dominguez Hills
Thia Wolf, California State University, Chico
Mark Wollaeger, Vanderbilt University

Valerie Wright, University of California, Irvine
Holly Zaitchik, Boston University
Diana Zilberman, Baltimore City Community College

For helping me see the strengths and weaknesses of the fifth edition, thanks go to the many instructors who took the time to answer a detailed questionnaire:

Kathryn Adams, Allan Hancock College; Paul Andrews, St. John's River Community College; Kim Baker, Roger Williams University; Carole Brown, Moravian College; N. Bradley Christie, Erksine College; Mattie Collins, Angelina College; Elizabeth Davis, Southern Arkansas University; Rosemary Day, Albuquerque TVI Community College; Matthew DeVoll, Washington University; Marylynne Diggs, Clark College; John Doyle, Quinnipiac College; Robert Dunne, Central Connecticut State University; Gwyn Enright, San Diego City College; Larry Frazier, College of the Redwoods; Kimberley Gibson, St. Mary's University; Carl Glover, Mount St. Mary's College; Carol Hansen, College of San Mateo; Carol Howard, Warren Wilson College; John Jebb, University of Delaware; Deborah Kinder, University of Wisconsin, Platteville; Deborah Kirkman, University of Kentucky; Dara Llewellyn, Asheville Biltmore Technical Community College; Grace McLaughlin, Portland Community College; Jean Moore, Northwest Mississippi Community College; Carolyn Poor, Wharton County Junior College; Eugene Richie, Pace University; MeMe Riordan, City College of San Francisco; Edwin Sams, San Jose State University; Marjorie Task, University of Dayton; Thomas Thompson, The Citadel; Lynda Vannice, Umpqua Community College; Elizabeth Westgard, Saint Mary-of-the-Woods College; Rosalie Winston, California State University, Dominguez Hills; Carla Witcher, Montgomery College, Germantown

Writing a handbook is truly a collaborative effort. Librarian Barbara Fister helped me reorganize the research sections and bring them up to date (no small feat). William Peirce assisted with the sections on argument, Lloyd Shaw helped me improve the research sections, and Julia Sullivan contributed to the section on writing about literature. For the book's companion Web site, Carolyn Lengel has created several well-written grammar exercises on a variety of interesting topics.

Thanks are due to the authors of the book's ancillaries: to Leigh Ryan for her insightful *Bedford Guide for Writing Tutors;* to Glenn Blalock for his carefully edited *Background Readings;* to Wanda Van Goor and Mitch Evich for their work on *Quizzes and Diagnostic Tests;* to Wanda Van Goor for her creative *Developmental Exercises;* to Barbara Fister for her expert contribution to *Research and Documentation in the Electronic Age;* and to Barbara Sloan and Carolyn Christensen West and to Ellen Shull and Paula Tran for their useful guides *Preparing for the CLAST* and *Preparing for the TASP,* respectfully.

I am indebted to the students whose essays appear in this edition — Ned Bishop, Angela Daly, LaShawn Freeman, Andrew Knutson, Dan Larson, Paul Levi, Margaret Peel, Karen Shaw, Matt Watson, and Tom Weitzel — not only for permission to use their work but for allowing me to adapt it for pedagogical purposes as well. My thanks also go to the students who granted me permission to use their paragraphs: Celeste Barrus, Diana Crawford, Jim Drew, Connie Hailey, William G. Hill, Linda Lavelle, Kathleen Lewis, Chris Mileski, Julie Reardon, Kevin Smith, Margaret Smith, Margaret Stack, John Clyde Thatcher, and David Warren.

Several talented editors have contributed to the book. Leasa Burton directed the project, both the book and its companion Web site, with spirited good humor; her understanding of technology proved invaluable as we worked to keep pace with changing realities in the classroom. Ellen Thibault provided me with a wealth of useful materials as I revised the book's research sections, and in addition to orchestrating development of the *Instructor's Annotated Edition,* she edited *Research and Documentation in the Electronic Age* and *Background Readings.* Sara Eaton worked enthusiastically with the authors of *The Bedford Guide for Writing Tutors* and *Developmental Exercises,* and she contributed to the book's companion Web site, especially its Links Library. Editorial assistant Christine Turnier-Vallecillo has helped me field e-mail queries in a timely and professional manner, and she has handled other matters too numerous to mention. This team—Leasa, Ellen, Sara, and Christine—worked under the adroit leadership of editor in chief Karen Henry, who stepped in occasionally to help me solve especially thorny rhetorical problems.

Book editor Anne Noonan has expertly steered the book through production under impossible deadlines with the help of Thomas Crehan, Helaine Denenberg, Kerri Cardone, and Dobrota Pucherova and under the direction of managing editor Elizabeth Schaaf. Designer Claire Seng-Niemoeller has retained the clean, uncluttered look of the book's pages while adding new visuals and color-coded sections on MLA, APA, and *Chicago* papers. Copyeditor Barbara Flanagan has once again brought grace and consistency to the final manuscript. In addition, she played a significant role in the development of *The Electronic Bedford Handbook.*

I would also like to thank marketing manager Richard Cadman and director of marketing Karen Melton for promoting my book so enthusiastically and for helping to guide its revision in light of the needs of instructors and their students.

Special thanks are due to publishers Chuck Christensen and Joan Feinberg. Eighteen years ago Chuck took a chance on an unknown community college instructor with an inexplicable urge to write a handbook. I am deeply grateful to him for giving me this opportunity. In retrospect, I suppose Chuck knew that almost anyone could learn to write a handbook under the guidance of Joan Feinberg. Certainly a better teacher-editor could not have been found.

Finally, for their support and encouragement, a note of thanks goes to my husband, Robert Hacker; to the families of Greg and Joyce Tarvin, Jeff and Eileen Hacker, Jack and Chris Dougherty, and Steve and Peggy Shearer; to Robbie Wallin, Austin Nichols, Elaine Pirozzi, Kate Miller, Jessica Webner, Rima Koyler, Greg Krakower, Betty Renshaw, Bill Fry, John Bodnar, Sandra Kurtinitis, Joanne Amberson, Margaret Van de Ree, Joyce Neff, Christine McMahon, and Joan Naake; to the English department at Prince George's Community College; and to the many students over the years who have taught me that errors, a natural by-product of the writing process, are simply problems waiting to be solved.

Diana Hacker
Prince George's Community College

How to Use This Book and Its Web Site

Though it is small enough to hold in your hand, *The Bedford Handbook* will answer most of the questions you are likely to ask as you plan, draft, and revise a piece of writing: How do I choose and narrow a topic? What can I do if I get stuck? How do I know when to begin a new paragraph? Should I write *none was* or *none were*? When does a comma belong before *and*? What is the difference between *accept* and *except*? How do I cite a source from the Web?

The book's companion Web site provides opportunities for you to practice the skills covered in the book.

How to find information with an instructor's help

When you are revising an essay that has been marked by your instructor, tracking down information is simple. If your instructor marks problems with a number such as *16* or a number and letter such as *12e*, you can turn directly to the appropriate section of the handbook. Just flip through the colored tabs on the upper corners of the right-hand pages until you find the number in question. The number *16*, for example, leads you to the rule "Tighten wordy sentences," and *12e* takes you to the subrule "Repair dangling modifiers." If your instructor uses an abbreviation such as *w* or *dm* instead of a number, consult the list of abbreviations and symbols on the page right before the endpapers. There you will find the names of the problems (*wordy; dangling modifier*) and the number of the section to consult.

How to find information on your own

With a little practice, you will be able to find information in this book without an instructor's help — usually by tracking the icons that appear in the brief menu inside the front cover. At times, you may want to consult the detailed menu inside the back cover, the index, the Glossary of Usage, or one of the directories to the documentation models.

THE FRONT ENDPAPERS   Usually the brief menu on the inside front cover is the fastest way into the book. Let's say you are having problems with run-on sentences. Your first step is to find the appropriate section — in this case "Grammatical Sentences," which is represented by a check mark icon. Next, find the appropriate numbered item: "20 Run-on sentences." You can flip directly to the page number given (p. 251), or you can use the icon tabs on the left-hand pages and section number tabs on the right-hand pages to help you find section 20.

THE BACK ENDPAPERS   When the numbered section you're looking for is broken up into quite a few lettered subsections, try consulting the detailed menu on the inside back cover.

THE INDEX   If you aren't sure which topic to choose from one of the menus, consult the index at the back of the book. For example, you may not realize that the issue of *is* versus *are* is a matter of subject-verb agreement (section 21). In that case, simply look up "*is* versus *are*" in the index and you will be directed to the exact pages you need.

THE GLOSSARY OF USAGE   When in doubt about the correct use of a particular word (such as *affect* and *effect, among* and *between,* or *hopefully*), consult the Glossary of Usage at the back of the book. This glossary explains the difference between commonly confused words; it also lists colloquialisms and jargon that are inappropriate in formal written English.

DIRECTORIES TO DOCUMENTATION MODELS   When you are documenting a research paper with MLA, APA, or *Chicago* style, you can find documentation models by consulting the appropriate directories. The MLA directories to in-text citation models and to works cited models are easy to find: Just look for the pages marked with a vertical band of red. The APA directories appear on pages marked with a vertical band of teal. And the *Chicago* directories appear on pages marked with a vertical band of khaki.

How to use this book and its Web site for self-study

In a composition class, most of your time should be spent writing. Therefore it is unlikely that you will want to study all of the chapters in this book in detail. Instead you should focus on the problems that tend to crop up in your own writing. Your instructor (or your college's writing center) will be glad to help you plan an individual program of self-study.

The Bedford Handbook has been designed so that you can learn from it on your own. By providing answers to some exercise sentences, it allows you to test your understanding of the material. Most exercise sets begin with five sentences lettered a–e and conclude with five sentences numbered 1–5. Answers to the five lettered sentences appear near the end of the book.

ON THE WEB

Throughout *The Bedford Handbook,* Sixth Edition, "On the Web" boxes direct you to relevant resources on the book's companion Web site.

Simply go to **www.dianahacker.com/bedhandbook** and click on

▶ **Electronic Writing Exercises**
    Interactive exercises on topics such as choosing a thesis statement and conducting peer review

▶ **Electronic Grammar Exercises**
    Interactive exercises on grammar, style, and punctuation skills

▶ **Electronic Research Exercises**
    Interactive exercises on topics such as integrating quotations and documenting sources in MLA style

▶ **Language Debates**
    Mini-essays exploring controversial issues of grammar and usage, such as split infinitives

▶ **Links Library**
    Carefully selected and annotated links to additional online resources for every part of the book

▶ **Model Papers**
    Annotated sample papers in MLA, APA, *Chicago,* and CBE styles with guidelines for both formatting and documenting papers

▶ **Research and Documentation Online**
    Advice on finding sources and up-to-date guidelines for documenting print and online sources in MLA, APA, *Chicago,* and CBE styles

▶ **Additional Resources**
    Print-format versions of the exercises in the book

The chart on the previous page describes the features on the book's companion Web site (www.dianahacker.com/bedhandbook). Each feature — whether an electronic exercise or a language debate — has been developed for you to use on your own whenever you need it.

Diana Hacker

Tutorials

The following tutorials will give you practice using the book's menus, index, Glossary of Usage, and MLA directory. Answers to the tutorials begin on page 833.

TUTORIAL 1   Using the menus

Each of the following "rules" violates the principle it expresses. Using the brief menu inside the front cover or the more detailed menu inside the back cover, find the section in *The Bedford Handbook* that explains the principle. Then fix the problem. Examples:

▶ *Tutors in*
~~In~~ the writing center, ~~they~~ say that vague pronoun reference
  ^
is unacceptable.   *23*

▶   *come*
Be alert for irregular verbs that have ~~came~~ to you in the
                                      ^
wrong form.   *27a*

1. A verb have to agree with its subject.
2. Each pronoun should agree with their antecedent.
3. About sentence fragments. You should avoid them.

4. Its important to use apostrophe's correctly.
5. Check for *-ed* verb endings that have been drop.
6. Discriminate careful between adjectives and adverbs.
7. If your sentence begins with a long introductory word group use a comma to separate the word group from the rest of the sentence.
8. Don't write a run-on sentence, you must connect independent clauses with a comma and a coordinating conjunction or with a semicolon.
9. For clarity, a writer must be careful not to shift your point of view.
10. Do not capitalize a Word just to make it look important.

TUTORIAL 2   Using the index

Assume that you have written the following sentences and want to know the answers to the questions in brackets. Use the index at the back of the book to locate the information you need, and edit the sentences if necessary.

1. Each of the candidates have agreed to participate in tonight's debate. [Should the verb be *have* or *has* to agree with *Each*?]
2. We had intended to go surfing but spent most of our vacation lying on the beach. [Should I use *lying* or *laying*?]
3. We only looked at two houses before buying the house of our dreams. [Is *only* in the right place?]
4. In Saudi Arabia it is considered ill mannered for you to accept a gift. [Is it okay to use *you* to mean "anyone in general"?]
5. In Canada, Joanne picked up several bottles of maple syrup for her sister and me. [Should I write *me* or *I*?]

TUTORIAL 3   Using the menus or the index

Imagine that you are in the following situations. Using either the menus or the index, find the information you need.

1. You are Ray Farley, a community college student who has been out of high school for ten years. You recall learning to punctu-

ate items in a series by putting a comma between all items except the last two. In your college readings, however, you have noticed that most writers use a comma between all items. You're curious about the current rule. Which section of *The Bedford Handbook* will you consult?

2. You are Maria Sanchez, an honors student working in your university's writing center. Mike Lee, who speaks English as a second language, has come to you for help. He is working on a rough draft that contains a number of problems involving the use of articles (*a, an,* and *the*). You know how to use articles, but you aren't able to explain the rather complicated rules on their correct use. Which section of *The Bedford Handbook* will you and Mike Lee consult?

3. You are John Pell, engaged to marry Jane Dalton. In a note to Jane's parents, you have written "Thank you for giving Jane and myself such a generous contribution toward our honeymoon trip to Hawaii." You wonder if you should write "Jane and I" or "Jane and me" instead. Upon consulting *The Bedford Handbook,* what do you learn?

4. You are Selena Young, an intern supervisor at a housing agency. Two of your interns, Jake Gilliam and Susan Green, have writing problems involving -*s* endings on verbs. Jake tends to drop -*s* endings; Susan tends to add them where they don't belong. You suspect that both problems stem from nonstandard dialects spoken at home.

   Susan and Jake are in danger of losing their jobs because your boss thinks that anyone who writes "the tenant refuse" or "the landlords agrees" is beyond hope. You disagree. Susan and Jake are more intelligent than your boss supposes, and they have asked for your help. Where in *The Bedford Handbook* can they find the rules they need?

5. You are Joe Thompson, a first-year college student. Your friend Samantha, who has completed two years of college, seems to enjoy correcting your English. Just yesterday she corrected your sentence "I felt badly about her death" to "I felt bad about her death." You're sure you've heard many educated persons, including professors, say "I felt badly." Upon consulting *The Bedford Handbook,* what do you discover?

TUTORIAL 4   Using the Glossary of Usage

Consult the Glossary of Usage to see if the italicized words are used correctly. Then edit any sentences containing incorrect usage. Example:

> *an*
> The pediatrician gave my daughter ~~a~~ injection for her allergy.

1. Changing attitudes *toward* alcohol have *effected* the beer industry.
2. It is *mankind's* nature to think wisely and act foolishly.
3. This afternoon I plan to *lie* out in the sun and work on my tan.
4. Everyone in our office is *enthused* about this project.
5. Most sleds are pulled by no *less* than two dogs and no more than ten.

TUTORIAL 5   Using the directory to MLA works cited models

Assume that you have written a short research paper on the growth of gambling operations on Indian reservations. You have cited the following sources in your paper, using MLA documentation, and you are ready to type your list of works cited. Turn to page 604 and use the MLA directory to locate the appropriate models. Then write a correct entry for each source and arrange the entries in a properly formatted list of works cited. *Note:* Do not number the entries in a list of works cited.

> A book by Jeff Benedict entitled *Without Reservation: The Making of America's Most Powerful Indian Tribe and the World's Largest Casino.* The book was published in New York by Harper in 2000.

> An article by Jerry Useem entitled "The Big Game: Have American Indians Found Their New Buffalo?" from the biweekly magazine *Fortune.* The article appears on nonconsecutive pages beginning with page 22 of the October 2, 2000, issue of the magazine.

> An e-mail with the subject line "Casinos on reservations in the Northeast," sent to you by Helen Codoga on April 10, 2001.

A journal article by Susan Johnson entitled "From Wounded Knee to Capitol Hill." The article appears in *State Legislatures,* which is paginated by issue. The volume number is 24, the issue number is 9, and the year is 1998. You found this article using the InfoTrac database *Expanded Academic ASAP* at the University of Pittsburgh library on April 6, 2001.

A short web document entitled "Tribal Gaming Myths and Facts" written by the National Indian Gaming Association and published in 2000 on the group's Web site at http://www.indiangaming.org/info/pr/myths.shtml. You found the document on April 4, 2001.

A radio segment entitled "Indian Gaming" from the program *All Things Considered* hosted by Robert Siegel. The program was produced by National Public Radio on March 5, 2001. You listened to the program on WDUQ in Pittsburgh.

Contents

PART II
Document Design 101

PART IV
Word Choice   203

PART V
Grammatical Sentences — 239

PART VI
ESL Trouble Spots   345

PART VII
Punctuation   381

PART VIII
Mechanics   443

PART IX
Critical Thinking — 477

PART X
Researched Writing   519

The Writing Process

Since it's not possible to think about everything all at once, most experienced writers handle a piece of writing in stages. Roughly speaking, those stages are planning, drafting, and revising. You should generally move from planning to drafting to revising, but be prepared to circle back to earlier stages whenever the need arises.

1

Generate ideas and sketch a plan.

Before attempting a first draft, spend some time generating ideas. Mull over your subject while listening to music or driving to work, jot down inspirations on scratch paper, and explore your insights with anyone willing to listen. At this stage you should be collecting information and experimenting with ways of focusing and organizing it to best reach your readers.

1a   Assess the writing situation.

Begin by taking a look at the writing situation in which you find yourself. The key elements of the writing situation include your subject, the sources of information available to you, your purpose, your audience, and constraints such as length, document design, review sessions, and deadlines.

It is unlikely that you will make final decisions about all of these matters until later in the writing process — after a first draft, for example. Nevertheless, you can save yourself time by thinking about as many of them as possible in advance. For a quick checklist, see pages 4–5.

Subject

Frequently your subject will be given to you. In a psychology class, for example, you might be asked to explain Bruno Bettelheim's Freudian analysis of fairy tales. Or in a course on the history of filmmaking, you might be assigned an essay on the political impact of D. W. Griffith's silent film *The Birth of a Nation.* In the business world, your assignment might be to draft a quarterly sales report or craft a diplomatic e-mail to a customer who has complained about your firm's computer software.

In a composition class, assignments often ask you to respond to readings. At times, though, you will be free to choose your own subject. Then you will be wise to select a subject that you already know something about or one that you can reasonably investigate in the time you have. Students in composition classes have written successfully on all of the subjects listed here, most of which were later narrowed into topics suitable for essays of 500–750 words. By browsing through the lists, perhaps you can pick up some ideas of your own.

Education: computers in the classroom, an inspiring teacher, sex education in junior high school, magnet schools, a learning disability such as dyslexia, programmed instruction, parochial schools, teacher certification, a local program to combat adult illiteracy, creative means of funding a college education

Careers and the workplace: working in an emergency room, the image versus the reality of a job such as lifeguarding, a police officer's workday, advantages of flextime for workers and employers, company-sponsored day care, mandatory drug testing by employers, sex or racial discrimination on the job, the psychological effects of unemployment, the rewards of a part-time job such as camp counseling, e-mail privacy issues

The writing process

Checklist for assessing the writing situation

At the beginning of the writing process, you may not be able to answer all of the questions on this checklist. That's fine. Just be prepared to think about them later.

NOTE: It is not necessary to think about the elements of a writing situation in the exact order listed in this chart.

SUBJECT

— Has a subject (or a range of possible subjects) been given to you, or are you free to choose your own?

— Why is your subject worth writing about? How might readers benefit from reading about it?

— How broadly can you cover the subject? Do you need to narrow it to a more specific topic (because of length restrictions, for instance)?

— How detailed should your coverage be?

SOURCES OF INFORMATION

— Where will your information come from: Personal experience? Direct observation? Interviews? Questionnaires? Reading?

— If your information comes from reading, what sort of documentation is required?

PURPOSE

— Why are you writing: To inform readers? To persuade them? To entertain them? To call them to action? Some combination of these?

Assessing the writing situation (continued)

AUDIENCE

— How well informed are your readers about the subject? What do you want them to learn about the subject?

— How interested and attentive are they likely to be? Will they resist any of your ideas?

— What is your relationship to them: Employee to supervisor? Citizen to citizen? Expert to novice? Scholar to scholar?

— How much time are they willing to spend reading?

— How sophisticated are they as readers? Do they have large vocabularies? Can they follow long and complex sentences?

LENGTH AND DOCUMENT DESIGN

— Are you working within any length specifications? If not, what length seems appropriate, given your subject, your purpose, and your audience?

— Must you use a particular design for your document? If so, do you have guidelines or examples that you can consult?

REVIEWERS AND DEADLINES

— Who will be reviewing your draft in progress — your instructor, a writing center tutor, your classmates, a friend, someone in your family?

— What are your deadlines? How much time will you need to allow for the various stages of writing, including proofreading the final draft?

Families: an experience with adoption, a portrait of a family member who has aged well, the challenges facing single parents, living with an alcoholic, a portrait of an ideal parent, growing up in a large family, the problems of split custody, an experience with child abuse, the depiction of parent-child relationships in a popular TV series, expectations versus the reality of marriage, overcoming sibling rivalry, the advantages or disadvantages of being a twin, overseeing a child's access to the World Wide Web

Health: a vegetarian diet, weight loss through hypnotism, a fitness program for the elderly, reasons not to smoke, the rights of smokers or nonsmokers, overcoming an addiction, Prozac as a treatment for depression, the side effects of a particular treatment for cancer, life as a diabetic, the benefits of an aerobic exercise such as swimming, caring for a person with AIDS, the effectiveness of herbal supplements

Sports and hobbies: an unusual sport such as free-fall parachuting or bungee jumping, surviving a wilderness program, bodybuilding, a sport from another culture, the philosophy of karate, the language of sports announcers, pros and cons of banning boxing, coaching a Little League team, cutting the costs of an expensive sport such as skiing, a portrait of a favorite sports figure, sports for the handicapped, the discipline required for a sport such as gymnastics, the rewards of a hobby such as woodworking, salary caps for professional athletes

The arts: working behind the scenes at a theater, censorship of rap lyrics, photography as an art form, the Japanese tea ceremony, the influence of African art on Picasso, the appeal of a local art museum, a portrait of a favorite musician or artist, performing as a musician, a high school for the arts, science fiction as a serious form of literature, a humorous description of romance novels or hard-boiled detective thrillers

Social justice: an experience with racism or sexism, affirmative action, reverse discrimination, making public transportation accessible for the physically handicapped, an experience as a juror, a local program to aid the homeless, discrimination against homosexuals, pros and cons of a national drinking age of twenty-one

Death and dying: working on a suicide hotline, the death of a loved one, a brush with death, caring for terminally ill patients, assisted suicide, the Buddhist view of death, explaining death to a child, passive euthanasia, death with dignity, an out-of-body experience

Violence and crime: an experience with a gun, a wartime experience, violence on television news programs, visiting a friend in prison, alternative sentencing for first offenders, victims' rights, a successful program to eliminate violence in a public high school, Internet fraud, capital punishment, preventing terrorist attacks, domestic violence and the courts

Nature and ecology: safety of nuclear power plants, solar energy, wind energy, air pollution in the national parks, forest fires on the California coast, grizzly bears in Yellowstone, communication among dolphins, organic gardening, backpacking in the Rockies, marine ecology, cleaning up Boston Harbor, the preservation of beaches in Delaware

Science and technology: genetic engineering, an experimental farming technique, a medical breakthrough, free speech and the Internet, the search for extraterrestrial life

Many of these subjects are too broad. Part of your challenge as a writer will be whittling broad subjects down to manageable topics. If you are limited to a few pages, for example, you could not possibly do justice to a subject as broad as "sports for the handicapped." You would be wise to restrict your paper to a topic more manageable in the space allowed—perhaps a description of the Saturday morning athletic program your college offers for handicapped children. The chart on page 8 suggests specific ways to narrow a subject to a topic.

The writing process

Ways to narrow a subject to a topic

SUBDIVIDING YOUR SUBJECT

Many subjects can be subdivided. Instead of writing about censorship of popular songs, for example, you might select a subdivision of this general subject: government labeling of CDs for content. Or instead of writing about homelessness in general, you might focus on the homeless in a particular city.

RESTRICTING YOUR PURPOSE

Often you can restrict your purpose. For example, if your subject is drug testing in the workplace, you might at first hope to persuade readers that it should be banned in all situations. Upon further reflection, however, you might realize that this goal is more than you could hope to accomplish, given your word limit. By adopting a more limited purpose — to show that drug testing is unreliable, to argue that its use by private employers should be banned, or to demonstrate that it violates an innocent person's right to privacy — you would have a better chance of success.

RESTRICTING YOUR AUDIENCE

Consider writing for a particular audience. For example, instead of writing to a general audience on a subject such as teenage pregnancy, you might address persons with a special interest in the subject: young people, parents, or counselors working for Planned Parenthood.

CONSIDERING THE INFORMATION AVAILABLE TO YOU

Look at the information you have collected. If you have gathered a great deal of information on one aspect of your subject (for example, discrimination against persons with AIDS) and less information on other aspects (such as the causes of AIDS or promising treatments for AIDS), you may have found your topic.

Sources of information

Where will your facts, details, and examples come from? Can your topic be illustrated by personal experience, or will you need to search out relevant information through direct observation, interviews, questionnaires, or reading?

PERSONAL EXPERIENCE   You can develop many topics wholly through personal experience, depending of course on your own life experiences. The students who wrote about life-guarding, learning disabilities, weight loss through hypnotism, and free-fall parachuting all spoke with the voice of experience, as did those who wrote about flextime, coaching a Little League team, and company-sponsored day care. When narrowing their subjects, those students chose to limit themselves to information they had at hand. For example, instead of writing about company-sponsored day care in general—a subject that would have required a great deal of research—one student limited her discussion to the successful day care center at the company for which she worked.

DIRECT OBSERVATION   Direct observation is an excellent means of collecting information about a wide range of subjects, such as male-female relationships on the television program *Dawson's Creek,* the clichéd language of sports announcers, or the appeal of a local art museum. For such subjects, do not rely on your memory alone; your information will be fresher and more detailed if you actively collect it, with a notebook or tape recorder in hand. As writer Stuart Chase advises young journalists assigned to report on their city's water system, "You will write a better article if you heave yourself out of a comfortable chair and go down in tunnel 3 and get soaked."

INTERVIEWS AND QUESTIONNAIRES   Interviews and questionnaires can supply you with detailed and interesting information on a variety of subjects. A nursing student interested in the care of terminally ill patients might interview nurses at a hospice; a political science major might speak with a local judge to learn about alternative sentencing for first offenders; a future teacher might conduct a survey on the classroom use of computers in local elementary schools.

It is a good idea to tape interviews to preserve any lively quotations that you might want to weave into your essay. Keep questionnaires simple and specify a deadline to ensure that you get a reasonable number of responses. (See also 49g.)

READING   Reading will be your primary source of information for many college assignments, which will generally be of two kinds: (1) analytical assignments that call for a close reading of one book, essay, or literary work and (2) research assignments that ask you to find and consult a variety of sources on a particular topic.

For analytical essays, you can usually assume that your reader is familiar with the work and has a copy of it at hand. You select details from the work not to inform readers but to support an interpretation. When you quote from the work, page references are often sufficient. For research papers, however, you cannot assume that your reader is familiar with your sources or has them close at hand. This means that you must formally document all quoted and summarized or paraphrased material (see 52). When in doubt about the need for documentation, consult your instructor.

Purpose

Your purpose will often be dictated by the specific writing situation that faces you. Perhaps you have been asked to take minutes for a club meeting, to draft a letter requesting payment from a client, or to describe the results of a biology experiment. Even though your overall purpose is fairly obvious in such situations, a close look at that purpose can help you make a variety of necessary decisions. How detailed should the minutes be? Is your purpose to summarize the meeting or to establish a careful record of discussion in case future controversies arise? How firmly should your letter request payment? Do you need the money at all costs, or do you hope to get it without risking loss of the client's business? How technical does your biology professor want your report to be?

In many writing situations, part of your challenge will be discovering a purpose. Consider, for example, the topic of magnet schools—schools that draw students from different neighborhoods because of features such as advanced science classes or late-afternoon day care. Your purpose could be to inform parents of the options available in your county. Or you might argue that the county's magnet schools are not promoting racial integration as had been planned. Or you might propose that the board of education create a magnet high school for the arts on your college campus.

Although no precise guidelines will lead you to a purpose, you can begin by asking yourself which one or more of the following aims you hope to accomplish.

PURPOSES FOR WRITING

to inform	to evaluate
to persuade	to recommend
to call readers to action	to request
to change attitudes	to propose
to analyze	to provoke thought
to argue	to express feelings
to theorize	to entertain
to summarize	to give aesthetic pleasure

It is surprising how often writers misjudge their own purposes: informing, for example, when they should be recommending; summarizing when they should be analyzing; or expressing feelings about problems instead of proposing solutions. Before beginning any writing task, therefore, pause to ask, "Why am I communicating with my readers?" And this question will lead you to another important question: "Just who are those readers?"

Audience

Audience analysis can often lead you to an effective strategy for reaching your readers. One writer, whose purpose was to persuade teenagers not to smoke, jotted down the following observations about her audience:

dislike lectures, especially from older people

have little sense of their own mortality

are concerned about physical appearance and image

want to be socially accepted

have limited budgets

This analysis led the writer to focus more on the social aspects of smoking (she pointed out, for instance, that kissing a smoker is like licking an ashtray) than on the health risks. Her audience analysis also warned her against adopting a preachy tone that her readers might find offensive. Instead of lecturing to her audience, she decided to draw examples from her own experience as a hooked smoker: burning holes in her best sweater, driving in zero-degree weather late at night in search of an open tavern to buy cigarettes, rummaging through ashtrays for stale butts, and so on. The result was an essay that reached its readers instead of alienating them.

Of course, in some writing situations the audience will not be neatly defined for you. Nevertheless, many of the choices that you make as you write will tell readers who you think they are (novices or experts, for example), so it is best to be consistent—even if this means creating an audience that is in some sense a fiction.

For an audience checklist, see the chart on page 5.

BUSINESS AUDIENCES   Writers in the business world often find themselves writing for multiple audiences. A letter to a client, for instance, might be distributed to sales representatives as well. Readers of a report may include persons with and without technical expertise or readers who want details and those who prefer a quick overview.

To satisfy the demands of multiple audiences, business writers have developed a variety of strategies: attaching cover letters to detailed reports, adding boldface headings, placing summaries in the left margin, and so on.

ACADEMIC AUDIENCES   In the academic world, considerations of audience can be more complex than they seem at first. Your professor will read your essay, of course, but most professors play multiple roles while reading. Their first and most obvious roles are as coach and judge; less obvious is their role as an intelligent and objective reader, the kind of person who might reasonably be informed, convinced, entertained, or called to action by what you have to say.

Some professors create writing assignments that specify an audience, such as a hypothetical supervisor, readers of a local newspaper, or fellow academics in a particular field of study. Other professors expect you to imagine an audience appropriate to your purpose and your subject. Still others prefer that you write for a general audience of educated readers—nonspecialists who can be expected to read with an intelligent, critical eye. When in doubt about an appropriate audience for a particular assignment, check with your professor.

Length and document design

Writers seldom have complete control over length and document design. Journalists usually write within strict word limits set by their editors, businesspeople routinely aim for conciseness, and most college assignments specify an approximate length.

Certain document designs may also be required by your writing situation. Specific formats are used in the business world for documents such as letters, memos, reports, budget analyses, and personnel records. In the academic world, you may need to learn precise conventions for lab reports, critiques, research papers, and so on. For most undergraduate essays, a standard format is acceptable (see 6a).

In some writing situations, you will be free to create your own document design, complete with headings, displayed lists, and perhaps even visuals, such as charts and graphs. Quite sophisticated results are now possible with software, and both writers and readers are becoming increasingly interested in designs that improve readability. For a discussion of the principles of document design, see 5.

Reviewers and deadlines

Professional and business writers rarely work alone. They work with reviewers, often called editors, who offer advice throughout the writing process. In college classes, too, the use of reviewers is increasingly common. Some instructors will play the role of reviewer for you; others may ask you to visit your college's writing center. Still others schedule peer review sessions in class (sometimes conducted online, in a networked classroom). Such sessions give you a chance to hear what other students think about your draft in progress — and to play the role of reviewer yourself.

Deadlines are a key element of any writing situation. They tell you what is possible and help you plan your time. For complex writing projects, such as research papers, you'll need to plan your time quite carefully. By working backward from the final deadline, you can create a schedule of target dates for completing various parts of the process. (See p. 520 for an example.)

EXERCISE 1-1

Choose one of the subject areas mentioned on pages 6–7 and add at least five subjects to those already on the list. If other members of your class have also done this exercise, pool the results.

EXERCISE 1-2

Narrow five of the following subjects into topics that would be manageable for an essay of two to five pages.

1. Working behind the scenes at a theater
2. A sport from another culture
3. Domestic violence and the courts
4. The advantages or disadvantages of being a twin
5. An experience with adoption
6. The side effects of a particular treatment for cancer
7. Computers in the classroom
8. Parochial schools
9. Performing as a musician
10. An experience with racism or sexism

EXERCISE 1-3

Which of the following subjects might be illustrated wholly by personal experience? For the others, suggest possible sources of information: direct observation, interviews, questionnaires, or reading.

1. The problems of split custody
2. Working in an emergency room
3. Backpacking in the Rockies
4. The influence of African art on Picasso
5. Violence on television news programs
6. The discipline required for a sport such as gymnastics
7. Photography as an art form
8. Online marketing techniques

9. A local program to aid the homeless
10. Visiting a friend in prison

EXERCISE 1–4

Suggest a purpose and an audience for five of the following subjects.

1. A vegetarian diet
2. Cutting the costs of an expensive sport such as skiing
3. The challenges facing single parents
4. Advantages of flextime for workers and employers
5. Growing up in a large family
6. Pros and cons of a national speed limit
7. Science fiction as a serious form of literature
8. An unusual sport such as bungee jumping
9. A police officer's workday
10. Working on a suicide hotline

ON THE WEB

For an electronic exercise on considering purpose and audience, go to
www.dianahacker.com/bedhandbook

and click on ▶ **Electronic Writing Exercises**
  ▶ **E-ex 1–1**

1b   Experiment with ways to explore your subject.

Instead of just plunging into a first draft, experiment with one or more techniques for exploring your subject, perhaps one of these:

listing	annotating texts and taking notes
clustering	freewriting
asking questions	keeping a journal
responding to prompts	talking and listening

You can use most of these techniques whether you are work-ing with pencil and paper or entering ideas into a computer.

Whatever technique you turn to, the goal is the same: to generate a wealth of ideas. At this early stage of the writing process, you should aim for quantity, not necessarily qual-ity, of ideas. If an idea proves to be off the point, trivial, or too far-fetched, you can always throw it out later.

Listing

You might begin by simply listing ideas, putting them down in the order in which they occur to you—a technique some-times known as *brainstorming.* Here, for example, is a list one student writer jotted down:

The Phillips Collection

Washington, D.C.

1612 21st Street, close to Mass. Ave.

near Dupont Circle, in an interesting neighborhood

hard to find a parking space; better to take subway

elegant red brick townhouse, once home of Duncan and Marjorie Phillips (art collectors)

turned into a museum in 1918

facade reminds me of a bygone era—teas and debutante balls

free concerts on Sundays

mostly Impressionists, Postimpressionists, and modern masters

Renoir's *Luncheon of the Boating Party*—warm and joyful—you can almost smell the breeze off the Seine and hear the hum of conversation

you can wander through small rooms filled with paintings by van Gogh, Degas, Cézanne, Bonnard, and Klee

the Rothko room, with huge color paintings—pulsating, sen-suous reds, yellows, blues, greens the new wing—no more bygone era—clean and uncluttered lines appropriate for modern masters like Picasso, Pollock, Dalí, Braque

a walled garden

The ideas appear here in the order in which they first occurred to the writer. Later she felt free to rearrange them, to cluster them under general categories, to delete some, and to add others. In other words, she treated her initial list as a source of ideas and a springboard to new ideas, not as an outline.

Clustering

Unlike listing, the technique of clustering highlights relationships among ideas. To cluster ideas, write your topic in the center of a sheet of paper, draw a circle around it, and surround that with related ideas connected to it with lines. If

some of the satellite ideas lead to more specific clusters, write them down as well. The writer of the diagram on page 18 was exploring ideas for an essay on home uses for computers.

Asking questions

By asking relevant questions, you can generate many ideas — and you can make sure that you have adequately surveyed your subject. When gathering material for a story, journalists routinely ask themselves Who? What? When? Where? Why? and How? In addition to helping journalists get started, these questions ensure that they will not overlook an important fact: the date of a prospective summit meeting, for example, or the exact location of a neighborhood burglary.

Whenever you are writing about events, whether current or historical, the journalist's questions are one way to get started. One student, whose subject was the negative reaction in 1915 to D. W. Griffith's silent film *The Birth of a Nation,* began exploring her topic with this set of questions:

Who objected to the film?

What were the objections?

When were protests first voiced?

Where were protests most strongly expressed?

Why did protesters object to the film?

How did protesters make their views known?

In the academic world, scholars often generate ideas with questions related to a specific discipline: one set of questions for analyzing short stories, another for evaluating experiments in social psychology, still another for reporting field experiences in anthropology. If you are writing in a particular discipline, try to discover the questions that scholars typically explore.

Responding to prompts

Composition students are sometimes asked to respond to software (or online) prompts as a way of getting started on an assignment. Here, for example, is a screen from a pre-writing program designed to help students begin work on a descriptive essay.

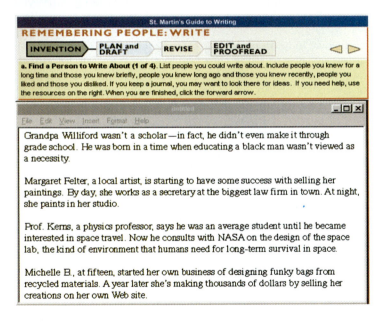

St. Martin's Guide to Writing

REMEMBERING PEOPLE: WRITE

INVENTION ▷ PLAN and DRAFT ▷ REVISE ▷ EDIT and PROOFREAD   ◁ ▷

a. Find a Person to Write About (1 of 4). List people you could write about. Include people you knew for a long time and those you knew briefly, people you knew long ago and those you knew recently, people you liked and those you disliked. If you keep a journal, you may want to look there for ideas. If you need help, use the resources on the right. When you are finished, click the forward arrow.

untitled   _ □ ×

File Edit View Insert Format Help

Grandpa Williford wasn't a scholar—in fact, he didn't even make it through grade school. He was born in a time when educating a black man wasn't viewed as a necessity.

Margaret Felter, a local artist, is starting to have some success with selling her paintings. By day, she works as a secretary at the biggest law firm in town. At night, she paints in her studio.

Prof. Kerns, a physics professor, says he was an average student until he became interested in space travel. Now he consults with NASA on the design of the space lab, the kind of environment that humans need for long-term survival in space.

Michelle B., at fifteen, started her own business of designing funky bags from recycled materials. A year later she's making thousands of dollars by selling her creations on her own Web site.

Annotating texts and taking notes

When you write about reading, one of the best ways to explore ideas is to mark up the text—on the pages themselves if you own the work, on photocopies if you don't. For examples of annotated texts, see pages 479–82. In addition to annotating texts, you will often want to take notes on your reading (see 51c).

Freewriting

In its purest form, freewriting is simply nonstop writing. You set aside ten minutes or so and write whatever comes to you, without pausing to think about word choice, spelling, or even meaning. If you get stuck, you can write about being stuck, but you should keep your pencil moving. The point is to loosen up, relax, and see what happens. Even if nothing much happens, you have lost only ten minutes. It's more likely, though, that something interesting will emerge on paper—perhaps an eloquent sentence, an honest expression of feeling, or a line of thought worth exploring.

To explore ideas on a particular topic, consider using a technique known as *focused freewriting.* Again, you write quickly and freely—without regard for word choice, spelling, punctuation, or even paragraphing—but this time you focus on a subject and pay some attention to meaning.

Keeping a journal

A journal is a collection of personal, exploratory writings. An entry in a journal can be any length—from a single sentence to several pages—and it is likely to be informal and experimental.

In a journal, meant for your eyes only, you can take risks. In one entry, for example, you might do some freewriting or focused freewriting. In another, you might pose a series of interesting questions, whether or not you have the answers. In still another, you might play around with language for the sheer fun of it: writing "purple prose," for instance, or parodying the style of a favorite author or songwriter.

Keeping a journal can be an enriching experience in its own right, since it allows you to explore issues of concern to you without worrying about what someone else thinks. A journal can also serve as a sourcebook of ideas to draw on in future essays; on rare occasions, in fact, a journal entry may emerge as a polished essay of interest to readers other than yourself. Some writers find that they do their best work when writing for themselves, deliberately ignoring the constraints of a formal writing situation.

Should you decide to keep a journal, here are some prompts to help you get started.

SOME IDEAS FOR JOURNAL WRITINGS

—Record some stories from your family's history.

—Write about a moral dilemma that you (or a friend or relative) once faced or that you now face.

—Write a history of your involvement with a hobby or an art form; or write about current projects.

—Write an imaginary dialogue between two major historical figures you have read about, or a scientist and a philosopher, or characters in different novels.

—Comment on an interesting idea encountered in one of your college classes—a historical interpretation, a psychological theory, a new biological breakthrough.

—Parody the style of a favorite author or songwriter. Or mimic the style of a genre with which you are familiar (such as romances, hard-boiled detective novels, or sports writing).

Talking and listening

The early stages of the writing process need not be lonely. Many writers begin a writing project by brainstorming ideas in a group, debating a point with friends, or engaging in conversation with a professor. Others turn to themselves for company—by talking nonstop into a tape recorder.

Some writers "virtually converse" by exchanging ideas through e-mail, by joining an Internet chat group, or by following a mailing list discussion. If you are part of a networked classroom, you may be encouraged to exchange ideas with your classmates and instructor in an electronic workshop. One advantage of engaging in such discussions is that while you are "talking" you are actually writing. That writing might prove useful later. For example, a student who participated in the following chat was able to cut and paste some of her own words into an essay.

Bay State University - Bay State University - Bay State University - Bay State

The Composition Chat Room

User Name:

[   ]

Password:

[   ]

[Log In]

Forgot your password?

[Help]

[Quit]

Chat Message:

[   ] [Submit]

Yvette Reid (10:47:42 AM): Tony, my essay on working with refugees is too short. Any ideas?

Anthony Rivera (10:47:55 AM): Yvette, why not write more about real refugee families you've worked with?

Yvette Reid (10:48:25 AM): Good idea. Maybe I could use Tran Luc's family to show how hard it is to help refugee children adapt to our school system. Both parents were at first too respectful of authority to contact Tran's teacher. When I first met them, they even viewed me as an authority!

There are **2** users logged on.

Talking can be a good way to get to know your audience. If you're planning to write a narrative, for instance, you can test its dramatic effect on a group of friends. Or if you hope to advance a certain argument, you can try it out on listeners who hold a different view.

As you have no doubt discovered, conversation can deepen and refine your ideas before you even begin to set them down on paper. Our first thoughts are not necessarily our wisest thoughts; by talking and listening to others we can all stretch our potential as thinkers and as writers.

EXERCISE 1–5

Generate a list of at least fifteen items for one of the subjects listed on pages 6–7.

EXERCISE 1–6

Using the technique of clustering or freewriting, explore one of the subjects listed on pages 6–7.

1c   Settle on a tentative focus.

As you explore your subject, you will begin to see possible ways to focus your material. At this point, try to settle on a tentative central idea. The more complex your subject, the more your initial central idea will change as your drafts evolve.

For many types of writing, your central idea can be asserted in one sentence, a generalization preparing readers for the supporting details that will follow. Such a sentence, which will ordinarily appear in the opening paragraph of your finished essay, is called a *thesis.* A successful thesis—like the following, all taken from articles in *Smithsonian*—points both the writer and the reader in a definite direction.

> Much maligned and the subject of unwarranted fears, most bats are harmless and highly beneficial.

Geometric forms known as fractals may have a profound effect on how we view the world, not only in art and film but in many branches of science and technology, from astronomy to economics to predicting the weather.

Aside from his more famous identities as colonel of the Rough Riders and president of the United States, Theodore Roosevelt was a lifelong professional man of letters.

The thesis sentence usually contains a key word or controlling idea that limits its focus. The preceding sentences, for example, prepare for essays that focus on the *beneficial* aspects of bats, the *effect* of fractals on how we view the world, and Roosevelt's identity as a writer, or *man of letters.*

It's a good idea to formulate a thesis early in the writing process, perhaps by jotting it on scratch paper, by putting it at the head of a rough outline, or by attempting to write an introductory paragraph that includes the thesis. Your tentative thesis will probably be less graceful than the thesis you include in the final version of your essay. Here, for example, is one student's early effort:

Although they both play percussion instruments, drummers and percussionists are very different.

The thesis that appeared in the final draft of the student's paper was more polished:

Two types of musicians play percussion instruments—drummers and percussionists—and they are as different as Quiet Riot and the New York Philharmonic.

Don't worry too soon about the exact wording of your thesis, however, because your main point may change as you refine your ideas.

For a more detailed discussion of the thesis, see 2a.

1d   Sketch a tentative plan.

Once you have generated some ideas and formulated a tentative thesis, you may want to sketch an informal outline. Informal outlines can take many forms. Perhaps the most common is simply the thesis followed by a list of major supporting ideas.

> Hawaii is losing its cultural identity.
>
> — pure-blooded Hawaiians increasingly rare
>
> — native language diluted
>
> — natives forced off ancestral lands
>
> — little emphasis on native culture in schools
>
> — customs exaggerated and distorted by tourism

Clustering diagrams, often used to generate ideas, can also serve as rough outlines (see p. 18). And if you began by jotting down a list of ideas (see pp. 17–18), you may be able to turn the list into a rough outline by crossing out some ideas, adding others, and numbering the ideas to create a logical order.

Planning with headings

When writing a relatively long college paper or business document, consider using headings to guide readers. In addition to helping readers follow the organization of your final draft, headings can be a powerful planning tool, especially if you are working on a computer. You can type in your tentative thesis and then experiment with possible headings; once you have settled on the headings that work best, you can begin typing in chunks of text beneath each heading.

Here, for example, is what one student typed into his computer when planning a long history paper. The headings, written in the form of questions, are centered.

> Although we will never know whether Nathan Bedford
> Forrest directly ordered the massacre of Union
> troops at Fort Pillow, evidence strongly suggests
> that he was responsible for it.
>
> What happened at Fort Pillow?
> Did Forrest order the massacre?
> Did the men have reason to think Forrest
> wanted a massacre?

For more detailed advice about using headings, see pages 104–07. For examples of papers that use headings, see pages 716–26 and 759–63.

When to use a formal outline

Early in the writing process, rough outlines have certain advantages over their more formal counterparts: They can be produced more quickly, they are more obviously tentative, and they can be revised more easily should the need arise. However, a formal outline may be useful later in the writing process, after you have written a rough draft, especially if your subject is complex.

The following formal outline brought order to a complex subject, methods for limiting and disposing of nuclear waste. Notice that the student's thesis is an important part of the outline. Everything else in the outline supports it, either directly or indirectly.

Thesis: Although various methods for limiting or disposing of nuclear wastes have been proposed, each has serious drawbacks.

I.   The process of limiting nuclear waste through partitioning and transmutation has serious drawbacks.

  A. The process is complex and costly.

  B. Nuclear workers' exposure to radiation would increase.

II. Antarctic ice sheet disposal is problematic for scientific and legal reasons.

  A. Our understanding of the behavior of ice sheets is too limited.

  B. An international treaty prohibits disposal in Antarctica.

III. Space disposal is unthinkable.

  A. The risk of an accident and resulting worldwide disaster is great.

  B. The cost is prohibitive.

  C. The method would be unpopular at home and abroad.

IV. Seabed disposal is unwise because we do not know enough about the procedure or its impact.

  A. Scientists have not yet solved technical difficulties.

  B. We do not fully understand the impact of such disposal on the ocean's ecology.

V.   Deep underground disposal endangers public safety and creates political problems.

  A. Geologists disagree about the safest disposal sites, and no sites are completely safe.

  B. There is much political pressure against the plan from citizens who do not want their states to become nuclear dumps.

Guidelines for constructing an outline

1. Put the thesis at the top.
2. Make items at the same level of generality as parallel as possible (see 9).
3. Use sentences unless phrases are clear.
4. Use the conventional system of numbers and letters for the levels of generality.

    I.
    - A.
    - B.
        1.
        2.
            - a.
            - b.

    II.
    - A.
    - B.
        1.
        2.
            - a.
            - b.

5. Always use at least two subdivisions for a category, since nothing can be divided into fewer than two parts.
6. Limit the number of major sections in the outline; if the list of roman numerals begins to look like a laundry list, find some way of clustering the items into a few major categories with more subcategories.
7. Be flexible; in other words, be prepared to change your outline as your drafts evolve.

2

Rough out an initial draft.

As you rough out an initial draft, keep your planning materials—lists, diagrams, outlines, and so on—close at hand. With your earlier thoughts close by, you won't need to stare at a blank page or screen in search of ideas. In addition to helping you get started, those notes and blueprints will encourage you to keep moving. Writing tends to flow better when it is drafted relatively quickly, without many starts and stops. The trick, of course, is to relax—to overcome the fear that grips many of us as we face that blank page.

LOOKING AT YOURSELF AS A WRITER
Writer's block

At one time or another, we all experience writer's block, but if writer's block is a chronic problem for you, consider some common causes and cures.

CAUSE   You expect your ideas to emerge full-blown, like Athena from the head of Zeus.

CURE   Look at writing as a process of discovery, not just a means of expressing fixed thoughts. As Joan Didion puts it, "I write entirely to find out what I'm thinking, what I'm looking at, what I see, and what it means."

CAUSE   You demand that your sentences all be stylish and perfectly grammatical right from the start.

CURE   Don't be so hard on yourself. Follow the practice of Jacques Barzun, who lets his rough draft sentences be "as stupid" as they wish.

Writer's block (continued)

CAUSE   You cling to what writing teacher Mike Rose calls rigid rules—such as "Don't use *I* or *you*" or "Be descriptive."

CURE   Treat most rules as "rules of thumb"—guidelines that can be violated at least some of the time. The *I* and *you* points of view can be effective, and not every paper needs to dazzle readers with vivid sensory details.

CAUSE   You always begin with the hardest part, the introduction, and you feel that you must get it just right before moving on.

CURE   Try drafting the easiest paragraph first. By the time you have drafted it, you may begin to gain confidence. You can always return to the introduction later, once you have loosened up.

CAUSE   You're confused about the assignment or about the best way to get started on it.

CURE   You might call or visit your instructor during office hours. Tutors at your school's writing center might also help; they have been trained to analyze assignments and give you tips on getting started. They can also help later in the writing process—after you have written a rough draft.

ON THE WEB

For links to online writing labs and other resources that will help you with the writing process, go to
www.dianahacker.com/bedhandbook

and click on   ▶ **Links Library**
                    ▶ **The Writing Process**

2a   For most types of writing, draft an introduction that includes a thesis.

The introduction announces the main point; the body develops it, usually in several paragraphs; the conclusion drives it home. You can begin drafting, however, at any point. If you find it difficult to introduce a paper that you have not yet written, you can write the body first and save the introduction for later.

For most writing tasks, your introduction will be a paragraph of 50 to 150 words. Perhaps the most common strategy is to open the paragraph with a few sentences that engage the reader and to conclude it with a statement of the essay's main point. The sentence stating the main point is called a *thesis.* (See also 1c.) In the following examples, the thesis has been italicized.

> To the Australian aborigines, the Dreamtime was the time of creation. It was then that the creatures of the earth, including man, came into being. There are many legends about that mystical period, but unfortunately, the koala does not fare too well in any of them. *Slow-witted though it is in life, the koala is generally depicted in myth and folklore as a trickster and a thief.*
> —Roger Caras, "What's a Koala?"

> When I was sixteen, I married and moved to a small town to live. My new husband nervously showed me the house he had rented. It was after dark when we arrived there, and I remember wondering why he seemed so apprehensive about my reaction to the house. I thought the place seemed shabby but potentially cozy and quite livable inside. The morning sun revealed the reason for his anxiety by exposing the squalor outdoors. Up to that point, my contact with any reality but that of my own middle-class childhood had come from books. *The next four years in a small Iowa town taught me that reading about poverty is a lot different from living with it.*
> —Julie Reardon, student

Ideally, the sentences leading to the thesis should hook the reader, perhaps with one of the following:

a startling statistic or unusual fact

a vivid example

a description

a paradoxical statement

a quotation or bit of dialogue

a question

an analogy

a joke or an anecdote

Such hooks are particularly important when you cannot assume your reader's interest in the subject. Hooks are less necessary in scholarly essays and other writing aimed at readers with a professional interest in the subject.

Although the thesis frequently appears at the end of the introduction, it can just as easily appear at the beginning. Much work-related writing, in which a straightforward approach is most effective, commonly begins with the thesis.

> *Flextime scheduling, which has proved its effectiveness at the Library of Congress, should be introduced on a trial basis at the main branch of the Montgomery County Public Library.* By offering flexible work hours, the library can boost employee morale, cut down on absenteeism, and expand its hours of operation. —David Warren, student

For some types of writing, it may be difficult or impossible to express the central idea in a thesis sentence; or it may be unwise or unnecessary to put a thesis sentence in the essay itself. A personal narrative, for example, may have a focus too subtle to be distilled in a single sentence, and such a sentence might ruin the story. Strictly informative writing, like that found in many business memos, may be difficult to summarize in a thesis. In such instances, do not try to force the central idea into a thesis sentence. Instead, think in terms of an overriding purpose, which may or may not be stated directly.

Characteristics of an effective thesis

An effective thesis should be a generalization, not a fact; it should be limited, not too broad; and it should be sharply focused, not too vague.

Because a thesis must prepare readers for facts and details, it cannot itself be a fact. It must always be a generalization demanding proof or further development.

TOO FACTUAL   The first polygraph was developed by Dr. John A. Larson in 1921.

REVISED   Because the polygraph has not been proved reliable, even under the most controlled conditions, its use by private employers should be banned.

Although a thesis must be a generalization, it must not be *too* general. You will need to narrow the focus of any thesis that you cannot adequately develop in the space allowed. Unless you were writing a book or a very long research paper, the following thesis would be too broad.

TOO BROAD   Many drugs are now being used successfully to treat mental illnesses.

You would need to restrict the thesis, perhaps like this:

REVISED   Despite its risks and side effects, Prozac is an effective treatment for depression.

Finally, a thesis should be sharply focused, not too vague. Beware of any thesis containing a fuzzy, hard-to-define word such as *interesting, good,* or *disgusting.*

TOO VAGUE   Many of the songs played on station WXQP are disgusting.

The word *disgusting* is needlessly vague. To sharpen the focus of this thesis, the writer should be more specific.

> **REVISED** Of the songs played on station WXQP, all too many depict sex crudely, sanction the beating or rape of women, or foster gang violence.

In the process of making a too-vague thesis more precise, you may find yourself outlining the major sections of your paper, as in the preceding example. This technique, known as *blueprinting,* helps readers know exactly what to expect as they read on. It also helps you, the writer, control the shape of your essay.

The thesis sentence is central to so many types of writing that it is discussed in several other sections of this book:

— in 46, writing about texts

— in 47, writing arguments

— in 57, MLA research papers

— in 58, MLA literature papers

— in 59 and 60, APA and *Chicago* research papers

LOOKING AT YOURSELF AS A WRITER
The thesis sentence

In much college writing, you will need to state a thesis in your introduction and to support the thesis in the body of your essay. Although the thesis is usually only one sentence long, it can be surprisingly hard to write. When you have trouble formulating a good thesis, consider possible causes and cures for your difficulties.

CAUSE You are trying to write the thesis sentence by itself.
CURE Try drafting the whole introduction, placing the thesis sentence in context (usually at the end of the introduction).

The thesis sentence *(continued)*

CAUSE Once you have written a thesis, you tend to cling to it, even if the body of the essay doesn't exactly support it.

CURE View your initial thesis as tentative. As you draft an essay, you may discover a main idea that is more interesting than the one you began with. As writer E. M. Forster put it, "How do I know what I think until I see what I say?"

CAUSE You underestimate the importance of a clear thesis statement because you are unfamiliar with the academic world in which you are trying to write.

CURE Develop an appreciation for the goals of academic writing: to seek the truth, to argue a point, to propose solutions, to deepen insights, to clarify a theory, to challenge conventional wisdom. To reach any of these goals, you will need to articulate a thesis.

CAUSE You feel that a thesis sentence will not be significant unless it makes a grand, sweeping statement about life. But you lack the evidence to back up such a sweeping statement.

CURE Aim to do less, and you will accomplish more. As Darcy O'Brien advises writers, "Do not be grand. Try to get the ordinary into your writing. . . . Middletown today, not Mankind through the ages."

CAUSE You fear that a thesis sentence will sound too blunt. Perhaps this is because you come from a culture that values a more indirect approach. Or maybe you feel uncomfortable being assertive or lack the confidence to be assertive.

CURE Try to be flexible—to adapt to the needs of readers in your particular writing situation. You might also experiment with strategies for softening the tone of a thesis sentence without sacrificing clarity. With practice, writers can learn to assert a main idea simply and directly without sounding too blunt.

EXERCISE 2–1

In each of the following pairs, which sentence might work well as a thesis for a paper based on personal experience (not on reading)? What is the problem with the other one? Is it too factual? Too broad? Too vague?

1a. By networking with friends, a single parent can manage to strike a balance among work, school, a social life, and family.

 b. Single parents face many challenges as they try to juggle all of their responsibilities.

2a. From the time I was a young child, I have always had at least three cats.

 b. In addition to being the perfect size to be kept indoors, cats are clean, loving, graceful, and surprisingly intelligent animals.

3a. At the Special Olympics, disabled athletes are taught that with hard work and support from others they can accomplish anything: that they can indeed be winners.

 b. Working with the Special Olympics program is rewarding.

4a. Immigrants from many lands have made major contributions to American culture.

 b. When Uncle Jacob stepped onto Ellis Island with only a small suitcase and the clothes on his back, no one could have predicted that one day his stone carvings would grace many buildings and monuments in our nation's capital.

5a. History 201, taught by Professor Brown, is offered at 10 A.M. on Tuesdays and Thursdays.

 b. Whoever said that history is nothing but polishing tombstones must have missed History 201, because in Professor Brown's class history is very much alive.

EXERCISE 2–2

In each of the following pairs, which sentence might work well as a thesis for a paper based on reading? What is the problem with the other one? Is it too factual? Too broad? Too vague?

1a. So far, research suggests that zero-emissions vehicles are not a sensible solution to the problem of steadily increasing air pollution.

b. Because air pollution is of serious concern to many people in the world today, several government agencies in the United States have implemented plans to begin solving the problem.

2a. Anorexia nervosa is a dangerous, sometimes deadly eating - disorder found mainly in young, upper-middle-class teen-agers.

b. The eating disorder anorexia nervosa is rarely cured by one treatment alone; only by combining drug therapy with psy-chotherapy and family therapy can the patient begin the long, torturous journey to wellness.

3a. Although we cannot fully harness the powers that nature wields, we can manage most naturally occurring forest fires to benefit our national parks.

b. The Yellowstone fires of 1988 taught many lessons to many people.

4a. Marijuana is classified by the Drug Enforcement Agency as a Schedule I drug.

b. If marijuana was legalized for medical purposes, we could re-lieve some of the suffering associated with AIDS, cancer, and glaucoma.

5a. On July 22, 1934, a man identified as John Dillinger was killed in the alley next to the Biograph Theater in Chicago.

b. Sweeping across the Midwest in the early 1930s, the Dillinger gang's crime wave epitomized the lawlessness of the era.

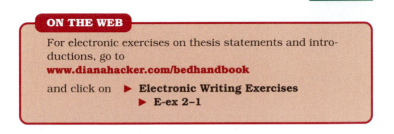

ON THE WEB

For electronic exercises on thesis statements and introductions, go to

www.dianahacker.com/bedhandbook

and click on ▶ **Electronic Writing Exercises**
▶ **E-ex 2–1**

2b Fill out the body.

Before drafting the body of an essay, take a careful look at
your introduction, focusing especially on your thesis sentence. What does the thesis promise readers? Try to keep
this focus in mind.

It's a good idea to have a plan in mind as well. If your
thesis sentence outlines a plan (see 2a) or if you have
sketched a preliminary outline, try to block out your paragraphs accordingly. If you do not have a plan, you would be
wise to pause for a moment and sketch one (see 1d). Of
course it is also possible to begin without a plan—assuming
you are prepared to treat your first attempt as a "discovery
draft" that will almost certainly be tossed (or radically
rewritten) once you discover what you really want to say.

For more detailed advice about paragraphs in the body
of an essay, see section 4.

2c Attempt a conclusion.

The conclusion should echo the main idea, without dully repeating it. Often the concluding paragraph can be relatively
short. By the end of the essay, readers should already understand your main point; your conclusion simply drives it
home and perhaps suggests its significance.

In addition to echoing your main idea, a conclusion might summarize the essay's key points, pose a question for future study, offer advice, or propose a course of action. To end an essay detailing the social skills required of a bartender, one writer concludes with some advice:

> If someone were to approach me one day looking for the secret to running a good bar, I suppose I would offer the following advice: Get your customers to pour out their ideas at a greater rate than you pour out the liquor. You will both win in the end.   — Kathleen Lewis, student

To make the conclusion memorable, you might include a detail, example, or image from the introduction to bring readers full circle; a quotation or bit of dialogue; an anecdote; or a humorous, witty, or ironic comment. To end a narrative describing a cash register holdup, one student uses an anecdote that includes some dialogue:

> It took me a long time to get over that incident. Countless times I found myself gasping as someone "pointed" a dollar bill at me. On one such occasion, a jovial little man buying a toy gun for his son came up to me and said in a Humphrey Bogart impression, "Give me all your money, Sweetheart." I didn't laugh. Instead, my heart skipped a beat, for I had heard those words before.   — Diana Crawford, student

Whatever concluding strategy you choose, avoid introducing wholly new ideas at the end of an essay. Also avoid apologies and other limp, indeterminate endings. The essay should end crisply, preferably on a positive note.

Do not become discouraged if the perfect conclusion eludes you at the rough-draft stage of the writing process. Because the conclusion is so closely tied to the rest of the essay in both content and tone, you may well decide to rework it (or even replace it) as your drafts evolve.

3

Make global revisions; then revise sentences.

Global revisions affect blocks of text longer than a sentence. They include improvements in focus, organization, content, and overall strategy. You will save yourself time if you handle global revisions before turning to sentence-level issues, because in the process of revising globally you may decide to delete sentences, paragraphs, or even larger chunks of text. There is little sense in revising sentences that may not even appear in your final draft.

Many of us resist global revisions because we find it difficult to distance ourselves from a draft. We tend to view our work from our own, not from our audience's, perspective. To distance yourself from a draft, put it aside for a while, preferably overnight or even longer. When you return to it, try to play the role of your audience as you read. If possible, enlist the help of reviewers — persons willing to play the role of audience for you.

Professors often set aside class time for peer review sessions in which students respond to one another's drafts in written comments, discussions, or both. In some courses, students use e-mail or other forms of electronic communication to send and receive comments on one another's rough drafts.

A checklist for reviewers appears on page 55, and guidelines for reviewers appear in the chart on page 44.

ON THE WEB

For an electronic exercise on responding to another student's writing, go to
www.dianahacker.com/bedhandbook

and click on ▶ **Electronic Writing Exercise**
▶ **E-ex 3–1**

The writing process

EXAMPLE OF GLOBAL REVISIONS

> Sports on TV--A Win or a Loss?
>
> Team sports are as much a part of Americain life as Mom and apple pie, and they have a good tendency to bring people together. They encourage team members to cooperate with one another, they also create shared enthusiasm among fans. Thanks to television, this togetherness now seems available to nearly all of us at the flick of a switch. We do not have to buy tickets, and travel to a stadium, to see the World Series or the Super Bowl, these games are on television. We can enjoy the game in the comfort of our own living room. ~~After Thanksgiving or Christmas dinner, the whole family may gather around the TV set to watch football together.~~ It would appear that television has done us a great service. But is this really the case?

Although television does make sports more accessible, it also creates a distance between the sport and the fans and between athletes and the teams they play for.

The advantage of television is that it provides sports fans with greater convenience.

[insert]
We can see more games than if we had to attend each one in person, and we can follow greater varieties of sports.

EXAMPLE OF SENTENCE-LEVEL REVISIONS

Televised
Sports ~~on TV~~--A Win or a Loss?

Team sports, ~~are~~ as much a part of American
tend
life as Mom and apple pie, ~~and they have a good~~
us
~~tendency~~ to bring ~~people~~ together. They encourage
and
team members to cooperate with one another, they
Because of
~~also~~ create shared enthusiasm among fans. ~~Thanks to~~
television, this togetherness now seems available
~~to nearly all of us~~ at the flick of a switch. ~~It~~
~~would appear that television has done us a great~~
~~service.~~ But is this really the case? Although
makes
television ~~does make~~ sports more accessible, it also
creates a distance between the sport and the fans
their
and between athletes and ~~the~~ teams. ~~they play for.~~

The advantage of television is that it provides
sports fans with greater convenience. We do not
have to buy tickets / and travel to a stadium / to
but
see the World Series or the Super Bowl / ~~these games~~
any
~~are on television. We~~ can enjoy ~~the~~ game in the
rooms.
comfort of our own living ~~room.~~ We can see more
games than if we had to attend each one in person,
a   *variety*
and we can follow greater ~~varieties~~ of sports.

Guidelines for peer reviewers

VIEW YOURSELF AS A COACH, NOT A JUDGE.

Think of yourself as a proposer of possibilities, not a dictator of revisions. It is the writer, after all, who will have to grapple with the task of improving the essay.

MAKE AT LEAST SOME DESCRIPTIVE COMMENTS.

Not all comments need to be evaluative. Sometimes it's helpful just to describe your response. For example, if the writer's subject is physical disabilities, you might comment, "I think your point is that many adults are insensitive and patronizing when they encounter persons with physical disabilities."

WHERE POSSIBLE, COMPLIMENT THE WRITER. BE SPECIFIC.

Vague compliments (such as "I liked your essay") sound insincere—and they aren't helpful. Point out specific successes. For example, you might mention that the writer's second paragraph contains a powerful example of insensitivity toward people with physical disabilities.

LINK SUGGESTIONS FOR IMPROVEMENT TO THE WRITER'S GOALS.

Criticism is constructive when it is offered in the right spirit. For example, you might advise the writer to put the most dramatic example last, where it will have the maximum impact on readers. Or you might suggest that a passage would gain power if abstractions were replaced with concrete details.

TELL THE WRITER WHERE YOU WOULD LIKE TO HEAR MORE.

When you indicate an interest in hearing more about a topic, the writer is often inspired to come up with useful and vivid details—such as a bit of dialogue that perfectly illustrates just how patronizing some people can be toward those with physical disabilities.

EXPRESS INTEREST IN READING THE NEXT DRAFT.

When your interest is sincere, expressing it can be a powerful motivation for a writer.

3a   Approach global revision in cycles.

Global revisions address the larger elements of writing. Frequently they can be quite dramatic. Whole paragraphs
might be dropped, others added. Material once stretched
over two or three paragraphs might be condensed into one.
Entire sections might be rearranged. Even the content may
change dramatically, for the process of revision stimulates
thought.

Major revising can be difficult, sometimes even painful.
You might discover, for example, that an essay's first three
paragraphs are nothing but padding, that its central argument tilts the wrong way, and that you sound like a stuffed
shirt throughout. But the sheer fact that you can see such
problems in your own writing is a sign of hope. Those opening paragraphs can be dropped, the argument's slant re-
aligned, the voice made more human.

Because the process of global revision can be overwhelming, it is best to approach it in cycles, with each cycle
encompassing a particular purpose for revising. Five common cycles of global revision are discussed in this section:

— Sharpening the focus
— Improving the organization
— Strengthening the content
— Clarifying the point of view
— Engaging the audience

You can handle these cycles in nearly any order, and you
may be able to skip or combine some of them. A chart summarizing these cycles appears on page 54.

If someone has reviewed your draft, you have already
begun to see which of these cycles most need your attention.
And by giving some thought to your overall purpose and audience, you'll discern even more clearly where your essay
does — and does not — need revision.

NOTE: When working on a computer, print out a hard copy so that you can read the draft as a whole rather than screen by screen. Once you have decided what global revisions may be needed, the computer, of course, is an excellent tool. In fact, because the computer saves time, it encourages you to experiment with global revisions. Should you combine two paragraphs? Would your conclusion make a good introduction? Might several paragraphs be rearranged for greater impact? With little risk, you can explore the possibilities. When a revision misfires, it is easy to restore your original draft.

Sharpening the focus

A draft is clearly focused when it fixes the reader's attention on one central idea and does not stray from that idea. You can sharpen the focus of a draft by clarifying the introduction (especially the thesis) and by deleting any text that is off the point.

CLARIFYING THE INTRODUCTION First you will want to make sure that your introduction looks and reads like an introduction. Can readers tell where the introduction stops and the body of the essay begins? Have you perhaps included material in the introduction that really belongs in the body of the essay? Is your introduction long-winded?

Next check to see whether the introduction focuses on the essay's main point. Does it let readers know what to expect as they read on? Does it make the significance of the subject clear so that readers will want to read on?

The most important sentence in the introduction is the thesis. (See 2a.) If your essay lacks a thesis, make sure that you have a good reason for not including one. If your thesis is poorly focused or if it doesn't accurately state the real point of the essay, you'll need to revise it.

DELETING TEXT THAT IS OFF THE POINT Compare the essay's introduction, particularly its thesis statement, with the body of the essay. Does the body of the essay fulfill the promise of the introduction? If not, one or the other must be adjusted. Either rebuild the introduction to fit the body of the paper or keep the introduction and delete any sentences or paragraphs that stray from its point.

Improving the organization

A draft is well organized when its major divisions are logical and easy for readers to follow. To improve the organization of your draft, consider taking one or more of the following actions: adding or sharpening topic sentences, moving blocks of text, reparagraphing, and inserting headings.

ADDING OR SHARPENING TOPIC SENTENCES   Topic sentences, as you probably know, state the main ideas of the paragraphs in the body of an essay. (See 4a.) Topic sentences act as signposts for readers, announcing ideas to come.

You can review the organization of a draft by reading only the topic sentences. Do they clearly support the essay's main idea? Do they make a reasonable sentence outline of the paper? If your draft lacks topic sentences, make sure you have a good reason for omitting these important signposts.

MOVING BLOCKS OF TEXT   Improving the organization of a draft can be as simple as moving a few sentences from one paragraph to another or switching the order of paragraphs. Often, however, the process is more complex. As you move blocks of text, you may need to supply transitions to make them fit smoothly in the new positions; you may also need to rework topic sentences to make your new organization clear.

Before moving text, consider sketching a revised outline. Divisions in the outline might become topic sentences in the restructured essay. (See 1d.)

REPARAGRAPHING AND INSERTING HEADINGS   Occasionally you can clarify the organization of a draft simply by combining choppy paragraphs or by dividing those that are too long for easy reading. (See 4f.)

The writing process

In long documents, such as research papers or business reports, headings can help readers follow your organization. Possible headings include phrases, declarative or imperative sentences, and questions. To draw attention to headings, you can center them, put them in boldface, underline them, use all capital letters, or some combination of these. (See also pp. 104–07.)

Strengthening the content

In reviewing the content of a draft, consider whether any text (sentences, paragraphs, or longer passages) should be added or deleted, keeping in mind your readers' needs. Then, if your purpose is to argue a point, consider how persuasively you have proved your point to an intelligent, discerning audience. When necessary, rethink your argument.

ADDING TEXT   If any paragraphs or sections of the essay are developed too skimpily to be clear and convincing (a common flaw in rough drafts), you will need to add specific facts, details, and examples. This necessity will take you back to the beginning of the writing process: listing specifics, brainstorming ideas with friends or classmates, perhaps doing more research.

DELETING TEXT   Look for sentences and paragraphs that can be cut without serious loss of meaning. Perhaps you have repeated yourself or strayed from your point. Maybe you have given undue emphasis to minor ideas. Cuts may also be necessitated by word limits, such as those imposed by a college assignment or by the realities of the business world, where readers are often pressed for time.

RETHINKING YOUR ARGUMENT   A first draft presents you with an opportunity for rethinking your argument. You can often deepen your ideas about a subject by asking yourself some hard questions. Is your claim more sweeping than the evidence allows? Have you left out an important step in the argument? Have you dealt with the arguments of the opposition? Is your draft free of faulty reasoning? The more challenging your subject, the more likely you will find yourself adjusting your early thoughts. (For more about argumentative writing, see 7.)

Clarifying the point of view

If the point of view of a draft shifts confusingly or if it seems not quite appropriate for your purpose, audience, and subject, consider adjusting it.

There are three basic points of view to choose from: the first person (*I* or *we*), the second person (*you*), and the third person (*he/she/it/one* or *they*). Each point of view is appropriate in at least some contexts, and you may need to experiment before discovering which one best suits your needs.

THE THIRD-PERSON POINT OF VIEW   Much academic and professional writing is best presented from the third-person point of view (*he/she/it/one* or *they*), which puts the subject in the foreground. The *I* point of view is usually inappropriate in such contexts because, by focusing attention on the writer, it pushes the subject into the background. Consider, for example, one student's first-draft description of the behavior of a species of frog that he had observed in the field.

> Each frog that *I* was able to locate in trees remained in its given tree during the entirety of *my* observation period. However, *I* noticed that there was considerable movement within the home tree.

Here the *I* point of view is distracting, as the student himself noticed when he began to revise his report. His revision focuses more on the frogs, less on himself.

> Each frog located in a tree remained in that tree through-
> out the observation period. The frogs moved about consider-
> ably, however, within their home trees.

Just as the first-person pronoun *I* can draw too much
attention to the writer, the second-person pronoun *you* can
focus unnecessarily on the reader. In the following sentence
from a memo, for example, a supervisor writing to a sales
manager needlessly draws attention to the reader.

> When *you* look at the numbers, *you* can clearly see that travel
> expenses must be cut back.

This sentence would be clearer and more direct if presented
without the distraction of the *you* point of view.

> The numbers clearly show that travel expenses must be cut
> back.

Although the third-person point of view is often a better
choice than the *I* or *you* point of view, it is by no means
trouble-free. Writers who choose it can run into problems
when they want to use singular pronouns in an indefinite
sense. For example, when the Muppets character Miss Piggy
says that a reason for jogging is "to improve *one's* emotional
health and make *one* feel better about *oneself*," one wishes
she wouldn't use quite so many *one*s, doesn't one? The
trouble is that American English, unlike British English,
does not allow this pronoun to echo unself-consciously
throughout a sentence. The repetitions sound stuffy.

Some years ago Americans would have said "to improve
a person's emotional health and to make *him* feel better
about *himself*," with the understanding that *him* really
meant *him or her*. Today, however, this use of *him* is offensive
to many readers and is best avoided. But "to make *him or
her* feel better about *himself or herself*" is distinctly awkward. So what is poor Miss Piggy to say?

Her only hope, it turns out, is a flexible and inventive mind. She might switch to the plural: *Joggers run to improve their emotional health and to make them feel better about themselves.* Or she could restructure the sentence altogether: *Jogging improves a person's emotional health and self-image.* (See 17f and 22a.)

THE SECOND-PERSON POINT OF VIEW The *you* point of view, which puts the reader in the foreground, is appropriate if the writer is advising readers directly, as in giving tips on raising children or instructions on flower arranging. All imperative sentences, such as the advice for writers in this book, are written from the *you* point of view, although the word itself is frequently omitted and understood. "Sketch a plan" means "*You* should sketch a plan"; everyone knows this, so the *you* is not expressed.

In the course of giving advice or instructions, the actual word *you* may be appropriate and even desired. In advising gardeners about walkways, for example, newspaper columnist Henry Mitchell feels free to use the words *you* and *your* as the need arises:

> If *your* main walk is less than four feet wide, and if it is
> white concrete, then widen it, no matter what has to be sacri-
> ficed . . . and resurface it with brick, stone, or something less
> glaring and dull. Three flowers against a good-looking pave-
> ment will do more for *you* than thirty flowers against white
> concrete. [Italics added.]

Mitchell might have written this passage from the third-person point of view instead ("If *the gardener's* walk is less than four feet wide . . ."), but the effect would have seemed oddly indirect. Even at the risk of sounding a bit bossy, Mitchell has wisely selected the imperative (*you*) approach instead.

Notice that Mitchell's *you* means "you, the reader." It does not mean "you, anyone in general." Indefinite uses of *you*, such as in the following example, are inappropriate in formal writing. (See 23d.)

> Young Japanese women wired together electronic products on a piece-rate system: The more *you* wired, the more *you* were paid.

Here the writer should have stayed with the third-person point of view.

> The more *they* wired, the more *they* were paid.

THE FIRST-PERSON POINT OF VIEW   If much of a writer's material comes from personal experience, the *I* point of view will prove most natural. It is difficult to imagine, for example, how James Thurber could have avoided the word *I* in describing his early university days:

> *I* passed all the other courses that *I* took at *my* university, but *I* could never pass botany. This was because all botany students had to spend several hours a week in a laboratory looking through a microscope at plant cells, and *I* could never see through a microscope. *I* never once saw a cell through a microscope. This used to enrage my instructor. [Italics added.]
>
> — "University Days"

Thurber's *I* point of view puts the writer in the foreground, and since the writer is in fact the subject, this makes sense.

Writers who are aware that the first-person point of view is sometimes viewed as inappropriate in academic writing often overgeneralize the rule. Concluding that the word *I* is never appropriate, they go to extreme lengths to avoid it:

> Mama read with such color and detail that *one* could fancy *oneself* as the hero of the story.

Since the paper in which this sentence appeared was a personal reminiscence, the entire paper sounded more natural once the writer allowed himself to use the word *I*.

> Mama read with such color and detail that *I* could fancy *myself* as the hero of the story.

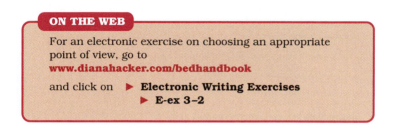

ON THE WEB

For an electronic exercise on choosing an appropriate point of view, go to
www.dianahacker.com/bedhandbook

and click on ▶ **Electronic Writing Exercises**
▶ **E-ex 3–2**

Engaging the audience

Considerations of audience often lead to global revision. Many rough drafts need a major overhaul because they are directed at no audience at all for no apparent purpose — written in a vacuum, so to speak. Readers are put off by such writing because when they don't know *why* they are reading, they suspect that a writer may be wasting their time. A good question to ask yourself about your own rough drafts, therefore, is the toughest question that a reader might ask: "So what?" If your draft can't pass the "So what?" test, you will need to rethink your entire approach; in fact, you may even decide to scrap the draft and start over.

Once you have made sure that your draft is directed at an audience — readers who stand to benefit in some way by reading it — you may still need to refine your tone. The tone of a piece of writing expresses the writer's feelings toward the audience, so it is important to get it right. If the tone

Cycles of global revision (for writers)

SHARPENING THE FOCUS

Look for opportunities

> — to clarify the introduction (especially the thesis)
> — to delete text that is off the point

IMPROVING THE ORGANIZATION

Look for opportunities

> — to add or sharpen topic sentences
> — to move blocks of text
> — to reparagraph and perhaps to add headings

STRENGTHENING THE CONTENT

Look for opportunities

> — to add specific facts, details, and examples
> — to emphasize major ideas
> — to rethink your argument or central insight

CLARIFYING THE POINT OF VIEW

Look for opportunities

> — to make the point of view more consistent
> — to use a more appropriate point of view

ENGAGING THE AUDIENCE

Look for opportunities

> — to let readers know why they are reading
> — to motivate readers to read on
> — to use a more appropriate tone

Checklist for global revision (for reviewers)

FOCUS

— Does the introduction focus on the main point?

— Is the thesis clear enough? (If there is no thesis, is there a good reason for omitting one?)

— Are any ideas off the point?

ORGANIZATION

— Does the writer give readers enough organizational cues (such as topic sentences or headings)?

— Should any text be moved?

— Are any paragraphs too long or short for easy reading?

CONTENT

— Are there enough facts, examples, and details to support major ideas?

— Are the parts proportioned sensibly? Do major ideas receive enough attention?

— How might the argument be strengthened?

POINT OF VIEW

— Is the draft free of distracting shifts in point of view?

— Is the point of view appropriate?

AUDIENCE APPEAL

— Does the draft accomplish its purpose — to inform us, to persuade us, to entertain us, to call us to action (or some combination of these)?

— Does the opening paragraph make us want to read on? Do we know why we are reading?

— Is the tone appropriate?

seems too self-centered — or too flippant, stuffy, bossy, patronizing, opinionated, or hostile — obviously it should be
modified.

Any piece of writing drafted in anger or frustration will
almost certainly need to be toned down. The following rough
draft, for example, was written by a secretary in response to
criticisms of a newsletter sent out by the organization for
which she worked.

> Dear Mr. Martin:
>
> I know our newsletter is crudely laid out, the reason
> being that I work under a tight deadline, and we can't afford
> any fancy desktop publishing equipment. Perhaps we'd do
> better if we had more funding.
>
> I think you were wrong to dismiss the offending review as
> bragging about *Nuclear War: What's in It for You?* The book
> was nominated for the prize, a fact worthy of mention despite
> the fact that it did not win.
>
> In any case, I am glad to hear that you liked the open
> letter to the president. Would that the *Philadelphia Inquirer*
> had liked it as well.
>
> Sincerely,
> Robbie Nichols

As she reached the last paragraph of the rough draft, the
writer saw the need to be more diplomatic. Later, in a calmer
and less defensive mood, she revised the letter like this:

> Dear Mr. Martin:
>
> We are glad to hear that you liked Roger Molander's "An
> Open Letter to the President." Would that the *Philadelphia
> Inquirer* had liked it as well.
>
> I do think you were wrong to dismiss the sentence about
> *Nuclear War: What's in It for You?* as "bragging." It is a fairly
> direct sentence, and there may well be those among the faith-
> ful who wouldn't otherwise have known about its nomination
> for the prize.

Your comments about the physical layout of the story were, in fact, echoed by the staff here. The layout could not be changed, however, because of the limitations of our current computers.

Thank you for writing. We hope that Roger's open letter will elicit serious thought about the president's March 23 address on weapons in space.

Sincerely,
Robbie Nichols

3b Revise and edit sentences; proofread the final draft.

When you revise sentences, you focus on effectiveness; when you edit, you check for correctness. Proofreading is a slow and careful reading in search of typos and other obvious mistakes.

Revising and editing sentences

As with global revision, sentence-level revision may be approached in cycles, with each cycle focusing on a different purpose for making changes. The main purposes for revising sentences—to strengthen, clarify, vary, and refine them—are detailed in the chart on page 60. A checklist on editing for grammar, punctuation, and mechanics appears on page 61.

Some writers handle most sentence-level revisions directly at the computer, experimenting on-screen with a variety of possible improvements. Other writers prefer to print out a hard copy of the draft, mark it up, and then return to the computer. Here, for example, is a rough-draft paragraph as one student edited it for a variety of sentence-level problems:

> *deciding*
> Finally ~~we decided~~ that perhaps our dream
>   ^
> needed ~~some~~ prompting, ~~and~~ we visited a fertility

doctor and began the expensive, time-consuming
                                    some
round of procedures that held out ~~the~~ promise of
our dream's fulfillment. Our efforts, however, were   *As*
~~fulfilling our dream. All this was~~ to no avail ~~/.~~ ~~and~~

~~as~~ we approached the sixth year of our marriage,
      could no longer
we ~~had reached the point where we couldn't~~ even

discuss our childlessness without becoming very

depressed. We questioned why this had happened to
                               such a
us ~~/.~~ Why had we been singled out for ~~this~~ major

disappointment?

The original paragraph was flawed by wordiness and an excessive reliance on structures connected with *and*. Such problems can be addressed through any number of acceptable revisions. The first sentence, for example, could have been changed like this:

     Finally we decided that perhaps our dream
                     After visiting
needed ~~some~~ prompting ~~/.~~ ~~and we visited~~ a fertility
     we
doctor, ~~and~~ began the expensive, time-consuming
                        promised hope
round of procedures that ~~held out the promise~~ of

fulfilling our dream.

Though some writers might argue about the effectiveness of these improvements compared with the previous revision, most would agree that both versions are better than the original.

Some of the paragraph's improvements involve less choice and are not so open to debate. The hyphen in *time-consuming* is necessary; a noun must be substituted for the pronoun *this* in the second sentence, which was being used more loosely than grammar allows; and the question mark in the next to last sentence must be changed to a period.

Proofreading

After revising and editing, you are ready to prepare the final manuscript. (See 5b for guidelines.) At this point, make sure to allow yourself enough time for proofreading—the final and most important step in manuscript preparation.

Proofreading is a special kind of reading: a slow and methodical search for misspellings, typographical mistakes, and omitted words or word endings. Such errors can be difficult to spot in your own work because you may read what you intended to write, not what is actually on the page. To fight this tendency, try proofreading out loud, articulating

GRAMMAR CHECKERS on your computer can help with some but by no means all of the sentence-level problems in a typical draft. Because so many problems—such as faulty parallelism, mixed constructions, and misplaced modifiers—lack mathematical precision, they slip right past the grammar checker. Even when the grammar checker has the capability of flagging a potential problem, such as the passive voice, you must still decide whether your sentence is effective.

Throughout this book, you will find grammar checker boxes that look like the one you are now reading. The boxes show you how well grammar checkers can flag specific problems such as dangling modifiers, run-on sentences, and so on. The information in these boxes is based on a large sample of correct and incorrect sentences that were run through two widely used grammar checker programs.

Cycles of sentence-level revision

The numbers in this chart refer to sections in this handbook.

STRENGTHENING SENTENCES

Look for opportunities

—to use more active verbs (8a)

—to prune excess words (16)

CLARIFYING SENTENCES

Look for opportunities

—to balance parallel ideas (9)

—to supply missing words (10)

—to untangle mixed constructions (11)

—to repair misplaced or dangling modifiers (12)

—to eliminate distracting shifts (13)

INTRODUCING VARIETY

Look for opportunities

—to combine choppy sentences (14b)

—to break up long sentences (14e)

—to vary sentence openings (15a)

REFINING THE STYLE

Look for opportunities

—to choose language more appropriate for the subject and audience (17)

—to choose more exact words (18)

An editing checklist

At first this checklist may seem overwhelming, but as your instructor responds to your writing and as you become familiar with the rules in this handbook, you'll begin to see which problems, if any, tend to cause you trouble. You can then devise a personal checklist of errors to look for as you edit. (The numbers in the chart refer to sections in this handbook.)

GRAMMAR

Sentence fragments (19)
Run-on sentences (20)
Subject-verb agreement (21)
Pronoun-antecedent agreement (22)
Pronoun reference (23)
Case of nouns and pronouns (24)
Case of *who* and *whom* (25)
Adjectives and adverbs (26)
Standard English verb forms (27)
Verb tense, mood, and voice (28)
ESL problems (29, 30, 31)

PUNCTUATION

The comma and unnecessary commas (32, 33)
The semicolon (34)
The colon (35)
The apostrophe (36)
Quotation marks (37)
End punctuation (38)
Other punctuation marks (39)

MECHANICS

Abbreviations and numbers (40, 41)
Italics (underlining) (42)
Spelling and the hyphen (43, 44)
Capital letters (45)

each word as it is actually written. You might also try proof-reading your sentences in reverse order, a strategy that takes your attention away from the meanings you intended and forces you to think about small surface features instead.

Although proofreading may be dull, it is crucial. Errors strewn throughout an essay are distracting and annoying. If the writer doesn't care about this piece of writing, thinks the reader, why should I? A carefully proofread essay, however, sends a positive message: It shows that you value your writing and respect your readers.

SPELL CHECKERS are much more reliable than grammar checkers, but they too must be used with caution. Many typographical errors (such as *quiet* for *quite*) and misused words (such as *effect* for *affect*) slip past the spell checker because the checker flags only words not found in its dictionary. See Exercise 43–1 on page 465 for an example of the kinds of errors that can remain once you have run your spell checker.

STUDENT ESSAY

Matt Watson, who wrote "Hooked on Credit Cards" (pp. 67–71), was responding to the following assignment:

> In an essay of 500–1,000 words, alert readers to a significant problem facing today's college students. Assume that your audience consists of general readers, not simply college students.
>
> If you use any sources, document them with MLA in-text citations and a list of works cited (see section 56 in *The Bedford Handbook*).

When he received the assignment, Watson considered several possibilities before settling on the topic of credit cards. He already knew something about the topic because his older sister had run up large credit card bills while in college and was working hard to pay them off.

To get started on his paper, Watson interviewed his sister over the phone and then typed the following list of ideas into his computer.

```
easy to get hooked on credit cards and run up huge
debts

Why do credit card companies try to sign up
students? Aren't we a bad risk? But they must be
profiting, or they'd stop. High interest rates.

advertisements for credit cards appear all over
campus and on the Web

using plastic--doesn't seem like spending money

tactics used by the companies--offering low inter-
est rates at first, setting high credit limits,
allowing a revolving balance

What happens to students who get in debt but don't
have parents who can bail them out?
```

With this list of ideas, Watson began writing a first draft. He wrote it quickly, focusing more on ideas than on grammar, style, and mechanics. Then he made some additions and deletions and fixed a few typos before submitting the draft for peer review in a networked classroom. Here is the draft he submitted, together with the most helpful comments he received from classmates. The peer reviewers were asked to comment on global issues—focus, organization, content, point of view, and audience appeal—and to ignore any problems with grammar and punctuation.

ROUGH DRAFT

Hooked on Credit Cards

Credit card companies love to extend credit to college students. You see ads for these cards on campus bulletin boards and also on the Web. Why do companies market their product to a population that has no job and lacks a substantial credit history? They seem to be trying to hook us on their cards; unfortunately many of us do get hooked on a cycle of spending that leads to financial ruin.

Banks require applicants for a loan to demonstrate a good credit history and some evidence of a source of income, but credit card companies don't. On campus, students are bombarded with offers of pre-approved credit cards. Then there are the Web sites. Sites with lots of student traffic are plastered with banner ads like this one: "To get a credit card, you need to establish credit. To establish credit, you need a credit card. Stop the vicious cycle! Apply for our student MasterCard."

Credit card companies often entice students with low interest rates, then they jack up the rates later. A student may not think about the cost of interest. That new stereo or back-to-school wardrobe can get pretty ex-

Some students do have jobs. (Sara)

Good question. What's the answer? (Mark)

The assignment asks for a general audience; your thesis shouldn't be about "us." (Sara)

Shouldn't your thesis focus more on how card companies hook students? (Tim)

Good point. The card companies are going too easy on students. (Sara)

Maybe you could also mention the solicitors who show up during orientation. (Mark)

This sentence sounds too informal. (Tim)

I like this example. (Mark)

Why not give us some numbers here? Just how low and how high? (Sara)

pensive at 17.9% interest if it's compounded over several months. Would you have bought that $600 item if you knew it would end up costing you $900?

Most cards allow the holder to keep a revolving balance, which means that they don't have to pay the whole bill, they just pay a minimum amount. The minimum is usually not too much, but a young person may be tempted to keep running up debt. The companies also give students an unrealistically high credit limit. I've heard of undergraduates who had a limit as high as $4,000.

Card companies make money not just from high interest rates. Often they charge fees for late payments. I've heard of penalties for going over the credit limit too.

Often students discover too late that they are thoroughly trapped. Some drop out of school, others graduate and then can't find a good job because they have a poor credit rating. There are psychological problems too. Your parents may bail you out of debt, but you'll probably feel guilty. On a Web site, I read that two students felt so bad they committed suicide.

Credit cards are a part of life these days, and everyone is probably wise to have a charge account for emergencies. But every college student must take a hard look at their financial picture. The very things that make those cards so convenient and easy to use can lead to a mountain of debt that will take years to pay off.

Margin comments:

The shift to "you" seems odd. (Sara)

Maybe you could get some statistics from the Internet. (Mark)

This paragraph seems sort of skimpy. (Tim)

Maybe you could find some facts to back up your points. (Mark)

Professor Mills won't like your shifts to "you" and "I" here.

Also, he wants us to cite our sources. (Sara)

Your paper focuses on the tactics that the companies use, but your conclusion doesn't mention them. (Tim)

After rereading his draft and considering the feedback from his classmates, Watson decided that his paper needed more facts. He located several Web sites and rejected those that were obviously promotional. He decided to rely on sites sponsored by two reputable organizations, Nellie Mae and the Consumer Federation of America.

In his next draft, Watson reworked his introduction and then strengthened his content by supplying more facts. While adding facts, he discovered ways of improving the organization. Then, when he was more or less satisfied with the paper as a whole, he worked to polish his sentences. Watson's final draft begins on the next page.

Watson 1

Matt Watson
Professor Mills
English 101
12 March 2001

Hooked on Credit Cards

Credit card companies love to extend credit to
college students, especially those just out of high
school. Ads for credit cards line campus bulletin
boards, flash across commercial Web sites for students, and get stuffed into shopping bags at college bookstores. Why do the companies market their
product so vigorously to a population that lacks a
substantial credit history and often has no steady
source of income? The answer is that significant
profits can be earned through high interest rates
and assorted penalties and fees. By granting college students liberal lending arrangements, credit
card companies often hook them on a cycle of spending that can ultimately lead to financial ruin.

Whereas banks require applicants for a loan to
demonstrate a good credit history and some evidence
of an income flow, credit card companies make no
such demands on students. On campus, students find
themselves bombarded with offers of pre-approved
cards--and not just on flyers pinned to bulletin
boards. Many campuses allow credit card vendors to
solicit applications during orientation week. In
addition to offering pre-approved cards, these

Introduction
orients readers
and ends with a
thesis.

Thesis
announces
the writer's
main point.

Clear topic
sentences guide
readers through
the body of the
paper.

The writing process

vendors often give away T-shirts or CDs to entice students to apply. Students are bombarded on the Web as well. Sites with heavy student traffic are emblazoned with banner ads like this one: "To get a credit card, you need to establish credit. To establish credit, you need a credit card. Stop the vicious cycle! Apply for our student MasterCard."

Body paragraphs are developed with details and examples.

Credit card companies often entice students with low "teaser" interest rates of 13% and later raise those rates to 18% or even higher. Others charge high rates up front, trusting that students won't read the fine print. Some young people don't think about the cost of interest, let alone the cost of interest compounding month after month. That back-to-school wardrobe can get pretty expensive at 17.9% interest compounded over several months. A $600 trip to Fort Lauderdale is not such a bargain when in the long run it costs $900 or more.

Transition serves as a bridge between paragraphs.

Summary of source is in the student's own words.

Source is documented with an MLA in-text citation.

In addition to charging high interest rates, credit card companies try to maximize the amount of interest generated. One tactic is to extend an unreasonably high credit limit to students. According to Nellie Mae statistics, in 1998 undergraduates were granted an average credit limit of $3,683; for graduate students, the figure jumped to $15,721. Nearly 10% of the students in the Nellie Mae study carried balances near or exceeding these credit limits (Blair).

Watson 3

Another tactic is to allow students to maintain a revolving balance. A revolving balance permits the debtor to pay only part of a current bill, often an amount just a little larger than the accumulated interest. The indebted student is tempted to keep on charging, paying a minimum amount every month, because there aren't any immediate consequences to doing so.

Once a student is hooked on a cycle of debt, the companies profit even further by assessing a variety of fees and penalties. According to a press release issued by Consumer Action and the Consumer Federation of America, many credit card companies charge late fees and "over the limit" penalties as high as $29 per month. In addition, grace periods are often shortened to ensure that late fees kick in earlier. Many companies also raise interest rates for those who fail to pay on time or exceed the credit limit. Those "penalty" rates can climb as high as 25% (1-2).

Often students discover too late that they are thoroughly hooked. The results can be catastrophic. Some students are forced to drop out of school and take low-paying full-time jobs. Others, once they graduate, have difficulty landing good jobs because of their poor credit rating. Many students suffer psychologically as well. Even those who have parents willing to bail them out of debt often experience a

The writer cites a Web article from a reputable source.

Watson 4

great deal of anxiety and guilt. Two students recently grew so stressed by their accumulating debt
that they committed suicide (Consumer Federation
of Amer. 3).

Credit cards are a part of life these days,
and there is nothing wrong with having one or two
of them. Before signing up for a particular card,
however, college students should take the time to
read the fine print and do some comparison shopping. Students also need to learn to resist the
many seductive offers that credit card companies
extend to them once they have signed up. Students
who can't "just say no" to temptations such as high
credit limits and revolving balances could well
become hooked on a cycle of debt from which there
is no easy escape.

Conclusion
echoes the
writer's main
idea.

Works Cited

Blair, Alan D. "A High Wire Act: Balancing Student
Loan and Credit Card Debt." <u>Nellie Mae</u>. 1999.
6 Nov. 2000 <http://www.nelliemae.com/
shared/bal.htm>.

Consumer Action and Consumer Federation of
America. "Card Issuers Hike Fees and Rates
to Bolster Profits." <u>Consumer Federation of
America</u>. 5 Nov. 1998. 5 pp. 6 Nov.
2000 <http://www.consumerfed.org/
cardissuerspr.pdf>.

Consumer Federation of America."Credit Card Debt
Imposes Huge Costs on Many College Students."
<u>Consumer Federation of America</u>. 8 June 1999.
7 pp. 6 Nov. 2000 <http://
www.consumerfed.org/ccstudent.pdf>.

Works cited
page follows
MLA format.

4

Build effective paragraphs.

Except for special-purpose paragraphs, such as introductions and conclusions (see 2a and 2c), paragraphs are clusters of information supporting an essay's main point (or advancing a story's action). Aim for paragraphs that are clearly focused, well developed, organized, coherent, and neither too long nor too short for easy reading.

4a   Focus on a main point.

A paragraph should be unified around a main point. The point should be clear to readers, and all sentences in the paragraph must relate to it.

Stating the main point in a topic sentence

As readers move into a paragraph, they need to know where they are—in relation to the whole essay—and what to expect in the sentences to come. A good topic sentence, a one-sentence summary of the paragraph's main point, acts as a signpost pointing in two directions: backward toward the thesis of the essay and forward toward the body of the paragraph.

Like a thesis statement (see 1c and 2a), a topic sentence is more general than the material supporting it. Usually the topic sentence comes first.

> *Nearly all living creatures manage some form of communication.* The dance patterns of bees in their hive help to point the way to distant flower fields or announce successful foraging. Male stickleback fish regularly swim upside-down to indicate outrage in a courtship contest. Male deer and lemurs

mark territorial ownership by rubbing their own body secretions on boundary stones or trees. Everyone has seen a frightened dog put his tail between his legs and run in panic. We, too, use gestures, expressions, postures, and movement to give our words point. [Italics added.]

—Olivia Vlahos, *Human Beginnings*

Sometimes the topic sentence is introduced by a transitional sentence linking it to earlier material. In the following paragraph, the topic sentence (italicized) has been delayed to allow for a transition.

But flowers are not the only source of spectacle in the wilderness. *An opportunity for late color is provided by the berries of wildflowers, shrubs, and trees.* Baneberry presents its tiny white flowers in spring but in late summer bursts forth with clusters of red berries. Bunchberry, a ground-cover plant, puts out red berries in the fall, and the red berries of wintergreen last from autumn well into winter. In California, the bright red, fist-sized clusters of Christmas berries can be seen growing beside highways for up to six months of the year. [Italics added.]

—James Crockett et al., *Wildflower Gardening*

Occasionally the topic sentence may be withheld until the end of the paragraph—but only if the earlier sentences hang together so well that the reader perceives their direction, if not their exact point. The opening sentences of the following paragraph state facts, so they are supporting material rather than topic sentences, but they strongly suggest a central idea. The topic sentence at the end is hardly a surprise.

Tobacco chewing starts as soon as people begin stirring. Those who have fresh supplies soak the new leaves in water and add ashes from the hearth to the wad. Men, women, and children chew tobacco and all are addicted to it. Once there was a shortage of tobacco in Kaobawa's village and I was plagued for a week by early morning visitors who requested

permission to collect my cigarette butts in order to make a
wad of chewing tobacco. Normally, if anyone is short of tobacco, he can request a share of someone else's already chewed
wad, or simply borrow the entire wad when its owner puts it
down somewhere. *Tobacco is so important to them that their
word for "poverty" translates as "being without tobacco."* [Italics
added.]
— Napoleon A. Chagnon, *Yanomamo: The Fierce People*

Although it is generally wise to use topic sentences, at
times they are unnecessary. A topic sentence may not be
needed if a paragraph continues developing an idea clearly
introduced in a previous paragraph, if the details of the
paragraph unmistakably suggest its main point, or if the
paragraph appears in a narrative of events where generalizations might interrupt the flow of the story.

Sticking to the point

Sentences that do not support the topic sentence destroy
the unity of a paragraph. If the paragraph is otherwise well
focused, such offending sentences can simply be deleted or
perhaps moved elsewhere. In the following paragraph describing the inadequate facilities in a high school, the information about the word processing instructor (in italics) is
clearly off the point.

As the result of tax cuts, the educational facilities of
Lincoln High School have reached an all-time low. Some of
the books date back to 1985 and have long since shed their
covers. The lack of lab equipment makes it necessary for four
to five students to work at one table, with most watching
rather than performing experiments. The few computers in
working order must share one dot matrix printer. *Also, the
word processing instructor left to have a baby at the beginning
of the semester, and most of the students don't like the substitute.* As for the furniture, many of the upright chairs have become recliners, and the desk legs are so unbalanced that they
play seesaw on the floor.

Sometimes the cure for a disunified paragraph is not as simple as deleting or moving material. Writers often wander into uncharted territory because they cannot think of enough evidence to support a topic sentence. Feeling that it is too soon to break into a new paragraph, they move on to new ideas for which they have not prepared the reader. When this happens, the writer is faced with a choice: Either find more evidence to support the topic sentence or adjust the topic sentence to mesh with the evidence that is available.

LOOKING AT YOURSELF AS A WRITER
Topic sentences

Professors and business supervisors often complain about the writing that is submitted to them, and one of their loudest complaints concerns topic sentences. Why, they wonder, do so many students and employees have trouble stating the point of a paragraph in its first sentence?

If you have difficulty writing topic sentences, ask yourself why. Here are some common causes and cures.

CAUSE   You haven't decided how to organize your draft, so you don't know what key idea to express in the topic sentence for each paragraph.

CURE   Jot down an informal outline and build a topic sentence for each key point in the outline. It's best to do this before drafting, but you can do it later as well.

CAUSE   You are focusing on details and forget the reader's need to see how the details fit into the overall structure of the essay. The forward flow of writing tempts nearly all of us to blur the structure while we are drafting.

CURE   As you revise a draft, pay special attention to organization, inserting (or sharpening) topic sentences as needed.

The writing process

Topic sentences (continued)

CAUSE You are trying to link the opening sentence of a new paragraph to the last sentence of the previous paragraph.

CURE When you move into a new paragraph, don't worry about subtle links between sentences. Pay attention instead to links between larger chunks of text — the move from one topic to another.

CAUSE You are aware that some professional writers, especially journalists and informal essayists, do not always use clear topic sentences.

CURE Develop a flexible approach to writing. In some contexts, topic sentences may not be so important. In the academic world, however, topic sentences are often necessary for clarifying the lines of an argument or reporting the research in a field. In the business world, topic sentences (along with headings) are essential, since readers often scan for information.

EXERCISE 4–1

Underline the topic sentence in the following paragraph and cross out any material that does not clarify or develop the central idea.

Historically, quilt making has served as an important means of social, political, and artistic expression for women. In the nineteenth century, especially, quilting circles provided one of the few opportunities for the women of a community to forge social bonds outside of their families. Once a week or more, they came together to sew as well as trade small talk, advice, and news. They used dyed cotton fabrics much like the fabrics quilters use today; surprisingly, quilters' basic materials haven't changed that much over the years. Sometimes the women joined their efforts in the support of a political cause, making quilts that would be raffled to raise money for temperance societies, hospitals for sick and wounded soldiers, and the fight against slavery. The abolitionist movement, in particular, led one activist, Sarah Grimké, to memorably express her hopes for herself and fellow quilters: "May the points of our needles prick the slave owner's conscience." Quilt making also afforded women a means of artistic expression at a time when they had few other creative outlets. Within their socially acceptable roles as homemakers, many quilters subtly—and perhaps subconsciously—pushed back at the restrictions placed on them by experimenting with color, design, and technique.

ON THE WEB

For an electronic exercise on topic sentences, go to
www.dianahacker.com/bedhandbook

and click on   ▶ **Electronic Writing Exercises**
                ▶ **E-ex 4–1**

4b Develop the main point.

Though an occasional short paragraph is fine, particularly if it functions as a transition or emphasizes a point, a series of brief paragraphs suggests inadequate development. How much development is enough? That varies, depending on the writer's purpose and audience.

For example, when she wrote a paragraph attempting to convince readers that it is impossible to lose fat quickly, health columnist Jane Brody knew that she would have to present a great deal of evidence because many dieters want to believe the opposite. She did *not* write:

> When you think about it, it's impossible to lose—as many diets suggest—10 pounds of *fat* in ten days, even on a total fast. Even a moderately active person cannot lose so much weight so fast. A less active person hasn't a prayer.

This three-sentence paragraph is too skimpy to be convincing. But the paragraph that Brody wrote contains enough evidence to convince even skeptical readers.

> When you think about it, it's impossible to lose — as many diets suggest— 10 pounds of *fat* in ten days, even on a total fast. A pound of body fat represents 3,500 calories. To lose 1 pound of fat, you must expend 3,500 more calories than you consume. Let's say you weigh 170 pounds and, as a moderately active person, you burn 2,500 calories a day. If your diet contains only 1,500 calories, you'd have an energy deficit of 1,000 calories a day. In a week's time that would add up to a 7,000-calorie deficit, or 2 pounds of real fat. In ten days, the accumulated deficit would represent nearly 3 pounds of lost body fat. Even if you ate nothing at all for ten days and maintained your usual level of activity, your caloric deficit would add up to 25,000 calories. . . . At 3,500 calories per pound of fat, that's still only 7 pounds of lost fat.
> — Jane Brody, *Jane Brody's Nutrition Book*

4c   Choose a suitable pattern of organization.

Although paragraphs (and indeed whole essays) may be patterned in any number of ways, certain patterns of organization occur frequently, either alone or in combination: examples and illustrations, narration, description, process, comparison and contrast, analogy, cause and effect, classification and division, and definition. There is nothing particularly magical about these patterns (sometimes called *methods of development*). They simply reflect some of the ways in which we think.

Examples and illustrations

Examples, perhaps the most common pattern of development, are appropriate whenever the reader might be tempted to ask, "For example?" Though examples are just selected instances, not a complete catalog, they are enough to suggest the truth of many topic sentences, as in the following paragraph.

> Normally my parents abided scrupulously by "The Budget," but several times a year Dad would dip into his battered, black strongbox and splurge on some irrational, totally satisfying luxury. Once he bought over a hundred comic books at a flea market, doled out to us thereafter at the tantalizing rate of two a week. He always got a whole flat of pansies, Mom's favorite flower, for us to give her on Mother's Day. One day a boy stopped at our house selling fifty-cent raffle tickets on a sailboat and Dad bought every ticket the boy had left—three books' worth.
> —Connie Hailey, student

Illustrations are extended examples, frequently presented in story form. Because they require several sentences apiece, they are used more sparingly than examples. When well selected, however, they can be a vivid and effective means of developing a point. The writer of the following paragraph uses illustrations to demonstrate that Harriet Tubman, famous conductor on the underground railroad for escaping slaves, was a genius at knowing how and when to retreat.

> Part of Harriet Tubman's strategy of conducting was, as in all battle-field operations, the knowledge of how and when to retreat. Numerous allusions have been made to her moves when she suspected that she was in danger. When she feared the party was closely pursued, she would take it for a time on a train southward bound. No one seeing Negroes going in this direction would for an instant suppose them to be fugitives. Once on her return she was at a railway station. She saw some men reading a poster and she heard one of them reading it aloud. It was a description of her, offering a reward for her capture. She took a southbound train to avert suspicion. At another time when Harriet heard men talking about her, she pretended to read a book which she carried. One man remarked, "This cannot be the woman. The one we want can't read or write." Harriet devoutly hoped the book was right side up.
> —Earl Conrad, *Harriet Tubman*

The writing process

Narration

A paragraph of narration tells a story or part of a story. Narrative paragraphs are usually arranged in chronological order, but they may also contain flashbacks, interruptions that take the story back to an earlier time. The following paragraph, from Jane Goodall's *In the Shadow of Man*, recounts one of the author's experiences in the African wild.

> One evening when I was wading in the shallows of the lake to pass a rocky outcrop, I suddenly stopped dead as I saw the sinuous black body of a snake in the water. It was all of six feet long, and from the slight hood and the dark stripes at the back of the neck I knew it to be a Storm's water cobra—a deadly reptile for the bite of which there was, at that time, no serum. As I stared at it an incoming wave gently deposited part of its body on one of my feet. I remained motionless, not even breathing, until the wave rolled back into the lake, drawing the snake with it. Then I leaped out of the water as fast as I could, my heart hammering.
>
> —Jane Goodall, *In the Shadow of Man*

Description

A descriptive paragraph sketches a portrait of a person, place, or thing by using concrete and specific details that appeal to one or more of our senses—sight, sound, smell, taste, and touch. Consider, for example, the following description of the grasshopper invasions that devastated the midwestern landscape in the late 1860s.

> They came like dive bombers out of the west. They came by the millions with the rustle of their wings roaring overhead. They came in waves, like the rolls of the sea, descending with a terrifying speed, breaking now and again like a mighty surf. They came with the force of a williwaw and they formed a huge, ominous, dark brown cloud that eclipsed the sun. They dipped and touched earth, hitting objects and people like hailstones. But they were not hail. These were live demons. They

popped, snapped, crackled, and roared. They were dark brown, an inch or longer in length, plump in the middle and tapered at the ends. They had transparent wings, slender legs, and two black eyes that flashed with a fierce intelligence.

—Eugene Boe, "Pioneers to Eternity"

Process

A process paragraph is patterned in time order, usually chronologically. A writer may choose this pattern either to describe a process or to show readers how to perform a process. The following paragraph describes what happens when water freezes.

In school we learned that with few exceptions the solid phase of matter is more dense than the liquid phase. Water, alone among common substances, violates this rule. As water begins to cool, it contracts and becomes more dense, in a perfectly typical way. But about four degrees above the freezing point, something remarkable happens. It ceases to contract and begins expanding, becoming less dense. At the freezing point the expansion is abrupt and drastic. As water turns to ice, it adds about one-eleventh to its liquid volume.

—Chet Raymo, "Curious Stuff, Water and Ice"

Here is a paragraph explaining how to perform a "roll cast," a popular fly fishing technique:

Begin by taking up a suitable stance, with one foot slightly in front of the other and the rod pointing down the line. Then begin a smooth, steady draw, raising your rod hand to just above shoulder height and lifting the rod to the 10:30 or 11:00 position. This steady draw allows a loop of line to form between the rod top and the water. While the line is still moving, raise the rod slightly, then punch it rapidly forward and down. The rod is now flexed and under maximum compression, and the line follows its path, bellying out slightly behind you and coming off the water close to your feet. As you power the rod down through the 3:00 position, the belly of the

line will roll forward. Follow through smoothly so that the line
unfolds and straightens above the water.

— *The Dorling Kindersley Encyclopedia of Fishing*

Comparison and contrast

To compare two subjects is to draw attention to their similarities, although the word *compare* also has a broader
meaning that includes a consideration of differences. To
contrast is to focus only on differences.

Whether a comparison-and-contrast paragraph stresses
similarities or differences, it may be patterned in one of two
ways. The two subjects may be presented one at a time,
block style, as in the following paragraph of contrast.

> So Grant and Lee were in complete contrast, representing
> two diametrically opposed elements in American life. Grant
> was the modern man emerging; beyond him, ready to come
> on the stage, was the great age of steel and machinery, of
> crowded cities and a restless burgeoning vitality. Lee might
> have ridden down from the old age of chivalry, lance in hand,
> silken banner fluttering over his head. Each man was the per-
> fect champion of his cause, drawing both his strengths and
> weaknesses from the people he led.
>
> — Bruce Catton, "Grant and Lee: A Study in Contrasts"

Or a paragraph may proceed point by point, treating the two
subjects together, one aspect at a time. The following paragraph uses the point-by-point method to contrast the
writer's academic experiences in an American high school
with those in an Irish convent.

> Strangely enough, instead of being academically inferior
> to my American high school, the Irish convent was superior.
> In my class at home, *Love Story* was considered pretty heavy
> reading, so imagine my surprise at finding Irish students who
> could recite passages from *War and Peace*. In high school we

complained about having to study *Romeo and Juliet* in one semester, whereas in Ireland we simultaneously studied *Macbeth* and Dickens's *Hard Times*, in addition to writing a composition a day in English class. In high school, I didn't even begin algebra until the ninth grade, while at the convent seventh graders (or their Irish equivalent) were doing calculus and trigonometry.

— Margaret Stack, student

Analogy

Analogies draw comparisons between items that appear to have little in common. Writers turn to analogies for a variety of reasons: to make the unfamiliar seem familiar, to provide a concrete understanding of an abstract topic, to argue a point, or to provoke fresh thoughts or changed feelings about a subject. In the following paragraph, physician Lewis Thomas draws an analogy between the behavior of ants and that of humans. Thomas's analogy helps us to understand the social behavior of ants and forces us to question the superiority of our own human societies.

Ants are so much like human beings as to be an embarrassment. They farm fungi, raise aphids as livestock, launch armies into wars, use chemical sprays to alarm and confuse enemies, capture slaves. The families of weaver ants engage in child labor, holding their larvae like shuttles to spin out the thread that sews the leaves together for their fungus gardens. They exchange information ceaselessly. They do everything but watch television.

— Lewis Thomas, "On Societies as Organisms"

Although analogies can be a powerful tool for illuminating a subject, they should be used with caution in arguments. Just because two things may be alike in one respect, we cannot conclude that they are alike in all respects. (See *false analogy*, p. 508.)

Cause and effect

When causes and effects are a matter of argument, they are too complex to be reduced to a simple pattern (see p. 508). However, if a writer wishes merely to describe a cause-and-effect relationship that is generally accepted, then the effect may be stated in the topic sentence, with the causes listed in the body of the paragraph.

> The fantastic water clarity of the Mount Gambier sinkholes results from several factors. The holes are fed from aquifers holding rainwater that fell decades—even centuries—ago, and that has been filtered through miles of limestone. The high level of calcium that limestone adds causes the silty detritus from dead plants and animals to cling together and settle quickly to the bottom. Abundant bottom vegetation in the shallow sinkholes also helps bind the silt. And the rapid turnover of water prohibits stagnation.
> —Hillary Hauser, "Exploring a Sunken Realm in Australia"

Or the paragraph may move from cause to effects, as in this paragraph from a student paper on the effects of the industrial revolution on American farms.

> The rise of rail transport in the nineteenth century forever changed American farming—for better and for worse. Farmers who once raised crops and livestock to sustain just their own families could now make a profit by selling their goods in towns and cities miles away. These new markets improved the living standard of struggling farm families and encouraged them to seek out innovations that would increase their profits. On the downside, the competition fostered by the new markets sometimes created hostility among neighboring farm families where there had once been a spirit of cooperation. Those farmers who couldn't compete with their neighbors left farming forever, facing poverty worse than they had ever known.
> —Chris Mileski, student

Classification and division

Classification is the grouping of items into categories according to some consistent principle. Philosopher Francis Bacon was using classification when he wrote that "some books are to be tasted, others to be swallowed, and some few to be chewed and digested." Bacon's principle for classifying books is the degree to which they are worthy of our attention, but books of course can be classified according to other principles. For example, an elementary school teacher might classify children's books according to their level of difficulty, or a librarian might group them by subject matter. The principle of classification that a writer chooses ultimately depends on the purpose of the classification.

The following paragraph classifies species of electric fish.

> Scientists sort electric fishes into three categories. The first comprises the strongly electric species like the marine electric rays or the freshwater African electric catfish and South American electric eel. Known since the dawn of history, these deliver a punch strong enough to stun a human. In recent years, biologists have focused on a second category: weakly electric fish in the South American and African rivers that use tiny voltages for communication and navigation. The third group contains sharks, nonelectric rays, and catfish, which do not emit a field but possess sensors that enable them to detect the minute amounts of electricity that leak out of other organisms.
>
> —Anne Rudloe and Jack Rudloe, "Electric Warfare: The Fish That Kill with Thunderbolts"

Division takes one item and divides it into parts. As with classification, division should be made according to some consistent principle. Dividing a tree into roots, trunk, branches, and leaves makes sense; listing its components as branches, wood, water, and sap does not, for the categories overlap.

The following passage describes the components that make up a baseball.

> Like the game itself, a baseball is composed of many layers. One of the delicious joys of childhood is to take apart a baseball and examine the wonders within. You begin by removing the red cotton thread and peeling off the leather cover—which comes from the hide of a Holstein cow and has been tanned, cut, printed, and punched with holes. Beneath the cover is a thin layer of cotton string, followed by several hundred yards of woolen yarn, which make up the bulk of the ball. Slice into the rubber and you'll find the ball's heart—a cork core. The cork is from Portugal, the rubber from southeast Asia, the covers are American, and the balls are assembled in Costa Rica.
>
> —Dan Gutman, *The Way Baseball Works*

Definition

A definition puts a word or concept into a general class and then provides enough details to distinguish it from others in the same class. For example, in one of its senses the term *grit* names the class of things that birds eat, but it is restricted to those items—such as small pebbles, eggshell, and ashes—that help the bird grind food.

Many definitions may be presented in a sentence or two, but abstract or difficult concepts may require a paragraph or even a full essay of definition. In the following paragraph, the writer defines envy as a special kind of desire.

> Envy is so integral and so painful a part of what animates human behavior in market societies that many people have forgotten the full meaning of the word, simplifying it into one of the synonyms of desire. It is that, which may be why it flourishes in market societies: democracies of desire, they might be called, with money for ballots, stuffing permitted. But envy is more or less than desire. It begins with the almost frantic sense of emptiness inside oneself, as if the pump of

one's heart were sucking on air. One has to be blind to perceive the emptiness, of course, but that's just what envy is, a
selective blindness. *Invidia,* Latin for envy, translates as "non-
sight," and Dante had the envious plodding along under cloaks
of lead, their eyes sewn shut with leaden wire. What they are
blind to is what they have, God-given and humanly nurtured,
in themselves.

— Nelson W. Aldrich Jr., *Old Money*

EXERCISE 4–2

Write a paragraph modeled on one of the patterns discussed in this
section. Some possible topics—most of which you'll need to restrict—are listed here.

Examples or illustrations: sexism in a comic strip, ways to include protein in a vegetarian diet, the benefits of a particular
summer job, community services provided by your college,
violence on the six o'clock news, educational software for
children

Narration: the active lifestyle of a grandparent, life with an alcoholic, working in an emergency room, the benefits (or problems) of intercultural dating, growing up in a large family, the
rewards of working in a nursing home, an experience that
taught you a lesson, a turning point in your life

Description: your childhood home, an ethnic neighborhood,
a rock concert, a favorite painting in an art gallery, a garden, a
classic car, a hideous building or monument, a style of dress,
a family heirloom (such as a crazy quilt or a collection of
Christmas tree ornaments), a favorite park or retreat

Process: how to repair something, how to develop a successful
job interview style, how to ask someone out on a date, how to
practice safe scuba diving, how to build a set for a play, how
to survive in the wilderness, how to train a dog, how to quit
smoking, how to make bread

Comparison and contrast: two neighborhoods, teachers, political candidates, colleges, products; country living versus city

living; the stereotype of a job versus the reality; a change in attitude toward your family's religion or ethnic background

Analogy: between a family reunion and a circus, between training for a rigorous sport and boot camp, between settling an argument and being a courtroom judge, between a dog-fight and a boxing match, between raising a child and tending a garden

Cause and effect: the effects of water pollution on a particular area, the effects of divorce on a child, the effects of an illegal drug, why a particular film or television show is popular, why an area of the country has high unemployment, why early training is essential for success as a ballet dancer, violinist, or athlete

Classification: types of clothing worn on your college campus, types of people who join online chat groups, types of dieters, types of television weather reports, types of rock bands, types of teachers

Definition: an Internet addict, an ideal parent or teacher, an authoritarian personality, an intellectual, a sexist, anorexia nervosa, a typical heroine in a Harlequin romance, a typical blind date

4d　Consider possible ways of arranging information.

In addition to choosing a pattern of development (or a combination of patterns), you may need to make decisions about arrangement. If you are developing a paragraph with examples, for instance, you'll need to decide how to order the examples. Or if you are contrasting two items point by point, you'll need to decide which points to discuss first, second, and so on. Often considerations of purpose and audience will help you make these choices.

Three of the most common ways of arranging information are treated in this section: time order, spatial order, and order of climax. Other possible arrangements include order of complexity (from simple to complex), order of familiarity (from most familiar to least familiar), and order of audience appeal (from "safe" ideas to those that may challenge the audience's views).

Order of time

Time order, usually chronological, is appropriate for a variety of purposes such as narrating a personal experience, telling an anecdote, describing an experiment, or explaining a process. The following paragraph, arranged in chronological order, is from an account of the author's travels on the back roads of America.

> Orion Saddle Road, after I was committed to it, narrowed to a single rutted lane affording no place to turn around; if I met somebody, one of us would have to back down. The higher I went, the more that idea unnerved me — the road was bad enough driving forward. The compass swung from point to point, and within five minutes it had touched each of the three hundred sixty degrees. The clutch started pushing back, and ruts and craters and rocks threw the steering wheel into nasty jerks that wrenched to the spine. I understood why, the day before, I'd thought there could be no road over the Chiricahuas; there wasn't. No wonder desperadoes hid in this inaccessibility.
> — William Least Heat Moon, *Blue Highways*

Time order need not be chronological. For example, you might decide to arrange events in the order in which they were revealed to you, not in the order in which they happened. Or you might choose to begin with a dramatic moment and then flash back to the events that led up to it.

Order of space

For descriptions of a location or a scene, a spatial arrangement will seem natural. Imagine yourself holding a video camera and you'll begin to see the possibilities. Might you

pan the scene from afar and then zoom to a close-up? Would
you rather sweep the camera from side to side—or from top
to bottom? Or should you try for a more impressionistic
effect, focusing the camera on first one and then another
significant feature of the scene?

The writer of the following paragraph describes the contents of a long, narrow pool hall by taking us from the front
to the back.

> The pool tables were in a line side by side from the front
> to the back of the long, narrow building. The first one was the
> biggest, and the best snooker players used it. Beyond it were
> the other tables used by lesser players, except for the last one.
> This was the bank's pool table, used only by the best players
> in the county.   —William G. Hill, student

Order of climax

When ideas are presented in the order of climax, they build
toward a conclusion. Consider the following paragraph describing the effects on workers of long-term blue-collar employment. All of the examples have an emotional impact, but
the final one—even though it might at first seem trivial—
is the most powerful. It shows us just how degrading blue-
collar work can become.

> I met people who taught me about human behavior. I
> saw people take amphetamines to keep up with ever-rising
> production rates. I saw good friends, and even relatives, physi-
> cally attack each other over job assignments that would mean
> a few cents' difference. I observed women cheating on their
> husbands and men cheating on their wives. I watched women
> hand over their entire paycheck to a bookie. I saw pregnant
> women, their feet too swollen for shoes, come to work in slip-
> pers. I saw women with colds stuff pieces of tissue up their
> nostrils so they wouldn't have to keep stopping to blow their
> nose.   —Linda Lavelle, student

Because the order of climax saves the most dramatic examples for the end, it is appropriate only when readers are likely to persist until the end. In much business writing, for example, you cannot assume that readers will read more than the first couple of sentences of a paragraph. In such cases, you will be wise to open with your most powerful examples, even at the risk of allowing the paragraph to fizzle at the end.

4e Make paragraphs coherent.

When sentences and paragraphs flow from one to another without discernible bumps, gaps, or shifts, they are said to be coherent. Coherence can be improved by strengthening the various ties between old information and new. A number of techniques for strengthening those ties are detailed in this section.

Linking ideas clearly

Readers expect to learn a paragraph's main point in a topic sentence early in the paragraph. Then, as they move into the body of the paragraph, they expect to encounter specific details, facts, or examples that support the topic sentence—either directly or indirectly. In the following paragraph, all of the sentences following the topic sentence directly support it.

> A passenger list of the early years of the Orient Express would read like a *Who's Who of the World,* from art to politics. Sarah Bernhardt and her Italian counterpart Eleonora Duse used the train to thrill the stages of Europe. For musicians there were Toscanini and Mahler. Dancers Nijinsky and Pavlova were there, while lesser performers like Harry Houdini and the girls of the Ziegfeld Follies also rode the rails. Violinists were allowed to practice on the train, and occasionally one might see trapeze artists hanging like bats from the baggage racks.
> —Barnaby Conrad III, "Train of Kings"

If a sentence does not support the topic sentence directly, readers expect it to support another sentence in the paragraph and therefore to support the topic sentence indirectly. The following paragraph begins with a topic sentence. The italicized sentences are direct supports, and the rest of the sentences are indirect supports.

> Though the open-space classroom works for many children, it is not practical for my son, David. *First, David is hyperactive.* When he was placed in an open-space classroom, he became distracted and confused. He was tempted to watch the movement going on around him instead of concentrating on his own work. *Second, David has a tendency to transpose letters and numbers, a tendency that can be overcome only by individual attention from the instructor.* In the open classroom he was moved from teacher to teacher, with each one responsible for a different subject. No single teacher worked with David long enough to diagnose the problem, let alone help him with it. *Finally, David is not a highly motivated learner.* In the open classroom, he was graded "at his own level," not by criteria for a certain grade. He could receive a B in reading and still be a grade level behind, because he was doing satisfactory work "at his own level."
>
> —Margaret Smith, student

Repeating key words

Repetition of key words is an important technique for gaining coherence. To prevent repetitions from becoming dull, you can use variations of a key word (*hike, hiker, hiking*), pronouns referring to the word (*gamblers . . . they*), and synonyms (*run, spring, race, dash*). In the following paragraph describing plots among indentured servants in the seventeenth century, historian Richard Hofstadter binds sentences together by repeating the key word *plots* and echoing it with a variety of synonyms (which are italicized).

Plots hatched by several servants to run away together occurred mostly in the plantation colonies, and the few recorded servant *uprisings* were entirely limited to those colonies. Virginia had been forced from its very earliest years to take stringent steps against *mutinous plots,* and severe punishments for *such behavior* were recorded. Most servant *plots* occurred in the seventeenth century: A contemplated *uprising* was nipped in the bud in York County in 1661; apparently led by some left-wing offshoots of the *Great Rebellion,* servants *plotted* an *insurrection* in Gloucester County in 1663, and four leaders were condemned and executed; some discontented servants apparently joined *Bacon's Rebellion* in the 1670s. In the 1680s the planters became newly apprehensive of discontent among the servants "owing to their great necessities and want of clothes," and it was feared that they would *rise up* and *plunder* the storehouses and ships; in 1682 there were plant-cutting *riots* in which servants and laborers, as well as some planters, took part. [Italics added.]

— Richard Hofstadter, *America at 1750*

Using parallel structures

Parallel structures are frequently used within sentences to underscore the similarity of ideas (see 9). They may also be used to bind together a series of sentences expressing similar information. In the following passage describing folk beliefs, anthropologist Margaret Mead presents similar information in parallel grammatical form.

Actually, almost every day, even in the most sophisticated home, something is likely to happen that evokes the memory of some old folk belief. The salt spills. A knife falls to the floor. Your nose tickles. Then perhaps, with a slightly embarrassed smile, the person who spilled the salt tosses a pinch over his left shoulder. Or someone recites the old rhyme, "Knife falls, gentleman calls." Or as you rub your nose you think, That means a letter. I wonder who's writing?

— Margaret Mead, "New Superstitions for Old"

A less skilled writer might have varied the structure, perhaps like this: *The salt gets spilled. Mother drops a knife on the floor. Your nose begins to tickle.* But these sentences are less effective; Mead's parallel structures help tie the passage together.

Maintaining consistency

Coherence suffers whenever a draft shifts confusingly from one point of view to another or from one verb tense to another. (See 13.) In addition, coherence can suffer when new information is introduced with the subject of each sentence. As a rule, a sentence's subject should echo a subject or object in the previous sentence.

The following rough-draft paragraph is needlessly hard to read because so few of the sentences' subjects are tied to earlier subjects or objects. The subjects appear in italics.

> *One* goes about trapping in this manner. At the very outset *one* acquires a "trapping" state of mind. A *library* of books must be read, and preferably *someone* with experience should educate the novice. *Preparing* for the first expedition takes several steps. The *purchase* of traps is first. A *pair* of rubber gloves, waterproof *boots*, and the grubbiest *clothes* capable of withstanding human use come next to outfit the trapper for his adventure. Finally, the *decision* has to be made on just what kind of animals to seek, what sort of bait to use, and where to place the traps.

Although the writer repeats a number of key words, such as *trapping*, the paragraph seems disconnected because new information is introduced with the subject of each sentence.

To improve the paragraph, the writer used the first-person pronoun as the subject of every sentence. The revision is much easier to read.

I went about trapping in this manner. To acquire a "trapping" state of mind, I read a library of books and talked at length with an experienced trapper, my father. Then I purchased the traps and outfitted myself by collecting a pair of rubber gloves, waterproof boots, and the grubbiest clothes capable of withstanding human use. Finally, I decided just what kinds of animals to seek, what sort of bait to use, and where to place my traps.

— John Clyde Thatcher, student

Notice that Thatcher combined some of his original sentences. By doing so, he was able to avoid excessive repetitions of the pronoun *I*. Notice, too, that he varied his sentence openings (most sentences do not begin with *I*) so that readers are not likely to find the repetitions tiresome.

Providing transitions

Transitions are bridges between what has been read and what is about to be read. Transitions help readers move from sentence to sentence; they also alert readers to more global connections of ideas—those between paragraphs or even larger blocks of text.

SENTENCE-LEVEL TRANSITIONS   Certain words and phrases signal connections between (or within) sentences. Frequently used transitions are included in the following list.

TO SHOW ADDITION
and, also, besides, further, furthermore, in addition, moreover, next, too, first, second

TO GIVE EXAMPLES
for example, for instance, to illustrate, in fact, specifically

TO COMPARE
also, in the same manner, similarly, likewise

The writing process

TO CONTRAST
but, however, on the other hand, in contrast, nevertheless, still, even though, on the contrary, yet, although

TO SUMMARIZE OR CONCLUDE
in other words, in short, in summary, in conclusion, to sum up, that is, therefore

TO SHOW TIME
after, as, before, next, during, later, finally, meanwhile, then, when, while, immediately

TO SHOW PLACE OR DIRECTION
above, below, beyond, farther on, nearby, opposite, close, to the left

TO INDICATE LOGICAL RELATIONSHIP
if, so, therefore, consequently, thus, as a result, for this reason, since

Skilled writers use transitional expressions with care, making sure, for example, not to use *consequently* when an *also* would be more precise. They are also careful to select transitions with an appropriate tone, perhaps preferring *so* to *thus* in an informal piece, *in summary* to *in short* for a scholarly essay.

In the following paragraph, taken from an argument that dinosaurs had the " 'right-sized' brains for reptiles of their body size," biologist Stephen Jay Gould uses transitions (italicized) with skill.

I don't wish to deny that the flattened, minuscule head of the large bodied "Stegosaurus" houses little brain from our subjective, top-heavy perspective, *but* I do wish to assert that we should not expect more of the beast. *First of all*, large animals have relatively smaller brains than related, small animals. The correlation of brain size with body size among kindred animals (all reptiles, all mammals, *for example*) is remarkably regular. *As* we move from small to large animals, from mice to elephants *or* small lizards to Komodo dragons, brain size increases, *but* not so fast as body size. *In other words,* bodies grow faster than brains, *and* large animals have low ratios of brain weight to body weight. *In fact,* brains grow only about two-thirds as fast as bodies. *Since* we have no reason to believe that large animals are consistently stupider than their smaller relatives, we must conclude that large animals require relatively less brain to do as well as smaller animals. *If* we do not recognize this relationship, we are likely to underestimate the mental power of very large animals, dinosaurs in particular. [Italics added.]

> —Stephen Jay Gould, "Were Dinosaurs Dumb?"

CAUTION: Do not be too self-conscious about plugging in transition words while you are drafting sentences; overuse of these signals can seem heavy-handed. Usually, you will use transitions quite naturally, just where readers need them. If you (or your reviewers) discover places where readers cannot easily move from sentence to sentence in your rough draft, you can always add transition words as you revise.

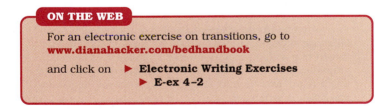

ON THE WEB

For an electronic exercise on transitions, go to
www.dianahacker.com/bedhandbook

and click on ▶ **Electronic Writing Exercises**
▶ **E-ex 4–2**

PARAGRAPH-LEVEL TRANSITIONS Paragraph-level transitions usually link the *first* sentence of a new paragraph with the *first* sentence of the previous paragraph. In other words, the topic sentences signal global connections.

Look for opportunities to allude to the subject of a previous paragraph (as summed up in its topic sentence) in the topic sentence of the next one. In his essay "Little Green Lies," Jonathan H. Alder uses this strategy in the following topic sentences, which appear in a passage describing the benefits of plastic packaging.

> Consider septic packaging, the synthetic packaging for the "juice boxes" so many children bring to school with their lunch. [*Rest of paragraph omitted.*]
>
> What is true for juice boxes is also true for other forms of synthetic packaging. [*Rest of paragraph omitted.*]

TRANSITIONS BETWEEN BLOCKS OF TEXT   In long essays, you will need to alert readers to connections between blocks of text more than one paragraph long. You can do this by inserting transitional sentences or short paragraphs at key points in the essay. Here, for example, is a transitional paragraph from a student research paper. It announces that the first part of her paper has come to a close and the second part is about to begin.

> Although the great apes have demonstrated significant language skills, one central question remains: Can they be taught to use that uniquely human language tool we call grammar, to learn the difference, for instance, between "ape bite human" and "human bite ape"? In other words, can an ape create a sentence?

Another strategy to help readers move from one block of text to another is to insert headings in your essay. Headings, which usually sit above blocks of text, allow you to announce a new topic boldly, without the need for subtle transitions. (See 5b.)

4f If necessary, adjust paragraph length.

Most readers feel comfortable reading paragraphs that range between 100 and 200 words. Shorter paragraphs force too much starting and stopping, and longer ones strain the reader's attention span. There are exceptions to this guideline, however. Paragraphs longer than 200 words frequently appear in scholarly writing, where they suggest seriousness and depth. Paragraphs shorter than 100 words occur in newspapers because of narrow columns; in informal essays to quicken the pace; and in business writing and Web sites, where readers routinely skim for main ideas.

In an essay, the first and last paragraphs will ordinarily be the introduction and conclusion. These special-purpose paragraphs are likely to be shorter than the paragraphs in the body of the essay. Typically, the body paragraphs will follow the essay's outline: one paragraph per point in short essays, a group of paragraphs per point in longer ones. Some ideas require more development than others, however, so it is best to be flexible. If an idea stretches to a length unreasonable for a paragraph, you should divide the paragraph, even if you have presented comparable points in the essay in single paragraphs.

Paragraph breaks are not always made for strictly logical reasons. Writers use them for the following reasons as well.

REASONS FOR BEGINNING A NEW PARAGRAPH

— to mark off the introduction and conclusion

— to signal a shift to a new idea

— to indicate an important shift in time or place

— to emphasize a point (by placing it at the beginning or the end, not in the middle, of a paragraph)

— to highlight a contrast

The writing process

— to signal a change of speakers (in dialogue)

— to provide readers with a needed pause

— to break up text that looks too dense

Beware of using too many short, choppy paragraphs, however. Readers want to see how your ideas connect, and they become irritated when you break their momentum by forcing them to pause every few sentences. Here are some reasons you might have for combining some of the paragraphs in a rough draft.

REASONS FOR COMBINING PARAGRAPHS

— to clarify the essay's organization

— to connect closely related ideas

— to bind together text that looks too choppy

Document Design

The term *document* is broad enough to describe anything you might write in an English class, in other classes across the curriculum, in the business world, and in everyday life. How you design a document (format it on the page) can affect how it is received.

Instructors have certain expectations about how a college paper should look (see 6a). Employers too expect documents such as business letters and memos to be formatted in standard ways (see 6b). And anyone who reads your e-mail and Web pages will appreciate an effective document design (see 7).

5

Become familiar with the principles of document design.

Good document design promotes readability, but what this means depends on your purpose and audience and perhaps on other elements of your writing situation, such as your subject and any length restrictions. (See the checklist on pp. 4–5.) All of your design choices—word processing options and use of headings, displayed lists, and other visuals—should be made in light of your specific writing situation.

5a Select appropriate format options.

Word processing programs present you with abundant format options. Before you print your final draft, make sure that your margins, line spacing, and alignment are set appropriately. Also decide which font (typeface style and size) is most appropriate for your purposes.

Margins and line spacing

For documents written on 8½" × 11" paper, leave a margin of between one and one and a half inches on all sides of the page. These margins prevent the text from looking too crowded, and they allow room for annotations, such as an instructor's comments or an editor's suggestions.

Most manuscripts-in-progress are double-spaced to allow room for editing. Final copy is often double-spaced as well, since single-spacing is less inviting to read. But at times the advantages of double-spacing are offset by other considerations. For example, most business and technical documents are single-spaced, with double-spacing between paragraphs. Single-spacing promotes quick scanning, and it also saves paper.

Alignment

Word processing programs allow you to align text and visuals on a page in four ways:

left justified

right justified

fully justified

centered

For most purposes, use left justification instead of full justification. Left-justified text lines up against the left margin but has a ragged right margin. When text is fully justified, all of the words line up against both the left and the right margins, as they do on a typeset page like the one you are now reading.

Unfortunately, text that has been fully justified on a computer can be hard to read. The problem is that extra space is added between words in some lines, creating "rivers" of white that can be distracting. The example at the top of the next page shows you how distracting extra space between words can be.

```
See   what   can   happen   when   you   choose   the   full
justification feature on a computer? Sometimes dis-
tracting gaps appear between words, making passages
needlessly hard to read.
```

Also, fully justified text may create a need for excessive hyphenation at the ends of lines. Unless your computer can create the real look of a typeset page, you will do readers a favor by turning off the full justification feature.

Fonts

If you have a choice of fonts, select a normal size (10 to 12 points) and a style that is not too offbeat. Although unusual styles of type, such as those that look handwritten, may seem attractive, they slow readers down. We all read more efficiently when a text meets our usual expectations.

CAUTION: Never write or type a college essay or any other document in all capital letters. Research shows that readers experience much frustration when they are forced to read more than a few consecutive words printed in all capital letters.

5b Consider using headings.

There is little need for headings in short essays, especially if the writer uses paragraphing and clear topic sentences to guide readers. In more complex documents, however, such as research papers, grant proposals, and business reports, headings can be a useful visual cue for readers.

Headings help readers see at a glance the organization of a document. If more than one level of heading is used, the headings also indicate the hierarchy of ideas—as they do throughout this book.

Headings serve a number of functions, depending on the needs of different readers. When readers are simply looking up information, headings will help them find it quickly. When readers are scanning, hoping to pick up the gist of things, headings will guide them. Even when readers are committed enough to read every word, headings can help. Efficient readers preview a document before they begin reading; when previewing and while reading, they are guided by any visual cues the writer provides.

CAUTION: Avoid using more headings (or more levels of headings) than you really need. Excessive use of headings can make a text choppy.

Phrasing headings

Headings should be as brief and as informative as possible. Certain styles of headings—the most common being *-ing* phrases, noun phrases, questions, and imperative sentences—work better for some purposes, audiences, and subjects than others.

Whatever style you choose, use it consistently for headings on the same level. In other words, headings on the same level of organization should be written in parallel structure (see 9), as in the following examples. The first set of headings appeared in a report written for an environmental think tank, the second in a history textbook, the third in a mutual fund brochure, and the fourth in a garden designer's newsletter.

***-ING* HEADINGS**
Safeguarding the earth's atmosphere

Charting the path to sustainable energy

Conserving global forests

Triggering the technological revolution

Strengthening international institutions

NOUN PHRASE HEADINGS
The economics of slavery

The sociology of slavery

Psychological effects of slavery

QUESTIONS AS HEADINGS
How do I buy shares?

How do I redeem shares?

What is the history of the fund's performance?

What are the tax consequences of investing in the fund?

IMPERATIVE SENTENCES AS HEADINGS
Fertilize roses in the fall.

Feed them again in the spring.

Prune roses when dormant and after flowering.

Spray roses during their growing season.

Placing and highlighting headings

Headings on the same level of organization should be positioned and highlighted in a consistent way. For example, you might center your first-level headings and print them in boldface; then you might place the second-level headings flush left (against the left margin) and underline them, like this:

First-level heading

Second-level heading

Most college papers should have only one level of heading, usually centered, as in the sample paper on pages 716–26. In business and technical writing, headings are usually placed flush left above flush-left text—without paragraph indents—to create strong alignment among elements on a page (see the memo on p. 124 for an example).

To highlight headings, you might use boldface, italics or underlining, all capital letters, color, a larger or smaller typeface than the text, a different font, or some combination of these:

boldface	color
italics	larger typeface
underlining	smaller typeface
ALL CAPITAL LETTERS	different font

On the whole, it is best to use restraint. Excessive highlighting results in a page that looks too busy, and it defeats its own purpose, since readers have trouble sorting out which headings are more important than others.

Important headings can be highlighted by using white space around them. Less important headings can be downplayed by using less white space or by running them into the text (as with the small all-capitals heading on p. 117).

5c   Consider using displayed lists.

Lists are easy to read or scan when they are displayed rather than run into your text. You might reasonably choose to display the following kinds of lists:

— steps in a process

— materials needed for a project

— parts of an object

— advice or recommendations

— items to be discussed

— criteria for evaluation (as in checklists)

Displayed lists should usually be introduced with an independent clause followed by a colon (see 35a and the preceding list). Periods are not used after items in a list unless the items are sentences.

Lists are most readable when they are presented in parallel grammatical form (see 9). In the preceding list, for instance, the items are all noun phrases. As with headings, some kinds of lists might be more appropriately presented as *-ing* phrases, as imperative sentences, or as questions.

To draw the reader's eye to a list, you might use bullets (circles or squares) or dashes if there is no need to number the items. If there is some reason to number the items, use an arabic number followed by a period for each item.

Although displayed lists can be a useful visual cue, they should not be overdone. Too many of them will give a document a choppy, cluttered look. And lists that are very long (sometimes called "laundry lists") should be avoided as well. Readers can hold only so many ideas in their short-term memory, so if a list grows too long, you should find some way of making it more concise or clustering similar items.

5d Consider adding visuals.

Visuals such as charts, graphs, tables, diagrams, maps, and photographs convey information concisely and vividly. In a student essay not intended for publication, you can use another person's visuals as long as you credit the borrowing (see 52). And with access to computer graphics, you can create your own visuals to enhance an essay, a report, or an electronic document.

This section suggests when charts, graphs, tables, and diagrams might be appropriate for your purposes. It also discusses where you might place such visuals.

Using charts, graphs, tables, and diagrams

In documents that help readers follow a process or make a decision, flow charts can be useful; for an example, see page 241 in this book. Pie charts are appropriate for indicating ratios or apportionment, as in the following example.

PIE CHART

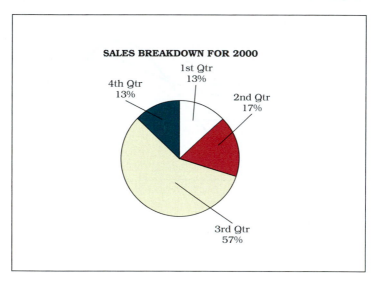

Line graphs and bar graphs illustrate disparities in numerical data. Line graphs (see page 110) are appropriate when you want to illuminate trends over a period of time, such as trends in sales, in unemployment, or in population growth. Bar graphs (see page 110) can be used for the same purpose. In addition, bar graphs are useful for highlighting comparisons, such as vote totals for rival political candidates or the number of refugees entering the United States during different time periods.

Tables are not as visually interesting as line graphs or charts, but they allow for inclusion of specific numerical data, such as exact percentages. The table on page 111 presents the responses of students and faculty to one question on a campus-wide questionnaire.

LINE GRAPH

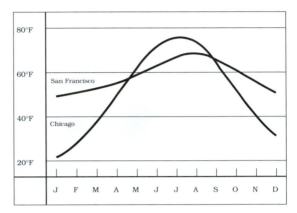

**MONTHLY MEAN TEMPERATURE IN
SAN FRANCISCO AND CHICAGO**

BAR GRAPH

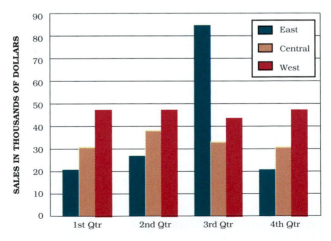

SALES BREAKDOWN BY REGION, 2000

TABLE

Is American education based too much on European history and values?

	PERCENT		
	NO	**UNDECIDED**	**YES**
Nonwhite students	21	25	54
White students	55	29	16
Nonwhite faculty	15	20	65
White faculty	57	27	16

Diagrams are useful—and sometimes indispensable—in scientific and technical writing. It is more concise, for example, to use the following diagram than to explain the chemical formula in words.

DIAGRAM

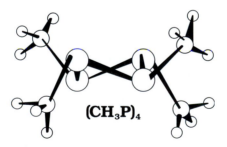

$(CH_3P)_4$

Placing visuals

A visual may be placed in the text of a document near a discussion to which it relates, or it can be put in an appendix, labeled, and referred to in the text.

Placing visuals in the text of a document can be tricky. Usually you will want the visual to appear close to the sentences that relate to it, but page breaks won't always allow this placement. At times you may need to insert the visual at a later point and tell readers where it can be found; sometimes, with the help of software, you can make the text flow around the visual.

In newsletters and in business and technical documents, page layout is both an art and a science. The best way to learn how to lay out pages is to work with colleagues who have had experience solving the many problems that can arise.

6

Use standard academic and business formats.

6a Use the manuscript format that is required by your academic discipline.

If your instructor provides formal guidelines for formatting an essay — or a more specialized document such as a lab report, a case study, or a research paper — you should of course follow them. Otherwise, use the manuscript format that is normally recommended for your academic discipline.

In most English and humanities classes, you will be asked to use the MLA (Modern Language Association) format. The following sample essay illustrates this format. For more detailed advice about MLA manuscript guidelines, along with a sample MLA research paper, see 57. If you have been asked to use APA (American Psychological Association) manuscript guidelines, see 59. *Chicago*-style guidelines appear in 60.

MLA ESSAY FORMAT

1"

½"
Weitzel 1

Tom Weitzel

Dr. Fry

English 101

18 April 2001

Double-spacing throughout

Title, centered

Who Goes to the Races?

½" indent

A favorite pastime of mine is observing people, and my favorite place to observe is at the horse races. After many encounters with the racing crowd, I have discovered that there are four distinct groups at the track: the once-a-year bunch, the professionals, the clubhouse set, and the unemployed.

The largest group at the track consists of those who show up once a year. They know little about horses or betting and rely strictly on racetrack gimmick sheets and newspaper predictions for selecting possible winners. If that strategy doesn't work, they use intuition, lucky numbers, favorite colors, or appealing names. They bet larger amounts as the day goes along, gambling on every race, including long-shot bets on exactas and daily doubles. The vast majority go home broke and frustrated.

1"

1"

More subtle and quiet are the professionals. They follow the horses from track to track and live in campers and motor homes. Many are married couples, some are retired, and all are easily spotted with their lunch sacks, water jugs, and binoculars. Since most know one another, they section themselves off in a particular area of the stadium. All rely on the racing form and on personal knowledge of each

1"

MLA ESSAY FORMAT *(continued)*

horse, jockey, and track in making the proper bet. They bet only on the smart races, rarely on the favorites. Never do they bet on exactas or daily doubles. More often than not they either break even or go home winners.

Isolated from the others is the clubhouse set. Found either at the cocktail lounge or in the restaurant, usually involved in business transactions, these racing fans rarely see a race in person; instead they do their betting via the waiter. It's difficult to tell whether they go home sad, happy, or in between. They keep their emotions to themselves.

The most interesting members of the racetrack population are the unemployed. They will be found not in the clubhouse, but right down at the rail next to the finish line. Here one can discover the real emotion of the racetrack--the screaming, the cursing, and the pushing. The unemployed are not in it for the sport. Betting is not a game for them, but a battle for survival. If they lose, they must borrow enough money to carry them until the next check comes in, and then, of course, they head right back to the track. This particular group arrives at the track beaten and leaves beaten.

I have probably lost more money than I have won at the track, but observing these four interesting groups of people makes it all worthwhile.

6b Use standard business formats.

This section provides guidelines for preparing business letters, résumés, and memos. For a more detailed discussion of these and other business documents—proposals, reports, executive summaries, and so on—consult a business writing textbook or look at examples currently being written at the organization for which you are writing.

Business letters

In writing a business letter, be direct, clear, and courteous, but do not hesitate to be firm if necessary. State your purpose or request at the beginning of the letter and include only pertinent information in the body. By being as direct and concise as possible, you show that you value your reader's time.

A sample business letter appears on page 116. This letter is typed in what is known as "modified block" style. The return address at the top and the close and signature at the bottom are lined up just to the right of the center of the width of the page. The inside address, the salutation, and the body of the letter are flush left (against the left margin). The paragraphs are not indented.

If you choose to indent your paragraphs, you are using "semiblock" style, which is considered less formal. If you choose to move all elements of the letter flush left, you are using the most formal style, "full block." This style is usually preferred when the letter is typed on letterhead stationery that gives the return address of the writer or the writer's company.

When writing to a woman, use the abbreviation *Ms.* in the salutation unless you know that the woman prefers another form of address. If you are not writing to a particular person, you can use the salutation *Dear Sir or Madam* or you can address the company itself—*Dear Solar Technology.*

BUSINESS LETTER IN MODIFIED BLOCK FORM

Return address → 121 Knox Road, #6
College Park, MD 20740
March 4, 2001

Linda Hennessee, Managing Editor
World Discovery
1650 K Street, NW
Washington, DC 20036 ← Inside address

Dear Ms. Hennessee: ← Salutation

Please accept my application for the summer editorial internship listed with the Career Development Center at the University of Maryland. Currently I am a junior at the University of Maryland, with a double major in English and Latin American studies.

Over the past three years I have gained considerable experience in newspaper and magazine journalism, as you will see on my enclosed résumé. I am familiar with the basic procedures of editing and photographic development, but my primary interests lie in feature writing and landscape photography. My professional goal is to work as a photojournalist with an international focus, preferably for a major magazine. I cannot imagine a better introduction to that career than a summer at *World Discovery*.

I am available for an interview almost any time and can be reached at 301-555-2651. My e-mail address is jrichard@umdcp.edu.

I look forward to hearing from you.

Close → Sincerely,

Signature → *Jeffrey Richardson*

Jeffrey Richardson

Enc.

Below the signature, flush left, you may include the abbreviation *Enc.* to indicate that something is enclosed with the letter or the abbreviation *cc* followed by a colon and the name of someone who is receiving a copy of the letter.

Résumés

An effective résumé gives relevant information in a clear and concise form. The trick is to present yourself in the best possible light without going on at length and wasting your reader's time.

When you send out your résumé, you should include a letter that tells what position you seek and where you learned about it (see p. 116). The letter should also summarize your education and past experience, relating them to the job you are applying for. End the letter with a suggestion for a meeting, and tell your prospective employer when you will be available.

You may be asked to produce a traditional résumé, a scannable résumé, or a Web résumé. Brief guidelines for each type of résumé appear in this section, along with examples.

TRADITIONAL RÉSUMÉS Traditional résumés are written on paper, and they are screened by people, not by computers. Because screening committees may face stacks of applications, they often spend very little time looking at each résumé. Therefore you will need to make your résumé as reader-friendly as possible. Here are a few guidelines to follow:

—Limit your résumé to one page if possible, two pages at the most.

—Organize your information into clear categories—Education, Experience, and so on.

—Present your educational and work experience in reverse chronological order to highlight your most recent accomplishments.

TRADITIONAL RÉSUMÉ

Jeffrey Richardson

121 Knox Road, #6
College Park, MD 20740
301–555–2651
jrichard@umdcp.edu

OBJECTIVE   To obtain an editorial internship with a magazine

EDUCATION
Fall 1998–   University of Maryland
present   • B.A. expected in June 2002
        • Double major: English and Latin American studies
        • GPA: 3.7 (on a 4-point scale)

EXPERIENCE
Fall 1999–   Photo editor, *The Diamondback*, college paper
present   • Shoot and print photographs
        • Select and lay out photographs and other visuals

Summer   Intern, *The Globe,* Fairfax, Virginia
2000   • Wrote stories about local issues and personalities
        • Interviewed political candidates
        • Edited and proofread copy
        • Contributed photographs
        • Coedited "The Landscapes of Northern Virginia:
          A Photoessay"

Summers   Tutor, Fairfax County ESL Program
1999,   • Tutored Latino students in English as a Second Language
2000   • Trained new tutors

ACTIVITIES   Photographers' Workshop, Spanish Club

REFERENCES   Available upon request

—Use bullets to draw the reader's eye to listed information.

—Use strong, active verbs to emphasize your accomplishments. (Use present-tense verbs, such as *manage,* for current activities and past-tense verbs, such as *managed,* for past activities.)

A sample traditional résumé appears on page 118.

SCANNABLE RÉSUMÉS   Scannable résumés are submitted on paper or via e-mail. The prospective employer puts the résumé through a scanner that enters the information from it into a database; the database matches keywords in a job description with keywords in the résumé. If a résumé survives the initial scan, it will later be reviewed by human beings.

As you can see from the sample on page 120, a scannable résumé looks considerably different from a traditional one. It must focus on keywords likely to be matched by the computer. (See the Keywords section at the bottom.) In addition, it must be very simply formatted so that the scanner can accurately pick up its content. In general, follow these guidelines when preparing a scannable résumé:

—Include a Keywords section that gives characteristics of your experience that match the job description. Use nouns, such as *manager,* not verbs such as *manage* or *managed.*

—Use standard résumé headings (for example, Education, Work Experience, References).

—Do not use graphic devices such as boldface or italics. To indicate italics, use an underscore before and after italicized words.

—Do not use word processor formatting, such as tabbed indents, columns, or bullets. Do not insert visuals.

—Use white, 8½" × 11" paper and a laser or an ink-jet printer. Avoid folding or stapling the document.

SCANNABLE RÉSUMÉ

Jeffrey Richardson
121 Knox Road, #6
College Park, MD 20740
301-555-2651
jrichard@umdcp.edu

OBJECTIVE
To obtain an editorial internship with a magazine

EDUCATION
Fall 1998–present
University of Maryland
B.A. expected in June 2002
Double major: English and Latin American studies
GPA: 3.7 (on a 4-point scale)

EXPERIENCE
Fall 1999–present
Photo editor, _The Diamondback_, college paper
Shoot and print photographs
Select and lay out photographs and other visuals

Summer 2000
Intern, _The Globe_, Fairfax, Virginia
Wrote stories about local issues and personalities
Interviewed political candidates
Edited and proofread copy
Contributed photographs
Coedited "The Landscapes of Northern Virginia: A Photoessay"

Summers 1999, 2000
Tutor, Fairfax County ESL Program
Tutored Latino students in English as a Second Language
Trained new tutors

ACTIVITIES
Photographers' Workshop, Spanish Club

REFERENCES
Available upon request

KEYWORDS
editorial internship, magazine, photo editor, layout, photographs,
writer, interviewer, editor, proofreader, tutor, trainer, Spanish

WEB RÉSUMÉS   A Web résumé makes it easy to provide prospective employers with recent information about your employment goals and accomplishments. It also allows you to present a number of details about yourself without overwhelming your readers. You can keep your opening screen simple and provide hyperlinks to take readers farther down the page. Readers can follow up on links as they choose.

Although Web résumés can vary considerably in scope and depth, you should generally adhere to the following guidelines:

— Put identifying information—your name, address, phone number, and e-mail address—at the top. Include a link to your e-mail address.

— Include a Keywords section. Keywords allow potential employers to find your résumé using a database.

— Be as concise as possible on the opening screen.

— Place links to sections such as Education and Experience high enough on the screen that readers won't need to scroll to see them.

— Limit your résumé to one printable "page." Offer a plain-text version that is easy to print (with no frames, for example).

— Keep your résumé current, and list the date on which you last updated it.

For a sample Web résumé, see page 122.

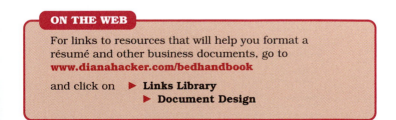

ON THE WEB

For links to resources that will help you format a résumé and other business documents, go to
www.dianahacker.com/bedhandbook

and click on   ▶ **Links Library**
                      ▶ **Document Design**

WEB RÉSUMÉ

Jeffrey Richardson
121 Knox Road, #6
College Park, MD 20740
301-555-2651
jrichard@umdcp.edu

Visible
on the
opening
screen

Objective
To obtain an editorial internship with a magazine

Summary of Qualifications
A current University of Maryland student and English major
with newspaper editorial and photography experience

More About My
Education | Experience | Activities | References

Portfolio
Photography
Examples of my published photos and other photos from
my personal portfolio
Writing
Samples of my published and unpublished writing

Education
Fall 1998-present
University of Maryland
B.A. expected in June 2002
Double major: English and Latin American studies
GPA: 3.7 (on a 4-point scale)

Experience
Fall 1999-present
Photo editor, *The Diamondback*, college paper
Shoot and print photographs
Select and lay out photographs and other visuals

Summer 2000
Intern, *The Globe*, Fairfax, Virginia
Wrote stories about local issues and personalities
Interviewed political candidates
Edited and proofread copy
Contributed photographs
Coedited "The Landscapes of Northern Virginia: A Photoessay"

Summers 1999, 2000
Tutor, Fairfax County ESL Proram
Tutored Latino students in English as a Second Language
Trained new tutors

Activities
Photographers' Workshop, Spanish Club

References
Available upon request

Keywords
editorial internship, magazine, photo editor, layout, photographs,
writer, interviewer, editor, proofreader, tutor, trainer, Spanish

Last Updated: April 4, 2001   **Printable Version**   **Back to Top**

Memos

Business memos (short for *memorandums*) are a form of communication used within a company or organization. Usually brief and to the point, a memo reports information, makes a request, or recommends an action. The format of a memo, which varies from company to company, is designed for easy distribution, quick reading, and efficient filing.

Most memos display the date, the name of the recipient, the name of the sender, and the subject on separate lines at the top of the page. Many companies have preprinted forms for memos, and some word processing programs allow you to call up a memo template that prints standard memo lines—"To," "cc" (for others receiving a copy of the memo), "From," and "Subject"—at the top of the page.

Because readers of memos are busy people, you cannot assume that they will read your memo word for word. Therefore the subject line should describe the subject as clearly and concisely as possible, and the introductory paragraph should get right to the point. In addition, the body of the memo should be well organized and easy to scan. To promote scanning, use headings where possible and display any items that deserve special attention by setting them off from the text. A sample memo with headings and a displayed list appears on page 124.

Document design

BUSINESS MEMO

Commonwealth Press

MEMORANDUM

February 26, 2001

To: Production, promotion, and editorial assistants

cc: Stephen Chapman

From: Helen Brown

Subject: New computers for staff

We will receive the new personal computers next week for the assistants in production, promotion, and editorial. In preparation, I would like you to take part in a training program and to rearrange your work areas to accommodate the new equipment.

Training Program

A computer consultant will teach in-house workshops on how to use our spreadsheet program. If you have already tried the program, be prepared to discuss any problems you have encountered.

Workshops for our three departments will be held in the training room at the following times:

- Production: Monday, March 5, 10:00 a.m. to 2:00 p.m.
- Promotion: Wednesday, March 7, 10:00 a.m. to 2:00 p.m.
- Editorial: Friday, March 9, 10:00 a.m. to 2:00 p.m.

Lunch will be provided in the cafeteria. If you cannot attend, please let me know by March 2.

Allocation and Setup

To give everyone access to a computer, we will set up the new computers as follows: two in the assistants' workspace in production; two in the area outside the conference room for the promotion assistants; and two in the library for the editorial assistants.

Assistants in all three departments should see me before the end of the week to discuss preparation of the spaces for the new equipment.

7

Create effective electronic documents.

7a Follow the conventions of e-mail.

As you are no doubt aware, e-mail is fast replacing snail mail in the business world and in most people's personal lives. E-mail is also being used in the academic world for communication between professors and their students and among students in a class.

As with all writing, you should keep your purpose and audience in mind as you draft e-mail. But you should also be aware of the special conventions of this fast-paced form of communication.

Keeping messages reader-friendly

Especially in business and academic contexts, you will want to show readers that you value their time. Your message may be just one of many that your reader has to wade through. Although you may need to spend more of your own time to create a reader-friendly e-mail, readers will appreciate the fact that you took that extra care.

Here are some strategies that you can use to make your messages reader-friendly:

— Fill in the subject line with a meaningful, concise subject to help the reader sort through messages and set priorities.

— Put the most important part of your message where it will be seen on the first screen.

— For long, detailed messages, consider providing a summary at the beginning.

— Write concisely, and keep paragraphs fairly short, especially if your audience is likely to read your message on the screen.

E-MAIL MESSAGE

Return-Path: <dportes@umass-boston.edu>
Date: Fri, 17 Nov 2000 22:31:45-0500
To: rdayson@newhoriz.org
cc: Helen Tran <htran@umass-boston.edu>
From: Danielle Portes <dportes@umass-boston.edu>
Subject: Telephone interview on Dec. 4

Dear Ms. Dayson:

Thank you for taking the time to speak with me last week about my research project. As we agreed, I am sending some questions for you to consider before our phone interview on December 4 at 2 p.m.

QUESTIONS ABOUT GUESTS

What symptoms of stress do guests--both women and their children--show when they first arrive at the shelter?

What problems, in addition to the abuse itself, must guests deal with (for example, lack of support from family or friends, financial concerns, problems in dealing with police and courts)?

Can you think of any past or current guests who might agree to an interview?

QUESTIONS ABOUT STAFFERS

What are the main stresses that staffers face? How do they cope with these stresses?

What do staffers see as the rewards as well as the drawbacks of the job?

On average, how many guests does each staffer work with every day? every week?

Can you think of any past or current staffers who might agree to an interview?

I appreciate your considering these questions and look forward to our interview.

Sincerely,
Danielle Portes
Phone: 617-555-7777

(In e-mails meant to be printed out, paragraphs can be some-what longer.)

—Avoid writing in all capital letters or all lowercase letters, a practice that is easy on the writer but hard on the reader.

—Keep in mind that a recipient's e-mail system may not accept attachments. When possible, include the text of an attach-ment in the body of the e-mail.

—Proofread for typos and obvious errors that are likely to slow down or annoy the reader.

For a sample e-mail message, see page 126.

Using an appropriate tone

Because e-mail is fast-paced and often informal, it is easy to strike an unprofessional tone if you are not careful. For ex-ample, if you omit the greeting line of an e-mail (such as *Hello, Gloria* or *Dear Professor Hart*), some readers may feel they are being treated unprofessionally. The same is true if you omit a brief closing (such as *Bye for now* or *Sincerely,* followed by your name). In the business and academic worlds, many readers are put off by flippant language or in-appropriate jokes. Even when a joke may be appropriate, you can't be sure that all readers will understand it in the spirit you intended it.

Some e-mailers use emoticons (combinations of symbols that look like faces turned sideways) and abbreviations (such as *TIA* for "thanks in advance"). Though these short-cuts are appropriate among friends, they may confuse or even annoy readers in business and academic contexts.

Obviously you should resist the temptation to "flame"—to spout off angry or insulting messages. One problem with e-mail is that it's so easy to press the send button—and then regret what you've done. When you have written a heated message, print it out and take a cool look at it. Chances are, you will decide to tone it down before sending it or you may choose not to send it at all.

Respecting privacy rights

E-mail programs make it easy to forward a message you received to another person or even to a large group of people. You should do this only when you are absolutely certain that the original sender would approve. It is always best to check first. If you decide to forward the message, send a copy to the sender who can then see exactly who has received it.

7b   Create effective Web sites.

Web sites in the academic and business worlds are usually aimed at audiences looking for ideas and information, not entertainment. You may have noticed that the most effective informational Web sites give you quick and easy access to what you're looking for.

As you are no doubt aware, a Web site consists of a home page and any number of internal pages linked to the home page. Deciding what to put on the home page and how to organize internal pages can present a challenge. When making such crucial decisions, consider your readers' needs and expectations:

—Why are they visiting your site?

—What are they expecting to find?

—What is their level of interest?

—Do they plan to read on-screen or to print hard copy?

The design of your site—from its home page, to its structure, to its page layout and even its writing style—will depend on the answers to such questions.

The home page

A home page consists of text and visuals on an opening screen and any other material that can be reached by scrolling. Because many Web users will resist scrolling—at least

SAMPLE HOME PAGE

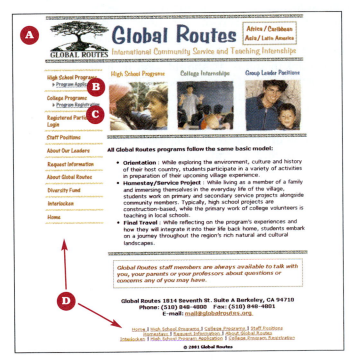

A The sponsoring organization and purpose of the site are clearly defined at the top of the page.

B By highlighting the main audiences for the site, this home page allows readers to skip information that is not relevant to their search.

C Appealing visual images emphasize the site's three main audiences.

D Links to internal pages are consistently placed on the left side of the screen and in the footer to help readers navigate the site.

initially—you will need to take advantage of the opening screen, sometimes called "prime real estate."

The opening screen of your home page should introduce visitors to the site, give them an overview of its contents, and show them that you have their needs (not your own agenda) in mind. It should also include navigational links, words or visual images that, at the click of the mouse, will send them to other locations or pages within the site. Usually these links are clustered together—often along the top of the screen or on one side—leaving room in the center for the name of the author or sponsor, the title, a relevant visual or two, and an indication of the purpose of the site. The example on page 129 illustrates a well-designed opening screen; the site sponsors community service and teaching internships for students.

The length of your home page depends on whether your visitors are likely to read onscreen or to print out and read hard copy. For onscreen readers, keep the page relatively short—an easily digested chunk of information—with links to equally brief internal pages. You can assume that visitors will read your text in a nonlinear manner, skipping some links but following others. If visitors to your site are more likely to print out information, you do not need to worry so much about the length of the home page.

Structure and navigation

Web sites consisting of more than one page usually have hierarchical structures: General pages link to more specific pages, which in turn may link to even more specific pages. On page 131 is an example of a Web site structure for a chain of fitness centers.

How shallow or how deep should your hierarchy be? In other words, how many levels make sense? The answer depends on the complexity of your material and your audience's needs, but two cautions are in order. A structure is too shallow if your readers must deal with long "laundry

SAMPLE WEB SITE STRUCTURE

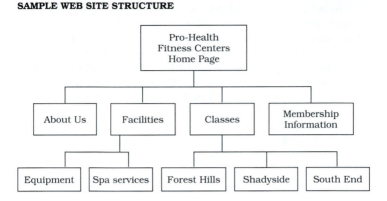

lists" of choices (unless they can be arranged alphabetically or by date). A structure is too deep if readers are needlessly forced to drill down through several layers of your hierarchy to reach what they need.

Visitors to your site will navigate it in different ways, depending on their interests. They will choose some links and ignore others, landing on internal pages in an order that you can't predict. Indeed, some visitors may arrive at one of your internal pages without having gone through your home page. Because of this unpredictability, provide as much context as possible for each internal page:

— Put key information on each internal page: a title, a link to the home page, and perhaps a list of links to other pages (such lists create context by outlining the site).

— Provide a brief overview that puts the internal page in context; make sure the content of the page can be understood on its own.

— Repeat design elements so that visitors will feel at home: Place navigational aids consistently, and use consistent background colors, fonts, visual motifs, and formatting.

In addition to providing links within your site, you may want to link to other sites. When you decide that an external link enhances the message of your site, create some context for it so that visitors will understand why it is worthwhile and what to expect if they follow it. Avoid external links that are distracting or unnecessary. Remember that an external link sends visitors into unfamiliar territory, where they may get lost or, worse, decide not to return.

Because a link to another site is an implicit endorsement of that site, you should evaluate potential sites before linking to them. As a courtesy to readers, periodically visit the sites you have links to; remove any links to sites that are nonfunctioning, and reroute links to sites that have moved.

Page layout and writing style

Don't expect Web site visitors to read in the traditional way: word by word. Most will scan your site, looking for information of interest and ignoring the rest. To keep the attention of a Web audience, make your page layout and writing style as user-friendly as possible.

EXCEPTION: If content on your site is scholarly work meant to be printed out, you can assume that your audience is motivated to read, not just to scan. Even so, visitors will appreciate a reader-friendly page layout and writing style.

PAGE LAYOUT To promote easy scanning, break up your text with headings and displayed lists and, when appropriate, display information with graphics such as clip art, photos, and charts. (See 5b–5d.)

Some common design practices make a site needlessly hard to read. If you are an experienced Web user, you no doubt could have written the following advice:

—Don't stretch lines of text across the full width of the screen. The reader's eye gets lost as it swoops from line to line.

— Don't make readers scroll sideways.

— Avoid ALL CAPS or *all italic* text. It slows readers down.

— Get rid of the busy background. The print is practically illegible.

— Turn off nonstop animations. They are distracting.

Graphics and other media, such as films and sound clips, can enhance a Web site, but they should be used thoughtfully — to support your message. For example, one student enhanced his Web site on Ralph Ellison's *The Invisible Man* by using a "dissolving" graphic, a visual representation of the novel's theme of invisibility. Too often, however, Web graphics and sound clips are used gratuitously, just for show. Most visitors to a site are annoyed by embellishments that take a long time to download and then turn out to be needless distractions.

In addition, consider how your text and visuals will look when printed out. To prevent some printers from chopping off words and images at the right margin, limit the width of your pages. If you've used a lot of graphics, provide a printable version of your text minus the graphics; graphics can be slow to print and may be irrelevant for your readers' purposes.

WRITING STYLE   Visitors to your Web site value their time. As a rule, they want concise, factual information that can be understood right away. For example, they expect to learn the key idea of a paragraph in its first sentence; if it's not there, they may well move on. They also prefer sentences that waste no words; a verbose, pseudointellectual style will send them elsewhere.

Web users are also sensitive to tone. There is so much promotional hype on the Web that many users have a keen ear for it. The tone of your site will vary, of course, depending on your purpose and audience, but in general aim for an objective — not a promotional — tone.

PROMOTIONAL

Our site tells you everything you want to know about hang gliding! Check out our awesome video clips and click on links to the coolest sites on the Web.

OBJECTIVE

Whether you're a beginning hang glider or a seasoned flier, this site will show you how and where to glide. Visit our Video Window for an animated bird's-eye view.

An objective tone enhances your credibility and makes it likely that readers will trust you enough to stay with you.

ON THE WEB

For links to html tutorials and other resources with technical advice about designing documents, go to
www.dianahacker.com/bedhandbook

and click on   ▶ **Links Library**
                 ▶ **Document Design**

Clear Sentences

8

Prefer active verbs.

As a rule, choose an active verb and pair it with a subject that names the person or thing doing the action. Active verbs express meaning more emphatically and vigorously than their weaker counterparts—forms of the verb *be* or verbs in the passive voice.

> **PASSIVE**   The pumps *were destroyed* by a surge of power.
>
> **BE VERB**   A surge of power *was* responsible for the destruction of the pumps.
>
> **ACTIVE**   A surge of power *destroyed* the pumps.

Verbs in the passive voice lack strength because their subjects receive the action instead of doing it. Forms of the verb *be* (*be, am, is, are, was, were, being, been*) lack vigor because they convey no action.

Although passive verbs and the forms of *be* have legitimate uses, if an active verb can carry your meaning, use it. Even among active verbs, some are more active—and therefore more vigorous and colorful—than others. Carefully selected verbs can energize a piece of writing.

▶   The goalie crouched low, ~~reached~~ out his stick, and ~~sent~~ the
    rebound away from the mouth of the net.

Corrections above: "reached" → swept, "sent" → hooked

Some speakers of English as a second language avoid the passive voice even when it is appropriate. For advice on transforming an active sentence to the passive, see 62c.

ESL

GRAMMAR CHECKERS are fairly good at flagging passive verbs, such as *were given*. However, because passive verbs are sometimes appropriate, you — not the computer program — must decide whether to make a passive verb active.

8a Use the active voice unless you have a good reason for choosing the passive.

In the active voice, the subject does the action; in the passive voice, the subject receives the action (see also 58c). Although both voices are grammatically correct, the active voice is usually more effective because it is simpler and more direct.

ACTIVE The Montgomery College Board of Trustees *reached* a decision.

PASSIVE A decision *was reached* by the Montgomery College Board of Trustees.

In passive sentences, the actor (in this case the Board of Trustees) frequently disappears from the sentence: *A decision was reached.*

In most cases, you will want to emphasize the actor, so you should use the active voice. To replace a passive verb with an active alternative, make the actor the subject of the sentence.

▶ *A bolt of lightning struck the transformer,*
~~The transformer was struck by a bolt of lightning,~~ plunging
us into darkness.

The active verb (*struck*) makes the point more forcefully than the passive verb (*was struck*).

> *The settlers stripped the land of timber before realizing the*
> ~~The land was stripped of timber before the settlers realized~~
>   ^
> ~~the~~ consequences of their actions.

The revision emphasizes the actors (*settlers*) by naming them in the subject.

> *We did not take down the*
> ~~The~~ Christmas decorations ~~were not taken down~~ until
>   ^
> Valentine's Day.

Often the actor does not appear in a passive-voice sentence. To turn such a sentence into the active voice, the writer must decide on an appropriate subject, in this case *We.*

Appropriate uses of the passive

The passive voice is appropriate if you wish to emphasize the receiver of the action or to minimize the importance of the actor.

APPROPRIATE PASSIVE	Many native Hawaiians *are forced* to leave their beautiful beaches to make room for hotels and condominiums.
APPROPRIATE PASSIVE	As the time for harvest approaches, the tobacco plants *are sprayed* with a chemical to retard the growth of suckers.

The writer of the first sentence wished to emphasize the receiver of the action, *Hawaiians.* The writer of the second sentence wished to focus on the tobacco plants, not on the people spraying them.

In much scientific writing, the passive voice properly emphasizes the experiment or process being described, not the researcher.

APPROPRIATE PASSIVE	The solution *was heated* to the boiling point, and then it *was reduced* in volume by 50 percent.

ON THE WEB

Rules on avoiding the passive voice have sparked debates. If you're interested in learning why, go to
www.dianahacker.com/bedhandbook

and click on ▶ **Language Debates**
           ▶ **Passive voice**

LOOKING AT YOURSELF AS A WRITER
The passive voice

If you are frequently tempted to use the passive voice in contexts where the active voice would be more effective, consider some common causes and cures.

CAUSE   In an attempt to avoid using the word *I* or *you*, you resort to the passive voice, like this: *In my excitement, my glass of iced tea was knocked over. Before a hard workout, warmup exercises are advised.*

CURE   Feel free to use the words *I* and *you* when they are appropriate: *In my excitement, I knocked over my glass of iced tea. Before a hard workout, you should do some warmup exercises.* (See pp. 51–53 for a discussion of appropriate uses of *I* and *you*.)

CAUSE   At work, you are surrounded by writers who use the passive voice, and you are picking up the habit from them.

CURE   Look at your co-workers' writing with a critical eye, noting when their use of the passive is effective — and when it is not. Then look at your own writing with an equally critical eye.

CAUSE   Your major is science or technology, disciplines in which use of the passive is often appropriate.

CURE   Shift gears when you are taking classes outside of your major. In most disciplines, the active voice usually emphasizes your point more clearly than the passive.

Clear sentences

8b Replace *be* verbs that result in dull or wordy sentences.

Not every *be* verb needs replacing. The forms of *be* (*be, am, is, are, was, were, being, been*) work well when you want to link a subject to a noun that clearly renames it or to an adjective that describes it: *History is a bucket of ashes. Scoundrels are always sociable.* And when used as helping verbs before present participles (*is flying, are disappearing*) to express ongoing action, *be* verbs are fine: *Derrick was plowing the field when his wife went into labor.* (See 29a.)

If using a *be* verb makes a sentence needlessly dull and wordy, however, consider replacing it. Often a phrase following the verb will contain a word (such as *violation*) that suggests a more vigorous, active alternative (*violate*).

▶ Burying nuclear waste in Antarctica would ~~be in violation of~~ *violate*

an international treaty.

Violate is less wordy and more vigorous than *be in violation of.*

▶ When Rosa Parks ~~was resistant to~~ *resisted* giving up her seat on the

bus, she became a civil rights hero.

Resisted is stronger than *was resistant to.*

8c As a rule, choose a subject that names the person or thing doing the action.

In weak, unemphatic prose, both the actor and the action may be buried in sentence elements other than the subject and the verb. In the following sentence, for example, the actor and the action both appear in prepositional phrases, word groups that do not receive much attention from readers.

WEAK   Exposure to Dr. Martinez's excellent teaching had the effect of inspiring me to major in education.

EMPHATIC   Dr. Martinez's excellent teaching inspired me to major in education.

Consider the subjects and verbs of the two versions — *exposure had* versus *teaching inspired.* Clearly the latter expresses the writer's point more emphatically.

▶ ~~The use of cocaine~~ *Cocaine used* by pregnant women can ~~be a major contributor to~~ *cause* severe brain damage in infants.

In the original version, the subject and verb — *use can be* — express the point blandly. *Cocaine can cause* alerts readers to the dangers of cocaine more emphatically than *use can be.*

EXERCISE 8–1

Revise any weak, unemphatic sentences by replacing *be* verbs or passive verbs with active alternatives and, if necessary, by naming in the subject the person or thing doing the action. Some sentences are emphatic; do not change them. Revisions of lettered sentences appear in the back of the book. Example:

> ~~The campfire was doused by the ranger before we were given~~ *The ranger doused the campfire before giving us* a ticket for unauthorized use of a campsite.

a. The Prussians were victorious over the Saxons in 1745.
b. The entire operation is managed by Ahmed, the producer.
c. Yellow flags were thrown down by all the referees.
d. At the crack of rocket and mortar blasts, I jumped from the top bunk and landed on my buddy below, who was crawling on the floor looking for his boots.
e. There were shouting protesters on the courthouse steps.

1. Just as the police were closing in, two shots were fired by the terrorists from the roof of the hotel.
2. Her letter was in acknowledgment of the student's participation in the literacy program.
3. The bomb bay doors rumbled open and freezing air whipped through the plane.
4. Listening to the music of Charlie Parker and John Coltrane had the effect of inspiring me to take up the saxophone.
5. The only responsibility I was given by my parents was putting gas in the brand-new Mitsubishi they bought me my senior year.

ON THE WEB

For electronic exercises on using active verbs, go to
www.dianahacker.com/bedhandbook

and click on ▶ **Electronic Grammar Exercises**
▶ **E-ex 8–1**

9

Balance parallel ideas.

If two or more ideas are parallel, they are easier to grasp when expressed in parallel grammatical form. Single words should be balanced with single words, phrases with phrases, clauses with clauses.

A kiss can be a comma, a question mark, or an exclamation

point.   — Mistinguett

This novel is not to be tossed lightly aside, but to be hurled

with great force.   — Dorothy Parker

In matters of principle, stand like a rock; in matters of taste,

swim with the current.   —Thomas Jefferson

Writers often use parallelism to create emphasis. (See pp. 194–95.)

GRAMMAR CHECKERS do not flag faulty parallelism. Because computer programs have no way of assessing whether two or more ideas are parallel in meaning, they fail to catch the faulty parallelism in sentences such as this: *In my high school, boys were either jocks, preppies, or studied constantly.*

9a   Balance parallel ideas in a series.

Readers expect items in a series to appear in parallel grammatical form. When one or more of the items violate readers' expectations, a sentence will be needlessly awkward.

▶ Abused children commonly exhibit one or more of the follow-

ing symptoms: withdrawal, rebelliousness, restlessness, and *depression.* ~~they are depressed.~~
   ^

The revision presents all of the items as nouns.

▶ Hooked on romance novels, I learned that there is nothing

more important than being rich, looking good, and *having* ~~to have~~ a
                                                       ^
good time.

The revision uses *-ing* forms for all items in the series.

▶ **After assuring us that he was sober, Sam drove down the**
　　　　　　　　　　　　　　　　　went through
　　middle of the road, ran one red light, and ~~two stop signs.~~
　　　　　　　　　　　　　　　　　　　　　　　　　^

The revision adds a verb to make the three items parallel:
drove . . . , ran . . . , went through. . . .

NOTE: In headings and lists, aim for as much parallelism as
the content allows. (See 5b and 5c.)

9b　Balance parallel ideas presented as pairs.

When pairing ideas, underscore their connection by expressing them in similar grammatical form. Paired ideas are
usually connected in one of these ways:

　—with a coordinating conjunction such as *and, but,* or *or*

　—with a pair of correlative conjunctions such as *either . . . or*
　　or *not only . . . but also*

　—with a word introducing a comparison, usually *than* or *as*

Parallel ideas linked with coordinating conjunctions

Coordinating conjunctions (*and, but, or, nor, for, so,* and *yet*)
link ideas of equal importance. When those ideas are closely
parallel in content, they should be expressed in parallel
grammatical form.

▶ **At Lincoln High School, vandalism can result in suspension**
　　　　　　　　　expulsion
　　or even ~~being expelled~~ from school.
　　　　　　　^

The revision balances the nouns *suspension* and *expulsion.*

▶ **Many states are reducing property taxes for home owners**
　　　　extending
　　and ~~extend~~ financial aid in the form of tax credits to renters.
　　　^

The revision balances the verb *reducing* with the verb *extending.*

Parallel ideas linked with correlative conjunctions

Correlative conjunctions come in pairs: *either . . . or, neither . . . nor, not only . . . but also, both . . . and, whether . . . or.* Make sure that the grammatical structure following the second half of the pair is the same as that following the first half.

▶ Thomas Edison was not only a prolific inventor but also ~~was~~

a successful entrepreneur.

The words *a prolific inventor* follow *not only,* so *a successful entrepreneur* should follow *but also.* Repeating *was* creates an unbalanced effect.

▶ I was advised either to change my flight or *to* take the train.

To change my flight, which follows *either,* should be balanced with *to take the train,* which follows *or.*

Comparisons linked with than or as

In comparisons linked with *than* or *as,* the elements being compared should be expressed in parallel grammatical structure.

▶ It is easier to speak in abstractions than ~~grounding~~ *to ground* one's

thoughts in reality.

▶ Mother could not persuade me that giving is as much a joy as

receiving.
~~to receive.~~

To speak in abstractions is balanced with *to ground one's thoughts in reality. Giving* is balanced with *receiving.*

NOTE: Comparisons should also be logical and complete. (See 10c.)

9c Repeat function words to clarify parallels.

Function words such as prepositions (*by*, *to*) and subordinating conjunctions (*that*, *because*) signal the grammatical nature of the word groups to follow. Although they can sometimes be omitted, include them whenever they signal parallel structures that might otherwise be missed by readers.

▶ Many smokers try switching to a brand they find distasteful
  to
  or a low tar and nicotine cigarette.
  ^

In the original sentence the prepositional phrase was too complex for easy reading. The repetition of the preposition *to* prevents readers from losing their way.

▶ The ophthalmologist told me that Julie was extremely far-
  that
  sighted but corrective lenses would help considerably.
  ^

A second subordinating conjunction helps readers sort out the two parallel ideas: *that* Julie was extremely farsighted and *that* corrective lenses would help.

NOTE: If it is possible to streamline the sentence, repetition of the function word may not be necessary.

▶ The board reported that its investments had done well in the

  first quarter but ~~that they~~ had since dropped in value.

Instead of linking two subordinate clauses beginning with *that*, the revision balances the two parts of a compound predicate— *had done well in the first quarter* and *had since dropped in value*.

EXERCISE 9–1

Edit the following sentences to correct faulty parallelism. Revisions of lettered sentences appear in the back of the book. Example:

> We began the search by calling the Department of Social
> Services and ~~requested~~ *requesting* a list of licensed day care centers in
> our area.

a. Police dogs are used for finding lost children, tracking criminals, and the detection of bombs and illegal drugs.

b. Roger explained to the immigration officer that his visa had expired and of his applying to have it renewed.

c. It is more difficult to sustain an exercise program than starting one.

d. During basic training, I was not only told what to do but also what to think.

e. Jan wanted to drive to the wine country or at least Sausalito.

1. Activities on Wednesday afternoons include fishing trips, dance lessons, and computers.

2. Tony found that it was faster to ride his bike than driving into the city.

3. The streets were not only too steep but also were too narrow for anything other than pedestrian traffic.

4. More plants fail from improper watering than any other cause.

5. The winner of the gluttony contest swallowed six large pancakes, slurped down a cream pie, gobbled six waffles, and four pastries in front of the dumbfounded judges.

ON THE WEB

For electronic exercises on parallelism, go to
www.dianahacker.com/bedhandbook

and click on ▶ **Electronic Grammar Exercises**
▶ **E-ex 9–1**

LOOKING AT YOURSELF AS A WRITER
Parallelism

Nearly all writers encounter occasional problems with parallelism. Here are some common causes and cures.

CAUSE   You don't realize how awkward faulty parallelism can sound to readers.

CURE   Read aloud some sentences containing faulty parallelism (sentences in 9 or in Exercise 9–1, for example) to hear how awkward they sound. You can use the same read-aloud strategy for your own drafts.

CAUSE   You worry so much about sentence variety that you introduce it in inappropriate contexts.

CURE   Learn to appreciate the power of parallelism. In your reading, notice how skilled writers use parallelism to emphasize connections among ideas. Shakespeare has Hamlet say "to die, to sleep, perchance to dream" (not "to die, to sleep, perchance some dreaming").

CAUSE   You can't think of the right word or you're not sure how to spell the word that's needed to complete your parallel ideas.

CURE   Check a thesaurus or a dictionary.

EXERCISE 9–2

Describe the parallel structure in the following passages and discuss how the use of parallelism contributes to the effectiveness of each. (Also see 14f, which discusses parallel structure.)

1. All respect we may have had for politicians, preachers, lawyers, governors, Presidents, senators, congressmen was utterly destroyed as we watched them temporizing and compromising

over right and wrong, over legality and illegality, over constitutionality and unconstitutionality. — Eldridge Cleaver

2. I learned three important things in college — to use a library, to memorize quickly and visually, to drop asleep at any time given a horizontal surface and fifteen minutes. What I could not learn was to think creatively on schedule. — Agnes de Mille

3. Knowing others is wisdom; knowing the self is enlightenment. Mastering others requires force; mastering the self needs strength. — Lao-tzu

4. How can I love the man who raped my mother, killed my father, enslaved my ancestors, dropped atomic bombs on Japan, killed off the Indians, and keeps me cooped up in the slums?
— Malcolm X

5. I don't want to achieve immortality through my work, I want to achieve it through not dying. — Woody Allen

10

Add needed words.

Do not omit words necessary for grammatical or logical completeness. Readers need to see at a glance how the parts of a sentence are connected.

Languages sometimes differ in the need for certain words. In particular, be alert for missing verbs, articles, subjects, or expletives. See 29e, 30, and 31a.

GRAMMAR CHECKERS do not flag the vast majority of missing words. They can, however, catch some missing verbs (see 27e). Although they can flag some missing articles (*a, an,* and *the*), they often suggest that an article is missing when in fact it is not. (See also 30.)

10a Add words needed to complete compound structures.

In compound structures, words are often omitted for economy: *Tom is a man who means what he says and [who] says what he means.* Such omissions are perfectly acceptable as long as the omitted words are common to both parts of the compound structure.

If the shorter version defies grammar or idiom because an omitted word is not common to both parts of the compound structure, the word must be put back in.

▶ Some of the regulars are acquaintances whom we see at work
　　who
　　or live in our community.
　　^

　　The word *who* must be included because *whom . . . live in our community* is not grammatically correct.

　　　　　　accepted
▶ Mayor Davis never has and never will accept a bribe.
　　　　　　　　　　　　　　^

　　Has . . . accept is not grammatically correct.

　　　　　　　　　　　　　in
▶ Many South Pacific islanders still believe and live by ancient
　　　　　　　　　　　　　^
　　laws.

　　Believe . . . by is not idiomatic in English. (For a list of common idioms, see 18d.)

NOTE: Even when the omitted word is common to both parts of the compound structure, occasionally it must be inserted to avoid ambiguity. The sentence *My favorite English professor and mentor influenced my choice of a career* suggests that the professor and mentor are the same person. If they are not, *my* must be repeated: *My favorite English professor and my mentor influenced my choice of a career.*

10b Add the word *that* if there is any danger of misreading without it.

If there is no danger of misreading, the word *that* may be omitted when it introduces a subordinate clause. *The value of a principle is the number of things* [*that*] *it will explain.* Occasionally, however, a sentence might be misread without *that*.

▶ Looking out the family room window, Sarah saw her favorite _∧*that*

tree, which she had climbed so often as a child, was gone.

Sarah didn't see the tree; she saw that the tree was gone.

▶ Many civilians believe _∧*that* the air force has a vigorous exercise

program.

The word *that* tells readers to expect a clause, not just *the air force*, as the direct object of *believe*.

10c Add words needed to make comparisons logical and complete.

Comparisons should be made between items that are alike. To compare unlike items is illogical and distracting.

▶ The forests of North America are much more extensive than *those of* _∧
Europe.

Forests must be compared with forests.

▶ ~~The graduation rate of~~ *Our* student athletes ~~is higher~~ *graduate at a higher rate* than

the rest of the student population.

Clear sentences

A rate cannot be logically compared to a population. The writer could revise the sentence by inserting *that of* after *than*, but the preceding revision is more concise.

▶ Some say that Ella Fitzgerald's renditions of Cole Porter's
songs are better than any other ~~singer~~.
   singer's.
   ^

Ella Fitzgerald's renditions cannot be logically compared with a singer. The revision uses the possessive form *singer's*, with the word *renditions* being implied.

Sometimes the word *other* must be inserted to make a comparison logical.

▶ Jupiter is larger than any planet in our solar system.
   other
   ^

Jupiter cannot be larger than itself.

Sometimes the word *as* must be inserted to make a comparison grammatically complete.

▶ The city of Lowell is as old, if not older than, the neighboring
   as
   ^
city of Lawrence.

The construction *as old* is not complete without a second *as*: *as old as . . . the neighboring city of Lawrence.*

Finally, comparisons should be complete enough to ensure clarity. The reader should understand what is being compared.

INCOMPLETE	Brand X is less salty.
COMPLETE	Brand X is less salty than Brand Y.

Also, there should be no ambiguity. In the following sentence, two interpretations are possible.

AMBIGUOUS	Ken helped me more than my roommate.
CLEAR	Ken helped me more than *he helped* my roommate.
CLEAR	Ken helped me more than my roommate *did.*

10d Add the articles *a, an,* and *the* where necessary for grammatical completeness.

Articles are sometimes omitted in recipes and other instructions that are meant to be followed while they are being read. Such omissions are inappropriate, however, in nearly all other forms of writing, whether formal or informal.

> Blood can be drawn only by $\overset{a}{\underset{\wedge}{}}$ doctor or by $\overset{an}{\underset{\wedge}{}}$ authorized person who has been trained in $\overset{the}{\underset{\wedge}{}}$ procedure.

It is not always necessary to repeat articles with paired items: *We bought a computer and printer.* However, if one of the items requires *a* and the other requires *an,* both articles must be included.

> We bought a computer and $\overset{an}{\underset{\wedge}{}}$ ink-jet printer.

Articles can cause special problems for speakers of English as a second language. See 30.

EXERCISE 10–1

Add any words needed for grammatical or logical completeness in the following sentences. Revisions of lettered sentences appear in the back of the book. Example:

> *that*
> The officer at the desk feared the prisoner in the interroga-
> ^
> tion room would escape.

a. A good source of vitamin C is a grapefruit or orange.
b. The women entering VMI can expect haircuts as short as the male cadets.
c. The driver went to investigate, only to find one of the supposedly new tires had blown.
d. Most of the spectators were unhappy and angered by the decision.
e. Reefs are home to more species than any ecosystem in the sea.

1. Very few black doctors were allowed to serve in the Civil War, and their qualifications had to be higher than white doctors.
2. Producers of violent video games are not capable or interested in regulating themselves.
3. David's cat Machiavelli likes me more than his master.
4. The inspection team saw many historic old buildings had been damaged by the earthquake.
5. American English has borrowed more words from Spanish than from any language.

ON THE WEB

For electronic exercises on adding needed words, go to
www.dianahacker.com/bedhandbook

and click on ▶ **Electronic Grammar Exercises**
              ▶ **E-ex 10–1**

11

Untangle mixed constructions.

A mixed construction contains parts that do not sensibly fit together. The mismatch may be a matter of grammar or of logic.

> **GRAMMAR CHECKERS** can flag *is when, is where,* and *reason . . . is because* constructions (11c), but they fail to identify nearly all other mixed constructions, including sentences as tangled as this one: *Depending on the number and strength of drinks, the amount of time that has passed, and one's body weight determines the concentration of alcohol in the blood.*

11a   Untangle the grammatical structure.

Once you head into a sentence, your choices are limited by the range of grammatical patterns in English. (See 62 and 63.) You cannot begin with one grammatical plan and switch without warning to another.

MIXED   For most drivers who have a blood alcohol content of .05 percent double their risk of causing an accident.

REVISED For most drivers who have a blood alcohol content of .05 percent, the risk of causing an accident is doubled.

REVISED Most drivers who have a blood alcohol content of .05 percent double their risk of causing an accident.

The writer began with a long prepositional phrase that was destined to be a modifier but then tried to press it into service as the subject of the sentence. This cannot be done. If the sentence is to begin with the prepositional phrase, the writer must finish the sentence with a subject and verb (*risk...is doubled*). The writer who wishes to stay with the original verb (*double*) must head into the sentence another way: *Most drivers....*

▶ ~~When an employee is~~ *Being* promoted without warning can be
^
alarming.

The adverb clause *When an employee is promoted without warning* cannot serve as the subject of the sentence. The revision replaces the adverb clause with a gerund phrase, a word group that can function as the subject. (See 63b and 63c.)

▶ Although the United States is one of the wealthiest nations in

the world, ~~but~~ almost 20 percent of our children live in poverty.

The *Although* clause is subordinate, so it cannot be linked to an independent clause with the coordinating conjunction *but*.

Occasionally a mixed construction is so tangled that it defies grammatical analysis. When this happens, back away from the sentence, rethink what you want to say, and then say it again as clearly as you can.

MIXED In the whole-word method children learn to recognize entire words rather than by the phonics method in which they learn to sound out letters and groups of letters.

REVISED The whole-word method teaches children to recognize entire words; the phonics method teaches them to sound out letters and groups of letters.

ESL

English does not allow double subjects; nor does it allow an object or an adverb to be repeated in an adjective clause. See 31b and 31c.

▶ The squirrel that came down our chimney ~~it~~ did much damage.

▶ Hearing screams, Serena ran over to the pool that her daughter was swimming in.~~it.~~
                                                                        ^

11b   Straighten out the logical connections.

The subject and the predicate should make sense together; when they don't, the error is known as *faulty predication.*

▶ We decided that *Tiffany* ~~Tiffany's welfare~~ would not be safe living
                      ^
with her mother.

Tiffany, not her welfare, may not be safe.

▶ Under the revised plan, the elderly, *double personal exemption for the* ~~who now receive a double~~
                                   ^
~~personal exemption,~~ will be abolished.

The exemption, not the elderly, will be abolished.

An appositive and the noun to which it refers should be logically equivalent. When they are not, the error is known as *faulty apposition.*

▶ *Tax accounting,*
 ~~The tax accountant,~~ a very lucrative field, requires
 ^

intelligence, patience, and attention to mathematical

detail.

The tax accountant is a person, not a field.

11c   Avoid *is when, is where,* and *reason...is because* constructions.

In formal English many readers object to *is when, is where,* and *reason...is because* constructions on either grammatical or logical grounds. Grammatically, the verb *is* (as well as *are, was,* and *were*) should be followed by a noun that renames the subject or by an adjective that describes it, not by an adverb clause beginning with *when, where,* or *because.* (See 62b and 63b.) Logically, the words *when, where,* and *because* suggest relations of time, place, and cause—relations that do not always make sense with *is, was,* or *were.*

▶ *a disorder suffered by people who,*
 Anorexia nervosa is ~~where people,~~ believing they are too fat,
 ^

diet to the point of starvation.

Anorexia nervosa is a disorder, not a place.

▶ ~~The reason~~ I missed the exam ~~is~~ because my motorcycle

broke down.

The writer might have changed *because* to *that* (*The reason I missed the exam is that my motorcycle broke down*), but the revision above is more concise.

LOOKING AT YOURSELF AS A WRITER
Mixed constructions

An occasional mixed construction is nothing to worry about; just revise oddly structured sentences when you encounter them. But if many of your sentences are spinning out of control, try to discover why. Here are some common causes of mixed constructions, each of which suggests its own cure.

CAUSE   You don't know what you want to say about your subject, so you wind up in a tangle of words.

CURE   Spend more time on prewriting activities (see 1b). Begin drafting only when you have some promising ideas to work with.

CAUSE   You are attempting to write in a style more sophisticated than you can handle.

CURE   Write in a simpler, more direct style. Readers appreciate plain English more than you may think. (See 17a and 17b.)

CAUSE   While drafting, you are overly conscious of style—of how you "sound" on paper.

CURE   Focus on your meaning and often the style will take care of itself. Besides, you can always improve the sound of your sentences later.

CAUSE   You cling to a particular sentence opening, even though you can't find the right words to finish the sentence.

CURE   Experiment with alternatives; maybe you should open the sentence another way. When handwriting, make cross-outs and insertions; when working on a computer, delete and insert text until you get the sentence you want.

Clear sentences

EXERCISE 11–1

Edit the following sentences to untangle mixed constructions. Revisions of lettered sentences appear in the back of the book. Example:

> ~~By~~ *L*oosening the soil around your jade plant will help the air
>
> and nutrients penetrate to the roots.

a. Using surgical gloves is a precaution now worn by dentists to prevent contact with patients' blood and saliva.
b. A physician, the career my brother is pursuing, requires at least ten years of challenging work.
c. The reason the pharaohs had bad teeth was because tiny particles of sand found their way into Egyptian bread.
d. The change in quality of service has worsened each year.
e. In this box contains the key to your future.

1. Early diagnosis of prostate cancer is often curable.
2. Depending on the number and strength of drinks, the amount of time that has passed since the last drink, and one's body weight determines the concentration of alcohol in the blood.
3. Dyslexia is where people have a learning disorder that impairs reading ability.
4. Even though Ellen had heard French spoken all her life, yet she could not speak it.
5. By obtaining the correct form is the first step in the application process.

ON THE WEB

For electronic exercises on mixed constructions, go to
www.dianahacker.com/bedhandbook

and click on ▶ **Electronic Grammar Exercises**
▶ **E-ex 11–1**

12

Repair misplaced and dangling modifiers.

Modifiers, whether they are single words, phrases, or clauses, should point clearly to the words they modify. As a rule, related words should be kept together.

GRAMMAR CHECKERS can flag split infinitives, such as *to carefully and thoroughly sift* (12d). However, they don't alert you to other misplaced modifiers or dangling modifiers, including danglers like this one: *When a young man, my mother enrolled me in tap dance classes, hoping I would become the next Gregory Hines.*

12a Put limiting modifiers in front of the words they modify.

Limiting modifiers such as *only, even, almost, nearly,* and *just* should appear in front of a verb only if they modify the verb: *At first, I couldn't even touch my toes, much less grasp them.* If they limit the meaning of some other word in the sentence, they should be placed in front of that word.

▶ Lasers ~~only~~ *only* destroy the target, leaving the surrounding
healthy tissue intact.

   Only limits the meaning of *the target*, not *destroy*.

▶ The turtle ~~only~~ *only* makes progress when it sticks its neck out.

   Only limits the meaning of the *when* clause.

Clear sentences

The limiting modifier *not* is frequently misplaced, suggesting a meaning the writer did not intend.

▶ In the United States in 1860, all black southerners were ~~not~~ *not* ^

slaves.

The original sentence says that no black southerners were slaves. The revision makes the writer's real meaning clear: Some (but not all) black southerners were slaves.

12b Place phrases and clauses so that readers can see at a glance what they modify.

Although phrases and clauses can appear at some distance from the words they modify, make sure your meaning is clear. When phrases or clauses are oddly placed, absurd misreadings can result.

MISPLACED   The king returned to the clinic where he had undergone heart surgery in 2000 in a limousine sent by the White House.

REVISED   Traveling in a limousine sent by the White House, the king returned to the clinic where he had undergone heart surgery in 2000.

The revision corrects the false impression that the king underwent heart surgery in a limousine.

▶ ~~There~~ *On the walls* are many pictures of comedians who have performed
^

at Gavin's. ~~on the walls.~~
^

The comedians weren't performing on the walls; the pictures were on the walls.

▶ The robber was described as a six-foot-tall man with a heavy
                                    ^
150-pound,

mustache. ~~weighing 150 pounds~~.
          ^

The robber, not the mustache, weighed 150 pounds. The revision makes this clear.

Occasionally the placement of a modifier leads to an ambiguity, in which case two revisions will be possible, depending on the writer's intended meaning.

AMBIGUOUS	The exchange students we met for coffee occasionally questioned us about our latest slang.
CLEAR	The exchange students we occasionally met for coffee questioned us about our latest slang.
CLEAR	The exchange students we met for coffee questioned us occasionally about our latest slang.

In the original version, it was not clear whether the meeting or the questioning happened occasionally. The revisions eliminate the ambiguity.

12c   Move awkwardly placed modifiers.

As a rule, a sentence should flow from subject to verb to object, without lengthy detours along the way. When a long adverbial element separates a subject from its verb, a verb from its object, or a helping verb from its main verb, the result is usually awkward.

▶ ~~Hong Kong,~~ ^A^ after more than 150 years of British rule, was ~~Hong Kong~~

transferred back to Chinese control in 1997.

There is no reason to separate the subject *Hong Kong* from the verb *was transferred* with a long phrase.

EXCEPTION: Occasionally a writer may choose to delay a verb or an object to create suspense. In the following passage, for example, Robert Mueller inserts the *after* phrase between the subject *women* and the verb *walk* to heighten the dramatic effect.

I asked a Burmese why women, after centuries of following their men, now walk ahead. He said there were many unexploded land mines since the war. —Robert Mueller

---

ESL

English does not allow an adverb to appear between a verb and its object. See 31d.

▶ Yolanda lifted ~~easily~~ the fifty-pound weight ^easily.^

12d Avoid split infinitives when they are awkward.

An infinitive consists of *to* plus a verb: *to think, to breathe, to dance.* When a modifier appears between *to* and the verb, an infinitive is said to be "split": *to carefully balance.*

When a long word or a phrase appears between the parts of the infinitive, the result is usually awkward.

▶ ~~The~~ patient should try to ~~if possible~~ avoid going up and down ^If possible, the^

stairs.

Attempts to avoid split infinitives can result in equally awkward sentences. When alternative phrasing sounds unnatural, most experts allow—and even encourage—splitting the infinitive.

> **AWKWARD** We decided actually to enforce the law.
>
> **BETTER** We decided to actually enforce the law.

At times, neither the split infinitive nor its alternative sounds particularly awkward. In such situations, you may want to unsplit the infinitive, especially in formal writing.

formally.

▶ The candidate decided to ~~formally~~ launch her campaign./
                                                          ^

ON THE WEB

The rules on avoiding split infinitives have sparked debates. If you're interested in learning why, go to
www.dianahacker.com/bedhandbook

and click on ▶ **Language Debates**
               ▶ **Split infinitives**

EXERCISE 12–1

Edit the following sentences to correct misplaced or awkwardly placed modifiers. Revisions of lettered sentences appear in the back of the book. Example:

in a telephone survey

Answering questions can be annoying . ~~in a telephone survey.~~
                             ^   ^

a. Our English professor asked us to very carefully reread the sonnet, looking for subtleties we had missed on a first reading.
b. The monarch arrived in a gold carriage at the gate pulled by four white horses.

c. By afternoon, Sam had almost painted the entire dining room.
d. Coronado, after being appointed leader of the expeditionary force by the Spanish viceroy, spent his time recruiting volunteers for the adventure.
e. All fresh vegetables are not salt free.

1. Carlos sat solemnly and didn't even smile once during the comedy.
2. The orderly confessed that he had given a lethal injection to the patient after ten hours of grilling by the police.
3. Several recent studies have encouraged heart patients to more carefully watch their cholesterol levels.
4. The recordings were all done at the studio of the late Jimi Hendrix named Electric Ladyland.
5. The old Marlboro ads depicted a man on a horse smoking a cigarette.

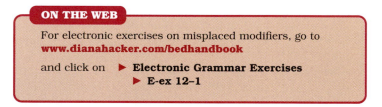

ON THE WEB

For electronic exercises on misplaced modifiers, go to
www.dianahacker.com/bedhandbook

and click on ▶ **Electronic Grammar Exercises**
▶ **E-ex 12–1**

12e   Repair dangling modifiers.

A dangling modifier fails to refer logically to any word in the sentence. Dangling modifiers are easy to repair, but they can be hard to recognize, especially in your own writing.

Recognizing dangling modifiers

Dangling modifiers are usually word groups (such as verbal phrases) that suggest but do not name an actor. When a sentence opens with such a modifier, readers expect the subject of the next clause to name the actor. If it doesn't, the modifier dangles.

▶ *When the driver opened*
~~Opening~~ the window to let out a huge bumblebee, the car
      ^

accidentally swerved into an oncoming car.

The car didn't open the window; the driver did.

                                    women have often been denied
▶ After completing seminary training, ~~women's~~ access to the
                                                ^

pulpit . ~~has often been denied~~.
       ^

The women (not their access to the pulpit) complete the training.

The following sentences illustrate four common kinds of dangling modifiers.

DANGLING   *Deciding to join the navy,* the recruiter enthusiastically pumped Joe's hand. [Participial phrase]

DANGLING   *Upon entering the doctor's office,* a skeleton
caught my attention. [Preposition followed by a
gerund phrase]

DANGLING   *To please the children,* some fireworks were set off
a day early. [Infinitive phrase]

DANGLING   *Though only sixteen,* UCLA accepted Martha's
application. [Elliptical clause with an understood
subject and verb]

These dangling modifiers falsely suggest that the recruiter decided to join the navy, that the skeleton entered the doctor's office, that the fireworks intended to please the children, and that UCLA is only sixteen years old.

Although most readers will understand the writer's intended meaning in such sentences, the inadvertent humor can be distracting, and it can make the writer appear somewhat foolish.

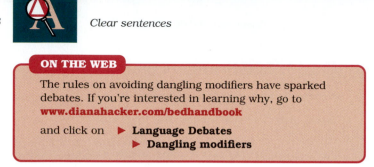

Repairing dangling modifiers

To repair a dangling modifier, you can revise the sentence in one of two ways:

1. Name the actor in the subject of the sentence, or
2. name the actor in the modifier.

Depending on your sentence, one of these revision strategies may be more appropriate than the other.

ACTOR NAMED IN SUBJECT

▶ Upon entering the doctor's office, a skeleton *I noticed*. ~~caught my attention.~~

▶ To please the children, *we set off* some fireworks ~~were set off~~ early.

ACTOR NAMED IN MODIFIER

▶ *When Joe decided* ~~Deciding~~ to join the navy, the recruiter enthusiastically pumped ~~Joe's~~ *his* hand.

▶ *Martha was* Though only sixteen, UCLA accepted ~~Martha's~~ *her* application.

NOTE: You cannot repair a dangling modifier just by moving it. Consider, for example, the sentence about the skeleton. If you put the modifier at the end of the sentence (*A skeleton caught my attention upon entering the doctor's office*), you are still suggesting—absurdly, of course—that the skeleton entered the office. The only way to avoid the problem is to put the word *I* in the sentence, either as the subject or in the modifier.

▶ Upon entering the doctor's office, a skeleton. *I noticed* ~~caught my~~ ^ ^ ~~attention.~~

▶ ~~Upon entering~~ *As I entered* the doctor's office, a skeleton caught my ^ attention.

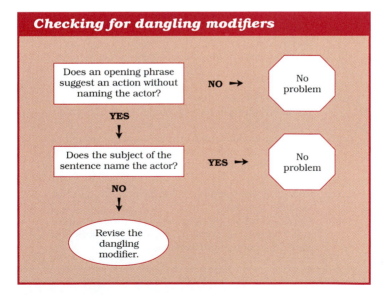

Checking for dangling modifiers

Does an opening phrase suggest an action without naming the actor? **NO** ➡ No problem

YES ↓

Does the subject of the sentence name the actor? **YES** ➡ No problem

NO ↓

Revise the dangling modifier.

Clear sentences

LOOKING AT YOURSELF AS A WRITER
Dangling modifiers

Most writers encounter occasional problems with dangling modifiers. Here are a few of the most common causes and cures.

CAUSE You are trying to avoid using the word *I*, so you write a sentence like this: *At the age of twenty, my father let me drive his restored Mustang.*

CURE Don't be afraid to use the word *I* in a personal narrative or in other writing that is clearly about you: *When I turned twenty, my father let me drive his restored Mustang.*

CAUSE You are writing in the passive voice, with the subject of your sentence receiving the action instead of doing it, like this: *To finance the rescue effort, thousands of dollars were donated.*

CURE Write in the active voice unless you have a good reason for choosing the passive: *To finance the rescue effort, citizens donated thousands of dollars.* (See 8a.)

CAUSE To achieve sentence variety, you are putting certain modifiers up front in a sentence—without noticing that they dangle.

CURE Keep the modifier up front, for variety, but add an actor to it. Or change the subject of the sentence so that it names the actor.

CAUSE You think your sentence is clear even though the modifier dangles.

CURE In fact, you may be right. Be aware, though, that some readers—especially English professors—find dangling modifiers distracting.

EXERCISE 12–2

Edit the following sentences to correct dangling modifiers. Most sentences can be revised in more than one way. Revisions of lettered sentences appear in the back of the book. Example:

> *a student must complete*
> **To acquire a degree in almost any field, two science courses.**
>   ^   ^
> ~~must be completed.~~

a. At the age of ten, my parents took me on my first balloon ride.
b. To show our appreciation for your patience, enclosed is a coupon that you may redeem for the book of your choice.
c. Nestled in the cockpit, the pounding of the engine was muffled only slightly by my helmet.
d. In choosing her bridesmaids' dresses, cost had to be considered a major factor.
e. When a young man, my mother enrolled me in tap dance classes, hoping I would become the next Gregory Hines.

1. While working as a ranger in Everglades National Park, a Florida panther crossed the road in front of my truck one night.
2. By following this new procedure, our mailing costs will be reduced significantly.
3. As president of the missionary circle, one of Grandmother's duties is to raise money for the church.
4. After becoming eligible to win these bonuses, a sales quota must be maintained for six consecutive months.
5. As a child growing up in Nigeria, my mother taught me to treat all elders with respect.

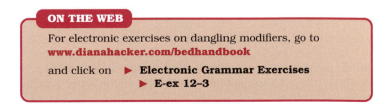

ON THE WEB

For electronic exercises on dangling modifiers, go to
www.dianahacker.com/bedhandbook

and click on   ▶ **Electronic Grammar Exercises**
                 ▶ **E-ex 12–3**

Clear sentences

13

Eliminate distracting shifts.

 GRAMMAR CHECKERS do not flag the shifts discussed in this section: shifts in point of view; shifts in verb tense, mood, or voice; and shifts between direct and indirect questions or quotations. Even the most obvious errors like this one will slip right past most grammar checkers: *My three-year-old fell into the pool and to my surprise she swims to the shallow end.*

13a Make the point of view consistent in person and number.

The point of view of a piece of writing is the perspective from which it is written: first person (*I* or *we*), second person (*you*), or third person (*he*/*she*/*it*/*one* or *they*).

The *I* (or *we*) point of view, which emphasizes the writer, is a good choice for informal letters and writing based primarily on personal experience. The *you* point of view, which emphasizes the reader, works well for giving advice or explaining how to do something. The third-person point of view, which emphasizes the subject, is appropriate in formal academic and professional writing.

Writers who are having difficulty settling on an appropriate point of view sometimes shift confusingly from one to another. The solution is to choose a suitable perspective and then stay with it.

▶ One week our class met in a junkyard to practice rescuing a

victim trapped in a wrecked car. We learned to dismantle the

car with the essential tools. ~~You~~ *We* were graded on ~~your~~ *our* speed

and ~~your~~ *our* skill in extricating the victim.

The writer should have stayed with the *we* point of view. *You* is
inappropriate because the writer is not addressing readers directly. *You* should not be used in a vague sense meaning "anyone." (See 23d.)

▶ ~~One needs~~ *You need* a password and a credit card number to access

this database. You will be billed at an hourly rate.

Here *You* is an appropriate choice because the writer is giving
advice directly to readers.

▶ ~~A police officer is~~ *Police officers are* often criticized for always being there when

they aren't needed and never being there when they are.

Although the writer might have changed *they* to *he or she* (to
match the singular *officer*), the revision in the plural is more
concise. (See also 17f and 22a.)

EXERCISE 13–1

Edit the following paragraph to eliminate distracting shifts in point
of view (person and number).

Many people my age grew up reading science fiction
books that told you about life in the twenty-first century. The
lives of the characters in these futuristic tales were often made
easier by all kinds of machines, especially robots. Every one of

Clear sentences

the kids I knew wanted to have their own robot someday. We thought that you wouldn't have to do any chores at home if you had a robot to do the work. Today some kinds of robots exist, but my childhood robot fantasies have not exactly come true. There are no robots like Rosie, the mechanized maid on the cartoon *The Jetsons.* Instead, robots for consumer use are more likely to be toys. For example, a child today might have their own Furby, an animatronic stuffed animal. A Furby is kind of amusing, I admit, but I'm still a little disappointed. They can talk and move, but they won't clean your room.

13b Maintain consistent verb tenses.

Consistent verb tenses clearly establish the time of the actions being described. When a passage begins in one tense and then shifts without warning and for no reason to another, readers are distracted and confused.

▶ There was no way I could fight the current and win. Just as I

was losing hope, a stranger ~~jumps~~ *jumped* off a passing boat and ~~swims~~ *swam*

toward me.

Writers often encounter difficulty with verb tenses when writing about literature. Because fictional events occur outside the time frames of real life, the past and the present tenses may seem equally appropriate. The literary convention, however, is to describe fictional events consistently in the present tense.

▶ The scarlet letter is a punishment sternly placed upon Hester's

breast by the community, and yet it ~~was~~ *is* an extremely fanciful

and imaginative product of Hester's own needlework.

EXERCISE 13-2

Edit the following paragraphs to eliminate distracting shifts in tense.

    The English colonists who settled in Massachusetts received assistance at first from the local Indian tribes, but by 1675, there had been friction between the English and the Indians for many years. On June 20 of that year, Metacomet, whom the colonists called Philip, leads the Wampanoag tribe in the first of a series of attacks on the colonial settlements. The war, known today as King Philip's War, rages on for over a year and leaves three thousand Indians and six hundred colonists dead. Metacomet's attempt to retain power in his native land failed. Finally he too is killed, and the victorious colonists sell his wife and children into slavery.

    The Indians did not leave records of their unfortunate encounters with the English settlers, but the settlers recorded some of their experiences at the hands of the Indians. One of the few accounts to survive was written by a captured colonist, Mrs. Mary Rowlandson. She is a minister's wife who is kidnapped by an Indian war party and held captive for eleven weeks in 1676. Her history, *A Narrative of the Captivity and Restoration of Mrs. Mary Rowlandson,* tells the story of her experiences with the Wampanoags. Although it did not paint a completely balanced picture of the Indians, Rowlandson's narrative, which is considered a classic early American text, showed its author to be a keen observer of life in an Indian camp.

13c   Make verbs consistent in mood and voice.

Unnecessary shifts in the mood of a verb can be as distracting as needless shifts in tense. There are three moods in English: the *indicative,* used for facts, opinions, and questions; the *imperative,* used for orders or advice; and the *subjunctive,* used in certain contexts to express wishes or conditions contrary to fact (see 28b).

The following passage shifts confusingly from the indicative to the imperative mood.

> ▶ The officers advised us against allowing anyone into our
> *They also suggested that we*
> homes without proper identification. ~~Also,~~ alert neighbors to
> vacation schedules.

Since the writer's purpose was to report the officers' advice, the revision puts both sentences in the indicative.

A verb may be in either the active voice (with the subject doing the action) or the passive voice (with the subject receiving the action). (See 8a.) If a writer shifts without warning from one to the other, readers may be left wondering why.

> ▶ When the tickets are ready, the travel agent notifies the
> *lists each ticket*
> client /, ~~Each ticket is then listed~~ on a daily register form , and
> *files*
> a copy of the itinerary. ~~is filed.~~

The passage began in the active voice (*agent notifies* and then switched to the passive (*ticket is listed, copy is filed*). Because the active voice is clearer and more direct, the writer changed all the verbs to the active voice.

13d Avoid sudden shifts from indirect to direct questions or quotations.

An indirect question reports a question without asking it: *We asked whether we could take a swim.* A direct question asks directly: *Can we take a swim?* Sudden shifts from indirect to direct questions are awkward. In addition, sentences containing such shifts are impossible to punctuate because indirect questions must end with a period and direct questions must end with a question mark. (See 38b.)

▶ I wonder whether the sister knew of the theft and, if so, ~~did~~
whether she reported
~~she report~~ it to the police.
　　∧

The revision poses both questions indirectly. The writer could also ask both questions directly: *Did the sister know of the theft and, if so, did she report it to the police?*

An indirect quotation reports someone's words without quoting word for word: *Annabelle said that she is a Virgo.* A direct quotation presents the exact words of a speaker or writer, set off with quotation marks: *Annabelle said, "I am a Virgo."* Unannounced shifts from indirect to direct quotations are distracting and confusing, especially when the writer fails to insert the necessary quotation marks, as in the following example.

　　　　　　　　　　　　　　　　　　asked me not to
▶ Mother said that she would be late for dinner and ~~please do~~
　　　　　　　　　　　　　　　came
~~not~~ leave for choir practice until Dad ~~comes~~ home.
　　　　　　　　　　　　　　　　　　　∧

The revision reports all of the mother's words. The writer could also quote directly: *Mother said, "I will be late for dinner. Please do not leave for choir practice until Dad comes home."*

LOOKING AT YOURSELF AS A WRITER
Shifts

Shifts in a rough draft alert you to choices you must make as a writer. Once you have made those choices—by deciding on an appropriate point of view or tense, for example—eliminating shifts in the final draft will be a simple matter.

Clear sentences

Shifts *(continued)*

Shifts in point of view

CAUSE You are trying to avoid the word *I* or the word *you* in a context where these pronouns may be appropriate.

CURE Consider drafting your essay from the *I* or the *you* point of view. For appropriate uses of these points of view, see pages 51–53.

CAUSE You are trying to avoid sexist language without resorting to the wordy *he or she* construction.

CURE Consider writing in the plural. (See 22a.)

CAUSE You have selected the pronoun *one* in an attempt to include both men and women, but repeating *one* seems awkward, so you shift to another pronoun such as *their* or *you*.

CURE You are right that repetitions of *one* sound awkward, at least to American ears: *One must watch one's pronouns.* Try another point of view instead: *Writers must watch their pronouns. You must watch your pronouns.*

Shifts in tense

CAUSE To make the action of a narrative more immediate, you are casting it in the present tense, but at times you shift to the past.

CURE Read your narrative to yourself twice—once using all present-tense verbs and once using all past-tense verbs. Then choose the tense that you feel sounds better. If you are still in doubt, ask another writer for advice.

CAUSE You are writing about events in a literary work, and you're not sure whether to use the present or the past tense.

CURE Choose the present tense, since that is the literary convention.

Shifts (continued)

Shifts from indirect to direct questions or quotations

CAUSE	By inserting direct questions or quotations, you hope to make your style more vivid, but you end up mixing direct and indirect questions or quotations.
CURE	You are right that adding direct questions or quotations can make your writing more lively. Consider revising your sentence to use the direct approach consistently.
CAUSE	In spoken English you hear such shifts all the time, and they don't seem to bother anyone.
CURE	Be aware that the standards for written English are stricter than those for spoken English.

EXERCISE 13–3

Edit the following sentences to eliminate distracting shifts. Revisions of lettered sentences appear in the back of the book. Example:

> For most people, quitting smoking is not easy once ~~you~~ *they* are
>
> hooked.

a. A courtroom lawyer has more than a touch of theater in their blood.

b. The interviewer asked if we had brought our proof of birth and citizenship and did we bring our passports.

c. A single parent often has only their ingenuity to rely on.

d. When the director travels, you will make the hotel and airline reservations and arrange for a rental car. A detailed itinerary must also be prepared.

e. Madame Defarge is a sinister figure in Dickens's *A Tale of Two Cities*. On a symbolic level, she represents fate; like the Greek Fates, she knitted the fabric of individual destiny.

1. Everyone should protect yourself from the sun, especially on the first day of extensive exposure.
2. Our neighbors told us that the island was being evacuated because of the coming storm. Also, take the northern route to the mainland.
3. Rescue workers put water on her face and lifted her head gently onto a pillow. Finally, she opens her eyes.
4. The polygraph examiner will ask you if you have ever stolen goods on the job, if you have ever taken drugs, and have you ever killed or threatened to kill anyone.
5. The artist has often been seen as a threat to society, especially when they refuse to conform to conventional standards of taste.

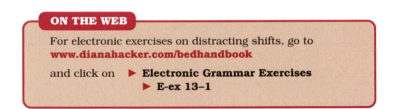

ON THE WEB

For electronic exercises on distracting shifts, go to
www.dianahacker.com/bedhandbook

and click on ▶ **Electronic Grammar Exercises**
 ▶ **E-ex 13–1**

14

Emphasize key ideas.

Within each sentence, emphasize your point by expressing it in the subject and verb of an independent clause, the words that receive the most attention from readers (see 14a–e).

Within longer stretches of prose, you can draw attention to ideas deserving special emphasis by using a variety of techniques, often involving an unusual twist or some element of surprise (see 14f).

14a Coordinate equal ideas; subordinate minor ideas.

When combining two or more ideas in one sentence, you have two choices: coordination or subordination. Choose coordination to indicate that the ideas are equal or nearly equal in importance. Choose subordination to indicate that one idea is less important than another.

> **GRAMMAR CHECKERS** do not catch the problems with coordination and subordination discussed in this section. Not surprisingly, computer programs have no way of sensing the relative importance of ideas.

Coordination

Coordination draws attention equally to two or more ideas. To coordinate single words or phrases, join them with a coordinating conjunction or with a pair of correlative conjunctions (see 61g). To coordinate independent clauses—word groups that could stand alone as a sentence—join them with a comma and a coordinating conjunction or with a semicolon:

| , and | , but | , or | , nor |
| , for | , so | , yet | ; |

The semicolon is often accompanied by a conjunctive adverb such as *moreover, furthermore, therefore,* or *however* or by a transitional phrase such as *for example, in other words,* or *as a matter of fact.* (See the chart on p. 183 for a more complete list.)

Assume, for example, that your intention is to draw equal attention to the following two ideas.

Grandmother lost her sight. Her hearing sharpened.

To coordinate these ideas, you can join them with a comma and the coordinating conjunction *but* or with a semicolon and the conjunctive adverb *however.*

> Grandmother lost her sight, but her hearing sharpened.

> Grandmother lost her sight; however, her hearing sharpened.

It is important to choose a coordinating conjunction or conjunctive adverb appropriate to your meaning. In the preceding example, the two ideas contrast with one another, calling for *but* or *however.*

Subordination

To give unequal emphasis to two or more ideas, express the major idea in an independent clause and place any minor ideas in subordinate clauses or phrases. (For specific subordination strategies, see the chart on p. 184.)

Deciding which idea to emphasize is not a matter of right and wrong but is determined by the meaning you intend. Consider the two ideas about Grandmother's sight and hearing.

> Grandmother lost her sight. Her hearing sharpened.

If your purpose is to stress your grandmother's acute hearing rather than her blindness, subordinate the idea about her blindness.

> *As she lost her sight,* Grandmother's hearing sharpened.

To focus on your grandmother's growing blindness, subordinate the idea about her hearing.

> *Though her hearing sharpened,* Grandmother gradually lost her sight.

Using coordination to combine sentences of equal importance

1. Consider using a comma and a coordinating conjunction. (See 32a.)

    , and   , but   , or   , nor
    , for   , so   , yet

▶ In Orthodox Jewish funeral ceremonies, the shroud is
    a simple linen vestment/,*and the* ~~The~~ coffin is plain wood with

    no adornment.

2. Consider using a semicolon and a conjunctive adverb or transitional phrase. (See 34b.)

also	in addition	now
as a result	in fact	of course
besides	in other words	on the other hand
consequently	in the first place	otherwise
finally	meanwhile	still
for example	moreover	then
for instance	nevertheless	therefore
furthermore	next	thus
however		

▶ Alicia scored well on the SAT/ *; moreover, she* ~~She also~~ had excellent

    high school grades and a record of community service.

3. Consider using a semicolon alone. (See 34a.)

▶ In youth we learn/; *in* ~~In~~ age we understand.

Using subordination to combine sentences of unequal importance

1. Consider putting the less important idea in a subordinate clause beginning with one of the following words. (See 63b.)

after	before	that	which
although	even though	unless	while
as	if	until	who
as if	since	when	whom
because	so that	where	whose

▶ ~~My~~ **When my** son asked his great-grandmother if she had been a
slave**/**, ~~She~~ **she** became very angry.

▶ My sister owes much of her recovery to a bodybuilding
program**/ that she** ~~She~~ began ~~the program~~ three years ago.

2. Consider putting the less important idea in an appositive phrase. (See 63d.)

▶ Karate**,** ~~is~~ a discipline based on the philosophy of non-
violence**/,** ~~It~~ teaches the art of self-defense.

3. Consider putting the less important idea in a participial phrase. (See 63c.)

▶ ~~I noticed~~ **Noticing** that smoke had filled the backyard**/,** I ran out
to see where it was coming from.

▶ ~~Alvin was~~ **E**ncouraged by his professor to apply for the
job**/,** ~~He~~ **Alvin** filed an application on Monday morning.

14b Combine choppy sentences.

Short sentences demand attention, so you should use them primarily for emphasis. Too many short sentences, one after the other, make for a choppy style.

If an idea is not important enough to deserve its own sentence, try combining it with a sentence close by. Put any minor ideas in subordinate structures such as phrases or subordinate clauses.

▶ We keep our use of insecticides, herbicides, and fungicides
to a minimum/ ~~We~~ *because we* are concerned about their effect on the
environment.

A minor idea is now expressed in a subordinate clause beginning with *because.*

▶ The Chesapeake and Ohio Canal, ~~is~~ a 184-mile waterway
constructed in the 1800s/, ~~It~~ was a major source of
transportation for goods during the Civil War.

A minor idea is now expressed in an appositive phrase (*a 184-mile waterway constructed in the 1800s*).

▶ ~~Sister Consilio was~~ *E*nveloped in a black robe with only her
face and hands visible/, ~~She~~ *Sister Consilio* was an imposing figure.

A minor idea is now expressed in a participial phrase beginning with *Enveloped.*

Although subordination is ordinarily the most effective technique for combining short, choppy sentences, coordination is appropriate when the ideas are equal in importance.

▶ The hospital decides when patients will sleep and wake~~,~~ **/,** ~~It~~

and

dictates what and when they will eat~~,~~ **/,** ~~It~~ tells them when they

may be with family and friends.

Equivalent ideas are expressed in a coordinate series.

ESL

When combining sentences, do not repeat the subject of the sentence; also do not repeat an object or adverb in an adjective clause. See 31b and 31c.

▶ The apartment that we moved into ~~it~~ needed many

repairs.

▶ Tanya climbed into the tree house that the boys were

playing in**,** ~~it.~~

LOOKING AT YOURSELF AS A WRITER
Choppy sentences

Combining choppy sentences is a natural part of revision for most writers, but if your writing style is unusually choppy, ask yourself why. Here are three common causes and cures.

CAUSE You are afraid of writing run-on sentences, so you play it safe by keeping your sentences short.

CURE You are right to be concerned about run-on sentences, but try not to worry about them while drafting. Often you can fix a run-on sentence by subordinating minor ideas—the same strategy that usually works for combining choppy sentences. (See 20d.)

Choppy sentences (continued)	

CAUSE You aren't sure how to punctuate sentences that contain subordinate clauses and phrases, so you keep your sentences simple.

CURE Take a few risks when drafting. You can get help with punctuation later—from your instructor or your school's writing center or by consulting Part VII of *The Bedford Handbook.*

CAUSE You are not yet comfortable with the subordination strategies that are necessary for a smooth writing style.

CURE When combining choppy sentences in your drafts, consult the chart on page 184, which gives examples of subordination strategies.

EXERCISE 14–1

Combine the following sentences by subordinating minor ideas or by coordinating ideas of equal importance. You must decide which ideas are minor because the sentences are given out of context. Revisions of lettered sentences appear in the back of the book. Example:

Agnes, ~~was~~ another girl I worked with/, ~~She~~ was a hyperactive child.

a. The lift chairs were going around very fast. They were bumping the skiers into their seats.

b. Our waitress was costumed in a kimono. She had painted her face white. She had arranged her hair in an upswept lacquered beehive.

c. Student volunteers from Baltimore City Community College help the younger children with reading and math. These are the children's weakest subjects.

d. Shore houses were flooded up to the first floor. Beaches were washed away. Brant's Lighthouse was swallowed by the sea.

e. Mary will graduate from high school in June. She has not yet decided on a college.

1. I noticed that the sky was glowing orange and red. I bent down to crawl into the bunker.

2. The Market Inn is located at 2nd and E Streets. It doesn't look very impressive from the outside. The food, however, is excellent.

3. He walked up to the pitcher's mound. He dug his toe into the ground. He swung his arm around backward and forward. Then he threw the ball and struck the batter out.

4. On one of my solo runs, I met a six-year-old boy. His name was Timmy. He was in the hospital for treatment of leukemia.

5. The first football card set was released by the Goudey Gum Company in 1933. The set featured only three football players. They were Red Grange, Bronko Nagurski, and Knute Rockne.

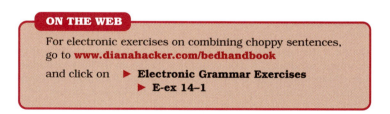

ON THE WEB

For electronic exercises on combining choppy sentences, go to **www.dianahacker.com/bedhandbook**

and click on ▶ **Electronic Grammar Exercises**
　　　　　　　 ▶ **E-ex 14–1**

14c Avoid ineffective or excessive coordination.

Coordinate structures are appropriate only when you intend to draw the reader's attention equally to two or more ideas: *Professor Naake praises loudly, and she criticizes softly.* If one idea is more important than another — or if a coordinating conjunction does not clearly signal the relation between the ideas — you should subordinate the less important idea.

INEFFECTIVE	Closets were taxed as rooms, and most colonists stored their clothes in chests or clothes presses.
IMPROVED	Because closets were taxed as rooms, most colonists stored their clothes in chests or clothes presses.

The revision subordinates the less important idea by putting it in a subordinate clause. Notice that the subordinating conjunction *Because* signals the relation between the ideas more clearly than the coordinating conjunction *and.*

Because it is so easy to string ideas together with *and,* writers often rely too heavily on coordination in their rough drafts. The cure for excessive coordination is simple: Look for opportunities to tuck minor ideas into subordinate clauses or phrases.

When
► Jason walked over to his new Miata, ~~and~~ he saw that its
 ^
 windshield had been smashed.

The minor idea has become a subordinate clause beginning with *When.*

 noticing
► My uncle, ~~noticed~~ my frightened look, ~~and~~ told me that
 ^   ^
 Grandma had to feel my face because she was blind.

The less important idea has become a participial phrase modifying the noun *uncle.*

After four hours,
► ~~Four hours went by, and~~ a rescue truck finally arrived, but by
 ^
 that time we had been evacuated in a helicopter.

Three independent clauses were excessive. The least important idea has become a prepositional phrase.

Clear sentences

EXERCISE 14–2

In the following sentences, ideas have been coordinated (joined with a coordinating conjunction or a semicolon). Restructure the sentences by subordinating minor ideas. You must decide which ideas are minor because the sentences are given out of context. Revisions of lettered sentences appear in the back of the book. Example:

> The crew team finally returned to shore, ~~and~~ had a party on $^{where\ they}$ the beach ~~and celebrated~~ the start of the season. $^{to\ celebrate}$

a. These particles are known as "stealth liposomes," and they can hide in the body for a long time without detection.

b. Cocaine is an addictive drug; it can seriously harm you both physically and mentally, if death doesn't get you first.

c. Students, textile workers, and labor unions have loudly protested sweatshop abuses, so apparel makers have been forced to examine their labor practices.

d. IRC (Internet Relay Chat) was developed in a European university; it was created as a way for a group of graduate students to talk about projects from their dorm rooms.

e. The cafeteria's new menu has an international flavor, and it includes everything from enchiladas and pizza to pad thai and sauerbraten.

1. We arrived at the Capital Center, and to my dismay we had to pay five dollars for parking.

2. Iguanas are dependent on ultraviolet rays from the sun, so in the winter months they must be put under ultraviolet-coated lights that can be purchased at most pet stores.

3. The Civil War Trust was founded in 1991; it spearheads a nationwide campaign to protect America's Civil War battlefields.

4. We did not expect to receive so many large orders so quickly, and we are short on inventory.

5. I am certain that Mother spread her love equally among us all, but she had a way of making each of us feel very special in our own way.

14d Do not subordinate major ideas.

If a sentence buries its major idea in a subordinate construction, readers may not give the idea enough attention. Express the major idea in an independent clause and subordinate any minor ideas.

▶ Lanie, who now walks with the help of braces*/*. had polio as a child. *had polio as a child,*

The writer wanted to focus on Lanie's ability to walk, but the original sentence buried this information in an adjective clause. The revision puts the major idea in an independent clause and tucks the less important idea into an adjective clause (*who had polio as a child*).

▶ *As* I was driving home from my new job, heading down Ranchitos Road, when my car suddenly overheated.

The writer wanted to emphasize that the car overheated, not the fact of driving home. The revision expresses the major idea in an independent clause, the less important idea in an adverb clause (*As I was driving home from my new job*).

14e Do not subordinate excessively.

In attempting to avoid short, choppy sentences, writers sometimes go to the opposite extreme, putting more subordinate ideas into a sentence than its structure can bear. If a sentence collapses of its own weight, occasionally it can be restructured. More often, however, such sentences must be divided.

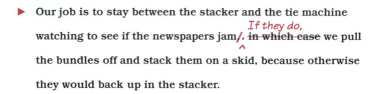

▶ Our job is to stay between the stacker and the tie machine

watching to see if the newspapers jam*/.* ~~in which case~~ we pull

If they do,

the bundles off and stack them on a skid, because otherwise

they would back up in the stacker.

EXERCISE 14–3

In each of the following sentences, the idea that the writer wished to emphasize is buried in a subordinate construction. Restructure each sentence so that the independent clause expresses the major idea and lesser ideas are subordinated. Revisions of lettered sentences appear in the back of the book. Example:

Although
Catherine has weathered many hardships, ~~although~~ she has

rarely become discouraged. [*Emphasize that Catherine has*

rarely become discouraged.]

a. Gina worked as an aide for the relief agency, distributing food and medical supplies. [*Emphasize distributing food and medical supplies.*]

b. For the past three years, Ms. Brooks has been an attorney at Pepco, where she has done an excellent job. [*Emphasize that Ms. Brooks has done an excellent job.*]

c. The visiting period was nearly over when the prison guard tapped me on the shoulder. [*Emphasize the guard's tapping the writer on the shoulder.*]

d. My grandfather, who raised his daughters the old-fashioned way, was born eighty years ago in Puerto Rico. [*Emphasize how the grandfather raised his daughters.*]

e. The Narcan reversed the depressive effect of the drug, saving the patient's life. [*Emphasize that the patient's life was saved.*]

1. The ivy-covered dormitories, located about a mile from most of the classrooms, date from the early nineteenth century. [*Emphasize where the dormitories are located.*]
2. I was losing consciousness when my will to live kicked in. [*Emphasize the will to live.*]
3. Louis's team worked with the foreign mission by building new churches and restoring those damaged by hurricanes. [*Emphasize the building and restoring.*]
4. The rotor hit, gouging a hole about an eighth of an inch deep in my helmet. [*Emphasize that the rotor gouged a hole in the helmet.*]
5. Sophia's country kitchen, which overlooks a field where cattle graze among old tombstones, was formerly a lean-to porch. [*Emphasize that the kitchen overlooks the field.*]

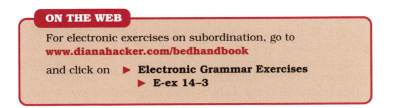

ON THE WEB

For electronic exercises on subordination, go to
www.dianahacker.com/bedhandbook

and click on ▶ **Electronic Grammar Exercises**
▶ **E-ex 14–3**

14f Experiment with techniques for gaining special emphasis.

By experimenting with certain techniques, usually involving some element of surprise, you can draw attention to ideas that deserve special emphasis. Use such techniques sparingly, however, or they will lose their punch. The writer who tries to emphasize everything ends up emphasizing nothing.

Using sentence endings for emphasis

You can highlight an idea simply by withholding it until the end of a sentence. The technique works something like a punch line. In the following example, the sentence's meaning is not revealed until its very last word.

> The only completely consistent people are the dead.
> —Aldous Huxley

Two types of sentences that withhold information until the end deserve special mention: the inversion and the periodic sentence. The *inversion* reverses the normal subject-verb order, placing the subject at the end, where it receives unusual emphasis. (Also see 15c.)

> In golden pots are hidden the most deadly poisons.
> —Thomas Draxe

The *periodic* sentence opens with a pile-up of modifiers and withholds the subject and verb until the end. It draws attention to itself because it contrasts with the cumulative sentence, which is used more frequently. A *cumulative* sentence begins with the subject and verb and adds modifying elements at the end.

PERIODIC

Twenty-five years ago, at the age of thirteen, while hiking in the mountains near my hometown of Vancouver, Washington, I came face to face with the legendary Goat Woman of Livingston Mountain. —Tom Weitzel, student

CUMULATIVE

A metaphysician is one who goes into a dark cellar at midnight without a light, looking for a black cat that is not there. —Baron Bowan of Colwood

Using parallel structure for emphasis

Parallel grammatical structure draws special attention to paired ideas or to items in a series. (See 9.) When parallel ideas are paired, the emphasis falls on words that underscore comparisons or contrasts, especially when they occur at the end of a phrase or clause.

> We must *stop talking* about the *American dream* and *start listening* to the *dreams of Americans.* —Reubin Askew

In a parallel series, the emphasis falls at the end, so it is generally best to end with the most dramatic or climactic item in the series.

> Sister Charity enjoyed passing out writing punishments: translate the Ten Commandments into Latin, type a thousand-word essay on good manners, copy the New Testament with a quill pen. —Marie Visosky, student

Using punctuation for emphasis

Obviously the exclamation point can add emphasis, but you should not overuse it. As a rule, the exclamation point is more appropriate in dialogue than in ordinary prose.

> I oozed a glob of white paint onto my palette, whipped some medium into it, loaded my brush, and announced to the class, "Move over, Michelangelo. Here I come!" —Carolyn Goff, student

A dash or a colon may be used to draw attention to word groups worthy of special attention. (See sections 35a, 35b, and 39a.)

> The middle of the road is where the white line is—and that's the worst place to drive. —Robert Frost

> I turned to see what the anemometer read: The needle had pegged out at 106 knots. —Jonathan Shilk, student

Occasionally, a pair of dashes may be used to highlight a word or an idea.

> [My friend] was a gay and impudent and satirical and delight-ful young black man—a slave—who daily preached sermons from the top of his master's woodpile, with me for sole audience.
> —Mark Twain

Using an occasional short sentence for emphasis

Too many short sentences in a row will fast become monoto-nous (see 14b), but an occasional short sentence, when played off against longer sentences in the same passage, will draw attention to an idea.

> The great secret, known to internists and learned early in marriage by internists' wives [or husbands], but still hidden from the general public, is that most things get better by themselves. Most things, in fact, are better by morning.
> —Lewis Thomas

EXERCISE 14–4

Discuss the methods used to achieve emphasis in the following paragraphs.

> Unseen in the jungle, but present, are tapirs, jaguars, many species of snake and lizard, ocelots, armadillos, mar-mosets, howler monkeys, toucans and macaws and a hundred other birds, deer, bats, peccaries, capybaras, agoutis, and sloths. Also present in this jungle, but variously distant, are Texaco derricks and pipelines, and some of the wildest Indians in the world, blowgun-using Indians, who killed missionaries in 1956 and ate them.
> —Annie Dillard

My Uncle Tom worked as a blacksmith in the B & O yards near Harpers Ferry. That was a good job too. Though he walked the four-mile round trip to and from the shop daily in sooty railroader's clothes, Uncle Tom was well off. His house contained a marvel I had never seen before: an indoor bathroom. This was enough to mark Uncle Tom a rich man, but in addition he had a car. And such a car. It was an Essex, with windows that rolled up and down with interior hand cranks, not like my father's Model T with the isinglass windows in side curtains that had to be buttoned onto the frame in bad weather. Uncle Tom's Essex even had cut-glass flower vases in sconces in the backseat. He was a man of substance. When he rolled up in his Essex for Ida Rebecca's command appearances on Sunday afternoons in Morrisonville, wearing a white shirt and black suit, smoking his pipe, his pretty red-haired wife Goldie on the seat beside him, I felt pride in kinship to so much grandeur.

— Russell Baker

15

Provide some variety.

When a rough draft is filled with too many same-sounding sentences, try injecting some variety — as long as you can do so without sacrificing clarity or ease of reading.

GRAMMAR CHECKERS are of little help with sentence variety. It takes a human ear to know when and why sentence variety is needed.

Some programs tell you when you have used the same word to open several sentences, but sometimes it is a good idea to do so — if you are trying to highlight parallel ideas, for example (see p. 93).

Clear sentences

15a Vary your sentence openings.

Most sentences in English begin with the subject, move to the verb, and continue along to the object, with modifiers tucked in along the way or put at the end. For the most part, such sentences are fine. Put too many of them in a row, however, and they become monotonous.

Adverbial modifiers, being easily movable, can often be inserted ahead of the subject. Such modifiers might be single words, phrases, or clauses.

▶ *Eventually a*
A few drops of sap ~~eventually~~ began to trickle into the
bucket.

Like most adverbs, *eventually* does not need to appear close to the verb it modifies (*began*).

▶ *Just as the sun was coming up, a*
A pair of black ducks flew over the blind. ~~just as the sun was~~
~~coming up.~~

The adverb clause, which modifies the verb *flew*, is as clear at the beginning of the sentence as it is at the end.

Adjectives and participial phrases can frequently be moved to the beginning of a sentence without loss of clarity.

▶ *Dejected and withdrawn,*
Edward, ~~dejected and withdrawn,~~ nearly gave up his search
for a job.

▶ *A* *John and I*
~~John and I,~~ anticipating a peaceful evening, sat down at the
campfire to brew a cup of coffee.

CAUTION: When beginning a sentence with an adjective or a participial phrase, make sure that the subject of the sentence names the person or thing described in the introductory phrase. If it doesn't, the phrase will dangle. (See 12e.)

15b Use a variety of sentence structures.

A writer should not rely too heavily on simple sentences and compound sentences, for the effect tends to be both monotonous and choppy. (See 14b and 14c.) Too many complex or compound-complex sentences, however, can be equally monotonous. If your style tends to one or the other extreme, try to achieve a better mix of sentence types.

The major sentence types are illustrated in the following sentences, all taken from Flannery O'Connor's "The King of the Birds," an essay describing the author's pet peafowl.

SIMPLE	Frequently the cock combines the lifting of his tail with the raising of his voice.
COMPOUND	Any chicken's dusting hole is out of place in a flower bed, but the peafowl's hole, being the size of a small crater, is more so.
COMPLEX	The peacock does most of his serious strutting in the spring and summer when he has a full tail to do it with.
COMPOUND-COMPLEX	The cock's plumage requires two years to attain its pattern, and for the rest of his life, this chicken will act as though he designed it himself.

For a fuller discussion of sentence types, see 64a.

15c Try inverting sentences occasionally.

A sentence is inverted if it does not follow the normal subject-verb-object pattern (see 62c). Many inversions sound artificial and should be avoided except in the most formal contexts. But if an inversion sounds natural, it can provide a welcome touch of variety.

▶ *Opposite the produce section is a*
A refrigerated case of mouth-watering cheeses; is opposite
  ^   ^
the produce section; a friendly attendant will cut off just the

amount you want.

The revision inverts the normal subject-verb order by moving the verb, *is,* ahead of its subject, *case.*

▶ *Set at the top two corners of the stage were huge*
Huge lavender hearts outlined in bright white lights. were set
  ^   ^
at the top two corners of the stage.

In the revision the subject, *hearts,* appears after the verb, *were set.* Notice that the two parts of the verb are also inverted — and separated from one another — without any awkwardness or loss of meaning.

Inverted sentences are used for emphasis as well as for variety (see 14f).

15d Consider adding an occasional question or quotation.

An occasional question can provide a welcome change of pace, especially at the beginning of a paragraph, where it engages the reader's interest.

Virginia Woolf, in her book *A Room of One's Own,* wrote that in order for a woman to write fiction she must have two things, certainly: a room of her own (with key and lock) and enough money to support herself.

What then are we to make of Phillis Wheatley, a slave, who owned not even herself? This sickly, frail black girl who required a servant of her own at times—her health was so precarious—and who, had she been white, would have been easily considered the intellectual superior of all the women and most of the men in the society of her day. [Italics added.]
—Alice Walker

Quotations can also provide variety, for they add other people's voices to your own. These other voices might be bits of dialogue.

When we got back upstairs, Dr. Haney and Captain Shiller, the head nurse, were waiting for us by the elevator. As the nurse hurried off, pushing Todd, the doctor explained to us what would happen next.

"Mrs. Barrus," he began, "this last test is one we do only when absolutely necessary. It is very painful and hard on the patient but we have no other choice." Apologetically, he went on. "I cannot give him an anesthetic." He waited for the statement to sink in.   —Celeste L. Barrus, student

Or they might be quotations from written sources.

Even when she enters the hospital on the brink of death, the anorexic will refuse help from anyone and will continue to deny needing help, especially from a doctor. At this point, reports Dr. Steven Levenkron, the anorexic is most likely "a frightened, cold, lonely, starved, and physically tortured, exhausted person—not unlike an actual concentration camp inmate" (29). In this condition she is ultimately force-fed through a tube inserted in the chest.   —Jim Drew, student

Notice that the quotation from a written source is documented with a citation in parentheses. (See 54a.)

EXERCISE 15–1

Edit the following paragraph to increase sentence variety.

> I have spent thirty years of my life on a tobacco farm, and I cannot understand why people smoke. The whole process of raising tobacco involves deadly chemicals. The ground is treated for mold and chemically fertilized before the tobacco seed is ever planted. The seed is planted and begins to grow, and then the bed is treated with weed killer. The plant is then transferred to the field. It is sprayed with poison to kill worms about two months later. Then the time for harvest approaches, and the plant is sprayed once more with a chemical to retard the growth of suckers. The tobacco is harvested and hung in a barn to dry. These barns are havens for birds. The birds defecate all over the leaves. After drying, these leaves are divided by color, and no feces are removed. They are then sold to the tobacco companies. I do not know what the tobacco companies do after they receive the tobacco. I do not need to know. They cannot remove what I know is in the leaf and on the leaf. I don't want any of it to pass through my mouth.

EXERCISE 15–2

Discuss how the writer of the following paragraph provides variety.

> I was then a listening child, careful to hear the very different sounds of Spanish and English. Wide-eyed with hearing, I'd listen to sounds more than to words. First, there were English (*gringo*) sounds. So many words were still unknown to me that when the butcher or the lady at the drugstore said something, exotic polysyllabic sounds would bloom in the midst of their sentences. Often the speech of people in public seemed to me very loud, booming with confidence. The man behind the counter would literally ask, "What can I do for you?" But by being so firm and clear, the sound of his voice said that he was a *gringo*; he belonged in public society.
> —Richard Rodriguez

PART IV

Word Choice

Word choice

16

Tighten wordy sentences.

In a rough draft we are rarely economical: We repeat ourselves, we belabor the obvious, we cushion our thoughts in
verbiage. As a general rule, advises writer Sidney Smith,
"run a pen through every other word you have written; you
have no idea what vigor it will give your style."

Long sentences are not necessarily wordy, nor are short
sentences always concise. A sentence is wordy if it can be
tightened without loss of meaning.

GRAMMAR CHECKERS can flag some, but not all, wordy
constructions. Most programs alert you to common redundancies, such as *true fact,* and empty or inflated phrases,
such as *in my opinion* or *in order that.* In addition, they
alert you to wordiness caused by passive verbs, such as *is
determined.* (See also 8a.) They are less helpful in identifying sentences with needlessly complex structures.

16a   Eliminate redundancies.

Writers often repeat themselves unnecessarily. Afraid, perhaps, that they won't be heard the first time, they insist that
a teacup is small *in size* or yellow *in color,* that married
people should cooperate *together,* that a fact is not just a fact
but a *true* fact. Such redundancies may seem at first to add
emphasis. In reality they do just the opposite, for they divide
the reader's attention.

▶ Black slaves were ~~thought of or~~ stereotyped as lazy even

   though they were the main labor force of the South.

▶ Daniel ~~is now employed~~ at a private rehabilitation center ^works^

~~working~~ as a registered physical therapist.

Though modifiers ordinarily add meaning to the words they modify, occasionally they are redundant.

▶ Sylvia ~~very hurriedly~~ scribbled her name, address, and phone number on the back of a greasy napkin.

▶ Joel was determined ~~in his mind~~ to lose weight.

The words *scribbled* and *determined* already contain the notions suggested by the modifiers *very hurriedly* and *in his mind.*

16b Avoid unnecessary repetition of words.

Though words may be repeated deliberately, for effect, repetitions will seem awkward if they are clearly unnecessary. When a more concise version is possible, choose it.

▶ Our fifth patient, in room six, is *a* mentally ill. ~~patient.~~

▶ The best teachers help each student to ~~become a better~~ ^grow^ ~~student~~ both academically and emotionally.

16c Cut empty or inflated phrases.

An empty phrase can be cut with little or no loss of meaning. Common examples are introductory word groups that apologize or hedge: *in my opinion, I think that, it seems that, one must admit that,* and so on.

▶ ~~In my opinion,~~ *O*ur current immigration policy is misguided

on several counts.

▶ ~~It seems that~~ *Lonesome Dove* is one of Larry McMurtry's

most ambitious novels.

Readers understand without being told that they are hearing the writer's opinion or educated guess.

Inflated phrases can be reduced to a word or two without loss of meaning.

INFLATED	CONCISE
along the lines of	like
as a matter of fact	in fact
at all times	always
at the present time	now, currently
at this point in time	now, currently
because of the fact that	because
by means of	by
by virtue of the fact that	because
due to the fact that	because
for the purpose of	for
for the reason that	because
have the ability to	be able to, can
in light of the fact that	because
in order to	to
in spite of the fact that	although, though
in the event that	if
in the final analysis	finally
in the nature of	like
in the neighborhood of	about
until such time as	until

▶ We will file the appropriate papers ~~in the event that~~ *if* we are

unable to meet the deadline.

w

16d Simplify the structure.

If the structure of a sentence is needlessly indirect, try simplifying it. Look for opportunities to strengthen the verb.

▶ The financial analyst claimed that because of volatile market

conditions she could not ~~make an~~ estimate ~~of~~ the company's

future profits.

The verb *estimate* is more vigorous and more concise than *make an estimate of.*

The colorless verbs *is, are, was,* and *were* frequently generate excess words.

monitors and balances
▶ The secretary ~~is responsible for monitoring and balancing~~
                    ^
the budgets for travel, contract services, and personnel.

The revision is more direct and concise. Actions originally appearing in subordinate structures have become verbs replacing *is.*

The expletive constructions *there is* and *there are* (or *there was* and *there were*) can also generate excess words. The same is true of expletive constructions beginning with *it.* (See 62c.)

                  A
▶ ~~There is~~ another module ~~that~~ tells the story of Charles

Darwin and introduces the theory of evolution.

                  All   *must*
▶ ~~It is imperative that all~~ police officers follow strict
                          ^   ^
procedures when apprehending a suspect.

Expletive constructions do have legitimate uses, however. For example, they are appropriate when a writer has a good reason for delaying the subject. (See 62c.)

Finally, verbs in the passive voice may be needlessly indirect. When the active voice expresses your meaning as well, use it. (See 8a.)

▶ All too often, athletes with marginal academic skills. ~~have been recruited by our coaches.~~
  our coaches have recruited

16e   Reduce clauses to phrases, phrases to single words.

Word groups functioning as modifiers can often be made more compact. Look for any opportunities to reduce clauses to phrases or phrases to single words.

▶ We took a side trip to Monticello, ~~which was~~ the home of

Thomas Jefferson.

▶ For her birthday we gave Jess a stylish vest. ~~made of silk.~~
  silk

EXERCISE 16–1

Edit the following sentences for wordiness. Revisions of lettered sentences appear in the back of the book. Example:

The Wilsons moved into the house ~~in spite of the fact that~~
  even though
the back door was only ten yards from the train tracks.

a. Martin Luther King Jr. was a man who set a high standard for future leaders to meet.

b. Coach Becker loves to work with the young people of today.
c. In my opinion, Bloom's race for the governorship is a futile exercise.
d. What a casualty call officer does is assist the bereaved family in many ways.
e. Your task will be the deliverance of correspondence to all employees in the company.

1. Seeing the barrels, the driver immediately slammed on his brakes.
2. The thing data sets are used for is communicating with other computers.
3. The opening words of the Declaration of Independence, which sum up in total America's entire rationale for its very existence, were the subject of considerable debate in 1776.
4. A typical autocross course consists of at least two straightaways, and the rest of the course is made up of numerous slaloms and several sharp turns.
5. You will be the departmental travel coordinator for all members of the department.

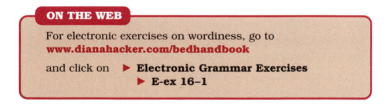

ON THE WEB

For electronic exercises on wordiness, go to
www.dianahacker.com/bedhandbook

and click on   ▶ **Electronic Grammar Exercises**
                 ▶ **E-ex 16–1**

EXERCISE 16–2

Edit the following business memo for wordiness.

To:	District managers
From:	Margaret Davenport, Vice President
Subject:	Customer files

It has recently been brought to my attention that a percentage of our sales representatives have been failing to log reports of their client calls on our electronic customer file each and every day. I have also learned that some representatives are not checking the customer file on a routine basis.

Our clients sometimes receive a multiple number of sales calls from us when a sales representative is not cognizant of the fact that the client has been contacted at a previous time. Repeated telephone calls from our representatives annoy our customers. These repeated telephone calls also portray our company as one that is lacking in organization.

Effective as of immediately, direct your representatives to do the following:

—Record each and every customer contact on the electronic file at the end of each day, without fail.
—Check the electronic file at the very beginning of each day to ensure that telephone communications will not be initiated with clients who have already been called.

Let me extend my appreciation to you for cooperating in this important matter.

LOOKING AT YOURSELF AS A WRITER
Wordy sentences

Editing for wordiness is a natural part of the writing process, especially in the business world, where conciseness (without loss of meaning) is highly valued. In the academic world, you may be tempted to adopt a wordy style for the following reasons.

CAUSE	You are padding your essay to reach the word limit established in the assignment.
CURE	Find an approach to the assignment that interests you; then do prewriting activities such as listing or clustering before you begin drafting. (See pp. 17–18.)
CAUSE	You are mimicking the indirect, wordy style that is unfortunately common in academic textbooks and journal articles.

Wordy sentences (continued)	
CURE	Try not to be impressed by intelligent people who write badly. In your reading, notice that the best writers waste no words; they make each word count.
CAUSE	You fear that a simple, direct style will not sound intelligent—that more words will suggest a greater depth of ideas.
CURE	Look at yourself as a reader. Don't you resent having to wade through wordy sentences? Do you view them as a sign of the writer's intelligence?

17

Choose appropriate language.

Language is appropriate when it suits your subject, engages your audience, and blends naturally with your own voice.

To some extent, your choice of language will be governed by the conventions of the genre in which you are writing. When in doubt about the conventions of a particular genre— lab reports, informal essays, business memos, and so on— take a look at models written by experts in the field.

17a Stay away from jargon.

Jargon is specialized language used among members of a trade, profession, or group. Use jargon only when readers will be familiar with it; even then, use it only when plain English will not do as well.

Sentences filled with jargon are likely to be long and lumpy. To revise such sentences, you must rewrite them, usually in fewer words.

JARGON For years the indigenous body politic of South Africa attempted to negotiate legal enfranchisement without result.

REVISED For years the indigenous people of South Africa negotiated in vain for the right to vote.

Though a political scientist might feel comfortable with the original version, jargon such as *body politic* and *legal enfranchisement* is needlessly complicated for ordinary readers.

Broadly defined, jargon includes puffed-up language designed more to impress readers than to inform them. The following are common examples from business, government, higher education, and the military, with plain English translations in parentheses.

ameliorate (improve)   indicator (sign)
commence (begin)   optimal (best, most favorable)
components (parts)   parameters (boundaries, limits)
endeavor (try)   peruse (read, look over)
exit (leave)   prior to (before)
facilitate (help)   utilize (use)
factor (consideration, cause) viable (workable)
impact (v.) (affect)

Sentences filled with jargon are hard to read, and they are often wordy as well.

▶ All ~~employees functioning in the capacity of~~ work-study
students ~~are required to give evidence of current enrollment.~~
must prove that they are currently enrolled.

▶ Mayor Summers will ~~commence~~ his term of office by
begin
~~ameliorating~~ living conditions in ~~economically deprived zones.~~
improving   *poor neighborhoods.*

17b   Avoid pretentious language, most euphemisms, and "doublespeak."

Hoping to sound profound or poetic, some writers embroider their thoughts with large words and flowery phrases, language that in fact sounds pretentious. Pretentious language is so ornate and often so wordy that it obscures the thought that lies beneath.

> ▶ When our ~~progenitors reach their silver-haired and golden~~ *parents become old,*
>   *entomb*   *old-age homes*
>   ~~years,~~ we frequently ~~ensepulcher~~ them in ~~homes for~~
>   *dead.*
>   ~~senescent beings~~ as if they were already among the ~~deceased.~~

The writer of the original sentence had turned to a thesaurus (a dictionary of synonyms and antonyms) in an attempt to sound educated. When such a writer gains enough confidence to speak in his or her own voice, pretentious language disappears.

Related to pretentious language are euphemisms, nice-sounding words or phrases substituted for words thought to sound harsh or ugly. Like pretentious language, euphemisms are wordy and indirect. Unlike pretentious language, they are sometimes appropriate. It is our social custom, for example, to use euphemisms when speaking or writing about death (*Her sister passed on*), excretion (*I have to go to the bathroom*), sexual intercourse (*They did not sleep together until they were married*), and the like. We may also use euphemisms out of concern for someone's feelings. Telling parents, for example, that their daughter is "unmotivated" is more sensitive than saying she's lazy. Tact or politeness, then, can justify an occasional euphemism.

Most euphemisms, however, are needlessly evasive or even deceitful. Like pretentious language, they obscure the intended meaning.

Word choice

EUPHEMISM	PLAIN ENGLISH
adult entertainment	pornography
preowned automobile	used car
economically deprived	poor
selected out	fired
negative savings	debts
strategic withdrawal	retreat or defeat
revenue enhancers	taxes
chemical dependency	drug addiction
downsize	lay off
correctional facility	prison

The term *doublespeak,* coined by George Orwell in his novel *1984,* applies to any deliberately evasive or deceptive language, including euphemisms. Doublespeak is especially common in politics, where missiles are named "Peace-keepers," airplane crashes are termed "uncontrolled contact with the ground," and a military retreat is described as "tactical redeployment." Business also gives us its share of doublespeak. When the manufacturer of a pacemaker writes that its product "may result in adverse health consequences in pacemaker-dependent patients as a result of sudden 'no output' failure," it takes an alert reader to grasp the message: The pacemakers might suddenly stop functioning and cause a heart attack or even death.

GRAMMAR CHECKERS can be helpful in identifying jargon and pretentious language. For example, they commonly advise against using words such as *utilize, finalize, facilitate,* and *effectuate.* You may find, however, that a program advises you to "simplify" language that is not jargon or pretentious language and may in fact be appropriate in academic writing. Sometimes you can direct the program to change the style level from standard to formal.

EXERCISE 17–1

Edit the following sentences to eliminate jargon, pretentious or flowery language, euphemisms, and doublespeak. You may need to make substantial changes in some sentences. Revisions of lettered sentences appear in the back of the book. Example:

> After two weeks in the legal department, Sue has ~~worked~~ *mastered*
> ~~into~~ the routine**,** ~~of the office,~~ and her ~~functional and self-~~
> *office*   *performance has*
> ~~management skills have~~ exceeded all expectations.

a. In my youth, my family was under the constraints of difficult material circumstances.

b. In order that I may increase my expertise in the area of delivery of services to clients, I feel that participation in this conference will be beneficial.

c. Have you ever been accused of flagellating a deceased equine?

d. Health educators facilitate lifestyle changes in their recipients of service.

e. Passengers should endeavor to finalize the customs declaration form prior to exiting the aircraft.

1. We learned that the mayor had been engaging in a creative transfer of city employees' pension funds.

2. As I approached the edifice of confinement where my brother was incarcerated, several inmates loudly vocalized a number of lewd remarks.

3. The nurse announced that there had been a negative patient-care outcome due to a therapeutic misadventure on the part of the surgeon.

4. Dan's early work hours leave him free to utilize afternoons for errands and for helping the children with their homework.

5. The bottom line is that the company is experiencing a negative cash flow.

EXERCISE 17-2

Edit the following e-mail message to eliminate jargon.

Dear Ms. Jackson:

We members of the Nakamura Reyes team value our external partnering arrangements with Creative Software, and I look forward to seeing you next week at the trade show in Fresno. Per Mr. Reyes, please let me know when you'll have some downtime there so that he and I can conduct a strategizing session with you concerning our production schedule. It's crucial that we all be on the same page re our 2001–2002 product release dates.

Before we have a face-to-face, however, I have some findings to share. Our customer-centric approach to the new products will necessitate that user testing periods trend upward. The enclosed data should help you effectuate any adjustments to your timeline; let me know asap if you require any additional information to facilitate the above.

Before we convene in Fresno, Mr. Reyes and I will agendize any further talking points. Thanks for your help.

Sincerely,

Sylvia Nakamura

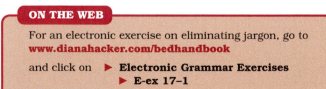

ON THE WEB

For an electronic exercise on eliminating jargon, go to
www.dianahacker.com/bedhandbook

and click on ▶ **Electronic Grammar Exercises**
▶ **E-ex 17–1**

LOOKING AT YOURSELF AS A WRITER
Jargon and pretentious language

In the academic and business worlds, you may be tempted to use jargon and pretentious language for several reasons.

CAUSE You're surrounded by jargon and pretentious language—at work or in your academic field—so you are picking it up, by osmosis.

CURE Develop an appreciation for good writing. Notice that the best writers can manage an elevated style without losing their human voices.

CAUSE You're afraid that if you present your ideas clearly, they will seem too simple.

CURE Give clear writing a try—and see if it sells. You can usually tell which professors or supervisors value a straightforward style and which are impressed by pompous language.

CAUSE Having discovered a thesaurus, you are using it for the wrong reason.

CURE Use a thesaurus or a dictionary to choose the best word, not necessarily the fanciest one. (See pp. 227–28.)

CAUSE You are experimenting with style, and your attempts at creativity and sophistication sometimes backfire.

CURE Continue to experiment, but be prepared—in the words of one writer—to "murder your darlings."

17c Avoid obsolete and invented words.

Although dictionaries list obsolete words such as *recomfort* and *reechy*, these words are not appropriate for current use. Invented words (also called *neologisms*) are too recently created to be part of standard English. Many invented words fade out of use without becoming standard. *Palimony* and *technobabble* are neologisms that may not last. *Printout* and *flextime* are no longer neologisms; they have become standard English. Avoid using invented words in formal writing unless they are given in the dictionary as standard or unless no other word expresses your meaning.

17d   In most contexts, avoid slang, regional expressions, and nonstandard English.

Slang is an informal and sometimes private vocabulary that expresses the solidarity of a group such as teenagers, rock musicians, or football fans; it is subject to more rapid change than standard English. For example, the slang teenagers use to express approval changes every few years; *cool, groovy, neat, awesome, phat,* and *money* have replaced one another within the last three decades. Sometimes slang becomes so widespread that it is accepted as standard vocabulary. *Jazz,* for example, started out as slang but is now generally accepted to describe a style of music.

Although slang has a certain vitality, it is a code that not everyone understands, and it is very informal. Therefore, it is inappropriate in most written work.

▶ If we don't begin studying for the final, a whole semester's

    will be wasted.
  work ~~is going down the tubes.~~
    ^

                                                    disgust you.
▶ The government's "filth" guidelines for food will ~~gross you out.~~
                                                              ^

Regional expressions are common to a group in a geographical area. *Let's talk with the bark off* (for *Let's speak frankly*) is an expression in the southern United States, for example. Regional expressions have the same limitations as slang and are therefore inappropriate in most writing.

▶ John was four blocks from the house before he remembered

         turn on
  to ~~cut~~ the headlights~~. on.~~
     ^   ^

▶ I'm not ~~for~~ sure, but I think the dance has been postponed

until tomorrow.

Standard English is the language used in all academic, business, and professional fields. Nonstandard English is spoken by people with a common regional or social heritage. Although nonstandard English may be appropriate when spoken within a close group, it is out of place in most formal and informal writing.

          has
▶ The counselor ~~have~~ so many problems in her own life that
                ^
    doesn't
  she ~~don't~~ know how to advise anyone else.
   ^

If you speak a nonstandard dialect, try to identify the ways in which your dialect differs from standard English. Look especially for the following features of nonstandard English, which commonly cause problems in writing.

Misuse of verb forms such as *began* and *begun* (See 27a.)

Omission of *-s* endings on verbs (See 27c.)

Omission of *-ed* endings on verbs (See 27d.)

Omission of necessary verbs (See 27e.)

Double negatives (See 26d.)

17e　Choose an appropriate level of formality.

In deciding on a level of formality, consider both your subject and your audience. Does the subject demand a dignified treatment, or is a relaxed tone more suitable? Will readers be put off if you assume too close a relationship with them, or might you alienate them by seeming too distant?

For most college and professional writing, some degree of formality is appropriate. In a letter applying for a job, for example, it is a mistake to sound too breezy and informal.

> **TOO INFORMAL**　I'd like to get that receptionist's job you've got in the paper.
>
> **MORE FORMAL**　I would like to apply for the receptionist's position listed in the *Peoria Journal Star*.

Informal writing is appropriate for private letters, personal e-mail, and business correspondence between close associates. Like spoken conversation, it allows contractions (*don't, I'll*) and colloquial words (*kids, buddy*). Vocabulary and sentence structure are rarely complex.

In choosing a level of formality, above all be consistent. When a writer's voice shifts from one level of formality to another, readers receive mixed messages.

▶ Once a pitcher for the Cincinnati Reds, Bob shared with me the secrets of his trade. His lesson ~~commenced~~ *began* with his famous curveball, ~~implemented~~ *thrown* by tucking the little finger behind the ball instead of holding it straight out. Next he ~~elucidated~~ *revealed* the mysteries of the sucker pitch, a slow ball coming behind a fast windup.

Words such as *commenced* and *elucidated* are inappropriate for the subject matter, and they clash with informal terms such as *sucker pitch* and *fast windup*.

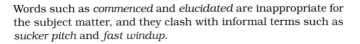

> **GRAMMAR CHECKERS** can flag slang and some informal language. Be aware, though, that they tend to be conservative on the matter of using contractions. If your ear tells you that a contraction such as *isn't* or *doesn't* strikes the right tone, stay with it.

EXERCISE 17–3

Edit the following paragraph to eliminate slang and maintain a consistent level of formality.

> The graduation speaker really blew it. He should have discussed the options and challenges facing the graduating class. Instead, he shot his mouth off at us and trashed us for being lazy and pampered. He did make some good points, however. Our profs have certainly babied us by not holding fast to deadlines, by dismissing assignments that the class ragged them about, by ignoring our tardiness, and by handing out easy C's like hotcakes. Still, we resented this speech as the final word from the college establishment. It should have been the orientation speech when we started college.

17f Avoid sexist language.

Sexist language is language that stereotypes or demeans men or women, usually women. Using nonsexist language is a matter of courtesy—of respect for and sensitivity to the feelings of others.

Word choice

Recognizing sexist language

Some sexist language is easy to recognize because it reflects genuine contempt for women: referring to a woman as a "broad," for example, or calling a lawyer a "lady lawyer," or saying in an advertisement, "If our new sports car were a lady, it would get its bottom pinched."

Other forms of sexist language are less blatant. The following practices, while they may not result from conscious sexism, reflect stereotypical thinking: referring to nurses as women and doctors as men, using different conventions when naming or identifying women and men, or assuming that all of one's readers are men.

STEREOTYPICAL LANGUAGE

After the nursing student graduates, *she* must face a difficult state board examination. [Not all nursing students are women.]

Running for city council are Jake Stein, an attorney, and *Mrs. Cynthia Jones*, a professor of English and *mother of three*. [The title *Mrs.* and the phrase *mother of three* are irrelevant.]

Wives of senior government officials are required to report any gifts they receive that are valued at more than $100. [Not all senior government officials are men.]

Still other forms of sexist language result from outmoded traditions. The pronouns *he, him,* and *his,* for instance, were traditionally used to refer generically to persons of either sex.

GENERIC *HE* OR *HIS*

When a senior physician is harassed by managed care professionals, *he* may be tempted to leave the profession.

A journalist is stimulated by *his* deadline.

Today, however, such usage is widely viewed as sexist because it excludes women and encourages sex-role stereotyping—the view that men are somehow more suited than women to be doctors, journalists, and so on.

Like the pronouns *he, him,* and *his,* the nouns *man* and *men* were once used indefinitely to refer to persons of either sex. Current usage demands gender-neutral terms for references to both men and women.

INAPPROPRIATE	APPROPRIATE
chairman	chairperson, moderator, chair, head
clergyman	member of the clergy, minister, pastor
congressman	member of Congress, representative, legislator
fireman	firefighter
foreman	supervisor
mailman	mail carrier, postal worker, letter carrier
mankind	people, humans
manpower	personnel
policeman	police officer
salesman	salesperson, sales associate, salesclerk, sales representative
to man	to operate, to staff
weatherman	weather forecaster, meteorologist
workman	worker, laborer

GRAMMAR CHECKERS are good at flagging sexist words, such as *mankind,* but they may also flag words, such as *girl* and *woman,* when they aren't being used in a sexist manner. It's sexist to call a woman a girl or a doctor a woman doctor, but you don't need to avoid the words *girl* and *woman* entirely and replace them with needlessly abstract terms like *female* and *individual.* All in all, just use your common sense. It's usually easy to tell when a word is offensive—and when it is not.

Although grammar checkers can flag sexist words, they cannot flag other kinds of sexist language, such as inconsistent treatment of men and women.

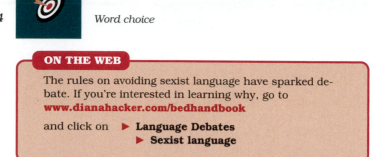

ON THE WEB

The rules on avoiding sexist language have sparked debate. If you're interested in learning why, go to
www.dianahacker.com/bedhandbook

and click on   ▶ **Language Debates**
                ▶ **Sexist language**

Revising sexist language

When revising sexist language, be sparing in your use of the wordy constructions *he or she* and *his or her.* Although these constructions are fine in small doses, they become awkward when repeated throughout an essay. A better revision strategy, many writers have discovered, is to write in the plural; yet another strategy is to recast the sentence so that the problem does not arise.

SEXIST
When a senior physician is harassed by managed care professionals, *he* may be tempted to leave the profession.

A journalist is stimulated by *his* deadline.

ACCEPTABLE BUT WORDY
When a senior physician is harassed by managed care professionals, *he or she* may be tempted to leave the profession.

A journalist is stimulated by *his or her* deadline.

BETTER: USING THE PLURAL
When senior *physicians* are harassed by managed care professionals, *they* may be tempted to leave the profession.

Journalists are stimulated by *their* deadlines.

BETTER: RECASTING THE SENTENCE

When harassed by managed care professionals, *a senior physician* may be tempted to leave the profession.

A journalist is stimulated by *a* deadline.

For more examples of these revision strategies, see 22.

EXERCISE 17–4

Edit the following sentences to eliminate sexist language or sexist assumptions. Revisions of lettered sentences appear in the back of the book. Example:

Scholarship athletes
A scholarship athlete must be as concerned about ~~his~~ *their*
academic performance as ~~he is~~ *they are* about ~~his~~ *their* athletic

performance.

a. Mrs. Geralyn Farmer, who is the mayor's wife, is the chief surgeon at University Hospital. Dr. Paul Green is her assistant.
b. Every applicant wants to know how much he will make.
c. An elementary school teacher should understand the concept of nurturing if she intends to be a success.
d. The vice president for community affairs asked Elizabeth and Joseph to serve as cochairmen for the Red Cross blood drive.
e. If man does not stop polluting his environment, mankind will perish.

1. A fireman must always be on call even when he is off duty.
2. If a high school graduate makes a career in the armed forces, he can retire with a comfortable pension before the age of fifty.
3. In the gubernatorial race, Lena Weiss, a defense lawyer and mother of two, easily defeated Harvey Tower, an architect.
4. My brother hired a lady lawyer who is a partner in the firm of Harris and Porter.

5. A secretary must be willing to sacrifice some of her spare time in the evenings and on the weekends if she expects to advance within this company.

ON THE WEB

For an electronic exercise on avoiding sexist language, go to **www.dianahacker.com/bedhandbook**

and click on ▶ **Electronic Grammar Exercises**
▶ **E-ex 17–2**

17g Revise language that may offend groups of people.

Obviously it is impolite to use offensive terms such as *Polack* or *redneck.* But biased language can take more subtle forms. Because language evolves over time, names once thought acceptable may become offensive. When describing groups of people, choose names that the groups currently use to describe themselves.

▶ North Dakota takes its name from the ~~Indian~~ Lakota word meaning

"friend" or "ally."

▶ Many ~~Oriental~~ Asian immigrants have recently settled in our small

town in Tennessee.

Negative stereotypes (such as "drives like a teenager" or "haggard as an old crone") are of course offensive. But you should avoid stereotyping a person or a group even if you believe your generalization to be positive.

▶ It was no surprise that Greer, ~~a Chinese American,~~ was
an excellent math and science student,
^

selected for the honors chemistry program.

18

Find the exact words.

Whatever you want to say, claimed French writer Gustave Flaubert, "there is but one word to express it, one verb to give it movement, one adjective to qualify it; you must seek until you find this noun, this verb, this adjective." Even if you are not reaching for such perfection in your writing, you will sometimes find yourself wishing for better words. The dictionary is the obvious first place to turn, a thesaurus the second.

A good dictionary—such as *The American Heritage Dictionary, The Random House College Dictionary, Merriam-Webster's Collegiate Dictionary,* or *Webster's New World Dictionary of the American Language*—lists synonyms and antonyms for many words, with helpful comments on shades of meaning. Under *fertile,* for example, *Webster's New World Dictionary* carefully distinguishes the meanings of *fertile, fecund, fruitful,* and *prolific*:

> SYN—*fertile* implies a producing, or power of producing, fruit or offspring, and may be used figuratively of the mind; *fecund* implies the abundant production of offspring or fruit, or, figuratively, of creations of the mind; *fruitful* specifically suggests the bearing of much fruit, but it is also used to imply fertility (of soil), favorable results, profitableness, etc.; *prolific,* a close synonym for *fecund,* more often carries derogatory connotations of overly rapid production or reproduction—ANT. *sterile, barren*

If the dictionary doesn't yield the word you need, try a book of synonyms and antonyms such as *Roget's International Thesaurus* (or its online equivalent). Look up (or click on) the adjective *still,* for example, and you will find synonyms such as *tranquil, quiet, quiescent, reposeful, calm, pacific,* and *halcyon.* Unless your vocabulary is better than average, the list will contain words you've never heard or with which you are only vaguely familiar. Whenever you are tempted to use one of these words, look it up in the dictionary first to avoid misusing it.

On discovering the thesaurus, many writers use it for the wrong reasons, so a word of caution is in order. Do not turn to a thesaurus in search of exotic, fancy words—such as *halcyon*—with which to embellish your essays. Look instead for words that exactly express your meaning. Most of the time these words will be familiar to both you and your readers. The first synonym on the list—*tranquil*—was probably the word you were looking for all along.

GRAMMAR CHECKERS can flag some nonstandard idioms, such as *comply to,* and many clichés, such as *leave no stone unturned.* In addition, they can flag commonly confused words such as *principal* and *principle* or *affect* and *effect,* although you must decide which word is correct in your context. Grammar checkers are less helpful with the other problems discussed in 18: choosing words with appropriate connotations, using concrete language, and using figures of speech appropriately.

18a   Select words with appropriate connotations.

In addition to their strict dictionary meanings (or *denotations*), words have *connotations,* emotional colorings that affect how readers respond to them. The word *steel* denotes "made of or resembling commercial iron that contains carbon," but it also calls up a cluster of images associated with steel, such as the sensation of touching it. These associations give the word its connotations—cold, smooth, unbending.

If the connotation of a word does not seem appropriate for your purpose, your audience, or your subject matter, you should change the word. When a more appropriate synonym does not come quickly to mind, consult a dictionary or a thesaurus.

▶ The model was ~~skinny~~ *slender* and fashionable.

The connotation of the word *skinny* is too negative.

▶ As I covered the boats with marsh grass, the ~~perspiration~~ *sweat* I

had worked up evaporated in the wind, and the cold morning

air seemed even colder.

The term *perspiration* is too dainty for the context, which suggests vigorous exercise.

EXERCISE 18–1

Use a dictionary and a thesaurus to find at least four synonyms for each of the following words. Be prepared to explain any slight differences in meaning.

1. decay (verb)
2. difficult (adjective)
3. hurry (verb)
4. pleasure (noun)
5. secret (adjective)
6. talent (noun)

EXERCISE 18–2

For each of the words italicized in the following passages, consider alternatives that the writer might have chosen instead. (A dictionary and a thesaurus will lead to other possibilities.) Then discuss why the author probably selected the word he or she did.

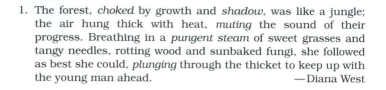

1. The forest, *choked* by growth and *shadow,* was like a jungle; the air hung thick with heat, *muting* the sound of their progress. Breathing in a *pungent steam* of sweet grasses and tangy needles, rotting wood and sunbaked fungi, she followed as best she could, *plunging* through the thicket to keep up with the young man ahead.   —Diana West

2. A change of just a few degrees in atmospheric temperature over the next century would be *catastrophic.* A *parade* of scientists appearing before a Senate committee in June *painted a graphic* picture of what that could mean: melting icecaps and rising sea levels that would *inundate* seaboard cities and drown thousands in *fierce* storms; rainfall shifts that would make the deserts *bloom* and turn *breadbaskets* into *dustbowls;* and, of course, heat everywhere.   —Matthew L. Wald

18b Prefer specific, concrete nouns.

Unlike general nouns, which refer to broad classes of things, specific nouns point to definite and particular items. *Film,* for example, names a general class, *science fiction film* names a narrower class, and *Jurassic Park* is more specific still. Other examples: *team, football team, Denver Broncos; music, symphony, Beethoven's Ninth.*

Unlike abstract nouns, which refer to qualities and ideas (*justice, beauty, realism, dignity*), concrete nouns point to immediate, often sensory experience and to physical objects (*steeple, asphalt, lilac, stone, garlic*).

Specific, concrete nouns express meaning more vividly than general or abstract ones. Although general and abstract language is sometimes necessary to convey your meaning, ordinarily prefer specific, concrete alternatives.

▶ The senator spoke about the challenges of the future:
   of famine, pollution, dwindling resources, and terrorism.
   problems ~~concerning the environment and world peace.~~
                  ^

Nouns such as *thing, area, aspect, factor,* and *individual* are especially dull and imprecise.

▶ A career in transportation management offers many ~~things.~~ *rewards.*

▶ Try pairing a trainee with an ~~individual with technical experience.~~ *experienced technician.*

18c Do not misuse words.

If a word is not in your active vocabulary, you may find yourself misusing it, sometimes with embarrassing consequences. Imagine the chagrin of the young woman who wrote that the "aroma of pumpkin pie and sage stuffing acted as an *aphrodisiac*" when she learned that aphrodisiacs are drugs or foods stimulating sexual desire. Such blunders are easily prevented: When in doubt, check the dictionary.

▶ The fans were ~~migrating~~ *climbing* up the bleachers in search of seats.

▶ Mrs. Johnson tried to fight but to no ~~prevail.~~ *avail.*

▶ Drugs have so ~~diffused~~ *permeated* our culture that they touch all segments of society.

Be especially alert for misused word forms—using a noun such as *absence, significance,* or *persistence,* for example, when your meaning requires the adjective *absent, significant,* or *persistent.*

▶ Most dieters are not ~~persistence~~ *persistent* enough to make a permanent change in their eating habits.

EXERCISE 18-3

Edit the following sentences to correct misused words. Revisions of lettered sentences appear in the back of the book. Example:

The training required for a ballet dancer is ~~all-absorbent.~~ *all-absorbing.*

a. We regret this delay; thank you for your patients.
b. Ada's plan is to require education and experience to prepare herself for a position as property manager.
c. Tiger Woods, the penultimate competitor, has earned millions of dollars just in endorsements.
d. When Robert Frost died at age eighty-eight, he left a legacy of poems that will make him immoral.
e. I would not advice anyone to pass up a chance to study geology.

1. Waste, misuse of government money, security and health violations, and even pilfering have become major dilemmas at the FBI.
2. Did you understand the significant of the list?
3. Grand Isle State Park is surrounded on three sides by water.
4. The Old World nuance of the restaurant intrigued us.
5. Trifle, a popular English dessert, contains a ménage of ingredients that do not always appeal to American tastes.

LOOKING AT YOURSELF AS A WRITER
Misused words

Most writers choose the wrong word now and then, but if you find yourself misusing a great many words, consider why. Here are some common causes and cures.

CAUSE	You have a fondness for fancy words, such as *penultimate,* that are not in your active vocabulary.
CURE	Write in a simpler style. Readers appreciate plain English more than you may think. (See 17a and 17b.) *Penultimate* probably isn't in their active vocabulary either.

Misused words (continued)

CAUSE You tend to mix up easily confused words such as *accept* and *except*.

CURE Turn to the Glossary of Usage at the back of this book whenever you are in doubt about such words. Or consult a dictionary.

CAUSE Your vocabulary is not as strong as you'd like it to be.

CURE This cure will take time. The best way to improve your vocabulary is to read, and the best way to develop the habit of reading is to choose articles and books that you enjoy. Seeing new words used properly, in context, will help you learn to use them in your own writing.

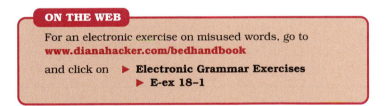

ON THE WEB

For an electronic exercise on misused words, go to
www.dianahacker.com/bedhandbook

and click on ▶ **Electronic Grammar Exercises**
▶ **E-ex 18–1**

18d Use standard idioms.

Idioms are speech forms that follow no easily specified rules. The English say "Maria went *to hospital*," an idiom strange to American ears, which are accustomed to hearing *the* in front of *hospital.* Native speakers of a language seldom have problems with idioms, but prepositions sometimes cause trouble, especially when they follow certain verbs and adjectives. When in doubt, consult a dictionary.

UNIDIOMATIC	IDIOMATIC
abide with (a decision)	abide by (a decision)
according with	according to
agree to (an idea)	agree with (an idea)
angry at (a person)	angry with (a person)
capable to	capable of
comply to	comply with
desirous to	desirous of
different than (a person or thing)	different from (a person or thing)
intend on doing	intend to do
off of	off
plan on doing	plan to do
preferable than	preferable to
prior than	prior to
superior than	superior to
sure and	sure to
try and	try to
type of a	type of

ESL

Because idioms follow no particular rules, you must learn them individually. You may find it helpful to keep a list of idioms that you frequently encounter in conversation and in reading.

EXERCISE 18–4

Edit the following sentences to eliminate errors in the use of idiomatic expressions. If a sentence is correct, write "correct" after it. Answers to lettered sentences appear in the back of the book. Example:

           by
We agreed to abide ~~with~~ the decision of the judge.

a. Queen Anne was so angry at Sarah Churchill that she refused to see her again.

b. Prior to the Russians' launching of *Sputnik, -nik* was not an English suffix.

c. The parade moved off of the street and onto the beach.

d. For the frightened refugees, the dangerous trek across the mountains was preferable than life in a war zone.

e. What type of a wedding are you planning?

1. Be sure and report on the danger of releasing genetically engineered bacteria into the atmosphere.

2. Why do you assume that embezzling bank assets is so different than robbing the bank?

3. Most of the class agreed to Sylvia's view that domestic terrorism is a very dangerous problem.

4. I refuse to abide by a decision I had no part in making.

5. Andrea intends on joining the Peace Corps after graduation.

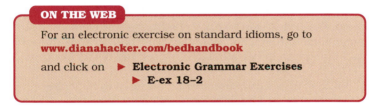

ON THE WEB

For an electronic exercise on standard idioms, go to
www.dianahacker.com/bedhandbook

and click on ▶ **Electronic Grammar Exercises**
                  ▶ **E-ex 18–2**

18e   Do not rely heavily on clichés.

The frontiersman who first announced that he had "slept like a log" no doubt amused his companions with a fresh and unlikely comparison. Today, however, that comparison is a cliché, a saying that has lost its dazzle from overuse. No longer can it surprise.

To see just how dully predictable clichés are, put your hand over the right-hand column on the following page and then finish the phrases on the left.

cool as a	cucumber
beat around	the bush
blind as a	bat
busy as a	bee, beaver
crystal	clear
dead as a	doornail
out of the frying pan and	into the fire
light as a	feather
like a bull	in a china shop
playing with	fire
nutty as a	fruitcake
selling like	hotcakes
starting out at the bottom	of the ladder
water under the	bridge
white as a	sheet, ghost
avoid clichés like the	plague

The cure for clichés is frequently simple: Just delete them. When this won't work, try adding some element of surprise. One student, for example, who had written that she had butterflies in her stomach, revised her cliché like this:

> If all of the action in my stomach is caused by butterflies, there must be a horde of them, with horseshoes on.

The image of butterflies wearing horseshoes is fresh and unlikely, not dully predictable like the original cliché.

ON THE WEB

The rules on avoiding clichés have sparked debates. If you're interested in learning why, go to
www.dianahacker.com/bedhandbook

and click on ▶ **Language Debates**
　　　　　　　▶ **Clichés**

18f   Use figures of speech with care.

A figure of speech is an expression that uses words imagina-
tively (rather than literally) to make abstract ideas concrete.
Most often, figures of speech compare two seemingly unlike
things to reveal surprising similarities.

In a *simile,* the writer makes the comparison explicitly,
usually by introducing it with *like* or *as:* "By the time cotton
had to be picked, grandfather's neck was as red as the clay
he plowed." In a *metaphor,* the *like* or *as* is omitted, and the
comparison is implied. For example, in the Old Testament
Song of Solomon, a young woman compares the man she
loves to a fruit tree: "With great delight I sat in his shadow,
and his fruit was sweet to my taste."

Although figures of speech are useful devices, writers
sometimes use them without thinking through the images
they evoke. This can result in a *mixed metaphor,* the combination of two or more images that don't make sense
together.

▶ Crossing Utah's salt flats in his new Corvette, my father flew
   at jet speed.
   ~~under a full head of steam.~~
   ˄

   Flew suggests an airplane, while *under a full head of steam*
   suggests a steamboat or a train. To clarify the image, the writer
   should stick with one comparison or the other.

▶ Our office had decided to put all controversial issues on a

   back burner. ~~in a holding pattern.~~
         ˄

   Here the writer is mixing stoves and airplanes. Simply deleting
   one of the images corrects the problem.

EXERCISE 18–5

Edit the following sentences to replace worn-out expressions and clarify mixed figures of speech. Revisions of lettered sentences appear in the back of the book. Example:

> *the color drained from his face.*
> When he heard about the accident, ~~he turned white as a~~
> ^
> ~~sheet.~~

a. John stormed into the room like a bull in a china shop.
b. The president thought that the scientists were using science as a sledgehammer to grind their political axes.
c. The Cubs easily beat the Mets, who were in the soup early in the game today at Wrigley Field.
d. We ironed out the sticky spots in our relationship.
e. Sasha told us that he wasn't willing to put his neck out on a limb.

1. Once she had sunk her teeth into it, Helen burned through the assignment.
2. The interrogators were raking him over the ropes.
3. The dean of students acted like a big fish in a little pond.
4. There are too many cooks in the broth here at corporate headquarters.
5. Juanita told Kyle that keeping skeletons in the closet would be playing with fire.

ON THE WEB

For an electronic exercise on clichés and figures of speech, go to **www.dianahacker.com/bedhandbook**

and click on ▶ **Electronic Grammar Exercises**
▶ **E-ex 18–3**

PART V

Grammatical Sentences

19

Repair sentence fragments.

A sentence fragment is a word group that pretends to be a sentence. Sentence fragments are easy to recognize when they appear out of context, like these:

> On the old wooden stool in the corner of my grandmother's kitchen.

> And immediately popped their flares and life vests.

When fragments appear next to related sentences, however, they are harder to spot.

> On that morning I sat in my usual spot. On the old wooden stool in the corner of my grandmother's kitchen.

> The pilots ejected from the burning plane, landing in the water not far from the ship. And immediately popped their flares and life vests.

Recognizing sentence fragments

To be a sentence, a word group must consist of at least one full independent clause. An independent clause has a subject and a verb, and it either stands alone or could stand alone.

To test a word group for sentence completeness, use the flow chart on page 241. For example, by using the flow chart, you can see exactly why *On the old wooden stool in the corner of my grandmother's kitchen* is a fragment: It lacks both a subject and a verb. *And immediately popped their flares and life vests* is a fragment because it lacks a subject.

Test for sentence completeness

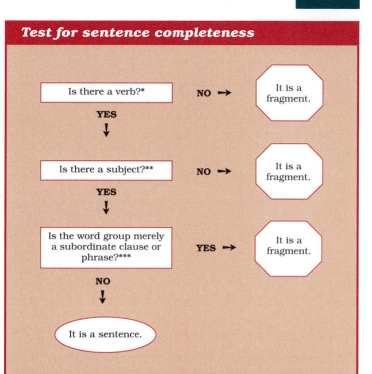

Is there a verb?*   NO → It is a fragment.

YES ↓

Is there a subject?**   NO → It is a fragment.

YES ↓

Is the word group merely a subordinate clause or phrase?***   YES → It is a fragment.

NO ↓

It is a sentence.

* Do not mistake verbals for verbs. (See 63c.)

** The subject of a sentence may be *you,* understood. (See 62a.)

*** A sentence may open with a subordinate clause, but the sentence must also include an independent clause. (See 63c.)

If you find any fragments, try one of these methods of revision:

1. Attach the fragment to a nearby sentence.
2. Turn the fragment into a sentence.

ESL

Unlike some languages, English does not allow omission of subjects (except in imperative sentences); nor does it allow omission of verbs. See 31a and 29e.

GRAMMAR CHECKERS can flag as many as half of the sentence fragments in a sample; but that means, of course, that they miss half or more of them. If fragments are a serious problem for you, you will still need to proofread for them.

Sometimes you will get "false positives," sentences that have been flagged but are not fragments. For example, one program flagged this complete sentence as a possible fragment: *I bent down to crawl into the bunker.* When a program spots a possible fragment, you should check to see if it is really a fragment. You can do this by using the flow chart on page 241.

Repairing sentence fragments

You can repair most fragments in one of two ways: Either pull the fragment into a nearby sentence or turn the fragment into a sentence.

▶ On that morning I sat in my usual spot/, ~~On~~ the old wooden
                                     on

  stool in the corner of my grandmother's kitchen.

▶ The pilots ejected from the burning plane, landing in the
                        They

  water not far from the ship. ~~And~~ immediately popped their

  flares and life vests.

19a   Attach fragmented subordinate clauses or turn them into sentences.

A subordinate clause is patterned like a sentence, with both a subject and a verb, but it begins with a word that marks it as subordinate. The following words commonly introduce subordinate clauses:

after	even though	so that	when	whom
although	how	than	where	whose
as	if	that	whether	why
as if	in order that	though	which	
because	rather than	unless	while	
before	since	until	who	

Subordinate clauses function within sentences as adjectives, as adverbs, or as nouns. They cannot stand alone. (See 63b.)

Most fragmented clauses beg to be pulled into a sentence nearby.

▶ Normally the bride-price consists of cattle and sheep**/**
   because
   ~~Because~~ money has little value to these isolated people.
   ^

   Because introduces a subordinate clause. (For punctuation of a subordinate clause appearing at the end of a sentence, see 33f.)

                                                          at
▶ Although we seldom get to see wildlife in the city**/,** ~~At~~ the zoo
                                                          ^

   we can still find some of our favorites.

   Although introduces a subordinate clause. (For punctuation of subordinate clauses appearing at the beginning of a sentence, see 32b.)

Grammatical sentences

If a fragmented clause cannot be attached to a nearby sentence or if you feel that attaching it would be awkward, try turning the clause into a sentence. The simplest way to do this is to delete the opening word or words that mark it as subordinate:

▶ Population increases and uncontrolled development are taking a deadly toll on the environment. ~~So that in~~ *In* many parts of the world, fragile ecosystems are collapsing.

19b Attach fragmented phrases or turn them into sentences.

Like subordinate clauses, phrases function within sentences as adjectives, as adverbs, or as nouns. They cannot stand alone. Fragmented phrases are often prepositional or verbal phrases; sometimes they are appositives, words or word groups that rename nouns or pronouns. (See 63a, 63c, and 63d.)

Often a fragmented phrase may simply be pulled into a nearby sentence.

▶ The archaeologists worked slowly/, ~~Examining~~ *examining* and labeling every pottery shard they uncovered.

The word group beginning with *Examining* is a verbal phrase.

▶ Mary is suffering from agoraphobia/, ~~A~~ *a* fear of the outside world.

A fear of the outside world is an appositive renaming the noun *agoraphobia*. (For punctuation of appositives, see 32e.)

If a fragmented phrase cannot be pulled into a nearby sentence effectively, turn the phrase into a sentence. You may need to add a subject, a verb, or both.

▶ In the computer training session, Eugene explained how to
install our new software. ~~Also~~ how to organize our files,
(inserted above: *He also taught us*)

connect to the Internet, and back up our hard drives.

The revision turns the fragmented phrase into a sentence by adding a subject and a verb.

19c   Attach other fragmented word groups or turn them into sentences.

Other word groups that are commonly fragmented include parts of compound predicates, lists, and examples introduced by *such as, for example,* or similar expressions.

Parts of compound predicates

A predicate consists of a verb and its objects, complements, and modifiers (see 62b). A compound predicate includes two or more predicates joined by a coordinating conjunction such as *and, but,* or *or.* Because the parts of a compound predicate share the same subject, they should appear in the same sentence.

▶ The woodpecker finch of the Galápagos Islands carefully
selects a twig of a certain size and shape. ~~And~~ then uses this
(inserted above: *and*)

tool to pry out grubs from trees.

Notice that no comma appears between the parts of a compound predicate. (See 33a.)

Grammatical sentences

Lists

When a list is mistakenly fragmented, it can often be attached to a nearby sentence with a colon or a dash. (See 35a and 39a.)

▶ It has been said that there are only three indigenous American art forms/: ~~Musical~~ *musical* comedy, jazz, and soap opera.

Examples introduced by such as, for example, *or similar expressions*

Expressions that introduce examples (or explanations) can lead to unintentional fragments. Although you may begin a sentence with some of the following words or phrases, make sure that what you have written is a sentence, not a fragment.

also	for instance	or
and	in addition	such as
but	like	that is
especially	mainly	
for example	namely	

Sometimes fragmented examples can be attached to the preceding sentence.

▶ The South has produced some of our greatest twentieth-century writers/, ~~Such~~ *such* as Flannery O'Connor, William Faulkner, Alice Walker, Tennessee Williams, and Thomas Wolfe.

At times, however, it may be necessary to turn the fragment into a sentence.

▶ If Eric doesn't get his way, he goes into a fit of rage. For
          he lies   *opens*
  example, ~~lying~~ on the floor screaming or ~~opening~~ the cabinet
                ^   *slams*   ^
  doors and then ~~slamming~~ them shut.
               ^

The writer corrected this fragment by adding a subject — *he* —
and substituting verbs for the verbals *lying, opening,* and
slamming.

LOOKING AT YOURSELF AS A WRITER
Sentence fragments

An occasional sentence fragment, used deliberately, can be
effective, but unintentional sentence fragments are serious
errors. If you tend to write unintentional fragments, try to
discover why.

CAUSE   You worry that you will write a run-on sentence
            (a comma splice or a fused sentence).

CURE   You are right to be concerned about run-on sen-
            tences, but you may be worrying too much about
            them while drafting. When you reach the editing
            stage of the writing process, try proofreading for
            both fragments and run-ons by using the flow
            charts on pages 241 and 252.

CAUSE   Feeling that a sentence should be a certain length,
            you insert a period at some convenient point when
            it has reached that length.

CURE   Make punctuation decisions based on sentence
            structure, not length. The following comma rules
            tell you when to use a comma (or no punctuation)
            instead of a period: 32b, 32e, 33e, and 33f.

CAUSE   You are trying to emphasize the idea in the
            fragment by putting it in its own sentence.

CURE   Consider using other strategies for emphasis, such
            as the dash or the colon. (See 19c.)

19d   Exception: Occasionally a fragment may be used deliberately, for effect.

Skilled writers occasionally use sentence fragments for the following special purposes.

FOR EMPHASIS	Following the dramatic Americanization of their children, even my parents grew more publicly confident. *Especially my mother.*
	—Richard Rodriguez
TO ANSWER A QUESTION	Are these new drug tests 100 percent reliable? *Not in the opinion of most experts.*
AS TRANSITION	*And now the opposing arguments.*
EXCLAMATIONS	*Not again!*
IN ADVERTISING	*Fewer calories. Improved taste.*

Although fragments are sometimes appropriate, writers and readers do not always agree on when they are appropriate. That's why you will find it safer to write in complete sentences.

EXERCISE 19–1

Repair any fragment by attaching it to a nearby sentence or by rewriting it as a complete sentence. If a word group is correct, write "correct" after it. Revisions of lettered sentences appear in the back of the book. Example:

> One Greek island that should not be missed is Mykonos/. A̶ *a*
>
> vacation spot for Europeans and a playpen for the rich.

a. The shock of bereavement is often followed by a succession of emotions. Denial, sorrow, anger, despair, guilt, remorse, and longing.

b. Cortés and his soldiers were astonished when they looked down from the mountains and saw Tenochtitlán. The magnificent capital of the Aztecs.

c. Although my spoken Spanish is not very good. I can read the language with ease.

d. There are several reasons for not eating meat. One reason being that dangerous chemicals are used throughout the various stages of meat production.

e. To give my family a comfortable, secure home life. That is my most important goal.

1. The panther lay quite motionless behind the rock. Waiting silently for its prey.

2. Mother loved to play all our favorite games. Canasta, Monopoly, hide-and-seek, and even kick-the-can.

3. With machetes, the explorers cut their way through the tall grasses to the edge of the canyon. Then they began to lay out the tapes for the survey.

4. The geologists were interested in visiting the Seychelles. The only midocean islands in the world that are formed of granite.

5. If a woman from the desert tribe showed anger toward her husband, she was whipped in front of the whole village. And shunned by the rest of the women.

EXERCISE 19–2

Repair each fragment in the following paragraphs by attaching it to a sentence nearby or by rewriting it as a complete sentence.

Surfing the Internet now competes with watching television as our national pastime. People, it seems, have a natural ability to sit for hour upon hour. Passively watching images flit before their eyes. Whether these appear on a TV screen or a computer screen doesn't seem to make much difference. What counts are the images themselves. Not where they come from.

Web surfing is the cyber-age equivalent of channel surfing. Both of which appeal to us because of their constant promise of something better around the corner. When 1950s

TV viewers got bored with Howdy Doody, they turned off the set. Or switched to a channel with no programming and stared at the test pattern. Today, with eighty or more channels to choose from, the demanding spectator is no longer forced to watch anything uninteresting. The Internet is the next logical step in this constant broadening of choice. Taking us from eighty channels to an almost infinite number of screens.

But there is at least one major risk of a culture based on images. That the written word may become an endangered species. As our brains eventually adapt to greater and greater levels of stimulation. Will we continue to be able to focus on a page of print? Already, members of the TV generation have a much harder time reading than their parents did. What, many people are wondering, will become of the Internet generation?

Before we send out too many alarms, however, we should remember that the Internet is still in its infancy. Already, Web browsers are helping us limit the dizzying number of choices that face us on the World Wide Web. By giving us powerful search tools that zero in on whatever aspect of a topic we are most interested in. And there is some evidence that those who spend time surfing the Net are doing more, not less, reading. Unlike TV viewers. Some Net surfers prefer to run their eyes over the words on the screen. An activity that is, after all, reading. Others download information and read the printouts. While it is true that television has reduced our nation's level of literacy, the Internet could well advance it. Only the future will tell.

ON THE WEB

For electronic exercises on sentence fragments, go to
www.dianahacker.com/bedhandbook

and click on   ▶ **Electronic Grammar Exercises**
                 ▶ **E-ex 19–1**

20

Revise run-on sentences.

Run-on sentences are independent clauses that have not been joined correctly. An independent clause is a word group that can stand alone as a sentence. (See 64.) When two independent clauses appear in one sentence, they must be joined in one of these ways:

— with a comma and a coordinating conjunction (*and, but, or, nor, for, so, yet*)

— with a semicolon (or occasionally with a colon or a dash)

Recognizing run-on sentences

There are two types of run-on sentences. When a writer puts no mark of punctuation and no coordinating conjunction between independent clauses, the result is called a *fused sentence.*

FUSED

INDEPENDENT CLAUSE

Gestures are a means of communication for everyone

INDEPENDENT CLAUSE

they are essential for the hearing-impaired.

A far more common type of run-on sentence is the *comma splice*— two or more independent clauses joined by a comma without a coordinating conjunction. In some comma splices, the comma appears alone.

COMMA Gestures are a means of communication for everyone,
SPLICE they are essential for the hearing-impaired.

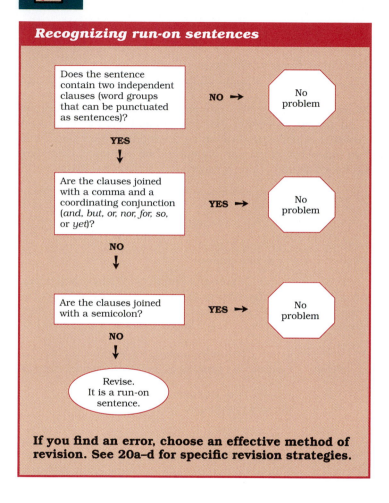

Recognizing run-on sentences

Does the sentence contain two independent clauses (word groups that can be punctuated as sentences)?

NO → No problem

YES
↓

Are the clauses joined with a comma and a coordinating conjunction (*and, but, or, nor, for, so,* or *yet*)?

YES → No problem

NO
↓

Are the clauses joined with a semicolon?

YES → No problem

NO
↓

Revise. It is a run-on sentence.

If you find an error, choose an effective method of revision. See 20a–d for specific revision strategies.

In other comma splices, the comma is accompanied by a joining word that is *not* a coordinating conjunction. There are only seven coordinating conjunctions in English: *and, but, or, nor, for, so,* and *yet.* Notice that all of these words are short—only two or three letters long.

> **COMMA**   Gestures are a means of communication for everyone,
> **SPLICE**   however, they are essential for the hearing-impaired.

However is a transitional expression, not a coordinating conjunction (see 20b).

To review your writing for possible run-on sentences, use the flow chart on page 252.

ON THE WEB

The rules on avoiding comma splices have sparked debates. If you're interested in learning why, go to
www.dianahacker.com/bedhandbook

and click on   ▶ **Language Debates**
                        ▶ **Comma splices**

GRAMMAR CHECKERS can flag only about 20 to 50 percent of the run-on sentences in a sample. The programs tend to be cautious, telling you that you "may have" a run-on sentence; you will almost certainly get a number of "false positives," sentences that have been flagged but are not run-ons. For example, a grammar checker flagged the following acceptable sentence as a possible run-on: *They believe that requiring gun owners to purchase a license is sufficient.*

If you have a problem with run-ons, you will need to proofread for them even after using a grammar checker. Also, if your program spots a "possible" run-on, you should check to see if it is in fact a run-on, perhaps by using the flow chart on page 252.

Revising run-on sentences

To revise a run-on sentence, you have four choices.

1. Use a comma and a coordinating conjunction (*and, but, or, nor, for, so, yet*).

▶ Gestures are a means of communication for everyone, ^{but} they

   are essential for the hearing-impaired.

2. Use a semicolon (or, if appropriate, a colon or a dash). A semicolon may be used alone; it can also be accompanied by a transitional expression.

▶ Gestures are a means of communication for everyone ; they

   are essential for the hearing-impaired.

▶ Gestures are a means of communication for everyone ^{; however,} they

   are essential for the hearing-impaired.

3. Make the clauses into separate sentences.

▶ Gestures are a means of communication for everyone . ^{They} ~~they~~

   are essential for the hearing-impaired.

4. Restructure the sentence, perhaps by subordinating one of the clauses.

▶ *Although gestures* ~~Gestures~~ are a means of communication for everyone, they

   are essential for the hearing-impaired.

One of these revision techniques usually works better than the others for a particular sentence. The fourth technique, the one requiring the most extensive revision, is often the most effective.

20a Consider separating the clauses with a comma and a coordinating conjunction.

There are seven coordinating conjunctions in English: *and, but, or, nor, for, so,* and *yet.* When a coordinating conjunction joins independent clauses, it is usually preceded by a comma. (See 32a.)

▶ The paramedic asked where I was hurt, _^ *and* as soon as I told him, he cut up the leg of my favorite pair of jeans.

▶ Many government officials privately admit that the polygraph is unreliable, ~~however~~ *yet* _^ they continue to use it as a security measure.

However is a transitional expression, not a coordinating conjunction, so it cannot be used with only a comma to join independent clauses. (See 20b.)

20b Consider separating the clauses with a semicolon (or, if appropriate, with a colon or a dash).

When the independent clauses are closely related and their relation is clear without a coordinating conjunction, a semicolon is an acceptable method of revision. (See 34a.)

▶ Tragedy depicts the individual confronted with the fact of

death**/;** comedy depicts the adaptability and ongoing survival
⌃

of human society.

A semicolon is required between independent clauses that have been linked with a transitional expression (such as *however, therefore, moreover, in fact,* or *for example*). For a longer list, see 34b.

▶ The timber wolf looks much like a large German shepherd**/;**
⌃

however, the wolf has longer legs, larger feet, a wider head,

and a long, bushy tail.

▶ Everyone in my outfit had a specific job**/;** as a matter of fact,
⌃

most of the officers had three or four duties.

If the first independent clause introduces the second or if the second clause summarizes or explains the first, a colon or a dash may be an appropriate method of revision. (See 35b and 39a.) In formal writing, the colon is usually preferred to the dash.

▶ Nuclear waste is hazardous ~~this~~ **: This** is an indisputable fact.
⌃

▶ The female black widow spider is often a widow of her own

making**/** she has been known to eat her partner after mating.
⌃

If the first independent clause introduces a quoted sentence, a colon is an appropriate method of revision.

▶ Feminist writer and scholar Carolyn Heilbrun has this to
say about the future*/:* "Today's shocks are tomorrow's
conventions."

20c Consider making the clauses into separate sentences.

▶ Why should we spend money on expensive space
exploration*/? We* ~~we~~ have enough underfunded programs here
on Earth.

Since one independent clause is a question and the other is a
statement, they should be separate sentences.

▶ I gave the necessary papers to the police officer*. Then* ~~then~~ he said
I would have to accompany him to the police station, where
a counselor would talk with me and call my parents.

Because the second independent clause is quite long, a sensible revision is to use separate sentences.

NOTE: When two quoted independent clauses are divided by
explanatory words, make each clause its own sentence.

▶ "It's always smart to learn from your mistakes," quipped my
supervisor*/. "It's* ~~"it's~~ even smarter to learn from the mistakes of
others."

20d   Consider restructuring the sentence, perhaps by subordinating one of the clauses.

If one of the independent clauses is less important than the other, turn it into a subordinate clause or phrase. (For more about subordination, see 14, especially the chart on p. 184.)

▶   Of the many geysers in Yellowstone National Park, the most
     which
     famous is Old Faithful, ~~it~~ sometimes reaches 150 feet in
                          ^
     height.

     Although many
▶   ~~Many~~ scholars dismiss the abominable snowman of the
   ^
     Himalayas as a myth, others claim it may be a kind of ape.

▶   Mary McLeod Bethune, ~~was~~ the seventeenth child of former
                        ^
     slaves, ~~she~~ founded the National Council of Negro Women in

     1935.

Minor ideas in these sentences are now expressed in subordinate clauses or phrases.

LOOKING AT YOURSELF AS A WRITER
Run-on sentences

Run-on sentences are considered serious errors because they suggest that the writer doesn't understand basic sentence structure. Unfortunately, the errors are fairly common, even among writers who are otherwise reasonably proficient. If you frequently write run-on sentences, consider the following possible causes and cures.

Run-on sentences *(continued)*

CAUSE Because you want your writing to flow smoothly from one idea to the next, you tend to string ideas together with commas. Run-on sentences sound better to you than a series of short, choppy sentences or a chain of ideas strung together with *and*s.

CURE You are right to want your writing to flow, but you'll need to turn to other strategies for making this happen. One of the best strategies for achieving sentence flow is subordination. (See 20d, 14b, and 14c.)

CAUSE Feeling that a sentence should be a certain length, you tend to keep it going until it has reached that length.

CURE Make punctuation decisions based on sentence structure, not length. The following punctuation rules show you ways of joining independent clauses correctly: 32a, 34a, 34b, 35b, 39a.

CAUSE You enjoy using formal-sounding transitional expressions like *therefore, however,* and *moreover,* and you confuse these words with coordinating conjunctions meaning the same thing (*so, but, and*).

CURE In most contexts, prefer the simpler coordinating conjunctions (*and, but, or, nor, for, so, yet*), which do not create run-on sentences.

CAUSE You are confused by the term "comma splice," which focuses your attention on the comma and prevents you from seeing several possibilities for revision.

CURE You are right that the term "comma splice" is confusing, especially since some revision strategies do not use a comma. Consider all four strategies (see 20a–20d).

Grammatical sentences

EXERCISE 20–1

Revise any run-on sentences using the method of revision suggested in brackets. Revisions of lettered sentences appear in the back of the book. Example:

> *Because*
> Orville had been obsessed with his weight as a teenager, he
> ^
> rarely ate anything sweet and delicious. [*Restructure the*
>
> *sentence.*]

a. The city had one public swimming pool, it stayed packed with children all summer long. [*Restructure the sentence.*]
b. The building is being renovated, therefore at times we have no heat, water, or electricity. [*Use a comma and a coordinating conjunction.*]
c. The neighborhood was ruled by gangs, what kind of environment was this for my ten-year-old son? [*Make two sentences.*]
d. Suddenly there was a loud silence, the shelling had stopped. [*Use a semicolon.*]
e. The car was hardly worth trading, the frame was twisted and the block was warped. [*Restructure the sentence.*]

1. The city government had good reason to fear a major earthquake, most of the business district was built on a landfill. [*Restructure the sentence.*]
2. The next time an event is canceled because of bad weather, don't blame the meteorologist, blame nature. [*Make two sentences.*]
3. Mr. Romero is an excellent linguist he has been studying Chinese dialects for twenty years. [*Restructure the sentence.*]
4. The president of Algeria was standing next to the podium he was waiting to be introduced. [*Restructure the sentence.*]
5. There was one major reason for John's wealth, his grandfather had been a multimillionaire. [*Use a colon.*]

EXERCISE 20–2

Revise any run-on sentences using a technique that you find effective. If a sentence is correct, write "correct" after it. Revisions of lettered sentences appear in the back of the book. Example:

> Crossing so many time zones on an eight-hour flight, I knew
>
> I would be tired when I arrived, ~~however,~~ *but* I was too excited
>
> to sleep on the plane.

a. Wind power for the home is a supplementary source of energy, it can be combined with electricity, gas, or solar energy.
b. The duck hunter set out his decoys in the shallow bay and then settled in to wait for the first real bird to alight.
c. In the Middle Ages, the streets of London were dangerous places, it was safer to travel by boat along the Thames.
d. "He's not drunk," I said, "he's in a state of diabetic shock."
e. Are you able to endure boredom, isolation, and potential violence, then the army may well be the adventure for you.

1. Death Valley National Monument, located in southern California and Nevada, is one of the hottest places on earth, temperatures in this desert area have soared as high as 134 degrees Fahrenheit.
2. If one of the dogs should happen to fall through the ice, it would be cut loose from the team and left to its fate, the sled drivers could not endanger the rest of the team for just one dog.
3. Nuclear power plants produce energy by fission, a process that generates radioactive waste.
4. The center of the French Quarter of New Orleans is Jackson Square, this square is one of the most beautiful urban spaces in the United States.
5. The neurosurgeon explained that the medication could have one side effect, it might cause me to experience a temporary memory loss.

EXERCISE 20–3

In the following rough draft, revise any run-on sentences.

Some parents and educators argue that requiring uniforms in public schools would improve student behavior and performance. They think that uniforms give students a more professional attitude toward school, moreover they believe that uniforms help create a sense of community among students from diverse backgrounds. Parents and educators holding these views are well meaning, however they should take a second look at the arguments against requiring school uniforms in public schools.

Uniforms do create a sense of community, they do this, however, by stamping out individuality. People spend most of their working lives having to conform to one dress code or another. Youth is a time to express originality, it is a time to develop a sense of self. One important way young people express their identities is through the clothes they wear. Of course, it could be argued that the self-patrolled dress code of high school students is ultimately stricter than that of any company, nevertheless, trying to control dress habits from above will only lead to resentment or to mindless conformity.

If children are going to act like adults, they need to be treated like adults, they need to be made responsible for their own choices. Telling young people what to wear to school merely prolongs their childhoods. Education is not just a matter of learning facts and figures, it also involves growing up and understanding how to function in the real world.

Most public schools must take everyone who applies, this includes students and parents who are opposed to school uniforms. Uniforms may be a good idea for private schools, they may even be a good idea for a few public "alternative" schools that parents and their children can choose. In most public schools, however, school uniforms should not be required.

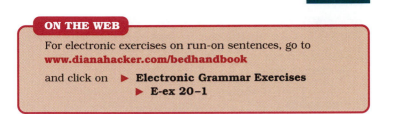

ON THE WEB

For electronic exercises on run-on sentences, go to
www.dianahacker.com/bedhandbook

and click on ▶ **Electronic Grammar Exercises**
          ▶ **E-ex 20–1**

21

Make subjects and verbs agree.

Native speakers of standard English know by ear that *he talks, she has,* and *it doesn't* (not *he talk, she have,* and *it don't*) are standard subject-verb combinations. For such speakers, problems with subject-verb agreement arise only in certain tricky situations, which are detailed in 21b–21k.

If you don't trust your ear—perhaps because you speak English as a second language, perhaps because you speak or hear nonstandard English in your community—you will need to learn the standard forms explained in 21a. Even if you do trust your ear, take a quick look at 21a to see what "subject-verb agreement" means.

21a Consult this section for standard subject-verb combinations.

In the present tense, verbs agree with their subjects in number (singular or plural) and in person (first, second, or third). The present-tense ending *-s* (or *-es*) is used on a verb if its subject is third-person singular; otherwise the verb takes no

Subject-verb agreement at a glance

PRESENT-TENSE FORMS OF *LOVE*
(A TYPICAL VERB)

	SINGULAR		PLURAL	
FIRST PERSON	I	love	we	love
SECOND PERSON	you	love	you	love
THIRD PERSON	he/she/it	loves	they	love

PRESENT-TENSE FORMS OF *HAVE*

	SINGULAR		PLURAL	
FIRST PERSON	I	have	we	have
SECOND PERSON	you	have	you	have
THIRD PERSON	he/she/it	has	they	have

PRESENT-TENSE FORMS OF *DO*

	SINGULAR		PLURAL	
FIRST PERSON	I	do/don't	we	do/don't
SECOND PERSON	you	do/don't	you	do/don't
THIRD PERSON	he/she/it	does/doesn't	they	do/don't

PRESENT-TENSE AND PAST-TENSE
FORMS OF *BE*

	SINGULAR		PLURAL	
FIRST PERSON	I	am/was	we	are/were
SECOND PERSON	you	are/were	you	are/were
THIRD PERSON	he/she/it	is/was	they	are/were

ending. Consider, for example, the present-tense forms of the verb *love,* given at the beginning of the chart on this page.

    The verb *be* varies from this pattern; unlike any other verb, it has special forms in *both* the present and the past tense. These forms appear at the end of the chart on this page.

When to use the -s (or -es) form of a present-tense verb

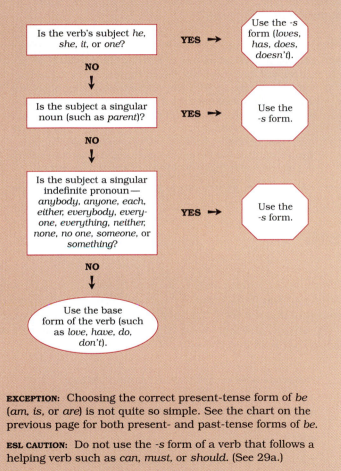

Is the verb's subject *he, she, it,* or *one*? → **YES** → Use the *-s* form (*loves, has, does, doesn't*).

NO ↓

Is the subject a singular noun (such as *parent*)? → **YES** → Use the *-s* form.

NO ↓

Is the subject a singular indefinite pronoun— *anybody, anyone, each, either, everybody, everyone, everything, neither, none, no one, someone,* or *something*? → **YES** → Use the *-s* form.

NO ↓

Use the base form of the verb (such as *love, have, do, don't*).

EXCEPTION: Choosing the correct present-tense form of *be* (*am, is,* or *are*) is not quite so simple. See the chart on the previous page for both present- and past-tense forms of *be.*

ESL CAUTION: Do not use the *-s* form of a verb that follows a helping verb such as *can, must,* or *should.* (See 29a.)

If you aren't confident that you know the standard forms, use the charts on pages 264 and 265 as you proofread for subject-verb agreement. You may also want to take a look at 27c, which discusses the matter of -s endings in some detail.

GRAMMAR CHECKERS attempt to flag faulty subject-verb agreement, but they have mixed success. They fail to flag many problems; in addition, they flag a number of correct sentences, usually because they have misidentified the subject, the verb, or both. For example, one program flagged the following correct sentence: *Nearly everyone on the panel favors the health care reform proposal.* The program identified the subject as *care* and the verb as *reform;* in fact, the subject is *everyone* and the verb is *favors.*

21b Make the verb agree with its subject, not with a word that comes between.

Word groups often come between the subject and the verb. Such word groups, usually modifying the subject, may contain a noun that at first appears to be the subject. By mentally stripping away such modifiers, you can isolate the noun that is in fact the subject.

The *samples* on the tray in the lab *need* testing.

▶ High levels of air pollution causes damage to the respiratory tract.

The subject is *levels,* not *pollution.* Strip away the phrase *of air pollution* to hear the correct verb: *levels cause.*

▶ The slaughter of pandas for their pelts ~~have~~ *has* caused the

panda population to decline drastically.

The subject is *slaughter,* not *pandas* or *pelts.*

NOTE: Phrases beginning with the prepositions *as well as, in addition to, accompanied by, together with,* and *along with* do not make a singular subject plural.

▶ The governor, as well as his press secretary, ~~were~~ *was* shot.

To emphasize that two people were shot, the writer could use *and* instead: *The governor and his press secretary were shot.*

21c Treat most subjects joined with *and* as plural.

A subject with two or more parts is said to be compound. If the parts are connected by *and,* the subject is nearly always plural.

┌─────────────┐
Leon and Jan often *jog* together.

▶ Jill's natural ability and her desire to help others ~~has~~ *have* led to a

career in the ministry.

Ability and desire is a plural subject, so its verb should be *have.*

EXCEPTIONS: When the parts of the subject form a single unit or when they refer to the same person or thing, treat the subject as singular.

Grammatical sentences

Strawberries and cream was a last-minute addition to the menu.

Sue's friend and adviser was surprised by her decision.

When a compound subject is preceded by *each* or *every*, treat it as singular.

Each tree, shrub, and vine needs to be sprayed.

Every car, truck, and van is required to pass inspection.

This exception does not apply when a compound subject is followed by *each: Alan and Marcia each have different ideas.*

21d
With subjects joined with *or* or *nor* (or by *either . . . or* or *neither . . . nor*), make the verb agree with the part of the subject nearer to the verb.

A driver's *license* or credit *card is* required.

A driver's *license* or two credit *cards are* required.

▶ If a relative or neighbor ~~are~~ *is* abusing a child, notify the police immediately.

▶ Neither the lab assistant nor the students ~~was~~ *were* able to download the information.

The verb must be matched with the part of the subject closer to it: *neighbor is* in the first sentence, *students were* in the second.

NOTE: If one part of the subject is singular and the other is plural, put the plural one last to avoid awkwardness.

21e Treat most indefinite pronouns as singular.

Indefinite pronouns are pronouns that do not refer to specific persons or things. The following commonly used indefinite pronouns are singular:

anybody	each	everyone	nobody	somebody
anyone	either	everything	no one	someone
anything	everybody	neither	nothing	something

Many of these words appear to have plural meanings, and they are often treated as such in casual speech. In formal written English, however, they are nearly always treated as singular.

Everyone on the team *supports* the coach.

▶ Each of the furrows ~~have~~ *has* been seeded.

▶ Everybody who signed up for the ski trip ~~were~~ *was* taking lessons.

The subjects of these sentences are *Each* and *Everybody*. These indefinite pronouns are third-person singular, so the verbs must be *has* and *was*.

A few indefinite pronouns (*all, any, none, some*) may be singular or plural depending on the noun or pronoun they refer to.

Some of our *luggage was* lost. *None* of his *advice makes* sense.

Some of the *rocks are* slippery. *None* of the *eggs were* broken.

NOTE: When the meaning of *none* is emphatically "not one," *none* may be treated as singular: *None* [meaning "Not one"] *of the eggs was broken.* However, some experts advise using *not one* instead: *Not one of the eggs was broken.*

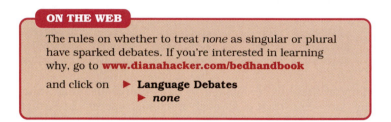

ON THE WEB

The rules on whether to treat *none* as singular or plural have sparked debates. If you're interested in learning why, go to **www.dianahacker.com/bedhandbook**

and click on   ▶ **Language Debates**
                ▶ *none*

21f   Treat collective nouns as singular unless the meaning is clearly plural.

Collective nouns such as *jury, committee, audience, crowd, class, troop, family,* and *couple* name a class or a group. In American English, collective nouns are nearly always treated as singular: They emphasize the group as a unit. Occasionally, when there is some reason to draw attention to the individual members of the group, a collective noun may be treated as plural. (Also see 22b.)

SINGULAR   The *class respects* the teacher.

PLURAL   The *class are* debating among themselves.

To underscore the notion of individuality in the second sentence, many writers would add a clearly plural noun such as *members.*

PLURAL   The class *members are* debating among themselves.

▶ The board of trustees ~~meet~~ in Denver on the first Tuesday of
  meets
  ^

each month.

The board as a whole meets; there is no reason to draw attention to its individual members.

▶ A young couple ~~was~~ arguing about politics while holding
  were
  ^

hands.

The meaning is clearly plural. Only individuals can argue and hold hands.

NOTE: The phrase *the number* is treated as singular, *a number* as plural.

SINGULAR   *The number* of school-age children *is* declining.

PLURAL   *A number* of children *are* attending the wedding.

NOTE: When units of measurement are used collectively, treat them as singular; when they refer to individual persons or things, treat them as plural.

SINGULAR   *Three-fourths* of the pie *has* been eaten.

PLURAL   *One-fourth* of the drivers *were* drunk.

21g Make the verb agree with its subject even when the subject follows the verb.

Verbs ordinarily follow subjects. When this normal order is reversed, it is easy to become confused. Sentences beginning with *there is* or *there are* (or *there was* or *there were*) are inverted; the subject follows the verb.

There *are* surprisingly few *children* in our neighborhood.

▶ There ~~was~~ a social worker and a crew of twenty volunteers at
  were
the scene of the accident.

The subject *worker and crew* is plural, so the verb must be
were.

Occasionally you may decide to invert a sentence for variety or effect. When you do so, check to make sure that
your subject and verb agree.

▶ At the back of the room ~~is~~ a small aquarium and an enormous
  are
terrarium.

The subject *aquarium and terrarium* is plural, so the verb must
be *are.* If the correct sentence seems awkward, begin with the
subject: *A small aquarium and an enormous terrarium are at the
back of the room.*

21h Make the verb agree with its subject, not with a subject complement.

One basic sentence pattern in English consists of a subject,
a linking verb, and a subject complement: *Jack is a securi-
ties lawyer.* Because the subject complement names or describes the subject (*Jack*), it is sometimes mistaken for the
subject. (See 62b on subject complements.)

These *exercises are* a way to test your ability to perform
under pressure.

▶ A tent and a sleeping bag are ~~is~~ the required equipment for all

campers.

Tent and bag is the subject, not *equipment*.

▶ A major force in today's economy is ~~are~~ women — as earners,

consumers, and investors.

Force is the subject, not *women*. If the corrected version seems awkward, make *women* the subject: *Women are a major force in today's economy — as earners, consumers, and investors.*

21i *Who, which,* and *that* take verbs that agree with their antecedents.

Like most pronouns, the relative pronouns *who, which,* and *that* have antecedents, nouns or pronouns to which they refer. Relative pronouns used as subjects of subordinate clauses take verbs that agree with their antecedents.

Take a *suit that travels* well.

Constructions such as *one of the students who* [or *one of the things that*] cause problems for writers. Do not assume that the antecedent must be *one.* Instead, consider the logic of the sentence.

▶ Our ability to use language is one of the things that sets us

apart from animals.

The antecedent of *that* is *things,* not *one.* Several things set us apart from animals.

When the word *only* comes before *one*, you are safe in assuming that *one* is the antecedent of the relative pronoun.

▶ Dr. Barker knew that Frank was the only one of his sons who
was
~~were~~ responsible enough to handle the estate.
^

The antecedent of *who* is *one*, not *sons*. Only one son was responsible enough.

ON THE WEB

The rules on *one of those who* constructions have sparked debates. If you're interested in learning why, go to
www.dianahacker.com/bedhandbook

and click on   ▶ **Language Debates**
                ▶ *one of those who* (or *that*)

LOOKING AT YOURSELF AS A WRITER
Subject-verb agreement

Subject-verb agreement causes trouble for most of us, largely because of the many tricky contexts that tempt us to choose the wrong verb. But if you find subject-verb agreement unusually troublesome, consider possible sources of your difficulties.

CAUSE   You are confused about the rules on when to use the *-s* form of a verb. For example, you may think that a "plural" verb takes an *-s* ending, just like most plural nouns. Or you may think that *all* singular subjects demand a verb with an *-s* ending, not just third-person singular subjects.

CURE   Trust the chart on page 264. Don't let yourself get confused by half-learned rules.

> **Subject-verb agreement (continued)**
>
> **CAUSE** You can't find the simple subject of the sentence (or clause).
>
> **CURE** You are at a serious disadvantage as a writer if you cannot find the subject of a sentence. Turn to 62a for help. If you need more practice, check with your instructor or a writing center tutor.
>
> **CAUSE** You aren't sure whether the subject is singular or plural.
>
> **CURE** Look up the appropriate rule in 21. There is no need to memorize all of these rules; just know where to find them.
>
> See also "Looking at Yourself as a Writer: Problems with *-s* endings on verbs" (pp. 328–29).

21j Words such as *athletics, economics, mathematics, physics, statistics, measles, mumps,* and *news* are usually singular, despite their plural form.

▶ Statistics ~~are~~ *is* among the most difficult courses in our program.

EXCEPTION: When they describe separate items rather than a collective body of knowledge, words such as *athletics, mathematics, physics,* and *statistics* are plural: *The statistics on school retention rates are impressive.*

21k Titles of works, company names, words mentioned as words, and gerund phrases are singular.

▶ *Lost Cities* ~~describe~~ *describes* the discoveries of many ancient civilizations.

Grammatical sentences

▶ Delmonico Brothers ~~specialize~~ *specializes* in organic produce and

additive-free meats.

▶ *Controlled substances* ~~are~~ *is* a euphemism for illegal drugs.

A gerund phrase consists of an *-ing* verb form followed by any objects, complements, or modifiers (see 63c). Treat gerund phrases as singular.

▶ Encountering busy signals ~~are~~ *is* troublesome to our clients, so

we have hired two new switchboard operators.

EXERCISE 21–1

Underline the subject (or compound subject) and then select the verb that agrees with it. (If you have difficulty identifying the subject, consult 62a.) Answers to lettered sentences appear in the back of the book. Example:

<u>Someone</u> in the audience ((has)/have) volunteered to partici-

pate in the experiment.

a. Your friendship over the years and your support on a wide variety of issues (has/have) meant a great deal to us.
b. Shelters for teenage runaways (offers/offer) a wide variety of services.
c. The main source of income for Trinidad (is/are) oil and pitch.
d. The chances of your being promoted (is/are) excellent.
e. There (was/were) a *Peanuts* cartoon and a few Mother Goose rhymes pinned to the bulletin board.

1. Neither the professor nor his assistants (was/were) able to solve the mystery of the eerie glow in the laboratory.

2. Four years of research (has/have) gone into making our software suitable for the Japanese market.
3. Discovered in the soil of our city garden (was/were) a button dating from the Civil War and three marbles dating from the turn of the century.
4. Every year, during the midsummer festival, the smoke of village bonfires (fills/fill) the sky.
5. When food supplies (was/were) scarce, the slaves had to make do with the less desirable parts of the animals.

EXERCISE 21–2

Edit the following sentences to eliminate problems with subject-verb agreement. If a sentence is correct, write "correct" after it. Answers to lettered sentences appear in the back of the book. Example:

> *were*
> **Jack's first days in the infantry ~~was~~ grueling.**

a. One of the main reasons for elephant poaching are the profits received from selling the ivory tusks.
b. Not until my interview with Dr. Hwang were other possibilities opened to me.
c. Of those who die in single-car wrecks, a majority is drunk.
d. Crystal chandeliers, polished floors, and a new oil painting has transformed Sandra's apartment.
e. The board of directors, ignoring the wishes of the neighborhood, has voted to allow further development.

1. Measles is a contagious childhood disease.
2. Of particular concern are penicillin and tetracycline, antibiotics used to make animals more resistant to disease.
3. The presence of certain bacteria in our bodies is one of the factors that determines our overall health.
4. Sheila is the only one of the many applicants who has the ability to step into this job.
5. Neither the explorer nor his companions was ever seen again.

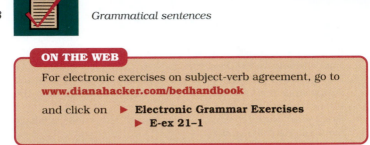

ON THE WEB

For electronic exercises on subject-verb agreement, go to
www.dianahacker.com/bedhandbook

and click on   ▶ **Electronic Grammar Exercises**
                 ▶ **E-ex 21–1**

22

Make pronouns and antecedents agree.

A pronoun is a word that substitutes for a noun. (See 61b.)
Many pronouns have antecedents, nouns or pronouns to
which they refer. A pronoun and its antecedent agree when
they are both singular or both plural.

> **SINGULAR**   *Dr. Samantha McQueen* finished *her*
> rounds.

> **PLURAL**   The hospital *interns* finished *their*
> rounds.

ESL

The pronouns *he, his, she, her, it,* and *its* must agree in
gender (masculine, feminine, or neuter) with their
antecedents, not with the words they modify.

Steve visited *his* [not *her*] sister in Seattle.

GRAMMAR CHECKERS do not flag problems with pronoun-antecedent agreement. It takes a human eye to see that a singular noun, such as *logger*, does not agree with a plural pronoun, such as *their*, in a sentence like this: *The logger in the Northwest relies on the old forest growth for their living.*

22a Do not use plural pronouns to refer to singular antecedents.

Writers are frequently tempted to use plural pronouns to refer to two kinds of singular antecedents: indefinite pronouns and generic nouns.

Indefinite pronouns

Indefinite pronouns refer to nonspecific persons or things. Even though some of the following indefinite pronouns may seem to have plural meanings, treat them as singular in formal English.

anybody	either	neither	somebody
anyone	everybody	nobody	someone
anything	everyone	no one	something
each	everything		

In class *everyone* performs at *his or her* [not *their*] own fitness level.

When a plural pronoun refers mistakenly to a singular indefinite pronoun, you can usually choose one of three options for revision:

1. Replace the plural pronoun with *he or she* (or *his or her*).

2. Make the antecedent plural.
3. Rewrite the sentence so that no problem of agreement exists.

▶ When someone has been drinking, ~~they are~~ *he or she is* likely to speed.

▶ When ~~someone has~~ *drivers have* been drinking, they are likely to speed.

▶ ~~When someone~~ *A driver who* has been drinking~~/ they are~~ *is* likely to speed.

Because the *he or she* construction is wordy, often the second or third revision strategy is more effective. Be aware that the traditional use of *he* (or *his*) to refer to persons of either sex is now widely considered sexist. (See 17f.)

Generic nouns

A generic noun represents a typical member of a group, such as a typical student, or any member of a group, such as any lawyer. Although generic nouns may seem to have plural meanings, they are singular.

Every *runner* must train rigorously if *he or she wants* [not *they want*] to excel.

When a plural pronoun refers mistakenly to a generic noun, you will usually have the same three revision options as just mentioned for indefinite pronouns.

▶ A medical student must study hard if ~~they want~~ *he or she wants* to succeed.

▶ ~~A medical student~~ *Medical students* must study hard if they want to succeed.

▶ A medical student must study hard ~~if they want~~ to succeed.

Choosing a revision strategy that avoids sexist language

Because many readers object to sexist language, avoid the use of *he, him,* and *his* to refer to both men and women. Also try to be sparing in your use of the wordy expressions *he or she* and *his or her.* Where possible, seek out more graceful alternatives.

USE AN OCCASIONAL *HE OR SHE* (OR *HIS OR HER*).

▶ In our office, everyone works at ~~their~~ own pace.
his or her

MAKE THE ANTECEDENT PLURAL.

▶ ~~An employee~~ on extended leave may continue their life insurance.
Employees

RECAST THE SENTENCE.

▶ The amount of annual leave a federal worker may accrue depends on ~~their~~ length of service.

▶ ~~If~~ a child ~~is~~ born to parents who are both bipolar, ~~they have~~ a high chance of being bipolar.
A ... *has*

▶ A year later someone finally admitted ~~that they were~~ involved in the kidnapping.
to being

▶ I was taught that no one could escape the fires of purgatory. ~~if they wanted to reach heaven.~~
who wanted to reach heaven

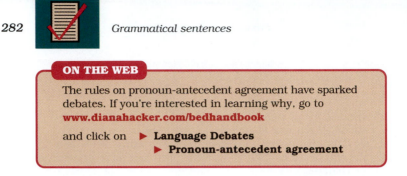

ON THE WEB

The rules on pronoun-antecedent agreement have sparked debates. If you're interested in learning why, go to **www.dianahacker.com/bedhandbook**

and click on ▶ **Language Debates**
                ▶ **Pronoun-antecedent agreement**

22b Treat collective nouns as singular unless the meaning is clearly plural.

Collective nouns such as *jury, committee, audience, crowd, class, troop, family, team,* and *couple* name a class or a group. Ordinarily the group functions as a unit, so the noun should be treated as singular; if the members of the group function as individuals, however, the noun should be treated as plural. (See also 21f.)

AS A UNIT The *committee* granted *its* permission to build.

AS INDIVIDUALS The *committee* put *their* signatures on the document.

▶ The jury has reached ~~their~~ decision.
                              its
                              ^

There is no reason to draw attention to the individual members of the jury, so *jury* should be treated as singular. Notice also that the writer treated the noun as singular when choosing the verb *has,* so for consistency the pronoun must be *its.*

▶ The audience shouted "Bravo" and stamped ~~its~~ feet.
                                              their
                                              ^

It is difficult to see how the audience as a unit can stamp *its* feet. The meaning here is clearly plural, requiring *their.*

22c Treat most compound antecedents connected by *and* as plural.

Jill and John moved to Luray, where *they* built a cabin.

22d With compound antecedents connected by *or* or *nor* (or by *either . . . or* or *neither . . . nor*), make the pronoun agree with the nearer antecedent.

Either *Bruce* or *Tom* should receive first prize for *his* poem.

Neither the *mouse* nor the *rats* could find *their* way through the maze.

NOTE: If one of the antecedents is singular and the other plural, as in the second example, put the plural one last to avoid awkwardness.

EXCEPTION: If one antecedent is male and the other female, do not follow the traditional rule. The sentence *Either Bruce or Ann should receive first prize for her poem* makes no sense. The best solution is to recast the sentence: *The prize for best poem should go to Bruce or Ann.*

EXERCISE 22–1

Edit the following sentences to eliminate problems with pronoun-antecedent agreement. Most of the sentences can be revised in more than one way, so experiment before choosing a solution. If a sentence is correct, write "correct" after it. Revisions of lettered sentences appear in the back of the book. Example:

> *Recruiters*
> ~~The recruiter~~ may tell the truth, but there is much that they
> ^
> choose not to tell.

Grammatical sentences

a. Every presidential candidate must appeal to a wide variety of ethnic and social groups if they want to win the election.
b. David lent his motorcycle to someone who allowed their friend to use it.
c. The instructor has asked everyone to bring their tools to carpentry class.
d. The parade committee was unanimous in its decision to allow all groups and organizations to join the festivities.
e. The applicant should be bilingual if they want to qualify for this position.

1. If a driver refuses to take a blood or breath test, he or she will have their licenses suspended for six months.
2. Why should we care about the timber wolf? One answer is that they have proven beneficial to humans by killing off weakened prey.
3. The National Rifle Association argues that current gun laws should be enforced. In the past, however, they have opposed nearly all proposed legislation affecting guns.
4. Seven qualified Hispanic agents applied, each hoping for a career move that would let them use their language and cultural training on more than just translations; the job went to a non-Hispanic who was taking a crash course in Spanish.
5. If anyone notices any suspicious activity, they should report it to the police.

EXERCISE 22–2

Edit the following paragraph to eliminate problems with pronoun-antecedent agreement or sexist language.

A common practice in businesses is to put each employee in their own cubicle. A typical cubicle resembles an office, but their walls don't reach the ceiling. Many office managers feel that a cubicle floor plan has its advantages. Cubicles make a large area feel spacious. In addition, they can be moved around so that each new employee can be accommodated in his own work area. Of course, the cubicle model also has problems. The typical employee is not as happy with a cubicle as they would be with a traditional office. Also, productivity can suffer. Neither a manager nor a frontline worker can ordinarily do their best work in a cubicle because of noise and lack of privacy. Each worker can hear his neighbors tapping on computer keyboards, making telephone calls, and muttering under their breath.

ON THE WEB

For electronic exercises on pronoun-antecedent agreement, go to **www.dianahacker.com/bedhandbook**

and click on ▶ **Electronic Grammar Exercises**
▶ **E-ex 22–1**

LOOKING AT YOURSELF AS A WRITER
Pronoun-antecedent agreement

Like all writers, at times you will find yourself wrestling with the problem of pronoun-antecedent agreement. Here is why the problem is so pervasive.

CAUSE   You hear faulty pronoun-antecedent agreement in speech all the time, and you probably don't see much wrong with it, since it rarely interferes with clarity.

CURE   Be aware that standards in writing tend to be stricter than those in speech.

CAUSE   You don't want to use sexist English, and you find *he or she* awkward — so you resort to using plural pronouns such as *their* with singular antecedents such as *swimmer.*

CURE   Choose plural antecedents or find a clever way around the problem. The chart on page 281 shows several possibilities.

23

Make pronoun references clear.

Pronouns substitute for nouns; they are a kind of short-hand. In a sentence like *After Andrew intercepted the ball, he kicked it as hard as he could,* the pronouns *he* and *it* substitute for the nouns *Andrew* and *ball.* The word a pronoun refers to is called its *antecedent.*

GRAMMAR CHECKERS do not flag problems with faulty pronoun reference. Although a computer program can identify pronouns, it has no way of knowing which words, if any, they refer to. For example, grammar checkers miss the fact that the pronoun *it* has an ambiguous reference in the following sentence: *The thief stole the woman's purse and her car and then destroyed it.* Did the thief destroy the purse or the car? It takes human judgment to realize that readers might be confused.

23a Avoid ambiguous or remote pronoun reference.

Ambiguous pronoun reference occurs when the pronoun could refer to two possible antecedents.

▶ *The pitcher broke when Gloria set it*
  ~~When Gloria set the pitcher~~ on the glass-topped table*/.* ~~it~~
   ^   ^
  ~~broke.~~

▶   *"You have*
  Tom told James*,* ~~that he had~~ won the lottery.*"*
                   ^   ^

What broke—the table or the pitcher? Who won the lottery—Tom or James? The revisions eliminate the ambiguity.

Remote pronoun reference occurs when a pronoun is too far away from its antecedent for easy reading.

▶ After the court ordered my ex-husband to pay child support, he refused. Approximately eight months later, we were back in court. This time the judge ordered him to make payments directly to the Support and Collections Unit, which would in turn pay me. For the first six months I received regular payments, but then they stopped. Again ~~he~~ was summoned to
  my ex-husband
  ^
appear in court; he did not respond.

The pronoun *he* was too distant from its antecedent, *ex-husband*, which appeared several sentences earlier.

23b Generally, avoid broad reference of *this, that, which,* and *it.*

For clarity, the pronouns *this, that, which,* and *it* should ordinarily refer to specific antecedents rather than to whole ideas or sentences. When a pronoun's reference is needlessly broad, either replace the pronoun with a noun or supply an antecedent to which the pronoun clearly refers.

▶ More and more often, especially in large cities, we are finding
  our fate
ourselves victims of serious crimes. We learn to accept ~~this~~
  ^
with minor gripes and groans.

For clarity the writer substituted a noun (*fate*) for the pronoun *this,* which referred broadly to the idea expressed in the preceding sentence.

▶ Romeo and Juliet were both too young to have acquired
  a fact
much wisdom, which accounts for their rash actions.
            ^

The writer added an antecedent (*fact*) that the pronoun *which* clearly refers to.

EXCEPTION: Many writers view broad reference as acceptable when the pronoun refers clearly to the sense of an entire clause.

> If you pick up a starving dog and make him prosperous, he will not bite you. *This* is the principal difference between a dog and a man. — Mark Twain

23c Do not use a pronoun to refer to an implied antecedent.

A pronoun should refer to a specific antecedent, not to a word that is implied but not present in the sentence.

                                      the braids
▶ After braiding Ann's hair, Sue decorated ~~them~~ with ribbons.
                                            ^

The pronoun *them* referred to Ann's braids (implied by the term *braiding*), but the word *braids* did not appear in the sentence.

Modifiers, such as possessives, cannot serve as antecedents. A modifier may strongly imply the noun that the pronoun might logically refer to, but it is not itself that noun.

                Euripides
▶ In ~~Euripides'~~ *Medea*, ~~he~~ describes the plight of a woman
                          ^
rejected by her husband.

The pronoun *he* cannot refer logically to the possessive modifier *Euripides'*. The revision substitutes the noun *Euripides* for the pronoun *he*, thereby eliminating the problem.

23d   Avoid the indefinite use of *they, it,* and *you.*

Do not use the pronoun *they* to refer indefinitely to persons who have not been specifically mentioned. *They* should always refer to a specific antecedent.

▶ Last year ~~they~~ shut down all government agencies for

   Congress
   ^

more than a month until the budget crisis was finally

resolved.

The word *it* should not be used indefinitely in constructions such as "It is said on television . . ." or "In the article it says that. . . ."

▶ ~~In the~~ encyclopedia ~~it~~ states that male moths can smell

   The
   ^

female moths from several miles away.

The pronoun *you* is appropriate when the writer is addressing the reader directly: *Once you have kneaded the dough, let it rise in a warm place for at least twenty-five minutes.* Except in informal contexts, however, the indefinite *you* (meaning "anyone in general") is inappropriate. (See pp. 51–52.)

▶ Ms. Pickersgill's *Guide to Etiquette* stipulates that
   a guest
   ~~you~~ should not arrive at a party too early or leave
   ^

   too late.

The writer could have replaced *you* with *one,* but in American English the pronoun *one* can seem stilted.

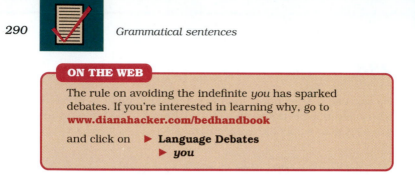

ON THE WEB

The rule on avoiding the indefinite *you* has sparked debates. If you're interested in learning why, go to **www.dianahacker.com/bedhandbook**

and click on   ▶ **Language Debates**
                 ▶ *you*

23e   To refer to persons, use *who, whom,* or *whose,* not *which* or *that.*

In most contexts, use *who, whom,* or *whose* to refer to persons, *which* or *that* to refer to animals or things. *Which* is reserved only for animals or things, so it is impolite to use it to refer to persons.

▶ When he heard about my seven children, four of ~~which~~ *whom*

   live at home, Ron smiled and said, "I love children."

Although *that* is sometimes used to refer to persons, many readers will find such references dehumanizing. It is more polite to use a form of *who*—a word reserved only for people.

▶ Fans wondered how an out-of-shape old man ~~that~~ *who* walked

   with a limp could play football.

NOTE: Occasionally *whose* may be used to refer to animals and things to avoid the awkward *of which* construction.

▶ A major corporation, ~~the name of which~~ *whose* will be in tomorrow's

   paper, has been illegally dumping toxic waste in the harbor.

ON THE WEB

The rule on avoiding *that* to refer to people has sparked debates. If you're interested in learning why, go to **www.dianahacker.com/bedhandbook**

and click on ▶ **Language Debates**
            ▶ *who* versus *which* or *that*

EXERCISE 23–1

Edit the following sentences to correct errors in pronoun reference. In some cases you will need to decide on an antecedent that the pronoun might logically refer to. Revisions of lettered sentences appear in the back of the book. Example:

> Following the breakup of AT&T, many other companies began to offer long-distance phone service. ~~This~~ *The competition* has led to lower long-distance rates.

a. They say that the *Challenger* disaster set the space program back five years.

b. She had decorated her living room with posters from chamber music festivals. This led her date to believe that she was interested in classical music, but actually she preferred rock.

c. In Ethiopia, you don't need much property to be considered well-off.

d. Marianne told Jenny that she was worried about her mother's illness.

e. Though Lewis cried for several minutes after scraping his knee, eventually it subsided.

1. Our German conversation group is made up of six people, three of which I had never met before.

2. Many people believe that the polygraph test is highly reliable if you employ a licensed examiner.

3. France receives nearly 80 percent of its electrical needs from nuclear power. They have not had a serious mishap to date, but will their luck continue?
4. Because of Paul Robeson's outspoken attitude toward fascism, he was labeled a Communist.
5. In the report it points out that lifting the ban on Compound 1080 would prove detrimental, possibly even fatal, to the bald eagle.

ON THE WEB

For electronic exercises on pronoun reference, go to
www.dianahacker.com/bedhandbook

and click on ▶ **Electronic Grammar Exercises**
             ▶ **E-ex 23–1**

24

Distinguish between pronouns such as *I* and *me*.

The personal pronouns in the following chart change what is known as case form according to their grammatical function in a sentence. Pronouns functioning as subjects (or subject complements) appear in the *subjective* case; those functioning as objects appear in the *objective* case; and those showing ownership appear in the *possessive* case.

	SUBJECTIVE CASE	OBJECTIVE CASE	POSSESSIVE CASE
SINGULAR	I	me	my
	you	you	your
	he/she/it	him/her/it	his/her/its

	SUBJECTIVE CASE	OBJECTIVE CASE	POSSESSIVE CASE
PLURAL	we	us	our
	you	you	your
	they	them	their

Pronouns in the subjective and objective case are frequently confused. Most of the rules in this section specify when to use one or the other of these cases (*I* or *me, he* or *him,* and so on). Rule 24g details a special use of pronouns and nouns in the possessive case.

GRAMMAR CHECKERS can flag some incorrect pronouns and explain the rules for using *I* or *me, he* or *him, she* or *her, we* or *us,* and *they* or *them.* For example, one grammar checker program correctly flagged *we* in the following sentence and advised using *us* instead: *I say it is about time for we parents to revolt.*

You should not assume, however, that a computer program will catch all incorrect pronouns. For example, grammar checkers did not flag *more than I* in this sentence, where the writer's meaning requires *me: I get a little jealous that our dog likes my neighbor more than I.*

24a Use the subjective case (*I, you, he, she, it, we, they*) for subjects and subject complements.

When personal pronouns are used as subjects, ordinarily your ear will tell you the correct pronoun. Problems sometimes arise, however, with compound word groups containing a pronoun, so it is not always safe to trust your ear.

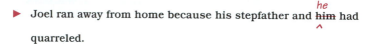

▶ Joel ran away from home because his stepfather and ~~him~~ ^he^ had

quarreled.

His stepfather and he is the subject of the verb *had quarreled.* If we strip away the words *his stepfather and,* the correct pronoun becomes clear: *he had quarreled* (not *him had quarreled*).

When a pronoun is used as a subject complement (a word following a linking verb), your ear may mislead you, since the incorrect form is frequently heard in casual speech. (See subject complement, 62b.)

▶ During the Lindbergh trial, Bruno Hauptmann repeatedly

denied that the kidnapper was ~~him.~~ ^he.^

If *kidnapper was he* seems too stilted, rewrite the sentence: *During the Lindbergh trial, Bruno Hauptmann repeatedly denied that he was the kidnapper.*

24b   Use the objective case (*me, you, him, her, it, us, them*) for all objects.

When a personal pronoun is used as a direct object, an indirect object, or the object of a preposition, ordinarily your ear will lead you to the correct pronoun. When an object is compound, however, you may occasionally become confused.

▶ Janice was indignant when she realized that the salesclerk

was insulting her mother and ~~she.~~ ^her.^

Her mother and her is the direct object of the verb *was insulting.* Strip away the words *her mother and* to hear the correct pronoun: *was insulting her* (not *was insulting she*).

▶ The most traumatic experience for her father and ~~I~~ *me* occurred

long after her operation.

Her father and me is the object of the preposition *for.* Strip away
the words *her father and* to test for the correct pronoun: *for me*
(not *for I*).

When in doubt about the correct pronoun, some writers
try to avoid making the choice by using a reflexive pronoun
such as *myself.* Such evasions are nonstandard, even though
they are used by some educated persons.

▶ The Egyptian cab driver gave my husband and ~~myself~~ *me* some

good tips on traveling in North Africa.

My husband and me is the indirect object of the verb *gave.* For
correct uses of *myself,* see the Glossary of Usage.

ON THE WEB

The rule on avoiding *myself* as a substitute for *I* or *me* has
sparked debates. If you're interested in learning why, go to
www.dianahacker.com/bedhandbook

and click on ▶ **Language Debates**
            ▶ *myself*

24c   Put an appositive and the word to which it refers in the same case.

Appositives are noun phrases that rename nouns or pronouns. A pronoun used as an appositive has the same function (usually subject or object) as the word(s) the appositive
renames.

▶ The chief strategists, Dr. Bell and ~~me,~~ *I,* could not agree on a

plan.

The appositive *Dr. Bell and I* renames the subject, *strategists.*
Test: *I could not agree* (not *me could not agree*).

▶ The reporter interviewed only two witnesses, the shopkeeper

and ~~I.~~ *me.*

The appositive *the shopkeeper and me* renames the direct
object, *witnesses.* Test: *interviewed me* (not *interviewed I*).

24d   Following *than* or *as,* choose the pronoun that expresses your meaning.

When a comparison begins with *than* or *as,* your choice of
a pronoun will depend on your intended meaning. Consider, for example, the difference in meaning between these
sentences.

My husband likes football better than I.

My husband likes football better than me.

Finish each sentence mentally and its meaning becomes
clear: *My husband likes football better than I* [*do*]. *My husband likes football better than* [*he likes*] *me.*

▶ Even though he is sometimes ridiculed by the other boys,

Norman is much better off than ~~them.~~ *they.*

They is the subject of the verb *are,* which is understood: *Norman is much better off than they* [*are*]. If the correct English
seems too formal, you can always add the verb.

▶ We respected no other candidate for the city council as

her.

much as ~~she.~~
^

This sentence means that we respected no other candidate as much as *we respected her. Her* is the direct object of an understood verb.

24e When deciding whether *we* or *us* should precede a noun, choose the pronoun that would be appropriate if the noun were omitted.

We

▶ ~~Us~~ tenants would rather fight than move.
^

us

▶ Management is short-changing ~~we~~ tenants.
^

No one would say *Us would rather fight than move* or *Management is short-changing we.*

24f Use the objective case for subjects and objects of infinitives.

An infinitive is the word *to* followed by the base form of a verb. (See 63c.) Subjects of infinitives are an exception to the rule that subjects must be in the subjective case. Whenever an infinitive has a subject, it must be in the objective case. Objects of infinitives also are in the objective case.

me *her*

▶ Ms. Wilson asked John and ~~I~~ to drive the senator and ~~she~~ to
^ ^

the airport.

John and me is the subject of the infinitive *to drive; senator and her* is the direct object of the infinitive.

Checking for problems with pronoun case

Look for the most common trouble spots; where possible, apply a test for the correct pronoun.

COMPOUND WORD GROUPS (24a, 24b)

Test: Mentally strip away the rest of the compound word group.

> While diving for pearls, [Ikiko and] *she* found a treasure chest full of gold bars.

> Geoffrey went with [my family and] *me* to King's Dominion.

PRONOUN AFTER *IS, ARE, WAS,* OR *WERE* (24a)

In formal English, remember to use the subjective-case pronouns *I, he, she, we,* and *they* after the linking verbs *is, are, was,* and *were.*

> The panel was shocked to learn that the undercover agent was *she.*

APPOSITIVES (24c)

Test: Mentally strip away the word group that the appositive renames.

> [Two actors], Chris and *I,* were selected to do the last scene of *King Lear.*

> The company could afford to send only [one of two researchers], Dr. Davis or *me,* to Paris.

Pronoun case (continued)

PRONOUN AFTER *THAN* OR *AS* (24d)

Test: Mentally complete the sentence.

> The supervisor claimed that she was much more experienced than *I* [was].

> Gloria admitted that she liked Greg's twin better than [she liked] *him.*

WE OR *US* BEFORE A NOUN (24e)

Test: Mentally delete the noun.

> *We* [women] really have come a long way.

> Sadly, discrimination against *us* [women] occurs in most cultures.

PRONOUN BEFORE OR AFTER AN INFINITIVE (24f)

Remember that both subjects and objects of infinitives take the objective case.

> Everyone expected Alan and *me* to defeat Tracy and *him* in the doubles tournament.

PRONOUN OR NOUN BEFORE A GERUND (24g)

Remember to use the possessive case when a pronoun modifies a gerund.

> There is only a small chance of *his* bleeding excessively because of this procedure.

Grammatical sentences

24g Use the possessive case to modify a gerund.

A pronoun that modifies a gerund or a gerund phrase should appear in the possessive case (*my, our, your, his/her/its, their*). A gerund is a verb form ending in *-ing* that functions as a noun. Gerunds frequently appear in phrases, in which case the whole gerund phrase functions as a noun. (See 63c.)

▶ The chances of ~~you~~ *your* being hit by lightning are about two

million to one.

Your modifies the gerund phrase *being hit by lightning.*

Nouns as well as pronouns may modify gerunds. To form the possessive case of a noun, use an apostrophe and an *-s* (*a victim's rights*) or just an apostrophe (*victims' rights*). (See 36a.)

▶ The old order in France paid a high price for the ~~aristocracy~~ *aristocracy's*

exploiting the lower classes.

The possessive noun *aristocracy's* modifies the gerund phrase *exploiting the lower classes.*

Gerund phrases should not be confused with participial phrases, which function as adjectives, not as nouns: *We saw Brenda driving a yellow convertible.* Here *driving a yellow convertible* is a participial phrase modifying the noun *Brenda.* (See 63c.)

Sometimes the choice between the objective or the possessive case conveys a subtle difference in meaning:

We watched *them* dancing.

We watched *their* dancing.

In the first sentence the emphasis is on the people; *dancing* is a participle modifying the pronoun *them.* In the second sentence the emphasis is on the dancing; *dancing* is a gerund, and *their* is a possessive pronoun modifying the gerund.

NOTE: Do not use the possessive if it creates an awkward effect. Try to reword the sentence instead.

AWKWARD   The president agreed to the applications' being reviewed by a faculty committee.

REVISED   The president agreed that the applications could be reviewed by a faculty committee.

REVISED   The president agreed that a faculty committee could review the applications.

ON THE WEB

The rule on using a possessive before a gerund has sparked debates. If you're interested in learning why, go to
www.dianahacker.com/bedhandbook

and click on   ▶ **Language Debates**
                ▶ **Possessive before a gerund**

EXERCISE 24–1

Edit the following sentences to eliminate errors in case. If a sentence is correct, write "correct" after it. Answers to lettered sentences appear in the back of the book. Example:

Grandfather cuts down trees for neighbors much younger
he.
than ~~him.~~
   ^

a. Rick applied for the job even though he heard that other candidates were more experienced than he.

b. The jury could not agree that the murderer was he.
c. She appreciated him telling the truth in such a difficult situation.
d. The director has asked you and I to draft a proposal for a new recycling plan.
e. Five close friends and myself rented a station wagon, packed it with food, and drove to Mardi Gras on a three-day weekend.

1. The chain stores are threatening the survival of us shopkeepers.
2. The mysterious old woman handed Natasha and he a gold coin each.
3. The patient began suffering from the delusion that him and his family were constantly being followed and observed.
4. My adjustment to a new career was compounded by me becoming a single parent.
5. The swirling cyclone caused he and his horse to race for shelter.

EXERCISE 24–2

Choose the correct pronoun in each set of parentheses.

(We / Us) adults who grew up on *Sesame Street* are familiar with the practice of using one product to sell another. Big Bird might not have been interrupted by ads, but wasn't he for sale at the local toy store? We may blame television, but in fact merchandising that capitalizes on a character's popularity with children predates television by decades. Raggedy Ann began as a child's rag doll, and a few years later books about (she / her) and her brother, Raggedy Andy, were published. A cartoonist named Johnny Gruelle painted a cloth face on a family doll and applied for a patent in 1915. Later Gruelle began writing and illustrating stories about Raggedy Ann, and in 1918 (he / him) and a publisher teamed up to publish the books and sell the dolls. He was not the only one to try to sell products linked to children's stories. Beatrix Potter created the beloved Peter Rabbit picture books, and no one was better

than (she / her) at making a living from spin-offs. After Peter
Rabbit and Benjamin Bunny became popular, Potter began
putting pictures of (they / them) and their little animal friends
on merchandise. Potter had fans all over the world, and she
understood (them / their) wanting to see Peter Rabbit not only
in books but also on teapots and plates and lamps and other
furnishings for the nursery. Potter and Gruelle, like countless
others before and since, knew that entertaining children could
be a profitable business.

ON THE WEB

For electronic exercises on pronoun case, go to
www.dianahacker.com/bedhandbook

and click on ▶ **Electronic Grammar Exercises**
▶ **E-ex 24–1**

25

Distinguish between *who* and *whom*.

The choice between *who* and *whom* (or *whoever* and *whomever*) occurs primarily in subordinate clauses and in questions. *Who* and *whoever,* subjective-case pronouns, are used
for subjects and subject complements. *Whom* and *whomever,* objective-case pronouns, are used for objects. (See 25a
and 25b.)

An exception to this general rule occurs when the pronoun functions as the subject of an infinitive (see 25c). See
also 24f.

GRAMMAR CHECKERS can flag some sentences with a misused *who* or *whom* and explain the nature of the error. For example, some grammar checkers flagged the subject pronoun *who* in the following sentence, suggesting correctly that the context calls for the object pronoun *whom: One of the women who Martinez hired became the most successful lawyer in the agency.*

However, at times the programs skip past a misused *who* or *whom,* as they did with this sentence: *Now that you have studied with both musicians, whom in your opinion is the better teacher?* The programs could not tell that the object pronoun *whom* functions as the subject of the verb *is.*

25a   In subordinate clauses, use *who* and *whoever* for subjects or subject complements, *whom* and *whomever* for all objects.

When *who* and *whom* (or *whoever* and *whomever*) introduce subordinate clauses, their case is determined by their function *within the clause they introduce.* To choose the correct pronoun, you must isolate the subordinate clause and then decide how the pronoun functions within it. (See subordinate clauses, 63b.)

In the following two examples, the pronouns *who* and *whoever* function as the subjects of the clauses they introduce.

▶ The prize goes to the runner ~~whom~~ *who* collects the most points.

The subordinate clause is *who collects the most points.* The verb of the clause is *collects,* and its subject is *who.*

▶ He tells that story to ~~whomever~~ will listen.
                              whoever
                              ^

> The writer selected the pronoun *whomever,* thinking that it was the object of the preposition *to.* However, the object of the preposition is the entire subordinate clause *whoever will listen.* The verb of the clause is *will listen,* and its subject is *whoever.*

Who occasionally functions as a subject complement in a subordinate clause. Subject complements occur with linking verbs (usually *be, am, is, are, was, were, being,* and *been).* (See 62b.)

▶ The receptionist knows ~~whom~~ you are.
                           who
                           ^

> The subordinate clause is *who you are.* Its subject is *you,* and its subject complement is *who.*

When functioning as an object in a subordinate clause, *whom* (or *whomever*) appears out of order, before both the subject and the verb. To choose the correct pronoun, you must mentally restructure the clause.

▶ You will work with our senior industrial engineers, ~~who~~ you
                                                        whom
                                                        ^
will meet later.

> The subordinate clause is *whom you will meet later.* The subject of the clause is *you,* the verb is *will meet,* and *whom* is the direct object of the verb. This becomes clear if you mentally restructure the clause: *you will meet whom.*

When functioning as the object of a preposition in a subordinate clause, *whom* is often separated from its preposition.

► *whom*
The tutor ~~who~~ I was assigned to was very supportive.
  ^

Whom is the object of the preposition *to*. In this sentence, the writer might choose to drop *whom: The tutor I was assigned to was very supportive.*

NOTE: Inserted expressions such as *they know, I think,* and *she says* should be ignored in determining whether to use *who* or *whom.*

► All of the show-offs, bullies, and tough guys in school want
who
to take on a big guy ~~whom~~ they know will not hurt them.
  ^

Who is the subject of *will hurt*, not the object of *know.*

25b In questions, use *who* and *whoever* for subjects, *whom* and *whomever* for all objects.

When *who* and *whom* (or *whoever* and *whomever*) are used to open questions, their case is determined by their function within the question. In the following example, *who* functions as the subject of the question.

► *Who*
~~Whom~~ was responsible for creating that computer virus?
^

When *whom* functions as the object of a verb or the object of a preposition in a question, it appears out of normal order. To choose the correct pronoun, you must mentally restructure the question.

► *Whom*
~~Who~~ did the Democratic Party nominate in 1976?
^

Whom is the direct object of the verb *did nominate*. This becomes clear if you restructure the question *The Democratic Party did nominate whom in 1976?*

Checking for problems with who and whom

Look for common trouble spots; where possible, apply a test for correct usage.

IN A SUBORDINATE CLAUSE

Isolate the subordinate clause. Then read its subject, verb, and any objects, restructuring the clause if necessary. Some writers find it helpful to substitute *he* for *who* and *him* for *whom*.

> Samuels hoped to become the business partner of (whoever / whomever) found the treasure.

> Test: . . . *whoever* found the treasure. [. . . *he* found the treasure.]

> Ada always seemed to be bestowing a favor on (whoever / whomever) she worked for.

> Test: . . . she worked for *whomever*. [. . . she worked for *him*.]

IN A QUESTION

Read the subject, verb, and any objects, rearranging the sentence structure if necessary.

> (Who / Whom) conferred with Roosevelt and Stalin at Yalta in 1945?

> Test: *Who* conferred . . . ?

> (Who / Whom) did the committee nominate?

> Test: The committee did nominate *whom*?

Whom
▶ ~~Who~~ did you enter into the contract with?
  ^

Whom is the object of the preposition *with*, as is clear if you recast the question: *You did enter into the contract with whom?*

25c   Use *whom* for subjects or objects of infinitives.

An infinitive is the word *to* followed by the base form of a verb. (See 63c.) Subjects of infinitives are an exception to the rule that subjects must be in the subjective case. Whenever an infinitive has a subject, it must be in the objective case. Objects of infinitives also are in the objective case.

▶ On the subject of health care, I don't know ~~who~~ *whom* to believe.

USAGE NOTE: In spoken English, *who* is frequently used when the correct *whom* sounds too stuffy. Even educated speakers are likely to say *Who* [not *Whom*] *did Joe replace?* Although some readers will accept such constructions in informal written English, it is safer to use *whom* in formal English: *Whom did Joe replace?*

ON THE WEB

The rules on using *who* and *whom* have sparked debates. If you're interested in learning why, go to
www.dianahacker.com/bedhandbook

and click on   ▶ **Language Debates**
              ▶ **who versus whom**

EXERCISE 25–1

Edit the following sentences to eliminate errors in the use of *who* and *whom* (or *whoever* and *whomever*). If a sentence is correct, write "correct" after it. Answers to lettered sentences appear in the back of the book. Example:

What is the name of the person ~~who~~ *whom* you are sponsoring for

membership in the club?

a. The roundtable featured several scholars who I had never heard of.
b. We had no idea who had shot whom.
c. Whom did you support in the last presidential election?
d. Daniel always gives a holiday donation to whomever needs it most.
e. So many of the candidates were overqualified that it was difficult to decide who to choose.

1. When medicine is scarce and expensive, physicians must give it to whomever has the best chance to survive.
2. Who was accused of receiving Mafia funds?
3. According to the Greek myth, the Sphinx devoured those who could not answer her riddles.
4. The only interstate travelers who get pulled over for speeding are the ones whom cannot afford a radar detector.
5. Who did the committee select?

ON THE WEB

For an electronic exercise on using *who* and *whom*, go to
www.dianahacker.com/bedhandbook

and click on ▶ **Electronic Grammar Exercises**
▶ **E-ex 25–1**

26

Choose adjectives and adverbs with care.

Adjectives ordinarily modify nouns or pronouns; occasionally they function as subject complements following linking verbs. Adverbs modify verbs, adjectives, or other adverbs. (See 61d and 61e.)

Many adverbs are formed by adding -*ly* to adjectives (*normal, normally; smooth, smoothly*). But don't assume that all words ending in *-ly* are adverbs or that all adverbs end in *-ly*. Some adjectives end in *-ly* (*lovely, friendly*) and some adverbs don't (*always, here, there*). When in doubt, consult a dictionary.

In English, adjectives are not pluralized to agree with the words they modify: *The red* [not *reds*] *roses were a wonderful surprise.*

ESL

GRAMMAR CHECKERS can flag a number of problems with adjectives and adverbs: some misuses of *bad* or *badly* and *good* or *well*; some double comparisons, such as *more meaner*; some absolute comparisons, such as *most unique*; and some double negatives, such as *can't hardly*. However, the programs slip past more problems than they find. Programs ignored errors like these: *could have been handled more professional* and *hadn't been bathed regular.*

26a   Use adverbs, not adjectives, to modify verbs, adjectives, and adverbs.

When adverbs modify verbs (or verbals), they nearly always answer the question When? Where? How? Why? Under what conditions? How often? or To what degree? When adverbs modify adjectives or other adverbs, they usually qualify or intensify the meaning of the word they modify. (See 61e.)

The incorrect use of adjectives in place of adverbs to modify verbs occurs primarily in casual or nonstandard speech.

▶ The arrangement worked out ~~perfect~~ *perfectly* for everyone.

▶ The manager must see that the office runs ~~smooth~~ and
smoothly
efficiently.
~~efficient.~~
^

The adverb *perfectly* modifies the verb *worked out*; the adverbs
smoothly and *efficiently* modify the verb *runs*.

The incorrect use of the adjective *good* in place of the adverb *well* is especially common in casual and nonstandard
speech.

▶ We were glad that Nemo had done ~~good~~ on the CPA exam.
well
^

The adverb *well* (not the adjective *good*) should be used to modify the verb *had done*.

NOTE: The word *well* is an adjective when it means "healthy,"
"satisfactory," or "fortunate": *I am very well, thank you. All is
well. It is just as well.*

Adjectives are sometimes used incorrectly to modify adjectives or adverbs.

▶ In the early 1970s, chances for survival of the bald eagle
really
looked ~~real~~ slim.
^

Only adverbs can be used to modify adjectives or other adverbs.
Really intensifies the meaning of the adjective *slim*.

ESL

Placement of adjectives and adverbs can be a tricky matter
for second language speakers. See 31d.

26b   Use adjectives, not adverbs, as complements.

Adjectives ordinarily precede nouns, but they can also function as subject complements or as object complements.

Subject complements

A subject complement follows a linking verb and completes the meaning of the subject. (See 62b.) When an adjective functions as a subject complement, it describes the subject.

Justice is blind.

Problems can arise with verbs such as *smell, taste, look,* and *feel,* which sometimes, but not always, function as linking verbs. If the word following one of these verbs describes the subject, use an adjective; if it modifies the verb, use an adverb.

ADJECTIVE   The detective looked *cautious.*

ADVERB   The detective looked *cautiously* for fingerprints.

The adjective *cautious* describes the detective; the adverb *cautiously* modifies the verb *looked.*

Linking verbs suggest states of being, not actions. Notice, for example, the different meanings of *looked* in the preceding examples. To look cautious suggests the state of being cautious; to look cautiously is to perform an action in a cautious way.

▶ The lilacs in our backyard smell especially ~~sweetly~~ *sweet* this year.

▶ Lori looked ~~well~~ *good* in her new raincoat.

The verbs *smell* and *looked* suggest states of being, not actions. Therefore, they should be followed by adjectives, not adverbs.

(Contrast with action verbs: *We smelled the flowers. Lori looked for her raincoat.*)

When the verb *feel* refers to the state of a person's health or emotions, it is a linking verb and should be followed by an adjective.

> *bad*
> ▶ We felt ~~badly~~ upon hearing of your grandmother's death.
>   ^

Another adjective, such as *saddened,* could be used in place of *bad.*

ON THE WEB

The rules on using *feel bad* and *feel badly* have sparked debates. If you're interested in learning why, go to
www.dianahacker.com/bedhandbook

and click on ▶ **Language Debates**
                  ▶ *feel bad* versus *feel badly*

Object complements

An object complement follows a direct object and completes its meaning. (See 62b.) When an adjective functions as an object complement, it describes the direct object.

Sorrow makes *us wise.*

Object complements occur with verbs such as *call, consider, create, find, keep,* and *make.* When a modifier follows the direct object of one of these verbs, it can function as an adjective describing the direct object or as an adverb modifying the verb.

ADJECTIVE	The referee called the plays *perfect.*
ADVERB	The referee called the plays *perfectly.*

Grammatical sentences

The first sentence means that the referee considered the plays to be perfect; the second means that the referee did an excellent job of calling the plays.

▶ God created all men and women ~~equally.~~ *equal.*

The adjective *equal* is an object complement describing the direct object *men and women*.

26c   Use comparatives and superlatives with care.

Most adjectives and adverbs have three forms: the positive, the comparative, and the superlative.

POSITIVE	COMPARATIVE	SUPERLATIVE
soft	softer	softest
fast	faster	fastest
careful	more careful	most careful
bad	worse	worst
good	better	best

Comparative versus superlative

Use the comparative to compare two things, the superlative to compare three or more.

▶ Which of these two brands of toothpaste is ~~best?~~ *better?*

▶ Though Shaw and Jackson are impressive, Hobbs is the ~~more~~ *most* qualified of the three candidates running for mayor.

Form of comparatives and superlatives

To form comparatives and superlatives of most one- and two-syllable adjectives, use the endings *-er* and *-est: smooth,* *smoother, smoothest; easy, easier, easiest.* With longer adjectives, use *more* and *most* (or *less* and *least* for downward comparisons): *exciting, more exciting, most exciting; helpful, less helpful, least helpful.*

Some one-syllable adverbs take the endings *-er* and *-est* (*fast, faster, fastest*), but longer adverbs and all of those ending in *-ly* form the comparative and superlative with *more* and *most* (or *less* and *least*).

The comparative and superlative forms of the following adjectives and adverbs are irregular: *good, better, best; well, better, best; bad, worse, worst; badly, worse, worst.*

▶ The Kirov is the ~~talentedest~~ *most talented* ballet company we have seen.

▶ Lloyd's luck couldn't have been ~~worser~~ *worse* than David's.

Double comparatives or superlatives

Do not use double comparatives or superlatives. When you have added *-er* or *-est* to an adjective or adverb, do not also use *more* or *most* (or *less* or *least*).

▶ Of all her family, Julia is the ~~most~~ happiest about the move.

▶ All the polls indicated that Dewey was more ~~likelier~~ *likely* to win

than Truman.

Absolute concepts

Avoid expressions such as *more straight, less perfect, very round,* and *most unique.* Either something is unique or it isn't. It is illogical to suggest that absolute concepts come in degrees.

▶ That is the most ~~unique~~ *unusual* wedding gown I have ever seen.

▶ The painting would have been even more ~~priceless~~ *valuable* had it

been signed.

ON THE WEB

The rule on avoiding absolute concepts in comparisons
has sparked debates. If you're interested in learning
why, go to **www.dianahacker.com/bedhandbook**

and click on   ▶ **Language Debates**
                  ▶ **Absolute concepts such as *unique***

26d   Avoid double negatives.

Standard English allows two negatives only if a positive
meaning is intended: *The orchestra was not unhappy with its
performance.* Double negatives used to emphasize negation
are nonstandard.

Negative modifiers such as *never, no,* and *not* should not
be paired with other negative modifiers or with negative
words such as *neither, none, no one, nobody,* and *nothing.*

▶ Management is not doing ~~nothing~~ *anything* to see that the trash is

picked up.

The double negative *not . . . nothing* is nonstandard.

The modifiers *hardly, barely,* and *scarcely* are considered negatives in standard English, so they should not be
used with negatives such as *not, no one,* or *never.*

▶ Maxine is so weak she ~~can't~~ *can* hardly climb stairs.

EXERCISE 26–1

Edit the following sentences to eliminate errors in the use of adjectives and adverbs. If a sentence is correct, write "correct" after it. Answers to lettered sentences appear in the back of the book. Example:

> When I watched Carl run the 440 on Saturday, I was amazed
>
> *well*
> at how ~~good~~ he paced himself.
>   ^

a. Did you do good on last week's chemistry exam?
b. With the budget deadline approaching, our office hasn't hardly had time to handle routine correspondence.
c. Some flowers smell surprisingly bad.
d. The customer complained that he hadn't been treated nice.
e. Of all my relatives, Uncle Roberto is the most cleverest.

1. When answering the phone, you should speak clearly and courteous.
2. Who was more upset about the loss? Was it the coach or the quarterback or the owner of the team?
3. The green bagels looked and tasted real peculiar.
4. After checking to see how bad I had been hurt, my sister dialed 911.
5. If the college's Web page had been updated more regular, students would have learned about the new course offerings.

ON THE WEB

For electronic exercises on using adjectives and adverbs, go to **www.dianahacker.com/bedhandbook**

and click on ▶ **Electronic Grammar Exercises**
              ▶ **E-ex 26–1**

27

Choose standard English verb forms.

In nonstandard English, spoken by those who share a regional or cultural heritage, verb forms sometimes differ from those of standard English. In writing, use standard English verb forms unless you are quoting nonstandard speech or using nonstandard forms for literary effect. (See 17d.)

Except for the verb *be*, all verbs in English have five forms. The following chart lists the five forms and provides a sample sentence in which each might appear.

BASE FORM	Usually I (*walk, ride*).
PAST TENSE	Yesterday I (*walked, rode*).
PAST PARTICIPLE	I have (*walked, ridden*) many times before.
PRESENT PARTICIPLE	I am (*walking, riding*) right now.
-S FORM	He / she / it (*walks, rides*) regularly.

Both the past-tense and past-participle forms of regular verbs end in *-ed* (*walked, walked*). Irregular verbs form the past tense and past participle in other ways (*rode, ridden*).

The verb *be* has eight forms instead of the usual five: *be, am, is, are, was, were, being, been.*

GRAMMAR CHECKERS can flag some misused irregular verbs in sentences, such as *I had drove the car only twice before* or *Lucia swum across the lake,* but they miss about twice as many errors as they find.

27a Use the correct forms of irregular verbs.

For all regular verbs, the past-tense and past-participle forms are the same (ending in *-ed* or *-d*), so there is no danger of confusion. This is not true, however, for irregular verbs, such as the following.

BASE FORM	PAST TENSE	PAST PARTICIPLE
go	went	gone
fight	fought	fought
fly	flew	flown

The past-tense form, which never has a helping verb, expresses action that occurred entirely in the past. The past participle is used with a helping verb—either with *has, have,* or *had* to form one of the perfect tenses or with *be, am, is, are, was, were, being,* or *been* to form the passive voice.

PAST TENSE	Last July, we *went* to Paris.
PAST PARTICIPLE	We have *gone* to Paris twice.

When you aren't sure which verb form to choose (*went* or *gone, began* or *begun,* and so on), consult the list of common irregular verbs that starts on the next page. Choose the past-tense form if the verb in your sentence doesn't have a helping verb; choose the past-participle form if it does.

In nonstandard English speech, the past-tense and past-participle forms may differ from those of standard English, as in the following sentences.

► Yesterday we ~~seen~~ *saw* an unidentified flying object.

► The reality of the situation finally ~~sunk~~ *sank* in.

The past-tense forms *saw* and *sank* are required because there are no helping verbs.

▶ The truck was apparently ~~stole~~ *stolen* while the driver ate lunch.

▶ By the end of the day, the stock market had ~~fell~~ *fallen* two hundred

points.

Because of the helping verbs, the past-participle forms are required: *was stolen, had fallen.*

When in doubt about the standard English forms of irregular verbs, consult the following list or look up the base form of the verb in the dictionary, which also lists any irregular forms. (If no additional forms are listed in the dictionary, the verb is regular, not irregular.)

Common irregular verbs

BASE FORM	PAST TENSE	PAST PARTICIPLE
arise	arose	arisen
awake	awoke, awaked	awaked, awoke
be	was, were	been
beat	beat	beaten, beat
become	became	become
begin	began	begun
bend	bent	bent
bite	bit	bitten, bit
blow	blew	blown
break	broke	broken
bring	brought	brought
build	built	built
burst	burst	burst
buy	bought	bought
catch	caught	caught
choose	chose	chosen
cling	clung	clung
come	came	come
cost	cost	cost
deal	dealt	dealt
dig	dug	dug

BASE FORM	PAST TENSE	PAST PARTICIPLE
dive	dived, dove	dived
do	did	done
drag	dragged	dragged
draw	drew	drawn
dream	dreamed, dreamt	dreamed, dreamt
drink	drank	drunk
drive	drove	driven
eat	ate	eaten
fall	fell	fallen
fight	fought	fought
find	found	found
fly	flew	flown
forget	forgot	forgotten, forgot
freeze	froze	frozen
get	got	gotten, got
give	gave	given
go	went	gone
grow	grew	grown
hang (suspend)	hung	hung
hang (execute)	hanged	hanged
have	had	had
hear	heard	heard
hide	hid	hidden
hurt	hurt	hurt
keep	kept	kept
know	knew	known
lay (put)	laid	laid
lead	led	led
lend	lent	lent
let (allow)	let	let
lie (recline)	lay	lain
lose	lost	lost
make	made	made
prove	proved	proved, proven
read	read	read
ride	rode	ridden
ring	rang	rung
rise (get up)	rose	risen
run	ran	run
say	said	said

BASE FORM	PAST TENSE	PAST PARTICIPLE
see	saw	seen
send	sent	sent
set (place)	set	set
shake	shook	shaken
shoot	shot	shot
shrink	shrank	shrunk
sing	sang	sung
sink	sank	sunk
sit (be seated)	sat	sat
slay	slew	slain
sleep	slept	slept
speak	spoke	spoken
spin	spun	spun
spring	sprang	sprung
stand	stood	stood
steal	stole	stolen
sting	stung	stung
strike	struck	struck, stricken
swear	swore	sworn
swim	swam	swum
swing	swung	swung
take	took	taken
teach	taught	taught
throw	threw	thrown
wake	woke, waked	waked, woken
wear	wore	worn
wring	wrung	wrung
write	wrote	written

27b   Distinguish among the forms of *lie* and *lay*.

Writers and speakers frequently confuse the various forms of *lie* (meaning "to recline or rest on a surface") and *lay* (meaning "to put or place something"). *Lie* is an intransitive verb; it does not take a direct object: *The tax forms lie on the table.* The verb *lay* is transitive; it takes a direct object: *Please lay the tax forms on the table.* (See 62b.)

In addition to confusing the meaning of *lie* and *lay*, writers and speakers are often unfamiliar with the standard English forms of these verbs.

BASE FORM	PAST TENSE	PAST PARTICIPLE	PRESENT PARTICIPLE
lie	lay	lain	lying
lay	laid	laid	laying

▶ Sue was so exhausted that she ~~laid~~ *lay* down for a nap.

The past-tense form of *lie* ("to recline") is *lay.*

▶ The patient had ~~laid~~ *lain* in an uncomfortable position all night.

The past-participle form of *lie* ("to recline") is *lain.* If the correct English seems too stilted, recast the sentence: *The patient had been lying in an uncomfortable position all night.*

▶ The prosecutor ~~lay~~ *laid* the pistol on a table close to the jurors.

The past-tense form of *lay* ("to place") is *laid.*

▶ Letters dating from the Civil War were ~~laying~~ *lying* in the corner of the chest.

The present participle of *lie* ("to rest on a surface") is *lying.*

ON THE WEB

The rules on using *lie* and *lay* have sparked debates. If you're interested in learning why, go to

www.dianahacker.com/bedhandbook

and click on ▶ **Language Debates**
          ▶ ***lie* versus *lay***

Grammatical sentences

EXERCISE 27–1

Edit the following sentences to eliminate problems with irregular verbs. If a sentence is correct, write "correct" after it. Answers to lettered sentences appear in the back of the book. Example:

> *saw*
> Was it you I ~~seen~~ last night at the concert?
> ^

a. When I get the urge to exercise, I lay down until it passes.
b. Grandmother had drove our new jeep to the sunrise church service on Savage Mountain, so we were left with the station wagon.
c. A pile of dirty rags was laying at the bottom of the stairs.
d. How did the detective know that the suspect had went to the office on the night of the murder?
e. Lincoln took good care of his legal clients; the contracts he drew for the Illinois Central Railroad could never be broke.

1. The burglar must have gone immediately upstairs, grabbed what looked good, and took off.
2. Have you ever dreamed that you were falling from a cliff or flying through the air?
3. I locked my brakes, leaned the motorcycle to the left, and laid it down to keep from slamming into the fence.
4. In her junior year, Cindy run the 440-yard dash in 51.1 seconds.
5. Larry claimed that he had drank a bad soda, but Esther suspected the truth.

ON THE WEB

For an electronic exercise on irregular verbs, go to
www.dianahacker.com/bedhandbook

and click on ▶ **Electronic Grammar Exercises**
▶ **E-ex 27–1**

27c Use -*s* (or -*es*) endings on present-tense verbs that have third-person singular subjects.

All singular nouns (*child, tree*) and the pronouns *he, she*, and *it* are third-person singular; indefinite pronouns such as *everyone* and *neither* are also third-person singular. When the subject of a sentence is third-person singular, its verb takes an -*s* or -*es* ending in the present tense. (See also 21.)

	SINGULAR		PLURAL	
FIRST PERSON	I	know	we	know
SECOND PERSON	you	know	you	know
THIRD PERSON	he/she/it	knows	they	know
	child	knows	parents	know
	everyone	knows		

In nonstandard speech, the -*s* ending required by standard English is sometimes omitted.

▶ Sulfur dioxide ~~turn~~ *turns* leaves yellow, ~~dissolve~~ *dissolves* marble, and ~~eat~~ *eats* away iron and steel.

The subject *sulfur dioxide* is third-person singular, so the verbs must end in -*s*.

CAUTION: Do not add the -*s* ending to the verb if the subject is not third-person singular.

The writers of the following sentences, knowing they sometimes dropped -*s* endings from verbs, overcorrected by adding the endings where they don't belong.

▶ I prepares program specifications and logic diagrams.

The writer mistakenly concluded that the -*s* ending belongs on present-tense verbs used with *all* singular subjects, not just *third-person* singular subjects. The pronoun *I* is first-person singular, so its verb does not require the *-s*.

▶   **The dirt floors requires continual sweeping.**

The writer mistakenly thought that the *-s* ending on the verb indicated plurality. The *-s* goes on present-tense verbs used with third-person *singular* subjects.

Has *versus* have

In the present tense, use *has* with third-person singular subjects; all other subjects require *have*.

	SINGULAR		**PLURAL**	
FIRST PERSON	I	have	we	have
SECOND PERSON	you	have	you	have
THIRD PERSON	he/she/it	has	they	have

In some dialects, *have* is used with all subjects. But standard English requires *has* for third-person singular subjects.

▶   **This respected musician almost always ~~have~~ _has_ a message to convey in his work.**

▶   **As for the retirement income program, it ~~have~~ _has_ finally been established.**

The subjects *musician* and *it* are third-person singular, so the verb should be *has* in each case.

CAUTION: Do not use *has* if the subject is not third-person singular. The writers of the following sentences were aware that they often wrote *have* when standard English requires *has.* Here they are using what appears to them to be the "more correct" form, but in an inappropriate context.

▶ My business law classes ~~has~~ *have* helped me to understand more about contracts.

▶ I ~~has~~ *have* much to be thankful for.

The subjects of these sentences—*classes* and *I*—are third-person plural and first-person singular, so standard English requires *have. Has* is used with third-person singular subjects only.

Does *versus* do *and* doesn't *versus* don't

In the present tense, use *does* and *doesn't* with third-person singular subjects; all other subjects require *do* and *don't*.

	SINGULAR		**PLURAL**	
FIRST PERSON	I	do/don't	we	do/don't
SECOND PERSON	you	do/don't	you	do/don't
THIRD PERSON	he/she/it	does/doesn't	they	do/don't

The use of *don't* instead of the standard English *doesn't* is a feature of many dialects in the United States. Use of *do* for *does* is rarer.

▶ Grandfather really ~~don't~~ *doesn't* have a place to call home.

▶ ~~Do~~ *Does* she know the correct procedure for setting up the experiment?

Grandfather and *she* are third-person singular, so the verbs should be *doesn't* and *does*.

Am, is, *and* are; was *and* were

The verb *be* has three forms in the present tense (*am, is, are*) and two in the past tense (*was, were*). Use *am* and *was* with first-person singular subjects; use *is* and *was* with third-person singular subjects. With all other subjects, use *are* and *were*.

	SINGULAR		**PLURAL**	
FIRST PERSON	I	am/was	we	are/were
SECOND PERSON	you	are/were	you	are/were
THIRD PERSON	he/she/it	is/was	they	are/were

▶ Judy wanted to borrow Tim's notes, but she ~~were~~ *was* too shy to

ask for them.

The subject *she* is third-person singular, so the verb should be *was*.

▶ Did you think you ~~was~~ *were* going to drown?

The subject *you* is second-person singular, so the verb should be *were*.

LOOKING AT YOURSELF AS A WRITER
Problems with -s endings on verbs

If *-s* verb forms are a serious problem for you, ask yourself why. Here are the most common causes and cures.

CAUSE	Your informal spoken English may differ from standard English in its use of *-s* forms.
CURE	Listen carefully to your own casual speech (or the casual speech of family and friends) and compare it with the chart on page 264. Make a list of any differences that you need to be alert to.

Problems with -s endings on verbs (continued)

CAUSE You may be confused about the rules on when to use the -s form of a verb. For example, you may mistakenly think that a "plural" verb takes an -s ending, just like most plural nouns.

CURE When proofreading, consult the chart on page 265, which shows when to use -s verb forms. Don't let yourself get confused by half-learned rules.

CAUSE When you proofread your final draft, you read for meaning, so you don't notice small surface features such as missing word endings.

CURE Proofread your draft out loud—slowly—articulating the words just as they are written on the page. If you still have trouble, ask your instructor or a writing center tutor for help.

CAUSE When it is difficult to pronounce an -s ending, you may have trouble hearing that the -s is needed—even when you proofread out loud. For example, many speakers do not articulate the -s in verbs like *costs* and *asks* and nouns like *tests* and *desks*.

CURE Be alert for words that give you difficulty. Probably they end in what grammarians call "consonant clusters." Here are some commonly used verbs and nouns that end in consonant clusters: *acts, asks, clasps, costs, crafts, desks, expects, grasps, lists, masks, risks, tests,* and *wasps.*

GRAMMAR CHECKERS can catch some missing -s endings on verbs and some misused -s forms of the verb. Unfortunately, they flag quite a few correct sentences, so you need to know how to interpret what the programs tell you. (See the grammar check advice on p. 266 for more detailed information.)

27d   Do not omit *-ed* endings on verbs.

Speakers who do not fully pronounce *-ed* endings sometimes omit them unintentionally in writing. Failure to pronounce *-ed* endings is common in many dialects and in informal speech even in standard English. In the following frequently used words and phrases, for example, the *-ed* ending is not always fully pronounced.

advised	developed	prejudiced	supposed to
asked	fixed	pronounced	used to
concerned	frightened	stereotyped	

When a verb is regular, both the past tense and the past participle are formed by adding *-ed* to the base form of the verb.

Past tense

Use an *-ed* or *-d* ending to express the past tense of regular verbs. The past tense is used when the action occurred entirely in the past.

▶ Over the weekend, Ed ~~fix~~ *fixed* his brother's skateboard and tuned up his mother's 1955 Thunderbird.

▶ Last summer my counselor ~~advise~~ *advised* me to ask my chemistry instructor for help.

Past participles

Past participles are used in three ways: (1) following *have, has,* or *had* to form one of the perfect tenses; (2) following *be, am, is, are, was, were, being,* or *been* to form the passive voice; and (3) as adjectives modifying nouns or pronouns.

The perfect tenses are listed on pages 336–37, and the passive voice is discussed in 8a. For a discussion of participles functioning as adjectives, see 63c.

▶ Robin has ~~ask~~ *asked* me to go to California with her.

Has asked is present perfect tense (*have* or *has* followed by a past participle).

▶ Though it is not a new phenomenon, domestic violence is ~~publicize~~ *publicized* more frequently than before.

Is publicized is a verb in the passive voice (a form of *be* followed by a past participle).

▶ All aerobics classes end in a cool-down period to stretch ~~tighten~~ *tightened* muscles.

The past participle *tightened* functions as an adjective modifying the noun *muscles*.

LOOKING AT YOURSELF AS A WRITER
Problems with -ed endings on verbs

If you have difficulty spotting missing *-ed* endings, consider possible sources of the problem.

CAUSE Like most people, you don't always pronounce *-ed* endings, so you tend not to hear them as you proofread.

CURE Try proofreading out loud in a formal-sounding voice. When speaking formally, most people enunciate word endings more clearly.

Problems with -ed endings on verbs (continued)

CAUSE   When you proofread a final draft, you read for meaning, so you don't notice small surface features such as missing word endings.

CURE   Again, reading out loud usually works. Read slowly, articulating the words just as they are written on the page. If you still have trouble, ask your instructor or a writing center tutor for help. Proofreading is a skill that can be learned.

CAUSE   You don't proofread your final draft carefully enough or you try to proofread for too many problems at once.

CURE   Take time to proofread. Until you become a skilled proofreader, you may need to go over your work several times.

GRAMMAR CHECKERS can catch some missing *-ed* endings, but they tend to slip past as many as they catch. For example, although some programs flagged *was accustom,* they ignored *has change* and *was pass.*

27e   Do not omit needed verbs.

Although standard English allows some linking verbs and helping verbs to be contracted, at least in informal contexts, it does not allow them to be omitted.

Linking verbs, used to link subjects to subject complements, are frequently a form of *be: be, am, is, are, was, were, being, been.* (See 62b.) Some of these forms may be contracted (*I'm, she's, we're, you're, they're*), but they should not be omitted altogether.

> *are*
> ▶ When we out there in the evening, we often hear the
>   ^
>
>   helicopters circling above.

> *is*
> ▶ Alvin a man who can defend himself.
>   ^

Helping verbs, used with main verbs, include forms of *be, do,* and *have* or the words *can, will, shall, could, would, should, may, might,* and *must.* (See 61c.) Some helping verbs may be contracted (*he's leaving, we'll celebrate, they've been told*), but they should not be omitted altogether.

> *have*
> ▶ We been in Chicago since last Thursday.
>   ^

> *would*
> ▶ Do you know someone who be good for the job?
>   ^

ESL

Speakers of English as a second language sometimes have problems with omitted verbs and correct use of helping verbs. See 29e and 29a.

GRAMMAR CHECKERS are fairly good at flagging omitted verbs, but they do not catch all of them. For example, programs caught the missing verb in this sentence: *He always talking.* But in the following, more complicated sentence, they did not catch the missing verb: *We often don't know whether he angry or just talking.*

EXERCISE 27–2

Edit the following sentences to eliminate problems with *-s* and *-ed* verb forms and with omitted verbs. If a sentence is correct, write "correct" after it. Answers to lettered sentences appear in the back of the book. Example:

> The Pell Grant sometimes cover the student's full tuition.

a. The cops was after my hot rod Lincoln. We was passing cars like they was standing still.
b. The museum visitors were not suppose to touch the exhibits.
c. Our church has all the latest technology, even a close-circuit television.
d. Christos didn't know about Marlo's promotion because he never listens. He always talking.
e. Most psychologists agree that no one performs well under stress.

1. Have there ever been a time in your life when you were too depressed to get out of bed?
2. My days in this department have taught me to do what I'm told without asking questions.
3. Last year, Darlene planned to major in computer science; this year she has change to accounting.
4. The training for security checkpoint screeners, which takes place in an empty airplane hangar, consist of watching out-of-date videos.
5. How would you feel if a love one had been a victim of a crime like this?

ON THE WEB

For electronic exercises on verb forms, go to
www.dianahacker.com/bedhandbook

and click on ▶ **Electronic Grammar Exercises**
▶ **E-ex 27–2**

28

Use verbs in the appropriate tense and mood.

28a   Choose the appropriate verb tense.

Tenses indicate the time of an action in relation to the time of the speaking or writing about that action.

The most common problem with tenses—shifting confusingly from one tense to another—is discussed in 13. Other problems with tenses are detailed in this section, after the following survey of tenses.

> **GRAMMAR CHECKERS** do not flag the problems with tense discussed in this section. Although some programs may tell you that *had had* is incorrect, in fact it is often correct. See page 339.

Survey of tenses

English has three simple tenses (past, present, and future) and three perfect tenses (present perfect, past perfect, and future perfect). In addition, there is a progressive form of each of these six tenses.

SIMPLE TENSES   The simple present tense is used primarily to describe habitual actions (*Jane walks to work*) or to refer to actions occurring at the time of speaking (*I see a cardinal in our maple tree*). It is also used to state facts or general truths and to describe fictional events in a literary work (see p. 338). The present tense may even be used to express future actions that are to occur at some specified time (*The semester begins tomorrow*).

The simple past tense is used for actions completed entirely in the past (*Yesterday Jane walked to work*).

The simple future tense is used for actions that will occur in the future (*Tomorrow Jane will walk to work*) or for actions that are predictable, given certain causes (*Meat will spoil if not properly refrigerated*).

In the following chart, the simple tenses are given for the regular verb *walk,* the irregular verb *ride,* and the highly irregular verb *be.*

SIMPLE PRESENT

SINGULAR		PLURAL	
I	walk, ride, am	we	walk, ride, are
you	walk, ride, are	you	walk, ride, are
he/she/it	walks, rides, is	they	walk, ride, are

SIMPLE PAST

SINGULAR		PLURAL	
I	walked, rode, was	we	walked, rode, were
you	walked, rode, were	you	walked, rode, were
he/she/it	walked, rode, was	they	walked, rode, were

SIMPLE FUTURE

I, you, he/she/it, we, they   will walk, ride, be

PERFECT TENSES   More complex time relations are indicated by the perfect tenses (which consist of a form of *have* plus the past participle). The present perfect tense is used for an action that began in the past and is still going on in the present (*Jane has walked to work for years*) or an action that began in the past and is finished by the time of speaking or writing (*Jane has discovered a new restaurant on Elm Street*).

The past perfect tense is used for an action already completed by the time of another past action (*Jane hailed a cab after she had walked several blocks in the rain*) or for an action already completed at some specific past time (*By 8:30, Jane had walked two miles*). (See also pp. 339–40.)

The future perfect tense is used for an action that will be completed before or by a certain future time (*Jane will have left Troy by the time Jo arrives*).

PRESENT PERFECT

| I, you, we, they | have walked, ridden, been |
| he/she/it | has walked, ridden, been |

PAST PERFECT

| I, you, he/she/it, we, they | had walked, ridden, been |

FUTURE PERFECT

| I, you, he/she/it, we, they | will have walked, ridden, been |

PROGRESSIVE FORMS The simple and perfect tenses already discussed have progressive forms that describe actions in progress. The present progressive form is used for actions currently in progress (*Jane is writing a letter*) or for future actions that are to occur at some specified time (*Jane is leaving for Chicago on Monday*).

The past progressive is used for past actions in progress (*Jane was writing a letter last night*).

The future progressive is used for future actions in progress (*Jane will be traveling next week*).

PRESENT PROGRESSIVE

I	am walking, riding, being
he/she/it	is walking, riding, being
you, we, they	are walking, riding, being

PAST PROGRESSIVE

| I, he/she/it | was walking, riding, being |
| you, we, they | were walking, riding, being |

FUTURE PROGRESSIVE

| I, you, he/she/it, we, they | will be walking, riding, being |

Like the simple tenses, the perfect tenses have progressive forms. The perfect progressive forms express the length of time an action is, was, or will be in progress: *Jane has been walking to work for five years* (present perfect progressive). *Jane had been walking to work until she was mugged* (past perfect progressive). *Jane will have been walking to work for five years by the end of this month* (future perfect progressive).

PRESENT PERFECT PROGRESSIVE

I, you, we, they	have been walking, riding, being
he/she/it	has been walking, riding, being

PAST PERFECT PROGRESSIVE
I, you, he/she/it, we, they had been walking, riding, being

FUTURE PERFECT PROGRESSIVE
I, you, he/she/it, we, they will have been walking, riding, being

ESL

The progressive forms are not normally used with mental activity verbs such as *believe*. See page 349.

Special uses of the present tense

Use the present tense when writing about events in a literary work, when expressing general truths, and when quoting, summarizing, or paraphrasing an author's views.

When writing about a work of literature, you may be tempted to use the past tense. The convention, however, is to describe fictional events in the present tense. (See also 13b.)

▶ In Masuji Ibuse's *Black Rain,* a child ~~reached~~ *reaches* for a pome-

granate in his mother's garden, and a moment later he ~~was~~ *is* dead, killed by the blast of the atomic bomb.

Scientific principles or general truths should appear in the present tense, unless such principles have been disproved.

▶ Galileo taught that the earth ~~revolved~~ ^revolves^ around the sun.

Since Galileo's teaching has not been discredited, the verb should be in the present tense. The following sentence, however, is acceptable: *Ptolemy taught that the sun revolved around the earth.*

When you are quoting, summarizing, or paraphrasing the author of a nonliterary work, use present-tense verbs such as *writes, reports, asserts,* and so on. (See p. 583 for a more complete list.) This convention is usually followed even when the author is dead (unless a date specifies the time of writing).

▶ Baron Bowan of Colwood ~~wrote~~ ^writes^ that a metaphysician is "one

who goes into a dark cellar at midnight without a light,

looking for a black cat that is not there."

EXCEPTION: When you are documenting a paper with the APA (American Psychological Association) style of in-text citations, which include a date after the author's name, use past-tense verbs such as *reported* or *demonstrated* or present perfect verbs such as *has reported* or *has demonstrated.* (See p. 686.)

E. Wilson (1996) reported that positive reinforcement alone was a less effective teaching technique than a mixture of positive reinforcement and constructive criticism.

The past perfect tense

The past perfect tense consists of a past participle preceded by *had* (*had worked, had gone, had had*). (See pp. 336–37.) This tense is used for an action already completed by the time of another past action or for an action already completed at some specific past time.

Grammatical sentences

Everyone *had spoken* by the time I arrived.

Everyone *had spoken* by 10:00 A.M.

Writers sometimes use the simple past tense when they should use the past perfect.

▶ We built our cabin high on a pine knoll, forty feet above an
abandoned quarry that ~~was~~ *had been* flooded in 1920 to create a lake.

The building of the cabin and the flooding of the quarry both occurred in the past, but the flooding was completed before the time of building.

▶ By the time we arrived at the party, the guest of honor *had* left.

The past perfect tense is needed because the action of leaving was completed at a specific past time (*by the time we arrived*).

Some writers tend to overuse the past perfect tense. Do not use the past perfect if two past actions occurred at the same time.

▶ When we arrived in Paris, Pauline ~~had~~ met us at the train

station.

Sequence of tenses with infinitives and participles

An infinitive is the base form of a verb preceded by *to.* (See 63c.) Use the present infinitive to show action at the same time as or later than the action of the verb in the sentence.

▶ The club had hoped to ~~have~~ *raise* ~~raised~~ a thousand dollars by

April 1.

The action expressed in the infinitive (*to raise*) occurred later than the action of the sentence's verb (*had hoped*).

Use the perfect form of an infinitive (*to have* followed by the past participle) for an action occurring earlier than that of the verb in the sentence.

▶ Dan would like to ~~join~~ the navy, but he did not pass the
    have joined
    ^

physical.

The liking occurs in the present; the joining would have occurred in the past.

Like the tense of an infinitive, the tense of a participle is also governed by the tense of the sentence's verb. Use the present participle (ending in *-ing*) for an action occurring at the same time as that of the sentence's verb.

Hiking the Appalachian Trail in early spring, we spotted many wildflowers.

Use the past participle (such as *given* or *helped*) or the present perfect participle (*having* plus the past participle) for an action occurring before that of the verb.

Discovered off the coast of Florida, the *Atocha* yielded many treasures.

Having worked her way through college, Melanie graduated debt-free.

28b Use the subjunctive mood in the few contexts that require it.

There are three moods in English: the *indicative,* used for facts, opinions, and questions; the *imperative,* used for orders or advice; and the *subjunctive,* used in certain contexts to express wishes, requests, or conditions contrary to fact.

Of these moods, only the subjunctive causes problems for writers.

Forms of the subjunctive

In the subjunctive mood, present-tense verbs do not change form to indicate the number and person of the subject (see 21). Instead, the subjunctive uses the base form of the verb (*be, drive, employ*) with all subjects.

> It is important that you *be* [not *are*] prepared for the interview.

> We asked that she *drive* [not *drives*] more slowly.

Also, in the subjunctive mood, there is only one past-tense form of *be: were* (never *was*).

> If I *were* [not *was*] you, I'd proceed more cautiously.

Uses of the subjunctive

The subjunctive mood appears only in a few contexts: in contrary-to-fact clauses beginning with *if* or expressing a wish; in *that* clauses following verbs such as *ask, insist, recommend, request,* and *suggest;* and in certain set expressions.

IN CONTRARY-TO-FACT CLAUSES BEGINNING WITH *IF* When a subordinate clause beginning with *if* expresses a condition contrary to fact, use the subjunctive mood.

▶ If I ~~was~~ *were* a member of Congress, I would vote for that bill.

▶ We could be less cautious if Jake ~~was~~ *were* more trustworthy.

The verbs in these sentences express conditions that do not exist: The writer is not a member of Congress, and Jake is not trustworthy.

Do not use the subjunctive mood in *if* clauses expressing conditions that exist or may exist.

If Dana *wins* the contest, she will leave for Barcelona in June.

IN CONTRARY-TO-FACT CLAUSES EXPRESSING A WISH In formal English, the subjunctive is used in clauses expressing a wish or desire; in informal speech, however, the indicative is more common.

FORMAL I wish that Dr. Kurtinitis *were* my professor.

INFORMAL I wish that Dr. Kurtinitis *was* my professor.

IN *THAT* CLAUSES FOLLOWING VERBS SUCH AS *ASK, INSIST, REQUEST,* AND *SUGGEST* Because requests have not yet become reality, they are expressed in the subjunctive mood.

▶ Professor Moore insists that her students ~~are~~ *be* on time.

▶ We recommend that Lambert ~~files~~ *file* form 1050 soon.

IN CERTAIN SET EXPRESSIONS The subjunctive mood, once more widely used, remains in certain set expressions: *Be that as it may, as it were, far be it from me,* and so on.

GRAMMAR CHECKERS rarely flag problems with the subjunctive mood. They may at times question your correct use of the subjunctive, since your correct use will seem to violate the rules of subject-verb agreement (see 21). For example, a program advised using *was* instead of *were* in this correct sentence: *This isn't my dog; if it were, I would feed it.*

EXERCISE 28–1

Edit the following sentences to eliminate errors in verb tense or mood. If a sentence is correct, write "correct" after it. Answers to lettered sentences appear in the back of the book. Example:

> *had been*
> After the path ~~was~~ plowed, we were able to walk through the
>   ^
> park.

a. The palace of Knossos in Crete is believed to have been destroyed by fire around 1375 B.C.E.

b. Watson and Crick discovered the mechanism that controlled inheritance in all life: the workings of the DNA molecule.

c. When Hitler decided to kill the Jews in 1941, did he know that Himmler and his SS had mass murder in mind since 1938?

d. This isn't the Waldorf; if it were, we wouldn't be here.

e. As soon as my aunt applied for the position of pastor, the post was filled by an inexperienced seminary graduate who had been so hastily snatched that his mortarboard was still in midair.

1. Don Quixote, in Cervantes's novel, was an idealist ill suited for life in the real world.

2. The hurricane tore up the palm trees, lifted them over the hotel roof, and had dropped them into the swimming pool.

3. I would like to have been on the *Mayflower* but not to have lived through the first winter.

4. When the doctor said "It's a girl," I was stunned. For nine months I dreamed about playing baseball with my son.

5. If men and women were angels, no government would be necessary.

ON THE WEB

For an electronic exercise on verb tense and mood, go to
www.dianahacker.com/bedhandbook

and click on ▶ **Electronic Grammar Exercises**
▶ **E-ex 28–1**

PART VI

ESL Trouble Spots

Part VI has a special audience: speakers of English as a second language (ESL) who have learned English but continue to have problems in a few trouble spots.

29

Be alert to special problems with verbs.

Both native and nonnative speakers of English encounter the following problems with verbs, which are treated elsewhere in this handbook:

problems with active and passive voice (8)

problems with subject-verb agreement (21)

misuse of verb forms (27)

problems with tense and mood (28)

This section focuses on features of the English verb system that cause special problems for multilingual speakers.

29a Match helping verbs and main verbs appropriately.

Only certain combinations of helping verbs and main verbs are allowed in English. The correct combinations are discussed in this section, after the following review of helping verbs and main verbs.

Review of helping verbs and main verbs

Helping verbs always appear before main verbs. (See 61c.)

     HV MV   **HV**   **MV**
We *will leave* for the picnic at noon. *Do* you *want* a ride?

Some helping verbs—*have, do,* and *be*—change form to indicate tense; others, known as modals, do not.

FORMS OF *HAVE, DO,* AND *BE*
have, has, had
do, does, did
be, am, is, are, was, were, being, been

MODALS
can, could, may, might, must, shall, should, will, would (*also* ought to)

Every main verb has five forms (except *be,* which has eight forms). The following list shows these forms for the regular verb *help* and the irregular verb *give.* (See 27a for a list of common irregular verbs.)

BASE FORM	help, give
PAST TENSE	helped, gave
PAST PARTICIPLE	helped, given
PRESENT PARTICIPLE	helping, giving
-S FORM	helps, gives

Modal + base form

After the modals *can, could, may, might, must, shall, should, will,* and *would,* use the base form of the verb.

▶ My cousin will send~~s~~ us photographs from her wedding.

▶ We could ~~spoke~~ *speak* Spanish when we were young.

CAUTION: Do not use *to* in front of a main verb that follows a modal. (*Ought to* is an exception.)

▶ Gina can ~~to~~ drive us home if we miss the bus.

Do, does, *or* did + *base form*

After helping verbs that are a form of *do,* use the base form of the verb.

The helping verbs *do, does,* and *did* are used in three ways: (1) to express a negative meaning with the adverb *not* or *never,* (2) to ask a question, and (3) to emphasize a main verb used in a positive sense.

▶ Mariko does not want~~s~~ any more dessert.

▶ Did Janice ~~bought~~ buy the gift for Katherine?

▶ We do ~~hoping~~ hope that you will come to the retirement

party.

Have, has, *or* had + *past participle (perfect tenses)*

After the helping verb *have, has,* or *had,* use the past participle to form one of the perfect tenses. (See 28a.) Past participles usually end in *-ed, -d, -en, -n,* or *-t.* (See 27a.)

▶ On cold nights many churches in the city have ~~offer~~ offered shelter

to the homeless.

▶ An-Mei has not ~~speaking~~ spoken Chinese since she was a young

child.

The helping verb *have* is sometimes preceded by a modal helping verb such as *will: By nightfall, we will have driven five hundred miles.* (See also perfect tenses, 28a.)

Form of be + *present participle (progressive forms)*

After the helping verb *be, am, is, are, was, were,* or *been,* use the present participle to express a continuing action. (See progressive forms, 28a.)

▶ Carlos is ~~build~~ his house on a cliff overlooking the Pacific
       building
       ^

Ocean.

▶ Uncle Roy was ~~driven~~ a brand-new red Corvette.
       driving
       ^

The helping verb *be* must be preceded by a modal (*can, could, may, might, must, shall, should, will,* or *would*): *Edith will be going to Germany soon.* The helping verb *been* must be preceded by *have, has,* or *had: Andy has been studying English for five years.* (See also progressive forms, 28a.)

CAUTION: Certain verbs are not normally used in the progressive sense in English. In general, these verbs express a state of being or mental activity, not a dynamic action. Common examples are *appear, believe, belong, contain, have, hear, know, like, need, see, seem, taste, think, understand,* and *want.*

▶ I ~~am wanting~~ to see August Wilson's *Fences* at Arena Stage.
       want
       ^

Some of these verbs, however, have special uses in which progressive forms are normal. (*We are thinking about going to the Bahamas.*) You will need to make a note of exceptions as you encounter them.

Form of be + *past participle (passive voice)*

When a sentence is written in the passive voice, the subject receives the action instead of doing it: *Melissa was given a special award.* (See 8a.)

To form the passive voice, use *be, am, is, are, was, were, being,* or *been* followed by a past participle (usually ending in *-ed, -d, -en, -n,* or *-t*).

▶ *Bleak House* was ~~write~~ by Charles Dickens.
   written

▶ The scientists were ~~honor~~ for their work with dolphins.
   honored

When the helping verb is *be, being,* or *been,* it must be preceded by another helping verb. *Be* must be preceded by a modal such as *will: Senator Dixon will be defeated. Being* must be preceded by *am, is, are, was,* or *were: The child was being teased. Been* must be preceded by *have, has,* or *had: I have been invited to a party.*

CAUTION: Although they may seem to have passive meanings, verbs such as *occur, happen, sleep, die,* and *fall* may not be used to form the passive voice because they are intransitive. Only transitive verbs, those that take direct objects, may be used to form the passive voice. (See transitive and intransitive verbs, 62b.)

▶ The earthquake ~~was~~ occurred last Wednesday.

EXERCISE 29–1

Revise any sentences in which helping and main verbs do not match. You may need to look at the list of irregular verbs in 27a to determine the correct form of some irregular verbs. Answers to lettered sentences appear in the back of the book. Example:

Maureen should finds an apartment closer to campus.

a. We will making this a better country.
b. There is nothing in the world that TV has not touch on.

c. Did the landlord told you that he's going to raise the rent?
d. If we can afford to, we will to spend our vacation in Canada next summer.
e. The child's innocent world has been taking away from him.

1. The swimming pool was fill early this year, on May 1.
2. A serious accident was happened at the corner of Main Street and First Avenue last night.
3. My family has going to Sam's restaurant ever since we moved to this neighborhood.
4. I have ate Thai food only once before.
5. How often does Sandy takes her daughter to the doctor?

ON THE WEB

For an electronic exercise on helping verbs and main verbs, go to **www.dianahacker.com/bedhandbook**

and click on ▶ **Electronic Grammar Exercises**
▶ **E-ex 29–1**

GRAMMAR CHECKERS can catch some mismatches of helping and main verbs. They can tell you, for example, that the base form of the verb should be used after certain helping verbs, such as *did* and *could*, in incorrect sentences like these: *Did you understood my question? Could Alan comes with us?*

Programs can also catch some, but not all, problems with main verbs following forms of *have* or *be*. For example, grammar checkers flagged *have spend*, explaining that the past participle *spent* is required. However, programs failed to flag problems in many sentences, such as these: *Sasha has change her major three times. The provisions of the contract were broke by both parties.*

ESL trouble spots

29b In conditional sentences, choose verbs with care.

Conditional sentences state that one set of circumstances depends on whether another set of circumstances exists. Choosing verbs in such sentences can be tricky, partly because two clauses are involved: usually an *if* or a *when* or an *unless* clause and an independent clause.

Three kinds of conditional sentences are discussed in this section: factual, predictive, and speculative.

Factual

Factual conditional sentences express factual relationships. These relationships might be scientific truths, in which case the present tense is used in both clauses.

> If water cools to 32°, it *freezes.*

Or they might be present or past relationships that are habitually true, in which case the same tense is used in both clauses.

> When Sue *bicycles* along the canal, her dog *runs* ahead of her.
>
> Whenever the coach *asked* for help, I *volunteered.*

Predictive

Predictive conditional sentences are used to predict the future or to express future plans or possibilities. In such a sentence, an *if* or *unless* clause contains a present-tense verb; the verb in the independent clause usually consists of the modal *will, can, may, should,* or *might* followed by the base form of the verb.

> If you *practice* regularly, your tennis game *will improve.*
>
> We *will lose* our remaining wetlands unless we *act* now.

Speculative

Speculative conditional sentences are used for three purposes: (1) to speculate about unlikely possibilities in the present or future, (2) to speculate about events that did not happen in the past, and (3) to speculate about conditions that are contrary to fact. Each of these purposes requires its own combination of verbs.

UNLIKELY POSSIBILITIES   Somewhat confusingly, English uses the past tense in an *if* clause to speculate about a possible but unlikely condition in the present or future. The verb in the independent clause consists of *would, could,* or *might* plus the base form of the verb.

> If I *had* the time, I *would travel* to Senegal.
>
> If Stan *studied* harder, he *could master* calculus.

In the *if* clause, the past-tense form *were* is used with subjects that would normally take *was: Even if I were* [not *was*] *invited, I wouldn't go to the picnic.* (See also 28b.)

EVENTS THAT DID NOT HAPPEN   English uses the past perfect tense in an *if* clause to speculate about an event that did not happen in the past or to speculate about a state of being that was unreal in the past. (See past perfect tense, 28a.) The verb in the independent clause consists of *would have, could have,* or *might have* plus the past participle.

> If I *had saved* enough money, I *would have traveled* to Senegal last year.
>
> If Aunt Grace *had been* alive for your graduation, she *would have been* very proud.

CONDITIONS CONTRARY TO FACT   To speculate about conditions that are currently unreal or contrary to fact, English usually uses the past-tense verb *were* (never *was*) in an *if* clause. (See 28b.) The verb in the independent clause consists of *would, could,* or *might* plus the base form of the verb.

> If Grandmother *were* alive today, she *would be* very proud of you.

> I *would make* children's issues a priority if I *were* president.

 GRAMMAR CHECKERS do not flag problems with conditional sentences. The programs miss even obvious errors, such as this one: *Whenever I washed my car, it rains.*

EXERCISE 29–2

Edit the following conditional sentences for problems with verbs. In some cases, more than one revision is possible. Suggested revisions of lettered sentences appear in the back of the book. Example:

> *had*
> If I ~~have~~ time, I would study both French and Russian next
> ^
> semester.

a. He would have won the election if he went to the inner city to campaign.
b. If Verena wins a scholarship, she would go to graduate school.
c. Whenever there is a fire in our neighborhood, everybody came out to watch.
d. We will lose our largest client unless we would update our computer system.
e. If I live in California, I wouldn't need to buy a winter coat.

1. If our daughter was an angel, we wouldn't need to discipline her.

2. If everyone has voted in the last election, the results would have been very different.
3. The tenants will not pay the rent unless the landlord fixed the furnace.
4. When dark gray clouds appeared on a hot summer afternoon, a thunderstorm often follows.
5. Our daughter would have drowned if Officer Blake didn't risk his life to save her.

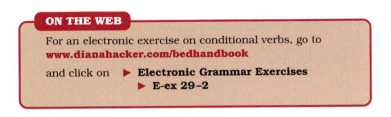

ON THE WEB

For an electronic exercise on conditional verbs, go to
www.dianahacker.com/bedhandbook

and click on ▶ **Electronic Grammar Exercises**
                ▶ **E-ex 29–2**

29c Become familiar with verbs that may be followed by gerunds or infinitives.

A gerund is a verb form that ends in *-ing* and is used as a noun: *sleeping, dreaming.* (See 63c.) An infinitive is the base form of the verb preceded by the word *to: to sleep, to dream.* The word *to* is not a preposition in this use but an infinitive marker. (See 63c.)

A few verbs may be followed by either a gerund or an infinitive; still others may be followed by an infinitive (either directly or with a noun or pronoun intervening) but not by a gerund.

Verb + gerund or infinitive

These commonly used verbs may be followed by a gerund or an infinitive, with little or no difference in meaning:

begin	continue	like	start
can't stand	hate	love	

I love *skiing.*   I love *to ski.*

With a few verbs, however, the choice of a gerund or infinitive changes the meaning dramatically:

forget	remember	stop	try

She stopped *speaking* to Lucia. [She no longer spoke to Lucia.]

She stopped *to speak* to Lucia. [She paused so that she could speak to Lucia.]

Verb + gerund

These verbs may be followed by a gerund but not by an infinitive:

admit	enjoy	postpone	resist
appreciate	escape	practice	risk
avoid	finish	put off	suggest
deny	imagine	quit	tolerate
discuss	miss	recall	

Have you finished *decorating* [not *to decorate*] the tree?

Bill enjoys *playing* [not *to play*] the piano.

Verb + infinitive

These verbs may be followed by an infinitive but not by a gerund:

agree	decide	manage	pretend	want
ask	expect	mean	promise	wish
beg	have	offer	refuse	
claim	hope	plan	wait	

We plan *to visit* [not *visiting*] the Yucatán next week.

Jill has offered *to water* [not *watering*] the plants while we are away.

Verb + noun or pronoun + infinitive

With certain verbs in the active voice, a noun or pronoun must come between the verb and the infinitive that follows it. The noun or pronoun usually names a person who is affected by the action.

advise	command	have	persuade	tell
allow	convince	instruct	remind	urge
cause	encourage	order	require	warn

The dean encourages *you to apply* for the scholarship.

The class asked *Luis to tell* the story of his escape.

A few verbs may be followed either by an infinitive directly or by an infinitive preceded by a noun or pronoun.

ask	expect	need	want	would like

We asked *to speak* to the congregation.

We asked *Rabbi Abrams to speak* to our congregation.

Verb + noun or pronoun + unmarked infinitive

An unmarked infinitive is an infinitive without *to*. A few verbs (known as "causative verbs") may be followed by a noun or pronoun and an unmarked (but not a marked) infinitive.

have ("cause")	let ("allow")	make ("force")

Absence makes *the heart grow* [not *to grow*] fonder.

Please let *me pay* [not *to pay*] for the tickets.

GRAMMAR CHECKERS can flag some, but not all, problems with gerunds and infinitives following verbs. For example, programs flagged many sentences with misused infinitives, such as this one: *Chris enjoys to play tennis.* Programs were less successful at flagging sentences with misused present participles, skipping past incorrect sentences like this one: *We want traveling to Hawaii next spring.*

EXERCISE 29–3

Form sentences by adding gerund or infinitive constructions to the following sentence openings. In some cases, more than one kind of construction may be possible. Possible sentences for lettered items appear in the back of the book. Example:

> Please remind *your sister to call me.*
>   ^

a. I enjoy
b. Will you help Samantha
c. The team hopes
d. Ricardo and his brothers miss
e. The babysitter let

1. Pollen makes
2. The club president asked
3. Next summer we plan
4. Waverly intends
5. Please stop

ON THE WEB

For an electronic exercise on verbs followed by gerunds or infinitives, go to
www.dianahacker.com/bedhandbook

and click on ▶ **Electronic Grammar Exercises**
            ▶ **E-ex 29–3**

29d Become familiar with commonly used two-word verbs.

Many verbs in English consist of a verb followed by a preposition or adverb known as a *particle.* (See 61c.) A two-word verb (also known as a *phrasal verb*) often expresses an idiomatic meaning that cannot be understood literally. Consider the verbs in the following sentences, for example:

> We *ran across* Professor Magnotto on the way to the bookstore.

> Calvin *dropped in* on his adviser this morning.

> Regina told me to *look* her *up* when I got to Seattle.

As you probably know, *ran across* means "encountered," *dropped in* means "paid an unexpected visit," and *look up* means "get in touch with." When you were first learning English, however, these two-word verbs must have suggested strange meanings.

Some two-word verbs are intransitive; they do not take direct objects. (See 62b.)

> This morning I *got up* at dawn.

Transitive two-word verbs (those that take direct objects) have particles that are either separable or inseparable. Separable particles may be separated from the verb by the direct object.

> Lucy *called* the wedding *off.*

When the direct object is a noun, a separable particle may also follow the verb immediately.

> At the last minute, Lucy *called off* the wedding.

When the direct object is a pronoun, however, the particle must be separated from the verb.

> Why was there no wedding? Lucy *called* it *off* [not *called off* it].

Inseparable particles must follow the verb immediately. A direct object cannot come between the verb and the particle.

> The police will *look into* the matter [not *look* the matter *into*].

29e   Do not omit needed verbs.

Some languages allow the omission of the verb when the meaning is clear without it; English does not.

▶ Jim ^is^ exceptionally intelligent.

▶ Many streets in San Francisco ^are^ very steep.

30

Use the articles *a, an,* and *the* appropriately.

Except for occasional difficulty in choosing between *a* and *an,* native speakers of English encounter few problems with articles. To speakers whose native language is not English, however, articles can prove troublesome, for the rules governing their use are surprisingly complex. This section summarizes those rules.

The definite article *the* and the indefinite articles *a* and *an* signal that a noun is about to appear. The noun may follow the article immediately or modifiers may intervene (see 61a and 61d).

the candidate, *the* exceptionally well qualified *candidate*

a sunset, *a* spectacular *sunset*

an apple, *an* appetizing *apple*

Articles are not the only words used to mark nouns. Other noun markers (sometimes called *determiners*) include possessive nouns (*Helen's*), numbers, and the following pronouns: *my, your, his, her, its, our, their, whose, this, that, these, those, all, any, each, either, every, few, many, more, most, much, neither, several, some.*

Usually an article is not used with another noun marker. Common exceptions include expressions such as *a few, the most,* and *all the.*

GRAMMAR CHECKERS can flag some missing or misused articles, pointing out, for example, that an article usually precedes a word such as *paintbrush* or *vehicle* or that the articles *a* and *an* are not usually used before a noncount noun such as *sugar* or *advice.*

However, the programs fail to flag many missing or misused articles. For example, in two paragraphs with eleven missing or misused articles, grammar checkers caught only two of the problems. In addition, the programs frequently suggest that an article is missing when it is not. For example, one program suggested that an article might be needed before *teacher* in this correct sentence: *My social studies teacher entered me in a public-speaking contest.*

30a Use *a* (or *an*) with singular count nouns whose specific identity is not known to the reader.

Count nouns refer to persons, places, or things that can be counted: *one girl, two girls; one city, three cities; one apple, four apples.* Noncount nouns refer to entities or abstractions that cannot be counted: *water, steel, air, furniture, patience, knowledge.* It is important to remember that noncount nouns vary from language to language. To see what nouns English categorizes as noncount nouns, refer to the list on page 363.

If a singular count noun names something not known to the reader — perhaps because it is being mentioned for the first time, perhaps because its specific identity is unknown even to the writer — the noun should be preceded by *a* or *an* unless it has been preceded by another noun marker. *A* (or *an*) usually means "one among many" but can also mean "any one."

▶ Mary Beth arrived in _∧ *a* limousine.

▶ We are looking for _∧ *an* apartment close to the lake.

NOTE: *A* is used before a consonant sound: *a banana, a tree, a picture, a hand, a happy child. An* is used before a vowel sound: *an eggplant, an occasion, an uncle, an hour, an honorable person.* Notice that words beginning with *h* can have either a consonant sound (*hand, happy*) or a vowel sound (*hour, honorable*). (See also the Glossary of Usage: *a, an.*)

30b Do not use *a* (or *an*) with noncount nouns.

A (or *an*) is not used to mark noncount nouns, such as *sugar, gold, honesty,* or *jewelry.* A list of commonly used noncount nouns is given in the chart on page 363.

Commonly used noncount nouns

FOOD AND DRINK

bacon, beef, bread, broccoli, butter, cabbage, candy, cauliflower, celery, cereal, cheese, chicken, chocolate, coffee, corn, cream, fish, flour, fruit, ice cream, lettuce, meat, milk, oil, pasta, rice, salt, spinach, sugar, tea, water, wine, yogurt

NONFOOD SUBSTANCES

air, cement, coal, dirt, gasoline, gold, paper, petroleum, plastic, rain, silver, snow, soap, steel, wood, wool

ABSTRACT NOUNS

advice, anger, beauty, confidence, courage, employment, fun, happiness, health, honesty, information, intelligence, knowledge, love, poverty, satisfaction, truth, wealth

OTHER

biology (and other areas of study), clothing, equipment, furniture, homework, jewelry, luggage, lumber, machinery, mail, money, news, poetry, pollution, research, scenery, traffic, transportation, violence, weather, work

NOTE: A few noncount nouns may also be used as count nouns, especially in informal English: *Bill loves chocolate; Bill offered me a chocolate. I'll have coffee; I'll have a coffee.*

▶ Claudia asked her mother for ~~an~~ advice.

If you want to express an approximate amount, you can often use one of the following quantifiers with a noncount noun.

QUANTIFIER	NONCOUNT NOUN
a great deal of	candy, courage
a little	salt, rain
any	sugar, homework
enough	bread, wood, money
less	meat, violence
little (*or* a little)	knowledge, time
more	coffee, information
much (*or* a lot of)	snow, pollution
plenty of	paper, lumber
some	tea, news, work

To express a more specific amount, you can often precede a noncount noun with a unit word that is typically associated with it. Here are some common combinations.

A OR *AN* + UNIT + *OF*	NONCOUNT NOUNS
a bottle of	water, vinegar
a carton of	ice cream, milk, yogurt
an ear of	corn
a head of	cabbage, lettuce
a loaf of	bread
a piece of	meat, furniture, advice
a pound of	butter, sugar
a quart of	milk, ice cream
a slice of	bread, bacon

CAUTION: Noncount nouns do not have plural forms, and they should not be used with numbers or words suggesting plurality (such as *several, many, a few, a couple of, a number of*).

▶ We need some informations̸ about rain forests.

▶ Do you have ~~many~~ *much* money with you?

30c Use *the* with most nouns whose specific identity is known to the reader.

The definite article *the* is used with most nouns whose iden-tity is known to the reader. (For exceptions, see 30d.) Usu-ally the identity will be clear to the reader for one of the following reasons:

—The noun has been previously mentioned.

—A phrase or a clause following the noun restricts its identity.

—A superlative such as *best* or *most intelligent* makes the noun's identity specific.

—The noun describes a unique person, place, or thing.

—The context or situation makes the noun's identity clear.

► A truck loaded with dynamite cut in front of our van.
                                                    the
  When truck skidded a few seconds later, we almost plowed
            ^
  into it.

  The noun *truck* is preceded by *A* when it is first mentioned. When the noun is mentioned again, it is preceded by *the* since readers now know the specific truck being discussed.

                                 the
► Bob warned me that gun on the top shelf of the cupboard was
                        ^
  loaded.

  The phrase *on the top shelf of the cupboard* identifies the spe-cific gun.

                                    the
► Our petite daughter dated tallest boy in her class.
                            ^
  The superlative *tallest* restricts the identity of the noun *boy.*

▶ During an eclipse, one should not look directly at ~~the~~ sun.

There is only one sun in our solar system, so its identity is clear.

▶ Please don't slam ~~the~~ door when you leave.

Both the speaker and the listener know which door is meant.

30d Do not use *the* with plural or noncount nouns meaning "all" or "in general"; do not use *the* with most singular proper nouns.

When a plural or a noncount noun means "all" or "in general," it is not marked with *the*.

▶ ~~The~~ *F*ountains are an expensive element of landscape design.

▶ In some parts of the world, ~~the~~ rice is preferred to all other grains.

As you probably know, proper nouns—which name specific people, places, or things—are capitalized. Although there are many exceptions, *the* is not used with most singular proper nouns, such as *Judge Hennessey, Spring Street,* or *Lake Huron.* However, *the* is used with plural proper nouns, such as *the United Nations, the Bahamas,* and *the Finger Lakes.*

Geographical names create problems because there are so many exceptions to the rules. When in doubt, consult the chart on the next page or ask a native speaker.

Geographical names

WHEN TO OMIT *THE*

streets, squares, parks	Ivy Street, Union Square, Denali National Park
cities, states, counties	Miami, Idaho, Bee County
most countries	Italy, Nigeria, China
continents	South America, Africa
bays, single lakes	Tampa Bay, Lake Geneva
single mountains, islands	Mount Everest, Crete

WHEN TO USE *THE*

united countries	the United States, the Republic of China
large regions, deserts	the East Coast, the Sahara
peninsulas	the Iberian Peninsula
oceans, seas, gulfs	the Pacific, the Dead Sea, the Persian Gulf
canals and rivers	the Panama Canal, the Amazon
mountain ranges	the Rocky Mountains, the Alps
groups of islands	the Solomon Islands

EXERCISE 30–1

Articles have been omitted from the following story, adapted from *Zen Flesh, Zen Bones,* compiled by Paul Reps. Insert the articles *a, an,* and *the* where English requires them and be prepared to explain the reasons for your choices.

Moon Cannot Be Stolen

Ryokan, who was Zen master, lived simple life in little hut at foot of mountain. One evening thief visited hut only to discover there was nothing in it to steal.

Ryokan returned and caught him. "You may have come long way to visit me," he told prowler, "and you should not return empty-handed. Please take my clothes as gift." Thief was bewildered. He took Ryokan's clothes and slunk away. Ryokan sat naked, watching moon. "Poor fellow," he mused, "I wish I could give him this beautiful moon."

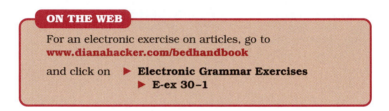

ON THE WEB

For an electronic exercise on articles, go to
www.dianahacker.com/bedhandbook

and click on ▶ **Electronic Grammar Exercises**
▶ **E-ex 30–1**

31

Be aware of other potential trouble spots.

31a   Do not omit subjects or the expletive *there* or *it*.

English requires a subject for all sentences except imperatives, in which the subject *you* is understood (*Give to the poor*). (See 62a.) If your native language allows the omission of an explicit subject in other sentences or clauses, be especially alert to this requirement in English.

▶ *I have*
~~Have~~ a large collection of baseball cards.
  ^

▶ Your Aunt Geraldine is very energetic; *she* seems young
                                              ^

for her age.

When the subject has been moved from its normal position before the verb, English sometimes requires an expletive (*there* or *it*) at the beginning of the sentence or clause. (See 62c.) *There* is used at the beginning of a sentence or clause to draw the reader's (or listener's) attention to the location or existence of something.

▶ *There is*
~~Is~~ an apple in the refrigerator.
 ^

▶ As you know, *there* are many religious sects in India.
 ^

Notice that the verb agrees with the subject that follows it: *apple is, sects are.* (See 21g.)

In one of its uses, the word *it* functions as an expletive, to call attention to a subject following the verb.

▶ *It is*
~~Is~~ healthy to eat fruit and grains.
 ^

▶ *It is*
~~Is~~ clear that we must change our approach.
 ^

The subjects of these sentences are *to eat fruit and grains* (an infinitive phrase) and *that we must change our approach* (a noun clause). (See 63c and 63b.)

As you probably know, the word *it* is also used as the subject of sentences describing the weather or temperature, stating the time, indicating distance, or suggesting an environmental fact.

It is raining in the valley, and it is snowing in the mountains.

In July, it is very hot in Arizona.

It is 9:15 A.M.

It is three hundred miles to Chicago.

It gets noisy in our dorm on weekends.

> **GRAMMAR CHECKERS** can flag some sentences with a
> missing expletive (*there* or *it*), but they often misdiagnose
> the problem, suggesting that if a sentence opens with a
> word such as *Is* or *Are*, it may need a question mark at the
> end. Consider this sentence, which grammar checkers
> flagged: *Are two grocery stores on Elm Street.* Clearly, the
> sentence doesn't need a question mark. What it needs is
> an expletive: *There are two grocery stores on Elm Street.*

31b Do not repeat the subject of a sentence.

English does not allow a subject to be repeated in its own
clause.

▶ **The doctor ~~she~~ advised me to cut down on salt.**

The pronoun *she* repeats the subject *doctor.*

The subject of a sentence should not be repeated even if a
word group intervenes between the subject and the verb.

▶ **The car that had been stolen ~~it~~ was found.**

The pronoun *it* repeats the subject *car.*

31c Do not repeat an object or an adverb in an adjective clause.

In some languages an object or an adverb is repeated later in
the adjective clause in which it appears; in English such
repetitions are not allowed. Adjective clauses begin with relative pronouns (*who, whom, whose, which, that*) or relative
adverbs (*when, where*), and these words always serve a

grammatical function within the clauses they introduce. (See 63b.) Another word in the clause cannot also serve that same grammatical function.

When a relative pronoun functions as the object of a verb or the object of a preposition, do not add another word with the same function later in the clause.

▶ The puppy ran after the car that we were riding in. ~~it.~~

The relative pronoun *that* is the object of the preposition *in*, so the object *it* is not allowed.

Even when the relative pronoun has been omitted, do not add another word with its same function.

▶ The puppy ran after the car we were riding in. ~~it.~~

The relative pronoun *that* is understood even though it is not present in the sentence.

Like a relative pronoun, a relative adverb should not be echoed later in its clause.

▶ The place where I work ~~there~~ is one hour from my apartment

in the city.

The adverb *there* should not echo the relative adverb *where*.

GRAMMAR CHECKERS usually fail to flag sentences with repeated subjects or objects. One program flagged some sentences with repeated subjects, such as this one: *The roses that they brought home they cost three dollars each.* However, the program misdiagnosed the problem, calling the sentence a run-on. The sentence is not a run-on; the problem is that the second *they* repeats the subject *roses*.

EXERCISE 31–1

In the following sentences, add needed subjects or expletives and delete any repeated subjects, objects, or adverbs. Answers to lettered sentences appear in the back of the book. Example:

> **Nancy is the woman whom I talked to ~~her~~ last week.**

a. Are some cartons of ice cream in the freezer.
b. I don't use the subway because am afraid.
c. The prime minister she is the most popular leader in my country.
d. We tried to get in touch with the same manager whom we spoke to him earlier.
e. Recently have been a number of earthquakes in Turkey.

1. We visited an island where several ancient ruins are being excavated there.
2. In this city is difficult to find a high-paying job.
3. Foreign tourists sometimes unhappy about the high prices here.
4. Is a banyan tree in our backyard.
5. The neighbor whom we trusted he was a thief.

ON THE WEB

For an electronic exercise on omitted and repeated words, go to **www.dianahacker.com/bedhandbook**

and click on   ▶ **Electronic Grammar Exercises**
                ▶ **E-ex 31–1**

31d   Place adjectives and adverbs with care.

Adjectives modify nouns or pronouns; adverbs modify verbs, adjectives, or other adverbs (see 61d and 61e). Both native and nonnative speakers encounter problems in the use of adjectives and adverbs (see 26). For nonnative speakers, the placement of adjectives and adverbs can also be troublesome.

Placement of adjectives

No doubt you have already learned that in English adjectives usually precede the nouns they modify and that they may also appear following linking verbs. (See 26b and 62b.)

Janine wore a *new* necklace. Janine's necklace was *new.*

When adjectives pile up in front of a noun, however, you may sometimes have difficulty arranging them. English is quite particular about the order of cumulative adjectives, those not separated by commas. (See 32d.)

> Janine was wearing a *beautiful antique silver* necklace [not *silver antique beautiful* necklace].

The chart on page 374 shows the order in which cumulative adjectives ordinarily appear in front of the noun they modify. This list is just a general guide; don't be surprised when you encounter exceptions.

NOTE: Long strings of cumulative adjectives tend to be awkward. As a rule, use no more than two or three of them between the article (or other noun marker) and the noun modified. Here are several examples:

> a beautiful old pine table
> two enormous French urns
> an exotic purple jungle flower
>
> Susan's large round painting
> some small blue medicine
>   bottles

Placement of adverbs

Adverbs modifying verbs appear in various positions: at the beginning or end of the sentence, before or after the verb, or between a helping verb and its main verb.

Usual order of cumulative adjectives

ARTICLE OR OTHER NOUN MARKER

a, an, the, her, Joe's, two, many, some

EVALUATIVE WORD

attractive, dedicated, delicious, ugly, disgusting

SIZE

large, enormous, small, little

LENGTH OR SHAPE

long, short, round, square

AGE

new, old, young, antique

COLOR

yellow, blue, crimson

NATIONALITY

French, Scandinavian, Vietnamese

RELIGION

Catholic, Protestant, Jewish, Muslim

MATERIAL

silver, walnut, wool, marble

NOUN/ADJECTIVE

tree (as in *tree* house), kitchen (as in *kitchen* table)

THE NOUN MODIFIED

house, sweater, bicycle, bread, woman, priest

Slowly, we drove along the rain-slick road.

Mia handled the teapot *very carefully.*

Martin *always* wins our tennis matches.

Christina is *rarely* late for our lunch dates.

My daughter has *often* spoken of you.

An adverb may not, however, be placed between a verb and its direct object.

▶ Mother wrapped ~~carefully~~ the gift/ *carefully.*

The adverb *carefully* may be placed at the beginning or at the end of this sentence or before the verb. It cannot appear after the verb because the verb is followed by the direct object *the gift.*

GRAMMAR CHECKERS do not flag problems with the placement of adjectives and adverbs. They can, however, flag a few other problems with adjectives and adverbs. See the grammar checker advice on page 310.

EXERCISE 31–2

Using the chart on page 374, arrange the following modifiers and nouns in their proper order. Answers to lettered items appear in the back of the book. Example:

> *two new French racing bicycles*
> **new, French, two, bicycles, racing**

a. woman, young, an, Vietnamese, attractive
b. dedicated, a, priest, Catholic
c. old, her, sweater, blue, wool
d. delicious, Joe's, Scandinavian, bread
e. many, cages, bird, antique, beautiful

1. round, two, marble, tables, large
2. several, yellow, tulips, tiny
3. a, sports, classic, car
4. courtyard, a, square, small, brick
5. charming, restaurants, Italian, several

ON THE WEB

For an electronic exercise on the order of cumulative adjectives, go to **www.dianahacker.com/bedhandbook**

and click on ▶ **Electronic Grammar Exercises**
▶ **E-ex 31–2**

31e Distinguish between present participles and past participles used as adjectives.

Both present and past participles may be used as adjectives. The present participle always ends in *-ing.* Past participles usually end in *-ed, -d, -en, -n,* or *-t.* (See 27a.)

> **PRESENT PARTICIPLES**   confusing, speaking
>
> **PAST PARTICIPLES**   confused, spoken

Participles used as adjectives can precede the nouns they modify; they can also follow linking verbs, in which case they describe the subject of the sentence. (See 62b.)

> It was a *depressing* movie. Jim was a *depressed* young man.
>
> The essay was *confusing.* The student was *confused.*

A present participle should describe a person or thing causing or stimulating an experience; a past participle should describe a person or thing undergoing an experience.

The lecturer was *boring* [not *bored*].

The audience was *bored* [not *boring*].

In the first example, the lecturer is causing boredom, not experiencing it. In the second example, the audience is experiencing boredom, not causing it.

The participles that cause the most trouble for nonnative speakers are those describing mental states:

annoying / annoyed	exhausting / exhausted
boring / bored	fascinating / fascinated
confusing / confused	frightening / frightened
depressing / depressed	satisfying / satisfied
exciting / excited	surprising / surprised

GRAMMAR CHECKERS do not flag problems with present and past participles used as adjectives. Not surprisingly, the programs have no way of knowing the meaning a writer intends. For example, both of the following sentences could be correct, depending on the writer's meaning: *My roommate was annoying. My roommate was annoyed.*

EXERCISE 31–3

Edit the following sentences for proper use of present and past participles. If a sentence is correct, write "correct" after it. Answers to lettered sentences appear in the back of the book. Example:

excited
Danielle and Monica were very ~~exciting~~ to be going to a
                                        ^
Broadway show for the first time.

a. Listening to everyone's complaints all day was irritated.
b. During the long lecture, many students appeared boring.
c. His skill at chess is amazing.

d. After a great deal of research, the scientist made a fascinated discovery.
e. That blackout was one of the most frightened experiences I've ever had.

1. I couldn't concentrate on my homework because I was distracted.
2. The directions to the new board game seem extremely complicating.
3. How interested are you in visiting Civil War battlefields?
4. The statistics on childhood poverty in the United States were depressing.
5. Even after the lecturer went over the main points again, the students were still confusing.

ON THE WEB

For an electronic exercise on present and past participles, go to **www.dianahacker.com/bedhandbook**

and click on ▶ **Electronic Grammar Exercises**
▶ **E-ex 31–3**

31f Become familiar with common prepositions that show time and place.

The most frequently used prepositions in English are *at, by, for, from, in, of, on, to,* and *with.* Each of these prepositions has a variety of uses that must be learned gradually, in context.

Prepositions that indicate time and place can be difficult to master because the differences among them are subtle and idiomatic. The chart in this section limits itself to four troublesome prepositions that show time and place: *at, on, in,* and *by.*

Not every possible use is listed in the chart, so don't be surprised when you encounter exceptions and idiomatic

At, on, in, *and* by *to show time and place*

Showing time

AT *at* a specific time: *at* 7:20, *at* dawn, *at* dinner

ON *on* a specific day or date: *on* June 4

IN *in* a part of a 24-hour period: *in* the afternoon, *in* the daytime [but *at* night]

    in a year or month: *in* 1999, *in* July

    in a period of time: finished *in* three hours

BY *by* a specific time or date: *by* 4:15, *by* Christmas

Showing place

AT *at* a meeting place or location: *at* home, *at* the club

    at the edge of something: sitting *at* the desk

    at the corner of something: turning *at* the intersection

    at a target: throwing the snowball *at* Lucy

ON *on* a surface: placed *on* the table, hanging *on* the wall

    on an electronic medium: *on* television, *on* the Internet

IN *in* an enclosed space: *in* the garage, *in* the envelope

    in a geographic location: *in* San Diego, *in* Texas

    in a print medium: *in* a book, *in* a magazine

BY *by* a landmark: *by* the fence, *by* the flagpole

uses that you must learn one at a time. For example, in English we ride *in* a car but *on* a bus, train, or subway. And when we fly *on* (not *in*) a plane, we are not sitting on top of the plane.

EXERCISE 31–4

In the following sentences, replace prepositions that are not used correctly. If a sentence is correct, write "correct" after it. Answers to lettered sentences appear in the back of the book. Example:

> *at*
> The play begins ~~on~~ 7:20 P.M.
> ^

a. Whenever we eat at the Centerville Diner, we sit at a small table on the corner of the room.

b. In the 1980s, the gap between the rich and the poor in the United States became wider.

c. In Wednesdays he leaves work early so he can lift weights at his health club.

d. Our rabbi moved to the Northwest in 1994 and has been with our temple at Seattle since 1996.

1. I don't feel safe walking on my neighborhood in night.

2. If the train is on time, it will arrive on six o'clock at the morning.

3. In the corner of the room there is a large bookcase with a pair of small Russian dolls standing at the top shelf.

4. She licked the stamp, stuck it in the envelope, put the envelope on her pocket, and walked to the nearest mailbox.

5. The mailbox was in the intersection of Laidlaw Avenue and Williams Street.

ON THE WEB

For an electronic exercise on prepositions showing time and place, go to **www.dianahacker.com/bedhandbook**

and click on   ▶ **Electronic Grammar Exercises**
                  ▶ **E-ex 31–4**

Punctuation

32

The comma

The comma was invented to help readers. Without it, sentence parts can collide into one another unexpectedly, causing misreadings.

> **CONFUSING**   If you cook Elmer will do the dishes.

> **CONFUSING**   While we were eating a rattlesnake approached our campsite.

Add commas in the logical places (after *cook* and *eating*), and suddenly all is clear. No longer is Elmer being cooked, the rattlesnake being eaten.

Various rules have evolved to prevent such misreadings and to speed readers along through complex grammatical structures. Those rules are detailed in this section. (Section 33 explains when not to use commas.)

32a   Use a comma before a coordinating conjunction joining independent clauses.

When a coordinating conjunction connects two or more independent clauses—word groups that could stand alone as separate sentences—a comma must precede it. There are seven coordinating conjunctions in English: *and, but, or, nor, for, so,* and *yet.*

A comma tells readers that one independent clause has come to a close and that another is about to begin.

▶ Nearly everyone has heard of love at first sight, but I fell in

   love at first dance.

GRAMMAR CHECKERS have mixed success in flagging missing or misused commas. They can tell you that a comma is usually used before *which* but not before *that* (see 32e), and they can flag some missing commas after an introductory word or word group or between items in a series. In general, however, the programs are unreliable. For example, in an essay with ten missing commas and five misused ones, a grammar checker spotted only one missing comma (after the word *therefore*).

EXCEPTION: If the two independent clauses are short and there is no danger of misreading, the comma may be omitted.

The plane took off and we were on our way.

CAUTION: As a rule, do *not* use a comma to separate coordinate word groups that are not independent clauses. (See 33a.)

▶ A good money manager controls expenses/ and invests

surplus dollars to meet future needs.

The word group following *and* is not an independent clause; it is the second half of a compound predicate.

32b Use a comma after an introductory clause or phrase.

The most common introductory word groups are clauses and phrases functioning as adverbs. Such word groups usually tell when, where, how, why, or under what conditions the main action of the sentence occurred. (See 63a–63c.)

A comma tells readers that the introductory clause or phrase has come to a close and that the main part of the sentence is about to begin.

▶ **When Irwin was ready to eat, his cat jumped onto the table.**
                                    ^

Without the comma, readers may have Irwin eating his cat. The comma signals that *his cat* is the subject of a new clause, not part of the introductory one.

▶ **Near a small stream at the bottom of the canyon, the park**
                                                        ^

rangers discovered an abandoned mine.

The comma tells readers that the introductory prepositional phrase has come to a close.

EXCEPTION: The comma may be omitted after a short adverb clause or phrase if there is no danger of misreading.

In no time we were at 2,800 feet.

Sentences also frequently begin with participial phrases describing the noun or pronoun immediately following them. The comma tells readers that they are about to learn the identity of the person or thing described; therefore, the comma is usually required even when the phrase is short. (See 63c.)

▶ **Thinking his motorcade drive through Dallas was routine,**
                                                          ^

President Kennedy smiled and waved at the crowds.

▶ **Buried under layers of younger rocks, the earth's oldest**
                                          ^

rocks contain no fossils.

NOTE: Other introductory word groups include transitional expressions and absolute phrases (see 32f).

EXERCISE 32-1

Add or delete commas where necessary in the following sentences. If a sentence is correct, write "correct" after it. Answers to lettered sentences appear in the back of the book. Example:

> **Because it rained all Labor Day, our picnic was rather soggy.**
> ⌃

a. Alisa brought the injured bird home, and fashioned a splint out of Popsicle sticks for its wing.
b. Considered the first Western philosopher Thales believed that water was the elemental principle underlying all things.
c. If you complete the enclosed card, and return it within two weeks, you will receive a free breakfast during your stay.
d. After retiring from the New York City Ballet in 1965, legendary dancer Maria Tallchief went on to found the Chicago City Ballet.
e. Uncle Swen's dulcimers disappeared as soon as he put them up for sale but he always kept one for himself.

1. When the runaway race car crashed the gas tank exploded.
2. He pushed the car beyond the tollgate, and poured a bucket of water on the smoking hood.
3. Lighting the area like a second moon the helicopter circled the scene.
4. As the concert began, we heard a tremendous explosion.
5. Many musicians of Bach's time played several instruments but few mastered them as early or played with as much expression as Bach.

32c Use a comma between all items in a series.

When three or more items are presented in a series, those items should be separated from one another with commas. Items in a series may be single words, phrases, or clauses.

▶ **Bubbles of air, leaves, ferns, bits of wood, and insects are**
⌃

often found trapped in amber.

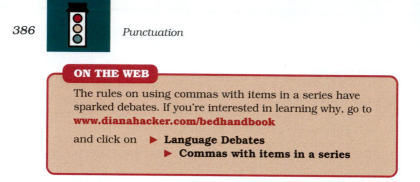

ON THE WEB

The rules on using commas with items in a series have sparked debates. If you're interested in learning why, go to

www.dianahacker.com/bedhandbook

and click on   ▶ **Language Debates**
                ▶ **Commas with items in a series**

Although some writers view the comma between the last two items as optional, most experts advise using the comma because its omission can result in ambiguity or misreading.

▶ Uncle David willed me all of his property, houses, and

warehouses.

Did Uncle David will his property *and* houses *and* warehouses—or simply his property, consisting of houses and warehouses? If the former meaning is intended, a comma is necessary to prevent ambiguity.

▶ The activities include a search for lost treasure, dubious

financial dealings, much discussion of ancient heresies, and

midnight orgies.

Without the comma, the activities seem to include discussing orgies, not participating in them. The comma makes it clear that *midnight orgies* is a separate item in the series.

32d   Use a comma between coordinate adjectives not joined with *and.* Do not use a comma between cumulative adjectives.

When two or more adjectives each modify a noun separately, they are coordinate.

Roberto is a *warm, gentle, affectionate* father.

Adjectives are coordinate if they can be joined with *and* (warm *and* gentle *and* affectionate).

Adjectives that do not modify the noun separately are cumulative.

Three large gray shapes moved slowly toward us.

Beginning with the adjective closest to the noun *shapes*, these modifiers lean on one another, piggyback style, with each modifying a larger word group. *Gray* modifies *shapes*, *large* modifies *gray shapes*, and *three* modifies *large gray shapes*. We cannot insert the word *and* between cumulative adjectives (three *and* large *and* gray shapes).

COORDINATE ADJECTIVES

▶ **Patients with severe, irreversible brain damage should not be**
         ^
put on life support systems.

Adjectives are coordinate if they can be connected with *and: severe and irreversible.*

CUMULATIVE ADJECTIVES

▶ **Ira ordered a rich/ chocolate/ layer cake.**

Ira didn't order a cake that was rich and chocolate and layer: He ordered a *layer cake* that was *chocolate*, a *chocolate layer cake* that was *rich.*

EXERCISE 32–2

Add or delete commas where necessary in the following sentences. If a sentence is correct, write "correct" after it. Answers to lettered sentences appear in the back of the book. Example:

We gathered our essentials, took off for the great outdoors**,**
∧

and ignored the fact that it was Friday the 13th.

a. The cold impersonal atmosphere of the university was unbearable.
b. An ambulance threaded its way through police cars, fire trucks and irate citizens.
c. The 1812 Overture is a stirring, magnificent piece of music.
d. After two broken arms, three cracked ribs and one concussion, Ken quit the varsity football team.
e. My cat's pupils had constricted to small black shining dots.

1. We prefer our staff to be orderly, prompt and efficient.
2. For breakfast the children ordered cornflakes, English muffins with peanut butter and cherry Cokes.
3. It was a small, unimportant part, but I was happy to have it.
4. Cyril was clad in a luminous orange rain suit and a brilliant white helmet.
5. Anne Frank and thousands like her were forced to hide in attics, cellars and secret rooms in an effort to save their lives.

32e Use commas to set off nonrestrictive elements. Do not use commas to set off restrictive elements.

Word groups describing nouns or pronouns (adjective clauses, adjective phrases, and appositives) are restrictive or nonrestrictive. A *restrictive* element defines or limits the meaning of the word it modifies and is therefore essential to the meaning of the sentence. Because it contains essential information, a restrictive element is not set off with commas.

> **RESTRICTIVE** For camp the children needed clothes *that were washable.*

If you remove a restrictive element from a sentence, the meaning changes significantly, becoming more general than you intended. The writer of the example sentence does not mean that the children needed clothes in general. The intended meaning is more limited: the children needed *wash-able* clothes.

A *nonrestrictive* element describes a noun or pronoun whose meaning has already been clearly defined or limited. Because it contains nonessential or parenthetical information, a nonrestrictive element is set off with commas.

> **NONRESTRICTIVE**   For camp the children needed sturdy shoes, *which were expensive.*

If you remove a nonrestrictive element from a sentence, the meaning does not change dramatically. Some meaning is lost, to be sure, but the defining characteristics of the person or thing described remain the same as before. The children needed *sturdy shoes,* and these happened to be expensive.

NOTE: Often it is difficult to tell whether a word group is restrictive or nonrestrictive without seeing it in context and considering the writer's meaning. Both of the following sentences are grammatically correct, but their meaning is slightly different.

> The dessert made with fresh raspberries was delicious.

> The dessert, made with fresh raspberries, was delicious.

In the example without commas, the phrase *made with fresh raspberries* tells readers which of two or more desserts the writer is referring to. In the example with commas, the phrase merely adds information about the particular dessert served with the meal.

Adjective clauses

Adjective clauses are patterned like sentences, containing subjects and verbs, but they function within sentences as modifiers of nouns or pronouns. They always follow the word they modify, usually immediately. Adjective clauses

Punctuation

begin with a relative pronoun (*who, whom, whose, which, that*) or with a relative adverb (*where, when*).

Nonrestrictive adjective clauses are set off with commas; restrictive adjective clauses are not.

NONRESTRICTIVE CLAUSE

▶ Ed's house, which is located on thirteen acres, was completely

furnished with bats in the rafters and mice in the kitchen.

The adjective clause *which is located on thirteen acres* does not restrict the meaning of *Ed's house,* so the information is nonessential.

RESTRICTIVE CLAUSE

▶ An office manager for a corporation/ that had government

contracts/ asked her supervisor whether she could

reprimand her co-workers for smoking.

Because the adjective clause *that had government contracts* identifies the corporation, the information is essential.

NOTE: Use *that* only with restrictive clauses. Many writers prefer to use *which* only with nonrestrictive clauses, but usage varies.

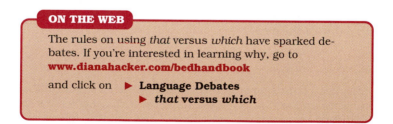

ON THE WEB

The rules on using *that* versus *which* have sparked debates. If you're interested in learning why, go to
www.dianahacker.com/bedhandbook

and click on ▶ **Language Debates**
▶ ***that* versus *which***

Phrases functioning as adjectives

Prepositional or verbal phrases functioning as adjectives may be restrictive or nonrestrictive. Nonrestrictive phrases are set off with commas; restrictive phrases are not.

NONRESTRICTIVE PHRASE

▶ The helicopter, with its 100,000-candlepower spotlight illuminating the area, circled above.

The *with* phrase is nonessential because its purpose is not to specify which of two or more helicopters is being discussed.

RESTRICTIVE PHRASE

▶ One corner of the attic was filled with newspapers/ dating from the turn of the century.

Dating from the turn of the century restricts the meaning of *newspapers,* so the comma should be omitted.

Appositives

An appositive is a noun or noun phrase that renames a nearby noun. Nonrestrictive appositives are set off with commas; restrictive appositives are not.

NONRESTRICTIVE APPOSITIVE

▶ Darwin's most important book, *On the Origin of Species,* was the result of many years of research.

Most important restricts the meaning to one book, so the appositive *On the Origin of Species* is nonrestrictive.

RESTRICTIVE APPOSITIVE

▶ The song/ "Fire It Up/ was blasted out of amplifiers ten feet tall.

Once they've read *song*, readers still don't know precisely which song the writer means. The appositive following *song* restricts its meaning.

EXERCISE 32–3

Add or delete commas where necessary in the following sentences. If a sentence is correct, write "correct" after it. Answers to lettered sentences appear in the back of the book. Example:

My youngest sister, who plays left wing on the team, now lives at The Sands, a beach house near Los Angeles.

a. Choreographer Alvin Ailey's best-known work *Revelations* is more than just a crowd pleaser.
b. Twyla Tharp's contemporary ballet *Push Comes to Shove* was made famous by Russian dancer Baryshnikov. [Tharp has written more than one contemporary ballet.]
c. The woman running for the council seat in the fifth district has a long history of community service.
d. A member of an organization, that provides housing for AIDS patients, was also appointed to the commission.
e. A 1911 fire at the Triangle Shirtwaist Company which killed 146 sweatshop workers led to reforms in working conditions.

1. I had the pleasure of talking to a woman who had just returned from India where she had lived for ten years.
2. Sally's best friend Sid Phillips has been playing the guitar since the age of seven.
3. The gentleman waiting for the prescription is Mr. Rhee.

4. *Where the Wild Things Are,* the 1964 Caldecott Medal winner, is my nephew's favorite book.
5. The flame crawled up a few blades of grass to reach a low-hanging palmetto branch which quickly ignited.

32f Use commas to set off transitional and parenthetical expressions, absolute phrases, and elements expressing contrast.

Transitional expressions

Transitional expressions serve as bridges between sentences or parts of sentences. They include conjunctive adverbs such as *however, therefore,* and *moreover* and transitional phrases such as *for example, as a matter of fact,* and *in other words.* (For more complete lists, see 34b.)

When a transitional expression appears between independent clauses in a compound sentence, it is preceded by a semicolon and is usually followed by a comma. (See 34b.)

▶ Minh did not understand our language; moreover, he was
        ^
unfamiliar with our customs.

When a transitional expression appears at the beginning of a sentence or in the middle of an independent clause, it is usually set off with commas.

▶ As a matter of fact, American football was established by
        ^
fans who wanted to play a more organized game of rugby.

▶ Natural foods are not always salt free; celery, for example,
        ^   ^
contains more sodium than most people would imagine.

EXCEPTION: If a transitional expression blends smoothly with the rest of the sentence, calling for little or no pause in reading, it does not need to be set off with a comma. Expressions such as *also, at least, certainly, consequently, indeed, of course, moreover, no doubt, perhaps, then,* and *therefore* do not always call for a pause.

> Alice's bicycle is broken; *therefore* you will need to borrow Sue's.

NOTE: The conjunctive adverb *however* always calls for a pause, but it should not be confused with *however* meaning "no matter how," which does not: *However hard Bill tried, he could not match his previous record.*

Parenthetical expressions

Expressions that are distinctly parenthetical should be set off with commas. Providing supplemental information, they interrupt the flow of a sentence or appear at the end as afterthoughts.

▶ Evolution**,** as far as we know**,** doesn't work this way.

▶ The bass weighed about twelve pounds**,** give or take a few ounces.

Absolute phrases

An absolute phrase, which modifies the whole sentence, usually consists of a noun followed by a participle or participial phrase. (See 63e.) Absolute phrases may appear at the beginning or at the end of a sentence. Wherever they appear, they should be set off with commas.

▶ Our grant having been approved, we were at last able to begin the archaeological dig.

▶ Elvis Presley made music industry history in the 1950s, his records having sold more than ten million copies.

CAUTION: Do not insert a comma between the noun and participle of an absolute construction.

▶ The next day/ being a school day, we turned down the invitation.

Contrasted elements

Sharp contrasts beginning with words such as *not, never,* and *unlike* are set off with commas.

▶ The Epicurean philosophers sought mental, not bodily, pleasures.

▶ Unlike Robert, Celia loved dance contests.

32g Use commas to set off nouns of direct address, the words *yes* and *no*, interrogative tags, and mild interjections.

▶ Forgive us, Dr. Spock, for reprimanding Jason.

▶ Yes, the loan will probably be approved.

▶ The film was faithful to the book, wasn't it?

▶ Well, cases like these are difficult to decide.

Punctuation

32h Use commas with expressions such as *he said* to set off direct quotations. (See also 37f.)

▶ Naturalist Arthur Cleveland Bent remarked, "In part the peregrine declined unnoticed because it is not adorable."

▶ "Convictions are more dangerous foes of truth than lies," wrote philosopher Friedrich Nietzsche.

32i Use commas with dates, addresses, titles, and numbers.

Dates

In dates, the year is set off from the rest of the sentence with a pair of commas.

▶ On December 12, 1890, orders were sent out for the arrest of Sitting Bull.

EXCEPTIONS: Commas are not needed if the date is inverted or if only the month and year are given.

The recycling plan went into effect on 15 April 2001.

January 2001 was an extremely cold month.

Addresses

The elements of an address or place name are separated by commas. A zip code, however, is not preceded by a comma.

▶ John Lennon was born in Liverpool, England, in 1940.

▶ **Please send the package to Greg Tarvin at 708 Spring Street,**

Washington, Illinois 61571.

Titles

If a title follows a name, separate it from the rest of the sentence with a pair of commas.

▶ **Sandra Belinsky, M.D., has been appointed to the board**

of trustees.

Numbers

In numbers more than four digits long, use commas to separate the numbers into groups of three, starting from the right. In numbers four digits long, a comma is optional.

> 3,500 [*or* 3500]
> 100,000
> 5,000,000

EXCEPTIONS: Do not use commas in street numbers, zip codes, telephone numbers, or years.

32j Use a comma to prevent confusion.

In certain contexts, a comma is necessary to prevent confusion. If the writer has omitted a word or phrase, for example, a comma may be needed to signal the omission.

▶ **To err is human; to forgive, divine.**

If two words in a row echo each other, a comma may be needed for ease of reading.

▶ All of the catastrophes that we had feared might happen, happened.

Sometimes a comma is needed to prevent readers from grouping words in ways that do not match the writer's intention.

▶ Patients who can, walk up and down the halls several times a day.

EXERCISE 32–4: Major uses of the comma

This exercise covers the major uses of the comma listed in the chart on page 399. Add or delete commas where necessary. If a sentence is correct, write "correct" after it. Answers to lettered sentences appear in the back of the book. Example:

Although we invited him to the party, Gerald decided to spend another late night in the computer room.

a. Cricket, which originated in England is also popular in Australia, South Africa and India.
b. At the sound of a starting pistol the horses surged forward toward the first obstacle, a sharp incline three feet high.
c. After the passage of the Civil Rights Act of 1964 the Ku Klux Klan went underground for a few years but the group's racist views did not change.
d. Jan's costume was completed with bright red, snakeskin sandals.
e. Computers must be manufactured in clean climate-controlled rooms.

1. Research on Andean condors has shown that high levels of the chemical pesticide chlorinated hydrocarbon can cause the thinning of eggshells.
2. Founded in 1868 Hampton University was one of the first colleges for African Americans.
3. Aunt Emilia was an impossible demanding guest.

Major uses of the comma

**BEFORE A COORDINATING CONJUNCTION
JOINING INDEPENDENT CLAUSES (32a)**

> No grand idea was ever born in a conference, but a lot
> of foolish ideas have died there.   —F. Scott Fitzgerald

AFTER AN INTRODUCTORY CLAUSE OR PHRASE (32b)

> If thought corrupts language, language can also cor-
> rupt thought.   —George Orwell

BETWEEN ALL ITEMS IN A SERIES (32c)

> All the things I really like to do are either immoral, ille-
> gal, or fattening.   —Alexander Woollcott

BETWEEN COORDINATE ADJECTIVES (32d)

> There is a mighty big difference between good, sound
> reasons and reasons that sound good.   —Burton Hillis

TO SET OFF NONRESTRICTIVE ELEMENTS (32e)

> Silence, which will save me from shame, will also deprive
> me of fame.   —Igor Stravinsky

---

4. The French Mirage, the fastest airplane in the Colombian air
   force, was an astonishing machine to fly.
5. In the showroom sat a brand-new, red convertible Porsche, a
   car no driver can resist.

EXERCISE 32–5: All uses of the comma

Add or delete commas where necessary in the following sentences. If
a sentence is correct, write "correct" after it. Answers to lettered
sentences appear in the back of the book. Example:

> **"Yes, Virginia, there is a Santa Claus," wrote the editor.**

Punctuation

a. On January 15, 1996 our office moved to 29 Commonwealth Avenue, Mechanicsville Virginia 19607.
b. The coach having bawled us out thoroughly, we left the locker room with his harsh words ringing in our ears.
c. Ms. Carlson you are a valued customer whose satisfaction is very important to us.
d. Mr. Mundy was born on July 22, 1939 in Arkansas, where his family had lived for four generations.
e. Swords flashing, our heroes dashed into action.

1. President Lincoln's original intention was to save the Union, not to destroy slavery.
2. For centuries people believed that Greek culture had developed in isolation from the world. Today however scholars are acknowledging the contributions made by Egypt and the Middle East.
3. Eating raw limpets, I found out, is like trying to eat art gum erasers.
4. Fortunately science is creating many alternatives to research performed on animals.
5. While the machine was printing the oversized paper jammed.

ON THE WEB

For electronic exercises on using commas, go to
www.dianahacker.com/bedhandbook

and click on ▶ **Electronic Grammar Exercises**
▶ **E-ex 32–1**

33

Unnecessary commas

Many common misuses of the comma result from an incomplete understanding of the major comma rules presented in 32. In particular, writers frequently form misconceptions about rules 32a–32e, either extending the rules inappropriately or misinterpreting them. Such misconceptions can lead to the errors described in 33a–33e; rules 33f–33h list other common misuses of the comma.

33a Do not use a comma between compound elements that are not independent clauses.

Though a comma should be used before a coordinating conjunction joining independent clauses (see 32a), this rule should not be extended to other compound word groups.

▶ Marie Curie discovered radium**/** and later applied her work

on radioactivity to medicine.

And links two verbs in a compound predicate: *discovered* and *applied.*

▶ Jake still doesn't realize that his illness is serious**/** and that

he will have to alter his diet to improve his chances of survival.

And links two subordinate clauses, each beginning with *that.*

33b Do not use a comma after a phrase that begins an inverted sentence.

Though a comma belongs after most introductory phrases (see 32b), it does not belong after phrases that begin an inverted sentence. In an inverted sentence, the subject follows the verb, and a phrase that ordinarily would follow the verb is moved to the beginning (see 62c).

▶ At the bottom of the sound**/** lies a ship laden with treasure.

56

33c   Do not use a comma before the first or after the last item in a series.

Though commas are required between items in a series (32c), do not place them either before or after the whole series.

▶ Other causes of asthmatic attacks are/ stress, change in

temperature, humidity, and cold air.

▶ Ironically, this job that appears so glamorous, carefree, and

easy/ carries a high degree of responsibility.

33d   Do not use a comma between cumulative adjectives, between an adjective and a noun, or between an adverb and an adjective.

Commas are required between coordinate adjectives (those that can be joined with *and*), but they do not belong between cumulative adjectives (those that cannot be joined with *and*). (For a full discussion, see 32d.)

▶ In the corner of the closet we found an old/ maroon hatbox

from Sears.

A comma should never be used between an adjective and the noun that follows it.

▶ It was a senseless, dangerous/ mission.

Nor should a comma be used between an adverb and an adjective that follows it.

▶ The Hurst Home is unsuitable as a mental facility for

severely**/** disturbed youths.

33e Do not use commas to set off restrictive or mildly parenthetical elements.

Restrictive elements are modifiers or appositives that restrict the meaning of the nouns they follow. Because they are essential to the meaning of the sentence, they are not set off with commas. (For a full discussion of both restrictive and nonrestrictive elements, see 32e.)

▶ Drivers**/** who think they own the road**/** make cycling a

dangerous sport.

The modifier *who think they own the road* restricts the meaning of *Drivers* and is therefore essential to the meaning of the sentence. Putting commas around the *who* clause falsely suggests that all drivers think they own the road.

▶ Margaret Mead's book**/** *Coming of Age in Samoa***/** stirred up

considerable controversy when it was published.

Since Mead wrote more than one book, the appositive contains information essential to the meaning of the sentence.

Although commas should be used with distinctly parenthetical expressions (see 32f), do not use them to set off elements that are only mildly parenthetical.

▶ Charisse believes that the Internet is**/** essentially**/** a bastion

of advertising.

33f Do not use a comma to set off a concluding adverb clause that is essential to the meaning of the sentence.

When adverb clauses introduce a sentence, they are nearly always followed by a comma (see 32b). When they conclude a sentence, however, they are not set off by commas if their content is essential to the meaning of the earlier part of the sentence. Adverb clauses beginning with *after, as soon as, because, before, if, since, unless, until,* and *when* are usually essential.

▶ **Don't visit Paris at the height of the tourist season/ unless**

  you have booked hotel reservations.

  Without the *unless* clause, the meaning of the sentence might at first seem broader than the writer intended.

When a concluding adverb clause is nonessential, it should be preceded by a comma. Clauses beginning with *although, even though, though,* and *whereas* are usually nonessential.

▶ **The lecture seemed to last only a short time, although the**

  clock said it had gone on for more than an hour.

33g Do not use a comma to separate a verb from its subject or object.

A sentence should flow from subject to verb to object without unnecessary pauses. Commas may appear between these major sentence elements only when a specific rule calls for them.

▶ Zoos large enough to give the animals freedom to roam/ are
becoming more popular.

▶ Francesca explained to him/ that she was busy and would
see him later.

In the first sentence, the comma should not separate the subject,
Zoos, from the verb, *are becoming.* In the second sentence, the
comma should not separate the verb, *explained,* from its object,
the subordinate clause *that she was busy and would see him later.*

33h Avoid other common misuses of the comma.

Do not use a comma in the following situations.

**AFTER A COORDINATING CONJUNCTION (*AND, BUT, OR, NOR,
FOR, SO, YET*)**

▶ Occasionally soap operas are performed live, but/ more often
they are taped.

AFTER *SUCH AS* OR *LIKE*

▶ Many shade-loving plants, such as/ begonias, impatiens, and
coleus, can add color to a shady garden.

BEFORE *THAN*

▶ Touring Crete was more thrilling for us/ than visiting the
Greek islands frequented by rich Europeans.

AFTER *ALTHOUGH*

▶ Although/ the air was balmy, the water was too cold for
swimming.

BEFORE A PARENTHESIS

▶ At MCI Sylvia began at the bottom**/** (with only three and a half walls and a swivel chair), but within five years she had been promoted to supervisor.

TO SET OFF AN INDIRECT (REPORTED) QUOTATION

▶ Samuel Goldwyn once said**/** that a verbal contract isn't worth the paper it's written on.

WITH A QUESTION MARK OR AN EXCLAMATION POINT

▶ "Why don't you try it?**/**" she coaxed. "You can't do any worse than the rest of us."

EXERCISE 33–1

Delete commas where necessary in the following sentences. If a sentence is correct, write "correct" after it. Answers to lettered sentences appear in the back of the book. Example:

Loretta Lynn has paved the way for artists such as**/** Reba

McEntire and Wynonna Judd.

a. As a child growing up in Jamaica, I often daydreamed about life in the United States.

b. He wore a thick, black, wool coat over army fatigues.

c. Often public figures, (Michael Jackson is a good example) go to great lengths to guard their private lives.

d. She loved early spring flowers such as, crocuses, daffodils, forsythia, and irises.

e. On Pam's wrist, was a tattoo of a dragon chasing a tiger.

LOOKING AT YOURSELF AS A WRITER
The comma and unnecessary commas

It is not necessary to learn all of the comma rules in 32 and 33; just know where to find them. If commas cause you a great deal of difficulty, however, you may want to consider possible causes and cures of your problems.

CAUSE   You insert a comma whenever you take a breath.
CURE   The "breath" method is too unreliable; learn to punctuate by the rules instead.

CAUSE   You oversimplify the rules by focusing on words. For example, because a comma goes before *and* some of the time, you conclude that it belongs before *and* all of the time.
CURE   Make a conscious effort to unlearn oversimplified rules. If the word *and* gives you problems, for example, consult 32a and 33a to see whether you need the comma.

CAUSE   Two of the most important comma rules (32a and 32b) refer to two different kinds of clauses — independent and subordinate — and you've never really understood clauses.
CURE   You can probably grasp the rules by focusing on the examples in 32a and 32b, together with the brief definitions of clauses that are given in those sections. If not, turn to 63b and 64a for a quick review of clauses.

CAUSE   You are confused about the difference between restrictive and nonrestrictive word groups (32e and 33e).
CURE   You are not alone. Most writers find this distinction tricky because it requires us to think carefully about our intended meaning. When in doubt, ask two or three "test readers" to tell you how the presence or absence of commas affects your meaning.

1. Mesquite, the hardest of the softwoods, grows primarily in the Southwest.
2. Male supremacy was assumed by my father, and accepted by my mother.
3. The lieutenant reported to his captain, that all of his men were present and accounted for.
4. The streets that three hours later would be bumper to bumper with commuters, were quiet and empty except for a few prowling cats.
5. Most of the citizens in the United States, expect their elected officials to be truthful.

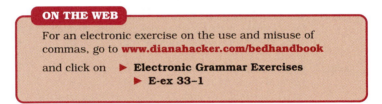

ON THE WEB

For an electronic exercise on the use and misuse of commas, go to **www.dianahacker.com/bedhandbook**

and click on ▶ **Electronic Grammar Exercises**
▶ **E-ex 33–1**

34

The semicolon

The semicolon is used to connect major sentence elements of equal grammatical rank.

GRAMMAR CHECKERS flag some, but not all, misused semicolons (34d). In addition, they can alert you to some run-on sentences (34a). However, they miss more run-on sentences than they identify, and they sometimes flag correct sentences as possible run-ons. (See also the grammar checker advice on p. 253.)

34a Use a semicolon between closely related independent clauses not joined with a coordinating conjunction.

When related independent clauses appear in one sentence,
they are ordinarily linked with a comma and a coordinating
conjunction (*and, but, or, nor, for, so, yet*). The coordinating
conjunction signals the relation between the clauses. If the
clauses are closely related and the relation is clear without a
conjunction, they may be linked with a semicolon instead.

> Injustice is relatively easy to bear; what stings is justice.
> —H. L. Mencken

> When I was a boy, I was told that anybody could become pres-
> ident; I'm beginning to believe it.   —Clarence Darrow

A semicolon must be used whenever a coordinating conjunction has been omitted between independent clauses. To
use merely a comma creates a kind of run-on sentence
known as a comma splice. (See 20.)

▶ In 1800, a traveler needed six weeks to get from New York

City to Chicago**/;** in 1860, the trip by railroad took only

two days.

CAUTION: Do not overuse the semicolon as a means of revising run-on sentences. For other revision strategies, see 20a,
20c, and 20d.

34b Use a semicolon between independent clauses
linked with a transitional expression.

Transitional expressions include conjunctive adverbs and
transitional phrases.

CONJUNCTIVE ADVERBS

accordingly	furthermore	moreover	subsequently
also	hence	nevertheless	then
anyway	however	next	therefore
besides	incidentally	nonetheless	thus
certainly	indeed	otherwise	
consequently	instead	similarly	
conversely	likewise	specifically	
finally	meanwhile	still	

TRANSITIONAL PHRASES

after all	even so	in fact
as a matter of fact	for example	in other words
as a result	for instance	in the first place
at any rate	in addition	on the contrary
at the same time	in conclusion	on the other hand

When a transitional expression appears between independent clauses, it is preceded by a semicolon and usually followed by a comma.

▶ Many corals grow very gradually/; in fact, the creation of a

coral reef can take centuries.

When a transitional expression appears in the middle or at the end of the second independent clause, the semicolon goes *between the clauses.*

▶ Most singers gain fame through hard work and dedication/;

Evita, however, found other means.

Transitional expressions should not be confused with the coordinating conjunctions *and, but, or, nor, for, so,* and *yet,* which are preceded by a comma when they link independent clauses. (See 32a.)

34c   Use a semicolon between items in a series containing internal punctuation.

▶ Classic science fiction sagas are *Star Trek,* with Mr. Spock
and his large pointed ears**/;** *Battlestar Galactica,* with its
Cylon Raiders**/;** and *Star Wars,* with Han Solo, Luke
Skywalker, and Darth Vader.

Without the semicolons, the reader would have to sort out the major groupings, distinguishing between important and less important pauses according to the logic of the sentence. By inserting semicolons at the major breaks, the writer does this work for the reader.

34d   Avoid common misuses of the semicolon.

Do not use a semicolon in the following situations.

BETWEEN A SUBORDINATE CLAUSE AND THE REST OF THE SENTENCE

▶ Unless you brush your teeth within ten or fifteen minutes
after eating**/,** brushing does almost no good.

BETWEEN AN APPOSITIVE AND THE WORD IT REFERS TO

▶ The scientists were fascinated by the species *Argyroneta
aquatica***/,** a spider that lives underwater.

TO INTRODUCE A LIST

▶ Some of my favorite film stars have home pages on the Web**/:**
John Travolta, Susan Sarandon, Brad Pitt, and Emma
Thompson.

Punctuation

BETWEEN INDEPENDENT CLAUSES JOINED BY *AND*, *BUT*, *OR*, *NOR*, *FOR*, *SO*, OR *YET*

▶ Five of the applicants had worked with spreadsheets**;** but

only one was familiar with database management.

EXCEPTIONS: If at least one of the independent clauses contains internal punctuation, you may use a semicolon even though the clauses are joined with a coordinating conjunction.

> As a vehicle [the model T] was hard-working, commonplace, and heroic; and it often seemed to transmit those qualities to the person who rode in it.   — E. B. White

Although a comma would also be correct in this sentence, the semicolon is more effective, for it indicates the relative weights of the pauses.

Occasionally, a semicolon may be used to emphasize a sharp contrast or a firm distinction between clauses joined with a coordinating conjunction.

> We hate some persons because we do not know them; and we will not know them because we hate them.
>   — Charles Caleb Colton

EXERCISE 34–1

Add commas or semicolons where needed in the following well-known quotations. If a sentence is correct, write "correct" after it. Answers to lettered sentences appear in the back of the book. Example:

> If an animal does something**,** we call it instinct**;** if we do the
>
> same thing**,** we call it intelligence.   — Will Cuppy

a. Do not ask me to be kind just ask me to act as though I were.

—Jules Renard

b. When men talk about defense they always claim to be protecting women and children but they never ask the women and children what they think. —Pat Schroeder

c. When I get a little money I buy books if any is left I buy food and clothes. —Desiderius Erasmus

d. America is a country that doesn't know where it is going but is determined to set a speed record getting there.

—Lawrence J. Peter

e. Wit has truth in it wisecracking is simply calisthenics with words. —Dorothy Parker

1. Everyone is a genius at least once a year a real genius has his [or her] original ideas closer together. —G. C. Lichtenberg

2. When choosing between two evils, I always like to try the one I've never tried before. —Mae West

3. Once the children were in the house the air became more vivid and more heated every object in the house grew more alive.

—Mary Gordon

4. We don't know what we want but we are ready to bite someone to get it. —Will Rogers

5. I've been rich and I've been poor rich is better.

—Sophie Tucker

EXERCISE 34–2

Edit the following sentences to correct errors in the use of the comma and the semicolon. If a sentence is correct, write "correct" after it. Answers to lettered sentences appear in the back of the book. Example:

> **Love is blind; envy has its eyes wide open.**
> ^

a. Strong black coffee will not sober you up, the truth is that time is the only way to get alcohol out of your system.

b. It is not surprising that our society is increasingly violent, after all, television desensitizes us to brutality at a very early age.

c. There is often a fine line between right and wrong; good and bad; truth and deception.

d. At Weight Watchers, we believe that being fat is not hereditary; it is a choice.

e. Severe, unremitting pain is a ravaging force; especially when the patient tries to hide it from others.

1. Another delicious dish is the chef's special; a roasted duck rubbed with spices and stuffed with wild rice.

2. Martin Luther King Jr. had not intended to be a preacher, initially, he had planned to become a lawyer.

3. We all assumed that the thief had been Jean's boyfriend; even though we had seen him only from the back.

4. The Victorians avoided the subject of sex but were obsessed with death, our contemporaries are obsessed with sex but avoid thinking about death.

5. Some educators believe that African American history should be taught in separate courses, others prefer to see it integrated into survey courses.

ON THE WEB

For electronic exercises on using semicolons, go to
www.dianahacker.com/bedhandbook

and click on ▶ **Electronic Grammar Exercises**
                ▶ **E-ex 34-1**

35

The colon

The colon is used primarily to call attention to the words that follow it. In addition, the colon has some conventional uses.

GRAMMAR CHECKERS do not flag missing or misused colons. For example, they failed to catch the misused colon in this sentence: *Uncle Carlos left behind: his watch, his glasses, and his favorite pen.* Occasionally grammar checkers flag misused semicolons in contexts where a colon is required.

35a Use a colon after an independent clause to direct attention to a list, an appositive, or a quotation.

A LIST
The daily routine should include at least the following: twenty knee bends, fifty sit-ups, fifteen leg lifts, and five minutes of running in place.

AN APPOSITIVE
My roommate is guilty of two of the seven deadly sins: gluttony and sloth.

A QUOTATION
Consider the words of John F. Kennedy: "Ask not what your country can do for you; ask what you can do for your country."

For other ways of introducing quotations, see "Introducing quoted material" on pages 428–30.

35b Use a colon between independent clauses if the second summarizes or explains the first.

Faith is like love: It cannot be forced.

Punctuation

NOTE: When an independent clause follows a colon, it may begin with a lowercase or a capital letter.

35c Use a colon after the salutation in a formal letter, to indicate hours and minutes, to show proportions, between a title and subtitle, and between city and publisher in bibliographic entries.

Dear Sir or Madam:

5:30 P.M. (or p.m.)

The ratio of women to men was 2:1.

The Glory of Hera: Greek Mythology and the Greek Family

Boston: Bedford, 2001

NOTE: In biblical references, a colon is ordinarily used between chapter and verse (Luke 2:14). The Modern Language Association recommends a period instead (Luke 2.14).

35d Avoid common misuses of the colon.

A colon must be preceded by a full independent clause. Therefore, avoid using it in the following situations.

BETWEEN A VERB AND ITS OBJECT OR COMPLEMENT

▶ Some important vitamins found in vegetables are: vitamin A, thiamine, niacin, and vitamin C.

BETWEEN A PREPOSITION AND ITS OBJECT

▶ The heart's two pumps each consist of: an upper chamber, or atrium, and a lower chamber, or ventricle.

AFTER *SUCH AS, INCLUDING,* OR *FOR EXAMPLE*

▶ The trees on our campus include many fine Japanese speci-

mens such as:/ black pines, ginkgos, and weeping cherries.

EXERCISE 35–1

Edit the following sentences to correct errors in the use of the comma, the semicolon, or the colon. If a sentence is correct, write "correct" after it. Answers to lettered sentences appear in the back of the book. Example:

> Smiling confidently, the young man stated his major goal in
>
> life:/: to be secretary of agriculture before he was thirty.
>   ^

a. Minds are like parachutes: They function only when open.
b. If we have come to fight, we are far too few, if we have come to die, we are far too many.
c. The travel package includes: a round-trip ticket to Athens, a cruise through the Cyclades, and all hotel accommodations.
d. The media like to portray my generation as lazy; although polls show that we work as hard as the twentysomethings before us.
e. Fran Lebowitz has this advice for parents, "Never allow your child to call you by your first name. He hasn't known you long enough."

1. Kay survived for one reason, the medics got to her in time.
2. While traveling through France, Fiona visited: the Loire Valley, Chartres, the Louvre, and the McDonald's stand at the foot of the Eiffel Tower.
3. There are three types of leave; annual leave, used for vacations, sick leave, used for medical appointments and illness, and personal leave, used for a variety of personal reasons.
4. Carl Sandburg once asked three important questions, "Who paid for my freedom? What was the price? And am I somehow beholden?"
5. Robin sorts the crabs into three groups: males, females, and crabs about to molt.

ON THE WEB

For an electronic exercise on using colons, go to
www.dianahacker.com/bedhandbook

and click on ▶ **Electronic Grammar Exercises**
▶ **E-ex 35–1**

36

The apostrophe

GRAMMAR CHECKERS can flag some, but not all, missing or misused apostrophes. They can catch missing apostrophes in common contractions, such as *don't*. They can also flag some problems with possessives, although they miss others. The programs usually phrase their advice cautiously, telling you that you have a "possible possessive error" in a phrase such as *a days work* or *sled dogs feet*. Therefore, you—not the grammar checker—must decide whether to add an apostrophe and, if so, whether to put it before or after the *-s*.

36a Use an apostrophe to indicate that a noun is possessive.

Possessive nouns usually indicate ownership, as in *Tim's hat* or *the lawyer's desk*. Frequently, however, ownership is only loosely implied: *the tree's roots, a day's work*. If you are not sure whether a noun is possessive, try turning it into an *of* phrase: *the roots of the tree, the work of a day*.

When to add -'s

1. If the noun does not end in -s, add -'s.

   Roy managed to climb out on the driver's side.

   Thank you for refunding the children's money.

2. If the noun is singular and ends in -s, add -'s.

   Lois's sister spent last year in India.

EXCEPTION: If pronunciation would be awkward with the added -'s, some writers use only the apostrophe. Either use is acceptable.

   Sophocles' plays are among my favorites.

When to add only an apostrophe

If the noun is plural and ends in -s, add only an apostrophe.

   Both diplomats' briefcases were stolen.

Joint possession

To show joint possession, use -'s or (-s') with the last noun only; to show individual possession, make all nouns possessive.

   Have you seen Joyce and Greg's new camper?

   John's and Marie's expectations of marriage couldn't have been more different.

In the first sentence, Joyce and Greg jointly own one camper. In the second sentence, John and Marie individually have different expectations.

Compound nouns

If a noun is compound, use *-'s* (or *-s'*) with the last element.

My father-in-law's sculpture won first place.

36b Use an apostrophe and *-s* to indicate that an indefinite pronoun is possessive.

Indefinite pronouns refer to no specific person or thing: *everyone, someone, no one, something.* (See 61b.)

Someone's raincoat has been left behind.

36c Use an apostrophe to mark omissions in contractions and numbers.

In contractions the apostrophe takes the place of missing letters.

It's a shame that Frank can't go on the tour.

It's stands for *it is, can't* for *cannot.*
 The apostrophe is also used to mark the omission of the first two digits of a year (*the class of '95*) or years (*the '60s generation*).

We'll never forget the blizzard of '96.

36d An apostrophe is no longer recommended in plural numbers, letters, abbreviations, and words mentioned as words.

Traditionally, an apostrophe has been used to pluralize numbers, letters, abbreviations, and words mentioned as words. The trend, however, is toward omitting the apostrophe.

PLURAL NUMBERS   Although an apostrophe was once used to pluralize numbers (figure 8's, the 1920's), the apostrophe is usually omitted in current usage.

Peggy skated nearly perfect figure 8s.

The 1920s are known as the Jazz Age.

PLURAL LETTERS   Using an apostrophe to pluralize letters mentioned as letters is no longer widely recommended. Italicize the letter and use roman type for the *-s* ending.

Two large *J*s were painted on the door.

The Modern Language Association continues to recommend the apostrophe: *J*'s. Especially with the letters *A* and *I*, there is a good rationale for using the apostrophe. Because *A*s and *I*s are words, readers might be confused.

PLURAL ABBREVIATIONS   The trend is away from using an apostrophe to pluralize an abbreviation.

We collected only four IOUs out of forty.

PLURALS OF WORDS MENTIONED AS WORDS   Current usage is to omit the apostrophe when the word mentioned as a word is italicized; notice that the *-s* ending appears in roman type.

We've heard enough *maybe*s.

Words mentioned as words may also appear in quotation marks. When you choose this option, use the apostrophe.

We've heard enough "maybe's."

36e   Avoid common misuses of the apostrophe.

Do not use an apostrophe in the following situations.

WITH NOUNS THAT ARE NOT POSSESSIVE

▶ Some ~~outpatient's~~ *outpatients* are given special parking permits.

IN THE POSSESSIVE PRONOUNS *ITS, WHOSE, HIS, HERS, OURS, YOURS,* AND *THEIRS*

▶ Each area has ~~it's~~ *its* own conference room.

It's means "it is." The possessive pronoun *its* contains no apostrophe despite the fact that it is possessive.

▶ This course was taught by a professional florist ~~who's~~ *whose*

technique was Japanese.

Who's means "who is." The possessive pronoun is *whose.*

EXERCISE 36–1

Edit the following sentences to correct errors in the use of the apostrophe. If a sentence is correct, write "correct" after it. Answers to lettered sentences appear in the back of the book. Example:

Marietta lived above the only bar in town, Smiling
~~Jacks.~~ *Jack's.*

a. This diet will improve almost anyone's health.
b. The deed must be transferred to the purchasers name.
c. Each days menu features a different European country's dish.

d. Sue worked overtime to increase her families earnings.

e. Ms. Jacobs is unwilling to listen to students complaints about computer failures and damaged disks.

1. Siddhartha sat by the river and listened to its many voices.

2. Three teenage son's can devour about as much food as four full-grown field hands. The only difference is that they dont do half as much work.

3. We handle contracts with NASA and many other government agency's.

4. Luck is an important element in a rock musicians career.

5. My sister-in-law's quilts are being shown at the Fendrick Gallery.

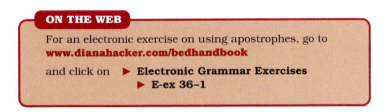

ON THE WEB

For an electronic exercise on using apostrophes, go to
www.dianahacker.com/bedhandbook

and click on ▶ **Electronic Grammar Exercises**
▶ **E-ex 36–1**

37

Quotation marks

GRAMMAR CHECKERS can tell you to put commas and periods inside quotation marks; they can also flag "unbalanced quotes," an opening quotation mark that is not balanced with a closing quotation mark. The programs can't tell you, however, when you should or shouldn't use quotation marks.

37a Use quotation marks to enclose direct quotations.

Direct quotations of a person's words, whether spoken or written, must be in quotation marks.

> "A foolish consistency is the hobgoblin of little minds," wrote Ralph Waldo Emerson.

CAUTION: Do not use quotation marks around indirect quotations. An indirect quotation reports someone's ideas without using that person's exact words.

> Ralph Waldo Emerson believed that consistency for its own sake is the mark of a small mind.

NOTE: In dialogue, begin a new paragraph to mark a change in speaker.

> "Mom, his name is Willie, not William. A thousand times I've told you, it's *Willie*."
> "Willie is a derivative of William, Lester. Surely his birth certificate doesn't have Willie on it, and I like calling people by their proper names."
> "Yes, it does, ma'am. My mother named me Willie K. Mason."
> — Gloria Naylor

If a single speaker utters more than one paragraph, introduce each paragraph with quotation marks, but do not use closing quotation marks until the end of the speech.

37b Set off long quotations of prose or poetry by indenting.

When a quotation of prose runs to more than four typed lines in your paper, set it off by indenting one inch (or ten spaces) from the left margin. Quotation marks are not required because the indented format tells readers that the quotation is taken word for word from a source. Long quotations are ordinarily introduced by a sentence ending with a colon.

> After making an exhaustive study of the historical
> record, James Horan evaluates Billy the Kid like
> this:
>
> > The portrait that emerges of [the
> > Kid] from the thousands of pages of
> > affidavits, reports, trial transcripts,
> > his letters, and his testimony is neither
> > the mythical Robin Hood nor the stereo-
> > typed adenoidal moron and pathological
> > killer. Rather Billy appears as a
> > disturbed, lonely young man, honest,
> > loyal to his friends, dedicated to his
> > beliefs, and betrayed by our institutions
> > and the corrupt, ambitious, and compro-
> > mising politicians in his time. (158)

The number in parentheses is a citation handled according to the Modern Language Association style. (See 55a.)

NOTE: When you quote two or more paragraphs from the source, indent the first line of each paragraph an additional one-half inch (or five spaces).

When you quote more than three lines of a poem, set the quoted lines off from the text by indenting one inch (or ten spaces) from the left margin. Use no quotation marks unless they appear in the poem itself. (To quote two or three lines of poetry, see 39e.)

```
Although many anthologizers "modernize" her punc-

tuation, Emily Dickinson relied heavily on dashes,

using them, perhaps, as a musical device. Here, for

example, is the original version of the opening

stanza from "The Snake":

              A narrow Fellow in the Grass

              Occasionally rides--

              You may have met Him--did you not

              His notice sudden is--
```

NOTE: APA and *Chicago* styles have slightly different guide-lines for setting off long quotations. (See pp. 688 and 737.)

37c   Use single quotation marks to enclose a quotation within a quotation.

According to Paul Eliott, Eskimo hunters "chant an ancient magic song to the seal they are after: 'Beast of the sea! Come and place yourself before me in the early morning!'"

37d   Use quotation marks around the titles of short works: newspaper and magazine articles, poems, short stories, songs, episodes of television and radio programs, and chapters or subdivisions of books.

Katherine Mansfield's "The Garden Party" provoked a lively discussion in our short-story class last night.

NOTE: Titles of books, plays, Web sites, television and radio programs, films, magazines, and newspapers are put in italics or underlined. (See 42a.)

37e Quotation marks may be used to set off words used as words.

Although words used as words are ordinarily underlined or italicized (see 42d), quotation marks are also acceptable. Just be sure to follow consistent practice throughout a paper.

> The words "accept" and "except" are frequently confused.

> The words *accept* and *except* are frequently confused.

37f Use punctuation with quotation marks according to convention.

This section describes the conventions used by American publishers in placing various marks of punctuation inside or outside quotation marks. It also explains how to punctuate when introducing quoted material.

Periods and commas

Place periods and commas inside quotation marks.

> "This is a stick-up," said the well-dressed young couple. "We want all your money."

This rule applies to single quotation marks as well as double quotation marks. (See 37c.) It also applies to all uses of quotation marks: for quoted material, for titles of works, and for words used as words.

EXCEPTION: In the Modern Language Association's style of parenthetical in-text citations (see 56a), the period follows the citation in parentheses.

Punctuation

James M. McPherson comments, approvingly, that the Whigs "were not averse to extending the blessings of American liberty, even to Mexicans and Indians" (48).

Colons and semicolons

Put colons and semicolons outside quotation marks.

Harold wrote, "I regret that I am unable to attend the fund-raiser for AIDS research"; his letter, however, came with a substantial contribution.

Question marks and exclamation points

Put question marks and exclamation points inside quotation marks unless they apply to the whole sentence.

Contrary to tradition, bedtime at my house is marked by "Mommy, can I tell you a story now?"

Have you heard the old proverb "Do not climb the hill until you reach it"?

In the first sentence, the question mark applies only to the quoted question. In the second sentence, the question mark applies to the whole sentence.

NOTE: Modern Language Association parenthetical citations create a special problem. According to MLA, the question mark or exclamation point should appear before the quotation mark, and a period should follow the parenthetical citation: *Rosie Thomas asks, "Is nothing in life ever straight and clear, the way children see it?" (77).*

Introducing quoted material

After a word group introducing a quotation, choose a colon, a comma, or no punctuation at all, whichever is appropriate in context.

FORMAL INTRODUCTION If a quotation has been formally introduced, a colon is appropriate. A formal introduction is a full independent clause, not just an expression such as *he said* or *she remarked.*

> Morrow views personal ads in the classifieds as an art form: "The personal ad is like a haiku of self-celebration, a brief solo played on one's own horn."

EXPRESSION SUCH AS *HE SAID* If a quotation is introduced with an expression such as *he said* or *she remarked*—or if it is followed by such an expression—a comma is needed.

> Stephan Leacock once said, "I am a great believer in luck, and I find the harder I work the more I have of it."

> "You can be a little ungrammatical if you come from the right part of the country," writes Robert Frost.

BLENDED QUOTATION When a quotation is blended into the writer's own sentence, either a comma or no punctuation is appropriate, depending on the way in which the quotation fits into the sentence structure.

> The future champion could, as he put it, "float like a butterfly and sting like a bee."

> Charles Hudson notes that the prisoners escaped "by squeezing through a tiny window eighteen feet above the floor of their cell."

BEGINNING OF SENTENCE If a quotation appears at the beginning of a sentence, set it off with a comma unless the quotation ends with a question mark or an exclamation point.

> "We shot them like dogs," boasted Davy Crockett, who was among Jackson's troops.

> "What is it?" I asked, bracing myself.

Punctuation

INTERRUPTED QUOTATION   If a quoted sentence is interrupted by explanatory words, use commas to set off the explanatory words.

> "A great many people think they are thinking," observed William James, "when they are merely rearranging their prejudices."

If two successive quoted sentences from the same source are interrupted by explanatory words, use a comma before the explanatory words and a period after them.

> "I was a flop as a daily reporter," admitted E. B. White. "Every piece had to be a masterpiece — and before you knew it, Tuesday was Wednesday."

37g   Avoid common misuses of quotation marks.

Do not use quotation marks to draw attention to familiar slang, to disown trite expressions, or to justify an attempt at humor.

▶   Between Thanksgiving and Super Bowl Sunday, many American wives become *"*football widows*."*

Do not use quotation marks around indirect quotations. (See also 37a.)

▶   After leaving the scene of the domestic quarrel, the officer said that *"*he was due for a coffee break*."*

Do not use quotation marks around the title of your own essay.

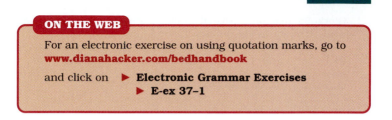

ON THE WEB

For an electronic exercise on using quotation marks, go to
www.dianahacker.com/bedhandbook

and click on ▶ **Electronic Grammar Exercises**
▶ **E-ex 37–1**

EXERCISE 37–1

Add or delete quotation marks as needed and make any other necessary changes in punctuation in the following sentences. If a sentence is correct, write "correct" after it. Answers to lettered sentences appear in the back of the book. Example:

> Bill Cosby once said, "I don't know the key to success, but
>   ^
> the key to failure is trying to please everyone."
>   ^

a. As for the advertisement "Sailors have more fun", if you consider chipping paint and swabbing decks fun, then you will have plenty of it.
b. Even after forty minutes of discussion, our class could not agree on an interpretation of Robert Frost's "The Road Not Taken."
c. After winning the lottery, Juanita said that "she would give half the money to charity."
d. After the movie Vicki said, "The reviewer called this flick "trash of the first order." I guess you can't believe everything you read."
e. "Cleaning your house while your kids are still growing," quipped Phyllis Diller, "is like shoveling the walk before it stops snowing."

1. "Order in the court! Order in the court!", shouts the judge, banging her wooden spoon on the kitchen table.
2. "Kick the tires and light the fires" exclaimed the pilot, giving me my cue to start the engines.

3. Gloria Steinem once twisted an old proverb like this, "A woman without a man is like a fish without a bicycle."
4. "Even when freshly washed and relieved of all obvious confections," says Fran Lebowitz, "children tend to be sticky."
5. Have you heard the Cowboy Junkies' rendition of Hank Williams's "I'm So Lonesome I Could Cry?"

38

End punctuation

 GRAMMAR CHECKERS occasionally flag sentences beginning with words like *Why* or *Are* and suggest that a question mark may be needed. On the whole, however, grammar checkers are of little help with end punctuation. Most notably, they neglect to tell you when your sentence is missing end punctuation.

38a   The period

Use a period to end all sentences except direct questions or genuine exclamations. Also use periods in abbreviations according to convention.

To end sentences

Everyone knows that a period should be used to end most sentences. The only problems that arise concern the choice between a period and a question mark or between a period and an exclamation point.

If a sentence reports a question instead of asking it directly, it should end with a period, not a question mark.

▶ **Celia asked whether the picnic would be canceled~~?~~.**
　　　　　　　　　　　　　　　　　　　　　　　　　　^

If a sentence is not a genuine exclamation, it should end with a period, not an exclamation point.

▶ **After years of working her way through school, Pat finally**

　graduated with high honors~~!~~.
　　　　　　　　　　　　　　　^

In abbreviations

A period is conventionally used in abbreviations such as these:

Mr.	B.A.	B.C.	i.e.	A.M. (or a.m.)
Mrs.	M.A.	B.C.E.	e.g.	P.M. (or p.m.)
Ms.	Ph.D.	A.D.	etc.	
Dr.	R.N.	C.E.		

A period is not used in U.S. Postal Service abbreviations for states: MD, TX, CA.

Ordinarily a period is not used in abbreviations of organization names:

NATO	UNESCO	UCLA	PUSH	IBM
TVA	IRS	AFL-CIO	NBA	FTC
USA (*or* U.S.A.)	NAACP	SEC	FCC	NIH

Usage varies, however. When in doubt, consult a dictionary, a style manual, or a publication by the agency in question. Even the yellow pages can help.

NOTE: If a sentence ends with a period marking an abbreviation, do not add a second period.

38b The question mark

Obviously a direct question should be followed by a question mark.

> What is the horsepower of a 747 engine?

If a polite request is written in the form of a question, it may be followed by a period.

> Would you please send me your catalog of lilies.

CAUTION: Do not use a question mark after an indirect question, one that is reported rather than asked directly. Use a period instead.

> ▶ He asked me who was teaching the mythology course⁇.
> ⌃

NOTE: Questions in a series may be followed by question marks even when they are not complete sentences.

> We wondered where Calamity had hidden this time. Under the sink? Behind the furnace? On top of the bookcase?

38c The exclamation point

Use an exclamation point after a word group or sentence that expresses exceptional feeling or deserves special emphasis.

> When Gloria entered the room, I switched on the lights and we all yelled, "Surprise!"

CAUTION: Do not overuse the exclamation point.

▶ **In the fisherman's memory the fish lives on, increasing in length and weight with each passing year, until at last it is big enough to shade a fishing boat/.**
                                                          ^

This sentence doesn't need to be pumped up with an exclamation point. It is emphatic enough without it.

▶ **Whenever I see Venus lunging forward to put away an overhead smash, it might as well be me/. She does it just**
                                              ^
the way that I would!

The first exclamation point should be deleted so that the second one will have more force.

EXERCISE 38–1

Add appropriate end punctuation in the following paragraph.

    Although I am generally rational, I am superstitious I never walk under ladders or put shoes on the table If I spill the salt, I go into frenzied calisthenics picking up the grains and tossing them over my left shoulder As a result of these curious activities, I've always wondered whether knowing the roots of superstitions would quell my irrational responses Superstition has it, for example, that one should never place a hat on the bed This superstition arises from a time when head lice were quite common and placing a guest's hat on the bed stood a good chance of spreading lice through the host's bed Doesn't this make good sense And doesn't it stand to reason that if I know that my guests don't have lice I shouldn't care where their hats go Of course it does It is fair to ask, then, whether I have changed my ways and place hats on beds Are you kidding I wouldn't put a hat on a bed if my life depended on it

39

Other punctuation marks: the dash, parentheses, brackets, the ellipsis mark, the slash

GRAMMAR CHECKERS rarely flag problems with the punctuation marks in this section: the dash, parentheses, brackets, the ellipsis mark, and the slash. (For a general discussion of what grammar checkers can and cannot do, see p. 59.)

39a The dash

When typing, use two hyphens to form a dash (--). Do not put spaces before or after the dash. (If your word processing program has what is known as an "em-dash," you may use it instead, with no space before or after it.) Dashes are used for the following purposes.

To set off parenthetical material that deserves emphasis

> Everything that went wrong—from the peeping Tom at her window last night to my head-on collision today—was blamed on our move.

To set off appositives that contain commas

An appositive is a noun or noun phrase that renames a nearby noun. Ordinarily most appositives are set off with commas (32e), but when the appositive contains commas, a pair of dashes helps the readers see the relative importance of all the pauses.

In my hometown the basic needs of people—food, clothing, and shelter—are less costly than in Los Angeles.

To prepare for a list, a restatement, an amplification, or a dramatic shift in tone or thought

Along the wall are the bulk liquids—sesame seed oil, honey, safflower oil, and that half-liquid "peanuts only" peanut butter.

Consider the amount of sugar in the average person's diet—104 pounds per year, 90 percent more than that consumed by our ancestors.

Everywhere we looked there were little kids—a box of Cracker Jacks in one hand and mommy's or daddy's sleeve in the other.

Kiere took a few steps back, came running full speed, kicked a mighty kick—and missed the ball.

In the first two examples, the writer could also use a colon. (See 35a.) The colon is more formal than the dash and not quite as dramatic.

CAUTION: Unless there is a specific reason for using the dash, avoid it. Unnecessary dashes create a choppy effect.

▶ Insisting that students use computers as instructional

tools—for information retrieval—makes good sense. Herding

them—sheeplike—into computer technology does not.

39b Parentheses

Use parentheses to enclose supplemental material, minor digressions, and afterthoughts.

After taking her temperature, pulse, and blood pressure (routine vital signs), the nurse made Becky as comfortable as possible.

The weights James was first able to move (not lift, mind you) were measured in ounces.

Use parentheses to enclose letters or numbers labeling items in a series.

Regulations stipulated that only the following equipment could be used on the survival mission: (1) a knife, (2) thirty feet of parachute line, (3) a book of matches, (4) two ponchos, (5) an *E* tool, and (6) a signal flare.

CAUTION: Do not overuse parentheses. Rough drafts are likely to contain more afterthoughts than necessary. As writers head into a sentence, they often think of additional details, occasionally working them in as best they can with parentheses. Usually such sentences should be revised so that the additional details no longer seem to be afterthoughts.

▶   Researchers have said that ~~ten million (estimates run as high as fifty million)~~ *from ten to fifty million* Americans have hypoglycemia.

39c Brackets

Use brackets to enclose any words or phrases that you have inserted into an otherwise word-for-word quotation.

Audubon reports that "if there are not enough young to balance deaths, the end of the species [California condor] is inevitable."

The sentence quoted from the *Audubon* article did not contain the words *California condor* (since the context made clear what species was meant), so the writer needed to add the name in brackets.

The Latin word "sic" in brackets indicates that an error in a quoted sentence appears in the original source.

> According to the review, k. d. lang's performance was brilliant, "exceding [sic] the expectations of even her most loyal fans."

Do not overuse "sic," however, since calling attention to others' mistakes can appear snobbish. The preceding quotation, for example, might have been paraphrased instead: *According to the review, even k. d. lang's most loyal fans were surprised by the brilliance of her performance.*

39d The ellipsis mark

The ellipsis mark consists of three spaced periods. Use an ellipsis mark to indicate that you have deleted words from an otherwise word-for-word quotation.

> Reuben reports that "when the amount of cholesterol circulating in the blood rises over . . . 300 milligrams per 100, the chances of a heart attack increase dramatically."

If you delete a full sentence or more in the middle of a quoted passage, use a period before the three ellipsis dots.

> "Most of our efforts," writes Dave Erikson, "are directed toward saving the bald eagle's wintering habitat along the Mississippi River. . . . It's important that the wintering birds have a place to roost, where they can get out of the cold wind."

CAUTION: Ordinarily, do not use the ellipsis mark at the beginning or at the end of a quotation. Readers will understand that the quoted material is taken from a longer passage. If you have cut some words from the end of the final sentence quoted, however, MLA requires an ellipsis mark, as in the first example on page 585.

In quoted poetry, use a full line of ellipsis dots to indicate that you have dropped a line or more from the poem.

> Had we but world enough, and time,
> This coyness, lady, were no crime.
> ....
> But at my back I always hear
> Time's winged chariot hurrying near;   —Andrew Marvell

The ellipsis mark may also be used to indicate a hesitation or interruption in speech or to suggest unfinished thoughts.

> "The apartment building next door . . . it's going up in flames!" yelled Marcia.

> Before falling into a coma, the victim whispered, "It was a man with a tattoo on his . . ."

39e The slash

Use the slash to separate two or three lines of poetry that have been run in to your text. Add a space both before and after the slash.

> In the opening lines of "Jordan," George Herbert pokes gentle fun at popular poems of his time: "Who says that fictions only and false hair / Become a verse? Is there in truth no beauty?"

More than three lines of poetry should be handled as an indented quotation. (See 37b.)

The slash may occasionally be used to separate paired terms such as *pass/fail* and *producer/director.* Do not use a space before or after the slash.

Roger, the producer/director, announced a casting change.

Be sparing, however, in this use of the slash. In particular, avoid the use of *and/or, he/she,* and *his/her.*

EXERCISE 39–1

Edit the following sentences to correct errors in punctuation, focusing especially on appropriate use of the dash, parentheses, brackets, ellipsis mark, and slash. If a sentence is correct, write "correct" after it. Answers to lettered sentences appear in the back of the book. Example:

> **Social insects/— bees, for example/— are able to**
>
> **communicate quite complicated messages to one another.**

a. A client has left his/her cell phone in our conference room.
b. The thousand dollars that we invested in the stock market— just ten years ago—has tripled in value.
c. Samantha selected the pass/fail option for Chemistry 101.
d. The child sang her way through the alphabet—*A, B, C, ... Z*— and then waited for our applause.
e. Of the three basic schools of detective fiction, the tea-and-crumpet, the hardboiled detective, and the police procedural, I find the quaint, civilized quality of the tea-and-crumpet school the most appealing.

1. The old Valentine verse we used to chant says it all: "Sugar is sweet, /And so are you."
2. In studies in which mothers gazed down at their infants in their cribs but remained facially unresponsive, for example, not smiling, laughing, or showing any change of expression, the infants responded with intense weariness and eventual withdrawal.
3. There are three points of etiquette in poker: 1. always allow someone to cut the cards, 2. don't forget to ante up, and 3. never stack your chips.

4. In *Lifeboat,* Alfred Hitchcock appears [some say without his knowledge] in a newspaper advertisement for weight loss.
5. When he was informed that fewer than 20 percent of the panelists scheduled for the 1986 PEN conference were women, Norman Mailer gave this explanation: "There are more men who are deeply interested in intellectual matters than women. . . . [If we put more women on the panel], all we'd be doing is lowering the level of discussion."

ON THE WEB

For an electronic exercise on using the dash, parentheses, brackets, the ellipsis mark, and the slash, go to **www.dianahacker.com/bedhandbook**

and click on   ▶ **Electronic Grammar Exercises**
                    ▶ **E-ex 39–1**

PART VIII

Mechanics

40

Abbreviations

> **GRAMMAR CHECKERS** can flag a few inappropriate abbreviations, such as *Xmas* and *e.g.,* but do not assume that a program will catch all problems with abbreviations.

40a Use standard abbreviations for titles immediately before and after proper names.

TITLES BEFORE PROPER NAMES	**TITLES AFTER PROPER NAMES**
Mr. Rafael Zabala	William Albert Sr.
Ms. Nancy Linehan	Thomas Hines Jr.
Mrs. Edward Horn	Anita Lor, Ph.D.
Dr. Margaret Simmons	Robert Simkowski, M.D.
the Rev. John Stone	Margaret Chin, LL.D.
Prof. James Russo	Polly Stein, D.D.S.

Do not abbreviate a title if it is not used with a proper name.

> My history ~~prof.~~ *professor* was an expert on America's use of the atomic bomb in World War II.

Avoid redundant titles such as *Dr. Amy Day, M.D.* Choose one title or the other: *Dr. Amy Day* or *Amy Day, M.D.*

40b Use abbreviations only when you are sure your readers will understand them.

Familiar abbreviations, often written without periods, are acceptable:

CIA	FBI	AFL-CIO	NAACP
NBA	UPI	NEA	CD-ROM
YMCA	CBS	USA (*or* U.S.A.)	ESL

While in Washington the schoolchildren toured the FBI.

The YMCA has opened a new gym close to my office.

NOTE: When using an unfamiliar abbreviation (such as NASW for National Association of Social Workers) throughout a paper, write the full name followed by the abbreviation in parentheses at the first mention of the name. Then use the abbreviation throughout the rest of the paper.

40c Use B.C., A.D., A.M., P.M., No., and $ only with specific dates, times, numbers, and amounts.

The abbreviation B.C. ("before Christ") follows a date, and A.D. ("*anno Domini*") precedes a date. Acceptable alternatives are B.C.E. ("before the common era") and C.E. ("common era"), both of which follow a date.

40 B.C. (or 40 B.C.E.)	4:00 A.M. (or a.m.)	No. 12 (or no. 12)
A.D. 44 (or 44 C.E.)	6:00 P.M. (or p.m.)	$150

Avoid using A.M., P.M., No., or $ when not accompanied by a specific figure.

▶ We set off for the lake early in the ~~A.M.~~ *morning.*

40d Be sparing in your use of Latin abbreviations.

Latin abbreviations are acceptable in footnotes and bibliographies and in informal writing for comments in parentheses.

> cf. (Latin *confer,* "compare")
> e.g. (Latin *exempli gratia,* "for example")
> et al. (Latin *et alia,* "and others")
> etc. (Latin *et cetera,* "and so forth")
> i.e. (Latin *id est,* "that is")
> N.B. (Latin *nota bene,* "note well")
>
> Harold Simms et al., *The Race for Space*
>
> Alfred Hitchcock directed many classic thrillers (e.g., *Psycho, Rear Window,* and *Vertigo*).

In formal writing use the appropriate English phrases.

▶ Many obsolete laws remain on the books, ~~e.g.,~~ *for example,* a law in Vermont forbidding an unmarried man and woman to sit closer than six inches apart on a park bench.

40e Avoid inappropriate abbreviations.

In formal writing, abbreviations for the following are not commonly accepted: personal names, units of measurement, days of the week, holidays, months, courses of study, divisions of written works, states, and countries (except in addresses and except Washington, D.C.). Do not abbreviate *Company* and *Incorporated* unless their abbreviated forms are part of an official name.

PERSONAL NAME	Charles (not Chas.)
UNITS OF MEASUREMENT	pound (not lb.)

DAYS OF THE WEEK   Monday (not Mon.)

HOLIDAYS   Christmas (not Xmas)

MONTHS   January, February, March (not Jan., Feb., Mar.)

COURSES OF STUDY   political science (not poli. sci.)

DIVISIONS OF WRITTEN WORKS   chapter, page (not ch., p.)

STATES AND COUNTRIES   Massachusetts (not MA or Mass.)

PARTS OF A BUSINESS NAME   Adams Lighting Company (not Adams Lighting Co.); Kim and Brothers, Inc. (not Kim and Bros., Inc.)

▶ Eliza promised to buy me one ~~lb.~~ of Godiva chocolate for my *[pound]* birthday, which was last ~~Fri.~~ *[Friday.]*

EXERCISE 40–1

Edit the following sentences to correct errors in abbreviations. If a sentence is correct, write "correct" after it. Answers to lettered sentences appear in the back of the book. Example:

> This year ~~Xmas~~ will fall on a ~~Tues.~~ *[Christmas]* *[Tuesday.]*

a. Since its inception, the BBC has maintained a consistently high standard of radio and television broadcasting.

b. A no. of govt. officials have been reviewing the records of some small brokerage firms in the area.

c. "Mahatma" Gandhi has inspired many modern leaders, including Martin Luther King Jr.

d. How many lbs. have you lost since you began running four miles a day?

e. Denzil spent all night studying for his psych. exam.

1. My favorite prof., Dr. Barker, is on sabbatical this semester.

2. When she arrived in Poughkeepsie to work at IBM, Pauline was overwhelmed by the sophistication and variety of product prototypes.

3. Some historians think that the New Testament was completed by A.D. 100.
4. My mother's birthday was on Fri. the 13th this year.
5. Many girls fall prey to a cult worship of great entertainers—e.g., in my mother's generation, girls worshiped the Beatles.

ON THE WEB

For an electronic exercise on using abbreviations, go to **www.dianahacker.com/bedhandbook**

and click on ▶ **Electronic Grammar Exercises**
▶ **E-ex 40–1**

41

Numbers

GRAMMAR CHECKERS can tell you to spell out certain numbers, such as *thirty-three* and numbers that begin a sentence, but they won't help you understand when it is acceptable to use figures.

41a Spell out numbers of one or two words or those that begin a sentence. Use figures for numbers that require more than two words to spell out.

▶ Now, some ~~8~~ *eight* years later, Muffin is still with us.

▶ I counted ~~one hundred seventy-six~~ *176* CDs on the shelf.

If a sentence begins with a number, spell out the number or rewrite the sentence.

One hundred fifty
▶ ~~150~~ children in our program need expensive dental treatment.
  ^

Rewriting the sentence will also correct the error and may be less awkward if the number is long: *In our program 150 children need expensive dental treatment.*

EXCEPTIONS: In technical and some business writing, figures are preferred even when spellings would be brief, but usage varies. When in doubt, consult the style guide of the organization for which you are writing.

When several numbers appear in the same passage, many writers choose consistency rather than strict adherence to the rule.

When one number immediately follows another, spell out one and use figures for the other: three 100-meter events, 125 four-poster beds.

41b   Generally, figures are acceptable for dates, addresses, percentages, fractions, decimals, scores, statistics and other numerical results, exact amounts of money, divisions of books and plays, pages, identification numbers, and the time.

DATES   July 4, 1776, 56 B.C., A.D. 30

ADDRESSES   77 Latches Lane, 519 West 42nd Street

PERCENTAGES   55 percent (or 55%)

FRACTIONS, DECIMALS   ½, 0.047

SCORES   7 to 3, 21–18

STATISTICS   average age 37, average weight 180

SURVEYS   4 out of 5

EXACT AMOUNTS OF MONEY $105.37, $106,000

DIVISIONS OF BOOKS   volume 3, chapter 4, page 189

DIVISIONS OF PLAYS   act 3, scene 3 (or act III, scene iii)

IDENTIFICATION NUMBERS   serial number 10988675

TIME OF DAY   4:00 P.M., 1:30 A.M.

▶ Several doctors put up ~~two hundred fifty-five thousand~~ *$255,000*

~~dollars~~ for the construction of a golf course.

NOTE: When not using A.M. or P.M., write out the time in words (*two o'clock in the afternoon, twelve noon, seven in the morning*).

EXERCISE 41–1

Edit the following sentences to correct errors in the use of numbers. If a sentence is correct, write "correct" after it. Answers to lettered sentences appear in the back of the book. Example:

By the end of the evening Ashanti had only ~~three dollars and~~ *$3.06*

~~six cents~~ left.

a. We have ordered 4 azaleas, 3 rhododendrons, and 2 mountain laurels for the back area of the garden.
b. The program's cost is well over one billion dollars.
c. The score was tied at 5–5 when the momentum shifted and carried the Standards to a decisive 12–5 win.
d. 8 students in the class had been labeled "learning disabled."
e. The Vietnam Veterans Memorial in Washington, D.C., had fifty-eight thousand one hundred thirty-two names inscribed on it when it was dedicated in 1982.

1. One of my favorite scenes in Shakespeare is the property division scene in act 1 of *King Lear.*
2. The botany lecture will begin at precisely 3:30 P.M.
3. 12 percent of all American marriages occur in June.
4. In nineteen hundred and forty-one, the United States entered World War II.
5. On a normal day, I spend at least 4 to 5 hours surfing the Internet.

ON THE WEB

For an electronic exercise on using numbers, go to
www.dianahacker.com/bedhandbook

and click on ▶ **Electronic Grammar Exercises**
　　　　　　　 ▶ **E-ex 41–1**

42

Italics (underlining)

Italics, a slanting typeface used in printed material, can be produced by word processing programs. In handwritten or typed papers, underlining is used instead. Some instructors prefer underlining even though their students can produce italics.

NOTE: Some e-mail systems do not allow for italics or underlining. Many people indicate words that should be italicized by preceding and ending them with underscore marks or asterisks. Punctuation should follow the coding.

```
I am planning to write my senior thesis on _Anna
Karenina_.
```

Mechanics

In less formal e-mail messages, normally italicized words aren't marked at all.

```
I finally finished reading Anna Karenina--what a
masterpiece!
```

CAUTION: In World Wide Web documents, underlining indicates a hot link. When creating a Web document, use italics, not underlining, for the conventions described in this section.

GRAMMAR CHECKERS do not flag problems with italics or underlining. (For a general discussion of what grammar checkers can and cannot do, see p. 59.)

42a Underline or italicize the titles of works according to convention.

Titles of the following works should be underlined or italicized.

TITLES OF BOOKS   *The Great Gatsby, A Distant Mirror*

MAGAZINES   *Time, Scientific American*

NEWSPAPERS   the *St. Louis Post-Dispatch*

PAMPHLETS   *Common Sense, Facts about Marijuana*

LONG POEMS   *The Waste Land, Paradise Lost*

PLAYS   *King Lear, A Raisin in the Sun*

FILMS   *Casablanca, The Matrix*

TELEVISION PROGRAMS   *Dawson's Creek, 60 Minutes*

RADIO PROGRAMS   *All Things Considered*

MUSICAL COMPOSITIONS   Gershwin's *Porgy and Bess*

CHOREOGRAPHIC WORKS   Twyla Tharp's *Brief Fling*

WORKS OF VISUAL ART   Rodin's *The Thinker*

COMIC STRIPS   *Dilbert*

SOFTWARE   *WordPerfect, Acrobat Reader*

WEB SITES   *Barron's Online, ZDNet*

The titles of other works, such as short stories, essays, episodes of radio and television programs, songs, and short poems, are enclosed in quotation marks. (See 37d.)

NOTE: Do not use underlining or italics when referring to the Bible, titles of books in the Bible (Genesis, not *Genesis*), or titles of legal documents (the Constitution, not the *Constitution*). Do not underline the title of your own paper.

42b   Underline or italicize the names of spacecraft, aircraft, ships, and trains.

Challenger, Spirit of St. Louis, Queen Elizabeth II, Silver Streak

▶ The success of the Soviets' Sputnik galvanized the U.S.

space program.

42c   Underline or italicize foreign words used in an English sentence.

▶ Although Joe's method seemed to be successful, I decided to

establish my own modus operandi.

Mechanics

EXCEPTION: Do not underline or italicize foreign words that have become a standard part of the English language — "laissez-faire," "fait accompli," "habeas corpus," and "per diem," for example.

42d   Underline or italicize words mentioned as words, letters mentioned as letters, and numbers mentioned as numbers.

▶ Tim assured us that the howling probably came from
   his bloodhound, Hill Billy, but his <u>probably</u> stuck in
   our minds.

▶ Sarah called her father by his given name, Johnny, but she
   was unable to pronounce <u>J</u>.

▶ A big <u>3</u> was painted on the door.

NOTE: Quotation marks may be used instead of underlining or italics to set off words mentioned as words. (See 37e.)

42e   Avoid excessive underlining or italics for emphasis.

Underlining or italicizing to emphasize words or ideas is distracting and should be used sparingly.

▶ In-line skating is a popular sport that has almost become
   an addiction.

EXERCISE 42–1

Edit the following sentences to correct errors in the use of italics. If a sentence is correct, write "correct" after it. Answers to lettered sentences appear in the back of the book. Example:

> <u>Leaves of Grass</u> by Walt Whitman was quite controversial
>
> when it was published a century ago.

a. Howard Hughes commissioned the Spruce Goose, a beautifully built but thoroughly impractical wooden aircraft.
b. The old man *screamed* his anger, *shouting* to all of us, "I will not leave my money to you worthless layabouts!"
c. I learned the Latin term ad infinitum from an old nursery rhyme about fleas: "Great fleas have little fleas upon their back to bite 'em, / Little fleas have lesser fleas and so on ad infinitum."
d. Cinema audiences once gasped at hearing the word *damn* in *Gone with the Wind.*
e. "The City and the Pillar" was an early novel by Gore Vidal.

1. Bernard watched as Eileen stood transfixed in front of Vermeer's Head of a Young Girl.
2. The monastery walls were painted with scenes described in the book of Genesis.
3. My per diem allowance was two hundred dollars.
4. In her first calligraphy lesson, Suzanne learned how to make a Romanesque B.
5. Redford and Newman in the movie "The Sting" were amateurs compared with the seventeen-year-old con artist who lives at our house.

ON THE WEB

For an electronic exercise on using italics, go to
www.dianahacker.com/bedhandbook

and click on ▶ **Electronic Grammar Exercises**
▶ **E-ex 42–1**

43

Spelling

You learned to spell from repeated experience with words in both reading and writing, but especially writing. Words have a look, a sound, and even a feel to them as the hand moves across the page. As you proofread, you can probably tell if a word doesn't look quite right. In such cases, the solution is obvious: Look up the word in the dictionary.

SPELL CHECKERS AND GRAMMAR CHECKERS are useful alternatives to a dictionary, but only to a point. A spell checker will not tell you how to spell words not listed in its dictionary; nor will it help you catch words commonly confused, such as *accept* and *except,* or some typographical errors, such as *own* for *won.* You will still need to proofread, and for some words you may need to turn to the dictionary.

Grammar checkers can flag commonly confused words such as *accept* and *except* or *principal* and *principle,* but they often do this when you have used the correct word. You will still need to think about the meaning you intend.

43a   Become familiar with your dictionary.

A good desk dictionary—such as *The American Heritage Dictionary of the English Language, The Random House College Dictionary, Merriam-Webster's Collegiate Dictionary,* or *Webster's New World Dictionary of the American Language*—is an indispensable writer's aid.

A sample dictionary entry, taken from *The American Heritage Dictionary*, appears below. Labels show where various kinds of information about a word can be found in that dictionary.

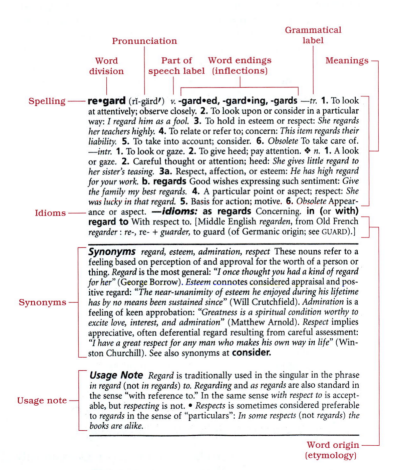

Pronunciation

Grammatical label

Word division

Part of speech label

Word endings (inflections)

Meanings

Spelling —— **re•gard** (rĭ-gärd*ʹ*) *v.* **-gard•ed, -gard•ing, -gards** —*tr.* **1.** To look at attentively; observe closely. **2.** To look upon or consider in a particular way: *I regard him as a fool.* **3.** To hold in esteem or respect: *She regards her teachers highly.* **4.** To relate or refer to; concern: *This item regards their liability.* **5.** To take into account; consider. **6.** *Obsolete* To take care of. —*intr.* **1.** To look or gaze. **2.** To give heed; pay attention. ❖ *n.* **1.** A look or gaze. **2.** Careful thought or attention; heed: *She gives little regard to her sister's teasing.* **3a.** Respect, affection, or esteem: *He has high regard for your work.* **b. regards** Good wishes expressing such sentiment: *Give the family my best regards.* **4.** A particular point or aspect; respect: *She was lucky in that regard.* **5.** Basis for action; motive. **6.** *Obsolete* Appearance or aspect. **—*idioms*: as regards** Concerning. **in (or with) regard to** With respect to. [Middle English *regarden*, from Old French *regarder* : *re-*, re- + *guarder*, to guard (of Germanic origin; see GUARD).]

Idioms ——

Synonyms ——

Synonyms *regard, esteem, admiration, respect* These nouns refer to a feeling based on perception of and approval for the worth of a person or thing. *Regard* is the most general: *"I once thought you had a kind of regard for her"* (George Borrow). *Esteem* connotes considered appraisal and positive regard: *"The near-unanimity of esteem he enjoyed during his lifetime has by no means been sustained since"* (Will Crutchfield). *Admiration* is a feeling of keen approbation: *"Greatness is a spiritual condition worthy to excite love, interest, and admiration"* (Matthew Arnold). *Respect* implies appreciative, often deferential regard resulting from careful assessment: *"I have a great respect for any man who makes his own way in life"* (Winston Churchill). See also synonyms at **consider.**

Usage note ——

Usage Note *Regard* is traditionally used in the singular in the phrase *in regard* (not *in regards*) *to. Regarding* and *as regards* are also standard in the sense "with reference to." In the same sense *with respect to* is acceptable, but *respecting* is not. • *Respects* is sometimes considered preferable to *regards* in the sense of "particulars": *In some respects* (not *regards*) *the books are alike.*

Word origin (etymology)

Spelling, word division, pronunciation

The main entry (*re•gard* in the sample entry) shows the correct spelling of the word. When there are two correct spellings of a word (as in *collectible, collectable,* for example), both are given, with the preferred spelling usually appearing first.

The main entry also shows how the word is divided into syllables. The dot between *re* and *gard* separates the word's two syllables and indicates where the word should be divided if it can't fit at the end of a line of type (see 44f). When a word is compound, the main entry shows how to write it: as one word (*crossroad*), as a hyphenated word (*cross-stitch*), or as two words (*cross section*).

The word's pronunciation is given just after the main entry. The accents indicate which syllables are stressed; the other marks are explained in the dictionary's pronunciation key. In some dictionaries this key appears at the bottom of every page or every other page.

Word endings and grammatical labels

When a word takes endings to indicate grammatical functions (called *inflections*), the endings are listed in boldface, as with *-garded, -garding,* and *-gards* in the sample entry.

Labels for the parts of speech and for other grammatical terms are abbreviated. The most commonly used abbreviations are these:

n.	noun	adj.	adjective
pl.	plural	adv.	adverb
sing.	singular	pron.	pronoun
v.	verb	prep.	preposition
tr.	transitive verb	conj.	conjunction
intr.	intransitive verb	interj.	interjection

Meanings, word origin, synonyms, and antonyms

Each meaning for the word is given a number. Occasionally a word's use is illustrated in a quoted sentence.

Sometimes a word can be used as more than one part of speech (*regard,* for instance, can be used as either a verb or a noun). In such a case, all the meanings for one part of speech are given before all the meanings for another, as in the sample entry. The entry also gives idiomatic uses of the word.

The origin of the word, called its *etymology,* appears in brackets after all the meanings (in some dictionaries it appears before the meanings).

Synonyms, words similar in meaning to the main entry, are frequently listed. In the sample entry, the dictionary draws distinctions in meaning among the various synonyms. Antonyms, which do not appear in the sample entry, are words having a meaning opposite from that of the main entry.

Usage

Usage labels indicate when, where, or under what conditions a particular meaning for a word is appropriately used. Common labels are *informal* (or *colloquial*), *slang, nonstandard, dialect, obsolete, archaic, poetic,* and *British.* In the sample entry, two meanings of *regard* are labeled *obsolete* because they are no longer in use.

Dictionaries sometimes include usage notes as well. In the sample entry, the dictionary offers advice on several uses of *regard* not specifically covered by the meanings. Such advice is based on the opinions of many experts and on actual usage in current magazines, newspapers, and books.

ON THE WEB

For links to online dictionaries and other resources that will help you with grammar, style, and punctuation, go to **www.dianahacker.com/bedhandbook**

and click on ▶ **Links Library**
▶ **Grammar, Style, and Punctuation**

43b Discriminate between words that sound alike but have different meanings.

Words that sound alike or nearly alike but have different meanings and spellings are called homophones. The following sets of words are so commonly confused that a good proofreader will double-check their every use.

affect (verb: "to exert an influence")
effect (verb: "to accomplish"; noun: "result")

its (possessive pronoun: "of or belonging to it")
it's (contraction for "it is")

loose (adjective: "free, not securely attached")
lose (verb: "to fail to keep, to be deprived of")

principal (adjective: "most important"; noun: "head of a school")
principle (noun: "a general or fundamental truth")

their (possessive pronoun: "belonging to them")
they're (contraction for "they are")
there (adverb: "that place or position")

who's (contraction for "who is")
whose (possessive form of "who")

your (possessive form of "you")
you're (contraction of "you are")

To check for correct use of these and other commonly confused words, consult the Glossary of Usage, which begins on page 815.

43c Become familiar with the major spelling rules.

i *before* e *except after* c

Use *i* before *e* except after *c* or when sounded like *ay*, as in *neighbor* and *weigh*.

I BEFORE E	relieve, believe, sieve, niece, fierce, frieze
E BEFORE I	receive, deceive, sleigh, freight, eight
EXCEPTIONS	seize, either, weird, height, foreign, leisure

Suffixes

FINAL SILENT -E Generally, drop a final silent -e when adding a suffix that begins with a vowel. Keep the final -e if the suffix begins with a consonant.

combine, combination	achieve, achievement
desire, desiring	care, careful
prude, prudish	entire, entirety
remove, removable	gentle, gentleness

Words such as *changeable, judgment, argument,* and *truly* are exceptions.

FINAL -Y When adding -s or -d to words ending in -y, ordinarily change -y to -ie when the -y is preceded by a consonant but not when it is preceded by a vowel.

| comedy, comedies | monkey, monkeys |
| dry, dried | play, played |

With proper names ending in -y, however, do not change the -y to -ie even if it is preceded by a consonant: *the Dougherty family, the Doughertys.*

FINAL CONSONANTS If a final consonant is preceded by a single vowel *and* the consonant ends a one-syllable word or a stressed syllable, double the consonant when adding a suffix beginning with a vowel.

| bet, betting | occur, occurrence |
| commit, committed | |

Mechanics

Spelling varies slightly among English-speaking countries. This can prove particularly confusing for ESL students, who may have learned British or Canadian English. Following is a list of some common words spelled differently in American and British English. Consult a dictionary for others.

AMERICAN	**BRITISH**
canceled, traveled	cancelled, travelled
color, humor	colour, humour
judgment	judgement
check	cheque
realize, apologize	realise, apologise
defense	defence
anemia, anesthetic	anaemia, anaesthetic
theater, center	theatre, centre
fetus	foetus
mold, smolder	mould, smoulder
civilization	civilisation
connection, inflection	connexion, inflexion
licorice	liquorice

Plurals

-S OR -ES   Add *-s* to form the plural of most nouns; add *-es* to singular nouns ending in *-s, -sh, -ch,* and *-x.*

table, tables	church, churches
paper, papers	dish, dishes

Ordinarily add *-s* to nouns ending in *-o* when the *-o* is preceded by a vowel. Add *-es* when it is preceded by a consonant.

radio, radios	hero, heroes
video, videos	tomato, tomatoes

OTHER PLURALS To form the plural of a hyphenated compound word, add the *-s* to the chief word even if it does not appear at the end.

mother-in-law, mothers-in-law

English words derived from other languages such as Latin or French sometimes form the plural as they would in their original language.

medium, media   chateau, chateaux
criterion, criteria

43d Be alert to commonly misspelled words.

absence	attendance	criticism	February
academic	basically	criticize	foreign
accidentally	beginning	decision	forty
accommodate	believe	definitely	fourth
achievement	benefited	descendant	friend
acknowledge	bureau	dictionary	government
acquaintance	business	disastrous	grammar
acquire	calendar	eighth	guard
address	candidate	eligible	harass
all right	cemetery	embarrass	height
amateur	changeable	emphasize	humorous
analyze	column	entirely	incidentally
answer	commitment	environment	incredible
apparently	committed	especially	indispensable
appearance	committee	exaggerated	inevitable
arctic	competitive	exercise	intelligence
argument	conceivable	exhaust	irrelevant
arithmetic	conferred	existence	irresistible
arrangement	conqueror	extraordinary	knowledge
ascend	conscience	extremely	license
athlete	conscientious	familiar	lightning
athletics	conscious	fascinate	loneliness

maintenance	phenomenon	quizzes	subtly
maneuver	physically	receive	succeed
marriage	picnicking	referred	surprise
mathematics	playwright	restaurant	thorough
mischievous	practically	rhythm	tragedy
necessary	precede	roommate	transferred
noticeable	preference	sandwich	tries
occasion	preferred	schedule	truly
occurred	prejudice	seize	unnecessarily
occurrence	prevalent	separate	usually
pamphlet	privilege	sergeant	vacuum
parallel	proceed	siege	vengeance
particularly	professor	similar	villain
pastime	pronunciation	sincerely	weird
permissible	quiet	sophomore	whether
perseverance	quite	strictly	writing

LOOKING AT YOURSELF AS A WRITER
Spelling

If spelling is a problem for you, consider possible sources of
your difficulties. Here are some causes and cures.

CAUSE   You have trouble with a few commonly misspelled
words, and because these words occur so often,
your spelling problem seems worse than it is.

CURE   Ask someone to dictate words from the list of commonly misspelled words on pages 463–64, and write
the words as they are read to you. Once you have
identified your "spelling demons," practice writing
the words correctly.

CAUSE   You tend to confuse words that sound alike.

CURE   Keep a list of the commonly confused words that
give you trouble. When they occur in a draft, consult the Glossary of Usage at the back of this book.

Spelling (continued)

CAUSE   Your handwriting is so poor that the words don't
flow smoothly onto the paper. (Spelling is to some
extent kinesthetic—a matter of how a word "feels"
as you form it.)

CURE   Try typing your drafts. The words may flow more
smoothly as you type, reducing your misspellings.
Another advantage of typing is that you'll have
access to a spell checker.

CAUSE   You have a learning disability. Maybe you have
trouble distinguishing between sounds, or perhaps
your eyes scramble or reverse letters.

CURE   If possible, consult an expert on learning disabilities. With the expert's help, you can diagnose
the cause of your problem and devise ways to overcome it—or work around it. Almost certainly the
expert will advise you to write on a computer with a
spell checker.

EXERCISE 43–1

The following memo has been run through a spell checker. Proofread it carefully, editing the spelling and typographical errors that
remain.

November 1, 2001

To: Patricia Wise

cc: Richard Chang

Form: Constance Mayhew

Subject: Express Tours annual report

Mechanics

Thank you for agreeing to draft the annual report for Express Tours. Before you begin you're work, let me outline the initial steps.

First, its essential for you to include brief profiles of top management. Early next week, I'll provide profiles for all manages accept Samuel Heath, who's biographical information is being revised. You should edit these profiles carefully, than format them according to the enclosed instructions. We may ask you to include other employee's profiles at some point.

Second, you should arrange to get complete financial information for fiscal year 2001 from our comptroller, Richard Chang. (Helen Boyes, to, can provide the necessary figures.) When you get this information, precede according tot he plans we discuss in yesterday's meeting. By the way, you will notice from the figures that the sale of our Charterhouse division did not significantly effect net profits.

Third, you should submit first draft of the report by December 15. I assume that you won a laser printer, but if you don't, you can submit a disk and we'll print out a draft here. Of coarse, you should proofread you writing.

I am quiet pleased that you can take on this project. If I or anyone else at Express Tours can answers questions, don't hesitate to call.

44

The hyphen

GRAMMAR CHECKERS can flag some, but not all, missing or misused hyphens. For example, the programs can often tell you that a hyphen is needed in compound numbers, such as *sixty-four*. They can also tell you how to spell certain compound words, such as *breakup* (not *break-up*).

44a Consult the dictionary to determine how to treat a compound word.

The dictionary will tell you whether to treat a compound word as a hyphenated compound (*water-repellent*), one word (*waterproof*), or two words (*water table*). If the compound word is not in the dictionary, treat it as two words.

▶ The prosecutor chose not to cross-examine any witnesses.

▶ Grandma kept a small notebook in her apron pocket.

▶ Alice walked through the looking-glass into a backward world.

44b Use a hyphen to connect two or more words functioning together as an adjective before a noun.

▶ Mrs. Douglas gave Toshiko a seashell and some newspaper-wrapped fish to take home to her mother.

▶ Priscilla Hood is not yet a well-known candidate.

Newspaper-wrapped and *well-known* are adjectives used before the nouns *fish* and *candidate*.

Generally, do not use a hyphen when such compounds follow the noun.

▶ After our television campaign, Priscilla Hood will be well known.

Do not use a hyphen to connect *-ly* adverbs to the words they modify.

▶ A slowly/moving truck tied up traffic.

NOTE: In a series, hyphens are suspended.

Do you prefer first-, second-, or third-class tickets?

44c Hyphenate the written form of fractions and of compound numbers from twenty-one to ninety-nine.

▶ One-fourth of my income goes to pay off the national debt.

44d Use a hyphen with the prefixes *all-*, *ex-* (meaning "former"), and *self-* and with the suffix *-elect*.

▶ The charity is funneling more money into self-help projects.

▶ Anne King is our club's president-elect.

44e A hyphen is used in some words to avoid ambiguity or to separate awkward double or triple letters.

Without the hyphen there would be no way to distinguish between words such as *re-creation* and *recreation.*

Bicycling in the country is my favorite recreation.

The film was praised for its astonishing re-creation of nineteenth-century London.

Hyphens are sometimes used to separate awkward double or triple letters in compound words (*anti-intellectual, cross-stitch*). Always check a dictionary for the standard form of the word.

44f If a word must be divided at the end of a line, divide it correctly.

1. Divide words between syllables.

▶ When I returned from overseas, I didn't ~~reco~~ ^recog-^
~~gnize~~ *nize* one face on the magazine covers. ^

2. Never divide one-syllable words.

▶ He didn't have the courage or the ~~stren~~
strength
~~gth~~ to open the door.
^

3. Never divide a word so that a single letter stands alone at the end of a line or fewer than three letters begin a line.

▶ She'll bring her brother with her when she comes ~~a~~
again.
~~gain.~~
^

▶ As audience to *The Mousetrap,* Hamlet is a ~~watch~~
watcher
~~er~~ watching watchers.
^

4. When dividing a compound word at the end of a line, either make the break between the words that form the compound or put the whole word on the next line.

▶ My niece is determined to become a long-~~dis~~
distance
~~tance~~ runner when she grows up.
^

5. To divide long e-mail and Internet addresses, do not use a hyphen. Break the address after a slash, like this:

> To find a zip code quickly, use the United States
> Postal Service Web site at <http://usps.gov/
> ncsc/lookup>.

EXERCISE 44–1

Edit the following sentences to correct errors in hyphenation. If a sentence is correct, write "correct" after it. Answers to lettered sentences appear in the back of the book. Example:

> **Zola's first readers were scandalized by his slice‸of‸life**
>
> **novels.**

a. Gold is the seventy-ninth element in the periodic table.
b. The swiftly-moving tugboat pulled alongside the barge and directed it away from the oil spill in the harbor.
c. The Moche were a pre-Columbian people who established a sophisticated culture in ancient Peru.
d. Your dog is well-known in our neighborhood.
e. Road-blocks were set up along all the major highways leading out of the city.

1. We knew we were driving too fast when our tires skidded on the rain slick surface.
2. The Black Death reduced the population of some medieval villages by two thirds.
3. The flight attendant asked us to fasten our seat belts before liftoff.
4. A well known actress who wishes to remain anonymous has contributed ten thousand dollars toward our scholarship fund.
5. Gail Sheehy writes that at age twenty five many people assume that the choices they make are irrevocable.

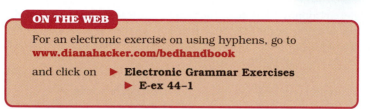

ON THE WEB

For an electronic exercise on using hyphens, go to
www.dianahacker.com/bedhandbook

and click on   ▶ **Electronic Grammar Exercises**
                ▶ **E-ex 44–1**

45

Capital letters

In addition to the rules in this section, you can use a good dictionary to tell you when to use capital letters.

GRAMMAR CHECKERS remind you that sentences should begin with capital letters and that some words, such as *Cherokee,* are proper nouns. Many words, however, should be capitalized only in certain contexts, and you must determine when to do so.

45a Capitalize proper nouns and words derived from them; do not capitalize common nouns.

Proper nouns are the names of specific persons, places, and things. All other nouns are common nouns. The following types of words are usually capitalized: names for the deity, religions, religious followers, sacred books; words of family relationship used as names; particular places; nationalities and their languages, races, tribes; educational institutions, departments, degrees, particular courses; government departments, organizations, political parties; historical movements, periods, events, documents; specific electronic sources; and trade names.

PROPER NOUNS	COMMON NOUNS
God (used as a name)	a god
Book of Jeremiah	a book
Uncle Pedro	my uncle
Father (used as a name)	my father
Lake Superior	a picturesque lake
the Capital Center	a center for advanced studies
the South	a southern state
Japan, a Japanese garden	an ornamental garden
University of Wisconsin	a good university
Geology 101	geology
Environmental Protection Agency	a federal agency
Phi Kappa Psi	a fraternity
a Democrat	an independent
the Enlightenment	the eighteenth century
the Declaration of Independence	a treaty
the World Wide Web, the Web	a home page
the Internet, the Net	a computer network
Kleenex	a tissue

Months, holidays, and days of the week are treated as proper nouns; the seasons and numbers of the days of the month are not.

Our academic year begins on a Tuesday in early September, right after Labor Day.

My mother's birthday is in early summer, on the second of June.

EXCEPTION: Capitalize Fourth of July (or July Fourth) when referring to the holiday.

Names of school subjects are capitalized only if they are names of languages. Names of particular courses are capitalized.

> This semester Austin is taking math, geography, geology, French, and English.

> Professor Anderson offers Modern American Fiction 501 to graduate students.

CAUTION: Do not capitalize common nouns to make them seem important: *Our company is currently hiring computer programmers* (not *Company, Computer Programmers*).

45b Capitalize titles of persons when used as part of a proper name but usually not when used alone.

> Professor Margaret Barnes; Dr. Harold Stevens; John Scott Williams Jr.; Anne Tilton, LL.D.

> District Attorney Marshall was reprimanded for badgering the witness.

> The district attorney was elected for a two-year term.

Usage varies when the title of an important public figure is used alone: *The president* [or *President*] *vetoed the bill.*

45c Capitalize the first, last, and all major words in titles and subtitles of works such as books, articles, songs, and online documents.

In both titles and subtitles, major words such as nouns, pronouns, verbs, adjectives, and adverbs should be capitalized. Minor words such as articles, prepositions, and coordinating conjunctions are not capitalized unless they are the first or last word of a title or subtitle. Capitalize the second part of a hyphenated term in a title if it is a major word but not if it is a minor word.

To see why some of the following titles are italicized and some are put in quotation marks, see 42a and 37d.

The Impossible Theater: A Manifesto
The F-Plan Diet
"Fire and Ice"
"I Want to Hold Your Hand"
The Canadian Green Page

Capitalize chapter titles and the titles of other major divisions of a work following the same guidelines used for titles of complete works.

"Work and Play" in Santayana's *The Nature of Beauty*

45d Capitalize the first word of a sentence.

Obviously the first word of a sentence should be capitalized.

When lightning struck the house, the chimney collapsed.

When a sentence appears within parentheses, capitalize its first word unless the parentheses appear within another sentence.

Early detection of breast cancer significantly increases survival rates. (See table 2.)

Early detection of breast cancer significantly increases survival rates (see table 2).

45e Capitalize the first word of a quoted sentence but not a quoted phrase.

In *Time* magazine Robert Hughes writes, "There are only about sixty Watteau paintings on whose authenticity all experts agree."

Russell Baker has written that in our country, sports are "the opiate of the masses."

If a quoted sentence is interrupted by explanatory words, do not capitalize the first word after the interruption. (See 37f.)

"If you wanted to go out," he said sharply, "you should have told me."

When quoting poetry, copy the poet's capitalization exactly. Many poets capitalize the first word of every line of poetry; a few contemporary poets dismiss capitalization altogether.

When I consider everything that grows
Holds in perfection but a little moment — Shakespeare

it was the week   that
i felt the city's narrow breezes rush about
me — Don L. Lee

45f Do not capitalize the first word after a colon unless it begins an independent clause, in which case capitalization is optional.

Most of the bar's patrons can be divided into two groups: the occasional after-work socializers and the nothing-to-go-home-to regulars.

This we are forced to conclude: The [*or* the] federal government is needed to protect the rights of minorities.

45g Capitalize abbreviations for departments and agencies of government, other organizations, and corporations; capitalize the call letters of radio and television stations.

EPA, FBI, OPEC, IBM, WCRB, KNBC-TV

EXERCISE 45–1

Edit the following sentences to correct errors in capitalization. If a sentence is correct, write "correct" after it. Answers to lettered sentences appear in the back of the book. Example:

On our trip to the West we visited the ~~g~~rand ~~c~~anyon and the
~~g~~reat ~~s~~alt ~~d~~esert.

a. District attorney Johnson was disgusted when the jurors turned in a verdict of not guilty after only one hour of deliberation.
b. Have you seen the Arena Stage production of *A Raisin in the Sun?*
c. Madeline is taking courses in geology, mathematics, french, and english.
d. My Grandfather and Grandmother emigrated from Lithuania in the mid-1960s.
e. I look forward every Spring to walking along the flower-lined paths in Boston's Public Garden.

1. Whenever my brother took us to the movies, he gave us three choices: A brainless beach party flick, a foreign fluff film, or a blood and lust adventure movie.
2. The grunion is an unremarkable fish except for one curious habit: It comes ashore to spawn.
3. In our family, aunt Sandra was notorious for her biting tongue.
4. Historians have described Robert E. Lee as the aristocratic south personified.
5. Because Eileen enjoys working with handicapped children, she is pursuing a degree in Special Education.

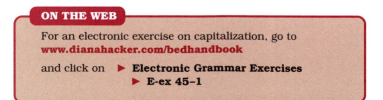

ON THE WEB

For an electronic exercise on capitalization, go to
www.dianahacker.com/bedhandbook

and click on   ▶ **Electronic Grammar Exercises**
                ▶ **E-ex 45–1**

PART IX

Critical Thinking

Most college assignments, especially those based on reading, call for critical thinking: an open-minded, reasoned response to a political or scholarly issue. At times you will be asked to write a researched essay in which you draw conclusions about a variety of sources advancing different points of view (see 49–52). Many assignments, however, ask you to respond critically to just one or two written texts (see 46) or to construct your own argument, which may or may not be based on reading (see 47 and 48).

46

Writing about texts

The word *texts* is general enough to refer to a variety of works: essays, periodical articles, government reports, books, Web sites, and even visuals such as cartoons or advertisements. Most assignments that ask you to respond to a text call for a summary or an analysis.

A summary is neutral in tone and demonstrates that you have understood the author's key ideas (or, in the case of Web sites and visuals, the creator's purpose and design). Assignments calling for an analysis of a text vary widely, but they will usually ask you to look at how the text's parts contribute to its central argument or purpose, often with the aim of judging its evidence or overall effect.

When you write about a text, obviously you need to read it first. Less obvious, perhaps, is the need to reread it and digest its full meaning. Two techniques will help you move beyond a superficial first reading: (1) annotating the text with your comments and insights and (2) outlining the text's key points.

46a   Read actively: Annotate the text.

When you annotate a text as you read, you are doing something—engaging with the work, not just letting the words slip past you. Although you may be fond of using a highlighter to interact with a text, consider using a pencil instead: A pencil promotes active reading in ways that a highlighter cannot. With a highlighter, you just identify key sentences, usually on a first reading; on a second reading, you are often tempted to read only what's highlighted. More important, you can't write down your thoughts, questions, and reactions with a highlighter.

A pencil offers greater flexibility. You can underline key concepts or you can draw an asterisk or other symbol in the margins to mark them. And you can scribble your insights all over the pages—not just on a first reading but on rereadings as well. Finally, if you change your mind while rereading, you can erase your early comments and replace them with fresh insights.

An article with a student's marginal annotations appears below. After annotating the article and later outlining it, the student, LaShawn Freeman, wrote both a summary and an analysis (see pp. 484–85 and pp. 487–91).

A Democrat and a Republican

One Lunch at a Time

GEORGE McGOVERN and ROBERT DOLE

In the summer of 1968, CBS television broadcast a powerful hour-long documentary titled "Hunger: USA." The cameras peered into the dismal pockets of hunger and misery populated by poor American families. Hollow cheeks and rickety legs plagued children and adults alike.

Title and visual suggest simplicity

Emotional appeals

The most moving scene was filmed in a school where all students—even those who were too poor to pay for a meal—were required to go to the cafeteria at lunchtime. One 9- or 10-year-old boy was asked how he felt standing at the rear of the room watching his better-off classmates eat. Lowering his head, the boy confessed softly, "I'm ashamed."

Thirty years later, a child going hungry in an American school is practically unheard of. That's because of the overwhelming success of bipartisan legislation we sponsored in the 1970s, while we were both U.S. senators, which ensures a nutritious meal at school for all children, including America's poorest. While hunger has not yet been eradicated in the United States, the lives of a whole generation of American schoolchildren have been improved thanks to that program.

Now we have the opportunity to reach an even higher goal: to implement a similar plan for the 300 million poor children in the world who either receive no meal at school or do not even attend class.

Once again we have jointly made a proposal, this time to establish a global school feeding program. It is currently being discussed among Washington policymakers and will soon be introduced in Congress. Building on a pilot program initiated this year, the bill commits an annual amount of American agricultural surpluses to provide nutritious meals to already enrolled students and to attract poorer children to school.

Studies show that when food is provided at schools in the developing world, attendance often doubles within a year, and within two years, academic performance can improve by as much as 40 percent. Students remain in school longer, and more of them graduate. Long-term studies indicate that increased literacy rates among girls and women mean they have fewer children. Of the estimated 130 million children who currently do not attend school, 60 percent are girls.

Link between literacy & birthrates

We are not talking about ordinary charity. Feeding children at school yields tangible results in their lives as well as long-term benefits for society as a whole. And in contrast to questionable mega-projects for development, school feeding focuses on the individual child. Reducing children's hunger and improving their educational opportunities creates the human infrastructure needed by nations if they are to prosper and become self-reliant.

Authors don't want to seem too liberal.

This global challenge can once again be met in the spirit of bipartisanship. By committing annual funds for a global school lunch program, we will not only dramatically improve the lives and futures of millions of poor children. We will also be helping out American farmers by increasing purchases of surplus food commodities.

Aren't both authors from farm states?

To use these surpluses, especially in periods when prices are down, strengthens our farmers' markets and takes some of the burden off storage capacities or selling surpluses off at rock-bottom prices. Overseas shipments of U.S. agricultural products also generate business for American processors, packers, shippers, railroads, stevedores and ocean carriers.

Issue of cost

Start-up costs to cover the first two years of a global program would be about $3 billion. As the leader of the effort, the U.S. government should commit half of that amount, the bulk of it in purchased surplus commodities.

How do we get them to do this?

As the program grows and more students enroll in participating schools, costs will increase, but it is hoped and expected that other countries will join in to help. Discussions with other governments have already begun. Rich nations that do not have farm surpluses could contribute cash, shipping, personnel, utensils and other educational inputs. Government costs could be further reduced or supplemented with contributions from private foundations, corporations, labor unions and individuals.

In order for the program to be sustainable, the benefiting governments should be expected to take over financing within five to 10 years. In the meantime, the initiative would be under the instructional and monitoring eyes of the World Food Program, which has nearly 40 years of school feeding experience. Working with other charities and aid groups, WFP can ensure that the other necessary aspects such as teacher training, sanitation and health inputs are coordinated.

I've never heard of this group. Look it up on the Web?

In an era of cynicism and weariness about Third World problems, using food surpluses to feed and help educate poor children may seem like a surprisingly simple way to make an impact. But a hot meal to a poor student today is key to helping him or her become a literate, self-reliant adult tomorrow. This could become the first generation in human history that is finally free from the scourge of hunger.

Again, the idea of simplicity. I don't buy it.

Former senator McGovern, the Democratic presidential nominee in 1972, is U.S. ambassador to the United Nations Agencies on Food and Agriculture in Rome. Former senator Dole was the Republican presidential nominee in 1996.

46b Try sketching a brief outline of the text.

After reading, rereading, and annotating a text, attempt to outline it. A brief outline serves as an X-ray of the text: It reveals the skeleton that lies beneath the words on the page.

As you sketch an outline, pay special attention to the text's thesis (central idea) and its topic sentences. The thesis usually appears in the introduction, often in the first or second paragraph. Topic sentences can be found at the beginnings of most paragraphs in the body of a text, where they announce a shift to a new topic. (See 2a and 4a.)

In your outline, put the author's thesis and key points in your own words. Here, for example, is the outline that LaShawn Freeman came up with as she prepared to write her summary and analysis of the text printed on pages 479–82. Notice that the outline does not simply trace the authors' ideas paragraph by paragraph; instead, it sums up the article's central points.

OUTLINE OF "ONE LUNCH AT A TIME"

Thesis: The United States should help fund worldwide school lunch programs for poor children.

I. The program would have significant benefits.
   A. It would feed hungry children and boost school attendance.
   B. Education leads to increased economic self-sufficiency, and when girls are educated they tend to have fewer children.
   C. U.S. farmers would benefit by selling food surpluses to the government, and our food processors and shippers would earn money as well.
II. The program is workable.
   A. A similar program has been successful in the United States.
   B. Costs of the program would be reasonable.
   C. Other wealthy countries and charities could share the costs.

46c Summarize to demonstrate your understanding.

Your goal in writing a summary is to articulate an author's main idea and key points as simply and briefly as possible, without sacrificing accuracy. Since most summaries must be fairly short, part of your challenge will be in deciding what *not* to include. That means making judgments about what is most important.

When you sit down to write a summary, don't get tangled up in details: Think big. Find the author's central idea for the whole piece — the thesis — and then try to divide the whole into a few major and perhaps minor ideas. If you have sketched a brief outline of the text (see 46b), refer to it as you draft your summary.

Here are some guidelines for writing a summary:

— In the first sentence, mention the title of the reading, the name of the author, and the author's thesis or central purpose.
— Use a neutral tone; be objective.
— Write from the third-person point of view, and use the present tense: *McGovern and Dole argue*...[not *I thought that* or *You will see that*].
— Keep your focus on the authors of the text (McGovern and Dole, for example). In other words, don't state the authors' argument as if it were your own.
— Put all or most of your summary in your own words; if you borrow a phrase or a sentence from the author, put it in quotation marks.
— Limit yourself to presenting the author's key points.
— Be concise; make every word count.

Following is a summary of the article by McGovern and Dole that is printed on pages 479–82.

In "One Lunch at a Time," George McGovern and Robert Dole propose that the United States help fund a worldwide school lunch program for poor children similar to the one in our country. The authors argue that in addition to feeding children, such a program would benefit poor countries in general. Lunches would attract children to schools, and education results in economic self-sufficiency. In addition, the education of girls leads to lower birthrates. American farmers would benefit from the program too, say the authors, since the government would purchase their surpluses. McGovern and Dole suggest that although their plan is ambitious, it is workable. They point to the fact that it has worked in the United States, and they argue that the costs would be reasonable. Start-up costs would be about $3 billion, with the U.S. paying only half of that, since charities and rich countries could be persuaded to cover the balance. The World Food Program, which has a successful track record, would coordinate the efforts. McGovern and Dole believe not only that the program would work: They think that its benefits would far outweigh its costs.

—LaShawn Freeman, student

NOTE: For advice on using summaries in researched writing, see 51c.

46d Analyze to demonstrate your critical thinking.

When an assignment calls for an analysis, read the whole assignment carefully, along with any models provided, to see what is required. The formal definition of *analysis*—the separation of the whole for the purpose of studying the parts —doesn't tell you much. Here are some questions that instructors may want you to address when they ask you to analyze a nonfiction reading:

— What is the author's thesis or central purpose? Who is the audience?

— How does the author structure the text? What are the key parts and how do they relate to one another and to the thesis?

— What strategies has the author used to generate interest in the argument and to persuade readers of its merit?

—What evidence is given in support of the thesis? How convincing is it?

—How effectively has the author addressed the concerns and assumptions of his or her audience? Does the author anticipate objections and counter opposing views? (See 47f.)

—Does the author fall prey to any faulty reasoning? (See 48.)

Depending on your assignment, it may not be necessary to address all of these questions. Also, there is no need to address the questions one at a time—or in just this order.

NOTE: An analysis of a work of literature is different, calling for an interpretation. (See 58.)

Following is an analysis of the article by McGovern and Dole that appears on pages 479–82.

Freeman 1

LaShawn Freeman
Professor Rubin
English 101
17 May 2001

"One Lunch at a Time":
Not as Simple as It Sounds

Former senators George McGovern and Robert
Dole have written the newspaper article "One Lunch
at a Time" hoping to generate public support for a
bold initiative: creating a worldwide school lunch
program for needy children. The authors skillfully
gain the attention of readers and generate interest
in their proposal; whether most readers will move
beyond interest to actual support, however, is
questionable. Although the authors successfully
describe the benefits of the plan, they do not
adequately demonstrate that it would be workable.

The fact that liberal Democrat McGovern and
conservative Republican Dole have teamed up to
write the article attracts readers' attention and
gains their respect. Knowing that the plan has bipartisan roots, conservative readers may be less
inclined to dismiss it as just one more left-wing
government program. Also, both authors have solid
credentials. Each has a reputation for integrity,
and together they bring experience to the subject.
As they write in their opening paragraphs, in the
1970s they cosponsored legislation creating the
U.S. school lunch program.

Opening sentences describe the purpose of the article.

Thesis expresses Freeman's evaluation of the article.

Freeman describes the authors' credibility.

Clear topic sentence announces shift to a new topic.

When describing the benefits of their plan, McGovern and Dole appeal to American idealism and self-interest. Their program's goals are idealistic: feeding hungry children, boosting school attendance, increasing literacy rates, reducing population growth, and spurring economic opportunities. Citing studies, the authors show how these goals are intertwined: When free school lunches are offered in poor communities, "attendance often doubles within a year, and within two years, academic performance can improve by as much as 40 percent" (A23). In addition, educated women tend to have fewer children. Finally, with an educated populace, countries in the developing world have a better chance of moving toward economic self-sufficiency.

Quotation is cited with an MLA in-text citation.

McGovern and Dole make clear that their program is not merely idealistic: "We are not talking about ordinary charity" (A23). America as a whole benefits by promoting stable and economically thriving societies around the world. American farmers benefit by selling their surpluses to the government for shipment overseas.

Question serves as a transition to the second section of the analysis.

Would the McGovern-Dole plan be workable? The authors attempt to persuade us that it would be feasible. The title of the article, "One Lunch at a Time," suggests simplicity, as does the sketch of a pair of hands clutching a full grocery bag. McGovern and Dole open their article with their

Freeman 3

most powerful evidence that the program might work:
A similar school lunch program has been highly successful in the United States. Because this program
was initiated by McGovern and Dole, readers are at
least tempted to think that the authors might be
able to take their plan worldwide.

Once the authors begin talking about specifics, however, many readers will become skeptical. McGovern and Dole focus primarily on costs,
arguing that they would be reasonable. They say
that the initial cost would be $3 billion, half
paid by the United States, half by charities and
other nations. They suggest that in the long run
the countries receiving the food would take over
the funding. Much of this seems like wishful
speculation.

Freeman
summarizes
the authors'
argument
about costs.

The authors pay little attention to the logistical problems their program would face. They do
mention that the World Food Program, which has a
long track record, might coordinate the efforts,
but they devote only a few sentences to this topic.
It is one thing to run a school lunch program in
the United States, a single country that is generally well off. It is quite another to establish
such programs in poor countries with varying cultural traditions and governmental structures. Imagine, for example, trying to work with the Taliban
government in Afghanistan or coordinating a program

Freeman asserts
her own skepti-
cism about the
authors' plan.

in war-torn Sierra Leone. The logistical problems
would be a nightmare.

Freeman treats
the authors
fairly.

To be fair, one must acknowledge that McGovern
and Dole have only a few columns in a newspaper in
which to sell readers on their program. They do a
fine job of generating public interest in their
proposal; in future writings and speeches, perhaps
they can make a better case that their program
might actually work.

Freeman 5

Work Cited

McGovern, George, and Robert Dole. "One Lunch at a
Time." <u>Washington Post</u> 1 May 2001: A23.

47

Constructing reasonable arguments

In argumentative writing, you take a stand on a debatable issue. The issue being debated might be a matter of public policy:

— Should religious groups be allowed to meet on public school property?

— What is the least dangerous way to dispose of nuclear waste?

— Should a state enact laws rationing medical care?

On such questions, reasonable people may disagree.

Reasonable men and women also disagree about many scholarly issues. Psychologists debate the validity of behaviorism; historians interpret causes of the Civil War quite differently; biologists conduct genetic experiments to challenge the conclusions of other researchers.

When you construct a *reasonable* argument, your goal is not simply to win or to have the last word. Your aim is to reveal your current understanding of the truth about a subject or to propose the best solution available for solving a problem—without being needlessly combative. Writing teacher Richard Fulkerson describes such aims well:

> The purpose of argumentation within a free society or within a research field is to reach the best conclusion possible at the time.   — *Teaching the Argument in Writing*

47a   Examine your issue's social and intellectual contexts.

Arguments appear in social and intellectual contexts. Public policy debates obviously arise in social contexts: Grounded in specific times and places, such debates are conducted among groups with competing values and interests. For example, the debate over nuclear power plants is currently being renewed in the United States in light of a perceived energy crisis—with environmentalists, the nuclear industry, consumers, and citizens worried about public safety all weighing in on the argument. Most public policy debates have intellectual dimensions that address scientific or theoretical concerns as well. In the case of the nuclear power issue, physicists, biologists, and economists all contribute their expertise.

Scholarly debates clearly play themselves out in intellectual contexts, but they have a social dimension too. Scholars and researchers rarely work in a vacuum: They respond to the contributions of other specialists in the field, often building on others' views and refining them, but at times challenging them. Social bonds develop among scholars who hold similar views, and bad feelings have been known to arise among those belonging to competing schools of thought.

Because many of your readers will be aware of the social and intellectual contexts in which your issue is grounded, you will be at a serious disadvantage if you are not informed. That's why it is a good idea to conduct some research before preparing your argument; consulting even a few sources can help. For example, the student whose paper appears on pages 501–05 became more knowledgeable about his issue—educating the children of illegal immigrants—after consulting just two brief print sources and one Web site. This student documented his sources using MLA style (see 56).

47b   View your audience as a panel of jurors.

Do not assume that your audience already agrees with you; instead, envision skeptical readers who, like a panel of jurors, will make up their minds after listening to all sides of the argument. If you are arguing a public policy issue, aim your paper at fellow citizens who represent a variety of opinions. In the case of the debate over nuclear power, for example, imagine a jury representative of those who have a stake in the matter: environmentalists, the nuclear industry, consumers, and citizens worried about public safety.

At times, of course, you can deliberately narrow your audience. If you are working within a word limit, for example, you might not have the space in which to address the concerns of all parties to the nuclear energy debate. Or you might be primarily interested in reaching one segment of a general audience, such as consumers. In such instances, you can still view your audience as a panel of jurors; the jury will simply be a less diverse group.

In the case of scholarly debates, you will be addressing readers who share your interest in an academic discipline such as literature or psychology. Such readers belong to what some have called a *discourse community*, a group with an agreed-upon way of investigating and talking about issues. Though they generally agree about procedures, scholars in an academic discipline often disagree about particular issues. Once you see how they disagree about your issue, it will be easy to imagine a jury that reflects the variety of opinions they hold.

47c   In your introduction, establish credibility and state your position.

In argumentative writing, your introduction should ordinarily end with a thesis sentence that states your position on the issue you have chosen to debate (see also 2a). In the sentences leading up to the thesis, establish your credibility with readers by showing that you are knowledgeable and fair-minded. If possible, build common ground with readers who may not be in initial agreement with your views.

In the following introduction, student Kevin Smith presents himself as someone worth listening to. His opening sentence shows that he is familiar with the legal issues surrounding school prayer. His next sentence reveals him to be fair-minded, and it builds common ground by showing that he, like many readers, believes in the value of prayer. Even Smith's thesis builds common ground: "Prayer is too important to be trusted to our public schools."

> Although the Supreme Court has ruled against prayer in public schools on First Amendment grounds, many people still feel that prayers should be allowed. These people, most of whom hold strong religious beliefs, are well intentioned. What they fail to realize is that the Supreme Court decision, although it was made on legal grounds, makes good sense on religious grounds as well. Prayer is too important to be trusted to our public schools.
>
> —Kevin Smith, student

Because Smith takes into consideration the values of those who disagree with him, readers are likely to approach his essay with an open mind.

47d Back up your thesis with persuasive lines of argument.

Arguments of any complexity contain lines of argument that, when taken together, might reasonably persuade readers that the thesis has merit. Here, for example, are the main lines of argument used by a student who opposes regulating use of cell phones while driving:

Thesis: We should not restrict the use of cell phones in moving vehicles.

—The risks of using a cell phone while driving have not been proved scientifically.

—Any risks must be weighed against the benefits of using a phone while driving.

> —Instead of restricting use of the phones, we can educate the public on using them responsibly and enforce laws on negligent and reckless driving.

If you sum up your main lines of argument, as in the example just given, you will have a rough outline of your essay. The outline will consist of your central claim—the thesis—and any subordinate claims that back it up. In your paper, you will provide evidence for each of these claims.

47e   Support your claims with specific evidence.

You will of course need to support your central claim and any subordinate claims with evidence: facts, statistics, examples and illustrations, expert opinion, and so on. Depending on the issue you have chosen to write about, you may or may not need to do some reading to gather evidence. Some argumentative topics, such as whether your college should continue to support its travel study program, can be developed through personal experience and research tools such as questionnaires and interviews. Most debatable topics, however, require that you consult some written sources.

If any of your evidence is based on reading, you must document your sources. Documentation gives credit to the authors and shows readers how to locate a source in case they want to assess its credibility or explore the issue further (see 52).

Using facts and statistics

A fact is something that is known with certainty because it has been objectively verified: The capital of Wyoming is Cheyenne. Carbon has an atomic weight of 12. John F. Kennedy was assassinated on November 22, 1963. Statistics are collections of numerical facts: Weather accounts for 65 percent of the delays at airports. Nearly nine out of ten U.S.

households currently own a VCR. As of 1999, North America held 8.4 percent of proven oil reserves; together, Iraq, Kuwait, and Saudi Arabia held 46 percent.

Most arguments are supported at least to some extent by facts and statistics. For example, in the following passage, the writer uses statistics to show that college students are granted unreasonably high credit limits:

> According to Nellie Mae statistics, in 1998 undergraduates were granted an average credit limit of $3,683; for graduate students the figure jumped to $15,721. Nearly 10% of the students in the Nellie Mae study carried balances near or exceeding these credit limits (Blair).

Writers and politicians often use statistics in selective ways to bolster their partisan views. If you suspect that a writer's handling of statistics is not quite fair, read authors with opposing views, who may give you a fuller understanding of the numbers. For example, one writer might argue that a capital gains tax cut would benefit the middle class because more than half the people earning capital gains have incomes less than $50,000 per year. By reading more about the subject, you might learn that the real beneficiaries of the tax cut would be millionaires, whose capital gains earnings are far greater than those of workers making under $50,000 per year.

Using examples and illustrations

Examples and illustrations (extended examples, often in story form) rarely prove a point by themselves, but when used in combination with other forms of evidence they flesh out an argument and bring it to life. Because they often have an emotional dimension, they can reach readers in ways that statistics cannot.

In a paper arguing in favor of restricting the use of cell phones while driving, student Angela Daly gives examples of four people who were killed in just one month because drivers were distracted by their phones (see p. 637). Daly supplements this emotionally powerful anecdotal evidence with an analysis of scientific investigations on the dangers of using cell phones while driving.

Citing expert opinion

Although they are no substitute for careful reasoning of your own, the views of an expert can contribute to the force of your argument. For example, in a paragraph describing the dangers of using a cell phone while driving, Angela Daly relies on expert Frances Bents:

> Frances Bents, an expert on the relation between cell phones and accidents, estimates that 450 to 1,000 crashes a year have some connection to cell phone use (Layton C9).

When you rely on expert opinion, make sure that your source is an expert in the field you are writing about. In some cases you may need to provide credentials showing why your source is worth listening to. When including expert testimony in your paper, you can summarize or paraphrase the expert's opinion or you can quote the expert's exact words. You will of course need to document the source, as in the example just given (see 52).

47f Anticipate objections; counter opposing arguments.

Readers who already agree with you need no convincing, although a well-argued case for their point of view is always welcome. But indifferent and skeptical readers may resist your arguments because they have minds of their own. To give up a position that seems reasonable, a reader has to see that there is an even more reasonable one. In addition to presenting your own case, therefore, you should review the opposing arguments and attempt to counter them.

There is no best place in an essay to deal with opposing views. Often it is useful to summarize the opposing position early in your essay. After stating your thesis but before developing your own arguments, you might have a paragraph beginning *Critics of this view argue that....* But sometimes a better plan is to anticipate objections as you develop your case paragraph by paragraph. Wherever you decide to deal with opposing arguments, do your best to counter them. Show that those who oppose you are not as persuasive as they claim because their arguments are flawed or because your arguments to the contrary have greater weight.

NOTE: Readers will judge the way you handle opposing views, so do your best to explain the arguments of others accurately and fairly (see 48c).

47g Build common ground.

As you counter opposing arguments, try to build common ground with readers who do not initially agree with your views. If you can show that you share your readers' values, they may be able to switch to your position without giving up what they feel is important. For example, to persuade people opposed to shooting deer, a state wildlife commission would have to show that it too cares about preserving deer and does not want them to die needlessly. Having established these values in common, the commission might be able to persuade critics that a carefully controlled hunting season is good for the deer population because it prevents starvation caused by overpopulation.

People believe that intelligence and decency support their side of an argument. To change sides, they must continue to feel intelligent and decent. Otherwise they will persist in their opposition.

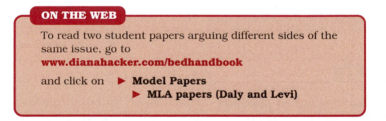

SAMPLE ARGUMENT PAPER

In the following paper, student Andrew Knutson argues that Americans should continue to educate the children of illegal immigrants. Notice that Knutson is careful to establish common ground with readers who may hold a different view. Notice too that he attempts to counter the arguments of the opposition.

In writing the paper, Knutson consulted two print sources and one Internet source. When he quotes from or uses statistics from a source, he cites the source with an MLA (Modern Language Association) in-text citation. Citations in the paper refer readers to the list of works cited at the end of the paper. (See 56.)

ON THE WEB

To read two student papers arguing different sides of the same issue, go to
www.dianahacker.com/bedhandbook

and click on ▶ **Model Papers**
▶ **MLA papers (Daly and Levi)**

Knutson 1

Andrew Knutson
Dr. Karr
English 102
8 March 2000

Why Educate the Children of Illegal Immigrants?

Immigration laws have been a subject of debate throughout American history, especially in states such as California and Texas, where immigrant populations are high. Recently, some citizens have been questioning whether we should continue to educate the children of illegal immigrants. While this issue is steeped in emotional controversy, we must not allow divisive "us against them" rhetoric to cloud our thinking. Yes, educating undocumented immigrants costs us, but not educating them would cost us much more.

Those who propose barring the children of illegal immigrants from our schools have understandable worries. They worry that their state taxes will rise as undocumented children crowd their school systems. They worry about the crowding itself, given the loss of quality education that comes with large class sizes. They worry that school resources will be deflected from their children because of the linguistic and social problems that many of the newcomers face. And finally, they worry that even more illegal immigrants will cross our borders because of the lure of free education.

Opening sentences establish credibility.

Thesis, at end of introductory paragraph, states the main point.

Writer addresses concerns of those who hold opposing views.

Critical thinking

Writer counters opposing arguments.

This last worry is probably unfounded. It is unlikely that many parents are crossing the borders solely to educate their children. More likely, they are in desperate need of work, economic opportunity, and possibly political asylum. As Charles Wheeler of the National Immigration Law Center asserts, "There is no evidence that access to federal programs acts as a magnet to foreigners or that further restrictions would discourage illegal immigrants" (qtd. in "Exploiting").

Quotation is cited using MLA style.

Reasonable tone keeps argument from sounding biased.

The other concerns are more legitimate, but they can be addressed by less drastic measures than barring children from schools. Currently the responsibility of educating about 75% of undocumented children is borne by just a few states-- California, New York, Texas, and Florida (Edmondson 1). One way to help these and other states is to have the federal government pick up the cost of educating undocumented children, with enough funds to alleviate the overcrowded classrooms that cause parents such concern. Such cost shifting could have a significant benefit, for if the federal government had to pay, it might work harder to stem the tide of illegal immigrants.

Statistic is cited using MLA style.

Writer uses evidence to support his thesis.

So far, attempts to bar undocumented children from public schools have failed. In the 1982 case of Plyler v. Doe, the Supreme Court ruled on the issue. In a 5-4 decision, it overturned a Texas law

that allowed schools to deny education to illegal
immigrants. Martha McCarthy reports that Texas had
justified its law as a means of "preserving financial resources, protecting the state from an influx
of illegal immigrants, and maintaining high quality
education for resident children" (128). The Court
considered these issues but concluded that in the
long run the costs of educating immigrant children
would pale in comparison to the costs--both to the
children and to society--of not educating them.

Quotation is
cited using
MLA style.

It isn't hard to figure out what the costs of
not educating these children would be. The costs to
innocent children are obvious: loss of the opportunity to learn English, to understand American culture and history, to socialize with other children
in a structured environment, and to grow up to be
successful, responsible adults.

Transitional
topic sentence
leads readers
to next part of
paper.

The costs to society as a whole are fairly
obvious as well. That is why we work so hard to
promote literacy and prevent students from dropping
out of school. An uneducated populace is dangerous
to the fabric of society, contributing to social
problems such as vandalism and crime, an underground economy, gang warfare, teenage pregnancy,
substance abuse, and infectious and transmissible
diseases. The health issue alone makes it worth our
while to educate the children of undocumented immigrants, for when children are in school, we can

Writer attempts
to build
common ground
with readers.

Knutson 4

make sure they are inoculated properly, and we can
teach them the facts about health and disease.

Conclusion
restates benefits
of educating
children of
illegal
immigrants.

Do we really want thousands of uneducated
children growing up on the streets, where we have
little control over them? Surely not. The lure of
the streets is powerful enough already. Only by
inviting all children into safe and nurturing and
intellectually engaging schools can we combat that
power. Our efforts will be well worth the cost.

Works Cited

Edmondson, Brad. "Life without Illegal Immigrants."
    American Demographics May 1996: 1.

"Exploiting Fears." Admissions Decisions: Should
    Immigration Be Restricted? 7 Oct. 1996.
    Public Agenda. 10 Feb. 2000 <http://
    www.vote-smart.org/issues/Immigration/
    chap2/imm2itx.html>.

McCarthy, Martha M. "Immigrants in Public Schools:
    Legal Issues." Educational Horizons 71 (1993):
    128-30.

Works cited
page is formatted
according to
MLA style.

Critical thinking

48

Evaluating arguments

In your reading and in your own writing, evaluate all arguments for logic and fairness. Many arguments can stand up to critical scrutiny. Often, however, a line of argument that at first seems reasonable turns out to be fallacious, unfair, or both.

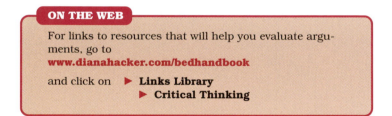

ON THE WEB

For links to resources that will help you evaluate arguments, go to
www.dianahacker.com/bedhandbook

and click on ▶ **Links Library**
▶ **Critical Thinking**

48a   Distinguish between reasonable and fallacious argumentative tactics.

A number of unreasonable argumentative tactics are known as *logical fallacies.* Most of the fallacies—such as hasty generalizations and false analogies—are misguided or dishonest uses of legitimate argumentative strategies. The examples in this section suggest when such strategies are reasonable and when they are not.

Generalizing (inductive reasoning)

Writers and thinkers generalize all the time. We look at a sample of data and conclude that data we have not observed will most likely conform to what we have seen before. From a spoonful of soup, we conclude just how salty the whole bowl will be. After numerous bad experiences with an airline, we decide to book future flights with one of its competitors instead.

When we draw a conclusion from an array of facts, we are engaged in inductive reasoning. Such reasoning deals in probability, not certainty. For a conclusion to be highly probable, it must be based on evidence that is sufficient, representative, and relevant. (See the chart on p. 509.)

The fallacy known as a *hasty generalization* is a conclusion based on insufficient or unrepresentative evidence.

HASTY GENERALIZATION
Deaths from drug overdoses in Metropolis have doubled in the past three years. Therefore, more Americans than ever are dying from drug abuse.

Data from one city do not justify a conclusion about the whole United States.

A *stereotype* is a hasty generalization about a group. Here are a few examples.

STEREOTYPES
Women are bad bosses.

Politicians are corrupt.

Asian students are exceptionally intelligent.

Stereotyping is common because of our human tendency to perceive selectively. We tend to see what we want to see; that is, we notice evidence confirming our already formed opinions and fail to notice evidence to the contrary. For example, if you have concluded that politicians are corrupt, your stereotype will be confirmed by news reports of legislators being indicted—even though every day the media describe conscientious officials serving the public honestly and well.

NOTE: Many hasty generalizations contain words like *all, ever, always,* and *never,* when qualifiers such as *most, many, usually,* and *seldom* would be more accurate.

Drawing analogies

An analogy points out a similarity between two things that are otherwise different. Analogies can be an effective means of arguing a point. In fact, our system of case law, which relies heavily on precedents, makes extensive use of reasoning by analogy. A prosecutor may argue, for example, that X is guilty because his actions resemble those of Y and Z, who were judged guilty in previous rulings. In response, the defense may maintain that the actions of X bear only a superficial resemblance to those of Y and Z and that in legally relevant respects they are in fact quite different.

It is not always easy to draw the line between a reasonable and an unreasonable analogy. At times, however, an analogy is clearly off-base, in which case it is called a *false analogy.*

> **FALSE ANALOGY**
> If we can put humans on the moon, we should be able to find a cure for the common cold.

The writer has falsely assumed that because two things are alike in one respect, they must be alike in others. Putting human beings on the moon and finding a cure for the common cold are both scientific challenges, but the technical problems confronting medical researchers are quite different from those solved by space scientists.

Tracing causes and effects

Demonstrating a connection between causes and effects is rarely a simple matter. For example, to explain why a chemistry course has a high failure rate, you would begin by listing possible causes: inadequate preparation of students,

Testing inductive reasoning

Though inductive reasoning leads to probable and not absolute truth, you can assess a conclusion's likely probability by asking three questions. This chart shows how to apply those questions to a sample conclusion based on a survey.

CONCLUSION The majority of students on our campus would subscribe to high-speed Internet access if it were available.

EVIDENCE In a recent survey, 923 of 1,515 students questioned say they would subscribe to high-speed Internet access.

1. Is the evidence sufficient?
   That depends. On a small campus (say, 3,000 students), the pool of students surveyed would be sufficient for market research, but on a large campus (say, 30,000), 1,515 students are only 5 percent of the population. If that 5 percent were known to be truly representative of the other 95 percent, however, even such a small sample would be sufficient (see question 2).

2. Is the evidence representative?
   The evidence is representative if those responding to the survey reflect the characteristics of the entire student population: age, sex, level of technical expertise, amount of disposable income, and so on. If most of those surveyed are majoring in technical fields, for example, the researchers would be wise to question the survey's conclusion.

3. Is the evidence relevant?
   The answer is yes. The survey question is directly linked to the conclusion. A question about the number of hours spent on the Internet, by contrast, would not be relevant, because it would not be about *subscribing to high-speed Internet access.*

poor teaching, large class size, lack of qualified tutors, and so on. Next you would investigate each possible cause. To see whether inadequate preparation contributes to the high failure rate, for instance, you might compare the math and science backgrounds of successful and failing students. To see whether large class size is a contributing factor, you might run a pilot program of small classes and compare grades in the small classes with those in the larger ones. Only after investigating the possible causes would you be able to weigh the relative impact of each cause and suggest appropriate remedies.

Because cause-and-effect reasoning is so complex, it is not surprising that writers frequently oversimplify it. In particular, writers sometimes assume that because one event follows another, the first is the cause of the second. This common fallacy is known as *post hoc,* from the Latin *post hoc, ergo propter hoc,* meaning "after this, therefore because of this."

> **POST HOC FALLACY**
> Since Governor Smith took office, unemployment of minorities in the state has decreased by 7 percent. Governor Smith should be applauded for reducing unemployment among minorities.

The writer must show that Governor Smith's policies are responsible for the decrease in unemployment; it is not enough to show that the decrease followed the governor's taking office.

Weighing options

Especially when reasoning about problems and solutions, writers must weigh options. To be fair, a writer should mention the full range of options, showing why one is superior to the others or might work well in combination with others.

It is unfair to suggest that there are only two alternatives when in fact there are more. Writers who set up a false choice between their preferred option and one that is clearly unsatisfactory are guilty of the *either...or* fallacy.

> **EITHER...OR FALLACY**
> Our current war against drugs has not worked. Either we should legalize drugs or we should turn the drug war over to our armed forces and let them fight it.

Clearly there are other options, such as increased funding for drug prevention and treatment.

Making assumptions

An assumption is a claim that is taken to be true—without the need of proof. Most arguments are based to some extent on assumptions, since writers rarely have the time and space to prove all of the conceivable claims on which the argument is based. For example, someone arguing about the best means of limiting population growth in developing countries might well assume that the goal of limiting population growth is worthwhile. For most audiences, there would be no need to articulate this assumption or to defend it.

There is a danger, however, in failing to spell out and prove a claim that is clearly controversial. Consider the following short argument, in which a key claim is missing.

> **ARGUMENT WITH MISSING CLAIM**
> Violent crime is increasing.
> Therefore, we should vigorously enforce the death penalty.

The writer seems to be assuming that the death penalty deters violent criminals—and that most audiences will agree. Obviously, neither is a safe assumption.

Critical thinking

When a missing claim is an assertion that few would agree with, we say that a writer is guilty of a *non sequitur* (Latin for "does not follow").

NON SEQUITUR
Mary loves good food; therefore she will be an excellent chef.

Few people would agree with the missing claim—that lovers of good food always make excellent chefs.

Deducing conclusions (deductive reasoning)

When we deduce a conclusion, we—like Sherlock Holmes—put things together. We establish that a general principle is true, that a specific case is an example of that principle, and that therefore a particular conclusion is a certainty. In real life, such absolute reasoning rarely happens. Approximations of it, however, sometimes occur.

Deductive reasoning can often be structured in a three-step argument called a *syllogism.* The three steps are the major premise, the minor premise, and the conclusion.

1. Anything that increases radiation in the environment is dangerous to public health. (Major premise)
2. Nuclear reactors increase radiation in the environment. (Minor premise)
3. Therefore, nuclear reactors are dangerous to public health. (Conclusion)

The major premise is a generalization. The minor premise is a specific case. The conclusion follows from applying the generalization to the specific case.

Deductive arguments break down if one of the premises is not true or if the conclusion does not logically follow from the premises. In the following short argument, the major premise is very likely untrue.

UNTRUE PREMISE
The police do not give speeding tickets to people driving less than five miles per hour over the limit. Sam is driving fifty-nine miles per hour in a fifty-five-mile-per-hour zone. Therefore, the police will not give Sam a speeding ticket.

The conclusion is true only if the premises are true. If the police sometimes give tickets for less than five-mile-per-hour violations, Sam cannot safely conclude that he will avoid a ticket.

In the following argument, both premises might be true, but the conclusion does not follow logically from them.

CONCLUSION DOES NOT FOLLOW
All members of our club ran in this year's Boston Marathon. Jay ran in this year's Boston Marathon. Therefore, Jay is a member of our club.

The fact that Jay ran a marathon is no guarantee that he is a member of the club. Presumably, many runners are nonmembers.

Assuming that both premises are true, the following argument holds up.

CONCLUSION FOLLOWS
All members of our club ran in this year's Boston Marathon. Jay is a member of our club. Therefore, Jay ran in this year's Boston Marathon.

48b Distinguish between legitimate and unfair emotional appeals.

There is nothing wrong with appealing to readers' emotions. After all, many issues worth arguing about have an emotional as well as a logical dimension. Even the Greek logician

Aristotle lists *pathos* (emotion) as a legitimate argumentative tactic.

In the article printed in 46a, George McGovern and Robert Dole have a good reason for tugging at readers' emotions: Their subject is hungry schoolchildren. In their introduction, McGovern and Dole appeal to readers' emotions by describing a scene from a documentary.

LEGITIMATE EMOTIONAL APPEAL

The most moving scene was filmed in a school where all students — even those who were too poor to pay for a meal — were required to go to the cafeteria at lunchtime. One 9- or 10-year-old boy was asked how he felt standing at the rear of the room watching his better-off classmates eat. Lowering his head, the boy confessed softly, "I'm ashamed."

As we all know, however, emotional appeals are frequently misused. Many of the arguments we see in the media, for instance, strive to win our sympathy rather than our intelligent agreement. A TV commercial suggesting that you will be thin and sexy if you drink a certain diet beverage is making a pitch to emotions. So is a political speech that recommends electing John D'Eau because he is a devoted husband and father who fought for his country in Desert Storm.

The following passage illustrates several types of unfair emotional appeals.

UNFAIR EMOTIONAL APPEALS

This progressive proposal to build a ski resort in the state park has been carefully researched by Western Trust, the largest bank in the state; furthermore, it is favored by a majority of the local merchants. The only opposition comes from narrow-minded, do-gooder environmentalists who care more about trees than they do about people; one of their leaders was actually arrested for disturbing the peace several years ago.

Words with strong positive or negative connotations, such as *progressive* and *do-gooder*, are examples of *biased language.* Attacking the persons who hold a belief (environmentalists) rather than refuting their argument is called *ad hominem,* a Latin term meaning "to the man." Associating a prestigious name (Western Trust) with the writer's side is called *transfer.* Claiming that an idea should be accepted because a large number of people are in favor (the majority of merchants) is called the *bandwagon appeal.* Bringing in irrelevant issues (the arrest) is a *red herring,* named after a trick used in fox hunts to mislead the dogs by dragging a smelly fish across the trail.

48c   Judge how fairly a writer handles opposing views.

The way in which a writer deals with opposing views is telling. Some writers address the arguments of the opposition fairly, conceding points when necessary and countering others, all in a civil spirit. Other writers will do almost anything to win an argument: either ignoring opposing views altogether or misrepresenting such views and attacking their proponents.

In your own writing, you build credibility by addressing opposing arguments fairly. (See also 47f.) In your reading, you can assess the credibility of your sources by looking at how they deal with views not in agreement with their own.

Describing the views of others

Writers and politicians often deliberately misrepresent the views of others. One way they do this is by setting up a "straw man," a character so weak that he is easily knocked down. The *straw man* fallacy consists of an oversimplification or outright distortion of opposing views. For example, in a California debate over attempts to control the mountain lion population, pro-lion groups characterized their opponents as trophy hunters bent on shooting harmless lions and sticking them on the walls of their dens. In truth, such hunters were only one faction of those who saw a need to control the lion population.

In response to the District of Columbia's request for voting representation, some politicians have set up a straw man, as shown in the following example.

> **STRAW MAN FALLACY**
> Washington, D.C., residents are lobbying for statehood. Giving a city such as the District of Columbia the status of a state would be unfair.

The straw man wants statehood. In fact, most District citizens are lobbying for voting representation in any form, not necessarily through statehood.

Quoting opposing views

Writers often quote the words of writers who hold opposing views. In general, this is a good idea, for it assures some level of fairness and accuracy. At times, though, both the fairness and accuracy are an illusion.

A source may be misrepresented when it is quoted out of context. All quotations are to some extent taken out of context, but a fair writer will explain that context to readers. To select a provocative sentence from a source and to ignore the more moderate sentences surrounding it is both unfair and misleading. Sometimes a source is deliberately distorted through the device of ellipsis dots. Ellipsis dots tell readers that words have been omitted from the original source. When those words are crucial to an author's meaning, omitting them is obviously unfair. (See also 39d.)

ORIGINAL SOURCE

Johnson's *History of the American West* is riddled with inaccuracies and astonishing in its blatantly racist description of the Indian wars.   —B. R., reviewer

MISLEADING QUOTATION

According to B. R., Johnson's *History of the American West* is "astonishing in its . . . description of the Indian wars."

EXERCISE 48–1

Explain what is illogical in the following brief arguments. It may be helpful to identify the logical fallacy or fallacies by name. Answers to lettered sentences appear in the back of the book.

a. All of my blind dates have been embarrassing disasters, so I know this one will be too.

b. If you're old enough to vote, you're old enough to drink. Therefore, the drinking age should be lowered to eighteen.

c. This country has been run too long by old, out-of-date, out-of-touch, entrenched politicians protecting the special interests that got them elected.

d. It was possible to feed a family of four on $100 a week before Governor Leroy took office and drove up food prices.

e. If you're not part of the solution, you're part of the problem.

1. Whenever I wash my car, it rains. I have discovered a way to end all droughts—get all the people to wash their cars.

2. Either learn how to build a Web site or you won't be able to get a decent job after college.

3. College professors tend to be sarcastic. Three of my five professors this semester make sarcastic remarks.

4. Although Ms. Bell's book on Joe DiMaggio was well researched, I doubt that an Australian historian can contribute much to our knowledge of an American baseball player.

5. Self-righteous nonsmoking fanatics have eroded our basic individual freedoms by railroading the passage of oppressive

antismoking laws that interfere with our natural right to make our own decisions.

6. If professional sports teams didn't pay athletes such high salaries, we wouldn't have so many kids breaking their legs at hockey and basketball camps.

7. Ninety percent of the students oppose a tuition increase; therefore, the board of trustees should not pass the proposed increase.

8. If the president had learned the lesson of Vietnam, he would realize that sending U.S. troops into a foreign country can only end in disaster.

9. A mandatory ten-cent deposit on bottles and cans will eliminate litter because everyone I know will return the containers for the money rather than throw them away.

10. Soliciting money to save whales and baby seals is irresponsible when thousands of human beings can't afford food and shelter.

PART X

Researched Writing

College research assignments are an opportunity for you to contribute to an intellectual inquiry or debate. Most college assignments ask you to pose a question worth exploring, to read widely in search of possible answers, to interpret what you read, to draw reasoned conclusions, and to support those conclusions with valid and well-documented evidence. Such assignments may at first seem overwhelming, but if you pose a question that intrigues you and approach it like a detective, with genuine curiosity, you will soon learn how rewarding research can be.

Admittedly, the process takes time: time for researching and time for drafting, revising, and documenting the paper in the style recommended by your instructor (see 52). Before beginning a research project, you should set a realistic schedule of deadlines. For example, one student constructed the following schedule for a paper assigned on October 1 and due October 31.

SCHEDULE	FINISHED BY
1. Choose a possible topic.	October 2
2. Talk with a reference librarian and plan a search strategy.	3
3. Locate sources.	5
4. Read and take notes.	10
5. Decide on a tentative thesis and outline.	11
6. Draft the paper.	16
7. Visit the writing center to get help with ideas for revision.	17
8. Do further research if necessary.	20
9. Revise the paper.	25
10. Prepare a list of works cited.	26
11. Type and proofread the final draft.	28

Notice that this student has budgeted more than a week for drafting and revising the paper. It's easy to spend too much of your available time gathering sources; make sure you allow a significant portion of your schedule for drafting and editing your work.

49

Conducting research

Throughout sections 49 and 50, you will encounter examples related to the three sample research papers in Part X:

—A paper on the issue of whether to limit use of cell phones while driving, written by a student in an English composition class (see pp. 637-45). The student, Angela Daly, uses the MLA (Modern Language Association) style of documentation.

—A paper on the extent to which apes have acquired language skills, written by a student in a psychology class (see pp. 716–26). The student, Karen Shaw, uses the APA (American Psychological Association) style of documentation.

—A paper on the extent to which Civil War general Nathan Bedford Forrest can be held responsible for the Fort Pillow massacre, written by a student in a history class (see pp. 759–63). The student, Ned Bishop, uses *Chicago*-style documentation, a style preferred by most historians.

49a Pose possible questions worth exploring.

Working within the guidelines of your assignment, pose a few questions that seem worth researching. Here, for example, are some preliminary questions jotted down by students enrolled in a variety of classes in different disciplines.

—Can a government-regulated rating system for television shows curb children's exposure to violent programming?

—Which geological formations are the safest repositories for nuclear waste?

—Will a ban on human cloning threaten important medical research?

—What was Marcus Garvey's contribution to the fight for racial equality?

—How can governments and zoos help preserve China's endangered panda?

—Why was amateur archaeologist Heinrich Schliemann such a controversial figure in his own time?

As you formulate possible questions, make sure that they are appropriate lines of inquiry for a research paper. Choose questions that are narrow (not too broad), challenging (not too bland), and grounded (not too speculative).

Choosing a narrow question

If your initial question is too broad, given the length of the paper you plan to write, look for ways to restrict your focus (see also p. 8). Here, for example, is how some students narrowed their initial questions.

TOO BROAD

—What are the hazards of fad diets?

—Is the military seriously addressing the problem of sexual harassment?

—What causes homelessness?

NARROWER

—What are the hazards of liquid diets?

—To what extent has the navy addressed the problem of sexual harassment since the Tailhook scandal?

—How has deinstitutionalization of the mentally ill contributed to the problem of homelessness?

Choosing a challenging question

Your research paper will be more interesting to both you and your audience if you base it on an intellectually challenging line of inquiry. Avoid bland questions that fail to provoke thought or engage readers in a debate.

TOO BLAND

—What is obsessive-compulsive disorder?

—Where is wind energy being used?

—How do lie detectors work?

CHALLENGING

—What treatments for obsessive-compulsive disorder show the most promise?

—Does investing in wind energy make economic sense?

—How reliable are lie detectors?

You may well need to address a bland question in the course of answering a more challenging one. For example, if you were writing about promising treatments for obsessive-compulsive disorder, you would no doubt answer the question "What is obsessive-compulsive disorder?" at some point in your paper. It would be a mistake, however, to use the bland question as the focus for the whole paper.

Choosing a grounded question

Finally, you will want to make sure that your research question is grounded, not too speculative. Although speculative questions—such as those that address philosophical, ethical, or religious issues—are worth asking and may receive some attention in a research paper, they are inappropriate central questions. The central argument of a research paper should be grounded in facts; it should not be based entirely on beliefs.

TOO SPECULATIVE

—Is capital punishment moral?

—Do medical scientists have the right to experiment on animals?

—What is the difference between a just and an unjust law?

GROUNDED

—Does capital punishment deter crime?

—How have technical breakthroughs made medical experiments on animals increasingly unnecessary?

—Should we adjust our laws so that penalties for possession of powdered cocaine and crack cocaine are comparable?

ON THE WEB

For an electronic exercise on choosing an appropriate research question, go to
www.dianahacker.com/bedhandbook

and click on　▶ **Electronic Research Exercises**
　　　　　　　▶ **E-ex 49–1**

49b　Map out a search strategy.

A search strategy is a systematic plan for tracking down sources. To create a search strategy appropriate for your research question, consult a reference librarian and perhaps take a look at your library's Web site, which will give you an overview of available resources.

Getting help

Reference librarians are information specialists who can save you time by steering you toward relevant and reliable sources. With the help of an expert, you can make the best use of electronic databases, Web search engines, and other reference tools.

When you ask a reference librarian for help, be prepared to answer a number of questions:

—What is your assignment?

—In which academic discipline are you writing?

—What is your tentative research question?

—How long will the paper be?

—How much time can you spend on the project?

It's a good idea to bring a copy of the assignment with you.

In addition to speaking with a reference librarian, you might log on to your library's Web site. Many libraries lead you to a wealth of information through their Web sites. On these sites, you will typically find links to the library's catalog and to a variety of databases and electronic sources. In addition, you may find links to other Web sites selected by librarians for their quality. While you will need to go to the library for some sources, you may be able to do much of your work from any computer that can connect to the campus network.

Many libraries provide online reference help. Researchers can communicate with a librarian via the Internet (sometimes

LIBRARY HOME PAGE

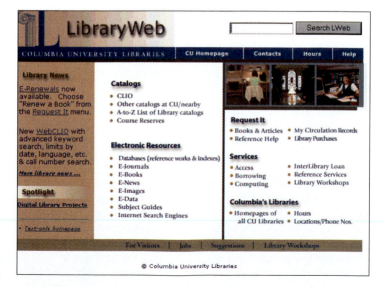

in real time) for help locating information. For example, students at Columbia University can go to their library's home page and click on Reference Help (see p. 525). In addition to helping you locate information, an online reference librarian may be able to link you to ask-an-expert services in a variety of subject areas.

Choosing an appropriate search strategy

There is no single search strategy that works for every topic. For some topics, it may be appropriate to search for information in newspapers, magazines, and Web sites. For others, the best sources might be found in scholarly journals and books and specialized reference works. Still other topics might be enhanced by field research—interviews, surveys, or direct observation, for example.

With the help of a reference librarian, each of the students mentioned on page 521 constructed a search strategy appropriate for his or her research question.

ANGELA DALY   Angela Daly's topic, the dangers of using cell phones while driving, was so current that books were an unlikely source (by the time a book is published, it is already dated). To find up-to-date information on her topic, Daly decided to

— search a general database for articles in magazines, newspapers, and journals

— use Web search engines, such as *Google,* to locate relevant sites, online articles, and government publications

KAREN SHAW   Karen Shaw's topic, the extent to which apes have learned language, has been the subject of psychological studies for many years, and it has been featured in the popular press (newspapers and magazines aimed at the general public). Thinking that both popular and scholarly works would be appropriate, Shaw decided to

—locate books through the library's online catalog

—check a specialized encyclopedia in psychology

—search a general database for popular articles

—search a specialized database, *PsycInfo,* for scholarly articles

NED BISHOP   Ned Bishop's topic, the role played by Nathan Bedford Forrest in the Fort Pillow massacre, is an issue that has been investigated and debated by professional historians. Given the nature of his historical topic, Ned Bishop decided to

—locate books through the library's online catalog

—locate scholarly articles by searching a specialized database, *America: History and Life*

—locate 1864 newspaper articles by using a print index

—search the Web for historical primary sources that have been posted online

49c   To locate articles, search a database or consult a print index.

Most college and public libraries subscribe to CD-ROM or Web-based databases (sometimes called *periodical indexes*). Students often have access to articles and other materials in these databases without charge. Many databases are limited to works published in the last ten to twenty years. To find older articles, you may need to consult a print index such as the *New York Times Index* or *Readers' Guide to Periodical Literature.*

NOTE: There is a difference between Web-based databases the library pays for through a subscription and those that are free to the public at large. Subscription sites provide edited material that has been scrutinized before being published. That isn't always the case with sites that are free.

What databases offer

Your library's databases will lead you to articles in periodicals such as newspapers, magazines, and scholarly or technical journals. Many of the databases also give you access to other sources, such as scholarly monographs, e-journals, and dissertations. Though each library is unique, here are some databases you might find available:

InfoTrac. A collection of databases. Some of them index periodical articles (many available in full text). Through *InfoTrac* your library may also subscribe to specialized databases in business, health, and other fields.

ProQuest. A database of periodical articles (many available in full text). Through *ProQuest* your library may also subscribe to databases in subjects such as nursing, biology, and psychology.

EBSCOhost. A database of periodical articles (many available in full text). Through *EBSCOhost* your library may also subscribe to a wide variety of subject-specific databases.

FirstSearch. A vast collection of specialized databases, including *WorldCat,* a database of library collections, and *ArticleFirst,* a database of journal articles. Some articles may be available in full text.

Lexis-Nexis Academic Universe. A set of databases that are particularly strong in coverage of news, business and legal matters, and congressional information. Nearly all of the material is available in full text.

ERIC. An education database covering articles from education journals and unpublished documents collected by a government clearinghouse. *ERIC* contains full-text articles, citations, and abstracts.

MLA Bibliography. A database of literary criticism, with references to articles, books, and dissertations.

PsycInfo. The most complete database of psychology research, including abstracts to articles in journals and books.

Refining keyword searches in databases and search engines

Although command terms and characters vary among electronic databases and Web search engines, some of the most commonly used functions are listed here.

— Use quotation marks around words that are part of a phrase: "Broadway musicals".

— Use AND to connect words that must appear in a document: Ireland AND peace. Some search engines require a plus sign instead: Ireland +peace.

— Use NOT in front of words that must not appear in a document: Titanic NOT movie. Some search engines require a minus sign (hyphen) instead: Titanic -movie.

— Use OR if only one of the terms must appear in a document: "mountain lion" OR cougar.

— Use an asterisk as a substitute for letters that might vary: "marine biolog*" (to find *marine biology* or *marine biologist,* for example).

— Use parentheses to group a search expression and combine it with another: (cigarettes OR tobacco OR smok*) AND lawsuits.

Many databases include the full text of at least some articles; others list only citations or citations with short summaries called *abstracts.* In the case of articles with full text, you may have the option to print an article, save it to a disk, or e-mail it to yourself.

When full text is not available, the citation will give you enough information to track down an article. You will need to find out if the library owns the periodical in which the article appears and, if so, where it is kept. If the library does not own the periodical, it may be possible to request a photocopy of the article through interlibrary loan service.

How to search a database

To find articles on your topic in a database, you will conduct a keyword search. If the first keyword you try results in no matches, don't give up; experiment with other keywords and perhaps ask a librarian for help. If your keyword search results in too many matches, narrow your search. The most common way to narrow a search is to connect two search terms with AND: *apes AND language.* This and other strategies for narrowing or broadening a search are included in the chart on page 529.

For her paper on the dangers of using a cell phone while driving, Angela Daly conducted a keyword search in a general periodical database. She typed in *"cell phones AND driving"* (see screen 1). This search brought up thirty-six possible articles, some of which looked promising (see screen 2). Daly sent several full-text articles to her e-mail

DATABASE SCREEN 1: KEYWORD SEARCH

DATABASE SCREEN 2: RESULTS OF A KEYWORD SEARCH

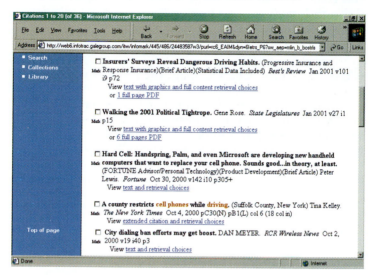

account and printed out citations to others so that she could locate them in the library.

For his history paper, Ned Bishop turned to a specialized database, *America: History and Life.* He found thirty items relevant to his topic of Nathan Bedford Forrest and the Fort Pillow massacre. Full texts of the articles were not available, but Bishop e-mailed abstracts of the articles to himself. Later he decided which articles were worth tracking down in the library.

When to use a print index

If you want to search for articles published before the 1980s, you may need to turn to a print index. For example, Ned Bishop consulted the *New York Times Index* to locate newspaper articles written in April 1864, just after the battle at

Fort Pillow. To find older magazine articles, consult *Readers' Guide to Periodical Literature* or *Poole's Index to Periodical Literature* or ask a librarian for help.

49d   To locate books, consult the library's catalog.

The books your library owns are listed in its computer catalog, along with other resources such as videos. You can search the catalog by author, title, or topic. Most of the time you will want to search by topic, especially at the beginning of a research project. The screens on pages 533 and 534 illustrate Karen Shaw's search of the library catalog.

Most catalogs offer two different ways to search by topic:

—A *keyword* (or *word*) search matches words in the titles or subject headings of books. (It does not search the full text, as a periodical database or Web search engine does.)

—A *subject* search matches subject headings, words that librarians have used to describe the subjects of books.

Don't be surprised if your first search calls up too few — or far too many — results. If you have too few results, experiment with other search terms or try broader concepts. If that doesn't work, ask a librarian for help or check the *Library of Congress Subject Headings,* large volumes usually placed near the catalog. These volumes tell you which terms librarians have used to catalog books on a wide variety of subjects.

If a search gives you too many results, you will need to narrow your search. Many catalogs offer a "limit search" option that will help you narrow your topic. When Karen Shaw, whose topic was apes and language, entered the term *apes* into the computer catalog, she was faced with eighty-seven hits, an unmanageable number. She narrowed her search by adding the term *language* and retrieved just twelve records. The first three records are displayed on screen 1.

COMPUTER CATALOG SCREEN 1: LIST OF BOOKS

APES is in 87 titles.
LANGUAGE is in 11277 titles.
Both "APES" and "LANGUAGE" are in 12 titles.
There are 12 entries with APES & LANGUAGE.

WORD | apes and language | Search

Num	Mark	WORDS (1-12 of 12)	Medium	Year
1	☐	Apes, language, and the human mind / Sue Savage-Rumbaugh, St		
		Main General, QL737.P96 S254 1998	text	1998
2	☐	Apes, men, and language		
		Main General, QL737.P96 L56	text	[1974]
3	☐	Aping language / Joel Wallman		
		Main General, QL737.P96 W35 1992	text	1992

Once you have narrowed your search to a list of relevant sources, you can display or print the complete record for each source, which includes its bibliographic information (author, title, publication data) and a call number. On page 534 is the complete record for title number 1 from the list generated by Shaw's search. The call number, which appears in the horizontal bar, is the book's address on the library shelf. When you're retrieving a book from the shelf, take the time to scan other books in the area since they are likely to be on the same topic.

LIBRARIAN'S TIP: The record for a book lists related subject headings. These headings are a good way to locate other books on your subject. For example, the record on page 534 lists the term *Human-animal communication* as an alternative to *apes and language.* By clicking on this new term, Karen Shaw found a few more books on her subject.

COMPUTER CATALOG SCREEN 2: COMPLETE RECORD FOR A BOOK

Author	Savage-Rumbaugh, E. Sue, 1946-
Title	**Apes, language, and the human mind / Sue Savage-Rumbaugh, Stuart G. Shanker, Talbot J. Taylor**
Publisher	New York : Oxford University Press, 1998

LOCATION	CALL #	STATUS
Main General	QL737.P96 S254 1998	DUE 06-27-01

Descript.	x, 244 p. : ill. ; 24 cm
Subject	Bonobo -- Psychology
	Kanzi (Bonobo)
	Human-animal communication
	Language acquisition
	Neurolinguistics
Alt author	Shanker, Stuart
	Taylor, Talbot J
Bibliog.	Includes bibliographical references (p. 233-239) and index
ISBN	0195109864 (alk. paper)
LCCN	98014600

49e   To locate a wide variety of sources, turn to the Web.

Especially for current topics, the Web is an excellent resource. For example, most government agencies post information on the Web, and federal and state governments use Web sites to communicate with citizens. The sites of many private organizations, such as the American Automobile Association and the Sierra Club, contain useful information about current issues. Even if your subject is not current, you may find the Web useful. Some historical primary sources are posted free on the Web: political speeches, treaties, classic literary texts, and so on.

Although the Web can be a rich source of information, some of which can't be found anywhere else, it lacks quality control. As you probably know, anyone can publish on the

Web, so you will need to evaluate online sources with special care (see 50c).

LIBRARIAN'S TIP: To date, the Web is not the best place to look for literary criticism, historical analysis, or reports of scholarly research, all of which are more likely to be published in traditional ways. However, your library may subscribe to Web-based databases that will give you access to some of these materials (see 49c).

This section describes the following Web resources: search engines, directories, archives, government and news sites, and Web and e-mail forums.

ON THE WEB

For live links to the sources listed in this section, go to
www.dianahacker.com/bedhandbook

and click on ▶ **Links Library**
▶ **Conducting Research**

Search engines

Search engines take your search terms and seek matches among millions of Web pages. Some search engines go into more depth than others, but none can search the entire Web. Often it is a good idea to try more than one search engine, since each locates sources in its own way.

For current information about search engines, visit *Search Engine Watch* at <http://www.searchenginewatch.com>. This site classifies search engines, evaluates them, and provides updates on new search features. Following are some popular search engines:

AltaVista <http://www.altavista.com>
Ask Jeeves <http://www.askjeeves.com>

Excite <http://www.excite.com>

Google <http://www.google.com>

HotBot <http://www.hotbot.lycos.com>

Lycos <http://www.lycos.com>

Metacrawler <http://www.metacrawler.com>

Northern Light <http://www.northernlight.com>

Yahoo! <http://www.yahoo.com>

In using a search engine, focus your search as narrowly as possible to prevent getting an impossible number of matches (or hits). You can sharpen your search by using many of the tips listed in the chart on page 529. For his paper on Nathan Bedford Forrest and the Fort Pillow massacre, Ned Bishop typed this into a search engine:

"Nathan Bedford Forrest" AND "Fort Pillow"

Of the resulting sixty-eight hits, several looked promising. In fact, the first source on the list, "Accounts of Fort Pillow," contained two useful primary sources: official reports of the incident by the Confederate and the Union commanders.

For her paper on using cell phones while driving, Angela Daly had difficulty restricting the number of hits. When she typed *cell phones* and *driving* into a search engine, she got over 40,000 matches. To narrow her search, Daly tried *cell phones while driving* and *accidents.* The result was 433 matches, still too many, so Daly clicked on Advanced Search. On the Advanced Search screen she restricted her search to government-sponsored sites with URLs ending in *.gov* (see screen 1, p. 537). The resulting list consisted of just 11 items, including promising sites sponsored by the National Highway Traffic Safety Administration (see screen 2, p. 538).

Later, Daly tried the same approach with the domain *.org* (organization) and retrieved 32 possible sources. Some of the sites sponsored by governments and organizations contained useful links to other relevant sites, such as a

SEARCH ENGINE SCREEN 1: ADVANCED SEARCH

commercial page sponsored by the radio program *Car Talk* and an education page sponsored by the Harvard Center for Risk Analysis.

Directories

Unlike search engines, which are powered by software known as *bots,* directories have a human touch. Directories are put together by information specialists who arrange sites by topic: education, health, public issues, and so on. Many search engines, such as *Google* and *Lycos,* offer a directory as an optional means of conducting a search.

Some directories are more selective and therefore more useful for scholarly research than the directories that typically accompany a search engine. For example, the directory for the *Internet Scout Project* was created with a research

SEARCH ENGINE SCREEN 2: RESULTS OF AN ADVANCED SEARCH

audience in mind; it includes annotations that are both descriptive and evaluative. The following list includes directories especially useful for scholarly research:

Argus Clearinghouse <http://www.clearinghouse.net>

Infomine <http://infomine.ucr.edu>

Internet Scout Project <http://www.scout.cs.wisc.edu/archives>

Librarian's Index to the Internet <http://www.lii.org>

World Wide Web Virtual Library <http://www.vlib.org>

Archives

Archives contain the texts of poems, books, speeches, political cartoons, and historically significant documents such as the Declaration of Independence and the Emancipation Proclamation. The materials in these sites are usually limited to older works because of copyright laws. The following online archives are impressive collections:

American Memory <http://memory.loc.gov>

Avalon Project <http://www.yale.edu/lawweb/avalon/avalon.htm>

Electronic Text Center <http://etext.lib.virginia.edu>

Eurodocs <http://library.byu.edu/~rdh/eurodocs>

Internet History Sourcebooks <http://www.fordham.edu/halsall/index.html>

Online Books Page <http://digital.library.upenn.edu/books/lists.html>

Government and news sites

For current topics, both government and news sites can prove useful. Many government agencies at every level provide online information. Government-maintained sites include resources such as legal texts, facts and statistics, government reports, and searchable reference databases. Here are just a few government sites (notice that the last one will lead you to others):

Census Bureau <http://www.census.gov>

Fedstats <http://www.fedstats.gov>

Thomas Legislative Information <http://thomas.loc.gov>

United Nations <http://www.un.org>

U.S. Federal Government Agencies Directory <http://www.lib.lsu.edu/gov/fedgov.html>

NOTE: You can access a state's Web site by putting the two-letter state abbreviation into a standard URL. For example, in the following URL, *ca* represents California: <http://www.state.ca.us>.

Many popular newsletters, magazines, and television networks offer up-to-date information on the Web. These online services often allow nonsubscribers to read current stories for free. Some allow users to log on as guests and search archives without cost, but to read actual articles users typically must pay a fee. The following are some news sites:

AJR NewsLink <http://ajr.newslink.org>

CNN <http://www.cnn.com>

Kidon Media-Link <http://www.kidon.com/media-link/index.html>

New York Times <http://www.nytimes.com>

NOTE: Your library may subscribe to *Lexis-Nexis* or other on-line databases with more full-text news sources than are available free on the Web (see 49c).

Web and e-mail forums

The Web offers ways of communicating with experts and others who have an interest in your topic. You might join an online mailing list, for example, to send and receive e-mail messages relevant to your topic. Or you may wish to search a particular newsgroup's postings. Newsgroups resemble bulletin boards on which messages are posted and connected through "threads" as others respond. To find mailing lists and newsgroups, go to one of these sites:

CataList <http://www.lsoft.com/catalist.html>

DejaNews <http://www.deja.com>

Directory of Scholarly and Professional E-Conferences <http://n2h2.com/KOVACS/>

Liszt <http://www.liszt.com>

In addition to mailing lists and newsgroups, you might log on to real-time discussion forums such as MUDs, MOOs, or chats.

NOTE: Be aware that many of the people you contact will not be experts on your topic. Although you are more likely to find serious and worthwhile commentary in moderated mailing lists and scholarly discussion forums than in more freewheeling newsgroups, it is difficult to guarantee the credibility of anyone you meet online.

49f   Consider other search tools.

In addition to articles, books, and Web sources, you may want to consult reference works such as encyclopedias and almanacs. Bibliographies (lists of works written on a topic) and citations in scholarly works are other useful tools.

Reference works

The reference section of the library holds both general and specialized encyclopedias, dictionaries, almanacs, atlases, and biographical references. Some are available in electronic format. Reference works provide information in easily digested nuggets; they often serve as a good overview of your subject. Check with a reference librarian to see which works are most appropriate for your topic.

GENERAL REFERENCE WORKS   General reference works are good places to check facts and get basic information. Here are a few frequently used general references that you might want to turn to:

Encyclopedia Americana

The New Encyclopaedia Britannica

The Oxford English Dictionary

World Almanac and Book of Facts

National Geographic Atlas of the World

Webster's New Biographical Dictionary

NOTE: Although general encyclopedias are often a good place to find background about your topic, you should rarely use them in your final paper. Most instructors expect you to rely on more specialized sources.

SPECIALIZED REFERENCE WORKS   Specialized reference works often go into a topic in depth, sometimes in the form of articles written by leading authorities. Many specialized works are available: *Encyclopedia of the Environment, Anchor Bible Dictionary, Almanac of American Politics, The Historical and Cultural Atlas of African Americans, Contemporary Artists,* and so on. Check with a reference librarian to see which works are available in your library.

ON THE WEB

For lists of specialized reference works, organized by academic discipline, go to
www.dianahacker.com/bedhandbook

and click on   ▶ **Research and Documentation Online**
                 ▶ **Finding Sources**

Bibliographies and scholarly citations

Bibliographies are lists of works written on a particular topic. They include enough information about each work (author's name, title, and publication data) so that you can locate the book or article. Many bibliographies are annotated: They contain abstracts giving a brief overview of each work's contents. You can find book-length bibliographies by adding the term *bibliography* to a catalog search. For example, Ned Bishop typed the search term *"Civil War" AND bibliography* and found a book that listed and described publications about all aspects of the Civil War. It included a section on the Fort Pillow massacre.

Bibliographies in book form are usually housed in the reference collection. A reference librarian can tell you which would be most useful for your topic and perhaps point you to relevant bibliographies on the Web.

As you read scholarly books and articles on your topic, you will encounter citations to other scholarly works. A list of the works the author has cited usually appears at the end of an article or a book. These lists of sources are useful short-cuts: Often the author of the work has done some of your research for you. For example, most of the scholarly articles Karen Shaw consulted contained citations to related research studies; through these citations, Shaw quickly located additional relevant sources on her topic, apes and language.

49g Consider doing field research.

For a composition class, you might want to visit your local historical society to research a paper on some aspect of your town's early history, such as the role it played in the underground railroad. For a sociology class, you might decide to study campus trends in classroom participation: Which students are most, and least, involved in class discussions, and why? At work you might need to learn how food industry executives are responding to reports that their companies have cut portions of some food products while increasing prices. Projects like these may be enhanced by, and sometimes centered on, your own field research.

Interviewing

Interviews can often shed some new light on a topic. Look for an expert who has firsthand knowledge of the subject or seek out someone whose personal experience provides an enlightening perspective on your topic. For example, for her paper on apes and language, Karen Shaw interviewed a professor who had spent seven months working with a gorilla who used sign language.

When asking for an interview, be clear about who you are, what the purpose of the interview is, and how you would prefer to conduct it: via e-mail, over the phone, or in person. Plan for an interview by writing down a series of questions. Try to avoid questions with yes or no answers or those that encourage vague rambling. Instead, ask questions that elicit facts, anecdotes, and opinions that will add a meaningful dimension to your paper.

INEFFECTIVE QUESTIONS
Did you use sign language to communicate with the gorilla Michael?

Was it interesting to work with a gorilla who knows sign language?

EFFECTIVE QUESTIONS
Was Michael's use of language creative? For example, do you think he was capable of joking and lying in sign language?

Accuracy is important. To ensure accuracy, you might want to ask for permission to tape the interview; if you cannot tape the interview, take careful notes. When quoting your source in your paper, you should of course be as accurate and fair as possible.

Surveying opinion

For some topics, you may find it useful to survey opinions through written questionnaires, telephone or e-mail polls, or questions posted on a Web forum. Many people are reluctant to fill out long questionnaires or answer long-winded telephone pollsters, so if you want a good response rate, you will need to limit your questions and frame them carefully.

When possible, ask yes/no questions or give multiple-choice options. Surveys with such queries can be filled out quickly, and they are easy to tabulate.

SAMPLE YES/NO QUESTION
Do you favor restricting the use of handheld cell phones while driving?

You may also want to ask a few open-ended questions to elicit more individual responses, some of which may be worth quoting in your paper.

> **SAMPLE OPEN-ENDED QUESTION**
> What, if any, close calls have you had with drivers distracted by cell phones?

Visiting sites

Your firsthand observations of a significant place—such as a museum, a park, or a historic site—can enhance a paper in a variety of classes in different disciplines. For example, while researching trends in contemporary American folk art, a student living in New York City went to an exhibit on folk art at the Museum of Modern Art. To gather information for a paper on nineteenth-century utopian experiments, a student from Peoria, Illinois, drove to nearby Bishop Hill, a commune founded in 1846 by Swedish refugees seeking religious freedom. A student studying in England visited Stonehenge and other ancient stone circles to make on-site observations to include in an essay for a course in physical anthropology.

Contacting organizations

Many organizations, both public and private, will mail you literature in response to a phone call, an e-mail, or a letter. Although this literature can provide up-to-date information, use it judiciously. Groups tend to promote their own interests; you can't always count on them to present a balanced view.

The Encyclopedia of Associations (available both electronically and in print) lists groups by their concerns, such as environment or family planning, and provides addresses and phone numbers. Many organizations are now publishing home pages on the Web; these pages can lead you to publications sponsored by an organization and, through links, to other publications as well.

50

Evaluating sources

With electronic search tools, you can often locate dozens or even hundreds of potential sources for your topic — far more than you will have time to read. Your challenge will be to home in on a reasonable number of quality sources, those truly worthy of your time and attention.

Later, once you have decided on some sources worth consulting, your challenge will be to read them with an open mind and a critical eye.

50a Select sources worth your time and attention.

Section 49 showed you how to restrict the number of "hits" that come up in the library's book catalog, in databases, and in search engines. This section shows you how to scan through the lists of hits looking for those that seem most promising. It also gives you tips on previewing possible sources — without actually reading them — to see whether they are likely to live up to your expectations.

Scanning lists of hits

As you scan through a list of hits, be alert for any clues indicating whether a source might be useful for your purposes. You will need to use somewhat different scanning strategies when looking at lists of hits from a book catalog, a database, or a Web search engine.

BOOK CATALOGS The library's book catalog will usually give you a fairly short list of hits (see p. 533 for an example). A book's title and date of publication will often be your first clues as to whether the book is worth consulting. If a title looks interesting, you can click on it for further information: the book's subject matter and its length, for example.

DATABASES   Most databases, such as *ProQuest* and *Lexis-Nexis*, list at least the following information, which can help you decide if a source is relevant, current, scholarly enough, and neither too short nor too long for your purposes.

Title and brief description (How relevant?)

Date (How current?)

Name of periodical (How scholarly?)

Length (How extensive in coverage?)

For example, consider just a few of the hits Ned Bishop came up with when he consulted a general database in search of articles on the Fort Pillow massacre, using the search term *Fort Pillow.*

☐ **Black, blue and gray: the other Civil War; African-American soldiers, sailors and**
Mark **spies were the unsung heroes.** *Ebony* Feb 1991 v46 n4 p96(6)
    View text and retrieval choices

☐ **The Civil War.** (movie reviews) Lewis Cole. *The Nation* Dec 3, 1990 v251 n19 p694(5)
Mark   View text and retrieval choices

☐ **The hard fight was getting into the fight at all.** (black soldiers in the Civil War)
Mark Jack Fincher. *Smithsonian* Oct 1990 v21 n7 p46(13)
    View text and retrieval choices

☑ **The Fort Pillow massacre: a statistical note.** John Cimprich, Robert C. Mainfort Jr..
Mark *Journal of American History* Dec 1989 v76 n3 p830(8)
    View extended citation and retrieval choices

By scanning the titles, Bishop saw that only one contained the words *Fort Pillow.* This title and the name of the periodical—*Journal of American History*—suggested that the source was scholarly. The 1989 publication date was not a problem, since currency is not necessarily a key issue for historical topics. The article's length (eight pages) is given in parentheses at the end of the citation. While the article may seem short, the topic—a statistical note—is narrow enough to ensure adequate depth of coverage. Bishop decided the article was worth consulting, even though it required a trip to the library because it was not available in full text.

Bishop chose not to consult the other sources. The first is a brief article in a popular magazine, the second is a movie review, and the third surveys a topic that is far too broad, "black soldiers in the Civil War."

WEB SEARCH ENGINES Anyone can publish on the Web, and unreliable sites often masquerade as legitimate sources of information. As you scan through a list of hits, look for the following clues about the probable relevance, currency, and reliability of a site — but be prepared to be disappointed, as the clues are by no means foolproof.

> Title, keywords, and lead-in text (How relevant?)
>
> A date (How current?)
>
> An indication of the site's sponsor or purpose (How reliable?)
>
> The URL, especially the domain name (How relevant? How reliable?)

On the next page are a few of the hits that Karen Shaw retrieved after typing the keywords *apes* and *language* into a search engine; she limited her search to works with these words in the title.

Shaw rejected the first source because it was just a message in an online mailing list, and she skipped the third one because it sounded too promotional. The last source looked promising because of its university affiliation, though in fact it turned out to be a student paper.

Shaw was uncertain about the second hit, which was a commercial site, but she clicked on it. It was an impressive site, nicely designed, well written, and documented with footnotes and a bibliography; the only problem was that its author was nowhere to be found. Reluctantly, she decided not to use the information in her paper.

LINGUIST List 7.144: Systemic-Functional WWW, **Apes** & **Language**
LINGUIST List 7.144. Tue Jan 30 1996. FYI: Systemic-Functional WWW,
Apes & **Language**. ... Message 2: **Apes** & **Language** syllabus. ...
www.linguistlist.org/issues/7/7-144.html - 11k - Cached - Similar pages

Can **Apes** Acquire **Language**?
Can **Apes** Acquire **Language**? Why have people embarked
on these Ape **language** studies? Some, it ...
www.fortunecity.com/greenfield/twyford/73/thoughts.html - 11k - Cached - Similar pages

YORK UNIVERSITY PROFESSOR'S BOOK PROVES **APES** CAPABLE OF ...
... to learn more about **language** in autistic and mentally handicapped children are
among those applauding the findings of **Apes**, **Language**, and the Human Mind. ...
www.yorku.ca/ycom/release/archive/080498.htm - 9k - Cached - Similar pages

Language in **Apes**
... Adams has some perceptive comments about "this business of trying to teach **apes language**"
(Adams & Carwardine 1993: 23). While sitting four feet away from a ...
Description: Introductory overview of ape **language** research, its history and its practice.
Category: Science > Social Sciences > Anthropology > Enculturated Apes
www.math.uwaterloo.ca/~dmswitze/apelang.html - 34k - Cached - Similar pages

Previewing sources

Once you have decided that a source looks promising, preview it quickly to see whether it lives up to its promise. If you
can reject irrelevant or unreliable sources before actually
reading them, you will save yourself time. Techniques for
previewing a book or an article are relatively simple; strategies for investigating the likely worth of a Web site are more
complicated.

PREVIEWING A BOOK As you preview a book, keep in
mind that even if the entire book is not worth your time,
parts of it may prove useful. For example, by using the indexes of several books on Civil War history, Ned Bishop
quickly located useful passages describing the Fort Pillow
massacre. As you preview a book, try any or all of the following techniques.

—Glance through the table of contents, keeping your research
  question in mind.

—Skim the preface in search of a statement of the author's purposes.

—Using the index, look up a few words related to your topic.

—If a chapter looks useful, read its opening and closing paragraphs and skim any headings.

—Consider the author's style and approach. Does the style suggest enough intellectual depth—or is the book too specialized for your purposes? Does the author present ideas in an unbiased way?

PREVIEWING AN ARTICLE   As with books, the techniques for previewing an article are fairly straightforward. In researching her paper on apes and language, for example, Karen Shaw spent no more than a few minutes scanning an article before deciding whether it was worth her time.

Here are a few strategies for previewing an article.

—Consider the publication in which the article is printed. Is it a scholarly journal? A popular magazine? A newspaper with a national reputation?

—For a magazine or journal article, look for an abstract or a statement of purpose at the beginning; also look for a summary at the end.

—For a newspaper article, focus on the headline and the opening, known as the *lead.*

—Skim any headings and take a look at any visuals—charts, graphs, diagrams, or illustrations—that might indicate the article's focus and scope.

PREVIEWING A WEB SITE   It is a fairly quick and easy job to track down numerous potentially useful sources on the Web, but evaluating those sources can require some detective work. Web sites can be put up by anyone, and their creators and purposes are not always readily apparent. In addition, there are no set standards for the design of Web sites, so you may need to do a fair amount of clicking and scrolling before locating clues about a site's reliability. In researching her paper on the dangers of using a cell phone while driving, Angela Daly spent considerable time previewing Web sites, many of which she rejected.

As you preview a Web site, check for relevance, reliability, and currency.

—Browse the home page. Do its contents and links seem relevant to your research question? What is the site trying to do: sell a product? promote an idea? inform the public? Is the site's purpose consistent with your research?

—Look for the name of an author or Webmaster, and if possible assess his or her credibility. Often a site's author is named at the end of the home page. If you have landed on an internal page of a site and no author is evident, try linking to the home page.

—Check for a sponsor name, and consider possible motives the organization might have in sponsoring the site. Is the group likely to look at one side of an issue only?

—Find out when the site was created or last updated. Is it current enough for your purposes?

NOTE: If a site gives very little information about its creators or sponsors, be suspicious. Do not rely on such sites when conducting academic research.

50b   Read with an open mind and a critical eye.

As you begin reading the sources you have chosen, keep an open mind. Do not let your personal beliefs prevent you from listening to new ideas and opposing viewpoints. Your research question—not a snap judgment about the question—should guide your reading.

CAUTION: When researching on the Web, it is easy to ignore views different from your own. Web pages that appeal to you will often link to other pages that support the same viewpoint. If your sources all seem to agree with you—and

with one another — seek out opposing views and try to evaluate them with an open mind.

When you read critically, you are not necessarily judging an author's work harshly; you are simply examining its
assumptions, assessing its evidence, and weighing its conclusions.

Distinguishing between primary and secondary sources

As you begin assessing evidence in a text, consider whether
you are reading a primary or a secondary source. Primary
sources are original documents such as letters, diaries, legislative bills, laboratory studies, field research reports, and
eyewitness accounts. Secondary sources are commentaries
on primary sources. A primary source for Ned Bishop was
Nathan Bedford Forrest's official report on the Battle of
Fort Pillow. Bishop also consulted a number of secondary
sources, some of which relied heavily on primary sources
such as letters.

Although a primary source is not necessarily more reliable than a secondary source, it has the advantage of being
a firsthand account. Naturally, you can better evaluate what
a secondary source says if you have first read any primary
sources it discusses.

Being alert for signs of bias

Both in print and online, some sources are more objective
than others. If you were exploring the conspiracy theories
surrounding John F. Kennedy's assassination, for example,
you wouldn't look to a supermarket tabloid, such as the
National Enquirer, for answers. Even publications that are
considered reputable can be editorially biased. For example,
USA Today, National Review, and *Ms.* are all credible
sources, but they are also likely to interpret events quite differently from one another. If you are uncertain about a periodical's special interests, check *Magazines for Libraries.* To

Evaluating all sources

CHECKING FOR SIGNS OF BIAS

— Does the author or publisher have political leanings or religious views that could affect objectivity?

— Is the author or publisher associated with a special-interest group, such as Greenpeace or the National Rifle Association, that might see only one side of an issue?

— How fairly does the author treat opposing views?

— Does the author's language show signs of bias?

ASSESSING AN ARGUMENT

— What is the author's central claim or thesis?

— How does the author support this claim—with relevant and sufficient evidence or with just a few anecdotes or emotional examples?

— Are statistics accurate? Have they been used fairly? (It is possible to "lie" with statistics by using them selectively or by omitting mathematical details.)

— Are any of the author's assumptions questionable?

— Does the author consider opposing arguments and refute them persuasively? (See 48c.)

— Does the author fall prey to any logical fallacies? (See 48a.)

check the reputation of a book, consult *Book Review Digest.* A reference librarian can help you locate these resources.

Like publishers, some authors are more objective than others. No authors are altogether objective, of course, since they are human beings with their own life experiences, values, and beliefs. But if you have reason to believe that an author is particularly biased, you will want to assess his or her arguments with special care. For a list of questions worth asking, see the chart above.

Assessing the author's argument

In nearly all subjects worth writing about, there is some element of argument, so don't be surprised to encounter experts who disagree. When you find areas of disagreement, you will want to read your source's arguments with special care, testing them with your own critical intelligence. Questions such as those in the chart on page 553 can help you weigh the strengths and weaknesses of each author's argument.

50c   Assess Web sources with special care.

As you have no doubt discovered, Web sources can be deceptive. Sophisticated-looking sites can be full of dubious information, and the identities of those who created a site are often hidden, along with their motives for having created it. Even hate sites may be cleverly disguised to look legitimate. In contrast, sites with reliable information can stand up to careful scrutiny. For a checklist on evaluating Web sources, see page 555.

Ned Bishop came across deceptive Web sources while researching his topic, the Fort Pillow massacre. This topic is of great interest to Civil War buffs, many of them amateurs and some still fighting the war. One site looked legitimate, but when Bishop went to the home page, he was not reassured by the Confederate flags emblazoned behind the title "The War for States' Rights." Another impressive-looking site turned out to have been created by a high school junior—an intelligent young man, no doubt, but by no means an authority on the subject.

In researching her topic on the dangers of using a cell phone while driving, Angela Daly encountered sites that raised her suspicions. In particular, some sites were sponsored by the wireless communications industry, which has

Evaluating Web sources

CAUTION: If the sponsorship and the authorship of a site are both unclear, be extremely suspicious of the site.

AUTHORSHIP

—Is there an author? You may need to do some clicking and scrolling to find the author's name. If you are on an internal page of a site, for example, you may need to go to the home page or click on an "about this site" link to learn the name of the author.

—If there is an author, can you tell whether he or she is knowledgeable and credible? When the author's qual-ifications aren't listed on the site itself, look for links to a home page, which may provide evidence of the author's interests and expertise.

SPONSORSHIP

—Who, if anyone, sponsors the site? The sponsor of a site is often named and described on the home page.

—What does the domain name tell you? The domain name often specifies the type of group hosting the site: commercial (.com), educational (.edu), nonprofit (.org), governmental (.gov), military (.mil), or network (.net).

PURPOSE AND AUDIENCE

—Why was the site created: to argue a position? to sell a product? to inform readers?

—Who is the site's intended audience? If you do not fit the audience profile, is information on the site still relevant to your topic?

(continued on page 556)

Evaluating Web sources (continued)

CURRENCY

—How current is the site? Check for the date of publication or the latest update.

—How current are the site's links? If many of the links no longer work, the site may be too dated for your purposes.

an obvious interest in preventing laws restricting use of their products. Even a site sponsored by the Harvard Center for Risk Analysis seemed somewhat suspect, since the wireless industry funded the center's study concluding that the risk of using a cell phone while driving is low compared with other risks.

Knowing that the creator of a site is an amateur or could be biased is not sufficient reason, however, to reject the site's information out of hand. For example, the Harvard Center for Risk Analysis offered evidence for its conclusions, and the high school junior had intelligent things to say about the Fort Pillow massacre. Nevertheless, when you know something about the creator of a site and have a sense of a site's purpose, you will be in a good position to evaluate the likely worth of its information.

ON THE WEB

For links to resources that will help you evaluate sources you find on the Web, go to
www.dianahacker.com/bedhandbook

and click on   ▶ **Links Library**
                      ▶ **Conducting Research**

51

Managing information; avoiding plagiarism

An effective researcher is a good record keeper. Whether you decide to keep records on paper or on your computer—or both—your challenge as a researcher will be to find systematic ways of managing information. More specifically, you will need methods for maintaining a working bibliography (see 51a), keeping track of source materials (see 51b), and taking notes without plagiarizing (stealing from) your sources (see 51c).

51a Maintain a working bibliography.

Keep a record of any sources you decide to consult. You will need this record, called a *working bibliography,* when you compile the list of works cited that will appear at the end of your paper. (The format of this list depends on the documentation style you are using. For MLA style, see 56b; for APA style, see 59d; for *Chicago* style, see 60d.) Your working bibliography will probably contain more sources than you will actually use and put in your list of works cited.

In the past, researchers recorded bibliographic information on 3″ × 5″ note cards. Today, however, most researchers print out this information from the library's computer catalog, periodical databases, and the Web. The printouts usually contain all the information you need to create the list of works cited. That information is given in the chart on page 558.

CAUTION: For Web sources, some bibliographic information may not be available, but spend time looking for it before assuming that it doesn't exist. Look especially for the author's

Information for a working bibliography

For books

— All authors; any editors or translators

— Title and subtitle

— Edition (if not the first)

— Publication information: city, publisher, and date

For periodical articles

— All authors of the article

— Title and subtitle of the article

— Title of the magazine, journal, or newspaper

— Date and volume, issue, and page numbers, if relevant

For Web sources

— All authors, editors, or translators of the work

— Editor or compiler of the Web site, if relevant

— Title and subtitle of the source and title of the longer work (if applicable)

— Title of the site, if available

— Publication information for the source, if available

— Date of publication (or latest update), if available

— Any page or paragraph numbers

— Name of the site's sponsoring organization

— Date you visited the site and the site's URL

For sources from electronic databases

— Publication information for the source

— Name of the database (along with an item number, if relevant)

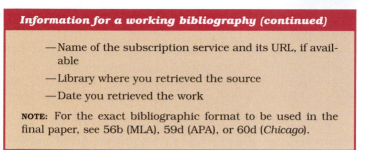

Information for a working bibliography (continued)

—Name of the subscription service and its URL, if available

—Library where you retrieved the source

—Date you retrieved the work

NOTE: For the exact bibliographic format to be used in the final paper, see 56b (MLA), 59d (APA), or 60d (*Chicago*).

name, the date of publication (or latest update), and the name of any sponsoring organization. Such information should not be omitted unless it is genuinely unavailable (see also 56a).

51b Keep track of source materials.

The best way to keep track of source materials is to photocopy them or print them out (except, of course, for books). Most libraries provide photocopy machines so you can copy pages from reference books and magazines and other sources that can't be removed from the library. In addition, many databases allow you to print the full text of articles, and of course you can easily print information from the Web.

Working with photocopies and printouts—as opposed to relying on memory or hastily written notes—has several benefits. It saves you time spent in the library. It allows you to highlight key passages, perhaps even color-coding passages to reflect topics in your outline. And you can annotate the text in the margins and get a head start on the process of taking notes. Finally, working with hard copy reduces the chances of unintentional plagiarism, since you will be able to compare your use of a source in your paper with the actual source, not just with your notes (see 51c).

NOTE: It's especially important to keep hard copies of Web sources, which may change or even become inaccessible. Make sure that your copy includes the site's URL and the date of access, information needed for your list of works cited.

When much of their material comes from the Web, some researchers prefer to organize their source material online — by downloading relevant material into files. This can be an efficient method of working, but it carries dangers. Although it is easy to patch information from downloaded files into your own paper, do so with caution. Some researchers have unwittingly plagiarized their sources because they lost track of which words came from sources and which were their own. To prevent unintentional plagiarism, put quotation marks around any text that you have patched into your own work. In addition, you might use a different color for text from your source so it stands out unmistakably as someone else's (not your own) writing.

51c As you take notes, avoid unintentional plagiarism.

You will discover that it is amazingly easy to borrow too much language from a source as you take notes. Do not allow this to happen. You are guilty of the academic offense known as *plagiarism* if you half-copy the author's sentences — either by mixing the author's phrases with your own without using quotation marks or by plugging your synonyms into the author's sentence structure. (For examples of this kind of plagiarism, see 54b, 59b, and 60b.)

To prevent unintentional borrowing, resist the temptation to look at the source as you take notes — except when you are quoting. Keep the source close by so you can check for accuracy, but don't try to put ideas in your own words with the source's sentences in front of you.

There are three kinds of note taking: summarizing, paraphrasing, and quoting. As you take notes, be sure to include exact page references, since you will need the page numbers later if you use the information in your paper.

Summarizing without plagiarizing

A summary condenses information, perhaps reducing a chapter to a short paragraph or a paragraph to a single sentence. A summary should be written in your own words; if you use phrases from the source, put them in quotation marks.

Here is a passage from an original source read by John Garcia in researching a paper on mountain lions. Following the passage is Garcia's summary of the source.

ORIGINAL SOURCE
In some respects, the increasing frequency of mountain lion encounters in California has as much to do with a growing *human* population as it does with rising mountain lion numbers. The scenic solitude of the western ranges is prime cougar habitat, and it is falling swiftly to the developer's spade. Meanwhile, with their ideal habitat already at its carrying capacity, mountain lions are forcing younger cats into less suitable terrain, including residential areas. Add that cougars have generally grown bolder under a lengthy ban on their being hunted, and an unsettling scenario begins to emerge.
— Rychnovsky, "Clawing into Controversy," p. 40

SUMMARY

Source: Rychnovsky, "Clawing into Controversy" (40)
Encounters between mountain lions and humans are on the rise in California because increasing numbers of lions are competing for a shrinking habitat. As the lions' wild habitat shrinks, older lions force younger lions into residential areas. These lions have lost some of their fear of humans because of a ban on hunting.

Researched writing

Paraphrasing without plagiarizing

Like a summary, a paraphrase is written in your own words; but whereas a summary reports significant information in fewer words than the source, a paraphrase retells the information in roughly the same number of words. If you retain occasional choice phrases from the source, use quotation marks so you will know later which phrases are your own.

As you read the following paraphrase of the original source on page 561, notice that the language is significantly different from that in the original.

PARAPHRASE

Source: Rychnovsky, "Clawing into Controversy" (40)
Californians are encountering mountain lions more
frequently because increasing numbers of humans and a
rising population of lions are competing for the same
territory. Humans have moved into mountainous regions
once dominated by the lions, and the wild habitat that
is left cannot sustain the current lion population.
Therefore, the older lions are forcing younger lions
out of the wilderness and into residential areas. And
because of a ban on hunting, these younger lions have
become bolder--less fearful of encounters with humans.

Using quotation marks to avoid plagiarizing

A quotation consists of the exact words from a source. In your notes, put all quoted material in quotation marks; do not trust yourself to remember later which words, phrases, and passages you have quoted and which are your own. When you quote, be sure to copy the words of your source exactly, including punctuation and capitalization. In the following example, John Garcia quotes from the original source on page 561.

QUOTATION

> Source: Rychnovsky, "Clawing into Controversy" (40)
> Rychnovsky explains that because the mountain lions'
> natural habitat can no longer sustain the population,
> older lions "are forcing younger cats into less suitable
> terrain, including residential areas."

52

Choosing a documentation style

The various academic disciplines use their own editorial style for citing sources and for listing the works that are cited in a paper. *The Bedford Handbook* describes three commonly used styles: MLA (section 56), APA (section 59), and *Chicago* (section 60). For a list of style manuals in a variety of disciplines, see 52b.

52a Select a style appropriate for your discipline.

In researched writing, sources are cited for several reasons. First, it is important to acknowledge the contributions of others. If you fail to credit sources properly, you are guilty of plagiarism, a serious academic offense. Second, choosing good sources will add credibility to your work; in a sense, you are calling on authorities to serve as expert witnesses. The more care you have taken in choosing reliable sources, the stronger your case will be. Finally—and most importantly—you are helping to build knowledge by showing readers where they can pursue your topic in greater depth.

All of the academic disciplines cite sources for these same reasons. Why, then, do they use different styles for citing those sources? The answer lies in the intellectual goals, along with the values, of scholars in different disciplines.

MLA and APA in-text citations

The Modern Language Association (MLA) style and the American Psychological Association (APA) style both use citations in the text of a paper that refer to a list of works at the end of the paper. The systems work somewhat differently, however, because MLA style was created for scholars in English composition and literature, and APA style was created for researchers in the social sciences.

MLA IN-TEXT CITATION

Brandon Conran argues that the story is written from "a bifocal point of view" (111).

APA IN-TEXT CITATION

Leakey and Lewin (1992) argued that in ape brains "the cognitive foundations on which human language could be built are already present" (p. 244).

While MLA and APA styles work in a similar way, some basic disciplinary differences show up in these key elements:

— author's name
— date of publication
— page numbers
— verb tense in signal phrases

MLA style, which gives the author's full name on first mention, reflects the respect that English scholars have for authors of written words. APA style uses last names only, not out of disrespect but to lend an air of scientific objectivity. APA style, which gives a date after the author's name, reflects the social scientist's concern with the currency of experimental results. MLA style omits the date because English scholars are less concerned with currency; what someone had to say a century ago may be as significant as the latest contribution to the field.

Although both styles include page numbers for quotations, MLA style requires page numbers for summaries and paraphrases as well, whereas APA does not. English scholars place great value on written texts, and with a page number readers can easily find the exact passage that has been summarized or paraphrased. Social scientists are less concerned about page numbers because they value an article's ideas and research results more than its written text.

One final point about the differences between the two styles: MLA style uses the present tense (such as *argues*) to introduce cited material, whereas APA style uses the past or present perfect tense (such as *argued* or *have argued*). The present tense evokes the timelessness of a literary text; the past or present perfect tense emphasizes that an experiment was conducted in the past.

Chicago-*style footnotes or endnotes*

Most historians and many scholars in the humanities use the style of footnotes or endnotes recommended by *The Chicago Manual of Style.* Historians base their work on a wide variety of primary and secondary sources, all of which must be cited. *Chicago*'s note system has the virtue of being relatively unobtrusive; even when a book or an article is thick with citations, readers will not be overwhelmed. In the text of the paper, only a raised number appears. Readers who are interested can consult the accompanying numbered note, which is given either at the foot of the page or on a separate page at the end of the paper.

TEXT

Historian Albert Castel quotes several eyewitnesses on both the Union and the Confederate sides as saying that Forrest ordered his men to stop firing.[7]

NOTE

    7. Albert Castel, "The Fort Pillow Massacre: A Fresh Examination of the Evidence," Civil War History 4 (1958): 44-45.

The *Chicago* system gives as much information as the MLA or APA system; the main difference is that less of that information is given in the text of the paper.

52b   If necessary, consult a style manual.

The Bedford Handbook describes three commonly used systems of documentation: MLA, used in English and the humanities (see 53–58); APA, used in psychology and the social sciences (see 59); and *Chicago* style, used in history and some humanities (see 60). Following is a list of style manuals used in a variety of disciplines.

BIOLOGY
Council of Biology Editors. *Scientific Style and Format: The CBE Manual for Authors, Editors, and Publishers.* 6th ed. New York: Cambridge UP, 1994.

BUSINESS
American Management Association. *The AMA Style Guide for Business Writing.* New York: AMACOM, 1996.

CHEMISTRY
Dodd, Janet S., ed. *The ACS Style Guide: A Manual for Authors and Editors.* 2nd ed. Washington: Amer. Chemical Soc., 1997.

ENGLISH AND THE HUMANITIES (SEE 53–58.)

Gibaldi, Joseph. *MLA Handbook for Writers of Research Papers.* 6th ed. New York: MLA, 2003.

GEOLOGY

Bates, Robert L., Rex Buchanan, and Marla Adkins-Heljeson, eds. *Geowriting: A Guide to Writing, Editing, and Printing in Earth Science.* 5th ed. Alexandria: Amer. Geological Inst., 1995.

GOVERNMENT DOCUMENTS

Garner, Diane L. *The Complete Guide to Citing Government Information Resources: A Manual for Writers and Librarians.* Rev. ed. Bethesda: Congressional Information Service, 1993.

United States Government Printing Office. *Style Manual.* Washington: GPO, 2000.

HISTORY (SEE 60.)

The Chicago Manual of Style. 14th ed. Chicago: U of Chicago P, 1993.

JOURNALISM

Goldstein, Norm, ed. *Associated Press Stylebook and Briefing on Media Law.* 35th ed. New York: Associated Press, 2000.

LAW

Harvard Law Review et al. *The Bluebook: A Uniform System of Citation.* 17th ed. Cambridge: Harvard Law Rev. Assn., 2000.

LINGUISTICS

Linguistic Society of America. "LSA Style Sheet." Published annually in the December issue of the *LSA Bulletin.*

MATHEMATICS

American Mathematical Society. *The AMS Author Handbook: General Instructions for Preparing Manuscripts.* Rev. ed. Providence: AMS, 1996.

MEDICINE

Iverson, Cheryl, et al. *American Medical Association Manual of Style: A Guide for Authors and Editors.* 9th ed. Baltimore: Williams, 1998.

MUSIC

Holoman, D. Kern, ed. *Writing about Music: A Style Sheet from the Editors of* 19th-Century Music. Berkeley: U of California P, 1988.

PHYSICS

American Institute of Physics. *Style Manual: Instructions to Authors and Volume Editors for the Preparation of AIP Book Manuscripts.* 5th ed. New York: AIP, 1995.

POLITICAL SCIENCE

American Political Science Association. *Style Manual for Political Science.* Rev. ed. Washington: APSA, 1993.

PSYCHOLOGY AND THE SOCIAL SCIENCES (SEE 59.)

American Psychological Association. *Publication Manual of the American Psychological Association.* 5th ed. Washington: APA, 2001.

SCIENCE AND TECHNICAL WRITING

American National Standard for the Preparation of Scientific Papers for Written or Oral Presentation. New York: Amer. Natl. Standards Inst., 1979.

Microsoft Corporation. *Microsoft Manual of Style for Technical Publications.* 2nd ed. Redmond: Microsoft, 1998.

Rubens, Philip, ed. *Science and Technical Writing: A Manual of Style.* 2nd ed. New York: Routledge, 2001.

SOCIAL WORK

National Association of Social Workers. *Writing for the NASW Press: Information for Authors.* Rev. ed. Washington: Natl. Assn. of Social Workers Press, 1995.

WRITING MLA PAPERS

Most English instructors and some humanities instructors will ask you to document your sources with the Modern Language Association (MLA) system of citations described in section 56. When writing an MLA paper that is based on sources, you face three main challenges: (1) supporting a thesis, (2) citing your sources and avoiding plagiarism, and (3) integrating quotations and other source material.

Examples in sections 53–55 are drawn from research two students conducted on the use of cell phones while driving. Angela Daly's research paper on this topic appears on pages 637–45. Daly calls for legislation restricting use of cell phones while driving. Paul Levi's paper opposing such legislation appears on the *Bedford Handbook* Web site (see p. 636).

If you are writing an MLA paper about literature (a short story, novel, play, film, or poem), see section 58.

53

Supporting a thesis

Most research assignments ask you to form a thesis, or main idea, and to support that thesis with well-organized evidence.

53a   Form a tentative thesis and sketch a rough outline.

Before you begin writing, you should decide on a tentative thesis and construct a preliminary outline. Remain flexible, however, because you may need to revise your approach later. Writing about a subject is a way of learning about it; as you write, your understanding of your subject will almost certainly deepen.

Tentative thesis

Once you have read a variety of sources and considered all sides of your issue, you are ready to form a tentative thesis: a one-sentence (or occasionally a two-sentence) statement of your central idea. (See also 2a and 53b.) The thesis expresses not just your opinion but your informed, reasoned judgment.

In a research paper, your thesis will answer the central research question that you posed earlier (see 49a). Here, for example, is Angela Daly's research question and her tentative thesis statement.

DALY'S RESEARCH QUESTION

Should states regulate use of cell phones in moving vehicles?

DALY'S TENTATIVE THESIS

States should regulate use of cell phones on the road because many drivers are using the phones irresponsibly and causing accidents.

After reading more about her topic, Daly revised her tentative thesis.

DALY'S REVISED THESIS

States must regulate use of cell phones on the road because drivers using phones are seriously impaired

and because laws on negligent and reckless driving
are not sufficient to punish offenders.

Rough outline

Before committing yourself to a detailed outline, create a
rough outline consisting of your thesis and the key ideas
that support the thesis. In the following rough outline, Paul
Levi supports his tentative thesis with sentences that sum
up the three main sections of his paper.

LEVI'S THESIS Instead of restricting use of cell phones
in moving vehicles, we should educate the
public about the dangers of driving while
phoning and prosecute irresponsible phone
users under laws on negligent and reckless
driving.

--Scientific studies haven't proved
a link between use of cell phones
and traffic accidents.

--The risks of using cell phones while
driving should be weighed against
the benefits.

--We need to educate drivers on using
cell phones responsibly and enforce
laws on negligent and reckless
driving.

ON THE WEB

For an electronic exercise on thesis statements, go to
www.dianahacker.com/bedhandbook

and click on ▶ **Electronic Research Exercises**
▶ **E-ex 53-1**

53b Include your thesis in the introduction.

In a research paper, readers are accustomed to seeing the thesis statement—the paper's main point—at the end of the first or second paragraph. The advantage of putting it in the first paragraph is that readers can immediately grasp your point. The advantage of delaying the thesis until the second paragraph is that you can provide a fuller context for your point.

As you draft your introduction, you may change your preliminary thesis, either because you have refined your thinking or because new wording fits more smoothly into the context you have provided for it. For example, Paul Levi's thesis became more complex as he drafted and polished his opening paragraph. Levi's thesis appears in the last sentence of his introduction:

> As of 2000, there were about ninety million cell phone users in the United States, with 85% of them using their phones while on the road (Sundeen 1). Because of evidence that cell phones impair drivers by distracting them, some states have considered laws restricting their use in moving vehicles. Proponents of legislation correctly point out that using phones while driving can be dangerous. The extent of the danger, however, is a matter of debate, and the benefits may outweigh the risks. Unless the risks of cell phones are shown to outweigh the benefits, we should not restrict their use in moving vehicles; instead, we should educate the public about the dangers of driving while phoning and prosecute irresponsible phone users under laws on negligent and reckless driving.

For Angela Daly's introduction and thesis, see page 637.

In addition to stating your thesis and establishing a context for it, an introduction should hook readers. For example, in your first sentence or two you might connect your topic to something recently in the news or allude to emerging trends in an academic discipline. Other strategies are to pose a puzzling problem or to cite a startling statistic. Paul Levi opens his paper with compelling statistics. Angela Daly begins her paper by linking her topic to everyday experiences: "When a cell phone goes off in a classroom or at a concert, we are irritated, but at least our lives are not endangered. When we are on the road, however, irresponsible cell phone users are more than irritating: They are putting our lives at risk."

53c Provide organizational cues.

Even if you are working with a good outline, your paper will appear disorganized unless you provide organizational cues: topic sentences, transitions between major sections of the paper, and perhaps headings. Paul Levi uses the following headings to set off the three sections of his paper:

— Assessing the risks
— Weighing risks and benefits
— Educating drivers and enforcing laws

Although Angela Daly does not use headings, her paper is easy to follow because she begins paragraphs with clear topic sentences and uses transitions to help readers move from one idea to the next. Some of the annotations in the margins of Daly's paper (pp. 637–45) draw attention to such organizational cues.

For more about topic sentences, transitions, and headings, see 4a, 4e, and 5b.

53d　Draft the paper in an appropriate voice.

A chatty, breezy voice is usually not welcome in a research paper, but neither is a stuffy, pretentious style or a timid, unsure one.

TOO CHATTY

Who says that cell phones and driving don't mix? Tell it to the cops who learn about wild or plastered drivers from callers dialing 911 while on the road.

BETTER

Cell phones contribute to traffic safety because drivers place 911 calls alerting police to accidents and reckless or drunk drivers.

TOO STUFFY

It has been concluded that many automotive mishaps are resultant from cell phone use.

BETTER

Research suggests that drivers using cell phones cause many traffic accidents.

TOO TIMID

I may not be an expert, but it seems to me that phoning while driving could be risky.

BETTER

Common sense tells us that phoning while driving presents a risk.

54

Citing sources; avoiding plagiarism

In a research paper, you will be drawing on the work of other writers, and you must document their contributions by citing your sources. Sources are cited for two reasons:

1. to tell readers where your information comes from — so that they can assess its reliability and, if interested, find and read the original source
2. to give credit to the writers from whom you have borrowed words and ideas

To borrow another writer's language or ideas without proper acknowledgment is a form of dishonesty known as *plagiarism.*

You must include a citation when you quote from a source, when you summarize or paraphrase, and when you borrow facts and ideas that are not common knowledge (see also 54b).

54a For most English papers, use the MLA system for citing sources. (See 56 for important details.)

Most English professors and some humanities professors require the MLA (Modern Language Association) system of in-text citations. Here, briefly, is how the MLA citation system usually works:

1. The source is introduced by a signal phrase that names its author.
2. The material being cited is followed by a page number in parentheses.

3. At the end of the paper, a list of works cited (arranged alphabetically according to the authors' last names) gives complete publication information about the source.

IN-TEXT CITATION

According to Donald Redelmeier and Robert Tibshirani, "The use of cellular telephones in motor vehicles is associated with a quadrupling of the risk of a collision during the brief period of a call" (453).

ENTRY IN THE LIST OF WORKS CITED

Redelmeier, Donald A., and Robert J. Tibshirani. "Association between Cellular-Telephone Calls and Motor Vehicle Collisions." New England Journal of Medicine 336 (1997): 453-58.

Handling an MLA citation is not always this simple. For a detailed discussion of possible variations, see 56.

54b Avoid plagiarism.

Your research paper is a collaboration between you and your sources. To be fair and ethical, you must acknowledge your debt to the writers of these sources. If you don't, you are guilty of plagiarism, a serious academic offense.

Three different acts are considered plagiarism: (1) failing to cite quotations and borrowed ideas, (2) failing to enclose borrowed language in quotation marks, and (3) failing to put summaries and paraphrases in your own words.

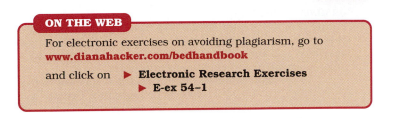

ON THE WEB

For electronic exercises on avoiding plagiarism, go to
www.dianahacker.com/bedhandbook

and click on ▶ **Electronic Research Exercises**
▶ **E-ex 54–1**

Citing quotations and borrowed ideas

You must of course document all direct quotations. You must also cite any ideas you borrow from a source: paraphrases of sentences, summaries of paragraphs or chapters, statistics and little-known facts, and tables, graphs, or diagrams.

The only exception is common knowledge — information your readers could find in any number of general sources because it is commonly known. For example, it is well known that Toni Morrison won the Nobel Prize in literature in 1993 and that Emily Dickinson published only a handful of her many poems during her lifetime.

As a rule, when you have seen information repeatedly in your reading, you don't need to cite it. However, when information has appeared in only one or two sources or when it is controversial, you should cite it. If a topic is new to you and you are not sure what is considered common knowledge or what is controversial, ask someone with expertise. When in doubt, cite the source.

Enclosing borrowed language in quotation marks

To indicate that you are using a source's exact phrases or sentences, you must enclose them in quotation marks unless they have been set off from the text by indenting (see p. 586). To omit the quotation marks is to claim — falsely — that the language is your own. Such an omission is plagiarism even if you have cited the source.

ORIGINAL SOURCE

Future cars will provide drivers with concierge services, web-based information, online e-mail capabilities, CD-ROM access, on-screen and audio navigation technology, and a variety of other information and entertainment services.

— Matt Sundeen, "Cell Phones and Highway Safety: 2000 State Legislative Update," p. 1

PLAGIARISM

Matt Sundeen points out that in cars of the future drivers will have concierge services, web-based information, online e-mail capabilities, CD-ROM access, on-screen and audio navigation technology, and a variety of other information and entertainment services (1).

BORROWED LANGUAGE IN QUOTATION MARKS

Matt Sundeen points out that in cars of the future drivers will have "concierge services, web-based information, online e-mail capabilities, CD-ROM access, on-screen and audio navigation technology, and a variety of other information and entertainment services" (1).

Putting summaries and paraphrases in your own words

A summary condenses information from a source; a paraphrase repeats this information in about the same number of words. When you summarize or paraphrase, it is not enough to name the source; you must restate the source's meaning using your own language. (See also 51c.) You are guilty of plagiarism if you half-copy the author's sentences—either by mixing the author's phrases with your own without using quotation marks or by plugging your synonyms into the author's sentence structure.

The first paraphrase of the following source is plagiarized—even though the source is cited—because too much of its language is borrowed from the original. The underlined strings of words have been copied word-for-word (without quotation marks). In addition, the writer has closely echoed the sentence structure of the source, merely plugging in some synonyms (*demonstrated* for *shown, devising* for *designing,* and *car* for *automotive*).

ORIGINAL SOURCE

The automotive industry has not shown good judgment in designing automotive features that distract drivers. A classic example is the use of a touch-sensitive screen to replace all the controls for radios, tape/CD players, and heating/cooling. Although an interesting technology, such devices require that the driver take his eyes off the road.

— Tom Magliozzi and Ray Magliozzi,
Letter to a Massachusetts state senator, p. 3

PLAGIARISM: UNACCEPTABLE BORROWING

Radio show hosts Tom and Ray Magliozzi argue that the automotive industry has not demonstrated good judgment in devising car features that distract drivers. One feature is a touch-sensitive screen that replaces controls for radios, tape/CD players, and heating/cooling. Although the technology is interesting, such devices require that a driver look away from the road (3).

To avoid plagiarizing an author's language, resist the temptation to look at the source while you are summarizing or paraphrasing. Close the book, write from memory, and then open the book to check for accuracy. This technique prevents you from being captivated by the words on the page.

TWO ACCEPTABLE PARAPHRASES

Radio show hosts Tom and Ray Magliozzi claim that
motor vehicle manufacturers do not always design
features with safety in mind. For example, when
designers replaced radio, CD player, and temperature control knobs with touch-sensitive panels,
they were forgetting one thing: To use the panels,
drivers would need to take their eyes off the
road (3).

Tom and Ray Magliozzi, hosts of the Car Talk radio
show, criticize the motor vehicle industry for contributing to driver distractions. They give the
example of new touch-sensitive technology for oper-
ating the radio, CD player, and tape deck and for
controlling temperature. Unlike old-fashioned
knobs, this new technology requires drivers to
look away from the road (3).

55

Integrating sources

With practice, you will learn to integrate information from
sources—quotations, summaries, paraphrases, and facts—
smoothly into your own text.

NOTE: If you are integrating quotations from a literary
source, see 58e.

ON THE WEB

For an electronic exercise on integrating quotations in MLA papers, go to **www.dianahacker.com/bedhandbook**

and click on ▶ **Electronic Research Exercises**
        ▶ **E-ex 55–1**

55a   Use signal phrases to introduce quotations; limit your use of quotations.

Using signal phrases

Readers need to move from your own words to the words of a source without feeling a jolt. Avoid dropping quotations into the text without warning. Instead, provide clear signal phrases, usually including the author's name, to prepare readers for a quotation.

DROPPED QUOTATION

In 2000, the legislature of Suffolk County passed a law restricting drivers' use of handheld phones. "The bill prohibits the use of a cell phone while driving unless it is equipped with an earpiece or can act like a speakerphone, leaving the driver's hands free" (Kelley 1).

QUOTATION WITH SIGNAL PHRASE

In 2000, the legislature of Suffolk County passed a law restricting drivers' use of handheld

```
phones. According to journalist Tina Kelley,
"The bill prohibits the use of a cell phone while
driving unless it is equipped with an earpiece or
can act like a speakerphone, leaving the driver's
hands free" (1).
```

To avoid monotony, try to vary both the language and the placement of your signal phrases. The models in the chart on page 583 suggest a range of possibilities.

When your signal phrase includes a verb, choose one that is appropriate in the context. Is your source arguing a point, making an observation, reporting a fact, drawing a conclusion, refuting an argument, or stating a belief? By choosing an appropriate verb, you can make your source's stance clear. See the chart for a list of verbs commonly used in signal phrases.

Limiting your use of quotations

Although it is tempting to insert many long quotations in your paper and to use your own words only for connecting passages, do not quote excessively. It is almost impossible to integrate numerous long quotations smoothly into your own text.

Except for the following legitimate uses of quotations, use your own words to summarize and paraphrase your sources and to explain your own ideas.

WHEN TO USE QUOTATIONS

—When language is especially vivid or expressive

—When exact wording is needed for technical accuracy

—When it is important to let the debaters of an issue explain their positions in their own words

—When the words of an important authority lend weight to an argument

Varying signal phrases in MLA papers

MODEL SIGNAL PHRASES

In the words of researchers Redelmeier and Tibshirani, "..."

As Matt Sundeen has noted, "..."

Patti Pena, mother of a child killed by a driver distracted by a cell phone, points out that "..."

"...," writes Christine Haughney, "..."

"...," claims wireless spokesperson Annette Jacobs.

Radio hosts Tom and Ray Magliozzi offer a persuasive counterargument: "..."

VERBS IN SIGNAL PHRASES

acknowledges	comments	endorses	reasons
adds	compares	grants	refutes
admits	confirms	illustrates	rejects
agrees	contends	implies	reports
argues	declares	insists	responds
asserts	denies	notes	suggests
believes	disputes	observes	thinks
claims	emphasizes	points out	writes

—When language of a source is the topic of your discussion (as in an analysis or interpretation)

It is not always necessary to quote full sentences from a source. To reduce your reliance on the words of others, you can often integrate a phrase from a source into your own sentence structure.

```
Redelmeier and Tibshirani found that hands-free
phones were not any safer in vehicles than other
cell phones. They suggest that crashes involving
```

cell phones may "result from a driver's limitations with regard to attention rather than dexterity" (456).

The Harvard Center for Risk Analysis argues that "because a significant percentage of cellular phone calls are made from vehicles during rush hour," accidents caused by the phones are less likely to be fatal than accidents caused by other risk factors (4-5).

Using the ellipsis mark and brackets

Two useful marks of punctuation, the ellipsis mark and brackets, allow you to keep quoted material to a minimum and to integrate it smoothly into your text.

THE ELLIPSIS MARK   To condense a quoted passage, you can use the ellipsis mark (three periods, with spaces between) to indicate that you have omitted words. What remains must be grammatically complete.

The University of North Carolina Highway Safety Research Center has begun a study assessing a variety of driver distractions. According to Allyson Vaughan, "The research . . . is intended to inject some empirical evidence into the debate over whether talking on wireless phones while driving leads to accidents" (1).

The writer has omitted the words *funded by the AAA Foundation for Traffic Safety,* which appeared in the source.

On the rare occasions when you want to omit one or more full sentences, use a period before the three ellipsis dots.

> Redelmeier and Tibshirani acknowledge that their
> study "indicates an association but not necessarily
> a causal relation between the use of cellular tele-
> phones while driving and a subsequent motor vehicle
> collision. . . . In addition, our study did not in-
> clude serious injuries . . ." (457).

Ordinarily, do not use an ellipsis mark at the beginning or at the end of a quotation. Your readers will understand that the quoted material is taken from a longer passage, so such marks are not necessary. The only exception occurs when words at the end of the final quoted sentence have been dropped. In such cases, put three ellipsis dots before the closing quotation mark and parenthetical reference, as in the previous example.

Obviously you should not use an ellipsis mark to distort the meaning of your source.

BRACKETS   Brackets allow you to insert your own words into quoted material. You can insert words in brackets to explain a confusing reference or to keep a sentence grammatical in your context.

> According to economists Robert Hahn and Paul
> Tetlock, "Some studies say they [hands-free phones]
> would have no impact on accidents, while others
> suggest the reductions could be sizable" (2).

To indicate an error in a quotation, insert [sic] after the error.

> Smith argues that "the dangers of driving while
> talking have not been exagerated [sic]"(4).

Setting off long quotations

When you quote more than four typed lines of prose or more than three lines of poetry, set off the quotation by indenting it one inch (or ten spaces) from the left margin. Use the normal right margin and do not single-space.

Long quotations should be introduced by an informative sentence, usually followed by a colon. Quotation marks are unnecessary because the indented format tells readers that the words are taken directly from the source.

```
Tom and Ray Magliozzi are not impressed by econo-
mists who conduct risk-benefit analyses of phone
use by drivers:

          Other critics [of regulation of cell
          phones]--some from prestigious "think
          tanks"--perform what appear to be erudite
          cost/benefit analyses. The problem here
          is that the benefits are always in units
          of convenience and productivity while
          the costs are in units of injuries and
          people's lives! (2)
```

Notice that at the end of an indented quotation the parenthetical citation goes outside the final mark of punctuation. (When a quotation is run into your text, the opposite is true. See the sample citation on p. 587.)

55b Use signal phrases to introduce most summaries and paraphrases.

Introduce most summaries and paraphrases with a signal phrase that names the author and places the material in

context. Readers will then understand that everything between the signal phrase and the parenthetical citation summarizes or paraphrases the cited source.

Without the signal phrase (underlined) in the following
example, readers might think that only the quotation at the
end is being cited, when in fact the whole paragraph is
based on the source.

> Alasdair Cain and Mark Burris report that
> scientific research on traffic accidents and cell
> phone use has been inconclusive. Many factors play
> a role: for example, the type of phone (hands-free
> or not), the extent to which the conversation is
> distracting, and the demographic profile of the
> driver. Although research suggests that phoning in
> a moving vehicle affects driver performance, stud-
> ies have failed to quantify the degree of driver
> impairment. Cain and Burris write that drivers
> using cell phones on the road "were anywhere from
> 34 percent to 300 percent more likely to have an
> accident" (1).

There are times, however, when a signal phrase naming
the author is not necessary. Readers will understand, for example, that the citation at the end of the following passage
applies to the entire paragraph, not just part of it:

> The American Automobile Association is
> funding a study on driver distractions, includ-
> ing cell phone use. In the summer of 2000,
> researchers at the University of North Carolina

Highway Safety Research Center began studying
144 drivers in Chapel Hill and Philadelphia to
determine which distractions--such as tuning the
radio, eating, and talking on the phone--most
affect the ability to drive. The drivers allowed
researchers to install cameras in their vehicles
to study their every movement while driving
(Vaughan 2).

55c   With statistics and other facts, a signal phrase may not be needed.

When you are citing a statistic or other specific fact, a signal phrase is often not necessary. In most cases, readers will understand that the citation refers to the statistic or fact (not the whole paragraph).

As of 2000, there were about ninety million cell
phone users in the United States, with 85% of them
using their phones while on the road (Sundeen 1).

There is nothing wrong, however, with using a signal phrase to introduce a statistic or other fact.

Matt Sundeen reports that as of 2000, there were
about ninety million cell phone users in the United
States, with 85% of them using their phones while
on the road (1).

Reviewing an MLA paper: Global revisions

FOCUS

—Is the thesis stated clearly enough? Is it placed where readers will notice it?

—Does each paragraph support the thesis?

ORGANIZATION

—Can readers follow the organization? Would headings help?

—Do topic sentences signal new ideas? Do transitions help readers move from one major group of paragraphs to another?

—Are ideas presented in a logical order?

CONTENT

—Is the supporting material persuasive? Are the arguments strong enough to stand up to arguments of those who disagree with the thesis?

—Are the parts proportioned sensibly? Do the major ideas receive enough attention?

—Is the draft concise—free of irrelevant, unimportant, or repetitious material?

STYLE

—Is the voice appropriate—not too chatty, too stuffy, or too timid?

—Are the sentences clear, emphatic, and varied?

Reviewing an MLA paper: Use of sources

USE OF QUOTATIONS

—Is quoted material enclosed within quotation marks (unless it has been set off from the text)? (See 54b.)

—Is quoted language word-for-word accurate? If not, do brackets or ellipsis marks indicate the changes or omissions? (See pp. 584–85.)

—Does a clear signal phrase (usually naming the author) prepare readers for each quotation? (See 55a.)

—Does a parenthetical citation follow each quotation? (See 56a.)

USE OF SUMMARIES AND PARAPHRASES

—Are summaries and paraphrases free of plagiarized wording—not copied or half-copied from the source? (See 54b.)

—Are summaries and paraphrases documented with parenthetical citations? (See 56a.)

—Do readers know where the material being cited begins? In other words, does a signal phrase mark the beginning of the cited material unless the context makes clear exactly what is being cited? (See 55b.)

USE OF STATISTICS AND OTHER FACTS

—Are statistics and facts (other than common knowledge) documented with parenthetical citations? (See 56a.)

—If there is no signal phrase, will readers understand exactly which facts are being cited? (See 55b.)

56

MLA documentation style

In English and in some humanities classes, you will be asked to use the MLA (Modern Language Association) system for documenting sources, which is set forth in the *MLA Handbook for Writers of Research Papers,* 6th ed. (New York: MLA, 2003). MLA recommends in-text citations that refer readers to a list of works cited.

An in-text citation names the author of the source, often in a signal phrase, and gives the page number in parentheses. At the end of the paper, a list of works cited provides publication information about the source; the list is alphabetized by authors' last names (or by titles for works without authors). There is a direct connection between the in-text citation and the alphabetical listing. In the following example, that link is highlighted in red.

IN-TEXT CITATION

Matt Sundeen notes that drivers with cell phones
place an estimated 98,000 emergency calls each day
and that the phones "often reduce emergency
response times and actually save lives" (1).

ENTRY IN THE LIST OF WORKS CITED

Sundeen, Matt. "Cell Phones and Highway Safety:
    2000 State Legislative Update." National
    Conference of State Legislatures. Dec. 2000.
    9 pp. 27 Feb. 2001 <http://ncsl.org/programs/
    esnr/cellphone.pdf>.

For a list of works cited that includes this entry, see pages
644–45.

Directory to MLA in-text citation models

BASIC RULES FOR PRINT AND ELECTRONIC SOURCES

1. Author named in a signal phrase, 594
2. Author named in parentheses, 595
3. Author unknown, 595
4. Page number unknown, 595
5. One-page source, 596

VARIATIONS ON THE BASIC RULES

6. Two or more titles by the same author, 597
7. Two or three authors, 598
8. Four or more authors, 598
9. Corporate author, 599
10. Authors with the same last name, 599
11. Indirect source (source quoted in another source), 599
12. Encyclopedia or dictionary, 599

56a MLA in-text citations

MLA in-text citations are made with a combination of signal phrases and parenthetical references. A signal phrase indicates that something taken from a source (such as a quotation, summary, or paraphrase) is about to be used; usually the signal phrase includes the author's name. The parenthetical reference includes at least a page number (unless the work has no page numbers or is organized alphabetically).

IN-TEXT CITATION

```
One driver, Peter Cohen, says that after he was
rear-ended, the guilty party emerged from his
vehicle still talking on the phone (127).
```

Readers can look up the author's last name in the alphabetized list of works cited, where they will find information about the work's title, publisher, and place and date of publication. When readers decide to consult the source, the page number will take them straight to the passage that has been cited.

Basic rules for print and electronic sources

The MLA system of in-text citations, which depends heavily on authors' names and page numbers, was created in the early 1980s with print sources in mind. Because some of today's electronic sources have unclear authorship and lack page numbers, they present a special challenge. Nevertheless, the basic rules are the same for both print and electronic sources.

The models in this section (items 1–5) show how the MLA system usually works and explain what to do if your source has no author or page numbers.

■ **1. AUTHOR NAMED IN A SIGNAL PHRASE** Ordinarily, introduce the material being cited with a signal phrase that includes the author's name. In addition to preparing readers for the source, the signal phrase allows you to keep the parenthetical citation brief.

> Christine Haughney reports that shortly after Japan made it illegal to use a handheld phone while driving, "accidents caused by using the phones dropped by 75 percent" (A8).

The signal phrase—"Christine Haughney reports that"—names the author; the parenthetical citation gives the page number where the quoted words may be found.

Notice that the period follows the parenthetical citation. When a quotation ends with a question mark or an exclamation point, leave the end punctuation inside the quotation mark and add a period after the parentheses: "...?" (8). (See also the note on p. 428.)

■ **2. AUTHOR NAMED IN PARENTHESES** If the signal phrase does not include the author's name (or if there is no signal phrase), the author's last name must appear in parentheses along with the page number.

```
Most states do not keep adequate records on the
number of times cell phones are a factor in acci-
dents; as of December 2000, only ten states were
trying to keep such records (Sundeen 2).
```

Use no punctuation between the name and the page number.

■ **3. AUTHOR UNKNOWN** If the author is unknown, either use the complete title in a signal phrase or use a short form of the title in parentheses. Titles of books are underlined (or italicized); titles of articles are put in quotation marks.

```
As of 2001, at least three hundred towns and munic-
ipalities had considered legislation regulating use
of cell phones while driving ("Lawmakers" 2).
```

CAUTION: Before assuming that a Web source has no author, do some detective work. Often the author's name is available but is not easy to find. For example, it may appear at the end of the source, in tiny print. Or it may appear on another page of the site, such as the home page.

NOTE: If a source has no author and is sponsored by a corporate entity, such as an organization or a government agency, name the corporate entity as the author (see item 9 on p. 599).

■ **4. PAGE NUMBER UNKNOWN** You may omit the page number if a work lacks page numbers, as is the case with many Web sources. Although printouts from Web sites usually show page numbers, different printers may provide different page breaks; for this reason, MLA recommends treating such sources as unpaginated.

> The California Highway Patrol opposes restrictions
> on the use of phones while driving, claiming that
> distracted drivers can already be prosecuted
> (Jacobs).

When the pages of a Web source are stable (as in pdf files), however, supply a page number in your in-text citation. (For example, the Web source by Sundeen cited in the example on p. 592 has stable pages, so a page number is included in the citation.)

NOTE: If a Web source uses paragraph or section numbers, give the abbreviation "par." or "sec." in the parentheses: (Smith, par. 4).

■ **5. ONE-PAGE SOURCE**   If the source is one page long, MLA allows (but does not require) you to omit the page number. Many instructors will want you to supply the page number because without it readers may not know where your citation ends or, worse yet, may not realize that you have provided a citation at all.

No page number given

> Milo Ippolito reports that the driver who struck
> and killed a two-year-old while using her cell
> phone got off with a light sentence even though
> she left the scene of the accident and failed to
> call 911 for help. In this and in similar cases,
> traffic offenders distracted by cell phones have

not been sufficiently punished under laws on reckless driving.

Page number given

Milo Ippolito reports that the driver who struck
and killed a two-year-old while using her cell
phone got off with a light sentence even though
she left the scene of the accident and failed to
call 911 for help (J1). In this and in similar
cases, traffic offenders distracted by cell phones
have not been sufficiently punished under laws on
reckless driving.

Variations on the basic rules

This section describes the MLA guidelines for handling a
variety of situations not covered by the basic rules just
given. Again, these rules on in-text citations are the same for
both traditional print sources and electronic sources.

■ **6. TWO OR MORE TITLES BY THE SAME AUTHOR** If your list
of works cited includes two or more titles by the same
author, mention the title of the work in the signal phrase or
include a short version of the title in the parentheses.

On December 6, 2000, reporter Jamie Stockwell wrote
that distracted driver Jason Jones had been charged
with "two counts of vehicular manslaughter . . . in
the deaths of John and Carole Hall" ("Phone" B1).
The next day Stockwell reported the judge's ruling:
Jones "was convicted of negligent driving and fined
$500, the maximum penalty allowed" ("Man" B4).

Titles of articles are placed in quotation marks, as in the example just given. Titles of books are underlined or italicized.

In the rare case when both the author's name and a short title must be given in parentheses, separate them with a comma.

> According to police reports, there were no skid
> marks indicating that the distracted driver who
> killed John and Carole Hall had even tried to stop
> (Stockwell, "Man" B4).

■ **7. TWO OR THREE AUTHORS** If your source has two or three authors, name them in the signal phrase, as in the following example, or include their last names in the parenthetical reference: (Redelmeier and Tibshirani 453).

> Redelmeier and Tibshirani found that "the risk of
> a collision when using a cellular telephone was
> four times higher than the risk when a cellular
> telephone was not being used" (453).

When three authors are named in the parentheses, separate the names with commas: (Alton, Davies, and Rice 56).

■ **8. FOUR OR MORE AUTHORS** If your source has four or more authors, you may name all of the authors or you may include only the first author's name followed by "et al." (Latin for "and others"). Make sure that your parenthetical citation matches the way you handle the entry in the list of works cited (see also item 2 on p. 606).

> The study was extended for two years, and only
> after results were reviewed by an independent panel
> did the researchers publish their findings (Blaine
> et al. 35).

■ **9. CORPORATE AUTHOR** When the author is a corporation or an organization, name the corporate author either in the signal phrase or in the parentheses.

> Researchers at the Harvard Center for Risk Analysis
> found that the risks of driving while phoning were
> small compared with other driving risks (3-4).

In the list of works cited, the Harvard Center for Risk Analysis is treated as the author and alphabetized under *H.*

■ **10. AUTHORS WITH THE SAME LAST NAME** If your list of works cited includes works by two or more authors with the same last name, include the first initial of the author in the signal phrase or parentheses. (If the authors share an initial as well as a last name, spell out the first name.)

> Estimates of the number of accidents caused by
> distracted drivers vary because little evidence
> is being collected (D. Smith 7).

■ **11. INDIRECT SOURCE (SOURCE QUOTED IN ANOTHER SOURCE)** When a writer's or a speaker's quoted words appear in a source written by someone else, begin the citation with the abbreviation "qtd. in."

> According to Richard Retting, "As the comforts of
> home and the efficiency of the office creep into the
> automobile, it is becoming increasingly attractive
> as a work space" (qtd. in Kilgannon A23).

■ **12. ENCYCLOPEDIA OR DICTIONARY** Unless an encyclopedia or a dictionary has an author, it will be alphabetized in the list of works cited under the word or entry that you consulted — not under the title of the reference work itself (see p. 610). Either in your text or in your parenthetical reference, mention the word or the entry. No page number is required, since readers can easily look up the word or entry.

```
The word crocodile has a surprisingly complex
etymology ("Crocodile").
```

■ **13. MULTIVOLUME WORK**   If your paper cites more than one volume of a multivolume work, indicate in the parentheses the volume you are referring to, followed by a colon and the page number.

```
Terman's studies of gifted children reveal a pattern
of accelerated language acquisition (2: 279).
```

If your paper cites only one volume of a multivolume work, you will include the volume number in the list of works cited and will not need to include it in the parentheses.

■ **14. TWO OR MORE WORKS**   When you want to document a particular point with more than one source, separate the citations with a semicolon.

```
The dangers of mountain lions to humans have been
well documented (Rychnovsky 40; Seidensticker 114;
Williams 30).
```

Multiple citations can be distracting, however, so you should not overuse the technique. If you want to alert readers to several sources that discuss a particular topic, consider using an information note instead (see 56c).

■ **15. AN ENTIRE WORK**   To cite an entire work, use the author's name in a signal phrase or a parenthetical reference. There is of course no need to use a page number.

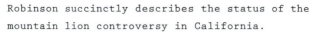

```
Robinson succinctly describes the status of the
mountain lion controversy in California.
```

■ **16. WORK IN AN ANTHOLOGY** Put the name of the author of the work (not the editor of the anthology) in the signal phrase or the parentheses.

```
In Susan Glaspell's "A Jury of Her Peers," Mrs.
Hale describes both a style of quilting and a
murder weapon when she utters the last words of the
story: "We call it--knot it, Mr. Henderson" (302).
```

In the list of works cited, the work is alphabetized under Glaspell, not under the name of the editor of the anthology.

```
Glaspell, Susan. "A Jury of Her Peers." Literature
      and Its Writers: An Introduction to Fiction,
      Poetry, and Drama. Ed. Ann Charters and Samuel
      Charters. 2nd ed. Boston: Bedford, 2001. 286-
      302.
```

Literary works and sacred texts

Literary works and sacred texts are usually available in a variety of editions. Your list of works cited will specify which edition you are using, and your in-text citation will usually consist of a page number from the edition you consulted (see item 17).

However, MLA suggests that when possible you should give enough information—such as book parts, play divisions, or line numbers—so that readers can locate the cited passage in any edition of the work (see items 18–20).

■ **17. LITERARY WORKS WITHOUT PARTS OR LINE NUMBERS** Many literary works, such as most short stories and many

novels and plays, do not have parts or line numbers that
you can refer to. In such cases, simply cite the page number.

```
At the end of Kate Chopin's "The Story of an Hour,"
Mrs. Mallard drops dead upon learning that her
husband is alive. In the final irony of the story,
doctors report that she has died of a "joy that
kills" (25).
```

■   **18. VERSE PLAYS AND POEMS**   For verse plays, MLA recommends omitting page numbers in the parenthetical citation. Instead, include act, scene, and line numbers that
can be located in any edition of the work. Use arabic
numerals, and separate the numbers with periods.

```
In his famous advice to players, Shakespeare's
Hamlet defines the purpose of theater, "whose
end, both at the first and now, was and is,
to hold, as 'twere, the mirror up to nature"
(3.2.21-23).
```

For a poem, cite the part (if there are a number of parts)
and the line numbers, separated by a period.

```
When Homer's Odysseus comes to the hall of Circe,
he finds his men "mild / in her soft spell, fed on
her drug of evil" (10.209-11).
```

For poems that are not divided into parts, use line numbers.
For a first reference, use the word "lines": (lines 5-8). There-
after use just the numbers: (12-13).

■   **19. NOVELS WITH NUMBERED DIVISIONS**   When a novel has
numbered divisions, put the page number first, followed by

a semicolon, and then indicate the book, part, or chapter in which the passage may be found. Use abbreviations such as "bk." and "ch."

> One of Kingsolver's narrators, teenager Rachel, pushes her vocabulary beyond its limits. For example, Rachel complains that being forced to live in the Congo with her missionary family is "a sheer tapestry of justice" because her chances of finding a boyfriend are "dull and void" (117; bk. 2, ch. 10).

■ **20. SACRED TEXTS**   When citing a sacred text such as the Bible or the Koran, name the edition you are using in your works cited entry (see p. 611). In your parenthetical citation, give the book, chapter, and verse (or their equivalent), separated by periods. Common abbreviations for books of the Bible are acceptable.

> Consider the words of Solomon: "If your enemies are hungry, give them food to eat. If they are thirsty, give them water to drink" (Holy Bible, Prov. 25.21).

ON THE WEB

For electronic exercises on using MLA documentation style, go to **www.dianahacker.com/bedhandbook**

and click on ▶ **Electronic Research Exercises**
                    ▶ **E-ex 56–1**

56b MLA list of works cited

An alphabetized list of works cited, which appears at the end of your research paper, gives publication information for each of the sources you have cited in the paper. (For information about preparing this list, see p. 635; for a sample list of works cited, see p. 644.)

NOTE: Unless your instructor asks for them, omit sources not actually cited in the paper, even if you read them.

Directory to MLA works cited entries

Directory to MLA works cited entries (continued)

General guidelines for listing authors

Alphabetize entries in the list of works cited by authors' last names (if a work has no author, alphabetize it by its title). The author's name is important because citations in the text of the paper refer to it and readers will be looking for it at the beginning of an entry in the alphabetized list.

NAME CITED IN TEXT

```
According to Matt Sundeen,...
```

BEGINNING OF WORKS CITED ENTRY

```
Sundeen, Matt.
```

The following examples show how to begin an entry for a work with (1) a single author, (2) multiple authors, (3) a corporate author, (4) an unknown author, and (5) multiple works by the same author. What comes after this first element of your citation will depend on the kind of source you are citing. (See items 6–56.)

NOTE: For a book, an entry in the works cited list will sometimes begin with an editor (see item 7).

■ **1. SINGLE AUTHOR** For a work with one author, begin the entry with the author's last name, followed by a comma; then give the author's first name, followed by a period.

```
Tannen, Deborah.
```

■ **2. MULTIPLE AUTHORS** For works with two or three authors, name the authors in the order in which they are listed in the source. Reverse the name of only the first author.

```
Walker, Janice R., and Todd Taylor.

Wilmut, Ian, Keith Campbell, and Colin Tudge.
```

For a work with four or more authors, either name all of the authors or name the first author, followed by "et al." (Latin for "and others").

```
Sloan, Frank A., Emily M. Stout, Kathryn Whetten-
     Goldstein, and Lan Liang.


Sloan, Frank A., et al.
```

■ **3. CORPORATE AUTHOR**   When the author of a print document or Web site is a corporation, a government agency, or some other organization, begin your entry with the name of the group.

```
Bank of Boston.

United States. Bureau of the Census.

American Automobile Association.
```

NOTE: Make sure that your in-text citation also treats the organization as the author (see item 9 on p. 599).

■ **4. UNKNOWN AUTHOR**   When the author of a work is unknown, begin with the work's title. Titles of articles and other short works are put in quotation marks. Titles of books and Web sites are underlined (or italicized). (For titles of works within Web sites, see items 28 and 29.)

Article

```
"Media Giants."
```

Book

```
Atlas of the World.
```

Web site

```
Caracol: The Official Website of the Caracol
    Archaeological Project.
```

Before concluding that the author of a work such as a Web source is unknown, check carefully (see the caution on p. 595). Also remember that an organization may be the author (see item 3).

■ **5. TWO OR MORE WORKS BY THE SAME AUTHOR** If your list of works cited includes two or more works by the same author, use the author's name only for the first entry. For other entries use three hyphens followed by a period. The three hyphens must stand for exactly the same name or names as in the first entry. List the titles in alphabetical order.

```
Atwood, Margaret. Alias Grace: A Novel. New York:
    Doubleday, 1996.

---. The Robber Bride. New York: Doubleday, 1993.
```

Books

Items 6–19 apply to print books. For online books, see item 29.

■ **6. BASIC FORMAT FOR A BOOK** For most books, arrange the information into three units, each followed by a period and one space: (1) the author's name; (2) the title and subtitle, underlined (or italicized); and (3) the place of publication, the publisher, and the date.

```
Tan, Amy. The Bonesetter's Daughter. New York:
    Putnam, 2001.
```

Take the information about the book from its title page and copyright page. You may use a short form of the publisher's name as long as it is easily identifiable; omit terms such as *Press, Inc.,* and *Co.* except when naming university presses (Harvard UP, for example). If the copyright page lists more than one date, use the most recent one.

■ **7. EDITORS** An entry for an editor is similar to that for an author except that the name is followed by a comma and the abbreviation "ed." for "editor" (or "eds." for "editors").

> Powell, Kevin, ed. Step into a World: A Global
> Anthology of the New Black Literature. New
> York: Wiley, 2000.

■ **8. AUTHOR WITH AN EDITOR** Begin with the author and title, followed by the name of the editor. In this case the abbreviation "Ed." means "Edited by," so it is the same for one or multiple editors.

> Plath, Sylvia. The Unabridged Journals of Sylvia
> Plath. Ed. Karen V. Kukil. New York:
> Anchor-Doubleday, 2000.

■ **9. AUTHOR WITH A TRANSLATOR** Begin with the name of the author. After the title, write "Trans." (for "Translated by") and the name of the translator.

> Allende, Isabel. Daughter of Fortune. Trans.
> Margaret Sayers Peden. New York: Harper, 2000.

■ **10. EDITION OTHER THAN THE FIRST** If you are citing an edition other than the first, include the number of the edition after the title: 2nd ed., 3rd ed., and so on.

> Boyce, David George. The Irish Question and British
>   Politics, 1868-1996. 2nd ed. New York: St.
>   Martin's, 1996.

■ **11. MULTIVOLUME WORK** Include the total number of volumes before the city and publisher, using the abbreviation "vols."

> Conway, Jill Ker, ed. Written by Herself. 2 vols.
>   New York: Random, 1996.

If your paper cites only one of the volumes, give the volume number before the city and publisher and give the total number of volumes after the date.

> Conway, Jill Ker, ed. Written by Herself. Vol. 2.
>   New York: Random, 1996. 2 vols.

■ **12. ENCYCLOPEDIA OR DICTIONARY ENTRY** When an encyclopedia or a dictionary is well known, simply list the author of the entry (if there is one), the title of the entry, the title of the reference work, the edition number (if any), and the date of the edition.

> Posner, Rebecca. "Romance Languages." The New
>   Encyclopaedia Britannica: Macropaedia. 15th
>   ed. 1987.

> "Sonata." The American Heritage Dictionary of the
>   English Language. 4th ed. 2000.

Volume and page numbers are not necessary because the entries in the source are arranged alphabetically and therefore are easy to locate.

If a reference work is not well known, provide full publication information as well.

■ **13. SACRED TEXT** Give the title of the edition of the sacred text (taken from the title page), underlined; the editor's name (if any); and publication information.

```
Holy Bible: New Living Translation. Wheaton:
     Tyndale, 1996.
```

■ **14. WORK IN AN ANTHOLOGY** Begin with the name of the author of the selection, not with the name of the editor of the anthology. Then give the title of the selection, the title of the anthology, the name of the editor, publication information, and the pages on which the selection appears.

```
Odell, Noell. "Mallory and Irvine's Attempt."
     Points Unknown: A Century of Great
     Exploration. Ed. David Roberts. New York:
     Norton, 2000. 161-72.
```

If an anthology gives the original publication information for a selection and if your instructor prefers that you use it, cite that information first. Follow with "Rpt. in" (for "Reprinted in") and the title of the anthology, along with the other information about the anthology as in the model just given.

```
Alvarez, Julia. "Picky Eater." Something to Declare.
     Chapel Hill: Algonquin, 1998. 75-86. Rpt. in
     The Norton Book of American Autobiography. Ed.
     Jay Parini. New York: Norton, 1999. 619-26.
```

■ **15. FOREWORD, INTRODUCTION, PREFACE, OR AFTERWORD**
Begin with the author of the foreword or other book part,

followed by the name of that part. Then give the title of the book; the author of the book, preceded by the word "By"; and the editor of the book (if any). After the publication information, give the page numbers for the part of the book being cited.

> Pipher, Mary. Foreword. Can't Buy My Love: How
>   Advertising Changes the Way We Think and Feel.
>   By Jean Kilbourne. New York: Touchstone-Simon,
>   1999. 11-13.

If the book part being cited has a title, include it immediately after the author's name.

> Ozick, Cynthia. "Portrait of the Essay as a Warm
>   Body." Introduction. The Best American Essays
>   1998. Ed. Ozick. Boston: Houghton, 1998. xv-xxi.

■ **16. BOOK WITH A TITLE WITHIN ITS TITLE** If the book contains a title normally underlined (or italicized), neither underline (or italicize) the internal title nor place it in quotation marks.

> Vanderham, Paul. James Joyce and Censorship: The
>   Trials of Ulysses. New York: New York UP, 1997.

If the title within is normally enclosed within quotation marks, retain the quotation marks and underline (or italicize) the entire title.

> Faulkner, Dewey R., ed. Twentieth Century
>   Interpretations of "The Pardoner's Tale."
>   Englewood Cliffs: Prentice, 1973.

■ **17. BOOK IN A SERIES** Before the publication information, cite the series name as it appears on the title page, followed by the series number, if any.

> Malena, Anne. The Dynamics of Identity in Francophone
> Caribbean Narrative. Francophone Cultures and
> Lits. Ser. 24. New York: Lang, 1998.

■ **18. REPUBLISHED BOOK** After the title of the book, cite the original publication date, followed by the current publication information. If the republished book contains new material, such as an introduction or afterword, include information about the new material after the original date.

> Dietz, Lew, and Kosti Ruohomaa. Night Train at
> Wiscasset Station. 1977. Foreword Andrew
> Wyeth. Camden: Down East, 1998.

■ **19. PUBLISHER'S IMPRINT** If a book was published by an imprint (a division) of a publishing company, link the name of the imprint and the name of the publisher with a hyphen, putting the imprint first.

> Truan, Barry. Acoustic Communication. Westport:
> Ablex-Greenwood, 2000.

Articles in periodicals

This section shows how to prepare works cited entries for articles in magazines, scholarly journals, and newspapers. In addition to consulting the models in this section, you will at times need to turn to other models as well:

—More than one author: see item 2

—Corporate author: see item 3

—Unknown author: see item 4

—Online article: see item 32

—Article from a subscription service: see item 31

NOTE: For articles appearing on consecutive pages, provide the range of pages (see items 21 and 22). When an article does not appear on consecutive pages, give the number of the first page followed by a plus sign: 32+.

■ **20. ARTICLE IN A MAGAZINE** List, in order, separated by periods, the author's name; the title of the article, in quotation marks; and the title of the magazine, underlined (or italicized). Then give the date and the page numbers, separated by a colon. If the magazine is issued monthly, give just the month and year. Abbreviate the names of the months except May, June, and July.

```
Kaplan, Robert D. "History Moving North." Atlantic
     Monthly Feb. 1997: 21+.
```

If the magazine is issued weekly, give the exact date.

```
Lord, Lewis. "There's Something about Mary Todd."
     U.S. News and World Report 19 Feb. 2001: 53.
```

■ **21. ARTICLE IN A JOURNAL PAGINATED BY VOLUME** Many scholarly journals continue page numbers throughout the year instead of beginning each issue with page 1; at the end of the year, the issues are collected in a volume. To find an article, readers need only the volume number, the year, and the page numbers.

```
Ryan, Katy. "Revolutionary Suicide in Toni
     Morrison's Fiction." African American Review
     34 (2000): 389-412.
```

■ **22. ARTICLE IN A JOURNAL PAGINATED BY ISSUE**   If each issue of the journal begins with page 1, you need to indicate the number of the issue. Simply place a period after the volume number and follow it with the issue number.

```
Wood, Michael. "Broken Dates: Fiction and the
     Century." Kenyon Review 22.3 (2000): 50-64.
```

■ **23. ARTICLE IN A DAILY NEWSPAPER**   Begin with the name of the author, if there is one, followed by the title of the article. Next give the name of the newspaper, the date, and the page number (including the section letter). Use a plus sign (+) after the page number if the article does not appear on consecutive pages.

```
Murphy, Sean P. "Decisions on Status of Tribes Draw
     Fire." Boston Globe 27 Mar. 2001: A2.
```

If the section is marked with a number rather than a letter, handle the entry as follows:

```
Wilford, John Noble. "In a Golden Age of Discovery,
     Faraway Worlds Beckon." New York Times 9 Feb.
     1997, late ed., sec. 1: 1+.
```

When an edition of the newspaper is specified on the masthead, name the edition after the date and before the page reference (eastern ed., late ed., natl. ed., and so on), as in the example just given.

■ **24. EDITORIAL IN A NEWSPAPER** Cite an editorial as you would an unsigned article, adding the word "Editorial" after the title.

> "All Wet." Editorial. Boston Globe 12 Feb. 2001: 14.

■ **25. LETTER TO THE EDITOR** Cite the writer's name, followed by the word "Letter" and the publication information for the newspaper or magazine in which the letter appears.

> Shrewsbury, Toni. Letter. Atlanta Journal-
>   Constitution 17 Feb. 2001: A13.

■ **26. BOOK OR FILM REVIEW** Cite first the reviewer's name and the title of the review, if any, followed by the words "Rev. of" and the title and author or director of the work reviewed. Add the publication information for the publication in which the review appears.

> Gleick, Elizabeth. "The Burdens of Genius." Rev. of
>   The Last Samurai, by Helen DeWitt. Time 4 Dec.
>   2000: 171.

> Denby, David. "On the Battlefield." Rev. of The
>   Hurricane, dir. Norman Jewison. New Yorker
>   10 Jan. 2000: 90-92.

Electronic sources

MLA's current guidelines for documenting electronic sources can be found in the *MLA Handbook for Writers of Research Papers* (6th ed., 2003). For more help with citing electronic sources in MLA style, see the list of frequently asked questions in the section "MLA Style" on MLA's Web site, <http://www.mla.org>.

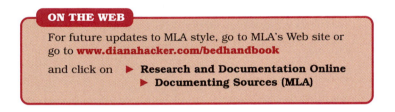

ON THE WEB

For future updates to MLA style, go to MLA's Web site or go to **www.dianahacker.com/bedhandbook**

and click on ▶ **Research and Documentation Online**
▶ **Documenting Sources (MLA)**

NOTE: When a Web address in a works cited entry must be divided at the end of a line, MLA recommends that you break it after a slash. Do not insert a hyphen.

■ **27. AN ENTIRE WEB SITE** Begin with the name of the author or corporate author (if known) and the title of the site, underlined (or italicized). Then give the names of any editors, the date of publication or last update, the name of any sponsoring organization, the date of access, and the URL in angle brackets. Provide as much of this information as is available.

With author

```
Peterson, Susan Lynn. The Life of Martin Luther.
     1999. 9 Mar. 2001 <http://pweb.netcom.com/
     ~supeters/luther.htm>.
```

With corporate (group) author

United States. Environmental Protection Agency.
     Values and Functions of Wetlands. 25 May 1999.
     24 Mar. 2001 <http://www.epa.gov-owow/
     wetlands/facts/fact2.html>.

Author unknown

Margaret Sanger Papers Project. 18 Oct. 2000.
     History Dept., New York U. 3 Apr. 2001
     <http://www.nyu.edu/projects/sanger/>.

With editor

Exploring Ancient World Cultures. Ed. Anthony F.
     Beavers. 1997. U of Evansville. 12 Mar. 2001
     <http://eawc.evansville.edu/index.htm>.

NOTE: If the site has no title, substitute a description, such as "Home page," for the title.

Block, Marylaine. Home page. 5 Mar. 2001. 12 Apr.
     2001 <http://www.marylaine.com>.

■ **28. SHORT WORK FROM A WEB SITE** "Short" works are those that appear in quotation marks in MLA style: articles, poems, and other documents that are not book length. For a short work from a Web site, include as many of the following elements as apply and as are available:

—Author's name

—Title of the short work, in quotation marks

—Title of the site, underlined (or italicized)

—Date of publication or last update

—Sponsor of the site (if not named as the author or given as the title of the site)

—Date you accessed the source

—The URL in angle brackets

Usually at least some of these elements will not apply or will be unavailable. For example, in the following model, no date of publication was available. (The date given is the date on which the researcher accessed the source.)

With author

```
Shiva, Vandana. "Bioethics: A Third World
    Issue." NativeWeb. 24 Feb. 2001
    <http://www.nativeweb.org/pages/legal/
    shiva.html>.
```

Author unknown

```
"Media Giants." Frontline: The Merchants of Cool.
    2001. PBS Online. 7 Mar. 2001 <http://
    www.pbs.org/wgbh/pages/frontline/shows/
    cool/giants>.
```

NOTE: When the URL for a short work from a Web site is very long, you may give the URL for the home page and indicate the path by which readers can access the source.

```
"Obesity Trends among U.S. Adults between 1985 and
    2001." Centers for Disease Control and Prevention.
    3 Jan. 2003. 17 Feb. 2003 <www.cdc.gov>. Path:
    Health Topics A-Z; Obesity Trends; U.S. Obesity
    Trends 1985 to 2001.
```

■ **29. ONLINE BOOK** When a book or a book-length work such as a play or a long poem is posted on the Web as its own site, give as much publication information as is available, followed by your date of access and the URL. (See also the models for print books: items 6–19.)

> Rawlins, Gregory J. E. <u>Moths to the Flame</u>. Cambridge: MIT P, 1996. 3 Apr. 2001 <http://mitpress.mit.edu/ e-books/Moths/contents.html>.

■ **30. PART OF AN ONLINE BOOK** Place the part title before the book's title. If the part is a short work such as a poem or an essay, put its title in quotation marks. If the part is an introduction or other division of the book, do not use quotation marks.

> Adams, Henry. "Diplomacy." <u>The Education of Henry Adams</u>. Boston: Houghton, 1918. <u>Bartleby.com: Great Books Online</u>. 1999. 17 Feb. 2003 <http://bartleby.com/159/8.html>.

■ **31. WORK FROM A SERVICE SUCH AS *INFOTRAC*** Libraries pay for access to databases through subscription services such as *InfoTrac.* For sources retrieved from such services, give as much of the following information as is available: (1) publication information for the source (see items 20–26); (2) the name of the database, underlined; (3) the name of the service; (4) the name and location of the library where you retrieved the article; (5) the date you accessed the source; and (6) the URL of the service.

The following models are for articles retrieved through three popular services: *InfoTrac, EBSCOhost,* and *ProQuest.* The first article is from a scholarly journal paginated by volume, the second from a bimonthly magazine, the third from a daily newspaper.

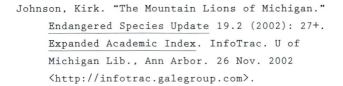

Johnson, Kirk. "The Mountain Lions of Michigan."
    Endangered Species Update 19.2 (2002): 27+.
    Expanded Academic Index. InfoTrac. U of
    Michigan Lib., Ann Arbor. 26 Nov. 2002
    <http://infotrac.galegroup.com>.

Darnovsky, Marcy. "Embryo Cloning and Beyond."
    Tikkun July-Aug. 2002: 29-32. Academic
    Search Premier. EBSCOhost. Portland Community
    Coll. Lib., Portland, OR. 1 Nov. 2002
    <http://search.epnet.com>.

Kolata, Gina. "Scientists Debating Future of
    Hormone Replacement." New York Times
    23 Oct. 2002: A20. ProQuest. Drew U Lib.,
    Madison, NJ. 26 Nov. 2002 <http://
    www.proquest.com>.

NOTE: When you access a work through a personal subscription service such as *America Online,* give the information about the source, the name of the service, the date of
access, and the keyword used to retrieve the source.

Conniff, Richard. "The House That John Built."
    Smithsonian Feb. 2001. America Online. 11 Mar.
    2001. Keyword: Smithsonian Magazine.

■ **32. ARTICLE IN AN ONLINE PERIODICAL** When citing online
articles, follow the guidelines for printed articles (see items
20–26), giving whatever information is available in the online
source. End the citation with your date of access and the URL.

NOTE: In some online articles, paragraphs are numbered. For such articles, include the total number of paragraphs in your citation, as in the next example.

From an online scholarly journal

Belau, Linda. "Trauma and the Material Signifier."
    Postmodern Culture 11.2 (2001): 37 pars. 30
    Mar. 2001 <http://jefferson.village.virginia.edu/
    pmc/current.issue/11.2belau.html>.

From an online magazine

Morgan, Fiona. "Banning the Bullies." Salon.com 15
    Mar. 2001. 2 Apr. 2001 <http://www.salon.com/
    news/feature/2001/03/15/bullying/index.html>.

From an online newspaper

Barabak, Mark Z. "Californians Endorse New Power
    Plants, Environmental Rules." Los Angeles
    Times 17 Feb. 2001. 18 Feb. 2001 <http://
    www.latimes.com/news/timespoll/state/
    lat_poll0010217.htm>.

■ **33. CD-ROM**   Treat a CD-ROM as you would any other source, but name the medium before the publication information.

"Pimpernel." The American Heritage Dictionary of
    the English Language. 4th ed. CD-ROM. Boston:
    Houghton, 2000.

Wattenberg, Ruth. "Helping Students in the Middle."
    American Educator 19.4 (1996): 2-18. ERIC.
    CD-ROM. SilverPlatter. Sept. 1996.

■ **34. E-MAIL** To cite an e-mail, begin with the writer's name and the subject line. Then write "E-mail to" followed by the name of the recipient. End with the date of the message.

> O'Donnell, Patricia. "Re: Interview questions."
>   E-mail to the author. 15 Mar. 2001.

■ **35. ONLINE POSTING** For an online posting, begin with the author's name, followed by the title or subject line (in quotation marks), the words "Online posting," the date of posting, the list or group name, the date of access, and the URL.

> Brown, Oliver. "Welcome." Online posting.
>   8 Oct. 2002. Chester Coll. Students Web
>   Forum. 20 Feb. 2003 <http://www.voy.com/
>   113243/>.

■ **36. REAL-TIME COMMUNICATION** To cite a real-time communication, include the writer's name (if relevant), a description and date of the event, the title of the forum, the date of access, and the URL.

> Carbone, Nick. Planning for the future. 1 Mar.
>   2001. TechRhet's Thursday night MOO. 1 Mar.
>   2001 <telnet://connections.moo.mud.org:3333>.

Multimedia sources

Multimedia sources include visuals (such as works of art), audio works (such as sound recordings), audiovisuals (such as films), and live events (such as the performance of a play).

MLA

When citing online multimedia sources, consult the appropriate model in this section and give whatever information is available for the online source; then end the citation with your date of access and the URL. (See item 37 for an example.)

■ **37. WORK OF ART**   Cite the artist's name, followed by the title of the artwork, usually underlined, and the institution and city in which the artwork can be found. If you want to indicate the work's date, include it after the title. For a work of art you viewed online, end your citation with your date of access and the URL.

> Constable, John. <u>Dedham Vale</u>. Victoria and Albert
>   Museum, London.

> van Gogh, Vincent. <u>The Starry Night</u>. 1889. Museum
>   of Mod. Art, New York. 27 Feb. 2001 <http://
>   www.moma.org/docs/collection/paintsculpt/
>   c58.htm>.

■ **38. CARTOON**   Begin with the cartoonist's name, the title of the cartoon (if it has one) in quotation marks, the word "Cartoon," and the publication information for the publication in which the cartoon appears.

> Rall, Ted. "Search and Destroy." Cartoon. <u>Village
>   Voice</u> 23 Jan. 2001: 6.

■ **39. ADVERTISEMENT**   Name the product or company being advertised, followed by the word "Advertisement." Give publication information for the source in which the advertisement appears.

Truth by Calvin Klein. Advertisement. <u>Vogue</u> Dec.
    2000: 95-98.

■ **40. MAP OR CHART**   Cite a map or chart as you would a
book or a short work within a longer work. Add the word
"Map" or "Chart" following the title.

<u>New Jersey</u>. Map. Chicago: Rand, 2000.

Joseph, Lori, and Bob Laird. "Driving While Phoning
    Is Dangerous." Chart. <u>USA Today</u> 16 Feb. 2001:
    1A.

■ **41. MUSICAL COMPOSITION**   Cite the composer's name,
followed by the title of the work. Underline the title of an
opera, a ballet, or a composition identified by name, but do
not underline or use quotation marks around a composition
identified by number or form.

Ellington, Duke. <u>Conga Brava</u>.

Haydn, Franz Joseph. Symphony no. 88 in G.

■ **42. SOUND RECORDING**   Begin with the name of the person
you want to emphasize: the composer, conductor, or per-
former. For a long work, give the title, underlined (or italicized),
followed by names of pertinent artists (such as performers,
readers, or musicians) and the orchestra and conductor (if
relevant). End with the manufacturer and the date.

Bizet, Georges. <u>Carmen</u>. Perf. Jennifer Laramore,
    Thomas Moser, Angela Gheorghiu, and Samuel

> Ramey. Bavarian State Orch. and Chorus. Cond.
>
> Giuseppe Sinopoli. Warner, 1996.

For a song, put the title in quotation marks. If you include the name of the album, underline it.

> Chapman, Tracy. "Paper and Ink." Telling Stories.
>
> Elektra, 2000.

■ **43. FILM OR VIDEO** Begin with the title, underlined (or italicized). For a film, cite the director and the lead actors or narrator ("Perf." or "Narr."), followed by the name of the distributor and the year of the film's release. For a videotape or DVD, add "Videocassette" or "DVD" before the name of the distributor.

> Chocolat. Dir. Lasse Hallström. Perf. Juliette
>
> Binoche, Judi Dench, Alfred Molina, Lena Olin,
>
> and Johnny Depp. Miramax, 2001.

> High Fidelity. Dir. Stephen Frears. Perf. John
>
> Cusack, Iben Hjejle, Jack Black, and Todd
>
> Louiso. 2000. Videocassette. Walt Disney
>
> Video, 2001.

■ **44. RADIO OR TELEVISION PROGRAM** Begin with the title of the radio segment or television episode (if there is one) in quotation marks, followed by the title of the program, underlined (or italicized). Next give relevant information about the program's writer ("By"), director ("Dir."), performers ("Perf."), or host ("Host"). Then name the network, the local station (if any), and the date the program was broadcast.

"American Limbo." This American Life. Host Ira
        Glass. Public Radio Intl. WBEZ, Chicago.
        9 Feb. 2001.

If there is a series title, include it after the title of the
program, neither underlined nor in quotation marks.

Mysteries of the Pyramids. On the Inside. Discovery
        Channel. 7 Feb. 2001.

■ **45. RADIO OR TELEVISION INTERVIEW** Begin with the
name of the person who was interviewed, followed by the
word "Interview." End with the information about the program as in item 44.

McGovern, George. Interview. Charlie Rose. PBS.
        WNET, New York. 1 Feb. 2001.

■ **46. LIVE PERFORMANCE OF A PLAY** Begin with the title of
the play, followed by the author ("By"). Then include
information about the performance: the director ("Dir."),
major actors ("Perf."), the theater company, the theater and
its location, and the date of the performance.

Mother Courage. By Bertolt Brecht. Dir. János
        Szász. Perf. Karen McDonald, Mirjana Jokovic,
        Jonathon Roberts, Tim Kang, and Amos Lichtman.
        Amer. Repertory Theatre, Cambridge. 18 Mar.
        2001.

■ **47. LECTURE OR PUBLIC ADDRESS** Cite the speaker's name,
followed by the title of the lecture (if any), the organization
sponsoring the lecture, the location, and the date.

Cohran, Kelan. "Slavery and Astronomy." Adler
        Planetarium, Chicago. 21 Feb. 2001.

■ **48. PERSONAL INTERVIEW** To cite an interview that you conducted, begin with the name of the person interviewed. Then write "Personal interview," followed by the date of the interview.

Shaikh, Michael. Personal interview. 22 Mar. 2001.

Other sources

This section includes a variety of traditional print sources not covered elsewhere. For sources obtained on the Web, consult the appropriate model in this section and give whatever information is available for the online source; then end the citation with the date on which you accessed the source and the URL. (See item 49 for an example.)

■ **49. GOVERNMENT PUBLICATION** Treat the government agency as the author, giving the name of the government followed by the name of the agency.

United States. Natl. Council on Disability. Promises
        to Keep: A Decade of Federal Enforcement of
        the Americans with Disabilities Act. Washing-
        ton: GPO, 2000.

For government documents published online, give as much publication information as is available and end your citation with the date of access and the URL.

United States. Dept. of Transportation. Natl.
        Highway Traffic Safety Administration. An
        Investigation of the Safety Implications of

Wireless Communications in Vehicles. Nov.
        1999. 20 May 2001 <http://www.nhtsa.dot.gov/
        people/injury/research/wireless>.

■ **50. LEGAL SOURCE** For most legal documents, cite the
name of the document (without underlining or quotation
marks), the article and section numbers, and the year if
relevant.

US Const. Art. 4, sec. 2.

For an act, include its Public Law number ("Pub. L."),
the date it was enacted, and its Statutes at Large number
("Stat.").

Electronic Freedom of Information Act Amendments
        of 1996. Pub. L. 104-418. 2 Oct. 1996. Stat.
        3048.

■ **51. PAMPHLET** Cite a pamphlet as you would a book.

Commonwealth of Massachusetts. Dept. of Jury
        Commissioner. A Few Facts about Jury Duty.
        Boston: Commonwealth of Massachusetts, 1997.

■ **52. DISSERTATION** Begin with the author's name, followed by the dissertation title in quotation marks, the
abbreviation "Diss.," the name of the institution, and the
year the dissertation was accepted.

Vallecillo, Maria Fernando. "At the Edge of the
        Abyss: The Concentration Camp Experience in
        the Novels of Jorge Semprún." Diss. U of North
        Carolina, 2001.

For dissertations that have been published in book form, underline the title. After the title and before the book's publication information, add the abbreviation "Diss.," the name of the institution, and the year the dissertation was accepted.

```
Damberg, Cheryl L. Healthcare Reform: Distributional
     Consequences of an Employer Mandate for Workers
     in Small Firms. Diss. Rand Graduate School,
     1995. Santa Monica: Rand, 1996.
```

■ **53. ABSTRACT OF A DISSERTATION**   Cite an abstract as you would an unpublished dissertation. After the dissertation date, give the abbreviation *DA* or *DAI* (for *Dissertation Abstracts* or *Dissertation Abstracts International*), followed by the volume number, the date of publication, and the page number.

```
Goldman, Dara. "Lost and Found: Insularity and the
     Construction of Subjectivity in Hispanic
     Caribbean Literature." Diss. Emory U, 2000.
     DAI 61 (2000): 1431A.
```

■ **54. PUBLISHED PROCEEDINGS OF A CONFERENCE**   Cite published conference proceedings as you would a book, adding information about the conference after the title.

```
Kartiganer, Donald M., and Ann J. Abadie. Faulkner
     at 100: Retrospect and Prospect. Proc. of
     Faulkner and Yoknapatawpha Conf., 27 July-
     1 Aug. 1997, U of Mississippi. Jackson: UP of
     Mississippi, 2000.
```

■ **55. PUBLISHED INTERVIEW**   Name the person interviewed, followed by the title of the interview (if there is one). If the interview does not have a title, include the word "Interview" followed by a period after the interviewee's name. Give publication information for the work in which the interview was published.

```
Renoir, Jean. "Renoir at Home: Interview with Jean
     Renoir." Film Quarterly 50.1 (1996): 2-8.
```

If the name of the interviewer is relevant, include it after the name of the interviewee, as in the following example.

```
Prince. Interview with Bilge Ebiri. Yahoo! Internet
     Life 7.6 (2001): 82-85.
```

■ **56. PERSONAL LETTER**   To cite a letter that you have received, begin with the writer's name and add the phrase "Letter to the author," followed by the date.

```
Coggins, Christopher. Letter to the author. 6 May
     2001.
```

56c MLA information notes (optional)

Researchers who use the MLA system of parenthetical documentation (see 56a) may also use information notes for one of two purposes:

1. to provide additional material that might interrupt the flow of the paper yet is important enough to include
2. to refer readers to any sources not discussed in the paper

Information notes may be either footnotes or endnotes. Footnotes appear at the foot of the page; endnotes appear on a separate page at the end of the paper, just before the list of works cited. For either style, the notes are numbered consecutively throughout the paper. The text of the paper contains a raised arabic numeral that corresponds to the number of the note.

TEXT

```
Local governments are more likely than state gov-
ernments to pass legislation against using a cell
phone while driving.[1]
```

NOTE

```
     [1] For a discussion of local laws banning cell
phone use, see Sundeen 8.
```

57

MLA manuscript format; sample MLA paper

57a MLA manuscript format

In most English and humanities classes, you will be asked to use MLA (Modern Language Association) guidelines for formatting a paper and preparing a list of the works you have cited. The following guidelines are consistent with advice given in the *MLA Handbook for Writers of Research Papers*, 5th ed. (New York: MLA, 1999). For a sample MLA paper, see 57b.

Formatting the paper

The following MLA recommendations have been endorsed by most English instructors.

MATERIALS   Use good-quality 8½″ × 11″ white paper. Secure the pages with a paper clip. Unless your instructor suggests otherwise, do not staple the pages together or use any sort of binder.

TITLE AND IDENTIFICATION   MLA does not require a title page. On the first page of your paper, place your name, your instructor's name, the course title, and the date on separate lines against the left margin. Then center your title. (See p. 637 for a sample first page.)

If your instructor requires a title page, ask for guidelines on formatting it. A format similar to the one on page 759 will most likely be acceptable.

PAGINATION   Put the page number preceded by your last name in the upper right corner of each page, one-half inch below the top edge. Use arabic numerals (1, 2, 3, and so on).

MARGINS, LINE SPACING, AND PARAGRAPH INDENTS   Leave margins of one inch on all sides of the page. Do not justify (align) the right margin.

Double-space throughout the paper. Do not add extra line spaces above or below the title of the paper or between paragraphs.

Indent the first line of each paragraph one-half inch (or five spaces) from the left margin.

LONG QUOTATIONS   When a quotation is longer than four typed lines of prose or three lines of verse, set it off from the text by indenting the entire quotation a full inch (or ten spaces) from the left margin. Double-space the indented quotation, and don't add extra space above or below it.

Quotation marks are not needed when a quotation has been set off from the text by indenting. See page 639 for an example.

WEB ADDRESSES   When a Web address mentioned in the text of your paper must be divided at the end of a line, do not insert a hyphen (a hyphen could appear to be part of the address). For MLA rules on dividing Web addresses in your list of works cited, see page 635.

HEADINGS   MLA neither encourages nor discourages the use of headings and currently provides no guidelines for their use. If you would like to insert headings in a long essay or research paper, check first with your instructor. Although headings are not used as frequently in English and the humanities as in other disciplines, the trend seems to be changing.

For a full discussion of headings, including their phrasing and placement, see 5b. A sample MLA paper with headings appears on *The Bedford Handbook*'s companion Web site; directions for finding the paper are given in the box on page 636.

VISUALS   MLA classifies visuals as tables and figures (figures include graphs, charts, maps, photographs, and drawings). Label each table with an arabic numeral (Table 1, Table 2, and so on) and provide a clear caption that identifies the subject. The label and caption should appear on separate lines above the table, flush left. Below the table, give its source in a note like this one:

Source: John M. Violanti, "Cellular Phones and Fatal Traffic Collisions," Accident Analysis and Prevention 30 (1998): 521.

For each figure, place a label and a caption below the figure, flush left. They need not appear on separate lines. The word "Figure" may be abbreviated to "Fig." Include source information following the caption.

Visuals should be placed in the text, as close as possible to the sentences that relate to them unless your instructor prefers them in an appendix. See page 639 for an example of a visual in the text of a paper.

Preparing the list of works cited

Begin the list of works cited on a new page at the end of the paper. Center the title Works Cited about one inch from the top of the page. Double-space throughout. See pages 644–45 for a sample list of works cited.

ALPHABETIZING THE LIST   Alphabetize the list by the last names of the authors (or editors); if a work has no author or editor, alphabetize by the first word of the title other than *A, An,* or *The.*

If your list includes two or more works by the same author, use the author's name only for the first entry. For subsequent entries use three hyphens followed by a period. List the titles in alphabetical order. See also page 608.

INDENTING   Do not indent the first line of each works cited entry, but indent any additional lines one-half inch (or five spaces). This technique highlights the names of the authors, making it easy for readers to scan the alphabetized list.

WEB ADDRESSES   Do not insert a hyphen when dividing a Web address at the end of a line. Break the line after a slash. Also insert angle brackets around the URL.

If your word processing program automatically turns Web addresses into hot links (by underlining them and highlighting them in color), turn off this feature. For advice on how to do this, visit the MLA Web site at <http://www.mla.org> and consult the list of frequently asked questions.

57b Sample research paper: MLA style

On the following pages is a research paper on the topic of cell phones and driving, written by Angela Daly, a student in a composition class. Daly's paper is documented with the MLA style of in-text citations and a list of works cited. Annotations in the margins of the paper draw your attention to features of special interest.

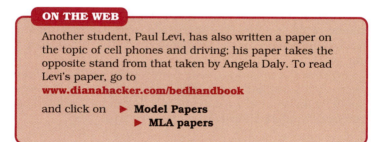

ON THE WEB

Another student, Paul Levi, has also written a paper on the topic of cell phones and driving; his paper takes the opposite stand from that taken by Angela Daly. To read Levi's paper, go to

www.dianahacker.com/bedhandbook

and click on ▶ **Model Papers**
▶ **MLA papers**

Daly 1

Angela Daly
Professor Chavez
English 101
14 March 2001

A Call to Action:

Regulate Use of Cell Phones on the Road

When a cell phone goes off in a classroom or
at a concert, we are irritated, but at least our
lives are not endangered. When we are on the road,
however, irresponsible cell phone users are more
than irritating: They are putting our lives at
risk. Many of us have witnessed drivers so distracted by dialing and chatting that they resemble
drunk drivers, weaving between lanes, for example,
or nearly running down pedestrians in crosswalks. A
number of bills to regulate use of cell phones on
the road have been introduced in state legislatures, and the time has come to push for their passage. Regulation is needed because drivers using
phones are seriously impaired and because laws on
negligent and reckless driving are not sufficient
to punish offenders.

No one can deny that cell phones have caused
traffic deaths and injuries. Cell phones were im-
plicated in three fatal accidents in November 1999
alone. Early in November, two-year-old Morgan Pena
was killed by a driver distracted by his cell
phone. Morgan's mother, Patti Pena, reports that

Title is centered.

Opening
sentences catch
readers' attention.

Thesis asserts
Angela Daly's
main point.

Daly uses a
clear topic
sentence.

Signal phrase
names the author
of the quotation
to follow.

No page number is available for this Web source.

the driver "ran a stop sign at 45 mph, broadsided my vehicle and killed Morgan as she sat in her car seat." A week later, corrections officer Shannon Smith, who was guarding prisoners by the side of the road, was killed by a woman distracted by a

Author's name is given in parentheses; no page number is available.

phone call (Besthoff). On Thanksgiving weekend that same month, John and Carole Hall were killed when a Naval Academy midshipman crashed into their parked car. The driver said in court that when he looked up from the cell phone he was dialing, he was three

Page number is given when available.

feet from the car and had no time to stop (Stock-well B8).

Clear topic sentences, like this one, are used throughout the paper.

Expert testimony, public opinion, and even cartoons suggest that driving while phoning is dangerous. Frances Bents, an expert on the relation between cell phones and accidents, estimates that between 450 and 1,000 crashes a year have some connection to cell phone use (Layton C9). In a survey published by Farmers Insurance Group, 87% of those polled said that cell phones affect a driver's ability, and 40% reported having close calls with drivers distracted by phones. Many cartoons have depicted the very real dangers of driving while distracted (see Fig. 1 for an example).

Summary and long quotation are introduced with a signal phrase naming the authors.

Scientific research confirms the dangers of using phones while on the road. In 1997 an important study appeared in the New England Journal of Medicine. The authors, Donald Redelmeier and Robert

Daly 3

Fig. 1. Chan Lowe, cartoon, <u>Washington Post</u> 22 July 2000: A21.

Illustration has figure number, label, and source information.

Tibshirani, studied 699 volunteers who made their cell phone bills available in order to confirm the times when they had placed calls. The participants agreed to report any nonfatal collision in which they were involved. By comparing the time of a collision with the phone records, the researchers assessed the dangers of driving while phoning. Here are their results:

> We found that using a cellular telephone was associated with a risk of having a

Long quotation is set off from the text; quotation marks are omitted.

Daly 4

motor vehicle collision that was about
four times as high as that among the same
drivers when they were not using their
cellular telephones. This relative risk
is similar to the hazard associated with
driving with a blood alcohol level at the
legal limit. (456)

In reports by news media, the latter claim was
exaggerated ("similar to" is not "equal to"), but
the comparison with drunk driving is startling
nonetheless.

A 1998 study focused on Oklahoma, one of the
few states to keep records on fatal accidents involving cell phones. Using police records, John M.
Violanti of the Rochester Institute of Technology
investigated the relation between traffic fatali-
ties in Oklahoma and the use or presence of a cell
phone. He found a ninefold increase in the risk of
fatality if a phone was being used and a doubled
risk simply when a phone was present in a vehicle
(522-23). The latter statistic is interesting, for
it suggests that those who carry phones in their
cars may tend to be more negligent (or prone to
distractions of all kinds) than those who do not.

Some groups have argued that state traffic
laws make legislation regulating cell phone use unnecessary. Sadly, this is not true. Laws on traffic
safety vary from state to state, and drivers dis-

Summary begins with a signal phrase naming the author and ends with page numbers in parentheses.

Daly counters an opposing argument.

tracted by cell phones can get off with light punishment even when they cause fatal accidents. For
example, although the midshipman mentioned earlier
was charged with vehicular manslaughter for the
deaths of John and Carole Hall, the judge was unable to issue a verdict of guilty. Under Maryland
law, he could only find the defendant guilty of
negligent driving and impose a $500 fine (Layton
C1). Such a light sentence is not unusual. The
driver who killed Morgan Lee Pena in Pennsylvania
received two tickets and a $50 fine--and retained
his driving privileges (Pena). In Georgia, a young
woman distracted by her phone ran down and killed a
two-year-old; her sentence was ninety days in boot
camp and five hundred hours of community service
(Ippolito J1). The families of the victims are un-
derstandably distressed by laws that lead to such
light sentences.

    When certain kinds of driver behavior are
shown to be especially dangerous, we wisely draft
special laws making them illegal and imposing specific punishments. Running red lights, failing to
stop for a school bus, and drunk driving are obvious examples; phoning in a moving vehicle should
be no exception. Unlike more general laws covering
negligent driving, specific laws leave little
ambiguity for law officers and for judges and
juries imposing punishments. Such laws have another

Facts are docu-
mented with in-
text citations:
authors' names
and page num-
bers (if available)
in parentheses.

Daly uses an
analogy to jus-
tify passing a
special law.

important benefit: They leave no ambiguity for drivers. Currently, drivers can tease themselves into thinking they are using their car phones responsibly because the definition of "negligent driving" is vague.

Daly explains why U.S. laws need to be passed on the state level.

As of December 2000, twenty countries were restricting use of cell phones in moving vehicles (Sundeen 8). In the United States, it is highly unlikely that legislation could be passed on the national level, since traffic safety is considered a state and local issue. To date, only a few counties and towns have passed traffic laws restricting cell phone use. For example, in Suffolk County, New York, it is illegal for drivers to use a handheld phone for anything but an emergency call while on the road (Haughney A8). The first town to restrict use of handheld phones was Brooklyn, Ohio (Layton C9). Brooklyn, the first community in the country to pass a seat belt law, has once again shown its concern for traffic safety.

Transition helps readers move from one paragraph to the next.

Daly cites an indirect source: words quoted in another source.

Laws passed by counties and towns have had some effect, but it makes more sense to legislate at the state level. Local laws are not likely to have the impact of state laws, and keeping track of a wide variety of local ordinances is confusing for drivers. Even a spokesperson for Verizon Wireless has said that statewide bans are preferable to a "crazy patchwork quilt of ordinances" (qtd. in

Daly 7

Haughney A8). Unfortunately, although a number of
bills have been introduced in state legislatures,
as of early 2001 no state law seriously restricting
use of the phones has passed--largely because of
effective lobbying from the wireless industry.

Despite the claims of some lobbyists, tough
laws regulating phone use can make our roads safer.
In Japan, for example, accidents linked to cell
phones fell by 75% just a month after the country
prohibited using a handheld phone while driving
(Haughney A8). Research suggests and common sense
tells us that it is not possible to drive an automobile at high speeds, dial numbers, and carry on
conversations without significant risks. When such
behavior is regulated, obviously our roads will be
safer.

Because of mounting public awareness of the
dangers of drivers distracted by phones, state legislators must begin to take the problem seriously.
"It's definitely an issue that is gaining steam
around the country," says Matt Sundeen of the
National Conference of State Legislatures (qtd. in
Layton C9). Lon Anderson of the American Automobile
Association agrees: "There is momentum building,"
he says, to pass laws (qtd. in Layton C9). The time
has come for states to adopt legislation restricting the use of cell phones in moving vehicles.

Daly counters a claim made by some opponents.

For variety Daly places a signal phrase after a brief quotation.

The paper ends with Daly's stand on the issue.

Daly 8

Works Cited

Besthoff, Len. "Cell Phone Use Increases Risk of
     Accidents, but Users Willing to Take the
     Risk." WRAL Online. 11 Nov. 1999. 12 Jan. 2001
     <http://www.wral-tv.com/news/wral/1999/
     1110-talking-driving/>.

Farmers Insurance Group. "New Survey Shows Driv-
     ers Have Had 'Close Calls' with Cell Phone
     Users." Farmers Insurance Group. 8 May 2000.
     12 Jan. 2001<http://www.farmersinsurance.com/
     news_cellphones.html>.

Haughney, Christine. "Taking Phones out of Drivers'
     Hands." Washington Post 5 Nov. 2000: A8.

Ippolito, Milo. "Driver's Sentence Not Justice, Mom
     Says." Atlanta Journal-Constitution 25 Sept.
     1999: J1.

Layton, Lyndsey. "Legislators Aiming to Disconnect
     Motorists." Washington Post 10 Dec. 2000: C1+.

Lowe, Chan. Cartoon. Washington Post 22 July 2000:
     A21.

Pena, Patricia N. "Patti Pena's Letter to Car
     Talk." Cars.com. Car Talk. 10 Jan. 2001
     <http://cartalk.cars.com/About/Morgan-Pena/
     letter.html>.

Redelmeier, Donald A., and Robert J. Tibshirani.
     "Association between Cellular-Telephone Calls
     and Motor Vehicle Collisions." New England
     Journal of Medicine 336 (1997): 453-58.

Heading is centered.

List is alphabetized by authors' last name (or by title when a work has no author).

First line of each entry is at the left margin; extra lines are indented 1/2" (or five spaces).

Double-spacing is used throughout.

Daly 9

Stockwell, Jamie. "Phone Use Faulted in Collision."
    Washington Post 6 Dec. 2000: B1+.
Sundeen, Matt. "Cell Phones and Highway Safety:
    2000 State Legislative Update." National
    Conference of State Legislatures. Dec. 2000.
    9 pp. 27 Feb. 2001 <http://ncsl.org/programs/
    esnr/cellphone.pdf>.
Violanti, John M. "Cellular Phones and Fatal
    Traffic Collisions." Accident Analysis and
    Prevention 30 (1998): 519-24.

The URL is broken
after a slash. No
hyphen is inserted.

58

Writing about literature

All good writing about literature attempts to answer a question, spoken or unspoken, about the text: "Why doesn't Hamlet kill his uncle sooner?" "How does street language function in Gwendolyn Brooks's 'We Real Cool'?" "What might the moth symbolize in Virginia Woolf's 'The Death of the Moth'?" "How does Dickens portray lawyers in *Great Expectations*?" "In what ways does James Joyce's 'The Dead' confront traditions of love and romance?"

The goal of a literature paper should be to answer such questions with a meaningful interpretation, presented forcefully and persuasively.

58a Get involved in the work; be an active reader.

Read the work closely and carefully. Think of the work as speaking to you: What is it telling you? Asking you? Trying to make you feel?

If the work provides an introduction and footnotes, read them attentively. They may be a source of important information. Use the dictionary to look up words unfamiliar to you or words with subtle nuances that may affect the work's meaning.

Rereading is a central part of the process. You should read short works several times, first to get an overall impression and then again to focus on meaningful details. With longer works, such as novels or plays, read the most important chapters or scenes more than once while keeping in mind the work as a whole.

As you read and reread, interact with the work by posing questions and looking for answers. The chart on pages

651–52 suggests some questions about literature that may help you become an active reader.

Annotating the work

Annotating the work is a way to focus your reading. The first time through, you may want to pencil a check mark next to passages you find especially significant. On a more careful rereading, pay particular attention to these passages and jot down your ideas and reactions in a notebook or (if the book is your own) in the margins of the page.

Here is one student's annotation of a poem by Shakespeare:

> Shall I compare <u>thee</u> to a summer's day? — *Who? (Must be a loved one.)*
> Thou art more lovely and more <u>temperate</u>: —
> Rough winds do shake the darling buds of May, — *Rhyming pattern of sonnet*
> And summer's lease hath all too short a date. — *Pleasant-natured (like pleasant weather)?*
> Sometime <u>too hot</u> the eye of heaven shines,
> And often is his <u>gold complexion</u> dimmed; — *Fair = beauty, or more than beauty?*
> And every (fair) from (fair) sometimes declines, — *Summer is fleeting and not always perfect. (But lover is perfect?)*
> By chance, or nature's changing course, untrimmed.
> But thy eternal summer shall not fade, — *What are "eternal lines to time"? Ask in class?*
> Nor lose possession of that fair thou ow'st
> Nor shall death brag thou wand'rest in his shade, — *Death would be proud to claim the lover but can't?*
> When in eternal lines to time thou grow'st.
> So long as men can breathe or eyes can see, — *Final couplet seems to signal a shift in thought.*
> So long lives <u>this</u>, and this gives life to thee.

This = the poem? (Art, like the writer's love, is eternal.)

Taking notes

Note taking is also an important part of rereading a work of literature. In your notes you can try out ideas and develop your perspective on the work. Here are some notes one student took on a story by Edgar Allan Poe:

"The Fall of the House of Usher"

House of Usher has two meanings — the building and the family

seeing the building has an emotional impact on the narrator: "with the first glimpse of the building, a sense of insufferable gloom pervaded my spirit"

narrator uses descriptive language that evokes his feelings — "dull," "dark," "soundless," "dreary," "melancholy," "insufferable gloom"

produces feeling of depression in reader too

Who is this narrator? What is his relationship to the Ushers?

Such notes are the raw material out of which you will build an interpretation.

Discussing the work

As you have no doubt discovered, class discussions can lead to interesting insights about a literary work, perhaps by calling attention to details in the work that you failed to notice on a first reading. Discussions don't always need to occur face to face. Many literature instructors are encouraging online discussion groups, where students can explore ideas without fear of embarrassment. Here, for example, is a set of networked postings about a character in Joyce Carol Oates's short story "Where Are You Going, Where Have You Been?"

JAKE   Do you think Arnold Friend represents the Devil? He sure seems like the incarnation of evil.

RIMA   I was wondering about that too, Jake. He seems to have supernatural powers. He knows all about Connie and even calls up a vision of her Aunt Tillie's barbecue miles away, complete with details about a fat woman.

BOB   There are places in the story that make me think
Arnold Friend is a wolf—maybe even the wolf in
"Little Red Riding Hood." Did you guys notice that he
was sniffing her like he was about to gobble her up?
And he has big teeth.

DAWN   I noticed that too, Bob, and near the end of the story
Arnold Friend says that Connie's house is so flimsy he
could knock it down. That sounds pretty close to the
fairy tale: "I'll huff and I'll puff and I'll blow your
house down."

RIMA   All I can say is that Arnold Friend is the kind of "wolf"
my mother has always warned me against—a fast-
talking older guy with nothing but sex on his mind.
Even before he begins making threats, Connie knows
she shouldn't get into a car with him. She keeps
repeating, "I don't even know you." And she's worried
about how old he is.

58b   Form an interpretation.

After rereading, jotting notes, and perhaps discussing the
work, you are ready to start forming an interpretation. At
this stage, try to focus on a central issue. Look through your
notes and annotations for recurring questions and insights
about a single aspect of the work.

Focusing on a central issue

In forming an interpretation, it is important to focus on a
central issue. In other words, avoid trying to do everything
at once. You may think, for example, that *Huckleberry Finn*
is a great book because it contains brilliant descriptions of
scenery, has a lot of humorous moments, but also tells a
serious story of one boy's development. This is a legitimate
response to the work, but your job in writing an essay will be

to close in on one issue that you can develop into a sustained, in-depth interpretation. For example, you might focus on ways in which the runaway slave Jim uses humor to preserve his dignity. Or you might focus on ironic discrepancies between what Huck says and what his heart tells him. Or you could choose just one or two minor characters, such as the Duke and the Dauphin, and show how they represent flaws in the society at large.

Asking questions that lead to an interpretation

Think of your interpretation as answering a question about the work. Some years ago, most interpretations answered questions about literary techniques, such as the writer's handling of plot, setting, and character (see p. 651). Today the concept of literary interpretation frequently includes questions about social context as well: what a work reveals about the time and culture in which it was written (see p. 651). Frequently you will find yourself writing about both technique and social context. For example, Margaret Peel, a student who wrote about Langston Hughes's poem "Ballad of the Landlord" (see pp. 669–72), addressed the following question, which touches on both language and race:

> How does the poem's language—through its four voices—
> dramatize the experience of a black man in a society
> dominated by whites?

In the introduction of your paper, you will usually announce your interpretation in a one- or two-sentence thesis. The thesis answers the central question that you posed. Here, for example, is Margaret Peel's two-sentence thesis:

> Langston Hughes's "Ballad of the Landlord" is narrated
> through four voices, each with its own perspective on the
> poem's action. These opposing voices—of a tenant, a landlord,
> the police, and the press—dramatize a black man's experi-
> ence in a society dominated by whites.

Questions to ask about literature

QUESTIONS ABOUT TECHNIQUE

Plot. What central conflicts drive the plot? Are they internal (within a character) or external (between characters or between a character and a force)? How are conflicts resolved? Why are events revealed in a particular order?

Setting. Does the setting (time and place) create an atmosphere, give an insight into a character, suggest symbolic meanings, or hint at the theme of the work?

Character. What seems to motivate the central characters? Do any characters change significantly? If so, what—if anything—have they learned from their experiences? Do sharp contrasts between characters highlight important themes?

Point of view. Does the point of view—the perspective from which the story is narrated or the poem is spoken—affect our understanding of events? Does the narration reveal the character of the speaker, or does the speaker merely observe others? Is the narrator perhaps innocent, naive, or deceitful?

Theme. Does the work have an overall theme (a central insight about people or a truth about life)? If so, how do details in the work illuminate this theme?

Language. Does language—such as formal or informal, standard or dialect, prosaic or poetic, cool or passionate—reveal the character of speakers? How do metaphors, similes, and sensory images contribute to the work? How do recurring images enrich the work and hint at its meaning? To what extent do sentence rhythms and sounds underscore the writer's meaning?

QUESTIONS ABOUT SOCIAL CONTEXT

Historical context. What does the work reveal about the time and place in which it was written? Does the work appear to

(continued on page 652)

promote or undermine a philosophy that was popular in its time, such as social Darwinism in the late nineteenth century?

Class. How does membership in a social class affect the characters' choices and their successes or failures? How does class affect the way characters view—or are viewed by —others? What do economic struggles reveal about power relationships in the society being depicted?

Race and culture. Are any characters portrayed as being caught between cultures: between the culture of home and work or school, for example, or between a traditional and an emerging culture? Are any characters engaged in a conflict with society because of their race or ethnic background? To what extent does the work celebrate a specific culture and its traditions?

Gender. Are any characters' choices restricted because of gender? What are the power relationships between the sexes, and do these change during the course of the work? Do any characters resist the gender roles society has assigned to them? Do other characters choose to conform to those roles?

Archetypes. Does a character, image, or plot fit a pattern—or archetype—that has been repeated in stories throughout history and across cultures? (For example, nearly every culture has stories about heroes, quests, redemption, and revenge.) How does an archetypal character, image, or plot line correspond to or differ from others like it?

58c Draft a thesis and sketch an outline.

Drafting a thesis

A thesis, which nearly always appears in the introduction, announces an essay's main point (see also 2a). In a literature paper, your thesis will answer the central question that you have asked about the work. In drafting your thesis, aim for a strong, assertive summary of your interpretation. Here, for example, are two successful theses taken from student essays, together with the central question each student had posed.

QUESTION
What does Stephen Crane's short story "The Open Boat" reveal about the relation between humans and nature?

THESIS
In Stephen Crane's gripping tale "The Open Boat," four men lost at sea discover not only that nature is indifferent to their fate but that their own particular talents make little difference as they struggle for survival.

QUESTION
In the Greek tragedy *Electra,* by Euripides, how do Electra and her mother, Clytemnestra, respond to the limitations society has placed on women?

THESIS
The experience of powerlessness has taught Electra and her mother two very different lessons: Electra has learned the value of traditional, conservative sex roles for women, but Clytemnestra has learned just the opposite.

As in other writing, the thesis of a literature paper cannot be too factual, too broad, or too vague (see 2a). For an essay on Mark Twain's *Huckleberry Finn,* for example, the following would all make poor thesis sentences.

TOO FACTUAL
As a runaway slave, Jim is in danger from the law.

TOO BROAD
In *Huckleberry Finn,* Mark Twain criticizes mid-nineteenth-century American society.

TOO VAGUE
Huckleberry Finn is Twain's most exciting work.

Here is a thesis about the novel that avoids these pitfalls.

> **ACCEPTABLE THESIS**
> Because Huckleberry Finn is a naive narrator, his comments on conventional religion are ironic at every turn, allowing Twain to poke fun at empty piety.

In a literature paper, your thesis should usually appear in your introductory paragraph. Often, however, you will want to present a context for the thesis and lead up to it, as in the following paragraph, which ends with the thesis (italicized).

> In *Electra,* Euripides depicts two women who have had too little control over their lives. Electra, ignored by her mother, Clytemnestra, has been married off to a farmer and treated more or less like a slave. Clytemnestra has fared even worse. Her husband, Agamemnon, has slashed the throat of their daughter Iphigenia as a sacrifice to the gods. *The experience of powerlessness has taught Electra and her mother two very different lessons: Electra has learned the value of traditional, conservative sex roles for women, but Clytemnestra has learned just the opposite.*

Sketching an outline

Your thesis may strongly suggest a method of organization, in which case you will have little difficulty jotting down your essay's key points. Consider, for example, the following informal outline, based on a thesis that leads naturally to a three-part organization.

> Thesis: George Bernard Shaw's *Major Barbara* depicts the ways in which three "religions" address the problem of poverty. The Established Church ignores poverty, the Salvation Army tries rather ineffectually to alleviate it, and a form of utopianism based on guns and money promises to eliminate it — but at a terrible cost.

—The Established Church (Lady Britomart)

—The Salvation Army (Major Barbara)

—Utopianism based on guns and money (Undershaft)

If your thesis does not by itself suggest a method of organization, turn to your notes and begin putting them into categories that relate to the thesis. For example, one student who was writing about Euripides' play *Medea* constructed the following formal outline from her notes.

Thesis: Although Medea professes great love for her children, Euripides gives us reason to suspect her sincerity: Medea does not hesitate to use the children as weapons in her bloody battle with Jason, and from the outset she displays little real concern for their fate.

  I. From the very beginning of the play, Medea is a less than ideal mother.
   A. Her first words about the children are hostile.
   B. Her first actions suggest indifference.
 II. In three scenes Medea appears to be a loving mother, but in each of these scenes we have reason to doubt her sincerity.
III. Throughout the play, as Medea plots her revenge, her overriding concern is not her children but her reputation.
   A. Fearing ridicule, she is proud of her reputation as one who can "help her friends and hurt her enemies."
   B. Her obsession with reputation may stem from the Greek view of reputation as a means of immortality.
IV. After she kills her children, Medea reveals her real concern.
   A. She shows no remorse.
   B. She revels in Jason's agony over their death.

Whether to use a formal or an informal outline is to some extent a matter of personal preference. For most purposes, you will probably find that an informal outline is sufficient, perhaps even preferable. (See 1d.)

58d Support your interpretation with evidence from the work; avoid simple plot summary.

Your thesis and tentative outline will point you toward details in the work relevant to your interpretation. As you begin filling out the body of your paper, make good use of those details.

Supporting your interpretation

As a rule, the topic sentence of each paragraph in the body of your paper should focus on some aspect of your overall interpretation. The rest of the paragraph should present details and perhaps quotations from the work that back up your interpretation. In the following paragraph, which develops part of the outline sketched on page 654, the topic sentence comes first. It sums up the religious views represented by Lady Britomart, a character in George Bernard Shaw's play *Major Barbara.*

> Lady Britomart, a member of the Established Church of England, reveals her superficial attitude toward religion in a scene that takes place in her fashionable London townhouse. Religion, according to Lady Britomart, is a morbid topic of conversation. She admonishes her daughter Barbara: "Really, Barbara, you go on as if religion were a pleasant subject. Do have some sense of propriety" (1.686–87). Religion is an unpleasant subject to Lady Britomart because, unlike Barbara, she finds no joy or humor within her religion. It is not simply that she is a humorless person, for she frequently displays a

sharp wit. But in Lady Britomart's upper-class world, religion has its proper place—a serious place bound by convention and cut off from the real world. When Undershaft suggests, for example, that religion can be a pleasant and profoundly important subject, Lady Britomart replies, "Well if you are determined to have it [religion], then I insist on having it in a proper and respectable way. Charles: ring for prayers" (1.690–93).

Notice that the writer has quoted dialogue from the play to lend both flavor and substance to her interpretation. Notice too that the writer is indeed *interpreting* the work: She is not merely summarizing the plot.

Avoiding simple plot summary

In a literature paper, it is tempting to rely heavily on plot summary and avoid interpretation. You can resist this temptation by paying special attention to your topic sentences. The following rough-draft topic sentence, for instance, led to a plot summary rather than an interpretation:

> As they drift down the river on a raft, Huck and the runaway slave Jim have many philosophical discussions.

The student's revised topic sentence, which announces an interpretation, is much better:

> The theme of dawning moral awareness is reinforced by the many philosophical discussions between Huck and Jim, the runaway slave, as they drift down the river on a raft.

Usually a little effort is all that is needed to make the difference between a plot summary that goes nowhere and a focused, forceful interpretation. As with all forms of writing, revision is key.

LOOKING AT YOURSELF AS A WRITER
Avoiding simple plot summary

When you write about a literary work that has a plot (such as a short story, a play, or a film), your instructor expects more than just a plot summary. If you — like many students — find it difficult to avoid veering off into plot summary, consider some common causes and cures.

CAUSE   You assume that your audience may not have read the work and either needs to hear the plot or wants to hear it. Or you enjoyed the story and want to share it with readers.

CURE   Unless you have been told otherwise, in academic writing you should assume that your readers have read the work. Your job is to share with them not the work itself but your own interpretation of it.

CAUSE   Time words such as *when* and *after*, which are natural and useful transitions in literature papers, tempt you to veer off into plot summary.

CURE   Continue to use these important transitions, but catch yourself if two or three sentences in a row move away from interpretation. Sometimes you can open a sentence with a subordinate clause beginning with a time word and put the interpretation in the main clause, like this: "When Sister says that the entire family has turned against her, she seems to be right, even though many of this narrator's other perceptions are not to be trusted."

CAUSE   Plot summaries appeal to you because you find a chronological organization of your paper easier to manage than other kinds of organization.

CURE   Although time order is indeed one of the easiest methods of organization, be aware that the easiest strategy is not always the best one.

Avoiding simple plot summary (continued)

CAUSE   Because you can't think of an interpretation, you turn to a plot summary.

CURE   Admittedly, interpretations are not always easy to come up with, but a variety of strategies may help. First, read the work more than once and pose questions that might lead to an interpretation (see the charts on pp. 651–52 for examples). Second, take a look at sample papers, such as the two at the end of this chapter or any that appear in your literary anthology. Third, discuss the work with classmates or friends. Finally, consider making an appointment with your instructor or visiting your college's writing center.

58e   Integrate quotations from the work.

Quotations from a literary work can lend vivid support to your argument, but keep most quotations fairly short. Excessive use of long quotations bores readers and interrupts the flow of your interpretation.

Integrating quotations smoothly into your own text can present a challenge. Because of the complexities of literature, do not be surprised to find yourself puzzling over the most graceful way to tuck in a short phrase or the clearest way to introduce a more extended passage from the work.

NOTE: The parenthetical citations at the ends of examples in this section tell readers where the quoted words can be found. They indicate the lines of a poem; the act, scene, and lines of a play; or the page number of a quotation from a short story or novel. For guidelines on using citations, see pages 601–03.

Introducing quotations

When writing about nonfiction essays and books, you have probably learned to introduce a quotation with a signal phrase naming the author: *According to Jane Doe, Jane Doe points out that, Jane Doe presents a compelling argument,* and so on.

When introducing quotations from a literary work, however, make sure that you don't confuse the author with the narrator of a story, the speaker of a poem, or a character in a play. Instead of naming the author, you can refer to the narrator or speaker — or to the work itself.

INAPPROPRIATE

Poet Andrew Marvell describes his fear of death like this: "But at my back I always hear / Time's wingèd chariot hurrying near" (21–22).

APPROPRIATE

Addressing his beloved in an attempt to win her sexual favors, the speaker of the poem argues that death gives them no time to waste: "But at my back I always hear / Time's wingèd chariot hurrying near" (21–22).

APPROPRIATE

The poem "To His Coy Mistress" says as much about fleeting time and death as it does about sexual passion. Its most powerful lines may well be "But at my back I always hear / Time's wingèd chariot hurrying near" (21–22).

In the last example, you could of course mention the author as well: *Marvell's poem "To His Coy Mistress" says as much. . . .* Although the author is mentioned, he is not being confused with the speaker of the poem.

If you are quoting the words of a character in a story or a play, you should name the character who is speaking and provide a context for the spoken words. In the following examples, the quoted dialogue is from Tennessee Williams's play *The Glass Menagerie* and Shirley Jackson's short story "The Lottery."

> Laura's life is so completely ruled by Amanda that when urged to make a wish on the moon, she asks, "What shall I wish for, Mother?" (1.5.140).

> When a neighbor suggests that the lottery should be abandoned, Old Man Warner responds, "There's *always* been a lottery" (284).

Avoiding shifts in tense

Because it is conventional to write about literature in the present tense (see p. 338) and because literary works often use other tenses, you will need to exercise some care when weaving quotations into your own text. A first-draft attempt may result in an awkward shift, as it did for one student who was writing about Nadine Gordimer's short story "Friday's Footprint."

TENSE SHIFT
When Rita sees Johnny's relaxed attitude, "she blushed, like a wave of illness" (159).

To avoid the distracting shift from present to past tense, the writer decided to include the reference to Rita's blushing in her own text and reduce the length of the quotation.

REVISED
When Rita sees Johnny's relaxed attitude, she blushes "like a wave of illness" (159).

The writer could have changed the quotation to present tense, using brackets to indicate the change, like this: *When Rita sees Johnny's relaxed attitude, "she blushe[s] like a wave of illness" (159).* However, using brackets around just one letter of a word can seem pedantic, so the earlier revision is preferable. (For advice on using brackets around a word or more, see 39c.)

Using quotations within quotations

In writing about literature, you may sometimes want to use a quotation with another quotation embedded in it—when you are quoting dialogue in a novel, for example. In such cases, set off the main quotation with double quotation marks, as you usually would, and set off the embedded quotation with single quotation marks. (See also 37c.) The following example from a student paper quotes lines from Amy Tan's novel *The Hundred Secret Senses.*

> Early in the novel the narrator's half-sister Kwan sees—or thinks she sees—ghosts: " 'Libby-ah' she'll say to me. 'Guess who I see yesterday, you guess.' And I don't have to guess she's talking about someone dead" (3).

Formatting quotations

Guidelines for formatting quotations from short stories (or novels), poems, and plays are slightly different.

SHORT STORIES OR NOVELS If a quotation from a short story or a novel takes up four or fewer typed lines, put it in quotation marks and run it into the text of your essay. Include a page number in parentheses after the quotation.

> The narrator of Eudora Welty's "Why I Live at the P.O.," known to us only as "Sister," makes many catty remarks about her enemies. For example, she calls Mr. Whitaker "this photographer with the pop-eyes" (46).

If a quotation from a short story or a novel is five typed lines or longer, set it off from the text by indenting one inch (or ten spaces) from the left margin; when you set a quotation off from the text, you should not use quotation marks around it. (See also 37b.) Put the page number in parentheses after the final mark of punctuation.

> Sister's tale begins with "I," and she makes every event revolve around herself, even her sister's marriage:
>
> > I was getting along fine with Mama, Papa-Daddy, and Uncle Rondo until my sister Stella-Rondo just separated from her husband and came back home again. Mr. Whitaker! Of course I went with Mr. Whitaker first, when he first appeared here in China Grove, taking "Pose Yourself" photos, and Stella-Rondo broke us up. (46)

POEMS Enclose quotations of three or fewer lines of poetry in quotation marks within your text, and indicate line breaks with a slash. (See also 39e.) Include line numbers in parentheses at the end of the quotation. (See also p. 602.)

> The opening lines of Frost's "Fire and Ice" strike a conversational tone: "Some say the world will end in fire, / Some say in ice" (1–2).

When you quote four or more lines of poetry, set the quotation off from the text by indenting one inch (or ten spaces) and omit the quotation marks. Put the line numbers in parentheses after the final mark of punctuation.

> The opening stanza of Louise Bogan's "Women" startles readers by presenting a negative stereotype of women:
>
> > Women have no wilderness in them,
> > They are provident instead,
> > Content in the tight hot cell of their hearts
> > To eat dusty bread. (1–4)

PLAYS If a quotation from a play takes up four or fewer typed lines and is spoken by only one character, put quotation marks around it and run it into the text of your essay. Whenever possible, include the act number, scene number, and line numbers in parentheses at the end of the quotation. Separate the numbers with periods, and use arabic numerals unless your instructor prefers roman numerals.

> Two attendants silently watch as the sleepwalking Lady Macbeth subconsciously struggles with her guilt: "Here's the smell of blood still. All the perfumes of Arabia will not sweeten this little hand" (5.1.50–51).

If a dramatic quotation by a single character is five lines or longer, set it off in the same way you would set off a long prose quotation. Include the act number, scene number, and line numbers after the final mark of punctuation.

When quoting dialogue between two or more characters in a play, no matter how many lines you use, set the quotation off from the text. Type the character's name in all capital letters at a one-inch (ten-space) indent from the left margin. Indent subsequent lines under the character's name an additional quarter inch (or three spaces).

> Throughout *The Importance of Being Earnest*, Algernon criticizes romance and the institution of marriage, as in the scene when he learns of Jack's intention to marry Gwendolen:
>
>> ALGERNON. My dear fellow, the way you flirt with Gwendolen is perfectly disgraceful. It is almost as bad as the way Gwendolen flirts with you.
>> JACK. I am in love with Gwendolen. I have come up to town expressly to propose to her.
>> ALGERNON. I thought you had come up for pleasure?—I call that business. (act 1)

58f Observe the conventions of literary papers.

When you are writing a literature paper, it is important to observe certain conventions so that your readers' attention will be focused directly on your interpretation, not on the details of your presentation.

Referring to authors and titles

The first time you make reference to authors, use their first and last names: *Virginia Woolf was one of England's most important novelists.* In subsequent references, use their last names only: *Woolf's early work was largely overlooked.* As a rule, do not use titles such as Mr. or Ms. or Dr.

Titles of short stories, essays, and most poems are put in quotation marks: "The Dead" by James Joyce; "The Death of the Moth" by Virginia Woolf; "High Windows" by Philip Larkin. (See 37d.) Titles of novels, nonfiction books, plays, and epics or other long poems are underlined or italicized: *Heart of Darkness* by Joseph Conrad; *I Know Why the Caged Bird Sings* by Maya Angelou; *Macbeth* by William Shakespeare; *Howl* by Allen Ginsberg. (See 42a.)

Referring to characters and events

Refer to each character by the name most often used for him or her in the work. If, for instance, a character's name is Lambert Strether and he is always referred to as "Strether," do not call him "Lambert" or "Mr. Strether." Similarly, write "Lady Macbeth," not "Mrs. Macbeth."

When describing fictional events in a work of literature, use the present tense: "Octavia *demands* blind obedience from James and from all of her children. When James and Ty *catch* two redbirds in their trap, they *want* to play with them; Octavia, however, *has* other plans for the birds." (See also 13b and 28a.)

Referring to parts of works

Be as accurate as possible when referring to subdivisions of a literary work. Avoid using phrases like *the part where.* Instead give specific references by using the appropriate descriptive terms: *the final stanza, the scene in which Hamlet confronts his mother, the passage that refers to Jane Austen,* and so on.

58g If you use secondary sources, document them appropriately and avoid plagiarism.

Many literature papers do not rely on secondary sources—works other than the literary text under discussion. (For an example of an essay without secondary sources, see pp. 669–71.)

Other literature papers use some ideas from sources such as articles or books of literary criticism, biographies of the author, the author's own essays and autobiography, and histories of the era in which the work was written. (For an example of a paper that uses secondary sources, see pp. 674–77.) Even if you use secondary sources, your main goal should always be to develop your own understanding and interpretation of the literary work.

Whenever you use secondary sources, you must document them and you must avoid plagiarism. Plagiarism is unacknowledged borrowing—whether intentional or unintentional—of a source's words or ideas. (See 54b.)

Documenting secondary sources

Most literature papers are documented with the system recommended by the Modern Language Association (MLA). This system of documentation is discussed in detail in 56, which is easy to find because its pages have a vertical band in red.

An MLA in-text citation usually combines a signal phrase with a page number in parentheses.

SAMPLE MLA IN-TEXT CITATION

Arguing that fate has little to do with the tragedy that befalls Oedipus, Bernard Knox writes that "the catastrophe of Oedipus is that he discovers his own identity; and for his discovery he is first and last responsible" (6).

The signal phrase names the author of the secondary source; the number in parentheses is the page on which the quoted words appear.

The in-text citation is used in combination with a list of works cited at the end of the paper. Anyone interested in knowing additional information about the secondary source can consult the list of works cited. Here, for example, is the works cited entry for the work referred to in the sample in-text citation.

SAMPLE ENTRY IN THE LIST OF WORKS CITED

Knox, Bernard. Oedipus at Thebes: Sophocles' Tragic Hero and His Time. New York: Norton, 1971.

As you document secondary sources with in-text citations, consult 56a; as you construct your list of works cited, consult 56b.

Avoiding plagiarism

The rules about plagiarism are the same for literary papers as for other research writing. It is wrong to use other writers' ideas or language without giving credit to your source. If an interpretation was suggested to you by another critic's work

or if an obscure point was clarified by someone else's research, it is your responsibility to cite the source. If you have borrowed any phrases or sentences from your source, you must put them in quotation marks and credit the author.

For important tips on avoiding plagiarism, see 54b.

58h Sample literature papers

Following are two sample essays. The first, by Margaret Peel, has no secondary sources. (Langston Hughes's "Ballad of the Landlord," the poem on which the essay is based, appears on p. 673.) Sample pages from the second essay, by Dan Larson, show a paper that uses secondary sources.

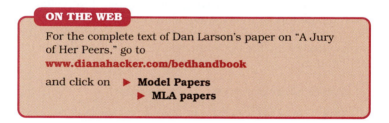

ON THE WEB

For the complete text of Dan Larson's paper on "A Jury of Her Peers," go to
www.dianahacker.com/bedhandbook

and click on ▶ **Model Papers**
▶ **MLA papers**

Margaret Peel
Professor Lin
English 102
20 April 2001

Opposing Voices in "Ballad of the Landlord"

Langston Hughes's "Ballad of the Landlord" is
narrated through four voices, each with its own
perspective on the poem's action. These opposing
voices--of a tenant, a landlord, the police, and
the press--dramatize a black man's experience in a
society dominated by whites.

The main voice in the poem is that of the
tenant, who, as the last line tells us, is black.
The tenant is characterized by his informal, nonstandard speech. He uses slang ("Ten Bucks"), contracted words ('member, more'n), and nonstandard
grammar ("These steps is broken down"). This colloquial English suggests the tenant's separation from
the world of convention, represented by the formal
voices of the police and the press, which appear
later in the poem.

Although the tenant uses nonstandard English,
his argument is organized and logical. He begins
with a reasonable complaint and a gentle reminder
that the complaint is already a week old: "My roof
has sprung a leak. / Don't you 'member I told you
about it / Way last week?" (lines 2-4). In the second
stanza, he appeals diplomatically to the landlord's

Thesis states
Peel's main idea.

Details from the
poem illustrate
Peel's point.

The first citation
to lines of the
poem includes
the word "lines."

Peel 2

Subsequent citations from the poem are cited with line numbers alone.

self-interest: "These steps is broken down. / When you come up yourself / It's a wonder you don't fall down" (6-8). In the third stanza, when the landlord has responded to his complaints with a demand for rent money, the tenant becomes more forceful, but his voice is still reasonable: "Ten Bucks you say is due? / Well, that's Ten Bucks more'n I'll pay you / Till you fix this house up new" (10-12).

Topic sentence focuses on an interpretation.

The fourth stanza marks a shift in the tone of the argument. At this point the tenant responds more emotionally, in reaction to the landlord's threats to evict him. By the fifth stanza, the tenant has unleashed his anger: "Um-huh! You talking high and mighty" (17). Hughes uses an exclamation point for the first time; the tenant is raising his voice at last. As the argument gets more heated, the tenant finally resorts to the language of violence: "You ain't gonna be able to say a word / If I land my fist on you" (19-20).

Transition prepares readers for the next topic.

These are the last words the tenant speaks in the poem. Perhaps Hughes wants to show how black people who threaten violence are silenced. When a new voice is introduced--the landlord's--the poem shifts to italics:

> Police! Police!
> Come and get this man!
> He's trying to ruin the government
> And overturn the land! (21-24)

Peel 3

This response is clearly an overreaction to a small threat. Instead of dealing with the tenant directly, the landlord shouts for the police. His hysterical voice--marked by repetitions and punctuated with exclamation points--reveals his disproportionate fear and outrage. And his conclusions are equally excessive: This black man, he claims, is out to "ruin the government" and "overturn the land." Although the landlord's overreaction is humorous, it is sinister as well, because the landlord knows that, no matter how excessive his claims are, he has the police and the law on his side.

Peel interprets the landlord's response.

In line 25, the regular meter and rhyme of the poem break down, perhaps showing how an arrest disrupts everyday life. The "voice" in lines 25-29 has two parts: the clanging sound of the police ("Copper's whistle! / Patrol bell!") and, in sharp contrast, the unemotional, factual tone of a police report ("Arrest. / Precinct Station. / Iron cell.").

Peel comments on meter and rhyme.

The last voice in the poem is the voice of the press, represented in newspaper headlines: "MAN THREATENS LANDLORD / TENANT HELD NO BAIL / JUDGE GIVES NEGRO 90 DAYS IN COUNTY JAIL" (31-33). Meter and rhyme return here, as if to show that once the tenant is arrested, life can go on as usual. The language of the press, like that of the police, is cold and distant, and it gives the tenant less and less status. In line 31, he is a "man"; in line 32,

he has been demoted to a "tenant"; and in line 33,
he has become a "Negro," or just another statistic.

Peel sums up her interpretation.

By using four opposing voices in "Ballad of
the Landlord," Hughes effectively dramatizes different views of minority assertiveness. To the
tenant, assertiveness is informal and natural, as
his language shows; to the landlord, it is a dangerous threat, as his hysterical response suggests.
The police response is, like the language that
describes it, short and sharp. Finally, the press's
view of events, represented by the headlines, is
distant and unsympathetic.

Peel concludes with an analysis of the poem's political significance.

By the end of the poem, we understand the
predicament of the black man. Exploited by the
landlord, politically oppressed by those who think
he's out "to ruin the government," physically re-
strained by the police and the judicial system, and
denied his individuality by the press, he is saved
only by his own sense of humor. The very title of
the poem suggests his--and Hughes's--sense of
humor. The tenant is singing a <u>ballad</u> to his
oppressors, but this ballad is no love song. It
portrays the oppressors, through their own voices,
in an unflattering light: the landlord as cowardly
and ridiculous, the police and press as dull and
soulless. The tenant may lack political power, but
he speaks with vitality, and no one can say he
lacks dignity or the spirit to survive.

Ballad of the Landlord

Landlord, landlord,
My roof has sprung a leak.
Don't you 'member I told you about it
Way last week?

Landlord, landlord,
These steps is broken down.
When you come up yourself
It's a wonder you don't fall down.

Ten Bucks you say I owe you?
Ten Bucks you say is due?
Well, that's Ten Bucks more'n I'll pay you
Till you fix this house up new.

What? You gonna get eviction orders?
You gonna cut off my heat?
You gonna take my furniture and
Throw it in the street?

Um-huh! You talking high and mighty.
Talk on — till you get through.
You ain't gonna be able to say a word
If I land my fist on you.

Police! Police!
Come and get this man!
He's trying to ruin the government
And overturn the land!

Copper's whistle!
Patrol bell!
Arrest.

Precinct Station.
Iron cell.
Headlines in press:

MAN THREATENS LANDLORD
TENANT HELD NO BAIL
JUDGE GIVES NEGRO 90 DAYS IN COUNTY JAIL

—Langston Hughes

Larson 1

Dan Larson
Professor Duncan
English 102
16 April 2001

The Transformation of Mrs. Peters:
An Analysis of "A Jury of Her Peers"

In Susan Glaspell's 1917 short story "A Jury
of Her Peers," two women accompany their husbands
and a county attorney to an isolated house where a
farmer named John Wright has been choked to death
in his bed with a rope. The chief suspect, Wright's
wife Minnie, is in jail awaiting trial. The
sheriff's wife, Mrs. Peters, has come along to
gather some personal items for Minnie, and Mrs.
Hale has joined her. Early in the story, Mrs. Hale
sympathizes with Minnie and objects to the way the
male investigators are "snoopin' round and criti-
cizin'" her kitchen (293). In contrast, Mrs. Peters
shows respect for the law, saying that the men are
doing "no more than their duty" (293). By the end
of the story, however, Mrs. Peters has joined Mrs.
Hale in a conspiracy of silence, lied to the men,
and committed a crime--hiding key evidence. What
causes this dramatic change?

One critic, Leonard Mustazza, argues that Mrs.
Hale recruits Mrs. Peters "as a fellow 'juror' in
the case, moving the sheriff's wife away from her
sympathy for her husband's position and towards

The opening lines name the story and estab-lish context.

Present tense is used to describe details from the story.

Quotations from the story are cited with page numbers in parentheses.

The opening paragraph ends with Larson's research ques-tion.

Quotation from a secondary source: author is named in a signal phrase; page number is given in paren-theses.

Larson 2

identification with the accused woman" (494). While
this is true, Mrs. Peters also reaches insights on
her own. Her observations in the kitchen lead her
to understand Minnie's grim and lonely plight as
the wife of an abusive farmer, and her identification with both Minnie and Mrs. Hale is strengthened
as the men conducting the investigation trivialize
the lives of women.

The thesis as-
serts Larson's
main point.

The first evidence that Mrs. Peters reaches
understanding on her own surfaces in the following
passage:

> The sheriff's wife had looked from the
> stove to the sink--to the pail of water
> which had been carried in from outside.
> ... That look of seeing into things,
> of seeing through a thing to something
> else, was in the eyes of the sheriff's
> wife now. (295)

A long quotation
is set off by
indenting; no
quotation marks
are needed;
ellipsis dots
indicate words
omitted from the
source.

Something about the stove, the sink, and the pail
of water connects with her own experience, giving
Mrs. Peters a glimpse into the life of Minnie
Wright. The details resonate with meaning.

Social historian Elaine Hedges argues that
such details, which evoke the drudgery of a farm
woman's work, would not have been lost upon
Glaspell's readers in 1917. Hedges tells us what
the pail and the stove, along with another detail
from the story--a dirty towel on a roller--would

Larson summa-
rizes ideas from
a secondary
source and then
quotes from that
source; he names
the author in a
signal phrase
and gives a page
number in
parentheses.

MLA papers

have meant to women of the time. Laundry was a dreaded all-day affair. Water had to be pumped, hauled, and boiled; then the wash was rubbed, rinsed, wrung through a wringer, carried outside, and hung on a line to dry. "What the women see, beyond the pail and the stove," writes Hedges, "are the hours of work it took Minnie to produce that one clean towel" (56).

Topic sentence focuses on Larson's interpretation.

    On her own, Mrs. Peters discovers clues about the motive for the murder. Her curiosity leads her to pick up a sewing basket filled with quilt pieces and then to notice something strange: a sudden row of badly sewn stitches. "What do you suppose she was so--nervous about?" asks Mrs. Peters (296). A short time later, Mrs. Peters spots another clue, an empty birdcage. Again she observes details on her own, in this case a broken door and hinge, suggesting that the cage has been roughly handled.

The complete text of the paper appears on *The Bedford Handbook* Web site. See page 668 for the address.

Works Cited

Ben-Zvi, Linda. "'Murder, She Wrote': The Genesis of Susan Glaspell's <u>Trifles</u>." <u>Theatre Journal</u> 44 (1992): 141-62. Rpt. in <u>Susan Glaspell: Essays on Her Theater and Fiction</u>. Ed. Linda Ben-Zvi. Ann Arbor: U of Michigan P, 1995. 19-48.

Glaspell, Susan. "A Jury of Her Peers." <u>Literature and Its Writers: An Introduction to Fiction, Poetry, and Drama</u>. Ed. Ann Charters and Samuel Charters. 2nd ed. Boston: Bedford, 2001. 286-302.

Hedges, Elaine. "Small Things Reconsidered: 'A Jury of Her Peers.'" <u>Women's Studies</u> 12 (1986): 89-110. Rpt. in <u>Susan Glaspell: Essays on Her Theater and Fiction</u>. Ed. Linda Ben-Zvi. Ann Arbor: U of Michigan P, 1995. 49-69.

Mustazza, Leonard. "Generic Translation and Thematic Shift in Susan Glaspell's <u>Trifles</u> and 'A Jury of Her Peers.'" <u>Studies in Short Fiction</u> 26 (1989): 489-96.

The works cited page lists the primary source (Glaspell's story) and secondary sources.

WRITING APA PAPERS

59

APA papers

Most writing assignments in the social sciences are either reports of original research or reviews of the literature written
about a particular research topic. Often an original research
report contains a "review of the literature" section that places
the writer's project in the context of previous research.

Most social science instructors will ask you to document
sources with the American Psychological Association (APA)
system of in-text citations and references described in this
section (see 59d). In addition to documenting your sources,
you face three main challenges when writing a social science
paper that draws on written sources: (1) supporting a thesis,
(2) citing your sources and avoiding plagiarism, and (3) integrating quotations and other source material.

59a   Supporting a thesis

A thesis, which usually appears at the end of the introduction, is a one-sentence (or occasionally a two-sentence) statement of your central idea. In a paper reviewing the literature on a topic, this thesis analyzes the often competing conclusions drawn by a variety of researchers.

Finding a thesis

You will be reading articles and other sources that address a central research question. Your thesis will express a reasonable answer to that question, given the current state of research in the field. Here, for example, is a research question and a thesis that answers it.

> **RESEARCH QUESTION**
> How and to what extent have the great apes—gorillas, chimpanzees, and orangutans—demonstrated language abilities akin to those of humans?

> **POSSIBLE THESIS**
> Researchers agree that apes have acquired fairly large vocabularies in American Sign Language and in artificial languages, but they have drawn quite different conclusions in addressing the following questions: (1) How spontaneously have apes used language? (2) How creatively have apes used language? (3) To what extent can apes create sentences? (4) What are some implications of the ape language studies?

Organizing your evidence

The American Psychological Association encourages the use of headings to help readers follow the organization of a paper. For an original research report, the major headings often follow a standard model: Method, Results, Discussion.

APA papers

The introduction is not given a heading; it consists of the material between the title of the paper and the first heading.

For a paper that is a review of the literature, headings will vary, depending on the topic. The student who wrote about apes and language used the four questions in her thesis as headings in her paper (see pp. 716–26).

NOTE: For APA's manuscript guidelines on placing and highlighting headings, see pages 712–13.

59b   Citing sources; avoiding plagiarism

In a research paper, you will be drawing on the work of other writers, and you must document their contributions by citing your sources. Sources are cited for two reasons:

1. to tell readers where your information comes from — so that they can assess its reliability and, if interested, find and read the original source
2. to give credit to the writers from whom you have borrowed words and ideas

To borrow another writer's language or ideas without proper acknowledgment is a form of dishonesty known as *plagiarism.*

Citing sources

Citations are required when you quote from a source, when you summarize or paraphrase a source, and when you borrow facts and ideas from a source (except for common knowledge). The American Psychological Association recommends an author-date style of citations. Here, very briefly, is how the author-date system often works. See 59d for a detailed discussion of variations.

1. The source is introduced by a signal phrase that includes the last names of the authors followed by the date of publication in parentheses.
2. The material being cited is followed by a page number in parentheses.
3. At the end of the paper, an alphabetized list of references gives complete publication information about the source.

IN-TEXT CITATION

Noting that the apes' brains are similar to those of our human ancestors, Leakey and Lewin (1992) argued that in ape brains "the cognitive foundations on which human language could be built are already present" (p. 244).

ENTRY IN THE LIST OF REFERENCES

Leakey, R., & Lewin, R. (1992). *Origins reconsidered: In search of what makes us human.* New York: Doubleday.

NOTE: APA recommends using a hanging indent, as just illustrated, in the list of references (see also p. 692).

Avoiding plagiarism

Your research paper is a collaboration between you and your sources. To be fair and ethical, you must acknowledge your debt to the writers of those sources. If you don't, you are guilty of plagiarism, a serious academic offense.

Three different acts are considered plagiarism: (1) failing to cite quotations and borrowed ideas, (2) failing to enclose borrowed language in quotation marks, and (3) failing to put summaries and paraphrases in your own words.

CITING QUOTATIONS AND BORROWED IDEAS   You must of course document all direct quotations. You must also cite any ideas borrowed from a source: paraphrases of sentences, summaries of paragraphs or chapters, statistics and little-known facts, and visuals such as cartoons, tables, graphs, or diagrams.

The only exception is common knowledge — information that your readers could find in any number of general sources because it is commonly known. For example, the current population of the United States is common knowledge in such fields as sociology and economics; Freud's theory of the unconscious is common knowledge in the field of psychology.

As a rule, when you have seen certain information repeatedly in your reading, you don't need to cite it. However, when information has appeared in only one or two sources or when it is controversial, you should cite it. If a topic is new to you and you are not sure what is considered common knowledge and what is considered controversial, ask your instructor or someone else with expertise. When in doubt, cite the source.

ENCLOSING BORROWED LANGUAGE IN QUOTATION MARKS   To indicate that you are using a source's exact phrases or sentences, you must enclose them in quotation marks. To omit the quotation marks is to claim — falsely — that the language is your own. Such an omission is plagiarism even if you have cited the source.

ORIGINAL SOURCE
No animal has done more to renew interest in animal intelligence than a beguiling, bilingual bonobo named Kanzi, who has the grammatical abilities of a 2½-year-old child and a taste for movies about cavemen.

— Linden, "Animals," p. 57

PLAGIARISM

According to Linden (1986), no animal has done
more to renew interest in animal intelligence than
a beguiling, bilingual bonobo named Kanzi, who
has the grammatical abilities of a 2-1/2-year-
old child and a taste for movies about cavemen
(p. 57).

BORROWED LANGUAGE IN QUOTATION MARKS

According to Linden (1986), "No animal has done
more to renew interest in animal intelligence than
a beguiling, bilingual bonobo named Kanzi, who
has the grammatical abilities of a 2-1/2-year-
old child and a taste for movies about cavemen"
(p. 57).

NOTE: When quoted sentences are set off from the text by indenting, quotation marks are not needed (see pp. 688–89).

PUTTING SUMMARIES AND PARAPHRASES IN YOUR OWN WORDS
When you summarize or paraphrase, you must restate the
source's meaning using your own language. You are guilty of
plagiarism if you half-copy the author's sentences—either
by mixing the author's well-chosen phrases without using
quotation marks or by plugging your own synonyms into
the author's sentence structure. The following paraphrases
are plagiarized—even though the source is cited—because
their language is too close to that of the source.

ORIGINAL SOURCE
If the existence of a signing ape was unsettling for linguists, it
was also startling news for animal behaviorists.
—Davis, *Eloquent Animals,* p. 26

UNACCEPTABLE BORROWING OF PHRASES

```
Davis (1976) observed that the existence of a
signing ape unsettled linguists and startled animal
behaviorists (p. 26).
```

UNACCEPTABLE BORROWING OF STRUCTURE

```
Davis (1976) observed that if the presence of a
sign-language-using chimp was disturbing for scien-
tists studying language, it was also surprising to
scientists studying animal behavior (p. 26).
```

To avoid plagiarizing an author's language, set the source aside, write from memory, and consult the source later to check for accuracy. This strategy prevents you from being captivated by the words on the page.

ACCEPTABLE PARAPHRASE

```
Davis (1976) observed that both linguists and
animal behaviorists were taken by surprise upon
learning of an ape's ability to use sign language
(p. 26).
```

59c   Integrating sources

The American Psychological Association recommends using past tense or present perfect tense in phrases that introduce quotations and other source material: *Davis noted that* or *Davis has noted that* (not *Davis notes that*). Use the present tense only for discussing the results of an experiment (*the results show*) or knowledge that has clearly been established (*researchers agree*).

It is generally acceptable in the social sciences to call authors by their last name only, even on a first mention. If your paper refers to two authors with same last name, use initials as well.

Integrating quotations

Readers need to move from your own words to the words of a source without feeling a jolt.

USING SIGNAL PHRASES   Avoid dropping quotations into the text without warning. Instead, provide clear signal phrases, usually including the author's name and the date of publication, to prepare readers for the quotation.

DROPPED QUOTATION

```
Perhaps even more significant is the pattern that
Kanzi developed on his own in combining various
lexigrams. "When he gave an order combining two
symbols for action--such as 'chase' and 'hide'--
it was important for him that the first action--
'chase'--be done first" (Gibbons, 1991, p. 1561).
```

QUOTATION WITH SIGNAL PHRASE

```
Perhaps even more significant is the pattern that
Kanzi developed on his own in combining various
lexigrams. According to Gibbons (1991), "When he
gave an order combining two symbols for action--
such as 'chase' and 'hide'--it was important for
him that the first action--'chase'--be done first"
(p. 1561).
```

To avoid monotony, try to vary the language and placement of your signal phrases. The models in the chart on the next page suggest a range of possibilities.

Varying signal phrases in APA papers

MODEL SIGNAL PHRASES

In the words of Terrace, ". . ."

As Davis has noted, ". . ."

The Gardners, Washoe's trainers, pointed out that ". . ."

". . . ," claimed linguist Noam Chomsky.

". . . ," wrote Eckholm, ". . ."

Psychologist H. S. Terrace has offered an odd argument for this view: ". . ."

Terrace answered these objections with the following analysis: ". . ."

VERBS IN SIGNAL PHRASES

admitted	contended	reasoned
agreed	declared	refuted
argued	denied	rejected
asserted	emphasized	reported
believed	insisted	responded
claimed	noted	suggested
compared	observed	thought
confirmed	pointed out	wrote

When the signal phrase includes a verb, choose one that is appropriate in the context. Is your source arguing a point, making an observation, reporting a fact, drawing a conclusion, refuting an argument, or stating a belief? By choosing an appropriate verb, you can make your source's stance clear. See the chart above for a list of verbs commonly used in signal phrases.

It is not always necessary to quote full sentences from a source. At times you may wish to borrow only a phrase or to weave part of a source's sentence into your own sentence structure.

Bower (1988) reported that Kanzi practiced "simple
grammatical ordering rules," such as putting
actions before objects (p. 140).

Perhaps the best summation of the early ape
language studies came from biologist Robert
Seyfarth (1982), who concluded that the line sep-
arating humans from other animals was "hazily
drawn, somewhere between the word and the sentence"
(p. 18).

USING THE ELLIPSIS MARK   To condense a quoted passage,
you can use the ellipsis mark (three periods, with spaces
between) to indicate that you have omitted words. What remains must be grammatically complete.

Eckholm (1985) reported that "a 4-year-old pygmy
chimpanzee . . . has demonstrated what scientists
say are the most humanlike linguistic skills ever
documented in another animal" (p. A1).

The writer has omitted the words *at a research center near
Atlanta,* which appeared in the original.

When you want to omit a full sentence or more, use a
period before the three ellipsis dots.

According to Wade (1980), the horse Clever Hans
"could apparently count by tapping out numbers with
his hoof. . . . Clever Hans owes his celebrity to his
master's innocence. Von Osten sincerely believed he
had taught Hans to solve arithmetical problems"
(p. 1349).

Ordinarily, do not use an ellipsis mark at the beginning or at the end of a quotation. Readers will understand that the quoted material is taken from a longer passage. The only exception occurs when you think that the author's meaning might be misinterpreted without ellipsis marks.

USING BRACKETS Brackets (square parentheses) allow you to insert words of your own into quoted material, perhaps to explain a confusing reference or to keep a sentence grammatical in your context.

    Seyfarth (1982) has written that "Premack [a
    scientist at the University of Pennsylvania] taught
    a seven-year-old chimpanzee, Sarah, that the word
    for 'apple' was a small, plastic triangle" (p. 13).

To indicate an error in a quotation, insert [*sic*] right after the error. Notice that the term *sic* is italicized and appears in brackets.

SETTING OFF LONG QUOTATIONS When you quote forty or more words, set off the quotation by indenting it one-half inch (or five spaces) from the left margin. Use the normal right margin and do not single-space.

Long quotations should be introduced by an informative sentence, usually followed by a colon. Quotation marks are unnecessary because the indented format tells readers that the words are taken directly from the source.

    Hart (1996) has described the kinds of linguistic
    signs and symbols used in the early ape language
    experiments:
        Researchers attempted to teach individual
        signs derived from American Sign Language

(ASL) to Washoe, a chimpanzee; Koko, a gorilla; and Chantek, an orangutan. Sarah, a chimpanzee, learned to manipulate arbitrary plastic symbols standing for words, and another chimpanzee, named Lana, used an early computer keyboard, with arbitrary symbols the researchers called lexigrams. (p. 108)

Integrating summaries and paraphrases

Summaries and paraphrases are written in your own words. A summary condenses information from a source; a paraphrase reports the information in about the same number of words. As with quotations, you should introduce most summaries and paraphrases with a signal phrase that mentions the author and the date of publication and places the material in context. Readers will then understand where the summary or paraphrase begins.

Without the signal phrase (underlined) in the following example, readers might think that only the last sentence is being cited, when in fact the whole paragraph is based on the source.

Recent studies at the Yerkes Primate Center in Atlanta are breaking new ground. <u>Researchers Greenfield and Savage-Rumbaugh (1990) reported that</u> the pygmy chimp Kanzi seemed to understand simple grammatical rules about lexigram order. For instance, Kanzi learned that in two-word utterances action precedes object, an ordering also used by human children at the two-word stage. What is impressive, noted Greenfield and Savage-Rumbaugh, is that in addition to being semantically related,

```
most of Kanzi's lexigram combinations are original
(p. 556).
```

There are times, however, when a signal phrase naming the author is not necessary. Most readers will understand, for example, that the citation at the end of the following passage applies to the entire anecdote, not just the last sentence.

```
     One afternoon, Koko the gorilla, who was often
bored with language lessons, stubbornly and repeat-
edly signaled "red" in American Sign Language when
asked the color of a white towel. She did this even
though she had correctly identified the color white
many times before. At last the gorilla plucked a
bit of red lint from the towel and showed it to her
trainer (Patterson & Linden, 1981, pp. 80-81).
```

Notice that when there is no signal phrase naming the author, the authors' names and the date must be included in the parentheses. Unless the work is short, also include the page number in the parentheses.

Integrating statistics and other facts

When you are citing a statistic or other specific fact, a signal phrase is often not necessary. In most cases, readers will understand that the citation refers to the statistic or fact (not the whole paragraph).

```
By the age of ten, Kanzi had learned to communicate
about two hundred symbols on his computerized board
(Lewin, 1991, p. 51).
```

There is nothing wrong, however, with using a signal phrase.

> Lewin (1991) reported that by the age of ten, Kanzi had learned to communicate about two hundred symbols on his computerized board (p. 51).

59d APA documentation style

In most social science classes, you will be asked to use the APA (American Psychological Association) system for documenting sources, which is set forth in the *Publication Manual of the American Psychological Association,* 5th ed. (Washington: APA, 2001). APA recommends in-text citations that refer readers to a list of references.

An in-text citation names the author of the source (often in a signal phrase), gives the date of publication, and at times includes a page number in parentheses. At the end of the paper, a list of references provides publication information about the source; the list is alphabetized by authors' last names (or by titles for works without authors). There is a direct link between the in-text citation and the alphabetical listing. In the following example, that link is highlighted in red.

IN-TEXT CITATION

> Rumbaugh (1995) reported that "Kanzi's comprehension of over 600 novel sentences of request was very comparable to Alia's; both complied with requests without assistance on approximately 70% of the sentences" (p. 722).

ENTRY IN THE LIST OF REFERENCES

Rumbaugh, D. (1995). Primate language and
    cognition: Common ground. *Social Research, 62,*
    711-730.

NOTE: Indent the entry in your list of references as shown here unless your instructor suggests otherwise (see pp. 713–14).

Directory to APA in-text citations

1. Basic format for a quotation, 693
2. Basic format for a summary or a paraphrase, 693
3. A work with two authors, 693
4. A work with three to five authors, 694
5. A work with six or more authors, 694
6. Unknown author, 695
7. Organization as author, 695
8. Two or more works in the same parentheses, 696
9. Authors with the same last name, 696
10. Personal communication, 696
11. An electronic document, 697

APA in-text citations

The APA's in-text citations provide at least the author's last name and the date of publication. For direct quotations and some paraphrases, a page number is given as well.

NOTE: In the models that follow, notice that APA style requires the use of the past tense or the present perfect tense in signal phrases introducing material that has been cited: *Smith reported, Smith has argued.*

■ **1. BASIC FORMAT FOR A QUOTATION** Ordinarily, introduce the quotation with a signal phrase that includes the author's last name followed by the date of publication in parentheses. Put the page number (preceded by "p.") in parentheses at the end of the quotation.

```
Hart (1996) wrote that some primatologists
"wondered if apes had learned Language, with a
capital L" (p. 109).
```

If the signal phrase does not name the author, place the author's name, the date, and the page number in parentheses at the end of the quotation. Use commas between items in the parentheses: (Hart, 1996, p. 109).

■ **2. BASIC FORMAT FOR A SUMMARY OR A PARAPHRASE** For a summary or a paraphrase, include the author's last name and the date either in a signal phrase or in parentheses at the end. A page number is not required for a summary or a paraphrase, but include one if it would help readers find the passage in a long work.

```
According to Hart (1996), researchers took
Terrace's conclusions seriously, and funding for
language experiments soon declined (p. 110).

Researchers took Terrace's conclusions seriously,
and funding for language experiments soon declined
(Hart, 1996, p. 110).
```

■ **3. A WORK WITH TWO AUTHORS** Name both authors in the signal phrase or parentheses each time you cite the work. In the parentheses, use "&" between the authors' names; in the signal phrase, use "and."

Greenfield and Savage-Rumbaugh (1990) have
acknowledged that Kanzi's linguistic development
was slower than that of a human child (p. 567).

Kanzi's linguistic development was slower than
that of a human child (Greenfield & Savage-
Rumbaugh, 1990, p. 567).

■ **4. A WORK WITH THREE TO FIVE AUTHORS** Identify all authors in the signal phrase or parentheses the first time you cite the source.

The chimpanzee Nim was raised by researchers who
trained him in American Sign Language by molding
and guiding his hands (Terrace, Petitto, Sanders,
& Bever, 1979, p. 891).

In subsequent citations, use the first author's name followed by "et al." in either the signal phrase or the parentheses.

Nim was able to string together as many as 16
signs, but their order appeared quite random
(Terrace et al., 1979, p. 895).

■ **5. A WORK WITH SIX OR MORE AUTHORS** Use only the first author's name followed by "et al." in the signal phrase or parentheses.

The ape language experiments are shedding light on
the language development of very young children and
children with linguistic handicaps (Savage-Rumbaugh
et al., 1993).

■ **6. UNKNOWN AUTHOR** If the author is unknown, mention the work's title in the signal phrase or give the first word or two of the title in the parenthetical citation. Titles of articles and chapters are put in quotation marks; titles of books and reports are italicized.

> Chimpanzees living in separate areas of Africa
> differ in a range of behaviors: in their methods
> of cracking nuts or gathering ants, for example, or
> in their grooming rituals. An international team of
> researchers has concluded that many of the differ-
> ing behaviors are cultural, not just responses to
> varying environmental factors ("Chimps," 1999).

NOTE: In the rare case when "Anonymous" is specified as the author, treat it as if it were a real name: (Anonymous, 2001). In the list of references, also use the name Anonymous as author.

■ **7. ORGANIZATION AS AUTHOR** If the author is a government agency or other corporate organization, give the full name of the organization in the signal phrase or in the parenthetical citation the first time you cite the source.

> According to the Language Research Center (2000),
> linguistic research with apes has led to new methods
> of treating humans with learning disabilities such
> as autism and dyslexia.

If the organization has a familiar abbreviation, you may include it in brackets the first time you cite the source and use the abbreviation alone in later citations.

FIRST CITATION   (National Institute of Mental
                          Health [NIMH], 2001)

LATER CITATIONS (NIMH, 2001)

■ **8. TWO OR MORE WORKS IN THE SAME PARENTHESES** When
your parenthetical citation names two or more works, put
them in the same order that they appear in the reference
list, separated by semicolons.

> Researchers argued that the apes in the early lan-
> guage experiments were merely responding to cues
> (Sebeok & Umiker-Sebeok, 1979; Terrace, 1979).

■ **9. AUTHORS WITH THE SAME LAST NAME** To avoid confusion, use initials with the last names if your reference list
includes two or more authors with the same last name.

> Research by E. Smith (1989) revealed that . . .

■ **10. PERSONAL COMMUNICATION** Interviews, memos, letters,
e-mail, and similar unpublished person-to-person communications should be cited by initials, last name, and precise
date.

> One of Patterson's former aides, who worked for
> seven months with the gorilla Michael, is convinced
> that he was capable of joking and lying in sign
> language (E. Robbins, personal communication,
> January 4, 2000).

It is not necessary to include personal communications in
the bibliographic references at the end of your paper.

■ **11. AN ELECTRONIC DOCUMENT**   When possible, cite an electronic document as you would any other document (using the author-date style).

```
R. Fouts and D. Fouts (1999) have explained one
benefit of ape language research: It has shown us
how to teach children with linguistic disabilities.
```

Electronic sources may lack authors' names or dates. In addition, they may lack page numbers (required in some citations). Here are APA's guidelines for handling sources without authors' names, dates, or page numbers.

Unknown author

If no author is named, mention the title of the document in a signal phrase or give the first word or two of the title in parentheses (see also item 6). (If an organization serves as the author, see item 7.)

```
According to the BBC article "Chimps Are Cultured
Creatures" (1999), chimpanzees at sites in West
Africa, Tanzania, and Uganda exhibit culture-
specific patterns of behavior when grooming one
another.
```

Unknown date

When the date is unknown, APA recommends using the abbreviation "n.d." (for "no date").

```
Attempts to return sign-language-using apes to the
wild have had mixed results (Smith, n.d.).
```

No page numbers

APA ordinarily requires page numbers for direct quotations, and it recommends them for summaries or paraphrases from long sources. When an electronic source lacks stable numbered pages, your citation should include—if possible—information that will help readers locate the particular passage being cited.

When an electronic document has numbered paragraphs, use the paragraph number preceded by the symbol ¶ or by the abbreviation "para.": (Hall, 2001, ¶ 5) *or* (Hall, 2001, para. 5). If neither a page nor a paragraph number is given and the document contains headings, cite the appropriate heading and indicate which paragraph under that heading you are referring to:

> According to Kirby (1999), some critics have accused activists in the Great Ape Project of "exaggerating the supposed similarities of the apes [to humans] to stop their use in experiments" (Shared Path section, para. 6).

NOTE: Some electronic sources post articles in files using portable document format (pdf). When such a file contains page numbers, give the page number in the parenthetical citation.

> Williams, Brakke, and Savage-Rumbaugh (1997) reported that three chimpanzees who were exposed to language after they were two years old could learn symbols but could not understand speech, even after years of hearing it (p. 302).

APA list of references

In APA style, the alphabetical list of works cited is titled "References." Following are models illustrating the form APA recommends for entries in the list of references. Observe all details: capitalization, punctuation, use of italics, and so on. For advice on preparing the reference list, see pages 713–15. For a sample reference list, see pages 725–26.

General guidelines for listing authors

Alphabetize entries in the list of references by authors' last names; if a work has no author, alphabetize it by its title. The first element of each entry is important because citations in the text of the paper refer to it and readers will be looking for it in the alphabetized list. The date of publication always appears immediately after the first element of the citation.

NAME AND DATE CITED IN TEXT

Duncan (2001) has reported that . . .

BEGINNING OF ENTRY IN THE LIST OF REFERENCES

Duncan, B. (2001).

Items 1–4 show how to begin an entry for a work with a single author, multiple authors, an organization as author, and an unknown author. Items 5 and 6 show how to begin an entry when your list includes two or more works by the same author or two or more works by the same author in the same year. What comes after the first element of your citation will depend on the kind of source you are citing (see items 7–30).

■ **1. SINGLE AUTHOR** Begin the entry with the author's last name, followed by a comma and the author's initial(s). Then give the date in parentheses.

```
Conran, G. (2001).
```

■ **2. MULTIPLE AUTHORS** List up to six authors by last names followed by initials. Use an ampersand (&) between the names of two authors or, if there are more than two authors, before the name of the last author.

```
Walker, J. R., & Taylor, T. (1998).

Sloan, F. A., Stout, E. M., Whetten-Goldstein, K.,
     & Liang, Lan. (2000).
```

If there are more than six authors, list the first six and "et al." (meaning "and others") to indicate that there are others.

■ **3. ORGANIZATION AS AUTHOR** When the author is an organization, begin with the name of the organization.

```
American Psychiatric Association. (2000).
```

NOTE: If the organization is also the publisher, see item 28.

■   **4. UNKNOWN AUTHOR**   Begin the entry with the work's title. Titles of books are italicized. Titles of articles are neither italicized nor put in quotation marks. (For rules on capitalization of titles, see p. 714.)

> *Oxford essential world atlas.* (1996).

> EMFs on the brain. (1995, January 21).

■   **5. TWO OR MORE WORKS BY THE SAME AUTHOR**   Use the author's name for all entries. List the entries by year, the earliest first.

> Schlechty, P. C. (1997).

> Schlechty, P. C. (2001).

■   **6. TWO OR MORE WORKS BY THE SAME AUTHOR IN THE SAME YEAR**   List the works alphabetically by title. In the parentheses, following the year, add lowercase letters beginning with "a," "b," and so on. Use these same designations when giving the year in the in-text citation.

> Kennedy, C. H. (2000a).

> Kennedy, C. H. (2000b).

These examples are for journal articles. For magazine or newspaper articles, give the full date in the reference list: (2002a, July 1). Give only the year in the in-text citation.

Articles in periodicals

This section shows how to prepare an entry for an article in a periodical such as a scholarly journal, a magazine, or a newspaper. In addition to consulting the models in this section, you may need to refer to items 1–6 (general guidelines for listing authors).

NOTE: For articles on consecutive pages, provide the range of pages. When an article does not appear on consecutive pages, give all page numbers (see item 10 for an example).

■ **7. ARTICLE IN A JOURNAL PAGINATED BY VOLUME** Many professional journals continue page numbers throughout the year instead of beginning each issue with page 1; at the end of the year, the issues are collected in a volume. After the italicized title of the journal, give the volume number (also italicized), followed by the page numbers.

    Morawski, J. (2000). Social psychology a century
        ago. *American Psychologist, 55,* 427-431.

■ **8. ARTICLE IN A JOURNAL PAGINATED BY ISSUE** When each issue of a journal begins with page 1, include the issue number in parentheses after the volume number. Italicize the volume number but not the issue number.

    Scruton, R. (1996). The eclipse of listening.
        The New Criterion, 15(3), 5-13.

■ **9. ARTICLE IN A MAGAZINE** In addition to the year of publication, list the month and, for weekly magazines, the day. If there is a volume number, include it following the title (italicized).

    Raloff, J. (2001, May 12). Lead therapy won't help
        most kids. *Science News, 159,* 292.

■ **10. ARTICLE IN A NEWSPAPER** Begin with the name of the author, if there is one, followed by the year, month, and day of publication. (For an article with an unknown author, see also item 4.) Page numbers are introduced with "p." (or "pp." for multiple pages).

```
Haney, D. Q. (1998, February 20). Finding eats at
    mystery of appetite. The Oregonian, pp. A1,
    A17.
```

■ **11. LETTER TO THE EDITOR**   Letters to the editor appear in scholarly journals, in magazines, and in newspapers. Follow the appropriate model and insert the words "Letter to the editor" in brackets before the name of the periodical.

```
Carter, R. (2000). New York, New York [Letter to
    the editor]. Scientific American, 238(1), 8.
```

■ **12. REVIEW**   Reviews of books and other media appear in a variety of periodicals. Follow the appropriate model for the periodical. For a book, give the title of the review (if there is one), followed by the words "Review of the book" and the title of the book in brackets.

```
Gleick, E. (2000, December 14). The burdens of
    genius [Review of the book The Last Samurai].
    Time, 156, 171.
```

For a film review, write "Review of the motion picture," and for a TV review, write "Review of the television program." Treat other media in a similar way.

Books

In addition to consulting the items in this section, you may need to turn to other models. See items 1–6 for general guidelines on listing authors.

■ **13. BASIC FORMAT FOR A BOOK**   Begin with the author's name followed by the date and the book's title. End with the place of publication and the name of the publisher.

```
Bernstein, N. (2001). The lost children of Wilder:
    The epic struggle to change foster care. New
    York: Pantheon.
```

■ **14. EDITORS**   For a book with an editor but no author, begin with the name of the editor (or editors) followed by the abbreviation "Ed." (or "Eds." for more than one editor) in parentheses.

```
Duncan, G. J., & Brooks-Gunn, J. (Eds.). (1997).
    Consequences of growing up poor. New York:
    Russell Sage Foundation.
```

For a book with an author and an editor, begin with the author's name. Give the editor's name in parentheses after the title of the book, followed by the abbreviation "Ed." (or "Eds.").

```
Plath, S. (2000). The unabridged journals
    (K. V. Kukil, Ed.). New York: Anchor.
```

■ **15. TRANSLATION**   After the title, name the translator, followed by the abbreviation "Trans.," in parentheses. Add the original date of the work's publication in parentheses at the end of the entry.

```
Singer, I. B. (1998). Shadows on the Hudson
    (J. Sherman, Trans.). New York: Farrar, Straus
    and Giroux. (Original work published 1957)
```

■ **16. EDITION OTHER THAN THE FIRST**   Include the number of the edition in parentheses after the title.

```
Helfer, M. E., Keme, R. S., & Drugman, R. D.
    (1997). The battered child (5th ed.). Chicago:
    University of Chicago Press.
```

■ **17. ARTICLE OR CHAPTER IN AN EDITED BOOK** Begin with the author, the year of publication, and the title of the article or chapter. Then write "In" and give the editor's name, followed by "Ed." in parentheses; the title of the book; and the page numbers of the article or chapter in parentheses. End with the book's publication information.

```
Luban, D. (2000). The ethics of wrongful obedience.
     In D. L. Rhode (Ed.), Ethics in practice:
     Lawyers' roles, responsibilities, and regula-
     tion (pp. 94-120). New York: Oxford University
     Press.
```

■ **18. MULTIVOLUME WORK** Give the number of volumes after the title.

```
Wiener, P. (Ed.). (1973). Dictionary of the history
     of ideas (Vols. 1-4). New York: Scribner's.
```

Electronic sources

The following guidelines for electronic sources are based on the 5th edition of the *Publication Manual of the American Psychological Association* (2001). Any updates will be posted on the APA Web site, <http://www.apastyle.org>.

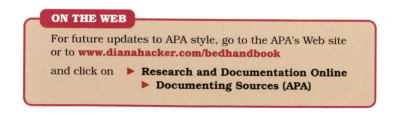

ON THE WEB

For future updates to APA style, go to the APA's Web site or to **www.dianahacker.com/bedhandbook**

and click on ▶ **Research and Documentation Online**
               ▶ **Documenting Sources (APA)**

■ **19. ARTICLE FROM AN ONLINE PERIODICAL** When citing online articles, follow the guidelines for printed articles (see items 7–12), giving whatever information is available in the online source. If the article also appears in a printed journal, a URL is not required; instead, include "Electronic version" in brackets after the title of the article.

```
Williams, S. L., Brakke, K. E., & Savage-Rumbaugh,
     E. S. (1977). Comprehension skills of
     language-competent and nonlanguage-competent
     apes [Electronic version]. Language and
     Communication, 17(4), 301-317.
```

If there is no print version, include the date you accessed the source and the article's URL.

```
Ashe, D. D., & McCutcheon, L. E. (2001). Shyness,
     loneliness, and attitude toward celebrities,
     Current Research in Social Psychology,
     6(9). Retrieved July 3, 2001,
     from http://www.uiowa.edu/~grpproc/crisp/
     crisp.6.9.htm
```

NOTE: When you have retrieved an article from a newspaper's searchable Web site, give the URL for the site, not for the exact source.

```
Cary, B. (2001, June 18). Mentors of the mind. Los
     Angeles Times. Retrieved July 5, 2001, from
     http://www.latimes.com
```

■ **20. ARTICLE FROM A DATABASE** Libraries pay for access to electronic databases such as *PsycINFO* and *JSTOR*, which are not otherwise available to the public. To cite an article from an electronic database, include the publication information from the source (see items 7–12). End the citation with your date of access, the name of the database, and the document number (if applicable).

```
Holliday, R. E., & Hayes, B. K. (2001).
        Dissociating automatic and intentional
        processes in children's eyewitness memory.
        Journal of Experimental Child Psychology,
        75(1), 1-5. Retrieved February 21, 2001, from
        Expanded Academic ASAP database (A59317972).
```

■ **21. NONPERIODICAL WEB DOCUMENT**   To cite a nonperiodical Web document, such as a report, list as many of the following elements as are available.

Author's name

Date of publication (if there is no date, use "n.d.")

Title of document (in italics)

Date you accessed the source

A URL that will take readers directly to the source

In the first model, the source has both an author and a date; in the second, the source lacks a date. If a source has no author, begin with the title.

```
Cain, A., & Burris, M. (1999, April). Investigation
        of the use of mobile phones while driving.
        Retrieved January 15, 2000, from http://
        www.cutr.eng.usf.edu/its/mobile_phone_text.htm

Archer, Z. (n.d.). Exploring nonverbal communica-
        tion. Retrieved July 18, 2001, from http://
        zzyx.ucsc.edu/~archer
```

NOTE: If you retrieved the source from a university program's Web site, name the program in your retrieval statement.

> Cosmides, L., & Tooby, J. (1997). *Evolutionary psychology: A primer.* Retrieved July 5, 2001, from the University of California, Santa Barbara, Center for Evolutionary Psychology Web site: http://www.psych.ucsb.edu/research/cep/primer.html

■ **22. CHAPTER OR SECTION IN A WEB DOCUMENT**   Begin with the author, the year of publication, and the title of the chapter or section. Then write "In" and give the title of the document, followed by any identifying information in parentheses. End with your date of access and the URL for the chapter or section.

> Heuer, R. J., Jr. (1999). Keeping an open mind. In *Psychology of intelligence analysis* (chap. 6). Retrieved July 7, 2001, from http://www.cia.gov/csi/books/19104/art9.html

■ **23. E-MAIL**   E-mail messages are personal communications and are not included in the list of references.

■ **24. ONLINE POSTING**   If an online posting cannot be retrieved (because the newsgroup or forum does not maintain archives), cite it as a personal communication in the text of your paper and do not include it in the list of references. If the posting can be retrieved from an archive, treat it as follows, giving as much information as is available.

> Eaton, S. (2001, June 12). Online transactions [Msg 2]. Message posted to news://sci.psychology.psychotherapy.moderated

APA documentation

■ **25. COMPUTER PROGRAM**   Add the words "Computer soft-ware" in brackets after the title of the program.

> Kaufmann, W. J., III, & Comins, N. F. (1998). Dis-
> covering the universe (Version 4.1) [Computer
> software]. New York: Freeman.

Other sources

■ **26. DISSERTATION ABSTRACT**

> Hu, X. (1996). Consumption and social inequality in
> urban Guangdong, China (Doctoral dissertation,
> University of Hawaii, 1996). *Dissertation*
> *Abstracts International, 57,* 3280A.

■ **27. GOVERNMENT DOCUMENT**

> U.S. Census Bureau. (2000). *Statistical abstract*
> *of the United States.* Washington, DC: U.S.
> Government Printing Office.

■ **28. REPORT FROM A PRIVATE ORGANIZATION**   If the publisher is the author, give the word "Author" as the publisher. If the report has an author, begin with the author's name, and name the publisher at the end.

> American Psychiatric Association. (2000). *Practice*
> *guidelines for the treatment of patients with*
> *eating disorders* (2nd ed.). Washington, DC:
> Author.

■ **29. CONFERENCE PROCEEDINGS**

> Schnase, J. L., & Cunnius, E. L. (Eds.). (1995).
> *Proceedings of CSCL '95: The First*

```
International Conference on Computer Support
    for Collaborative Learning. Mahwah, NJ:
    Erlbaum.
```

■ **30. MOTION PICTURE** To cite a motion picture in any format (film, video, or DVD), list the director and the producer (if available) and the year of the picture's release. Give the title, followed by "Motion picture" in brackets, the country where it was made, and the name of the studio. If the motion picture is difficult to find, include instead the name and address of its distributor.

```
Soderbergh, S. (Director). (2000). Traffic [Motion
    picture]. United States: Gramercy Pictures.
```

```
Donohew, P. (Producer/Director). (1999). Seven
    sisters: A Kentucky portrait [Motion picture].
    (Available from Sour Mash Films, 55 Cumberland
    Street, San Francisco, CA 94110)
```

59e APA manuscript format

The American Psychological Association makes a number of recommendations for formatting a paper and preparing a list of references. The following guidelines are consistent with advice given in the *Publication Manual of the American Psychological Association,* 5th ed. (Washington: APA, 2001).

Formatting the paper

APA guidelines for formatting a paper are endorsed by many instructors in the social sciences.

MATERIALS AND TYPEFACE Use good-quality 8½″ × 11″ white paper. Avoid a typeface that is unusual or hard to read.

TITLE PAGE The APA manual does not provide guidelines for preparing the title page of a college paper, but most instructors will want you to include one. See page 716 for an example.

PAGE NUMBERS AND RUNNING HEAD In the upper right-hand corner of each page, type a short version of your title, followed by five spaces and the page number. Number all pages, including the title page.

MARGINS, LINE SPACING, AND PARAGRAPH INDENTS Use margins of one inch on all sides of the page. Do not justify (align) the right margin.

Double-space throughout the paper, and indent the first line of each paragraph one-half inch (or five spaces).

LONG QUOTATIONS When a quotation is longer than forty words, set it off from the text by indenting it one-half inch (or five spaces) from the left margin. Double-space the quotation. Quotation marks are not needed when a quotation has been set off from the text. See page 722 for an example.

ABSTRACT If your instructor requires one, include an abstract immediately after the title page. Center the word Abstract one inch from the top of the page; double-space the abstract as you do the body of your paper.

An abstract is a 75-to-100-word paragraph that provides readers with a quick overview of your essay. It should express your main idea and your key points; it might also briefly suggest any implications or applications of the research you discuss in the paper.

HEADINGS Although headings are not always necessary, their use is encouraged in the social sciences. For most undergraduate papers, one or two levels of headings will usually be sufficient.

In APA style, major headings are centered and second-level headings are placed flush left and italicized. Capitalize the first word of the heading, along with all important words. Do not capitalize minor words—articles, short prepositions, and coordinating conjunctions—unless they are the first word.

VISUALS The APA classifies visuals as tables and figures (figures include graphs, charts, drawings, and photographs). Keep visuals as simple as possible. Label each table with an arabic numeral (Table 1, Table 2, and so on) and provide a clear title that identifies the subject. The label and title should appear on separate lines above the table, flush left. Below the table, give its source in a note like this one:

Note. From "Innovation Roles: From Souls of Fire to Devil's Advocates," by Marcy Meyer, 2000, *The Journal of Business Communication, 37,* p. 338.

For each figure, place a label and a caption below the figure, flush left. They need not appear on separate lines.

In the text of your paper, discuss the most significant features of each visual. Place the visual as close as possible to the sentences that relate to them unless your instructor prefers them in an appendix.

Preparing the list of references

Begin your list of references on a new page at the end of the paper. Center the title References about one inch from the top of the page. Double-space throughout. For a sample reference list, see pages 725–26.

INDENTING ENTRIES APA recommends using hanging indents, which highlight the authors' names and thus make it easy for readers to scan through the alphabetized list of references. To create a hanging indent, type the first line of an entry flush left and indent any additional lines one-half inch (or five spaces), as shown here.

```
Stoessinger, J. G. (1998). Why nations go to war
      (7th ed.). New York: St. Martin's Press.
```

Some instructors may prefer a paragraph-style indent, as in the following example.

```
      Stoessinger, J. G. (1998). Why nations go to
war (7th ed.). New York: St. Martin's Press.
```

ALPHABETIZING THE LIST   Alphabetize the reference list by the last names of the authors (or editors); when a work has no author or editor, alphabetize by the first word of the title other than *A, An,* or *The.*

If your list includes two or more works by the same author, arrange the entries by year, the earliest first. If your list includes two or more works by the same author in the same year, arrange them alphabetically by title. Add the lowercase letters "a," "b," and so on within the parentheses immediately following the year (see p. 702 for examples).

AUTHORS' NAMES   Invert all authors' names and use initials instead of first names. With two or more authors, use an ampersand (&) between the names. Separate the names with commas. Include names for the first six authors; if there are additional authors, end the list with "et al." (Latin for "and others") to indicate that there are others (see also p. 701).

TITLES OF BOOKS AND ARTICLES   Italicize the titles and subtitles of books; capitalize only the first word of the title and subtitle (and all proper nouns). Capitalize names of periodicals as you would capitalize them normally (see section 45).

ABBREVIATIONS FOR PAGE NUMBERS Abbreviations for "page" and "pages" ("p." and "pp.") are used before page numbers of newspaper articles and articles in edited books (see pp. 703–04 and 706) but not before page numbers of articles appearing in magazines and scholarly journals (see p. 703).

NOTE: The sample reference page (see p. 725) shows how to type your list of references.

BREAKING A URL When a URL must be divided, break it after a slash or before a period. Do not insert a hyphen.

For information about the exact format of each entry in your list, consult the models on pages 699–711.

59f Sample research paper: APA style

On the following pages is a research paper written by Karen Shaw, a student in a psychology class. Shaw's assignment was to write a "review of the literature" paper documented with APA-style citations and references.

In preparing her final manuscript, Shaw followed the APA guidelines. She did not include an abstract because her instructor did not require one.

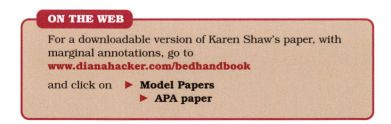

ON THE WEB

For a downloadable version of Karen Shaw's paper, with marginal annotations, go to
www.dianahacker.com/bedhandbook

and click on ▶ **Model Papers**
▶ **APA paper**

Short title and page number for student papers.

Full title, writer's name, name and section number of course, instructor's name, and date (all centered).

Apes and Language:

A Review of the Literature

Karen Shaw

Psychology 110, Section 2

Professor Verdi

March 2, 2001

Apes and Language:
A Review of the Literature

Over the past thirty years, researchers have demonstrated that the great apes (chimpanzees, gorillas, and orangutans) resemble humans in language abilities more than had been thought possible. Just how far that resemblance extends, however, has been a matter of some controversy. Researchers agree that the apes have acquired fairly large vocabularies in American Sign Language and in artificial languages, but they have drawn quite different conclusions in addressing the following questions:

1. How spontaneously have apes used language?
2. How creatively have apes used language?
3. Can apes create sentences?
4. What are the implications of the ape language studies?

This review of the literature on apes and language focuses on these four questions.

How Spontaneously Have
Apes Used Language?

In an influential article, Terrace, Petitto, Sanders, and Bever (1979) argued that the apes in language experiments were not using language spontaneously but were merely imitating their trainers, responding to conscious or unconscious cues. Terrace and his colleagues at Columbia University had

Full title, centered.

The writer sets up her organization in the introduction.

Headings, centered, help readers follow the organization.

A signal phrase names all four authors and gives date in parentheses.

trained a chimpanzee, Nim, in American Sign Language, so their skepticism about the apes' abilities
received much attention. In fact, funding for ape
language research was sharply reduced following
publication of their 1979 article "Can an Ape
Create a Sentence?"

In retrospect, the conclusions of Terrace et
al. seem to have been premature. Although some
early ape language studies had not been rigorously
controlled to eliminate cuing, even as early as the
1970s R. A. Gardner and B. T. Gardner were conducting double-blind experiments that prevented any pos-
sibility of cuing (Fouts, 1997, p. 99). Since 1979,
researchers have diligently guarded against cuing.

Perhaps the best evidence that apes are not
merely responding to cues is that they have signed
to one another spontaneously, without trainers
present. Like many of the apes studied, gorillas
Koko and Michael have been observed signing to one
another (Patterson & Linden, 1981). At Central
Washington University the baby chimpanzee Loulis,
placed in the care of the signing chimpanzee
Washoe, mastered nearly fifty signs in American
Sign Language without help from humans. "Interest-
ingly," wrote researcher Fouts (1997), "Loulis did
not pick up any of the seven signs that we [humans]
used around him. He learned only from Washoe and
[another chimp] Ally" (p. 244).

Because the author (Fouts) is not named in the signal phrase, his name and the date appear in parentheses, along with the page number.

An ampersand links the names of two authors in parentheses.

Brackets are used to indicate words not in original source.

A page number is required for a quotation.

The extent to which chimpanzees spontaneously use language may depend on their training. Terrace trained Nim using the behaviorist technique of operant conditioning, so it is not surprising that many of Nim's signs were cued. Many other researchers have used a conversational approach that parallels the process by which human children acquire language. In an experimental study, O'Sullivan and Yeager (1989) contrasted the two techniques, using Terrace's Nim as their subject. They found that Nim's use of language was significantly more spontaneous under conversational conditions.

The word "and" links the names of two authors in the signal phrase.

How Creatively Have
Apes Used Language?

There is considerable evidence that apes have invented creative names. One of the earliest and most controversial examples involved the Gardners' chimpanzee Washoe. Washoe, who knew signs for "water" and "bird," once signed "water bird" when in the presence of a swan. Terrace et al. (1979) suggested that there was "no basis for concluding that Washoe was characterizing the swan as a 'bird that inhabits water.'" Washoe may simply have been "identifying correctly a body of water and a bird, in that order" (p. 895).

When this article was first cited, all four authors were named. In subsequent citations of a work with three to five authors, "et al." is used after the first author's name.

Other examples are not so easily explained away. The bonobo Kanzi has requested particular films by combining symbols on a computer in a

APA papers

creative way. For instance, to ask for *Quest for Fire*, a film about early primates discovering fire, Kanzi began to use symbols for "campfire" and "TV" (Eckholm, 1985). The gorilla Koko, who learned American Sign Language, has a long list of creative names to her credit: "elephant baby" to describe a Pinocchio doll, "finger bracelet" to describe a ring, "bottle match" to describe a cigarette lighter, and so on (Patterson & Linden, 1981, p. 146). If Terrace's analysis of the "water bird" example is applied to the examples just mentioned, it does not hold. Surely Koko did not first see an elephant and then a baby before signing "elephant baby"--or a bottle and a match before signing "bottle match."

The writer interprets the evidence; she doesn't just report it.

Can Apes Create Sentences?

The early ape language studies offered little proof that apes could combine symbols into grammatically ordered sentences. Apes strung together various signs, but the sequences were often random and repetitive. Nim's series of sixteen signs is a case in point: "give orange me give eat orange me eat orange give me eat orange give me you" (Terrace et al., 1979, p. 895).

More recent studies with bonobos at the Language Research Center in Atlanta have broken new ground. Kanzi, a bonobo trained by Savage-Rumbaugh, seems to understand simple grammatical rules about

Apes and Language   6

word order. For instance, Kanzi learned that in
two-word utterances action precedes object, an
ordering also used by human children at the two-
word stage. In a major article reporting on their
research, Greenfield and Savage-Rumbaugh (1990)
wrote that Kanzi rarely "repeated himself or formed
combinations that were semantically unrelated"
(p. 556).

> The writer draws attention to an important article.

More important, Kanzi began on his own to create certain patterns that may not exist in English
but can be found among deaf children and in other
human languages. For example, Kanzi used his own
rules when combining action symbols. Symbols that
involved an invitation to play, such as "chase,"
would appear first; symbols that indicated what was
to be done during play ("hide") would appear second. Kanzi also created his own rules when combining gestures and symbols. He would use the symbol
first and then gesture, a practice often followed
by young deaf children (Greenfield & Savage-
Rumbaugh, 1990, p. 560).

In a later study, Kanzi's abilities to understand spoken language were shown to be similar to
those of a 2-1/2-year-old human, Alia. Rumbaugh
(1995) reported that "Kanzi's comprehension of over
600 novel sentences of request was very comparable
to Alia's; both complied with the requests without
assistance on approximately 70% of the sentences"

> The writer gives a page number for this sum-mary because the article is long.

(p. 722). A recent monograph provided examples of
the kinds of sentences both Kanzi and Alia were
able to understand:

A quotation
longer than
40 words is set
off from the
text. Quotation
marks are not
used.

> For example, the word *ball* occurred in 76 dif-
> ferent sentences, including such different re-
> quests as "Put the leaves in your ball," "Show
> me the ball that's on TV," "Vacuum your ball,"
> and "Go do ball slapping with Liz." Overall,
> 144 different content words, many of which
> were presented in ways that required syntactic
> parsing for a proper response (such as "Knife
> your ball" vs. "Put the knife in the hat"),
> were utilized in the study. (Savage-Rumbaugh
> et al., 2000, pp. 101-102)

The researchers concluded that neither Kanzi nor
Alia could have demonstrated understanding of
such requests without comprehending syntactical
relationships among the words in a sentence.

What Are the Implications of the Ape Language Studies?

Kanzi's linguistic abilities are so impressive
that they may help us understand how humans came
to acquire language. Pointing out that 99% of our
genetic material is held in common with the chimpanzees, Greenfield and Savage-Rumbaugh (1990) have
suggested that something of the "evolutionary root
of human language" can be found in the "linguistic
abilities of the great apes" (p. 540). Noting that

apes' brains are similar to those of our human ancestors, Leakey and Lewin (1992) argued that in ape brains "the cognitive foundations on which human language could be built are already present" (p. 244).

The suggestion that there is a continuity in the linguistic abilities of apes and humans has created much controversy. Linguist Noam Chomsky has strongly asserted that language is a unique human characteristic (Booth, 1990). Terrace has continued to be skeptical of the claims made for the apes, as have Petitto and Bever, coauthors of the 1979 article that caused such skepticism earlier (Gibbons, 1991).

> The writer presents a balanced view of the philosophical controversy.

Recently, neurobiologists have made discoveries that may cause even the skeptics to take notice. Ongoing studies at the Yerkes Primate Research Center have revealed remarkable similarities in the brains of chimpanzees and humans. Through brain scans of live chimpanzees, researchers have found that, as with humans, "the language-controlling PT [*planum temporale*] is larger on the left side of the chimps' brain than on the right. But it is not lateralized in monkeys, which are less closely related to humans than apes are" (Begley, 1998, p. 57).

Although the ape language studies continue to generate controversy, researchers have shown over

APA papers

Apes and Language   9

The tone of the
conclusion is
objective.

the past thirty years that the gap between the linguistic abilities of apes and humans is far less dramatic than was once believed.

References

Begley, S. (1998, January 19). Aping language.
     Newsweek, 131, 56-58.

Booth, W. (1990, October 29). Monkeying with lan-
     guage: Is chimp using words or merely aping
     handlers? *The Washington Post,* p. A3.

Eckholm, E. (1985, June 25). Kanzi the chimp: A
     life in science. *The New York Times,* pp. C1,
     C3.

Fouts, R. (1997). *Next of kin: What chimpanzees
     have taught me about who we are.* New York:
     William Morrow.

Gibbons, A. (1991). Déjà vu all over again: Chimp-
     language wars. *Science, 251,* 1561-1562.

Greenfield, P. M., & Savage-Rumbaugh, E. S. (1990).
     Grammatical combination in *Pan paniscus:*
     Processes of learning and invention in the
     evolution and development of language. In
     S. T. Parker & K. R. Gibson (Eds.), *"Language"
     and intelligence in monkeys and apes: Compara-
     tive developmental perspectives* (pp. 540-578).
     Cambridge: Cambridge University Press.

Leakey, R., & Lewin, R. (1992). *Origins reconsid-
     ered: In search of what makes us human.* New
     York: Doubleday.

O'Sullivan, C., & Yeager, C. P. (1989). Communica-
     tive context and linguistic competence: The

List of refer-
ences begins on
a new page.
Heading is
centered.

List is alphabet-
ized by authors'
names.

The first line of
an entry is at
the left margin;
subsequent
lines indent ½"
(or five spaces).

Double-spacing
is used
throughout.

effect of social setting on a chimpanzee's
conversational skill. In R. A. Gardner, B. T.
Gardner, & T. E. Van Cantfort (Eds.), *Teaching
sign language to chimpanzees* (pp. 269-279).
Albany: SUNY Press.

Patterson, F., & Linden, E. (1981). *The education
of Koko*. New York: Holt, Rinehart & Winston.

Rumbaugh, D. (1995). Primate language and cogni-
tion: Common ground. *Social Research, 62,*
711-730.

Savage-Rumbaugh, E. S., Murphy, J. S., Sevcik,
R. A., Brakke, K. E., Williams, S. L.,
Rumbaugh, D. M., et al. (2000). *Language
comprehension in ape and child: Monograph.*
Atlanta, GA: The Language Research Center.
Retrieved January 6, 2000, from the Language
Research Center Web site: http://www.gsu.edu/
~wwwlrc/monograph.html

Terrace, H. S., Petitto, L. A., Sanders, R. J.,
& Bever, T. G. (1979). Can an ape create a
sentence? *Science, 206,* 891-902.

WRITING *CHICAGO* PAPERS

60

Chicago papers

Most assignments in history and other humanities classes are based to some extent on reading. At times you will be asked to respond to one or two readings, such as essays or historical documents. At other times you may be asked to write a research paper that draws on a wide variety of sources.

Most history instructors and some humanities instructors require you to document sources with footnotes or endnotes based on *The Chicago Manual of Style,* 14th ed. (Chicago: U of Chicago P, 1993). (See 60d.) When you write a paper using sources, you face three main challenges in addition to documenting your sources: (1) supporting a thesis, (2) citing your sources and avoiding plagiarism, and (3) integrating quotations and other source material.

60a Supporting a thesis

Most assignments ask you to form a thesis, or main idea, and to support that thesis with well-organized evidence.

Finding a thesis

A thesis is a one-sentence (or occasionally a two-sentence) statement of your central idea. Usually your thesis will appear at the end of the first paragraph (as in the example on p. 760), but if you need to provide readers with considerable background information, you may place it in the second paragraph.

Although the thesis appears early in your paper, do not attempt to write it until fairly late in your reading and writing process. Early in the process, you can keep your mind open—yet focused—by posing questions. The thesis that you articulate later in the process will be a reasoned answer to the central question you pose, as in the following example.

RESEARCH QUESTION
To what extent was Confederate Major General Nathan Bedford Forrest responsible for the massacre of Union troops at Fort Pillow?

POSSIBLE THESIS
Although we will never know whether Nathan Bedford Forrest directly ordered the massacre of Union troops at Fort Pillow, evidence suggests that he was responsible for it.

Notice that the thesis expresses a view on a debatable issue—an issue about which intelligent, well-meaning people might disagree. The writer's job is to convince such readers that this view is worth taking seriously.

Organizing your evidence

The body of your paper will consist of evidence in support of your thesis. Instead of getting tangled up in a complex, formal outline, sketch an informal plan that organizes your evidence in bold strokes. The student who wrote about Fort Pillow used a simple list of questions as the blueprint for his paper. In the paper itself, these became headings that helped readers follow the writer's line of argument.

> What happened at Fort Pillow?
>
> Did Forrest order the massacre?
>
> Can Forrest be held responsible for the massacre?

60b Citing sources; avoiding plagiarism

In a research paper, you will be drawing on the work of other writers, and you must document their contributions by citing your sources. Sources are cited for two reasons:

1. to tell readers where your information comes from — so that they can assess its reliability and, if interested, find and read the original source
2. to give credit to the writers from whom you have borrowed words and ideas

To borrow another writer's language or ideas without proper acknowledgment is a form of dishonesty known as *plagiarism.*

Citing sources

Citations are required when you quote from a source, when you summarize or paraphrase a source, and when you borrow facts and ideas (except for common knowledge). (See also the next section, "Avoiding plagiarism.")

Chicago citations consist of numbered notes in the text of the paper that refer readers to notes with corresponding numbers either at the foot of the page (footnotes) or at the end of the paper (endnotes).

TEXT

```
Governor John Andrew was not allowed to recruit
black soldiers from out of state. "Ostensibly,"
writes Peter Burchard, "no recruiting was done out-
side Massachusetts, but it was an open secret that
Andrew's agents were working far and wide."[1]
```

NOTE

```
    1. Peter Burchard, One Gallant Rush: Robert
Gould Shaw and His Brave Black Regiment (New York:
St. Martin's Press, 1965), 85.
```

For detailed advice on using *Chicago*-style notes, see 60d. When you use footnotes or endnotes, you will usually need to provide a bibliography as well (see p. 741).

Avoiding plagiarism

Your research paper is a collaboration between you and your sources. To be fair and ethical, you must acknowledge your debt to the writers of these sources. If you don't, you are guilty of plagiarism, a serious academic offense.

Three different acts are considered plagiarism: (1) failing to cite quotations and borrowed ideas, (2) failing to enclose borrowed language in quotation marks, and (3) failing to put summaries and paraphrases in your own words.

CITING QUOTATIONS AND BORROWED IDEAS You must of course cite the source of all direct quotations. You must also cite any ideas borrowed from a source: paraphrases of sentences, summaries of paragraphs or chapters, statistics and little-known facts, and tables, graphs, or diagrams.

The only exception is common knowledge — information that your readers could find in any number of general sources because it is commonly known. For example, the current population of the United States is common knowledge in such fields as sociology and economics; the date of the Emancipation Proclamation is common knowledge in the fields of history and political science.

As a rule, when you have seen certain information repeatedly in your reading, you don't need to cite it. However, when information has appeared in only one or two sources or when it is controversial, you should cite it. If a topic is new to you and you are not sure what is considered common knowledge or what is a matter of controversy, ask someone with expertise. When in doubt, cite the source.

ENCLOSING BORROWED LANGUAGE IN QUOTATION MARKS To indicate that you are using a source's exact phrases or sentences, you must enclose them in quotation marks. To omit the quotation marks is to claim — falsely — that the language is your own. Such an omission is plagiarism even if you have cited the source.

ORIGINAL SOURCE
For many Southerners it was psychologically impossible to see a black man bearing arms as anything but an incipient slave uprising complete with arson, murder, pillage, and rapine.
— Dudley Taylor Cornish, *The Sable Arm: Negro Troops in the Union Army, 1861–1865,* p. 158

PLAGIARISM
```
According to Civil War historian Dudley Taylor
Cornish, for many Southerners it was psychologi-
cally impossible to see a black man bearing arms as
```

```
anything but an incipient slave uprising complete
with arson, murder, pillage, and rapine.²
```

BORROWED LANGUAGE IN QUOTATION MARKS

```
According to Civil War historian Dudley Taylor
Cornish, "For many Southerners it was psychologi-
cally impossible to see a black man bearing arms as
anything but an incipient slave uprising complete
with arson, murder, pillage, and rapine."²
```

NOTE: When quoted sentences are set off from the text by indenting, quotation marks are not needed (see pp. 737–38).

PUTTING SUMMARIES AND PARAPHRASES IN YOUR OWN WORDS
When you summarize or paraphrase, you must restate the source's meaning using your own language. In the following example, the paraphrase is plagiarized—even though the source is cited—because too much of its language is borrowed from the source without quotation marks. The underlined phrases have been copied word-for-word. In addition, the writer has closely followed the sentence structure of the original source, merely plugging in some synonyms (such as *fifty percent* for *half* and *savage hatred* for *fierce, bitter animosity*).

ORIGINAL SOURCE
Half of the force holding Fort Pillow were Negroes, former slaves now enrolled in the Union Army. Toward them Forrest's troops had the fierce, bitter animosity of men who had been educated to regard the colored race as inferior and who for the first time had encountered that race armed and fighting against white men. The sight enraged and perhaps terrified many of the Confederates and aroused in them the ugly spirit of a lynching mob.

—Albert Castel, "The Fort Pillow Massacre,"
pp. 46–47

PLAGIARISM: UNACCEPTABLE BORROWING

Albert Castel suggests that much of the brutality at Fort Pillow can be traced to racial attitudes. Fifty percent of the troops <u>holding Fort Pillow were Negroes, former slaves</u> who had joined the Union Army. <u>Toward them Forrest's</u> soldiers displayed the savage hatred <u>of men who had been</u> taught the inferiority of blacks <u>and who for the first time had</u> confronted them <u>armed and fighting against white men</u>. The vision angered and perhaps frightened the Confederates <u>and aroused in them the ugly spirit of a lynching mob</u>.³

To avoid plagiarizing an author's language, set the source aside, write from memory, and consult the source later to check for accuracy. This strategy prevents you from being captivated by the words on the page.

ACCEPTABLE PARAPHRASE

Albert Castel suggests that much of the brutality at Fort Pillow can be traced to racial attitudes. Nearly half of the Union troops were blacks, men whom the Confederates had been raised to consider their inferiors. The shock and perhaps fear of facing armed ex-slaves in battle for the first time may well have unleashed the fury that led to the massacre.³

60c Integrating sources

When using the *Chicago* style of documentation, use the present tense or present perfect tense in phrases that introduce quotations or other source materials from nonfiction

Chicago *papers*

sources: *Foote points out that* or *Foote has pointed out that* (not *Foote pointed out that*). If you have good reason to emphasize that the author's language or opinion was articulated in the past, however, the past tense is acceptable.

The first time you mention an author, use the full name: *Shelby Foote argues....*When you refer to the author again, you may use the last name only: *Foote raises an important question.*

Integrating quotations

Readers should be able to move from your own words to the words you quote from a source without feeling a jolt.

USING SIGNAL PHRASES   Avoid dropping quotations into the text without warning. Instead, provide clear signal phrases, usually including the author's name, to prepare readers for the source.

DROPPED QUOTATION

Not surprisingly, those testifying on the Union and Confederate sides recalled events at Fort Pillow quite differently. Unionists claimed that their troops had abandoned their arms and were in full retreat. "The Confederates, however, all agreed that the Union troops retreated to the river with arms in their hands."[4]

QUOTATION WITH SIGNAL PHRASE

Not surprisingly, those testifying on the Union and Confederate sides recalled events at Fort Pillow quite differently. Unionists claimed that their troops had abandoned their arms and were in full retreat. "The Confederates, however," writes histo-

Varying signal phrases in Chicago papers

MODEL SIGNAL PHRASES

In the words of historian James M. McPherson, ". . ."

As Dudley Taylor Cornish has argued, ". . ."

In a letter to his wife, a Confederate soldier who witnessed the massacre wrote that ". . ."

". . . ," claims Benjamin Quarles.

". . . ," writes Albert Castel, ". . ."

Shelby Foote offers an intriguing interpretation of these events:

VERBS IN SIGNAL PHRASES

admits	compares	insists	rejects
agrees	confirms	notes	reports
argues	contends	observes	responds
asserts	declares	points out	suggests
believes	denies	reasons	thinks
claims	emphasizes	refutes	writes

rian Albert Castel, "all agreed that the Union troops retreated to the river with arms in their hands."[4]

To avoid monotony, try to vary both the language and the placement of your signal phrases. The models in the chart above suggest a range of possibilities.

When the signal phrase includes a verb, choose one that is appropriate in the context. Is your source arguing a point, making an observation, reporting a fact, refuting an argument, or stating a belief? By choosing an appropriate verb, you can make your source's stance clear. See the chart above for a list of verbs commonly used in signal phrases.

It is not always necessary to quote full sentences from a source. At times you may wish to borrow only a phrase or to weave part of a source's sentence into your own sentence structure.

> As Hurst has pointed out, until there was "an out-
> cry in the northern press," even the Confederates
> did not deny that there had been a massacre at Fort
> Pillow.[5]

> Union surgeon Dr. Charles Fitch testified that
> after being taken prisoner by Forrest he saw
> Southern soldiers "kill every Negro who made his
> appearance in Federal uniform."[6]

USING THE ELLIPSIS MARK   To condense a quoted passage, you can use the ellipsis mark (three periods, with spaces between) to indicate that you have omitted words. The sentence that remains must be grammatically complete.

> Union surgeon Fitch's testimony that all women and
> children had been evacuated from Fort Pillow before
> the attack conflicts with Forrest's report: "We
> captured . . . about 40 negro women and children."[7]

The writer has omitted several words not relevant to the issue at hand: *164 Federals, 75 negro troops, and.*

When you want to omit a full sentence or more, use a period before the three ellipsis dots. For an example, see the long quotation on pages 737–38.

Ordinarily, do not use the ellipsis mark at the beginning or at the end of a quotation. Readers will understand that the quoted material is taken from a longer passage.

USING BRACKETS   Brackets allow you to insert words of
your own into quoted material, perhaps to explain a confusing reference or to keep a sentence grammatical in your context.

> According to Albert Castel, "It can be reasonably
> argued that he [Forrest] was justified in believing
> that the approaching steamships intended to aid the
> garrison [at Fort Pillow]."[8]

NOTE: Use [sic] to indicate that an error in a quoted sentence
appears in the original source. (An example appears at the
top of p. 738.) However, if a source is filled with errors, as is
the case with many historical documents, this use of [sic]
can become distracting and is best avoided.

SETTING OFF LONG QUOTATIONS   *Chicago* style allows you
some leeway in deciding whether to set off a quotation or
run it into your text. For emphasis you may want to set off a
quotation of more than four or five lines of text; almost certainly you should set off quotations of ten lines or more. To set
off a quotation, indent it one-half inch (or five spaces) from
the left margin and use the normal right margin. Double-space the indented quotation.

Long quotations should be introduced by an informative
sentence, usually followed by a colon. Quotation marks are
unnecessary because the indented format tells readers that
the words are taken directly from the source.

> In a letter home, Confederate officer Achilles
> V. Clark recounted what happened at Fort Pillow:
>> Words cannot describe the scene. The poor
>> deluded negroes would run up to our men fall
>> upon their knees and with uplifted hands

```
scream for mercy but they were ordered to
their feet and then shot down. The whitte
[sic] men fared but little better. . . . I
with several others tried to stop the butcher-
ing and at one time had partially succeeded,
but Gen. Forrest ordered them shot down like
dogs, and the carnage continued.9
```

Integrating summaries and paraphrases

Summaries and paraphrases are written in your own words. A summary condenses information from a source; a paraphrase reports the information in about the same number of words. As with quotations, you should introduce most summaries and paraphrases with a signal phrase that mentions the author and places the material in context. Readers will then understand that everything between the signal phrase and the numbered note summarizes or paraphrases the cited source.

Without the signal phrase (underlined) in the following example, readers might think that only the last sentence is being cited, when in fact the whole paragraph is based on the source.

```
According to Kenneth Davis, official Confederate
policy was that black soldiers were to be treated
as runaway slaves; in addition, the Confederate
Congress decreed that white Union officers command-
ing black troops be killed. Confederate Lieutenant
General Kirby Smith of Mississippi boldly announced
that he would kill all captured black troops.
Smith's policy never met with strong opposition
from the Richmond government.10
```

Integrating statistics and other facts

When you are citing a statistic or other specific fact, a signal phrase is often not necessary. In most cases, readers will understand that the citation refers to the statistic or fact (not the whole paragraph).

> Of the 295 white troops garrisoned at Fort Pillow, 168 were taken prisoner. Black troops fared much worse, with only 58 of 262 men being taken into custody and most of the rest presumably killed or badly wounded.[11]

There is nothing wrong, however, with using a signal phrase.

> Shelby Foote notes that of the 295 white troops garrisoned at Fort Pillow, 168 were taken prisoner but that black troops fared much worse, with only 58 of 262 men being taken into custody and most of the rest presumably killed or badly wounded.[11]

60d *Chicago* documentation style (footnotes or endnotes)

Professors in history and some humanities courses often require footnotes or endnotes based on *The Chicago Manual of Style*. When you use *Chicago*-style notes, you will usually be asked to include a bibliography at the end of your paper (see p. 763).

TEXT

> A Union soldier, Jacob Thomas, claimed to have seen Forrest order the killing, but when asked to

describe the six-foot-two general, he called him "a little bit of a man."[12]

FOOTNOTE OR ENDNOTE

12. Brian Steel Wills, <u>A Battle from the Start: The Life of Nathan Bedford Forrest</u> (New York: HarperCollins, 1992), 187.

BIBLIOGRAPHY ENTRY

Wills, Brian Steel. <u>A Battle from the Start: The Life of Nathan Bedford Forrest</u>. New York: HarperCollins, 1992.

First and subsequent references to a source

The first time you cite a source, the note should include publishing information for that work as well as the page number on which the passage being cited may be found.

1. Peter Burchard, <u>One Gallant Rush: Robert Gould Shaw and His Brave Black Regiment</u> (New York: St. Martin's Press, 1965), 85.

For subsequent references to a source you have already cited, give only the author's last name, followed by a comma and the page or pages cited.

4. Burchard, 31.

If you cite more than one work by the same author, include a short form of the title in subsequent citations. A short form of the title of a book is underlined or italicized; a short form of the title of an article is put in quotation marks.

8. Burchard, <u>One Gallant Rush</u>, 31.

10. Burchard, "Civil War," 10.

NOTE: *Chicago* style no longer requires the use of "ibid." to refer to the work cited in the previous note. The Latin abbreviations "op. cit." and "loc. cit." are also no longer used.

Chicago-*style bibliography*

A bibliography, which appears at the end of your paper, lists every work you have cited in your notes; in addition, it may include works that you consulted but did not cite. For advice on constructing the list, see pages 757–58. A sample bibliography appears on page 763.

Model notes and bibliography entries

The following models are consistent with guidelines set forth in *The Chicago Manual of Style,* 14th ed. For each type of source, a model note appears first, followed by a model bibliography entry. The model note shows the format you should use when citing a source for the first time. For subsequent citations of a source, use shortened notes (as just described).

Directory to **Chicago-*style notes and* bibliography *entries***

BOOKS

1. Basic format for a book, 743
2. Two or three authors, 743
3. Four or more authors, 743
4. Unknown author, 743
(continued on next page)

Books

1. BASIC FORMAT FOR A BOOK

1. William H. Rehnquist, The Supreme Court: A History (New York: Knopf, 2001), 204.

Rehnquist, William H. The Supreme Court: A History. New York: Knopf, 2001.

2. TWO OR THREE AUTHORS

2. Lesley Adkins and Roy Adkins, The Keys of Egypt: The Obsession to Decipher Egyptian Hieroglyphs (New York: HarperCollins, 2000), 117-23.

Adkins, Lesley, and Roy Adkins. The Keys of Egypt: The Obsession to Decipher Egyptian Hieroglyphs. New York: HarperCollins, 2000.

3. FOUR OR MORE AUTHORS

3. Joan N. Burstyn et al., Preventing Violence in Schools: A Challenge to American Democracy (Mahwah, N.J.: Lawrence Erlbaum, 2001), 22.

Burstyn, Joan N., et al. Preventing Violence in Schools: A Challenge to American Democracy. Mahwah, N.J.: Lawrence Erlbaum, 2001.

4. UNKNOWN AUTHOR

4. The Men's League Handbook on Women's Suffrage (London, 1912), 23.

The Men's League Handbook on Women's Suffrage. London, 1912.

■ **5. AUTHOR'S NAME IN TITLE**

5. <u>Long Walk to Freedom: The Autobiography of Nelson Mandela</u> (Boston: Little, Brown, 1995), 435.

Mandela, Nelson. <u>Long Walk to Freedom: The Auto-biography of Nelson Mandela</u>. Boston: Little, Brown, 1995.

■ **6. EDITED WORK WITHOUT AN AUTHOR**

6. Jon Meacham, ed., <u>Voices in Our Blood: America's Best on the Civil Rights Movement</u> (New York: Random House, 2001), 312.

Meacham, Jon, ed. <u>Voices in Our Blood: America's Best on the Civil Rights Movement</u>. New York: Random House, 2001.

■ **7. EDITED WORK WITH AN AUTHOR**

7. Ted Poston, <u>A First Draft of History</u>, ed. Kathleen A. Hauke (Athens: University of Georgia Press, 2000), 46.

Poston, Ted. <u>A First Draft of History</u>. Edited by Kathleen A. Hauke. Athens: University of Georgia Press, 2000.

■ **8. TRANSLATED WORK**

8. Sergei Nikolaevich Bulgakov, <u>Philosophy of Economy: The World as Household</u>, trans. Catherine Evtuhov (New Haven: Yale University Press, 2000), 167.

Bulgakov, Sergei Nikolaevich. Philosophy of
Economy: The World as Household. Translated by
Catherine Evtuhov. New Haven: Yale University
Press, 2000.

9. EDITION OTHER THAN THE FIRST

9. Andrew F. Rolle, California: A History,
5th ed. (Wheeling, Ill.: Harlan Davidson, 1998),
243-46.

Rolle, Andrew F. California: A History. 5th ed.
Wheeling, Ill.: Harlan Davidson, 1998.

10. UNTITLED VOLUME IN A MULTIVOLUME WORK

10. New Cambridge Modern History (Cambridge:
Cambridge University Press, 1957), 1:52-53.

New Cambridge Modern History. Vol. 1. Cambridge:
Cambridge University Press, 1957.

11. TITLED VOLUME IN A MULTIVOLUME WORK

11. Horst Boog et al., The Attack on the
Soviet Union, vol. 4 of Germany and the Second
World War (Cambridge: Oxford University Press,
1998), 70-72.

Boog, Horst, et al. The Attack on the Soviet
Union. Vol. 4 of Germany and the Second
World War. Cambridge: Oxford University
Press, 1998.

■ **12. WORK IN AN ANTHOLOGY**

12. Zora Neale Hurston, "From Dust Tracks on a Road," in The Norton Book of American Autobiography, ed. Jay Parini (New York: Norton, 1999), 336.

Hurston, Zora Neale. "From Dust Tracks on a Road." In The Norton Book of American Autobiography, edited by Jay Parini, 333-43. New York: Norton, 1999.

■ **13. LETTER IN A PUBLISHED COLLECTION**

13. Bartolomeo Vanzetti to Dante Sacco, 21 August 1927, Letters of the Century: America, 1900-1999, ed. Lisa Grunwald and Stephen J. Adler (New York: Dial, 1999), 180-81.

Vanzetti, Bartolomeo. Letter to Dante Sacco, 21 August 1927. In Letters of the Century: America, 1900-1999, edited by Lisa Grunwald and Stephen J. Adler, 180-81. New York: Dial, 1999.

■ **14. WORK IN A SERIES**

14. R. Keith Schoppa, The Columbia Guide to Modern Chinese History, Columbia Guides to Asian History (New York: Columbia University Press, 2000), 256-58.

Schoppa, R. Keith. The Columbia Guide to Modern Chinese History. Columbia Guides to Asian

History. New York: Columbia University Press, 2000.

15. ENCYCLOPEDIA OR DICTIONARY ENTRY

15. <u>Encyclopaedia Britannica</u>, 15th ed., s.v. "Monroe Doctrine."

NOTE: The abbreviation "s.v." is for the Latin *sub verbo* ("under the word").

Encyclopedias and dictionaries are usually not included in the bibliography.

16. BIBLICAL REFERENCE

16. Matt. 20.4-9 Revised Standard Version.

The Bible is usually not included in the bibliography.

Articles in periodicals

For articles in periodicals, a footnote or endnote should cite an exact page number. In the bibliography entry, include the page range for the entire article.

NOTE: If you accessed an article through an online database such as *Lexis-Nexis,* see also item 26.

17. ARTICLE IN A JOURNAL PAGINATED BY VOLUME

17. Virginia Guedea, "The Process of Mexican Independence," <u>American Historical Review</u> 105 (2000): 120.

Guedea, Virginia. "The Process of Mexican Independence." <u>American Historical Review</u> 105 (2000): 116-31.

■ **18. ARTICLE IN A JOURNAL PAGINATED BY ISSUE**

18. Jonathon Zimmerman, "Ethnicity and the History Wars in the 1920s," Journal of American History 87, no. 1 (2000): 101.

Zimmerman, Jonathon. "Ethnicity and the History Wars in the 1920s." Journal of American History 87, no. 1 (2000): 92-111.

■ **19. ARTICLE IN A MAGAZINE**

19. Joy Williams, "One Acre," Harper's, February 2001, 62.

Williams, Joy. "One Acre." Harper's, February 2001, 59-65.

■ **20. ARTICLE IN A NEWSPAPER**

20. Dan Barry, "A Mill Closes, and a Hamlet Fades to Black," New York Times, 16 February 2001, sec. A.

Barry, Dan. "A Mill Closes, and a Hamlet Fades to Black." New York Times, 16 February 2001, sec. A.

■ **21. UNSIGNED ARTICLE**

21. "Radiation in Russia," U.S. News and World Report, 9 August 1993, 41.

"Radiation in Russia." U.S. News and World Report, 9 August 1993, 40-42.

■ **22. BOOK REVIEW**

      22. Nancy Gabin, review of <u>The Other</u>
<u>Feminists: Activists in the Liberal Establishment</u>,
by Susan M. Hartman, <u>Journal of Women's History</u> 12
(2000): 230.

Gabin, Nancy. Review of <u>The Other Feminists:</u>
        <u>Activists in the Liberal Establishment</u>, by
        Susan M. Hartman. <u>Journal of Women's History</u>
        12 (2000): 227-34.

Electronic sources

Although *The Chicago Manual of Style* does not include guidelines for documenting online sources, the University of Chicago Press recommends following the system developed by Andrew Harnack and Eugene Kleppinger in *Online! A Reference Guide to Using Internet Sources* (Boston: Bedford/St. Martin's, 2000). The examples of online sources given in this section are based on Harnack and Kleppinger's guidelines.

ON THE WEB

To check for possible updates to *Chicago* style, go to
www.dianahacker.com/bedhandbook

and click on ▶ **Research and Documentation Online**
                 ▶ **Documenting Sources (*Chicago*)**

■   **23. AN ENTIRE WEB SITE**   Begin with the name of the author or corporate author (if known) and the title of the site (underlined). Then give the date of publication, the site's URL (in angle brackets), and the date of access (in parentheses).

```
    23. Kevin Rayburn, The 1920s, 9 April 2000,
<http://www.louisville.edu/~kprayb01/1920s.html>
(6 March 2001).
```

```
Rayburn, Kevin. The 1920s. 9 April 2000.
    <http://www.louisville.edu/~kprayb01/
    1920s.html> (6 March 2001).
```

■ **24. SHORT DOCUMENT FROM A WEB SITE**   "Short" works are those that appear in quotation marks in *Chicago* style: articles and other documents that are not book length. (For online books, see item 25.)

When citing a short work, include as many of the following elements as apply and as are available: author's name, title of the short work (in quotation marks), title of the site (underlined), date of publication, the URL (in angle brackets), date of access (in parentheses), and page number (if available). Many Web documents are not marked with page numbers; when possible, give the text division instead. In the following example, "Origins and Inspiration" is a heading breaking up the text of the article being cited.

With author

```
    24. Sheila Connor, "Historical Background,"
Garden and Forest, Library of Congress, 23 December
1999, <http://lcweb.loc.gov/preserv/prd/gardfor/
historygf.html> (20 January 2001), Origins and
Inspiration.
```

```
Connor, Sheila. "Historical Background." Garden and
    Forest. Library of Congress. 23 December 1999.
```

<http://lcweb.loc.gov/preserv/prd/gardfor/
historygf.html> (20 January 2001).

Author unknown

24. "Media Giants," The Merchants of Cool,
PBS Online, 2001,<http://www.pbs.org/wgbh/pages/
frontline/shows/cool/giants> (7 March 2001).

"Media Giants." The Merchants of Cool. PBS Online.
    2001. <http://www.pbs.org/wgbh/pages/
    frontline/shows/cool/giants> (7 March 2001).

■ **25. ONLINE BOOK** When a book or a book-length work is posted on the Web, give as much publication information as is available, followed by the URL (in angle brackets), your date of access (in parentheses), and page numbers.

25. Booker T. Washington, "Up from Slavery,"
in The Autobiographical Writings, vol. 1 of The
Booker T. Washington Papers, 2000, <http://
stills.nap.edu/btw/Vol.1/html/264.html> (16 Feb.
2001), 213.

Washington, Booker T. "Up from Slavery." In The
    Autobiographical Writings. Vol. 1 of The
    Booker T. Washington Papers, 2000, 211-388.
    <http://stills.nap.edu/btw/Vol.1/html/
    264.html> (16 Feb. 2001).

■ **26. DOCUMENT FROM A DATABASE** When you retrieve a document from an online database, give as much of the

following information as is available: publication information for the source, the name of the database (underlined), the name of the service, and the access date (in parentheses).

> 26. Anna Clark, "The New Poor Law and the
> Breadwinner Wage: Contrasting Assumptions," Journal
> of Social History 34, no. 2 (2000): 261. Expanded
> Academic ASAP, InfoTrac (20 March 2001).

> Clark, Anna. "The New Poor Law and the Breadwinner
>   Wage: Contrasting Assumptions." Journal of
>   Social History 34, no. 2 (2000): 261.
>   Expanded Academic ASAP, InfoTrac (20 March
>   2001).

■ **27. E-MAIL MESSAGE**   To cite an e-mail message, include
the writer's name, the subject line (in quotation marks), date
sent, and the type of e-mail (personal e-mail or distribution
list). End with the date you read it (in parentheses).

> 27. Kathleen Veslany, "Public Policy
> Initiative," 25 January 2001, personal e-mail
> (25 January 2001).

> Veslany, Kathleen. "Public Policy Initiative."
>   25 January 2001. Personal e-mail (25 January
>   2001).

■ **28. ONLINE POSTING**   To cite a posting to a Web forum,
an online mailing list, or a newsgroup, include the name of
the author, the title or subject of the posting (in quotation

marks), the date of the posting, the URL (in angle brackets), and the date of access (in parentheses).

> 28. Nancy Stegall, "Web Publishing and Censorship," 2 February 1997, <acw-1@ttacs6.ttu.edu> (18 March 1997).

> Stegall, Nancy. "Web Publishing and Censorship."
> 2 February 1997. <acw-1@ttacs6.ttu.edu>
> (18 March 1997).

■ **29. REAL-TIME COMMUNICATION**   Cite the name of the speaker or the site; the title, date, and description of the event; the URL (in angle brackets); and the date of access (in parentheses).

> 29. Diversity University MOO, 16 March 2001, group discussion, <http://moo.du.org> (16 March 2001).

> Diversity University MOO. 16 March 2001. Group discussion. <http://moo.du.org> (16 March 2001).

Other sources

■ **30. GOVERNMENT DOCUMENT**

> 30. U.S. Department of State, Foreign Relations of the United States: Diplomatic Papers, 1943 (Washington, D.C.: GPO, 1965), 562.

> U.S. Department of State. Foreign Relations of the United States: Diplomatic Papers, 1943. Washington, D.C.: GPO, 1965.

◼ **31. UNPUBLISHED DISSERTATION**

   31. Stephanie Lynn Budin, "The Origins of
Aphrodite (Greece)" (Ph.D. diss., University of
Pennsylvania, 2000), 301-2.

Budin, Stephanie Lynn. "The Origins of Aphrodite
   (Greece)." Ph.D. diss., University of
   Pennsylvania, 2000.

◼ **32. PERSONAL COMMUNICATION**

   32. Sara Lehman, letter to author, 13 August
2000.

Personal communications are not included in the bibliography.

◼ **33. INTERVIEW**

   33. Ron Haviv, interview by Charlie Rose,
The Charlie Rose Show, Public Broadcasting System,
12 February 2001.

Haviv, Ron. Interview by Charlie Rose. The Charlie
   Rose Show. Public Broadcasting System, 12 February 2001.

◼ **34. FILM OR VIDEOTAPE**

   34. North by Northwest, prod. and dir.
Alfred Hitchcock, 2 hr. 17 min., MGM/UA, 1959,
videocassette.

North by Northwest. Produced and directed by
   Alfred Hitchcock. 2 hr. 17 min. MGM/UA, 1959.
   Videocassette.

■ **35. SOUND RECORDING**

    35. Gustav Holst, The Planets, Royal Philharmonic, André Previn, Telarc compact disc 80133.

Holst, Gustav. The Planets. Royal Philharmonic. André Previn. Telarc compact disc 80133.

■ **36. SOURCE QUOTED IN ANOTHER SOURCE**

    36. George Harmon Knoles, The Jazz Age Revisited: British Criticism of American Civilization during the 1920s (Stanford: Stanford University Press, 1955), 31, quoted in C. Vann Woodward, The Old World's New World (Oxford: Oxford University Press, 1991), 46.

Knoles, George Harmon. The Jazz Age Revisited: British Criticism of American Civilization during the 1920s, 31. Stanford: Stanford University Press, 1955. Quoted in C. Vann Woodward, The Old World's New World (Oxford: Oxford University Press, 1991), 46.

60e *Chicago* manuscript format

The following guidelines for formatting a *Chicago*-style paper and preparing its endnotes and bibliography are based on *The Chicago Manual of Style,* 14th ed. For pages from a sample paper, see 60f.

Formatting the paper

Chicago manuscript guidelines are fairly generic, since they were not created with a specific type of writing in mind.

TITLE PAGE   On the title page, include the full title of your paper and your name. Your instructor will usually want you to include the course title, the instructor's name, and the date as well. Do not type a number on the title page but count it in the manuscript numbering; that is, the first page of the text will usually be numbered 2. See page 759 for a sample title page.

PAGINATION   Using arabic numerals, number all pages except the title page in the upper right corner. Depending on your instructor's preference, you may also use a short title or your last name before the page numbers to help identify pages in case they come loose from your manuscript.

MARGINS AND LINE SPACING   Leave margins of at least one inch at the top, bottom, and sides of the page. Double-space the entire manuscript, including long quotations that have been set off from the text.

LONG QUOTATIONS   When a quotation is fairly long, set it off from the text by indenting (see also pp. 737–38). Indent the full quotation one-half inch (five spaces) from the left margin. Quotation marks are not needed when a quotation has been set off from the text.

VISUALS   *The Chicago Manual* classifies visuals as tables and illustrations (illustrations, or figures, include drawings, photographs, maps, and charts). Keep visuals as simple as possible. Label each table with an arabic numeral (Table 1, Table 2, and so on) and provide a clear title that identifies the subject. The label and title should appear on separate lines above the table, flush left. Below the table, give its source in a note like this one:

    Source: Edna Bonacich and Richard P. Appelbaum,
    Behind the Label (Berkeley: University of
    California Press, 2000), 145.

For each figure, place a label and a caption below the figure, flush left. The label and caption need not appear on separate lines. The word "Figure" may be abbreviated to "Fig."

In the text of your paper, discuss the most significant features of each visual. Place visuals as close as possible to the sentences that relate to them unless your instructor prefers them in an appendix.

Preparing the endnotes

Begin the endnotes on a new page at the end of the paper. Center the title Notes about one inch from the top of the page, and number the pages consecutively with the rest of the manuscript. See page 762 for an example.

INDENTING AND NUMBERING Indent the first line of each entry one-half inch (or five spaces) from the left margin; do not indent additional lines in an entry. Begin the note with the arabic numeral that corresponds to the number in the text. Put a period after the number.

LINE SPACING Double-space throughout. Do not add extra lines of space between entries.

Preparing the bibliography

Typically, the notes in *Chicago*-style papers are followed by a bibliography, an alphabetically arranged list of all the works cited or consulted (see p. 763 for an example). Center the title Bibliography about one inch from the top of the page. Number bibliography pages consecutively with the rest of the paper.

ALPHABETIZING THE LIST   Alphabetize the bibliography by the last names of the authors (or editors); when a work has no author or editor, alphabetize by the first word of the title other than *A, An,* or *The.*

If your list includes two or more works by the same author, use three hyphens instead of the author's name in all entries after the first. You may arrange the entries alphabetically by title or chronologically; be consistent throughout the bibliography.

INDENTING AND LINE SPACING   Begin each entry at the left margin, and indent any additional lines one-half inch (or five spaces). Double-space throughout; do not add extra lines of space between entries.

60f   Sample pages from a research paper: *Chicago* style

Following are sample pages from a research paper by Ned Bishop, a student in a history class. Bishop was asked to document his paper using *Chicago*-style endnotes and a bibliography. In preparing his manuscript, Bishop also followed *Chicago* guidelines.

ON THE WEB

To read Ned Bishop's entire paper, go to
www.dianahacker.com/bedhandbook

and click on   ► **Model Papers**
                  ► *Chicago* **paper**

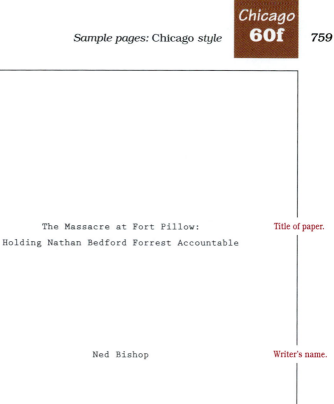

The Massacre at Fort Pillow:
Holding Nathan Bedford Forrest Accountable

Title of paper.

Ned Bishop

Writer's name.

History 214
Professor Citro
22 March 2001

Title of course,
instructor's
name, and date.

Although Northern newspapers of the time no
doubt exaggerated some of the Confederate atroci-
ties at Fort Pillow, most modern sources agree that
a massacre of Union troops took place there on 12
April 1864. It seems clear that Union soldiers,
particularly black soldiers, were killed after they
had stopped fighting or had surrendered or were
being held prisoner. Less clear is the role played
by Major General Nathan Bedford Forrest in leading
his troops. Although we will never know whether
Forrest directly ordered the massacre, evidence
suggests that he was responsible for it.

What happened at Fort Pillow?

Fort Pillow, Tennessee, which sat on a bluff
overlooking the Mississippi River, had been held
by the Union for two years. It was garrisoned by
580 men, 292 of them from the Sixth United States
Colored Heavy and Light Cavalry, 285 from the white
Thirteenth Tennessee Cavalry. Nathan Bedford
Forrest's troops numbered about 1,500 men.[1]

The Confederates attacked Fort Pillow on
12 April 1864 and had virtually surrounded the fort
by the time Forrest arrived on the battlefield. At
3:30 P.M., Forrest displayed a flag of truce and
sent in a demand for unconditional surrender of the
sort he had used before: "The conduct of the officers and men garrisoning Fort Pillow has been such
as to entitle them to being treated as prisoners of

Thesis asserts writer's main point.

Headings help readers follow the organization.

Statistics are cited with an endnote.

Bishop 3

war. . . . Should my demand be refused, I cannot be
responsible for the fate of your command."[2] Union
Major William Bradford, who had replaced Major
Booth, killed earlier by sharpshooters, asked for
an hour to consult. Forrest, worried that vessels
in the river were bringing in more troops, shortened the time to twenty minutes. Bradford refused
to surrender, and Forrest quickly ordered the attack.

The Confederates charged across the short distance between their lines and the fort, helping one
another scale the parapet, from which they fired
into the fort. Victory came quickly, with the Union
forces running toward the river or surrendering.
Shelby Foote describes the scene like this:

> Some kept going, right into the river, where a
> number drowned and the swimmers became targets
> for marksmen on the bluff. Others, dropping
> their guns in terror, ran back toward the Con-
> federates with their hands up, and of these
> some were spared as prisoners, while others
> were shot down in the act of surrender.[3]

Quotation is
cited with an
endnote.

Long quotation
is set off from
text by indent-
ing. Quotation
marks are
omitted.

The complete text of the paper appears on *The Bedford
Handbook* Web site. See page 758 for the address.

Notes

First line of each note is indented ½″ (or 5 spaces).

1. John Cimprich and Robert C. Mainfort Jr., "Fort Pillow Revisited: New Evidence about an Old Controversy," Civil War History 28 (1982): 293-94.

Note number is not raised and is followed by a period.

2. Quoted in Brian Steel Wills, A Battle from the Start: The Life of Nathan Bedford Forrest (New York: HarperCollins, 1992), 182.

Authors' names are not inverted.

3. Shelby Foote, The Civil War, a Narrative: Red River to Appomattox (New York: Vintage, 1986), 110.

4. Nathan Bedford Forrest, "Report of Maj. Gen. Nathan B. Forrest, C. S. Army, Commanding Cavalry, of the Capture of Fort Pillow," Shotgun's Home of the American Civil War, 7 January 1997, <http://www.civilwarhome.com/forrest.htm> (23 April 1999).

5. Jack Hurst, Nathan Bedford Forrest: A Biography (New York: Knopf, 1993), 174.

Last name refers to an earlier note by the same author.

6. Foote, 111.

7. Cimprich and Mainfort, 305.

8. Cimprich and Mainfort, 299.

9. Foote, 110.

10. Wills, 187.

Entries are double-spaced, with no extra spacing between entries.

11. Albert Castel, "The Fort Pillow Massacre: A Fresh Examination of the Evidence," Civil War History 4 (1958): 44-45.

12. Cimprich and Mainfort, 300.

13. Hurst, 177.

14. Hurst, 177.

Bishop 11

Bibliography

Castel, Albert. "The Fort Pillow Massacre: A Fresh
Examination of the Evidence." Civil War
History 4 (1958): 37-50.

Cimprich, John, and Robert C. Mainfort Jr. "Fort
Pillow Revisited: New Evidence about an Old
Controversy." Civil War History 28 (1982):
293-306.

Cornish, Dudley Taylor. The Sable Arm: Black Troops
in the Union Army, 1861-1865. Lawrence, Kans.:
University Press of Kansas, 1987.

Foote, Shelby. The Civil War, a Narrative: Red
River to Appomattox. New York: Vintage, 1986.

Forrest, Nathan Bedford. "Report of Maj. Gen.
Nathan B. Forrest, C. S. Army, Commanding
Cavalry, of the Capture of Fort Pillow."
Shotgun's Home of the American Civil War.
7 January 1997. <http://www.civilwarhome.com/
forrest.htm> (23 April 1999).

Hurst, Jack. Nathan Bedford Forrest: A Biography.
New York: Knopf, 1993.

McPherson, James M. Battle Cry of Freedom: The
Civil War Era. New York: Oxford University
Press, 1988.

Wills, Brian Steel. A Battle from the Start: The
Life of Nathan Bedford Forrest. New York:
HarperCollins, 1992.

Entries are alphabetized by authors' last names.

First line of entry is at left margin; additional lines are indented ½" (or 5 spaces).

Entries are double-spaced, with no extra space between entries.

Grammar Basics

61

Parts of speech

Traditional grammar recognizes eight parts of speech: noun, pronoun, verb, adjective, adverb, preposition, conjunction, and interjection. Many words can function as more than one part of speech. For example, depending on its use in a sentence, the word *paint* can be a noun (*The paint is wet*) or a verb (*Please paint the ceiling next*).

A quick-reference chart of the parts of speech appears on pages 781–83.

61a Nouns

As most schoolchildren can attest, a noun is the name of a person, place, or thing.

> **N**   **N**   **N**
> The *cat* in *gloves* catches no *mice.*

In addition to the traditional definition of a noun, grammarians describe a noun as follows:

—the kind of word that is often marked with an article (a *spoon*, an *apple*, the *newspaper*)

—the kind of word that can usually be made plural (one *cat*, two *cats*) or possessive (the *cat's* paw)

—the kind of word that when derived from another word typically takes one of these endings: play*er*, just*ice*, happi*ness*, divi*sion*, guid*ance*, refer*ence*, pave*ment*, child*hood*, king*dom*, agen*cy*, tour*ist*, sincer*ity*, censor*ship*

—the kind of word that can fill one of these slots in a sentence: subject, direct object, indirect object, subject complement, object complement, object of the preposition. (See 62.)

Nouns, in other words, may be identified as much by their form and function as by their meaning.

Nouns sometimes function as adjectives modifying other nouns. Because of their dual roles, nouns used in this manner may be called *noun/adjectives.*

      N/ADJ   **N/ADJ**
You can't make a *silk* purse out of a *sow's* ear.

Nouns are classified for a variety of purposes. When capitalization is the issue, we speak of *proper* versus *common nouns* (see 45a). If the problem is one of word choice, we may speak of *concrete* versus *abstract nouns* (see 18b). The distinction between *count nouns* and *noncount nouns* is useful primarily for nonnative speakers of English (see 30a and 30b). The term *collective noun* refers to a set of nouns that may cause problems with subject-verb or pronoun-antecedent agreement (see 21f and 22b).

EXERCISE 61–1

Underline the nouns (and noun/adjectives) in the following sentences. Answers to lettered sentences appear in the back of the book. Example:

    Idle <u>hands</u> are the <u>devil's</u> <u>workshop</u>.

a. The sun will set without your assistance.   —Hebrew proverb
b. Pride is at the bottom of all great mistakes.   —John Ruskin
c. Success breeds confidence.   —Beryl Markham
d. The ultimate censorship is the flick of the dial.

                —Tom Smothers
e. Our national flower is the concrete cloverleaf.

                —Lewis Mumford

1. Truthfulness so often goes with ruthlessness.   —Dodie Smith
2. Luck is a matter of preparation meeting opportunity.

                —Oprah Winfrey

3. Problems are only opportunities in work clothes.

—Henry Kaiser

4. A woman must have money and a room of her own.

—Virginia Woolf

5. Language helps form the limits of our reality. —Dale Spender

---

ON THE WEB

For an electronic exercise on identifying nouns, go to
www.dianahacker.com/bedhandbook

and click on ▶ **Electronic Grammar Exercises**
▶ **E-ex 61–1**

61b Pronouns

There are thousands of nouns, and new ones come into the language every year. This is not true of pronouns, which number about one hundred and are extremely resistant to change. Most of the pronouns in English are listed in this section.

A pronoun is a word used in place of a noun. Usually the pronoun substitutes for a specific noun, known as its *antecedent.*

When the *wheel* squeaks, *it* is greased.

Although most pronouns function as substitutes for nouns, some can function as adjectives modifying nouns.

This hanging will surely be a lesson to me.

Because they have the form of a pronoun and the function of an adjective, such pronouns may be called *pronoun/ adjectives.*

Pronouns are classified as personal, possessive, intensive and reflexive, relative, interrogative, demonstrative, indefinite, and reciprocal.

PERSONAL PRONOUNS   Personal pronouns refer to specific persons or things. They always function as noun equivalents.

Singular: I, me, you, she, her, he, him, it

Plural: we, us, you, they, them

POSSESSIVE PRONOUNS Possessive pronouns indicate ownership.

Singular: my, mine, your, yours, her, hers, his, its

Plural: our, ours, your, yours, their, theirs

Some of these possessive pronouns function as adjectives modifying nouns: *my, your, his, her, its, our, their.*

INTENSIVE AND REFLEXIVE PRONOUNS   Intensive pronouns emphasize a noun or another pronoun (The senator *herself* met us at the door). Reflexive pronouns, which have the same form as intensive pronouns, name a receiver of an action identical with the doer of the action (Paula cut *herself*).

Singular: myself, yourself, himself, herself, itself

Plural: ourselves, yourselves, themselves

RELATIVE PRONOUNS   Relative pronouns introduce subordinate clauses functioning as adjectives (The man *who robbed us* was never caught). In addition to introducing the clause, the relative pronoun, in this case *who,* points back to a noun or pronoun that the clause modifies (*man*). (See 63b.)

who, whom, whose, which, that

Some textbooks also treat *whichever, whoever, whomever, what,* and *whatever* as relative pronouns. These words introduce noun clauses; they do not point back to a noun or pronoun. (See 63b.)

INTERROGATIVE PRONOUNS   Interrogative pronouns introduce questions (*Who* is expected to win the election?).

who, whom, whose, which, what

DEMONSTRATIVE PRONOUNS   Demonstrative pronouns identify or point to nouns. Frequently they function as adjectives (*This* chair is my favorite), but they may also function as noun equivalents (*This* is my favorite chair).

this, that, these, those

INDEFINITE PRONOUNS   Indefinite pronouns refer to nonspecific persons or things. Most are always singular (*everyone, each*); some are always plural (*both, many*); a few may be singular or plural (see 21e). Most indefinite pronouns function as noun equivalents (*Something* is burning), but some can also function as adjectives (*All* campers must check in at the lodge).

all	anything	everyone	nobody	several
another	both	everything	none	some
any	each	few	no one	somebody
anybody	either	many	nothing	someone
anyone	everybody	neither	one	something

RECIPROCAL PRONOUNS   Reciprocal pronouns refer to individual parts of a plural antecedent (By turns, we helped *each other* through college).

each other, one another

NOTE: Pronouns cause a variety of problems for writers. See pronoun-antecedent agreement (22), pronoun reference (23), distinguishing between pronouns such as *I* and *me* (24), and distinguishing between *who* and *whom* (25).

EXERCISE 61–2

Underline the pronouns (and pronoun/adjectives) in the following sentences. Answers to lettered sentences appear in the back of the book. Example:

> Beware of persons who are praised by everyone.

a. He has every attribute of a dog except loyalty.   —Thomas Gore
b. A fall does not hurt those who fly low.   —Chinese proverb
c. I have written some poetry that I myself don't understand.
      —Carl Sandburg
d. I am firm. You are obstinate. He is a pig-headed fool.
      —Katherine Whitehorn
e. If you haven't anything nice to say about anyone, come and sit by me.   —Alice Roosevelt Longworth

1. Men are taught to apologize for their weaknesses, women for their strengths.   —Lois Wyse
2. Nothing is interesting if you are not interested.
      —Helen MacInness
3. We will never have friends if we expect to find them without fault.   —Thomas Fuller
4. The gods help those who help themselves.   —Aesop
5. I awoke one morning and found myself famous.   —Lord Byron

ON THE WEB

For an electronic exercise on identifying pronouns, go to
www.dianahacker.com/bedhandbook

and click on   ▶ **Electronic Grammar Exercises**
      ▶ **E-ex 61-2**

61c Verbs

The verb of a sentence usually expresses action (*jump,* *think*) or being (*is, become*). It is composed of a main verb possibly preceded by one or more helping verbs:

        MV
The best fish *swim* near the bottom.

        HV   **MV**
A marriage *is* not *built* in a day.

        HV HV   **MV**
Even God *has been defended* with nonsense.

Notice that words can intervene between the helping and the main verb (is *not* built).

Helping verbs

There are twenty-three helping verbs in English: forms of *have, do,* and *be,* which may also function as main verbs; and nine modals, which function only as helping verbs. The forms of *have, do,* and *be* change form to indicate tense; the nine modals do not.

FORMS OF *HAVE, DO,* AND *BE*
have, has, had

do, does, did

be, am, is, are, was, were, being, been

MODALS
can, could, may, might, must, shall, should, will, would

The phrase *ought to* is often classified as a modal as well.

Main verbs

The main verb of a sentence is always the kind of word that would change form if put into these test sentences:

BASE FORM	Usually I (*walk, ride*).
PAST TENSE	Yesterday I (*walked, rode*).
PAST PARTICIPLE	I have (*walked, ridden*) many times before.
PRESENT PARTICIPLE	I am (*walking, riding*) right now.
-S FORM	Usually he/she/it (*walks, rides*).

If a word doesn't change form when slipped into these test sentences, you can be certain that it is not a main verb. For example, the noun *revolution,* though it may seem to suggest an action, can never function as a main verb. Just try to make it behave like one (*Today I revolution . . . Yesterday I revolutioned . . .*) and you'll see why.

When both the past-tense and the past-participle forms of a verb end in *-ed,* the verb is regular (*walked, walked*). Otherwise, the verb is irregular (*rode, ridden*). (See 27a.)

The verb *be* is highly irregular, having eight forms instead of the usual five: the base form *be;* the present-tense forms *am, is,* and *are;* the past-tense forms *was* and *were;* the present participle *being;* and the past participle *been.*

Helping verbs combine with the various forms of main verbs to create tenses. For a survey of tenses, see 28a.

NOTE: Some verbs are followed by words that look like prepositions but are so closely associated with the verb that they are a part of its meaning. These words are known as *particles.* Common verb-particle combinations include *bring up, call off, drop off, give in, look up, run into,* and *take off.*

> A lot of parents *pack up* their troubles and *send* them *off* to camp. —Raymond Duncan

NOTE: Verbs cause many problems for writers. See active verbs (8), subject-verb agreement (21), standard English

774   *Grammar basics*

verb forms (27), verb tense and mood (28), and ESL problems with verbs (29).

EXERCISE 61–3

Underline the verbs in the following sentences, including helping verbs and particles. If a verb is part of a contraction (such as *is* in *isn't* or *would* in *I'd*), underline only the letters that represent the verb. Answers to lettered sentences appear in the back of the book. Example:

> **A full cup <u>must be carried</u> steadily.**

a. I can pardon everyone's mistakes except my own.   —Cato
b. There are no atheists on turbulent airplanes.   —Erica Jong
c. One arrow does not bring down two birds.   —Turkish proverb
d. Keep your talent in the dark, and you'll never be insulted.
                                                              —Elsa Maxwell
e. Throw a lucky man into the sea, and he will emerge with a fish in his mouth.   —Arab proverb

1. Do not scald your tongue in other people's broth.
                                                              —English proverb
2. Wrong must not win by technicalities.   —Aeschylus
3. Love your neighbor, but don't pull down the hedge.
                                                              —Swiss proverb
4. I'd rather have roses on my table than diamonds around my neck.   —Emma Goldman
5. He is a fine friend. He stabs you in the front.
                                                              —Leonard Louis Levinson

ON THE WEB

For electronic exercises on identifying verbs, go to
www.dianahacker.com/bedhandbook

and click on   ▶ **Electronic Grammar Exercises**
               ▶ **E-ex 61–3**

61d   Adjectives

An adjective is a word used to modify, or describe, a noun or pronoun. An adjective usually answers one of these questions: Which one? What kind of? How many?

> **ADJ**
> the *lame* elephant [Which elephant?]

> **ADJ**   **ADJ**
> *valuable old* stamps [What kind of stamps?]

> **ADJ**
> *sixteen* candles [How many candles?]

Grammarians also define adjectives according to their form and their typical position in a sentence, as follows:

— the kind of word that usually comes before a noun in a noun phrase (a *frisky* puppy, an *amiable young* man)

— the kind of word that can follow a linking verb and describe the subject (The ship was *unsinkable;* Talk is *cheap*) (See 62b.)

— the kind of word that when derived from another part of speech typically takes one of these endings: wonder*ful,* courte*ous,* luck*y,* fool*ish,* pleasur*able,* colon*ial,* help*less,* defens*ible,* urg*ent,* disgust*ing,* friend*ly,* spectacul*ar,* secret*ive*

The definite article *the* and the indefinite articles *a* and *an* are also classified as adjectives.

Some possessive, demonstrative, and indefinite pronouns can function as adjectives: *their, its, this* (see 61b).

NOTE: Writers sometimes misuse adjectives (see 26b). Speakers of English as a second language often encounter problems with the articles *a, an,* and *the* and occasionally have trouble placing adjectives correctly (see 30 and 31d).

61e   Adverbs

An adverb is a word used to modify, or qualify, a verb (or verbal), an adjective, or another adverb. It usually answers one of these questions: When? Where? How? Why? Under what conditions? To what degree?

Pull *gently* at a weak rope. [Pull how?]

Read the best books *first*. [Read when?]

Adverbs that modify a verb are also defined according to their form and their typical position in a sentence, as follows:

— the kind of word that can appear nearly anywhere in a sentence and is often movable (he *sometimes* jogged after work; *sometimes* he jogged after work)

— the kind of word that when derived from an adjective typically takes an *-ly* ending (nice, nice*ly*; profound, profound*ly*)

Adverbs modifying adjectives or other adverbs usually intensify or limit the intensity of the word they modify.

ADV   **ADV**

Be *extremely* good, and you will be *very* lonesome.

Adverbs modifying adjectives and other adverbs are not movable. We can't say "Be good *extremely*" or "*Extremely* be good."

The negators *not* and *never* are classified as adverbs. A word such as *cannot* contains the helping verb *can* and the adverb *not*. A contraction such as *can't* contains the helping verb *can* and a contracted form of the adverb *not*.

Adverbs can modify prepositional phrases (The budget is *barely* on target), subordinate clauses (We will try to attend, *especially* if you will be there), or whole sentences (*Certainly* Joe did not intend to insult you).

NOTE: Writers sometimes misuse adverbs (see 26a). Speakers of English as a second language may have trouble placing adverbs correctly (see 31d).

EXERCISE 61–4

Underline the adjectives and circle the adverbs in the following sentences. If a word is a pronoun in form but an adjective in function, treat it as an adjective. Also treat the articles *a, an,* and *the* as adjectives. Answers to lettered sentences are in the back of the book. Example:

A wild goose (never) laid a tame egg.

a. General notions are generally wrong.
— Lady Mary Wortley Montagu
b. The American public is wonderfully tolerant.
— Anonymous
c. Wildflowers sometimes grow in an uncultivated field, but they never bloom in an uncultivated mind.
— Anonymous
d. I'd rather be strongly wrong than weakly right.
— Tallulah Bankhead
e. Sleep faster. We need the pillows.   — Yiddish proverb

1. Success is a public affair; failure is a private funeral.
— Rosalind Russell
2. Their civil discussions were not interesting, and their interesting discussions were not civil.   — Lisa Alther
3. Money will buy a pretty good dog, but it will not buy the wag of its tail.   — Josh Billings
4. We cannot be too careful in the choice of our enemies.
— Oscar Wilde
5. Feelings are untidy.   — Esther Hautzig

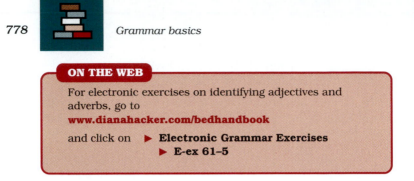

ON THE WEB

For electronic exercises on identifying adjectives and adverbs, go to

www.dianahacker.com/bedhandbook

and click on ▶ **Electronic Grammar Exercises**
▶ **E-ex 61–5**

61f Prepositions

A preposition is a word placed before a noun or pronoun to form a phrase modifying another word in the sentence. The prepositional phrase nearly always functions as an adjective or as an adverb.

P   P
The road *to hell* is usually paved *with good intentions.*

To hell functions as an adjective, modifying the noun *road; with good intentions* functions as an adverb, modifying the verb *is paved.* (For more about prepositional phrases, see 63a.)

There are a limited number of prepositions in English. The most common ones are included in the following list.

about	before	considering	like	over
above	behind	despite	near	past
across	below	down	next	plus
after	beside	during	of	regarding
against	besides	except	off	respecting
along	between	for	on	round
among	beyond	from	onto	since
around	but	in	opposite	than
as	by	inside	out	through
at	concerning	into	outside	throughout

till	under	until	upon	without
to	underneath	unto	with	
toward	unlike	up	within	

Some prepositions are more than one word long. *Along with, as well as, in addition to,* and *next to* are common examples.

NOTE: Except for certain idiomatic uses (see 18d), prepositions cause few problems for native speakers of English. For second-language speakers, however, prepositions can cause considerable difficulty (see 29d and 31f).

61g Conjunctions

Conjunctions join words, phrases, or clauses, and they indicate the relation between the elements joined.

COORDINATING CONJUNCTIONS A coordinating conjunction is used to connect grammatically equal elements. The coordinating conjunctions are *and, but, or, nor, for, so,* and *yet.*

> Poverty is the parent of revolution *and* crime.

> Admire a little ship, *but* put your cargo in a big one.

In the first sentence, *and* connects two nouns; in the second, *but* connects two independent clauses.

CORRELATIVE CONJUNCTIONS Correlative conjunctions come in pairs: *either...or; neither...nor; not only...but also; whether...or; both...and.* Like coordinating conjunctions, they connect grammatically equal elements.

> *Either* Jack Sprat *or* his wife could eat no fat.

SUBORDINATING CONJUNCTIONS A subordinating conjunction introduces a subordinate clause and indicates its relation to the rest of the sentence. (See 63b.) The most common subordinating conjunctions are *after, although, as, as if, because, before, even though, how, if, in order that, once, rather than, since, so that, than, that, though, unless, until, when, where, whether, while,* and *why.*

If you want service, serve yourself.

CONJUNCTIVE ADVERBS   A conjunctive adverb may be used with a semicolon to connect independent clauses; it usually serves as a transition between the clauses. The most common conjunctive adverbs are *consequently, finally, furthermore, however, moreover, nevertheless, similarly, then, therefore,* and *thus.* (See p. 346 for a more complete list.)

When we want to murder a tiger, we call it sport; *however,* when the tiger wants to murder us, we call it ferocity.

NOTE: The ability to distinguish between conjunctive adverbs and coordinating conjunctions will help you avoid run-on sentences and make punctuation decisions (see 20, 32a, and 32b). The ability to recognize subordinating conjunctions will help you avoid sentence fragments (see 19).

61h   Interjections

An interjection is a word used to express surprise or emotion (*Oh! Hey! Wow!*).

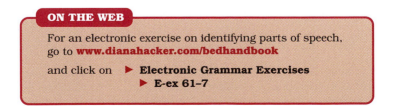

ON THE WEB

For an electronic exercise on identifying parts of speech, go to **www.dianahacker.com/bedhandbook**

and click on   ▶ **Electronic Grammar Exercises**
              ▶ **E-ex 61–7**

Parts of speech

A **NOUN** names a person, place, thing, or idea.

> N   N   N
> *Repetition* does not transform a *lie* into *truth*.

A **PRONOUN** substitutes for a noun.

>   PN   PN   PN
> When the gods wish to punish *us, they* heed *our* prayers.

Personal pronouns: I, me, you, he, him, she, her, it, we, us, they, them

Possessive pronouns: my, mine, your, yours, her, hers, his, its, our, ours, their, theirs

Intensive and reflexive pronouns: myself, yourself, himself, herself, itself, ourselves, yourselves, themselves

Relative pronouns: that, which, who, whom, whose

Interrogative pronouns: who, whom, whose, which, what

Demonstrative pronouns: this, that, these, those

Indefinite pronouns: all, another, any, anybody, anyone, anything, both, each, either, everybody, everyone, everything, few, many, neither, nobody, none, no one, nothing, one, several, some, somebody, someone, something

Reciprocal pronouns: each other, one another

A **HELPING VERB** comes before a main verb.

Modals: can, could, may, might, must, shall, should, will, would (*also* ought to)

Forms of be: be, am, is, are, was, were, being, been

Forms of have: have, has, had

Forms of do: do, does, did

Parts of speech (continued)

(The forms of *be, have,* and *do* may also function as main verbs.)

A **MAIN VERB** asserts action, being, or state of being.

       MV   **HV**   **MV**
Charity *begins* at home but *should* not *end* there.

A main verb will always change form when put into these positions in sentences:

Usually I _____ .	(*walk, ride*)
Yesterday I _____ .	(*walked, rode*)
I have _____ many times before.	(*walked, ridden*)
I am _____ right now.	(*walking, riding*)
Usually he _____ .	(*walks, rides*)

There are eight forms of the highly irregular verb *be: be, am, is, are, was, were, being, been.*

An **ADJECTIVE** modifies a noun or pronoun, usually answering one of these questions: Which one? What kind of? How many? The articles *a, an,* and *the* are also adjectives.

   ADJ   **ADJ**
Useless laws weaken *necessary* ones.

An **ADVERB** modifies a verb, adjective, or adverb, usually answering one of these questions: When? Where? Why? How? Under what conditions? To what degree?

     ADV   **ADV**
People think *too historically.*

A **PREPOSITION** indicates the relationship between the noun or pronoun that follows it and another word in the sentence.

Parts of speech (continued)

             P   P
A journey *of* a thousand miles begins *with* a single step.

Common prepositions: about, across, after, against, along, among, around, as, at, before, behind, below, beside, besides, between, beyond, but, by, concerning, considering, despite, down, during, except, for, from, in, inside, into, like, near, next, of, off, on, onto, opposite, out, outside, over, past, plus, regarding, respecting, round, since, than, through, throughout, till, to, toward, under, underneath, unlike, until, unto, up, upon, with, within, without

A **CONJUNCTION** connects words or word groups.

Coordinating conjunctions: and, but, or, nor, for, so, yet

Subordinating conjunctions: after, although, as, as if, because, before, even though, how, if, in order that, once, rather than, since, so that, than, that, though, unless, until, when, where, whether, while, why

Correlative conjunctions: either . . . or, neither . . . nor, not only . . . but also, both . . . and, whether . . . or

Conjunctive adverbs: accordingly, also, anyway, besides, certainly, consequently, conversely, finally, furthermore, hence, however, incidentally, indeed, instead, likewise, meanwhile, moreover, nevertheless, next, nonetheless, otherwise, similarly, specifically, still, subsequently, then, therefore, thus

An **INTERJECTION** expresses surprise or emotion. (*Oh! Wow! Hey! Hooray!*)

62

Sentence patterns

Most English sentences flow from subject to verb to any objects or complements. The vast majority of sentences conform to one of these five patterns:

> subject / verb / subject complement
>
> subject / verb / direct object
>
> subject / verb / indirect object / direct object
>
> subject / verb / direct object / object complement
>
> subject / verb

Adverbial modifiers (single words, phrases, or clauses) may be added to any of these patterns, and they may appear nearly anywhere—at the beginning, the middle, or the end.

Predicate is the grammatical term given to the verb plus its objects, complements, and adverbial modifiers.

For a quick-reference chart of sentence patterns, see page 791.

62a Subjects

The subject of a sentence names who or what the sentence is about. The *complete subject* is usually composed of a *simple subject,* always a noun or pronoun, plus any words or word groups modifying the simple subject.

The complete subject

To find the complete subject, ask Who? or What?, insert the verb, and finish the question. The answer is the complete subject.

┌─ **COMPLETE SUBJECT** ─┐
The purity of a revolution usually lasts about two weeks.

Who or what lasts about two weeks? *The purity of a revolution.*

┌──── **COMPLETE SUBJECT** ────┐
Historical books that contain no lies are extremely tedious.

Who or what are extremely tedious? *Historical books that contain no lies.*

COMPLETE SUBJECT
┌──┐
In every country the sun rises in the morning.

Who or what rises in the morning? *The sun.* Notice that *In every country the sun* is not a sensible answer to the question. *In every country* is a prepositional phrase modifying the verb *rises.* Since sentences frequently open with such modifiers, it is not safe to assume that the subject must always appear first in a sentence.

The simple subject

To find the simple subject, strip away all modifiers in the complete subject. This includes single-word modifiers such as *the* and *historical,* phrases such as *of a revolution,* and subordinate clauses such as *that contain no lies.*

┌─ **SS** ─┐
The purity of a revolution usually lasts about two weeks.

┌─ **SS** ─┐
Historical books that contain no lies are extremely tedious.

┌**SS**┐
In every country *the sun* rises in the morning.

A sentence may have a compound subject containing two or more simple subjects joined with a coordinating conjunction such as *and, but,* or *or.*

┌─ **SS** ─┐   ┌─ **SS** ─┐
Much industry and little conscience make us rich.

Understood subjects

In imperative sentences, which give advice or issue commands, the verb's subject is understood but not actually present in the sentence. The subject of an imperative sentence is understood to be *you,* as in the following example.

[*You*] Hitch your wagon to a star.

Subject after the verb

Although the subject ordinarily comes before the verb, occasionally it does not. When a sentence begins with *There is* or *There are* (or *There was* or *There were*), the subject follows the verb. The word *There* is an expletive in such constructions, an empty word serving merely to get the sentence started.

┌─ **SS** ─┐
There is *no substitute for victory.*

Occasionally a writer will invert a sentence for effect.

┌ **SS** ┐
Happy is *the nation that has no history.*

Happy is an adjective, so it cannot be the subject. Turn this sentence around and its structure becomes obvious: *The nation that has no history is happy.*

In questions, the subject frequently appears in an unusual position, sandwiched between parts of the verb.

┌**SS**┐
Do *married men* make the best husbands?

Turn the question into a statement, and the words will appear in their usual order: *Married men do make the best husbands.* (*Do make* is the verb.)

For more about unusual sentence patterns, see 62c.

NOTE: The ability to recognize the subject of a sentence will help you edit for a variety of problems such as sentence fragments (19), subject-verb agreement (21), and choice of pronouns such as *I* and *me* (24). If English is not your native language, see also 31a and 31b.

EXERCISE 62–1

In the following sentences, underline the complete subject and write *ss* above the simple subject(s). If the subject is an understood *you,* insert it in parentheses. Answers to lettered sentences appear in the back of the book. Example:

> *ss*　　　　　　　*ss*
> <u>Fools and their money</u> are soon parted.

a. Sticks and stones may break my bones, and words can sting like anything.　　　　　　　　　　　　　—Anonymous
b. In war, all delays are dangerous.　　　　　　—John Dryden
c. Speak softly and carry a big stick.　　—Theodore Roosevelt
d. There is nothing permanent except change.　　—Heraclitus
e. Most of the disputes in the world arise from words.
　　　　　　　　　　　　　　　　　　—Lord Mansfield

1. The structure of every sentence is a lesson in logic.
　　　　　　　　　　　　　　　　　　— J. S. Mill
2. Don't be humble. You're not that great.　　—Golda Meir
3. In the eyes of its mother, every beetle is a gazelle.
　　　　　　　　　　　　　　　　　　—Moorish proverb
4. The burden of proof lies on the plaintiff.　　—Legal maxim
5. There are no signposts in the sea.　　—Vita Sackville-West

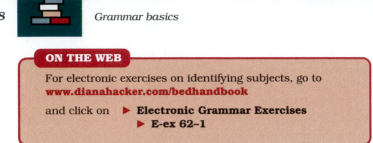

ON THE WEB

For electronic exercises on identifying subjects, go to
www.dianahacker.com/bedhandbook

and click on ▶ **Electronic Grammar Exercises**
▶ **E-ex 62–1**

62b Verbs, objects, and complements

Section 61c explains how to find the verb of a sentence, which consists of a main verb possibly preceded by one or more helping verbs. A sentence's verb is classified as linking, transitive, or intransitive, depending on the kinds of objects or complements the verb can (or cannot) take.

Linking verbs and subject complements

Linking verbs link the subject to a subject complement, a word or word group that completes the meaning of the subject by renaming or describing it. If the subject complement renames the subject, it is a noun or noun equivalent (sometimes called a *predicate noun*).

```
┌──────────── S ────────────┐ ┌─ V ─┐ ┌─ SC ─┐
The handwriting on the wall may be a forgery.
```

If the subject complement describes the subject, it is an adjective or adjective equivalent (sometimes called a *predicate adjective*).

S V SC
Love is blind.

Whenever they appear as main verbs (rather than helping verbs), the forms of *be — be, am, is, are, was, were, being, been*—usually function as linking verbs. In the preceding examples, for instance, the main verbs are *be* and *is*.

Verbs such as *appear, become, feel, grow, look, make, seem, smell, sound,* and *taste* are sometimes linking, depending on the sense of the sentence.

At the touch of love, everyone becomes a poet.

At first sight, original art often looks ugly.

When you suspect that a verb such as *becomes* or *looks* is linking, check to see if the word or words following it rename or describe the subject. In the same sentences, *a poet* renames *everyone,* and *ugly* describes *art.*

Transitive verbs and direct objects

A transitive verb takes a direct object, a word or word group that names a receiver of the action.

The little snake studies the ways of the big serpent.

In such sentences, the subject and verb alone will seem incomplete. Once we have read *The little snake studies,* for example, we want to know the rest: *The little snake studies what?* The answer to the question What? (or Whom?) is the complete direct object: *the ways of the big serpent.* The simple direct object is always a noun or pronoun, in this case *ways.* To find it, simply strip away all modifiers.

Transitive verbs usually appear in the active voice, with the subject doing the action and a direct object receiving the action. Active-voice sentences can be transformed into the passive voice, with the subject receiving the action instead. (See 62c.)

Transitive verbs, indirect objects, and direct objects

The direct object of a transitive verb is sometimes preceded by an indirect object, a noun or pronoun telling to whom or for whom the action of the sentence is done.

S   V   IO ┌ DO ┐   S┌─ V ─┐ IO ┌─ DO ┐
You show me a hero, and I will write you a tragedy.

The simple indirect object is always a noun or pronoun. To test for an indirect object, insert the word *to* or *for* before the word or word group in question. If the sentence makes sense, the word or word group is an indirect object.

You show [to] me a hero, and I will write [for] you a tragedy.

An indirect object may be turned into a prepositional phrase using *to* or *for: You show a hero to me, and I will write a tragedy for you.*
Only certain transitive verbs take indirect objects. Common examples are *ask, bring, find, get, give, hand, lend, offer, pay, pour, promise, read, send, show, teach, tell, throw,* and *write.*

Transitive verbs, direct objects, and object complements

The direct object of a transitive verb is sometimes followed by an object complement, a word or word group that completes the direct object's meaning by renaming or describing it.

┌─S─┐   ┌V┐┌─DO─┐┌──────── OC ────────┐
People now call a spade an agricultural implement.

┌─S─┐┌─V─┐┌──── DO ────┐┌─OC─┐
Love makes all hard hearts gentle.

When the object complement renames the direct object, it is a noun or pronoun (such as *implement*). When it describes the direct object, it is an adjective (such as *gentle*).

Sentence patterns

Subject / linking verb / subject complement

    ┌──── S ────┐ V ┌──── SC ────┐
Advertising is legalized lying. [*Legalized lying* renames *Advertising*.]

    ┌──── S ────┐ V ┌── SC ──┐
Great intellects are skeptical. [*Skeptical* describes *Great intellects*.]

Subject / transitive verb / direct object

    ┌── S ──┐┌── V ──┐┌ DO ┐
A stumble may prevent a fall.

Subject / transitive verb / indirect object / direct object

    S   V   IO ┌── DO ──┐
Fate gives us our relatives.

Subject / transitive verb / direct object / object complement

    ┌── S ──┐┌── V ──┐ DO   OC
Our fears do make us traitors. [*Traitors* renames *us*.]

    ┌── S ──┐ V ┌── DO ──┐ OC
The pot calls the kettle black. [*Black* describes *the kettle*.]

Subject / intransitive verb

    S   V
Time flies.

Intransitive verbs

Intransitive verbs take no objects or complements. Their pattern is subject/verb.

    S   V
Money talks.

     ┌────── **S** ──────┐   ┌**V**┐
Revolutions never go backward.

Nothing receives the actions of talking and going in these sentences, so the verbs are intransitive. Notice that such verbs may or may not be followed by adverbial modifiers. In the second sentence, *backward* is an adverb modifying *go.*

NOTE: The dictionary will tell you whether a verb is transitive or intransitive. Some verbs have both transitive and intransitive functions.

> **TRANSITIVE**   Sandra flew her Cessna over the canyon.
>
> **INTRANSITIVE**   A bald eagle flew overhead.

In the first example, *flew* has a direct object that receives the action: *her Cessna.* In the second example, the verb is followed by an adverb (*overhead*), not by a direct object.

EXERCISE 62–2

Label the subject complements and direct objects in the following sentences, using these labels: *sc, do.* If a subject complement or direct object consists of more than one word, bracket and label all of it. Example:

>   ┌────── *DO* ──────┐
> You can fool most of the people most of the time.

  a. Talk is cheap.   —English proverb
  b. An elephant never forgets an injury.   —American proverb
  c. A runaway monk never praises his convent.   —Italian proverb
  d. Religion is the opium of the people.   —Karl Marx
  e. Good medicine always tastes bitter.   —Japanese proverb

  1. You can say the nastiest things about yourself without offending anyone.   —Phyllis Diller
  2. The quarrels of friends are the opportunities of foes.   —Aesop
  3. Art is the signature of civilization.   —Beverly Sills

4. You can tell the ideals of a nation by its advertising.
   — Norman Douglas
5. You can never be too rich or too thin.
   — Wallis Warfield Simpson

EXERCISE 62–3

Each of the following sentences has either an indirect object followed by a direct object or a direct object followed by an object complement. Label the objects and complements, using these labels: *IO, DO, OC.* If an object or complement consists of more than one word, bracket and label all of it. Example:

$$\overbrace{\text{his own geese}}^{DO} \quad \text{swans.}^{OC}$$

Every man thinks his own geese swans.

a. Sorrow makes us wise.   — Alfred Lord Tennyson
b. Too many people make money their primary pursuit.
   — Anonymous
c. Make us happy and you make us good.   — Robert Browning
d. Ask me no questions, and I will tell you no lies. — Anonymous
e. Show me a good loser, and I will show you a failure.
   — Paul Newman

1. Give the devil his due.   — English proverb
2. God gives every bird its proper food, but all must fly for it.
   — Dutch proverb
3. A wide screen makes a bad film worse.   — Samuel Goldwyn
4. Trees and fields tell me nothing.   — Socrates
5. Necessity can make us surprisingly brave.   — Latin proverb

---

ON THE WEB

For electronic exercises on identifying objects and complements, go to
www.dianahacker.com/bedhandbook

and click on   ▶ **Electronic Grammar Exercises**
              ▶ **E-ex 62–3**

62c Pattern variations

Although most sentences follow one of the five patterns in the chart on page 791, variations of these patterns commonly occur in questions, commands, sentences with delayed subjects, and passive transformations.

Questions and commands

Questions are sometimes patterned in normal word order, with the subject preceding the verb.

> S ┌──V──┐
> Who will take the first step?

Just as frequently, however, the pattern of a question is inverted, with the subject appearing between the helping and main verbs or after the verb.

> HV S MV
> Will you take the first step?

> V ┌───S───┐
> Why is the first step so difficult?

In commands, the subject of the sentence is an understood *you.*

> [You] Keep your mouth shut and your eyes open.

Sentences with delayed subjects

Writers sometimes choose to delay the subject of a sentence to achieve a special effect such as suspense or humor.

> V ┌────S────┐
> Behind the phony tinsel of Hollywood lies the real tinsel.

The subject of the sentence is also delayed in sentences opening with the expletive *There* or *It.* When used as expletives, the words *There* and *It* have no strict grammatical function; they serve merely to get the sentence started.

V ⌐————— **S** —————⌐
There is no penalty for overachievement.

V   ⌐————— **S** —————⌐
It is not good to wake a sleeping lion.

The subject in the second example is an infinitive phrase. (See 63c.)

Passive transformations

Transitive verbs, those that can take direct objects, usually appear in the active voice. In the active voice, the subject does the action and a direct object receives the action.

⌐——— **S** ———⌐   **V** ⌐—— **DO** ——⌐
ACTIVE   The early bird sometimes catches the early worm.

Sentences in the active voice may be transformed into the passive voice, with the subject receiving the action instead.

⌐——— **S** ———⌐**HV**   **MV**
PASSIVE   The early worm is sometimes caught by the early bird.

What was once the direct object (*the early worm*) has become the subject in the passive-voice transformation, and the original subject appears in a prepositional phrase beginning with *by.* The *by* phrase is frequently omitted in passive-voice constructions.

PASSIVE   The early worm is sometimes caught.

Verbs in the passive voice can be identified by their form alone. The main verb is always a past participle, such as *caught* (see 61c), preceded by a form of *be* (*be, am, is, are, was, were, being, been*); *is caught.* Sometimes adverbs intervene (*is sometimes caught*).

NOTE: Writers sometimes use the passive voice when the active voice would be more appropriate (see 8a).

63

Subordinate word groups

Subordinate word groups include prepositional phrases, subordinate clauses, verbal phrases, appositives, and absolutes. Not all of these word groups are subordinate in quite the same way. Some are subordinate because they are modifiers; others function as noun equivalents, not as modifiers.

63a Prepositional phrases

A prepositional phrase begins with a preposition such as *at, by, for, from, in, of, on, to,* or *with* (see 61f) and usually ends with a noun or noun equivalent: *on the table, for him, with great fanfare.* The noun or noun equivalent is known as the *object of the preposition.*

Functions of prepositional phrases

Prepositional phrases function either as adjectives modifying a noun or pronoun or as adverbs modifying a verb, an adjective, or another adverb. When functioning as an adjective, a prepositional phrase nearby always appears immediately following the noun or pronoun it modifies.

Variety is the spice *of life.*

Adjective phrases usually answer one or both of the questions Which one? and What kind of? If we ask Which spice? or What kind of spice? we get a sensible answer: *the spice of life.*

Adverbial prepositional phrases that modify the verb can appear nearly anywhere in a sentence.

Do not *judge* a tree *by its bark.*

Tyranny will *in time lead* to revolution.

To the ant, a few drops of rain *are* a flood.

Adverbial word groups usually answer one of these questions: When? Where? How? Why? Under what conditions? To what degree?

Do not judge a tree *how? By its bark.*

Tyranny will lead to revolution *when? In time.*

A few drops of rain are a flood *under what conditions? To the ant.*

If a prepositional phrase is movable, you can be certain that it is adverbial; adjectival prepositional phrases are wedded to the words they modify. At least some of the time, adverbial modifiers can be moved to other positions in the sentence.

By their fruits you shall know them.

You shall know them *by their fruits.*

Objects of prepositions

Objects of prepositions range from a simple noun or pronoun (at *peace,* with *you,* and so on) to quite complex structures. For example, the object of the preposition might itself be modified by a prepositional phrase, with one phrase embedded in the other. In the following sentence, the complete object of *to* is *the top of the mountain;* the simple object is *top.* The prepositional phrase *of the mountain* modifies the noun *top.*

There are many paths *to the top of the mountain.*

The effect is something like Chinese eggs or Russian dolls nestled within one another. Consider the complexity of one such sentence:

> I am one individual
>> on a small planet
>>> in a little solar system
>>>> in one
>>>>> of the galaxies.

NOTE: In questions and subordinate clauses, a preposition may appear after its object.

> *What* are you afraid *of*?

> We avoided the bike trail *that* John had warned us *about*.

EXERCISE 63–1

Underline the prepositional phrases in the following sentences. Be prepared to explain the function of each phrase. Answers to lettered sentences appear in the back of the book. Example:

> **Communism is fascism with a human face.** *(Adjective phrase modifying fascism)*

a. On their side, the workers had only the Constitution. The other side had bayonets. —Mother Jones

b. Any mother could perform the job of several air traffic controllers with ease. —Lisa Alther

c. To my embarrassment, I was born in bed with a lady. —Wilson Mizner

d. Language is the road map of a culture. —Rita Mae Brown

e. In France, cooking is a serious art form and a national sport. —Julia Child

1. We know that the road to freedom has always been stalked by death. —Angela Davis
2. A society of sheep produces a government of wolves. —Bertrand de Jouvenal
3. Some people feel with their heads and think with their hearts. —G. C. Lichtenberg
4. By a small sample, we may know the whole piece. —Cervantes
5. You and I come by road or rail, but economists travel on infrastructure. —Margaret Thatcher

ON THE WEB

For electronic exercises on identifying prepositional phrases, go to **www.dianahacker.com/bedhandbook**

and click on ▶ **Electronic Grammar Exercises**
▶ **E-ex 63–1**

63b Subordinate clauses

Subordinate clauses are patterned like sentences, having subjects and verbs and sometimes objects or complements. But they function within sentences as adjectives, adverbs, or nouns. They cannot stand alone as complete sentences.

A subordinate clause usually begins with a subordinating conjunction or a relative pronoun.

SUBORDINATING CONJUNCTIONS

after	before	rather than	though	where
although	even though	since	unless	whether
as	how	so that	until	while
as if	if	than	when	why
because	in order that	that		

RELATIVE PRONOUNS

| that | who | whom | whose | which |

The chart on page 803 classifies these words according to the kinds of clauses (adjective, adverb, or noun) they introduce.

Adjective clauses

Like other word groups functioning as adjectives, adjective clauses modify nouns or pronouns. An adjective clause nearly always appears immediately following the noun or pronoun it modifies.

The arrow *that has left the bow* never returns.

Relatives are persons *who live too near and visit too often.*

To test whether a subordinate clause functions as an adjective, ask the adjective questions: Which one? What kind of? The answer should make sense. Which arrow? *The arrow that has left the bow.* What kind of persons? *Persons who live too near and visit too often.*

Most adjective clauses begin with a relative pronoun (*who, whom, whose, which,* or *that*), which marks them as grammatically subordinate. In addition to introducing the clause, the relative pronoun points back to the noun that the clause modifies.

The fur *that warms a monarch* once warmed a bear.

Relative pronouns are sometimes "understood."

The things [*that*] *we know best* are the things [*that*] *we haven't been taught.*

Occasionally an adjective clause is introduced by a relative adverb, usually *when, where,* or *why.*

Home is the place *where you slip in the tub and break your neck.*

The parts of an adjective clause are often arranged as in sentences (subject/verb/object or complement).

S   V   DO
We often forgive the people *who bore us.*

Frequently, however, the object or complement appears first, violating the normal order of subject/verb/object.

DO   S   V
We rarely forgive those *whom we bore.*

To determine the subject of a clause, ask Who? or What? and insert the verb. Don't be surprised if the answer is an echo, as in the first adjective clause above: Who bore us? *Who.* To find any objects or complements, read the subject and the verb and then ask Who? Whom? or What? Again, be prepared for a possible echo, as in the second adjective clause: We bore whom? *Whom.*

NOTE: For punctuation of adjective clauses, see 32e and 33e. If English is not your native language, see 31c for a common problem with adjective clauses.

Adverb clauses

Adverb clauses usually modify verbs, in which case they may appear nearly anywhere in a sentence—at the beginning, at the end, or in the middle. Like other adverbial word groups, they tell when, where, why, under what conditions, or to what degree an action occurred or a situation existed.

When the well is dry, we know the worth of water.

Venice would be a fine city *if it were only drained.*

When do we know the worth of water? *When the well is dry.* Under what conditions would Venice be a fine city? *If it were only drained.*

Unlike adjective clauses, adverb clauses are frequently movable. In the preceding example sentences, for instance, the adverb clauses can be moved without affecting the meaning of the sentences.

> We know the worth of water *when the well is dry.*

> *If it were only drained,* Venice would be a fine city.

When an adverb clause modifies an adjective or an adverb, it is not movable; it must appear next to the word it modifies. In the following examples the *because* clause modifies the adjective *angry,* and the *than* clause modifies the adverb *faster.*

> Angry *because the mayor had not kept his promises,* we worked for his defeat.

> Joan can run faster *than I can bicycle.*

Adverb clauses always begin with a subordinating conjunction (see the chart on p. 803 for a list). Subordinating conjunctions introduce clauses and express their relation to the rest of the sentence.

Adverb clauses are sometimes elliptical, with some of their words being "understood."

> When [*it is*] *painted,* the room will look larger.

Noun clauses

Because they do not function as modifiers, noun clauses are not subordinate in the same sense as are adjective and adverb clauses. They are called subordinate only because they cannot stand alone: They must function within a sentence, always as nouns.

A noun clause functions just like a single-word noun, usually as a subject, subject complement, direct object, or object of a preposition.

basic

Words that introduce subordinate clauses

WORDS INTRODUCING ADVERB CLAUSES

Subordinating conjunctions: after, although, as, as if, because, before, even though, if, in order that, rather than, since, so that, than, that, though, unless, until, when, where, whether, while

WORDS INTRODUCING ADJECTIVE CLAUSES

Relative pronouns: that, which, who, whom, whose

Relative adverbs: when, where, why

WORDS INTRODUCING NOUN CLAUSES

Relative pronouns: that, which, who, whom, whose

Other pronouns: whoever, whomever, what, whatever, whichever

Subordinating conjunctions: how, if, when, whenever, where, wherever, whether, why

┌─────── **S** ───────┐
Whoever gossips to you will gossip of you.

┌─────── **DO** ───────┐
We never forget *that we buried the hatchet.*

A noun clause begins with a word that marks it as subordinate (see the above for a list). The subordinating word may or may not play a significant role in the clause. In the preceding example sentences, *whoever* is the subject of its clause, but *that* does not perform a function in its clause.

As with adjective clauses, the parts of a noun clause may appear out of their normal order (subject/verb/object).

DO   S   V

Talent is *what you possess.*

The parts of a noun clause may also appear in their normal order.

S   V   DO

Genius is *what possesses you.*

EXERCISE 63–2

Underline the subordinate clauses in the following sentences. Be prepared to explain the function of each clause. Answers to lettered sentences appear in the back of the book. Example:

Dig a well <u>before you are thirsty</u>. *(Adverb clause modifying Dig)*

  a. It is hard to fight an enemy who has outposts in your head.
                                   —Sally Kempton
  b. A rattlesnake that doesn't bite teaches you nothing.
                                   —Jessamyn West
  c. If love is the answer, could you please rephrase the question?
                                   —Lily Tomlin
  d. Dreams say what they mean, but they don't say it in daytime language.   —Gail Godwin
  e. I generally avoid temptation unless I cannot resist it.
                                     —Mae West

  1. What history teaches us is that we have never learned anything from it.   —Georg Wilhelm Hegel
  2. When the insects take over the world, we hope that they will remember our picnics with gratitude.   —Anonymous
  3. A woman who will tell her age will tell anything.
                                —Rita Mae Brown
  4. If triangles had a god, it would have three sides.
                        —C. L. de Montesquieu
  5. He gave her a look that you could have poured on a waffle.
                                  —Ring Lardner

ON THE WEB

For electronic exercises on identifying subordinate
clauses, go to **www.dianahacker.com/bedhandbook**

and click on ▶ **Electronic Grammar Exercises**
▶ **E-ex 63–4**

63c Verbal phrases

A verbal is a verb form that does not function as the verb of
a clause. Verbals include infinitives (the word *to* plus the
base form of the verb), present participles (the *-ing* form of
the verb), and past participles (the verb form usually ending
in *-d, -ed, -n, -en,* or *-t*). (See 27a and 61c.)

INFINITIVE	PRESENT PARTICIPLE	PAST PARTICIPLE
to dream	dreaming	dreamed
to choose	choosing	chosen
to build	building	built
to grow	growing	grown

Instead of functioning as the verb of a clause, a verbal or
a verbal phrase functions as an adjective, a noun, or an
adverb.

ADJECTIVE	*Stolen* grapes are especially sweet.
NOUN	Continual *dripping* wears away a stone.
ADVERB	Were we born *to suffer?*

Verbals can take objects, complements, and modifiers to
form verbal phrases; the phrases usually lack subjects.

Living well is the best revenge.

Governments exist *to protect the rights of minorities.*

The verbal *Living* is modified by the adverb *well;* the verbal *to protect* is followed by a direct object, *the rights of minorities.*

Like single-word verbals, verbal phrases function as adjectives, nouns, or adverbs. In the sentences just given, for example, *living well* functions as a noun used as the subject of the sentence, and *to protect the rights of minorities* functions as an adverb, answering the question Why?

Verbal phrases are ordinarily classified as participles, gerunds, and infinitives. This classification is based partly on form (whether the verbal is a present participle, a past participle, or an infinitive) and partly on function (whether the whole phrase functions as an adjective, a noun, or an adverb).

NOTE: For advice on editing dangling verbal phrases, see 12e.

Participial phrases

Participial phrases always function as adjectives. Their verbals are either present participles, always ending in *-ing,* or past participles, frequently ending in *-d, -ed, -n, -en,* or *-t* (see 27a).

Participial phrases frequently appear immediately following the noun or pronoun they modify.

Congress shall make no law *abridging the freedom of speech or of the press.*

Truth *kept in the dark* will never save the world.

Unlike other adjectival word groups, however, which must always follow the noun or pronoun they modify, participial phrases are often movable. They can precede the word they modify.

Being weak, foxes are distinguished by superior tact.

They may also appear at some distance from the word they modify.

History is something that never happened, *written by someone who wasn't there.*

Gerund phrases

Gerund phrases are built around present participles (verb forms ending in *-ing*), and they always function as nouns: usually as subjects, subject complements, direct objects, or objects of a preposition.

    S
Justifying a fault doubles it.

    SC
The secret of education is *respecting the pupil.*

    DO
Kleptomaniacs can't help *helping themselves.*

    OBJ OF PREP
The hen is an egg's way of *producing another egg.*

Infinitive phrases

Infinitive phrases, usually constructed around *to* plus the base form of the verb (*to call, to drink*), can function as nouns, as adjectives, or as adverbs.

When functioning as a noun, an infinitive phrase may appear in almost any noun slot in a sentence, usually as a subject, subject complement, or direct object.

    S
To side with truth is noble.

```
    ┌─────── DO ───────┐
```
Never try *to leap a chasm in two jumps.*

Infinitive phrases functioning as adjectives usually appear immediately following the noun or pronoun they modify.

We do not have the right *to abandon the poor.*

The infinitive phrase modifies the noun *right.* Which right? *The right to abandon the poor.*

Adverbial infinitive phrases usually qualify the meaning of the verb, telling when, where, how, why, under what conditions, or to what degree an action occurred.

He cut off his nose *to spite his face.*

Why did he cut off his nose? *To spite his face.*

NOTE: In some constructions, the infinitive is unmarked; in other words, the *to* does not appear: *No one can make you [to] feel inferior without your consent.* (See 29c.)

EXERCISE 63-3

Underline the verbal phrases in the following sentences. Be prepared to explain the function of each phrase. Answers to lettered sentences appear in the back of the book. Example:

> **Do you want to be a writer? Then write.** *(Infinitive phrase used as direct object of Do want)*

a. Concealing a disease is no way to cure it.
                                    —Ethiopian proverb
b. The trouble with being punctual is that nobody is there to appreciate it.   —Franklin P. Jones
c. Fate tried to conceal him by naming him Smith.
                                —Oliver Wendell Holmes Jr.
d. Being weak, children quickly learn to beguile us with charm.
                                    —Anonymous

e. Wrestling with words gave me my moments of greatest meaning.
— Richard Wright

1. The thing generally raised on city land is taxes.
— C. D. Warner
2. Do not use a hatchet to remove a fly from your friend's forehead. — Chinese proverb
3. He has the gall of a shoplifter returning an item for a refund.
— W. I. E. Gates
4. Tact is the ability to describe others as they see themselves.
— Mary Pettibone Poole
5. He could never see a belt without hitting below it.
— Harriet Braiker

ON THE WEB

For electronic exercises on identifying verbal phrases, go to
www.dianahacker.com/bedhandbook

and click on ▶ **Electronic Grammar Exercises**
▶ **E-ex 63–7**

63d Appositive phrases

Though strictly speaking they are not subordinate word groups, appositive phrases function somewhat as adjectives do, to describe nouns or pronouns. Instead of modifying nouns or pronouns, however, appositive phrases rename them. In form they are nouns or noun equivalents.

Appositives are said to be "in apposition" to the nouns or pronouns they rename.

> Politicians, *acrobats at heart*, can sit on a fence and yet keep both ears to the ground.

Acrobats at heart is in apposition to the noun *politicians*.

63e   Absolute phrases

An absolute phrase modifies a whole clause or sentence, not just one word, and it may appear nearly anywhere in the sentence. It consists of a noun or noun equivalent usually followed by a participial phrase.

> *His words dipped in honey,* the senator mesmerized the crowd.
>
> The senator mesmerized the crowd, *his words dipped in honey.*

64

Sentence types

Sentences are classified in two ways: according to their structure (simple, compound, complex, and compound-complex) and according to their purpose (declarative, imperative, interrogative, and exclamatory).

64a   Sentence structures

Depending on the number and types of clauses they contain, sentences are classified as simple, compound, complex, or compound-complex.

Clauses come in two varieties: independent and subordinate. An independent clause is a full sentence pattern that does not function within another sentence pattern: It contains a subject and its modifiers plus a verb and any objects, complements, and modifiers of that verb, and it either stands alone or could stand alone. A subordinate clause is a full sentence pattern that functions within a sentence as an adjective, an adverb, or a noun but that cannot stand alone as a complete sentence. (See 63b.)

Simple sentences

A simple sentence is one independent clause with no subordinate clauses.

┌──────── **INDEPENDENT CLAUSE** ────────┐
Without music, life would be a mistake.

This sentence contains a subject (*life*), a verb (*would be*), a complement (*a mistake*), and an adverbial modifier (*Without music*).

A simple sentence may contain compound elements—a compound subject, verb, or object, for example—but it does not contain more than one full sentence pattern. The following sentence is simple because its two verbs (*enters* and *spreads*) share a subject (*Evil*).

┌──────────── **INDEPENDENT CLAUSE** ────────────┐
Evil enters like a needle and spreads like an oak.

Compound sentences

A compound sentence is composed of two or more independent clauses with no subordinate clauses. The independent clauses are usually joined with a comma and a coordinating conjunction (*and, but, or, nor, for, so, yet*) or with a semicolon. (See 14a.)

┌ **INDEPENDENT CLAUSE** ┐   ┌── **INDEPENDENT CLAUSE** ──┐
One arrow is easily broken, but you can't break a bundle of ten.

┌──────── **INDEPENDENT CLAUSE** ────────┐ ┌**INDEPENDENT**─
We are born brave, trusting, and greedy; most of us have

CLAUSE ────────┐
remained greedy.

Complex sentences

A complex sentence is composed of one independent clause with one or more subordinate clauses. (See 63b.)

Grammar basics

ADJECTIVE

SUBORDINATE
CLAUSE

They that sow in tears shall reap in joy.

ADVERB

SUBORDINATE
CLAUSE

If you scatter thorns, don't go barefoot.

NOUN

SUBORDINATE CLAUSE

What the scientists have in their briefcases is terrifying.

Compound-complex sentences

A compound-complex sentence contains at least two independent clauses and at least one subordinate clause. The following sentence contains two full sentence patterns that can stand alone.

INDEPENDENT CLAUSE   INDEPENDENT CLAUSE

Tell me what you eat, and I will tell you what you are.

And each independent clause contains a subordinate clause, making the sentence both compound and complex.

IND CL   IND CL
SUB CL   SUB CL

Tell me what you eat, and I will tell you what you are.

64b Sentence purposes

Writers use declarative sentences to make statements, imperative sentences to issue requests or commands, interrogative sentences to ask questions, and exclamatory sentences to make exclamations.

DECLARATIVE	The echo always has the last word.
IMPERATIVE	Love your neighbor.
INTERROGATIVE	Are second thoughts always wisest?
EXCLAMATORY	I want to wash the flag, not burn it!

EXERCISE 64–1

Identify the following sentences as simple, compound, complex, or compound-complex. Be prepared to identify the subordinate clauses and classify them according to their function: adjective, adverb, or noun. (See 63b.) Answers to lettered sentences appear in the back of the book. Example:

> **The frog in the well knows nothing of the ocean.** *(Simple)*

a. People who sleep like a baby usually don't have one.
                                                    —Leo Burke
b. My folks didn't come over on the *Mayflower;* they were there to meet the boat.   —Will Rogers
c. The impersonal hand of the government can never replace the helping hand of a neighbor.   —Hubert Humphrey
d. If you don't go to other people's funerals, they won't go to yours.
                                                    —Clarence Day
e. Tell us your phobias, and we will tell you what you are afraid of.
                                                    —Robert Benchley

1. The tragedy of life is that people don't change.
                                                    —Agatha Christie
2. Those who cannot remember the past are condemned to repeat it.   —George Santayana
3. The best mind-altering drug is truth.   —Lily Tomlin
4. Morality cannot be legislated, but behavior can be regulated.
                                                    —Martin Luther King Jr.
5. Science commits suicide when it adopts a creed.
                                                    —T. H. Huxley

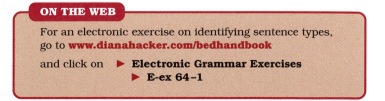

ON THE WEB

For an electronic exercise on identifying sentence types, go to **www.dianahacker.com/bedhandbook**

and click on ▶ **Electronic Grammar Exercises**
              ▶ **E-ex 64–1**

Glossary of Usage

This glossary includes words commonly confused (such as *accept* and *except*), words commonly misused (such as *aggravate*), and words that are nonstandard (such as *hisself*). It also lists colloquialisms and jargon. Colloquialisms are expressions that may be appropriate in informal speech but are inappropriate in formal writing. Jargon is needlessly technical or pretentious language that is inappropriate in most contexts. If an item is not listed here, consult the index. For irregular verbs (such as *sing, sang, sung*), see 27a. For idiomatic use of prepositions, see 18d.

ON THE WEB

Some matters of usage included in this glossary have sparked debates. If you are interested in learning why, go to **www.dianahacker.com/bedhandbook**

and click on ▶ **Language Debates**
  feel bad versus *feel badly*
  however at the beginning of a sentence
  lie versus *lay*
  myself
  that versus *which*
  Absolute concepts such as *unique*
  who versus *which* or *that*
  who versus *whom*
  you

a, an   Use *an* before a vowel sound, *a* before a consonant sound: *an apple, a peach.* Problems sometimes arise with words beginning with *h*. If the *h* is silent, the word begins with a vowel sound, so use *an*: *an hour, an heir, an honest senator, an honorable deed.* If the *h* is pronounced, the word begins with a consonant sound, so use *a*: *a hospital, a hymn, a historian, a hotel.* When an abbreviation or acronym begins with a vowel sound, use *an*: *an EKG, an MRI, an AIDS* patient.

accept, except   *Accept* is a verb meaning "to receive." *Except* is usually a preposition meaning "excluding." *I will accept all the packages except that one. Except* is also a verb meaning "to exclude." *Please except that item from the list.*

adapt, adopt   *Adapt* means "to adjust or become accustomed"; it is usually followed by *to. Adopt* means "to take as one's own." *Our family adopted a Vietnamese orphan, who quickly adapted to his new surroundings.*

adverse, averse   *Adverse* means "unfavorable." *Averse* means "opposed" or "reluctant"; it is usually followed by *to. I am averse to your proposal because it could have an adverse impact on the economy.*

advice, advise   *Advice* is a noun, *advise* a verb. *We advise you to follow John's advice.*

affect, effect   *Affect* is usually a verb meaning "to influence." *Effect* is usually a noun meaning "result." *The drug did not affect the disease, and it had adverse side effects. Effect* can also be a verb meaning "to bring about." *Only the president can effect such a change.*

aggravate   *Aggravate* means "to make worse or more troublesome." *Overgrazing aggravated the soil erosion.* In formal writing, avoid the colloquial use of *aggravate* meaning "to annoy or irritate." *Her babbling annoyed* (not *aggravated*) *me.*

agree to, agree with   *Agree to* means "to give consent." *Agree with* means "to be in accord" or "to come to an understanding." *He agrees with me about the need for change, but he won't agree to my plan.*

ain't   *Ain't* is nonstandard. Use *am not, are not* (*aren't*), or *is not* (*isn't*). *I am not* (not *ain't*) *going home for spring break.*

all ready, already   *All ready* means "completely prepared." *Already* means "previously." *Susan was all ready for the concert, but her friends had already left.*

all right   *All right* is written as two words. *Alright* is nonstandard.

all together, altogether   *All together* means "everyone gathered." *Altogether* means "entirely." *We were not altogether certain that we could bring the family all together for the reunion.*

allude   To *allude* to something is to make an indirect reference to it. Do not use *allude* to mean "to refer directly." *In his lecture the professor referred* (not *alluded*) *to several pre-Socratic philosophers.*

allusion, illusion   An *allusion* is an indirect reference. An *illusion* is a misconception or false impression. *Did you catch my allusion to Shakespeare? Mirrors give the room an illusion of depth.*

a lot   *A lot* is two words. Do not write *alot. We have had a lot of rain this spring.* See also *lots, lots of.*

among, between   See *between, among.*

amongst   In American English, *among* is preferred.

amoral, immoral   *Amoral* means "neither moral nor immoral"; it also means "not caring about moral judgments." *Immoral* means "morally wrong." *Until recently, most business courses were taught from an amoral perspective. Murder is immoral.*

amount, number   Use *amount* with quantities that cannot be counted; use *number* with those that can. *This recipe calls for a large amount of sugar. We have a large number of toads in our garden.*

an   See *a, an.*

and etc.   *Et cetera* (*etc.*) means "and so forth"; therefore, *and etc.* is redundant. See also *etc.*

and/or   Avoid the awkward construction *and/or* except in technical or legal documents.

angry at, angry with   To write that one is *angry at* another person is nonstandard. Use *angry with* instead.

ante-, anti-   The prefix *ante-* means "earlier" or "in front of"; the prefix *anti-* means "against" or "opposed to." *William Lloyd Garrison was a leader of the antislavery movement during the antebellum period. Anti-* should be used with a hyphen when it is followed by a capital letter or a word beginning with *i.*

anxious   *Anxious* means "worried" or "apprehensive." In formal writing, avoid using *anxious* to mean "eager." *We are eager* (not *anxious*) *to see your new house.*

anybody, anyone   *Anybody* and *anyone* are singular. (See 21e and 22a.)

anymore   Reserve the adverb *anymore* for negative contexts, where it means "any longer." *Moviegoers are rarely shocked anymore by profanity.* Do not use *anymore* in positive contexts. Use *now* or *nowadays* instead. *Interest rates are so low now* (not *anymore*) *that more people can afford to buy homes.*

anyone   See *anybody, anyone.*

anyone, any one   *Anyone,* an indefinite pronoun, means "any person at all." *Any one,* the pronoun *one* preceded by the adjective *any,* refers to a particular person or thing in a group. *Anyone from Chicago may choose any one of the games on display.*

anyplace   *Anyplace* is informal for *anywhere.* Avoid *anyplace* in formal writing.

anyways, anywheres   *Anyways* and *anywheres* are nonstandard. Use *anyway* and *anywhere.*

as   *As* is sometimes used to mean "because." But do not use it if there is any chance of ambiguity. *We canceled the picnic because* (not *as*) *it began raining. As* here could mean "because" or "when."

as, like   See *like, as.*

as to   *As to* is jargon for *about. He inquired about* (not *as to*) *the job.*

averse   See *adverse, averse.*

awful   The adjective *awful* and the adverb *awfully* are too colloquial for formal writing.

awhile, a while   *Awhile* is an adverb; it can modify a verb, but it cannot be the object of a preposition such as *for.* The two-word form *a while* is a noun preceded by an article and therefore can be the object of a preposition. *Stay awhile. Stay for a while.*

back up, backup   *Back up* is a verb phrase. *Back up the car carefully. Be sure to back up your hard drive. Backup* is a noun meaning "a duplicate of electronically stored data." *Keep your backup in a safe place. Backup* can also be used as an adjective. *I regularly create backup disks.*

bad, badly   *Bad* is an adjective, *badly* an adverb. (See 26a and 26b.) *They felt bad about being early and ruining the surprise. Her arm hurt badly after she slid headfirst into second base.*

being as, being that   *Being as* and *being that* are nonstandard expressions. Write *because* instead. *Because* (not *Being as*) *I slept late, I had to skip breakfast.*

beside, besides   *Beside* is a preposition meaning "at the side of" or "next to." *Annie Oakley slept with her gun beside her bed. Besides* is a preposition meaning "except" or "in addition to." *No one besides Terrie can have that ice cream. Besides* is also an adverb meaning "in addition." *I'm not hungry; besides, I don't like ice cream.*

between, among   Ordinarily, use *among* with three or more entities, *between* with two. *The prize was divided among several contestants. You have a choice between carrots and beans.*

bring, take   Use *bring* when an object is being transported toward you, *take* when it is being moved away. *Please bring me a glass of water. Please take these flowers to Mr. Scott.*

burst, bursted; bust, busted   *Burst* is an irregular verb meaning "to come open or fly apart suddenly or violently." Its principal parts are *burst, burst, burst.* The past-tense form *bursted* is nonstandard. *Bust* and *busted* are slang for *burst* and, along with *bursted*, should not be used in formal writing.

can, may   The distinction between *can* and *may* is fading, but some writers still observe it in formal writing. *Can* is traditionally reserved for ability, *may* for permission. *Can you ski down the advanced slope without falling? May I help you?*

capital, capitol   *Capital* refers to a city, *capitol* to a building where lawmakers meet. *Capital* also refers to wealth or resources. *The capitol has undergone extensive renovations. The residents of the state capital protested the development plans.*

censor, censure   *Censor* means "to remove or suppress material considered objectionable." *Censure* means "to criticize severely." *The library's new policy of censoring controversial books has been censured by the media.*

cite, site   *Cite* means "to quote as an authority or example." *Site* is usually a noun meaning "a particular place." *He cited the zoning law in his argument against the proposed site of the gas station.* Locations on the Internet are usually referred to as *sites. The library's Web site improves every week.*

climactic, climatic *Climactic* is derived from *climax,* the point of greatest intensity in a series or progression of events. *Climatic* is derived from *climate* and refers to meteorological conditions. *The climactic period in the dinosaurs' reign was reached just before severe climatic conditions brought on an ice age.*

coarse, course *Coarse* means "crude" or "rough in texture." *The coarse weave of the wall hanging gave it a three-dimensional quality. Course* usually refers to a path, a playing field, or a unit of study; the expression *of course* means "certainly." *I plan to take a course in car repair this summer. Of course, you are welcome to join me.*

compare to, compare with *Compare to* means "to represent as similar." *She compared him to a wild stallion. Compare with* means "to examine the ways in which two things are similar." *The study compared the language ability of apes with that of dolphins.*

complement, compliment *Complement* is a verb meaning "to go with or complete" or a noun meaning "something that completes." *Compliment* as a verb means "to flatter"; as a noun it means "flattering remark." *Her skill at rushing the net complements his skill at volleying. Mother's flower arrangements receive many compliments.*

conscience, conscious *Conscience* is a noun meaning "moral principles." *Conscious* is an adjective meaning "aware or alert." *Let your conscience be your guide. Were you conscious of his love for you?*

continual, continuous *Continual* means "repeated regularly and frequently." *She grew weary of the continual telephone calls. Continuous* means "extended or prolonged without interruption." *The broken siren made a continuous wail.*

could care less *Could care less* is a nonstandard expression. Write *couldn't care less* instead. *He couldn't* (not *could*) *care less about his psychology final.*

could of *Could of* is nonstandard for *could have. We could have* (not *could of*) *had steak for dinner if we had been hungry.*

council, counsel A *council* is a deliberative body, and a *councilor* is a member of such a body. *Counsel* usually means "advice" and can also mean "lawyer"; *counselor* is one who gives advice or guidance. *The councilors met to draft the council's position paper. The pastor offered wise counsel to the troubled teenager.*

criteria   *Criteria* is the plural of *criterion,* which means "a standard or rule or test on which a judgment or decision can be based." *The only criterion for the scholarship is ability.*

data   *Data* is a plural noun technically meaning "facts or propositions." But *data* is increasingly being accepted as a singular noun. *The new data suggest* (or *suggests*) *that our theory is correct.* (The singular *datum* is rarely used.)

different from, different than   Ordinarily, write *different from. Your sense of style is different from Jim's.* However, *different than* is acceptable to avoid an awkward construction. *Please let me know if your plans are different than* (to avoid *from what*) *they were six weeks ago.*

differ from, differ with   *Differ from* means "to be unlike"; *differ with* means "to disagree." *She differed with me about the wording of the agreement. My approach to the problem differed from hers.*

disinterested, uninterested   *Disinterested* means "impartial, objective"; *uninterested* means "not interested." *We sought the advice of a disinterested counselor to help us solve our problem. He was uninterested in anyone's opinion but his own.*

don't   *Don't* is the contraction for *do not. I don't want any. Don't* should not be used as the contraction for *does not,* which is *doesn't. He doesn't* (not *don't*) *want any.* (See 27c.)

each   *Each* is singular. (See 21e and 22a.)

effect   See *affect, effect.*

e.g.   In formal writing, replace the Latin abbreviation *e.g.* with its English equivalent: *for example* or *for instance.*

either   *Either* is singular. (See 21e and 22a.) (For *either . . . or* constructions, see 21d and 22d.)

elicit, illicit   *Elicit* is a verb meaning "to bring out" or "to evoke." *Illicit* is an adjective meaning "unlawful." *The reporter was unable to elicit any information from the police about illicit drug traffic.*

emigrate from, immigrate to   *Emigrate* means "to leave one country or region to settle in another." *In 1900, my grandfather emigrated from Russia to escape the religious pogroms. Immigrate* means "to enter another country and reside there." *Many Mexicans immigrate to the United States to find work.*

eminent, imminent   *Eminent* means "outstanding" or "distinguished." *We met an eminent professor of Greek history. Imminent* means "about to happen." *The announcement is imminent.*

enthused   Many people object to the use of *enthused* as an adjective. Use *enthusiastic* instead. *The children were enthusiastic* (not *enthused*) *about going to the circus.*

etc.   Avoid ending a list with *etc.* It is more emphatic to end with an example, and in most contexts readers will understand that the list is not exhaustive. When you don't wish to end with an example, *and so on* is more graceful than *etc.* See also *and etc.*

eventually, ultimately   Often used interchangeably, *eventually* is the better choice to mean "at an unspecified time in the future" and *ultimately* is better to mean "the furthest possible extent or greatest extreme." *He knew that eventually he would complete his degree. The existentialist considered suicide the ultimately rational act.*

everybody, everyone   *Everybody* and *everyone* are singular. (See 21e and 22a.)

everyone, every one   *Everyone* is an indefinite pronoun. *Every one,* the pronoun *one* preceded by the adjective *every,* means "each individual or thing in a particular group." *Every one* is usually followed by *of. Everyone wanted to go. Every one of the missing books was found.*

except   See *accept, except.*

expect   Avoid the colloquial use of *expect* meaning "to believe, think, or suppose." *I think* (not *expect*) *it will rain tonight.*

explicit, implicit   *Explicit* means "expressed directly" or "clearly defined"; *implicit* means "implied, unstated." *I gave him explicit instructions not to go swimming. My mother's silence indicated her implicit approval.*

farther, further   *Farther* usually describes distances. *Further* usually suggests quantity or degree. *Chicago is farther from Miami than I thought. You extended the curfew further than you should have.*

female, male   The terms *female* and *male* are jargon when used to refer to specific people. *Two women* (not *females*) *and one man* (not *male*) *applied for the position.*

fewer, less   *Fewer* refers to items that can be counted; *less* refers to general amounts. *Fewer people are living in the city. Please put less sugar in my tea.*

finalize   *Finalize* is jargon meaning "to make final or complete." Use ordinary English instead. *The architect prepared final drawings* (not *finalized the drawings*).

firstly   *Firstly* sounds pretentious, and it leads to the ungainly series *firstly, secondly, thirdly, fourthly,* and so on. Write *first, second, third* instead.

further   See *farther, further.*

get   *Get* has many colloquial uses. In writing, avoid using *get* to mean the following: "to evoke an emotional response" (*That music always gets to me*); "to annoy" (*After a while his sulking got to me*); "to take revenge on" (*I got back at him by leaving the room*); "to become" (*He got sick*); "to start or begin" (*Let's get going*). Avoid using *have got to* in place of *must. I must* (not *have got to*) *finish this paper tonight.*

good, well   *Good* is an adjective, *well* an adverb. (See 26.) *He hasn't felt good about his game since he sprained his wrist last season. She performed well on the uneven parallel bars.*

graduate   Both of the following uses of *graduate* are standard: *My sister was graduated from UCLA last year. My sister graduated from UCLA last year.* It is nonstandard, however, to drop the word *from: My sister graduated UCLA last year.* Though this usage is common in informal English, many readers object to it.

grow   Phrases such as *to grow the economy* or *to grow a business* are jargon. Usually the verb *grow* is intransitive (it does not take a direct object). *Our business has grown very quickly.* When *grow* is used in a transitive sense, with a direct object, it means "to cultivate" or "to allow to grow." *We plan to grow tomatoes this year. John is growing a beard.*

hanged, hung   *Hanged* is the past-tense and past-participle form of the verb *hang* meaning "to execute." *The prisoner was hanged at dawn. Hung* is the past-tense and past-participle form of the verb *hang* meaning "to fasten or suspend." *The stockings were hung by the chimney with care.*

hardly   Avoid expressions such as *can't hardly* and *not hardly,* which are considered double negatives. *I can* (not *can't*) *hardly describe my elation at getting the job.* (See 26d.)

has got, have got   *Got* is unnecessary and awkward in such constructions. It should be dropped. *We have* (not *have got*) *three days to prepare for the opening.*

he   At one time *he* was commonly used to mean "he or she." Today such usage is inappropriate. (See 17f and 22a.)

he/she, his/her   In formal writing, use *he or she* or *his or her*. For alternatives to these wordy constructions, see 17f and 22a.

hisself   *Hisself* is nonstandard. Use *himself*.

hopefully   *Hopefully* means "in a hopeful manner." *We looked hopefully to the future.* Some usage experts object to the use of *hopefully* as a sentence adverb, apparently on grounds of clarity. To be safe, avoid using *hopefully* in sentences such as the following: *Hopefully, your son will recover soon.* At least some educated readers will want you to indicate who is doing the hoping: *I hope that your son will recover soon.*

however   In the past, some writers objected to *however* at the beginning of a sentence, but current experts advise you to place the word according to your meaning and desired emphasis. Any of the following sentences is correct, depending on the intended contrast. *Pam decided, however, to attend Harvard. However, Pam decided to attend Harvard.* (She had been considering other schools.) *Pam, however, decided to attend Harvard.* (Unlike someone else, Pam opted for Harvard.)

hung   See *hanged, hung.*

i.e.   In formal writing, replace the Latin abbreviation *i.e.* with its English equivalent: *that is.*

if, whether   Use *if* to express a condition and *whether* to express alternatives. *If you go on a trip, whether it be to Nebraska or New Jersey, remember to bring traveler's checks.*

illusion   See *allusion, illusion.*

immigrate, emigrate   See *emigrate from, immigrate to.*

imminent   See *eminent, imminent.*

immoral   See *amoral, immoral.*

implement   *Implement* is a pretentious way of saying "do," "carry out," or "accomplish." Use ordinary language instead. *We carried out* (not *implemented*) *the director's orders with some reluctance.*

imply, infer   *Imply* means "to suggest or state indirectly"; *infer* means "to draw a conclusion." *John implied that he knew all about computers, but the interviewer inferred that John was inexperienced.*

in, into   *In* indicates location or condition; *into* indicates movement or a change in condition. *They found the lost letters in a box after moving into the house.*

individual   *Individual* is a pretentious substitute for *person*. *We invited a person* (not *an individual*) *from the audience to participate.*

ingenious, ingenuous   *Ingenious* means "clever." *Sarah's solution to the problem was ingenious. Ingenuous* means "naive" or "frank." *For a successful manager, Ed is surprisingly ingenuous.*

in regards to   *In regards to* confuses two different phrases: *in regard to* and *as regards*. Use one or the other. *In regard to* (or *As regards*) *the contract, ignore the first clause.*

irregardless   *Irregardless* is nonstandard. Use *regardless*.

is when, is where   These mixed constructions are often incorrectly used in definitions. *A run-off election is a second election held to break a tie* (not *is when a second election breaks a tie*). (See 11c.)

it is   *It is* is nonstandard when used to mean "there is." *There is* (not *It is*) *a fly in my soup.*

its, it's   *Its* is a possessive pronoun; *it's* is a contraction for *it is*. (See 36c and 36e.) *The dog licked its wound whenever its owner walked into the room. It's a perfect day to walk the twenty-mile trail.*

kind(s)   *Kind* is singular and should be treated as such. Don't write *These kind of chairs are rare*. Write instead *This kind of chair is rare*. *Kinds* is plural and should be used only when you mean more than one kind. *These kinds of chairs are rare.*

kind of, sort of   Avoid using *kind of* or *sort of* to mean "somewhat." *The movie was somewhat* (not *kind of*) *boring*. Do not put *a* after either phrase. *That kind of* (not *kind of a*) *salesclerk annoys me.*

lay, lie   See *lie, lay*.

lead, led   *Lead* is a noun referring to a metal. *Led* is the past tense of the verb *lead*. *He led me to the treasure.*

learn, teach   *Learn* means "to gain knowledge"; *teach* means "to impart knowledge." *I must teach* (not *learn*) *my sister to read.*

leave, let   *Leave* means "to exit." *Let* means "to permit." *Let* (not *Leave*) *me help you with the dishes.*

less   See *fewer, less*.

let, leave   See *leave, let*.

liable   *Liable* means "obligated" or "responsible." Do not use it to mean "likely." *You're likely* (not *liable*) *to trip if you don't tie your shoelaces.*

lie, lay   *Lie* is an intransitive verb meaning "to recline or rest on a surface." Its principal parts are *lie, lay, lain. Lay* is a transitive verb meaning "to put or place." Its principal parts are *lay, laid, laid.* (See 27b.)

like, as   *Like* is a preposition, not a subordinating conjunction. It can be followed only by a noun or a noun phrase. *As* is a subordinating conjunction that introduces a subordinate clause. In casual speech you may say *She looks like she hasn't slept* or *You don't know her like I do.* But in formal writing, use *as. She looks as if she hasn't slept. You don't know her as I do.* (See prepositions and subordinating conjunctions, 61f and 61g.)

loose, lose   *Loose* is an adjective meaning "not securely fastened." *Lose* is a verb meaning "to misplace" or "to not win." *Did you lose your only loose pair of work pants?*

lots, lots of   *Lots* and *lots of* are colloquial substitutes for *many, much,* or *a lot.* Avoid using them in formal writing.

male, female   See *female, male.*

mankind   Avoid *mankind* whenever possible. It offends many readers because it excludes women. Use *humanity, humans, the human race,* or *humankind* instead.

may   See *can, may.*

maybe, may be   *Maybe* is an adverb meaning "possibly." *May be* is a verb phrase. *Maybe the sun will shine tomorrow. Tomorrow may be a brighter day.*

may of, might of   *May of* and *might of* are nonstandard for *may have* and *might have. We may have* (not *may of*) *had too many cookies.*

media, medium   *Media* is the plural of *medium. Of all the media that cover the Olympics, television is the medium that best captures the spectacle of the events.*

most   *Most* is colloquial when used to mean "almost" and should be avoided. *Almost* (not *Most*) *everyone went to the parade.*

must of   See *may of.*

myself   *Myself* is a reflexive or intensive pronoun. Reflexive: *I cut myself.* Intensive: *I will drive you myself.* Do not use *myself* in place of *I* or *me. He gave the flowers to Melinda and me* (not *myself*). (See also 24.)

neither   *Neither* is singular. (See 21e and 22a.) For *neither...nor* constructions, see 21d and 22d.

none   *None* may be singular or plural. (See 21e.)

nowheres   *Nowheres* is nonstandard for *nowhere.*

number   See *amount, number.*

of   Use the verb *have,* not the preposition *of,* after the verbs *could, should, would, may, might,* and *must. They must have* (not *of*) *left early.*

off of   *Off* is sufficient. Omit *of. The ball rolled off* (not *off of*) *the table.*

OK, O.K., okay   All three spellings are acceptable, but in formal speech and writing avoid these colloquial expressions for consent or approval.

parameters   *Parameter* is a mathematical term that has become jargon for "fixed limit," "boundary," or "guideline." Use ordinary English instead. *The task force was asked to work within certain guidelines* (not *parameters*).

passed, past   *Passed* is the past tense of the verb *pass. Mother passed me another slice of cake. Past* usually means "belonging to a former time" or "beyond a time or place." *Our past president spoke until past midnight. The hotel is just past the next intersection.*

percent, per cent, percentage   *Percent* (also spelled *per cent*) is always used with a specific number. *Percentage* is used with a descriptive term such as *large* or *small,* not with a specific number. *The candidate won 80 percent of the primary vote. Only a small percentage of registered voters turned out for the election.*

phenomena   *Phenomena* is the plural of *phenomenon,* which means "an observable occurrence or fact." *Strange phenomena occur at all hours of the night in that house, but last night's phenomenon was the strangest of all.*

plus   *Plus* should not be used to join independent clauses. *This raincoat is dirty; moreover* (not *plus*), *it has a hole in it.*

precede, proceed   *Precede* means "to come before." *Proceed* means "to go forward." *As we proceeded up the mountain path, we noticed fresh tracks in the mud, evidence that a group of hikers had preceded us.*

principal, principle   *Principal* is a noun meaning "the head of a school or organization" or "a sum of money." It is also an adjective meaning "most important." *Principle* is a noun meaning "a basic truth or law." *The principal expelled her for three principal reasons. We believe in the principle of equal justice for all.*

proceed, precede   See *precede, proceed.*

quote, quotation   *Quote* is a verb; *quotation* is a noun. Avoid using *quote* as a shortened form of *quotation. Her quotations* (not *quotes*) *from Shakespeare intrigued us.*

raise, rise   *Raise* is a transitive verb meaning "to move or cause to move upward." It takes a direct object. *I raised the shades. Rise* is an intransitive verb meaning "to go up." It does not take a direct object. *Heat rises.*

real, really   *Real* is an adjective; *really* is an adverb. *Real* is sometimes used informally as an adverb, but avoid this use in formal writing. *She was really* (not *real*) *angry.* (See 26a.)

reason is because   Use *that* instead of *because. The reason I'm late is that* (not *because*) *my car broke down.* (See 11c.)

reason why   The expression *reason why* is redundant. *The reason* (not *The reason why*) *Jones lost the election is clear.*

relation, relationship   *Relation* describes a connection between things. *Relationship* describes a connection between people. *There is a relation between poverty and infant mortality. Our business relationship has cooled over the years.*

respectfully, respectively   *Respectfully* means "showing or marked by respect." *Respectively* means "each in the order given." *He respectfully submitted his opinion to the judge. John, Tom, and Larry were a butcher, a baker, and a lawyer, respectively.*

sensual, sensuous   *Sensual* means "gratifying the physical senses," especially those associated with sexual pleasure. *Sensuous* means "pleasing to the senses," especially those involved in the experience of art, music, and nature. *The sensuous music and balmy air led the dancers to more sensual movements.*

set, sit   *Set* is a transitive verb meaning "to put" or "to place." Its principal parts are *set, set, set. Sit* is an intransitive verb meaning "to be seated." Its principal parts are *sit, sat, sat. She set the dough in a warm corner of the kitchen. The cat sat in the warmest part of the room.*

shall, will   *Shall* was once used as the helping verb with *I* or *we: I shall, we shall, you will, he/she/it will, they will.* Today, however, *will* is generally accepted even when the subject is *I* or *we.* The word *shall* occurs primarily in polite questions (*Shall I find you a pillow?*) and in legalistic sentences suggesting duty or obligation (*The applicant shall file form 1080 by December 31*).

should of   *Should of* is nonstandard for *should have. They should have* (not *should of*) *been home an hour ago.*

since   Do not use *since* to mean "because" if there is any chance of ambiguity. *Since we won the game, we have been celebrating with a pitcher of beer. Since* here could mean "because" or "from the time that."

sit   See *set, sit.*

site, cite   See *cite, site.*

somebody, someone   *Somebody* and *someone* are singular. (See 21e and 22a.)

something   *Something* is singular. (See 21e.)

sometime, some time, sometimes   *Sometime* is an adverb meaning "at an indefinite or unstated time." *Some time* is the adjective *some* modifying the noun *time* and is spelled as two words to mean "a period of time." *Sometimes* is an adverb meaning "at times, now and then." *I'll see you sometime soon. I haven't lived there for some time. Sometimes I run into him at the library.*

suppose to   Write *supposed to.*

sure and   *Sure and* is nonstandard for *sure to. We were all taught to be sure to* (not *and*) *look both ways before crossing a street.*

take   See *bring, take.*

than, then   *Than* is a conjunction used in comparisons; *then* is an adverb denoting time. *That pizza is more than I can eat. Tom laughed, and then we recognized him.*

that   See *who, which, that.*

that, which   Many writers reserve *that* for restrictive clauses, *which* for nonrestrictive clauses. (See 32e.)

theirselves   *Theirselves* is nonstandard for *themselves. The two people were able to push the Volkswagen out of the way themselves* (not *theirselves*).

them   The use of *them* in place of *those* is nonstandard. *Please send those* (not *them*) *flowers to the patient in room 220.*

there, their, they're   *There* is an adverb specifying place; it is also an expletive. Adverb: *Sylvia is lying there unconscious.* Expletive: *There are two plums left.* *Their* is a possessive pronoun. *Fred and Jane finally washed their car.* *They're* is a contraction of *they are.* *They're later than usual today.*

they   The use of *they* to indicate possession is nonstandard. Use *their* instead. *Cindy and Sam decided to sell their* (not *they*) *1975 Corvette.*

this kind   See *kind(s).*

to, too, two   *To* is a preposition; *too* is an adverb; *two* is a number. *Too many of your shots slice to the left, but the last two were right on the mark.*

toward, towards   *Toward* and *towards* are generally interchangeable, although *toward* is preferred in American English.

try and   *Try and* is nonstandard for *try to. The teacher asked us all to try to* (not *and*) *write an original haiku.*

ultimately, eventually   See *eventually, ultimately.*

unique   Avoid expressions such as *most unique, more straight, less perfect, very round.* Something either is unique or it isn't. It is illogical to suggest degrees of uniqueness. (See 26c.)

usage   The noun *usage* should not be substituted for *use* when the meaning intended is "employment of." *The use* (not *usage*) *of computers dramatically increased the company's profits.*

use to   Write *used to.*

utilize   *Utilize* means "to make use of." It often sounds pretentious; in most cases, *use* is sufficient. *I used* (not *utilized*) *the best workers to get the job done fast.*

wait for, wait on   *Wait for* means "to be in readiness for" or "await." *Wait on* means "to serve." *We're only waiting for* (not *waiting on*) *Ruth to take us to the game.*

ways   *Ways* is colloquial when used to mean "distance." *The city is a long way* (not *ways*) *from here.*

weather, whether   The noun *weather* refers to the state of the atmosphere. *Whether* is a conjunction referring to a choice between alternatives. *We wondered whether the weather would clear up in time for our picnic.*

well, good   See *good, well.*

where Do not use *where* in place of *that*. *I heard that* (not *where*) *the crime rate is increasing.*

which See *that, which* and *who, which, that*.

while Avoid using *while* to mean "although" or "whereas" if there is any chance of ambiguity. *Although* (not *While*) *Gloria lost money in the slot machine, Tom won it at roulette.* Here *While* could mean either "although" or "at the same time that."

who, which, that Do not use *which* to refer to persons. Use *who* instead. *That*, though generally used to refer to things, may be used to refer to a group or class of people. *Fans wondered how an old man who* (not *that* or *which*) *walked with a limp could play football. The team that scores the most points in this game will win the tournament.* (See 23e.)

who, whom *Who* is used for subjects and subject complements; *whom* is used for objects. (See 25.)

who's, whose *Who's* is a contraction of *who is; whose* is a possessive pronoun. *Who's ready for more popcorn? Whose coat is this?* (See 36c and 36e.)

will See *shall, will*.

would of *Would of* is nonstandard for *would have*. *She would have* (not *would of*) *had a chance to play if she had arrived on time.*

you In formal writing, avoid *you* in an indefinite sense meaning "anyone." (See 23d.) *Any spectator* (not *You*) *could tell by the way John caught the ball that his throw would be too late.*

your, you're *Your* is a possessive pronoun; *you're* is a contraction of *you are. Is that your new motorcycle? You're on the list of finalists.* (See 36c and 36e.)

Answers to Tutorials and Lettered Exercises

Answers to Tutorial 1, page xxv

1. A verb has to agree with its subject. (21)
2. Each pronoun should agree with its antecedent. (22)
3. Avoid sentence fragments. (19)
4. It's important to use apostrophes correctly. (36)
5. Check for *-ed* verb endings that have been dropped. (27d)
6. Discriminate carefully between adjectives and adverbs. (26)
7. If your sentence begins with a long introductory word group, use a comma to separate the word group from the rest of the sentence. (32b)
8. Don't write a run-on sentence; you must connect independent clauses with a comma and a coordinating conjunction or with a semicolon. (20)
9. For clarity, a writer must be careful not to shift his or her [*not* their] point of view. *Or* For clarity, writers should be careful not to shift their point of view. (13a)
10. Do not capitalize a word just to make it look important. (45)

Answers to Tutorial 2, page xxvi

1. The index entry "each" mentions that the word is singular, so you might not need to look further to realize that the verb should be *has*, not *have*. The first page reference takes you to section 21, which explains in more detail why *has* is correct. The index entry "*has* versus *have*" also leads you to section 21.
2. The index entry "*lying* versus *laying*" takes you to section 27b, where you will learn that *lying* (meaning "reclining or resting on a surface") is correct.
3. Look up "*only*" and you will be directed to section 12a, which explains that limiting modifiers such as *only* should be placed before the words they modify. The sentence should read *We looked at only two houses before buying the house of our dreams.*

4. Looking up "*you,* inappropriate use of" leads you to section 23d and the Glossary of Usage, which explain that *you* should not be used to mean "anyone in general." You can revise the sentence by using *a person* or *one* instead of *you,* or you can restructure the sentence completely: *In Saudi Arabia, accepting a gift is considered ill mannered.*
5. The index entries "*I* versus *me*" and "*me* versus *I*" take you to section 24, which explains why *me* is correct.

Answers to Tutorial 3, page xxvi

1. Section 32c states that, although usage varies, most experts advise using a comma between all items in a series—to prevent possible misreadings or ambiguities. To find this section, Ray Farley would probably use the menu system.
2. Maria Sanchez and Mike Lee would consult section 30, on articles. This section is easy to locate in the menu system.
3. Section 24 explains why "Jane and me" is correct. To find section 24, John Pell could use the menu system if he knew to look under "Problems with pronouns." Otherwise, he could look up "*I* versus *me*" in the index. Pell could also look up "*myself*" in the index or he could consult the Glossary of Usage, where a cross reference would direct him to section 24.
4. Selena Young's employees could turn to sections 21 and 27c for help. Young could use the menu system to find these sections if she knew to look under "Subject-verb agreement" or "Standard English verb forms." If she wasn't sure about the grammatical terminology, she could look up "*-s,* as verb ending" or "Verbs, -s form of" in the index.
5. Section 26b explains why "I felt bad about her death" is correct. To find section 26b, Joe Thompson could use the menu system if he knew that *bad* versus *badly* is a choice between an adjective and an adverb. Otherwise he could look up "*bad, badly*" in the index or the Glossary of Usage.

Answers to Tutorial 4, page xxviii

1. Changing attitudes toward alcohol have *affected* the beer industry.
2. It is *human* nature to think wisely and act foolishly.
3. Correct
4. Everyone in our office is *enthusiastic* about this project.
5. Most sleds are pulled by no *fewer* than two dogs and no more than ten.

Answers to Tutorial 5, page xxviii

Benedict, Jeff. <u>Without Reservation: The Making of America's Most Powerful Indian Tribe and the World's Largest Casino</u>. New York: Harper, 2000.

Codoga, Helen. "Casinos on reservations in the
Northeast." E-mail to the author. 10 Apr.
2001.

"Indian Gaming." All Things Considered. Host
Robert Siegel. Natl. Public Radio. WDUQ,
Pittsburgh. 5 Mar. 2001.

Johnson, Susan. "From Wounded Knee to Capitol
Hill." State Legislatures 24.9 (1998).
Expanded Academic ASAP. InfoTrac. U of Pitts-
burgh Lib. 6 Apr. 2001.

National Indian Gaming Association. "Tribal
Gaming Myths and Facts." 2000. 4 Apr. 2001
<http://www.indiangaming.org/info/pr/
myths.shtml>.

Useem, Jerry. "The Big Game: Have American Indians
Found Their New Buffalo?" Fortune 2 Oct.
2000: 22+.

EXERCISE 8–1, page 141

Possible revisions:

a. The Prussians defeated the Saxons in 1745.
b. Ahmed, the producer, manages the entire operation.
c. All the referees threw down yellow flags.
d. Emphatic and active; no change
e. Protesters were shouting on the courthouse steps.

EXERCISE 9–1, page 147

Possible revisions:

a. Police dogs are used for finding lost children, tracking criminals, and de-
tecting bombs and illegal drugs.
b. Roger explained to the immigration officer that his visa had expired and
that he was applying to have it renewed.
c. It is more difficult to sustain an exercise program than to start one.
d. During basic training, I was told not only what to do but also what to
think.
e. Jan wanted to drive to the wine country or at least to Sausalito.

EXERCISE 10–1, page 154

Possible revisions:

a. A good source of vitamin C is a grapefruit or an orange.
b. The women entering VMI can expect haircuts as short as those of the male cadets.
c. The driver went to investigate, only to find that one of the supposedly new tires had blown.
d. Most of the spectators were unhappy with and angered by the decision.
e. Reefs are home to more species than any other ecosystem in the sea.

EXERCISE 11–1, page 160

Possible revisions:

a. Using surgical gloves is a precaution now taken by dentists to prevent contact with patients' blood and saliva.
b. A career in medicine, which my brother is pursuing, requires at least ten years of challenging work.
c. The pharaohs had bad teeth because tiny particles of sand found their way into Egyptian bread.
d. The quality of service has worsened each year.
e. This box contains the key to your future.

EXERCISE 12–1, page 165

Possible revisions:

a. Our English professor asked us to reread the sonnet very carefully, looking for subtleties we had missed on a first reading.
b. The monarch arrived at the gate in a gold carriage pulled by four white horses.
c. By afternoon, Sam had painted almost the entire dining room.
d. After being appointed leader of the expeditionary force by the Spanish viceroy, Coronado spent his time recruiting volunteers for the adventure.
e. Not all fresh vegetables are salt free.

EXERCISE 12–2, page 171

Possible revisions:

a. When I was ten, my parents took me on my first balloon ride.
b. To show our appreciation for your patience, we have enclosed a coupon that you may redeem for the book of your choice.
c. As I nestled in the cockpit, the pounding of the engine was muffled only slightly by my helmet.
d. In choosing her bridesmaids' dresses, she considered cost a major factor.
e. When I was a young man, my mother enrolled me in tap dance classes, hoping I would become the next Gregory Hines.

EXERCISE 13–3, page 179

Possible revisions:

a. Courtroom lawyers have more than a touch of theater in their blood.
b. The interviewer asked if we had brought our proof of birth and citizenship and our passports.
c. Single parents often have only their ingenuity to rely on.
d. When the director travels, you will make the hotel and airline reservations, arrange for a rental car, and prepare a detailed itinerary.
e. Madame Defarge is a sinister figure in Dickens's *A Tale of Two Cities*. On a symbolic level, she represents fate; like the Greek Fates, she knits the fabric of individual destiny.

EXERCISE 14–1, page 187

Possible revisions:

a. The lift chairs were going around so fast that they were bumping the skiers into their seats.
b. Our waitress, costumed in a kimono, had painted her face white and arranged her hair in an upswept lacquered beehive.
c. Student volunteers from Baltimore City Community College help the younger children with their weakest subjects, reading and math.
d. Shore houses were flooded up to the first floor, beaches were washed away, and Brant's Lighthouse was swallowed by the sea.
e. Although Mary will graduate from high school in June, she has not yet decided on a college.

EXERCISE 14–2, page 190

Possible revisions:

a. These particles, known as "stealth liposomes," can hide in the body for a long time without detection.
b. Cocaine, an addictive drug, can seriously harm you both physically and mentally, if death doesn't get you first.
c. Because students, textile workers, and labor unions have loudly protested sweatshop abuses, apparel makers have been forced to examine their labor practices.
d. Developed in a European university, IRC (Internet Relay Chat) was created as a way for a group of graduate students to talk about projects from their dorm rooms.
e. The cafeteria's new menu, which has an international flavor, includes everything from enchiladas and pizza to pad thai and sauerbraten.

EXERCISE 14–3, page 192

Possible revisions:

a. Working as an aide for the relief agency, Gina distributed food and medical supplies.

b. During her three years as an attorney at Pepco, Ms. Brooks has done an excellent job.
c. When the visiting period was nearly over, the prison guard tapped me on the shoulder.
d. My grandfather, who was born eighty years ago in Puerto Rico, raised his daughters the old-fashioned way.
e. By reversing the depressive effect of the drug, the Narcan saved the patient's life.

EXERCISE 16–1, page 208

Possible revisions:

a. Martin Luther King Jr. set a high standard for future leaders.
b. Coach Becker loves to work with young people.
c. Bloom's race for the governorship is futile.
d. A casualty call officer assists the bereaved family in many ways.
e. You will deliver mail to all employees.

EXERCISE 17–1, page 215

Possible revisions:

a. In my youth, my family was poor.
b. This conference will help me serve my clients better.
c. Have you ever been accused of beating a dead horse?
d. Health educators help people change their lifestyles.
e. Passengers should try to complete the customs declaration form before leaving the plane.

EXERCISE 17–4, page 225

Possible revisions:

a. Dr. Geralyn Farmer is the chief surgeon at University Hospital. Dr. Paul Green is her assistant.
b. All applicants want to know how much they will make.
c. Elementary school teachers should understand the concept of nurturing if they intend to be a success.
d. The vice president for community affairs asked Elizabeth and Joseph to serve as cochairs of the Red Cross blood drive.
e. If we do not stop polluting our environment, we will perish.

EXERCISE 18–3, page 232

Possible revisions:

a. We regret this delay; thank you for your patience.
b. Ada's plan is to acquire education and experience to prepare herself for a position as property manager.
c. Tiger Woods, the ultimate competitor, has earned millions of dollars just in endorsements.

d. When Robert Frost died at age eighty-eight, he left a legacy of poems that will make him immortal.
e. I would not advise anyone to pass up a chance to study geology.

EXERCISE 18–4, page 234

Possible revisions:

a. Queen Anne was so angry with Sarah Churchill that she refused to see her again.
b. Correct
c. The parade moved off the street and onto the beach.
d. For the frightened refugees, the dangerous trek across the mountains was preferable to life in a war zone.
e. What type of wedding are you planning?

EXERCISE 18–5, page 238

Possible revisions:

a. John stormed into the room like a hurricane.
b. The president thought that the scientists were using science as a grindstone to sharpen their political axes.
c. The Cubs easily beat the Mets, who were in trouble early in the game today at Wrigley Field.
d. We ironed out the wrinkles in our relationship.
e. Sasha told us that he wasn't willing to put his neck in a financial noose. [*or...* willing to go out on a limb—especially a rotten one.]

EXERCISE 19–1, page 248

Possible revisions:

a. The shock of bereavement is often followed by a succession of emotions: denial, sorrow, anger, despair, guilt, remorse, and longing.
b. Cortés and his soldiers were astonished when they looked down from the mountains and saw Tenochtitlán, the magnificent capital of the Aztecs.
c. Although my spoken Spanish is not very good, I can read the language with ease.
d. There are several reasons for not eating meat. One reason is that dangerous chemicals are used throughout the various stages of meat production.
e. To give my family a comfortable, secure home life is my most important goal.

EXERCISE 20–1, page 260

Possible revisions:

a. The city had one public swimming pool that stayed packed with children all summer long.
b. The building is being renovated, so at times we have no heat, water, or electricity.

c. The neighborhood was ruled by gangs. What kind of environment was this for my ten-year-old son?
d. Suddenly there was a loud silence; the shelling had stopped.
e. The car was hardly worth trading because the frame was twisted and the block was warped.

EXERCISE 20–2, page 261

Possible revisions:

a. Wind power for the home is a supplementary source of energy that can be combined with electricity, gas, or solar energy.
b. Correct
c. In the Middle Ages, when the streets of London were dangerous places, it was safer to travel by boat along the Thames.
d. "He's not drunk," I said. "He's in a state of diabetic shock."
e. Are you able to endure boredom, isolation, and potential violence? Then the army may well be the adventure for you.

EXERCISE 21–1, page 276

a. Subject: friendship and support; verb: have. b. Subject: Shelters; verb: offer. c. Subject: source; verb: is. d. Subject: chances; verb: are. e. Subject: cartoon and rhymes; verb: were.

EXERCISE 21–2, page 277

a. One of the main reasons for elephant poaching is the profits received from selling the ivory tusks.
b. Correct
c. Of those who die in single-car wrecks, a majority are drunk.
d. Crystal chandeliers, polished floors, and a new oil painting have transformed Sandra's apartment.
e. Correct

EXERCISE 22–1, page 283

Possible revisions:

a. To win the election, every presidential candidate must appeal to a wide variety of ethnic and social groups.
b. David lent his motorcycle to someone who allowed a friend to use it.
c. The instructor has asked all students to bring their tools to carpentry class.
d. Correct
e. Applicants should be bilingual if they want to qualify for this position.

EXERCISE 23–1, page 291

Possible revisions:

a. Some critics say that the *Challenger* disaster set the space program back five years.

b. Because she had decorated her living room with posters from chamber music festivals, her date thought she was interested in classical music, but actually she preferred rock.

c. In Ethiopia, a person doesn't need much property to be considered well-off.

d. Marianne told Jenny, "I am worried about your mother's illness." [*or* ". . . about my mother's illness."]

e. Though Lewis cried for several minutes after scraping his knee, eventually the pain subsided.

EXERCISE 24–1, page 301

a. Correct [But the writer could change the end of the sentence: . . . *than he is.*]

b. Correct [But the writer could change the end of the sentence: . . . *that he was the murderer.*]

c. She appreciated his telling the truth in such a difficult situation.

d. The director has asked you and me to draft a proposal for a new recycling plan.

e. Five close friends and I rented a station wagon, packed it with food, and drove to Mardi Gras on a three-day weekend.

EXERCISE 25–1, page 308

a. The roundtable featured several scholars whom I had never heard of. [*or* . . . scholars I had never heard of.]

b. Correct

c. Correct

d. Daniel always gives a holiday donation to whoever needs it most.

e. So many of the candidates were overqualified that it was difficult to decide whom to choose.

EXERCISE 26–1, page 317

Possible revisions:

a. Did you do well on last week's chemistry exam?

b. With the budget deadline approaching, our office has hardly had time to handle routine correspondence.

c. Correct

d. The customer complained that he hadn't been treated nicely.

e. Of all my relatives, Uncle Roberto is the cleverest.

EXERCISE 27–1, page 324

a. When I get the urge to exercise, I lie down until it passes.

b. Grandmother had driven our new jeep to the sunrise church service on Savage Mountain, so we were left with the station wagon.

c. A pile of dirty rags was lying at the bottom of the stairs.

d. How did the detective know that the suspect had gone to the office on the night of the murder?

e. Lincoln took good care of his legal clients; the contracts he drew for the Illinois Central Railroad could never be broken.

EXERCISE 27–2, page 334

a. The cops were after my hot rod Lincoln. We were passing cars like they were standing still.
b. The museum visitors were not supposed to touch the exhibits.
c. Our church has all the latest technology, even a closed-circuit television.
d. Christos didn't know about Marlo's promotion because he never listens. He is always talking.
e. Correct

EXERCISE 28–1, page 344

Possible revisions:

a. Correct
b. Watson and Crick discovered the mechanism that controls inheritance in all life: the workings of the DNA molecule.
c. When Hitler decided to kill the Jews in 1941, did he know that Himmler and his SS had had mass murder in mind since 1938?
d. Correct
e. Correct

EXERCISE 29–1, page 350

a. We will make this a better country.
b. There is nothing in the world that TV has not touched on.
c. Did the landlord tell you that he's going to raise the rent?
d. If we can afford to, we will spend our vacation in Canada next summer.
e. The child's innocent world has been taken away from him.

EXERCISE 29–2, page 354

Possible revisions:

a. He would have won the election if he had gone to the inner city to campaign.
b. If Verena wins a scholarship, she will go to graduate school.
c. Whenever there is a fire in our neighborhood, everybody comes out to watch.
d. We will lose our largest client unless we update our computer system.
e. If I lived in California, I wouldn't need to buy a winter coat.

EXERCISE 29–3, page 358

Possible answers:

a. I enjoy riding my motorcycle.
b. Will you help Samantha study for the test?
c. The team hopes to work hard and win the championship.
d. Ricardo and his brothers miss surfing during the winter.
e. The babysitter let Roger stay up until midnight.

EXERCISE 31–1, page 372

a. There are some cartons of ice cream in the freezer.
b. I don't use the subway because I am afraid.
c. The prime minister is the most popular leader in my country.
d. We tried to get in touch with the same manager whom we spoke to earlier.
e. Recently there have been a number of earthquakes in Turkey.

EXERCISE 31–2, page 375

a. an attractive young Vietnamese woman
b. a dedicated Catholic priest
c. her old blue wool sweater
d. Joe's delicious Scandinavian bread
e. many beautiful antique bird cages

EXERCISE 31–3, page 377

a. Listening to everyone's complaints all day was irritating.
b. During the long lecture, many students appeared bored.
c. Correct
d. After a great deal of research, the scientist made a fascinating discovery.
e. That blackout was one of the most frightening experiences I've ever had.

EXERCISE 31–4, page 380

a. Whenever we eat at the Centerville Diner, we sit at a small table in the corner of the room.
b. Correct
c. On Wednesdays he leaves work early so he can lift weights at his health club.
d. Our rabbi moved to the Northwest in 1994 and has been with our temple in Seattle since 1996.

EXERCISE 32–1, page 385

a. Alisa brought the injured bird home and fashioned a splint out of Popsicle sticks for its wing.
b. Considered the first Western philosopher, Thales believed that water was the elemental principle underlying all things.
c. If you complete the enclosed card and return it within two weeks, you will receive a free breakfast during your stay.
d. Correct
e. Uncle Swen's dulcimers disappeared as soon as he put them up for sale, but he always kept one for himself.

EXERCISE 32–2, page 387

a. The cold, impersonal atmosphere of the university was unbearable.
b. An ambulance threaded its way through police cars, fire trucks, and irate citizens.
c. Correct

d. After two broken arms, three cracked ribs, and one concussion, Ken quit the varsity football team.
e. Correct

EXERCISE 32–3, page 392

a. Choreographer Alvin Ailey's best-known work, *Revelations,* is more than just a crowd pleaser.
b. Correct
c. Correct
d. A member of an organization that provides housing for AIDS patients was also appointed to the commission.
e. A 1911 fire at the Triangle Shirtwaist Company, which killed 146 sweatshop workers, led to reforms in working conditions.

EXERCISE 32–4, page 398

a. Cricket, which originated in England, is also popular in Australia, South Africa, and India.
b. At the sound of a starting pistol, the horses surged forward toward the first obstacle, a sharp incline three feet high.
c. After the passage of the Civil Rights Act of 1964, the Ku Klux Klan went underground for a few years, but the group's racist views did not change.
d. Jan's costume was completed with bright red snakeskin sandals.
e. Computers must be manufactured in clean, climate-controlled rooms.

EXERCISE 32–5, page 399

a. On January 15, 1996, our office moved to 29 Commonwealth Avenue, Mechanicsville, Virginia 19607.
b. Correct
c. Ms. Carlson, you are a valued customer whose satisfaction is very important to us.
d. Mr. Mundy was born on July 22, 1939, in Arkansas, where his family had lived for four generations.
e. Correct

EXERCISE 33–1, page 406

a. Correct
b. He wore a thick black wool coat over army fatigues.
c. Often public figures (Michael Jackson is a good example) go to great lengths to guard their private lives.
d. She loved early spring flowers such as crocuses, daffodils, forsythia, and irises.
e. On Pam's wrist was a tattoo of a dragon chasing a tiger.

EXERCISE 34–1, page 412

a. Do not ask me to be kind; just ask me to act as though I were.

b. When men talk about defense, they always claim to be protecting women and children, but they never ask the women and children what they think.
c. When I get a little money, I buy books; if any is left, I buy food and clothes.
d. Correct
e. Wit has truth in it; wisecracking is simply calisthenics with words.

EXERCISE 34–2, page 413

a. Strong black coffee will not sober you up; the truth is that time is the only way to get alcohol out of your system.
b. It is not surprising that our society is increasingly violent; after all, television desensitizes us to brutality at a very early age.
c. There is often a fine line between right and wrong, good and bad, truth and deception.
d. Correct
e. Severe, unremitting pain is a ravaging force, especially when the patient tries to hide it from others.

EXERCISE 35–1, page 417

a. Correct
b. If we have come to fight, we are far too few; if we have come to die, we are far too many.
c. The travel package includes a round-trip ticket to Athens, a cruise through the Cyclades, and all hotel accommodations.
d. The media like to portray my generation as lazy, although polls show that we work as hard as the twentysomethings before us.
e. Fran Lebowitz has this advice for parents: "Never allow your child to call you by your first name. He hasn't known you long enough."

EXERCISE 36–1, page 422

a. Correct
b. The deed must be transferred to the purchaser's name.
c. Each day's menu features a different European country's dish.
d. Sue worked overtime to increase her family's earnings.
e. Ms. Jacobs is unwilling to listen to students' complaints about computer failures and damaged disks.

EXERCISE 37–1, page 431

a. As for the advertisement "Sailors have more fun," if you consider chipping paint and swabbing decks fun, then you will have plenty of it.
b. Correct
c. After winning the lottery, Juanita said that she would give half the money to charity.
d. After the movie Vicki said, "The reviewer called this flick 'trash of the first order.' I guess you can't believe everything you read."
e. Correct

EXERCISE 39–1, page 441

a. A client has left his or her cell phone in our conference room.
b. The thousand dollars that we invested in the stock market just ten years ago has tripled in value.
c. Correct
d. Correct
e. Of the three basic schools of detective fiction — the tea-and-crumpet, the hardboiled detective, and the police procedural — I find the quaint, civilized quality of the tea-and-crumpet school the most appealing.

EXERCISE 40–1, page 447

a. Correct
b. A number of government officials have been reviewing the records of some small brokerage firms in the area.
c. Correct
d. How many pounds have you lost since you began running four miles a day?
e. Denzil spent all night studying for his psychology exam.

EXERCISE 41–1, page 450

a. We have ordered four azaleas, three rhododendrons, and two mountain laurels for the back area of the garden.
b. Correct
c. Correct
d. Eight students in the class had been labeled "learning disabled."
e. The Vietnam Veterans Memorial in Washington, D.C., had 58,132 names inscribed on it when it was dedicated in 1982.

EXERCISE 42–1, page 455

a. Howard Hughes commissioned the *Spruce Goose,* a beautifully built but thoroughly impractical wooden aircraft.
b. The old man screamed his anger, shouting to all of us, "I will not leave my money to you worthless layabouts!"
c. I learned the Latin term *ad infinitum* from an old nursery rhyme about fleas: "Great fleas have little fleas upon their back to bite 'em, / Little fleas have lesser fleas and so on *ad infinitum.*"
d. Correct
e. *The City and the Pillar* was an early novel by Gore Vidal.

EXERCISE 44–1, page 470

a. Correct
b. The swiftly moving tugboat pulled alongside the barge and directed it away from the oil spill in the harbor.
c. Correct
d. Your dog is well known in our neighborhood.
e. Roadblocks were set up along all the major highways leading out of the city.

EXERCISE 45–1, page 476

a. District Attorney Johnson was disgusted when the jurors turned in a verdict of not guilty after only one hour of deliberation.
b. Correct
c. Madeline is taking courses in geology, mathematics, French, and English.
d. My grandfather and grandmother emigrated from Lithuania in the mid-1960s.
e. I look forward every spring to walking along the flower-lined paths in Boston's Public Garden.

EXERCISE 48–1, page 517

a. hasty generalization; b. false analogy; c. biased language; d. faulty cause-and-effect reasoning; e. *either . . . or* fallacy

EXERCISE 61–1, page 767

a. sun, assistance; b. Pride, bottom, mistakes; c. Success, confidence; d. censorship, flick, dial; e. flower, concrete (noun/adjective), cloverleaf

EXERCISE 61–2, page 771

a. He, every (pronoun/adjective); b. those, who; c. I, some (pronoun/adjective), that, I, myself; d. I, You, He; e. you, anything, anyone, me

EXERCISE 61–3, page 774

a. can pardon; b. are; c. does bring down; d. Keep, 'll [will] be insulted; e. Throw, will emerge

EXERCISE 61–4, page 777

a. Adjectives: General, wrong; adverb: generally; b. Adjectives: The (article), American, tolerant; adverb: wonderfully; c. Adjectives: an (article), uncultivated, an (article) uncultivated; adverbs: sometimes, never; d. Adjectives: wrong, right; adverbs: rather, strongly, weakly; e. Adjective: the (article); adverb: faster

EXERCISE 62–1, page 787

a. Complete subjects: Sticks and stones, words; simple subjects: Sticks, stones, words; b. Complete subject: all delays; simple subject: delays; c. Complete subject: (You); d. Complete subject: nothing except change; simple subject: nothing; e. Complete subject: Most of the disputes in the world; simple subject: Most

EXERCISE 62–2, page 792

a. Subject complement: cheap; b. Direct object: an injury; c. Direct object: his convent; d. Subject complement: the opium of the people; e. Subject complement: bitter

EXERCISE 62–3, page 793

a. Direct object: us; object complement: wise; b. Direct object: money; object complement: their primary pursuit; c. Direct objects: us, us; object complements: happy, good; d. Indirect objects: me, you; direct objects: no questions, no lies; e. Indirect objects: me, you; direct objects: a good loser, a failure

EXERCISE 63–1, page 798

a. On their side (adverb phrase modifying *had*); b. of several air traffic controllers (adjective phrase modifying *job*), with ease (adverb phrase modifying *could perform*); c. To my embarrassment (adverb phrase modifying *was born*), in bed (adverb phrase modifying *was born*), with a lady (adverb phrase modifying *was born*); d. of a culture (adjective phrase modifying *map*); e. In France (adverb phrase modifying *is*)

EXERCISE 63–2, page 804

a. who has outposts in your head (adjective clause modifying *enemy*); b. that doesn't bite (adjective clause modifying *rattlesnake*); c. If love is the answer (adverb clause modifying *could rephrase*); d. what they mean (noun clause used as direct object of *say*); e. unless I cannot resist it (adverb clause modifying *avoid*)

EXERCISE 63–3, page 808

a. Concealing a disease (gerund phrase used as subject), to cure it (infinitive phrase modifying *way*); b. being punctual (gerund phrase used as object of the preposition *with*), to appreciate it (infinitive phrase modifying *is*); c. to conceal him (infinitive phrase used as direct object), naming him Smith (gerund phrase used as the object of the preposition *by*); d. Being weak (participial phrase modifying *children*), to beguile us with charm (infinitive phrase used as direct object); e. Wrestling with words (gerund phrase used as subject)

EXERCISE 64–1, page 813

a. Complex; who sleep like a baby (adjective clause); b. Compound; c. Simple; d. Complex; If you don't go to other people's funerals (adverb clause); e. Compound-complex; what you are afraid of (noun clause)

(*continued from p. iv*)

Louise Bogan. "Women" opening stanza. From *The Blue Estuaries* by Louise Bogan. Copyright © 1968 by Louise Bogan. Copyright © renewed 1996 by Ruth Limmer. Reprinted by permission of Farrar, Straus & Giroux LLC.

Boston Public Library screen shot. Copyright © 1997–2001 Boston Public Library. Reprinted by permission.

Carleton College Library screen shot. Images provided courtesy of Carleton College, Northfield, MN.

Columbia University Libraries. "Library Web" screen shot. © Columbia University Libraries. Reprinted by permission.

Robert Frost. "Fire and Ice" excerpt. From *The Poetry of Robert Frost* edited by Edward Connery Lathem. © 1923, 1969 by Henry Holt and Company. © 1951 by Robert Frost. Reprinted by permission of Henry Holt and Company, LLC.

Gale Group screen shot. "Screen Image—Results of a Keyword Search." © Gale Group Inc. 2001. All Rights Reserved. Reprinted by permission of The Gale Group.

Global Routes screen shot. © 1999–2000 Global Routes. Reprinted by permission.

Google screen shot. © 2001 Google, Inc. Reprinted by permission.

Langston Hughes. "Ballad of the Landlord." From *Collected Poems* by Langston Hughes. Copyright © 1994 by the Estate of Langston Hughes. Reprinted by permission of Alfred A. Knopf, Inc. and Harold Ober Associates, Inc.

Chan Lowe. "Yep, got my cell" cartoon. © Tribune Media Services, Inc. All Rights Reserved. Reprinted with permission.

Barrie Maguire. Line drawing of shopping bag shown in "One Lunch at a Time." Copyright © Barrie Maguire/The Creative Workshop. From NewsArt on the Net: www.newsart.com. Reprinted by permission.

George McGovern and Robert Dole. "One Lunch at a Time." Article published in *The Washington Post,* May 1, 2001, p. A23. Reprinted by permission.

Webster's New World College Dictionary. Synonyms for "fertile, fecund, fruitful, and prolific." From *Webster's New World College Dictionary,* 4th Edition. Copyright © 2000, 1999 by Hungry Minds, Inc. All rights reserved. Reproduced by permission of the publisher.

Index

D

E

U

V

A complete section on major ESL problems:

ESL notes in other sections:

A List of Charts